THE REHNQUIST LEGACY

During the thirty-three years William Rehnquist has been on the Supreme Court, nineteen as Chief Justice, significant developments have defined the American legal landscape. This book is a legal biography of Chief Justice William Rehnquist of the United States Supreme Court and the legacy he created. It is an intensive examination of his thirty-three-year legacy as a Supreme Court Justice based on his Court opinions, primarily in the area of constitutional law. It is written by a group of legal scholars each of whom is a specialist in the area covered by his or her chapter. The focus of the book is on Rehnquist's own legacy, not necessarily that of the Court that he headed. Thus emphasis is placed not only on the goals that he achieved, but also on those that he failed to achieve.

Craig M. Bradley is the James Louis Calamaras Professor of Law at the Indiana University Law School in Bloomington, Indiana. Before entering teaching, Prof. Bradley served as an Assistant United States Attorney in Washington, D.C., as a law clerk to then-Justice William Rehnquist of the United States Supreme Court, and as Senior Trial Attorney in the Public Integrity Section of the U.S. Department of Justice. Since entering teaching Prof. Bradley has specialized in Criminal Procedure, Federal Criminal Law, and Comparative Criminal Procedure. His previous books include *The Failure of the Criminal Procedure Revolution* (U. of Pa. Press, 1993) and *Criminal Procedure: A Worldwide Study* (Carolina Academic Press, 1999). He has published over forty articles in such law journals as the *Harvard Law Review,* the *Supreme Court Review,* and many others. He also writes a bimonthly column on Supreme Court criminal procedure cases for *Trial* magazine, a publication of the American Association of Trial Lawyers. He is also the author of a forthcoming biographical essay on Chief Justice Rehnquist in Melvin I. Urofsky (ed.), *The Supreme Court Justices: A Biographical Dictionary* (CQ Press, 2d ed., 2006).

THE REHNQUIST LEGACY

Edited by

Craig M. Bradley

Indiana University

CAMBRIDGE
UNIVERSITY PRESS

CAMBRIDGE UNIVERSITY PRESS
Cambridge, New York, Melbourne, Madrid, Cape Town, Singapore, São Paulo

Cambridge University Press
40 West 20th Street, New York, NY 10011–4211, USA

Published in the United States of America by Cambridge University Press, New York

www.cambridge.org
Information on this title: www.cambridge.org/9780521859196

First published 2006

Printed in the United States of America

A catalog record for this book is available from the British Library

ISBN-13 978-0-521-85919-6 hardback
ISBN-10 0-521-85919-0 hardback

ISBN-13 978-0-521-68366-1 paperback
ISBN-10 0-521-68366-1 paperback

For Cindy, Derek, Kathleen, Snowy, and Wicca

CONTENTS

CONTRIBUTORS

Lʏɴɴ A. Bᴀᴋᴇʀ holds the Frederick M. Baron Chair in Law at the University of Texas School of Law in Austin, Texas. One of the United States' leading academic defenders of federalism and the rights of states, Baker has written extensively about the role of the spending power in federal–state relations. Among her most-cited works in this area are *Conditional Federal Spending after Lopez*, 95 Coʟᴜᴍ. L. Rᴇᴠ. 1911 (1995), and *Federalism and the Double Standard of Judicial Review*, 51 Dᴜᴋᴇ L.J. 75 (2001) (coauthored).

Dᴀᴠɪᴅ J. Bᴀʀʀᴏɴ is Professor of Law at Harvard University. A former law clerk to Judge Stephen Reinhardt of the U.S. Court of Appeals for the Ninth Circuit and Justice John Paul Stevens, Professor Barron is a graduate of Harvard College and Harvard Law School. Prior to teaching, he served as an attorney-advisor for the Office of Legal Counsel of the U.S. Department of Justice from 1996 to 1999. His research focuses on issues in administrative law, constitutional law, and the scope of state and local governmental power. His recent publications include *Reclaiming Home Rule*, 116 Hᴀʀᴠ. L. Rᴇᴠ. 2255 (2003) and *A Localist Critique of the New Federalism*, 51 Dᴜᴋᴇ L.J. 377 (2001). He is also the coauthor of a casebook, Lᴏᴄᴀʟ Gᴏᴠᴇʀɴᴍᴇɴᴛ Lᴀᴡ (3d ed. 2001) (with Gerald Frug and Richard Ford).

Cʀᴀɪɢ M. Bʀᴀᴅʟᴇʏ is the James Louis Calamaras Professor of Law at Indiana University, Bloomington. He has previously served as an Assistant United States Attorney in Washington, D.C., as Senior Trial Attorney, Public Integrity Section, U.S. Department of Justice, and as a law clerk to then–Justice William Rehnquist. He is the author of Tʜᴇ Fᴀɪʟᴜʀᴇ ᴏꜰ ᴛʜᴇ Cʀɪᴍɪɴᴀʟ Pʀᴏᴄᴇᴅᴜʀᴇ Rᴇᴠᴏʟᴜᴛɪᴏɴ (1993) and both editor and coauthor of Cʀɪᴍɪɴᴀʟ Pʀᴏᴄᴇᴅᴜʀᴇ: A Wᴏʀʟᴅᴡɪᴅᴇ Sᴛᴜᴅʏ (1999). He is also the author of a forthcoming biographical essay on Chief Justice Rehnquist in Melvin I. Urofsky (ed.), Tʜᴇ Sᴜᴘʀᴇᴍᴇ Cᴏᴜʀᴛ Jᴜsᴛɪᴄᴇs: A Bɪᴏɢʀᴀᴘʜɪᴄᴀʟ Dɪᴄᴛɪᴏɴᴀʀʏ (2d ed. 2006).

Rᴜᴛʜ Cᴏʟᴋᴇʀ is the Heck-Faust Memorial Chair in Constitutional Law at the Michael E. Moritz College of Law, The Ohio State University. She has published more than fifty law journal articles and is the author of numerous books, including Aᴍᴇʀɪᴄᴀɴ Lᴀᴡ ɪɴ ᴛʜᴇ Aɢᴇ ᴏꜰ Hʏᴘᴇʀᴄᴀᴘɪᴛᴀʟɪsᴍ (1998) and Dɪsᴀʙɪʟɪᴛʏ Pᴇɴᴅᴜʟᴜᴍ: Tʜᴇ Fɪʀsᴛ Dᴇᴄᴀᴅᴇ ᴏꜰ ᴛʜᴇ Aᴍᴇʀɪᴄᴀɴs ᴡɪᴛʜ Dɪsᴀʙɪʟɪᴛɪᴇs Aᴄᴛ (2005). She and Kevin M. Scott have compiled a database of all Rehnquist Court decisions.

DANIEL O. CONKLE is the Robert H. McKinney Professor of Law at Indiana University, Bloomington, as well as an Adjunct Professor of Religious Studies and Nelson Poynter Scholar. He clerked for Judge Edward Allen Tamm of the U.S. Court of Appeals for the D.C. Circuit and practiced with the Cincinnati law firm of Taft, Stettinius & Hollister before joining the Indiana University faculty in 1983. Professor Conkle has published extensively on constitutional law and theory, religious liberty, and the role of religion in American law, politics, and public life. His recent publications include a 2003 book, CONSTITUTIONAL LAW: THE RELIGION CLAUSES.

NEAL DEVINS is Goodrich Professor of Law and Professor of Government at the College of William and Mary. His books include THE DEMOCRATIC CONSTITUTION (with Louis Fisher), SHAPING CONSTITUTIONAL VALUES, and POLITICAL DYNAMICS OF CONSTITUTIONAL LAW (with Fisher). He is also the series editor for CONSTITUTIONAL CONFLICTS and coeditor of the volume FEDERAL ABORTION POLITICS (with Wendy L. Watson).

DANIEL A. FARBER is the Sho Sato Professor of Law at the University of California at Berkeley. He was formerly the McKnight Presidential Professor of Public Law at the University of Minnesota, where he taught for twenty years. He is the coauthor of a leading casebook on constitutional law (with Phil Frickey and Bill Eskridge) and of a reader on modern constitutional theory (with John Garvey and Alex Aleinikoff). He has also authored or coauthored several other books on constitutional themes, such as LINCOLN'S CONSTITUTION, THE FIRST AMENDMENT, and DESPERATELY SEEKING CERTAINTY: THE MISGUIDED QUEST FOR CONSTITUTIONAL FOUNDATIONS (with Suzanna Sherry). He was a law clerk for Justice John Paul Stevens during the 1976 Term.

PHILIP P. FRICKEY, the Richard W. Jennings Professor of Law at the University of California at Berkeley (Boalt Hall), is a nationally recognized scholar in the fields of statutory interpretation, legislative process, federal Indian law, and constitutional law. Frickey is the coauthor of widely adopted casebooks on legislation and constitutional law, as well as books on legislation and statutory interpretation, and on law and public choice. He is also a publication editor of Hart & Sacks's THE LEGAL PROCESS (1994), and the author or coauthor of numerous journal articles, essays, and book reviews. He is a member of the editorial boards of *Issues in Legal Scholarship*, an electronic journal, and *Court Review*, the quarterly journal of the American Judges Association.

RICHARD W. GARNETT is a Lilly Endowment Associate Professor of Law at Notre Dame Law School, where he teaches and writes about criminal law, capital punishment, religious freedom, and the freedom of speech. Before coming to Notre Dame, he served as law clerk to Chief Justice Rehnquist during October Term 1996 and to then–Chief Judge Richard S. Arnold of the U.S. Court of Appeals for the Eighth Circuit.

LINDA GREENHOUSE is the *New York Times*'s longtime Supreme Court correspondent and winner of a 1998 Pulitzer Prize in Journalism (beat reporting) for her coverage of the Court. She jas also received the Goldsmith Career Award for Excellence in Journalism from Harvard's Kennedy School of Government and the John Chancellor Award for Excellence in Journalism from the University of Pennsylvania's Annenberg School for Communication, both in 2004. Her most recent book is BECOMING JUSTICE BLACKMUN (2005).

JOSEPH L. HOFFMANN is the Harry Pratter Professor of Law at Indiana University, Bloomington. He has been teaching at Indiana since 1986, following one-year clerkships with the Honorable Phyllis A. Kravitch of the U.S. Court of Appeals for the Eleventh Circuit and then–Associate Justice William H. Rehnquist. He is a nationally recognized expert on criminal procedure, habeas corpus, and the law of the death penalty. He is a coauthor of COMPREHENSIVE CRIMINAL PROCEDURE (2005), and recently served as cochair of the Massachusetts Governor's Council on Capital Punishment.

DAWN JOHNSEN is Professor of Law at Indiana University, Bloomington. Prior to entering teaching she served as a law clerk to Judge Richard Cudahy of the U.S. Court of Appeals for the Seventh Circuit, as Legal Director of the National Abortion Rights Action League (1988–93), and as Deputy and then Acting Assistant Attorney General for the Office of Legal Counsel at the U.S. Department of Justice (1993–98).

YALE KAMISAR is Professor of Law at the University of San Diego and Professor of Law Emeritus at the University of Michigan, where he taught during 1965–2004 and was Clarence Darrow Distinguished University Professor of Law. Since he first started to write on the subject in 1963, Kamisar has written fourteen law review articles on the law of confessions, seven of which were collected in POLICE INTERROGATION AND CONFESSIONS: ESSAYS IN LAW AND POLICY (1980). He is also coauthor of all eleven editions of MODERN CRIMINAL PROCEDURE, the most widely used casebook in its field, and all nine editions of CONSTITUTIONAL LAW.

EARL M. MALTZ is Distinguished Professor of Law at Rutgers University School of Law in Camden, New Jersey. He is the author of four books and many articles dealing with constitutional law and constitutional history, among them THE CHIEF JUSTICESHIP OF WARREN BURGER (2000). He is also the editor of the recently published REHNQUIST JUSTICE: UNDERSTANDING THE COURT DYNAMIC (2003).

WILLIAM P. MARSHALL is the Kenan Professor of Law the University of North Carolina in Chapel Hill. He served as Associate Counsel and Deputy Counsel to the President during the Clinton administration, where he worked primarily on issues of constitutional policy. He has written extensively on constitutional law issues and published articles in such leading journals as the Virginia, Harvard, Chicago, Northwestern, and Illinois law reviews.

KEVIN M. SCOTT is Assistant Professor, Political Science Department, Texas Tech University. He and Ruth Colker have compiled a database of all of the Supreme Court decisions decided by the Rehnquist Court, and have published a preliminary assessment of this data, entitled *Dissing States?*, 88 VA. L. REV. 1301 (2002).

GEOFFREY R. STONE is the Harry Kalven, Jr., Distinguished Service Professor of Law at the University of Chicago. He served as a law clerk to Supreme Court Justice William Brennan. Stone has been a member of the faculty of the University of Chicago since 1973, and served as Dean of the Law School from 1987 to 1993 and as Provost of the University of Chicago from 1993 to 2001. Stone is the author or coauthor of many scholarly articles in the field of constitutional law and several books, including THE FIRST AMENDMENT, CONSTITUTIONAL LAW, ETERNALLY VIGILANT: FREE SPEECH IN THE MODERN ERA, and the award-winning PERILOUS TIMES: FREE SPEECH IN WARTIME (2004). He has served as an editor of the *Supreme Court Review* since 1991.

JAMES J. TOMKOVICZ is the Edward A. Howrey Professor of Law at the University of Iowa College of Law, where he has taught since 1982. He has also served as a visiting professor at the University of Michigan School of Law and the University of California, Los Angeles, School of Law. He is the author of THE RIGHT TO THE ASSISTANCE OF COUNSEL: A REFERENCE GUIDE TO THE UNITED STATES CONSTITUTION (2002) and the coauthor (with Professor Welsh White) of a casebook, CRIMINAL PROCEDURE: CONSTITUTIONAL CONSTRAINTS UPON INVESTIGATION AND PROOF (5th ed. 2004).

MARK TUSHNET is Carmack Waterhouse Professor of Constitutional Law at the Georgetown University Law Center. He served as a law clerk to Supreme Court Justice Thurgood Marshall. He is the coauthor of four casebooks, including the most widely used casebook on constitutional law. He has also written twelve books, including a two-volume work on the life of Justice Thurgood Marshall (1996–7) and A COURT DIVIDED: THE REHNQUIST COURT AND THE FUTURE OF CONSTITUTIONAL LAW (2005), and has edited four others. He was President of the Association of American Law Schools in 2003. In 2002 he was elected a Fellow of the American Academy of Arts and Sciences.

FOREWORD: THE THIRD REHNQUIST COURT

Linda Greenhouse

Two years ago, Professor Thomas Merrill published an influential article, based on his 2002 Childress Lecture at St. Louis University School of Law, entitled "The Making of the Second Rehnquist Court."[1] His starting premise was that the Supreme Court under the leadership of Chief Justice Rehnquist, then in its sixteenth year, could be divided into periods of roughly equal duration. From the beginning of the 1986 term until the end of October Term 1993, the Court experienced frequent changes in its membership and spent much of its time and energy spinning its wheels on hot-button social issues without being able, despite what appeared to be a conservative majority, to make much progress toward advancing the conservative agenda on such issues as abortion and school prayer. That was the first Rehnquist Court. Then, beginning with the summer of 1994, the Court experienced no turnover. The emphasis of the docket – a shrinking docket – shifted from the social issues to the structural, most notably to questions related to federalism, on which the conservative majority enjoyed striking – some might say startling – success. That was the second Rehnquist Court, and the Chief Justice appeared to be leading it with a sure hand.

I will leave the explanations to Professor Merrill, who has some very interesting ones (and to whom I apologize for having given such a superficial introduction to his complex and original argument), as well as to those who have drawn from his work, including Mark Tushnet's new book on the impact of the divisions within the Court's majority.[2] My point here is a different one. It is to suggest that we have passed from the second Rehnquist Court to a third, a Court that in fact came into being at just about the time Professor Merrill's article was at the printer's. In other words, rather than endeavor to explain what I view as the *past*, I will attempt first to describe the *present*, the current and in some ways quite surprising Rehnquist Court, and then to offer a possible explanation for

[1] Thomas W. Merrill, *The Making of the Second Rehnquist Court: A Preliminary Analysis*, 47 St. Louis L.J. 569 (2003).
[2] Mark Tushnet, *A Court Divided: The Rehnquist Court and the Future of Constitutional Law* (2005).

what may be driving the Court in directions that were not readily foreseeable as recently as two years ago.

This third and, undoubtedly, final phase of the Rehnquist Court has several characteristics that make it distinct. One is a reengagement with divisive social issues, including affirmative action, religion, and gay rights.[3] Another is the suggestion that the much-vaunted federalism revolution may have run its course.[4] And finally, there was the unmistakable indication in the Court's last term, carried forward into this one, that Chief Justice Rehnquist no longer speaks for a majority of the Court on many of the docket's most important issues.[5] The Court's membership has not changed, but its dynamic evidently has, as it has been drawn inexorably back to the themes that preoccupied the members of the first Rehnquist Court. Professor Merrill's assertion in the introduction to his article that "The second Rehnquist Court started in October 1994 and is still with us"[6] appears to have been overtaken by events.

Let me start by simply listing some of the decisions of the Court from which Chief Justice Rehnquist has dissented in the past two years: *Rasul v. Bush*,[7] asserting federal jurisdiction over the detainees at the Guantanamo Bay naval base; *Tennessee v. Lane*,[8] rejecting a state claim of Eleventh Amendment immunity from application of the Americans with Disabilities Act to courthouses; *Lawrence v. Texas*,[9] overturning state criminal sodomy laws and repudiating *Bowers v. Hardwick*;[10] *Grutter v. Bollinger*,[11] upholding affirmative action in higher education; *Blakely v. Washington*,[12] striking down state criminal-sentencing guidelines – the Chief Justice's dissenting vote there was of course essentially foreordained by the dissenting position he'd taken five years ago in *Apprendi*[13] and had maintained thereafter; *McConnell v. Federal Election Commission*,[14] upholding the McCain–Feingold federal campaign finance statute; *Newdow*, the Pledge of Allegiance

---

[3] *See* Grutter v. Bollinger, 539 U.S. 982 (2003), and Gratz v. Bollinger, 539 U.S. 244 (2003) (affirmative action); Elk Grove Unified School District v. Newdow, 124 S. Ct. 2301 (2004), Van Orden v. Perry, No. 03-1500, and McCreary County v. ACLU of Kentucky, No. 03-1693, both argued March 2, 2005, Cutter v. Wilkinson, No. 03-9877, argued March 21, 2005 (religion); Lawrence v. Texas, 539 U.S. 558 (2003) (gay rights).

[4] *See, e.g.,* Nevada Dept. of Human Resources v. Hibbs, 538 U.S. 721 (2003); Tennessee v. Lane, 541 U.S. 509 (2004); and Gonzales v. Raich, 125 S. Ct. 2195 (2005). *See also* Linda Greenhouse, *Will the Court Reassert National Authority?*, N.Y. Times, Sept. 30, 2001, § 4, at 14.

[5] *See* Linda Greenhouse, *The Year Rehnquist May Have Lost His Court*, N.Y. Times, July 4, 2004, at A1.

[6] Merrill, *supra* note 1, at 569.

[7] Rasul v. Bush, 124 S. Ct. 2686 (2004).

[8] Tennessee v. Lane, 541 U.S. 509 (2004).

[9] Lawrence v. Texas, 539 U.S. 558 (2003).

[10] Bowers v. Hardwick, 478 U.S. 186 (1986).

[11] Grutter v. Bollinger, 539 U.S. 982 (2003).

[12] Blakely v. Washington, 124 S. Ct. 2531 (2004).

[13] Apprendi v. New Jersey, 530 U.S. 466 (2000).

[14] McConnell v. Federal Election Commission, 540 U.S. 93 (2003).

case,[15] in which the Chief Justice would have found "under God" constitutional but the majority refused to reach the merits; *Brown v. Legal Foundation of Washington*,[16] in which the majority refused to characterize the operation of state IOLTA programs[17] as an unconstitutional taking; and *Sosa v. Alvarez-Machain*,[18] in which the majority kept the federal courthouse doors open to human rights claims by foreigners under the Alien Tort Statute. In last term's political gerrymandering case, *Vieth v. Jubelirer*,[19] the Chief Justice wanted to eliminate political gerrymandering as a justiciable claim, and thus to overrule *Davis v. Bandemer*,[20] but came up short. This term, of course, has found him in dissent in the juvenile death penalty case *Roper v. Simmons*.[21] And he was on the losing side in a major civil rights case, the Title IX retaliation decision *Jackson v. Birmingham Board of Education*,[22] in the medical marijuana case *Gonzales v. Raich*,[23] and in the eminent domain case *Kelo v. City of New London*.[24]

My list of Rehnquist dissenting votes is by no means complete; I simply listed cases that I thought were of special significance and that helped to define the terms during which they were decided. On a purely statistical measure, it is worth noting that of eighteen cases last term that were decided by five-Justice majorities, the Chief Justice was in the majority in only eight. Clearly, the Court's center of gravity lies where it so often has; Justice O'Connor was in the majority in thirteen of the eighteen.

But of course, that's not the whole story; if it were, the challenge of understanding, or even simply describing, the Rehnquist Court would not be nearly as interesting. Two of the most surprising decisions since Professor Merrill's article was published were *Nevada Department of Human Resources v. Hibbs*,[25] rejecting a state claim of Eleventh Amendment immunity from suit by its employees under the Family and Medical Leave Act of 1993, and *Locke v. Davey*,[26] rejecting a claim under the Free Exercise Clause that a state that provides tuition assistance for needy and worthy students to pursue a post–high school course of study must also subsidize those who wish to study for the ministry.

It is difficult to overstate the significance of these decisions. *Hibbs*, by characterizing the Family and Medical Leave Act (which obliges employers to grant up

---

[15] Elk Grove Unified School District v. Newdow, 542 U.S. 1 (2004).
[16] Brown v. Legal Foundation of Washington, 538 U.S. 216 (2003).
[17] Interest on Lawyers Trust Accounts (IOLTA).
[18] Sosa v. Alvarez-Machain, 124 S. Ct. 2739 (2004).
[19] Vieth v. Jubelirer, 541 U.S. 267 (2004).
[20] Davis v. Bandemer, 478 U.S. 109 (1986).
[21] Roper v. Simmons, 125 S. Ct. 1183 (March 1, 2005).
[22] Jackson v. Birmingham Board of Education, No. 02-1672, decided March 29, 2005.
[23] Gonzales v. Raich, 125 S. Ct. 2195 (2005).
[24] Kelo v. City of New London, No. 04-108, decided June 23, 2005.
[25] Nevada Dept. of Human Resources v. Hibbs, 538 U.S. 721 (2003).
[26] Locke v. Davey, 540 U.S. 712 (2004).

to twelve weeks of unpaid leave to enable employees to take care of family emergencies) as an exercise of Congress's power under Section 5 of the Fourteenth
Amendment to enforce constitutional protection against sex discrimination, effectively announced that state sovereignty would not, after all, trump Congress's
authority to legislate on behalf of classifications that receive heightened scrutiny
under traditional equal protection analysis. *Locke v. Davey* answered the question
left open two terms earlier by the Ohio voucher case,[27] in which the Court, in a
Rehnquist opinion, had invoked the principles of government neutrality and
private choice to reject an Establishment Clause challenge to the use of taxpayer
money for parochial school tuition.[28] If vouchers were constitutionally permissible, could they be constitutionally required? That was the logical next question
that *Locke v. Davey* raised. In answering in the negative, the Court in effect re-
mitted the voucher debate to the political process, where the "school choice"
movement faces very substantial obstacles and has made little headway.

The path from the Ohio voucher case in 2002 to *Locke v. Davey* in 2004 was
by no means obvious. In fact, in a commentary published along with Professor
Merrill's article in 2003, Professor John McGinnis characterized the Ohio case as
"surely one of the most important social issue decisions for our generation," one
that "changes the balance of power between secular and religious educational institutions."[29] While that claim could perhaps still be maintained as a doctrinal
matter after *Locke v. Davey*, as a practical matter it almost certainly could not be.

Both *Hibbs* and *Locke v. Davey* were Rehnquist opinions, and that, of course,
is my point in dwelling on them. Both were issued over the dissent of Justices
Scalia and Thomas; *Hibbs* drew an additional dissenting vote from Justice Kennedy. The author of *Hibbs*, in other words, was the very Justice who had been
leading the federalism charge for more than twenty-five years, since the long-ago
dissent in *Fry v. United States*[30] in which he first staked his ground. The author
of *Locke v. Davey* was the author of the opinion that only two years earlier had
seemed to promise so much to adherents of the school choice movement that
more than one advocate had compared it to *Brown v. Board of Education.*[31]

WHAT GOT INTO WILLIAM REHNQUIST?

What *Hibbs* and *Locke v. Davey* had in common, it seems to me, is that both cases
invited the Court to follow its recent precedents to their logical conclusions. Un-

---

[27] Zelman v. Simmons-Harris, 534 U.S. 1111 (2002).
[28] The Chief Justice thus brought to fruition the analysis he had first put forward in an earlier Establishment Clause case, *Mueller v. Allen*, 463 U.S. 388 (1983).
[29] John O. McGinnis, *Continuity and Coherence in the Rehnquist Court*, 47 St. Louis U. L.J. 875, 879
(2003).
[30] Fry v. United States, 421 U.S. 542 (1975).
[31] Brown v. Board of Education, 347 U.S. 483 (1954). On the use of the *Brown* analogy in the voucher context, *see* Linda Greenhouse, *Win the Debate, Not Just the Case*, N.Y. Times, July 14, 2002,
§ 4, at 4.

der Rehnquist's leadership, the Court declined the invitation in both cases. You can almost picture the majority peering over the cliff and deciding not to jump.

Doctrinally, jumping off the cliff would have been quite plausible, even principled. By the time *Hibbs* arrived at the Court, after all, Section 5 of the Fourteenth Amendment – which under Chief Justice Rehnquist's 1996 opinion for the Court in *Seminole Tribe v. Florida*[32] had become the only means by which Congress could abrogate the immunity of unconsenting states against private suits seeking damages in federal court – had acquired a new significance and quite a lot of fresh baggage.[33] In 1997, *City of Boerne v. Flores*[34] instructed that Section 5 legislation must show "congruence and proportionality between the injury to be prevented or remedied and the means adopted to that end."[35] During the following four years, in *Kimel v. Florida Board of Regents*[36] and again in *Board of Trustees of the University of Alabama v. Garrett*,[37] the Court applied this test to hold that Congress lacked the power to abrogate state immunity from suit under provisions of the Age Discrimination in Employment Act and the Americans with Disabilities Act. The Chief Justice's opinion for the Court in *Garrett* insisted that as the predicate for the exercise of Section 5 power, Congress had to have acquired a documented record that the states themselves were violating the judicially protected right to which the legislation was addressed – in all these cases, the right not to be discriminated against on the job.

If the ten years of hearings leading up to passage of the Americans with Disabilities Act could not provide Congress with enough of a record to meet that test in *Garrett*, then the Family and Medical Leave Act claim in *Hibbs* indeed appeared doomed. What saved it was the majority's interpretation of the Family and Medical Leave Act as an exercise of Congress's power under Section 5 to enforce the constitutional proscription against sex discrimination. By requiring employers to give time off to both men and women to deal with family emergencies, the Chief Justice explained, in words that Ruth Bader Ginsburg herself could not have written more forcefully, Congress was doing its part to eradicate the "pervasive sex-role stereotype that caring for family members is women's work." This, in turn, caused women to be perceived as less valuable employees or job seekers. This was, I should point out, not the only way to look at the Family and Medical Leave Act, which was, after all, a labor regulation and could well have been seen as a garden-variety Commerce Clause enactment. By treating the law as a Section 5, anti–sex discrimination enactment, the *Hibbs* opinion therefore stands for the proposition that when Congress acts within its core Section 5 authority to

---

[32] Seminole Tribe of Florida v. Florida, 517 U.S. 44 (1996).

[33] *See generally* Robert C. Post & Reva B. Siegel, *Legislative Constitutionalism and Section Five Power: Policentric Interpretation of the Family and Medical Leave Act*, 112 Yale L.J. 1943 (2003).

[34] City of Boerne v. Flores, 521 U.S. 507 (1997).

[35] *Id.* at 520.

[36] Kimel v. Florida Board of Regents, 528 U.S. 62 (2000).

[37] Board of Trustees of the University of Alabama v. Garrett, 531 U.S. 356 (2001).

combat discrimination that receives heightened scrutiny – not age, not disability, but in this instance sex – the Court will accede. As Robert Post pointed out in his analysis of *Hibbs* in his *Harvard Law Review* "Foreword,"[38] the decision to draw this line protected Title VII of the 1964 Civil Rights Act, thus avoiding the "major political confrontation"[39] with the ensuing damage to the Court that could otherwise have resulted had the majority exported the newly muscular Eleventh Amendment from rational basis territory into the land of heightened scrutiny.

If a contrary result in *Hibbs* would have been destabilizing, acceptance of the free exercise claim in *Locke v. Davey* to public tuition assistance for religious education might have been even more so. The Chief Justice's cryptic seventeen-paragraph majority opinion is not long on legal analysis, but its point is clear: "If any room exists between the two Religion Clauses, it must be here. We need not venture further into this difficult area. . . ."[40] The majority looked down from the cliff, and decided not to jump.

I'd like to propose that the third Rehnquist Court has been shaped by how its members have responded to the challenge of deciding whether to follow the precedents they established during the first two Rehnquist Courts to their logical conclusions. Clearly, Justices who made up the second Rehnquist Court's majority have found different stopping points, reflecting their different comfort levels as they balance the twin imperatives of consistency and pragmatism. Of course, pragmatism is not necessarily a positive value for all these Justices, and pragmatism does not have a single accepted meaning in any event. To borrow again from Robert Post, I suppose what I really mean here is that different Justices have different felt needs for the Court to engage in dialogue with the surrounding constitutional culture.[41]

And to take Professor Post's point perhaps beyond *his* comfort level, different Justices, sometimes implicitly and sometimes in terms of formal doctrine, appear to be defining constitutional culture differently. Clearly, in such decisions as *Lawrence v. Texas, Roper v. Simmons, Rasul v. Bush,* and, to a lesser extent, *Grutter v. Bollinger,* the majority envisioned itself in a dialogue with the wider world beyond the country's borders and cared a fair amount about how the Court, and through it, the country, looked to that world.

It is no accident that the Chief Justice dissented in each of those cases. That is not a dialogue that appears to matter to him. One might argue that a global constitutional culture is taking shape, or already exists, whether or not the Supreme Court of the United States chooses to acknowledge or engage with it. But I don't

---

[38] Robert C. Post, *Foreword: Fashioning the Legal Constitution: Culture, Courts, and the Law,* 117 Harv. L. Rev. 4 (2003).

[39] *Id.* at 22.

[40] *Locke,* 540 U.S. at 725.

[41] Post, *supra* note 38, at 8–9.

mean to join the current debate over the Court's increasing acknowledgment of foreign sources.[42] I offer these cases only as examples of instances when the majority responded to cues that the Chief Justice thought irrelevant or inappropriate. By perceptions of constitutional culture, I mean not a formal stance toward foreign law or any source of law in particular, but rather something much less formal, a more personal orientation on the part of individual Justices. Amid the cacophony of commentary, which voices – present or anticipated, formally expressed or simply part of the background music, within our borders or without – are most salient? At which point do various Justices decide that it is necessary in the Court's interest, or the country's, to subordinate "craft to outcome" and engage in "the sacrifice of cogency for wisdom," to borrow from John Jeffries's recent reappraisal[43] of Justice Powell's performance in *Bakke*.[44]

By a large majority, which included the Chief Justice, the Court decided that such a point had been reached in *Hibbs* and *Locke*. But in last term's *Tennessee v. Lane*,[45] another Eleventh Amendment state immunity case, the Chief Justice went one way and his *Hibbs* majority went the other. So it is worth pausing over *Tennessee v. Lane* for what it demonstrates about the third Rehnquist Court. Like *Garrett*, *Lane* presented a question of state immunity under the Americans with Disabilities Act, this time under Title II of the act, the public services provision, rather than Title I, which bars discrimination in employment. The issue was whether Congress's abrogation of state immunity from suit under Title II was a valid exercise of its Section 5 enforcement authority. With disability being subject only to rational basis analysis under the Equal Protection Clause, a point *Garrett* had reemphasized, the difficulty of the plaintiffs' task was obvious. The facts, however, were very much in their favor even if the law was not. The plaintiffs were two wheelchair users who had been unable to climb the stairs to reach courtrooms in Tennessee county courthouses that were not in compliance with the ADA. One of the plaintiffs, George Lane, had crawled up two flights of stairs the first time he needed to go to court. On his second visit, he refused to crawl or allow himself to be carried, and was arrested and jailed for "failure to appear" when he remained seated in his wheelchair in the lobby, asserting his legal right to an accessible courtroom.

The Sixth Circuit, affirming the District Court's denial of the state's motion to dismiss, threaded the needle by avoiding equal protection analysis entirely. It held that in making states liable to suit under Title II of the ADA, Congress had appropriately exercised its power to enforce a due process right of access to court.

---

[42] *See, e.g.*, Diane Marie Amann, *"Raise the Flag and Let It Talk,"* 2 Int'l J. Const. Law 597 (2004); Jess Bravin, *Congress May Fight Court on Global Front – Some Conservatives Worry That Jurists Too Often Cite International Precedents*, Wall St. J., March 21, 2005, at A4; Anne E. Kornblut, *Justice Ginsburg Backs Value of Foreign Law*, N.Y. Times, April 2, 2005, at A10.

[43] John C. Jeffries, Jr., Bakke *Revisited*, 2003 Sup. Ct. Rev. 1, at 24 and 21.

[44] Regents of the University of California v. Bakke, 438 U.S. 265 (1978).

[45] Tennessee v. Lane, 541 U.S. 509 (2004).

The Supreme Court affirmed, with a majority opinion by Justice Stevens that essentially limited the case to its facts:

> Whatever might be said about Title II's other applications, the question presented in this case is not whether Congress can validly subject the states to private suits for money damages for failing to provide reasonable access to hockey rinks, or even to voting booths, but whether Congress had the power under §5 to enforce the constitutional right of access to the courts. Because we find that Title II unquestionably is valid §5 legislation as it applies to the class of cases implicating the accessibility of judicial services, we need go no further.

Clearly, this was a majority mortified at the prospect of leaving Mr. Lane at the bottom of the courthouse stairs, without a remedy under what was arguably the most important federal civil rights enactment of the last quarter of the twentieth century. Crucially, that majority included Justice O'Connor, who had not previously departed from the Chief Justice's position in any of the state immunity or other federalism cases. This case challenged her comfort level. It did not challenge his.

Chief Justice Rehnquist's dissenting opinion objected to the majority's methodology as well to as its conclusion:

> . . . the majority posits a hypothetical statute, never enacted by Congress, that applies only to courthouses. The effect is to rig the congruence-and-proportionality test by artificially constricting the scope of the statute to closely mirror a recognized constitutional right. . . . [T]he majority's approach is not really an assessment of whether Title II is "appropriate *legislation*" at all, . . . but a test of whether the Court can conceive of a hypothetical statute narrowly tailored enough to constitute valid prophylactic legislation.

In other words, the fact that the majority had decided the case narrowly and saved the harder issues for another day bought it no credit with the Chief Justice; to the contrary, he stops just short of accusing the majority of having pulled off an intellectually dishonest trick. In the balance between pragmatism and consistency, which for him had tilted toward pragmatism a year earlier in *Hibbs*, consistency was the stronger value for the Chief Justice in *Tennessee v. Lane.*

So this is the third Rehnquist Court: a majority that has fractured over how far to go – over "when to hold 'em and when to fold 'em," in the words of the Kenny Rogers song,[46] over when to stop at the edge of the cliff and when to jump. This development should not, after all, surprise us. The second Rehnquist Court moved far and fast, reopening fundamental debates that had been settled for more than half a century. A pause to take stock, if not a regression to the mean, is quite natural. William Rehnquist has pushed, prodded, and questioned the received wisdom for all his years on the Court, so it is also quite natural that he is less ready to pause than some of those who have usually been his allies.

---

[46] "The Gambler," music and lyrics by Don Schlitz, recorded by Kenny Rogers, 1978.

I know I've offered more questions than answers. I look forward to the scholarship that will come out of this period, one chapter among so many in a fascinating and consequential career. History will evaluate the Rehnquist Court in all its phases, and I would be very surprised if the ambiguity of this final phase serves to cast doubt on the effectiveness or impact of a man who is already being proclaimed as one of the great Chief Justices.[47] If anything, the emergence of the third Rehnquist Court makes the first and especially the second all the more interesting. It challenges our understanding of the Supreme Court itself. What are we to make, after all, of a Court that changes even as its membership remains the same? As of Wednesday, April 6, it had been eleven years since Harry Blackmun, the last Justice to leave the Court, announced his retirement. We look at a Court that we think we know, and then we have to blink and look again. The only sure thing is that one of these days, we will find a new Justice, or two, or three, in place of those that have been so familiar – or so we thought – for so long, and the Court will move into still another cycle of continuity and change.

---

[47] *See, e.g.,* Jeffrey Rosen, *Rehnquist the Great?,* 295 Atlantic Monthly 79, at 79–90 (2005). For an appraisal contemporaneous with Professor Merrill's, see Linda Greenhouse, *The Last Days of the Rehnquist Court: The Rewards of Patience and Power,* 45 Ariz. L. Rev. 251 (2003).

INTRODUCTION

Craig M. Bradley

William Hubbs Rehnquist was born on October 1, 1924, and grew up in Milwaukee, Wisconsin. His father worked as a wholesale paper salesman, and his mother was a homemaker. After briefly attending Kenyon College in Ohio, he joined the Army Air Corps and was stationed in North Africa as a weather observer until the conclusion of World War II. Disdaining the midwestern climate after his experience in North Africa, he attended Stanford University, where he received a bachelor's and a master's degree in Political Science. He moved on to get a master's degree from Harvard, with an eye toward an academic career in Political Science. However, he became disenchanted with academics and decided to become a lawyer instead.

To that end, he returned to Stanford and finished first in his class at Stanford Law School in December of 1951. (Future Justice Sandra Day was third). In those days, a trip to Washington from California to interview for a Supreme Court clerkship was unthinkable, even for someone who was first in his class, and Rehnquist had not received an offer from Justice Douglas, who recruited in the West. However, as luck would have it, Justice Robert Jackson came to Stanford to dedicate a new Law School building. Phillip Neal, a former Jackson clerk who taught at Stanford, asked Rehnquist if he would like to interview with Jackson. Rehnquist readily accepted and was offered the job. He served as Jackson's clerk from February of 1952 through June of 1953.

From there, again influenced by climatic considerations, political as well as meteorological, he moved to Phoenix, where he engaged in private practice for the next sixteen years. He was active in Republican politics, including writing speeches for Barry Goldwater's 1964 presidential campaign. He also played poker with another prominent Arizona Republican, Richard Kleindienst. When Richard Nixon was elected President in 1968, Kleindienst became Deputy Attorney General and invited Rehnquist to become an Assistant Attorney General in charge of the Office of Legal Counsel. This is a highly respected office in the Justice Department that serves as "the President's lawyer" – offering legal opinions to the White

House and the Attorney General. Among Rehnquist's duties was the screening of potential Supreme Court nominees.

When two Supreme Court openings occurred in 1971 with the retirements of Justices Black and Harlan, Nixon was determined to appoint a woman and a southerner. To that end, he proposed Mildred Lillie, a California appellate judge, and Herschel Friday, a lawyer from Little Rock, Arkansas. However, the American Bar Association, which, in those days, had an informal veto power over nominees, rejected both as unqualified. Meanwhile Rehnquist had made a favorable impression on Attorney General Mitchell. Nixon was under pressure from Chief Justice Burger to fill the two vacant slots, so, rather at the last minute, Nixon chose the former Supreme Court clerk Rehnquist and Lewis Powell of Virginia, a onetime President of the ABA, whom they could hardly deem unqualified.[1]

Rehnquist took some heat during his confirmation hearings in the Senate concerning his activities as a Republican poll watcher who allegedly discouraged blacks and Hispanics from voting, and for a memo he wrote to Justice Jackson, while a law clerk, defending the turn-of-the-century case of *Plessy v. Ferguson,* in which the Supreme Court had upheld the "separate but equal" approach to racial segregation that was to be overruled in *Brown v. Board of Education.* (Rehnquist testified that his defense of *Plessy* was in the role of devil's advocate). However, Rehnquist was confirmed by a vote of 68–26 and took his seat in January of 1972. He became Chief Justice in September of 1986.

This book is a "legal biography" of Chief Justice Rehnquist. That is, it attempts to assess his legacy by analyzing his legal writings – mostly majority and dissenting opinions of the Supreme Court. No one book could possibly analyze with any care the hundreds of opinions he has written over his thirty-three-year career. Nor could any one author have the expertise to do so. Consequently this book is a collection of essays by noted law professors, each an expert in his or her field, of those areas of constitutional law in which Rehnquist is thought to have had the greatest impact. Thus it does not include many other areas of the law, such as administrative, military, or Indian law, in which Rehnquist has written key opinions. Nor does it include, for example, death penalty law. In this area, Rehnquist, while on the winning side of the battle over the constitutionality of the death penalty, did not author major decisions, and then was on the losing side in the recent cases striking down the death penalty for the retarded[2] and for juveniles.[3] This therefore would not be considered as one of the most significant parts of his legacy – though, but for constraints of space, it would have been a topic worthy of discussion in this book.

In order to determine Rehnquist's legacy, a reasonable starting point is to consider the goals he set for himself on the Court. He has directly stated only two,

---

[1] The confirmation process is described in John Dean, *The Rehnquist Choice* (2001).
[2] Atkins v. Virginia, 536 U.S. 304 (2002).
[3] Roper v. Simmons, 543 U.S. (2005).

rather modest, objectives. The first was "to call to a halt a number of the sweeping rulings of the Warren Court" in the area of criminal procedure.[4] As several chapters in this book make clear, he has certainly achieved this goal. Though he fell short of his ambitious desire to overrule both *Mapp v. Ohio*,[5] which required states to exclude evidence seized by police in violation of the Fourth Amendment, and *Miranda v. Arizona*,[6] which imposed the famous warnings requirement on state and local police, he certainly limited the impact of both of those decisions. In addition, his nearly complete reversal of the Warren Court's habeas corpus expansions severely restricted the opportunities for state criminal defendants to litigate violations of their rights in federal court.

The second goal, stated in an interview after he became Chief Justice, was to be remembered as a good administrator, "to run a relatively smoothly functioning Court."[7] In this he has clearly succeeded, being admired even by his political opponents on the Court. Justice Thurgood Marshall deemed him a "Great Chief Justice," and Justice William Brennan described him as "'the most all-around successful' chief he had known – including Earl Warren."[8]

The reasons for his success as Chief relate to his agreeable personality, his fairness in assigning opinions, based primarily on whether a Justice was up-to-date on his last assignment, and to the fact that he ran disciplined oral arguments, not allowing advocates at argument to exceed their allotted time. Likewise, at the conference where the Court meets to discuss recently heard cases, he ran a tight ship, giving each Justice a chance to state his or her views, in order of seniority. He did not allow debate among the Justices, being of the opinion that, since most had already made up their minds, extended discussion was a waste of time.[9]

Since assigning opinions (which he does whenever he votes in the majority at conference) and presiding over the conference and oral argument are the extent of a Chief Justice's formal powers over his fellow Justices, it is understandable that Brennan and Marshall might consider him a "great Chief Justice" while generally condemning his legal positions as misguided and even dangerous.[10] Another attribute that a Chief Justice might possess is the ability to sway fellow Justices toward his (or her) own position. Rehnquist, with his keen intelligence and

---

[4] Quoted in Craig Bradley, *William Hubbs Rehnquist*, in *The Supreme Court Justices: A Biographical Dictionary* 376 (M. Urofsky ed., 1994).

[5] 367 U.S. 643 (1961).

[6] 384 U.S. 436 (1966).

[7] Jeffrey Rosen, *Rehnquist the Great?*, 295 Atlantic Monthly 79, at 80 (2005).

[8] *Id.* at 80.

[9] *Id.* at 80–81.

[10] *See, e.g.*, Brennan's dissent in *California v. Greenwood*, 486 U.S. 35 (1988), where the majority, including Rehnquist, approved searches of trash without warrants or probable cause: "The Court paints a grim picture of our society. It depicts a society in which local authorities may . . . monitor (citizens) arbitrarily and without judicial oversight – a society that is not prepared to recognize as reasonable an individual's expectation of privacy in the most private of personal effects."

personableness, was surely as likely as any Chief Justice could have been to succeed in this endeavor. As I can attest from personal experience as his clerk, he had
a knack for explaining his views, with which I often disagreed, in ways that made
them seem eminently reasonable. However, he simply didn't believe in politick-
ing his fellow Justices, preferring to confine his arguments to the logic of the
opinions he drafted.

The Court has been dominated by his own party during his entire tenure. Justice Powell, who joined the Court the same day as Rehnquist, replacing Justice
Black, gave the Republicans a majority that they have never relinquished. Currently, the Republican majority is 7–2. Yet Rehnquist has found himself on the
losing side of cases striking down homosexual sodomy laws,[11] upholding the right
to abortion,[12] finding affirmative action constitutional,[13] disallowing school
prayer,[14] and placing limits on the death penalty, as well as his disappointments
in criminal procedure previously mentioned. While some conservatives may feel
that "allowing" this to happen was a failure of Rehnquist to lead his fellow Republicans, such a belief misunderstands the nature of the Supreme Court in
general, and of the current Court in particular.

As noted above, the Chief Justice has little formal power over his fellow Justices. He may be *primos inter pares,* but the emphasis is on the *pares.* Thus, no
Chief Justice is likely to exert much sway over the votes of his or her fellows. Rehnquist certainly didn't drive anybody out of his camp as Chief Justice Burger is
widely believed to have driven his fellow Minnesotan Harry Blackmun into the
welcoming arms of the liberals.[15] Sometimes, though, a Chief, or another senior
Justice, may be able to convince a new Justice, who is inexperienced in matters
of constitutional law, to come around to his point of view, as Chief Justice Warren
is alleged to have done with Justice Brennan.[16]

But look at the Court Rehnquist had to work with! On the current Court there
are three former Supreme Court clerks (Rehnquist, Breyer, and Stevens), three
former professors at elite law schools (Ginsburg, Breyer, and Scalia), and a Rhodes
Scholar (Souter). Moreover, Justices Thomas and Scalia joined the Court with
a conservative agenda to the right of Rehnquist. All the Justices hold law degrees
from top law schools, and all but two had had plenty of opportunity to form their
views on constitutional issues prior to joining the Court. The only exceptions
are O'Connor and Souter, whose prior positions as a state officials would not
have exposed them to much federal constitutional litigation.

O'Connor was also a longtime friend of Rehnquist's both from law school and
Phoenix. Rehnquist must have been particularly frustrated that she, tapped by

[11] Lawrence v. Texas, 123 S. Ct. 2472 (2003).
[12] Roe v. Wade, 410 U.S. 113 (1973); Planned Parenthood v. Casey, 505 U.S. 833 (1992).
[13] Grutter v. Bollinger, 539 U.S. 982 (2003).
[14] Lee v. Weisman, 505 U.S. 577 (1992).
[15] *See* Linda Greenhouse, *Becoming Justice Blackmun* 185–88 (2005) in this regard.
[16] *See* Kim Isaac Eisler, *A Justice for All* 103, 139–40 (1993).

the Reagan administration as a conservative appointee, did not join him in toe-ing the conservative line. But her single-mindedness on a number of critical cases have led some to call this "the O'Connor Court."[17] In other major cases, where he has held O'Connor's vote, he has lost Kennedy's. But to blame these defections on Rehnquist in any way would be misguided. Rather, it must be recognized that when someone becomes a Supreme Court Justice, his or her prior views may bend under the weight of the responsibility and the careful consideration of the issues that is part of a Justice's job. Had Rehnquist tried to twist the arms of these independent thinkers, he might have succeeded only in weakening his status as a Chief Justice whose *written* views were highly respected by his colleagues.

Leaving aside Rehnquist's role as Chief Justice (beyond the specific goals he named) and considering him as one of the nine, his vision of the Constitution was based on three principles: strict construction, judicial restraint, and federal-ism. He summarized this vision in a 1976 speech, "The Notion of a Living Con-stitution":

> It is almost impossible . . . to conclude that the [Founding Fathers] intended the Constitution itself to suggest answers to the manifold problems that they knew would confront succeeding generations. The Constitution that they drafted was in-tended to endure indefinitely, but the reason for this well-founded hope was the general language by which national authority was granted to Congress and the Pres-idency. These two branches were to furnish the motive power within the federal system, which was in turn to coexist with the state governments; the elements of government having a popular constituency were looked to for the solution of the numerous and varied problems that the future would bring.[18]

In other words, as he elaborated in a dissenting opinion in *Trimble v. Gordon*[19] in 1977: Nothing in the Constitution made "this Court (or the federal courts generally) into a council of revision, and they did not confer on this Court any authority to nullify state laws which were merely felt to be inimical to the Court's notion of the public interest."

It is difficult to believe, after all of the acrimony surrounding abortion rights in the past two decades that, in 1973, when *Roe v. Wade*[20] was decided, Rehnquist was (along with the Democrat Justice White), one of only two dissenters. He fur-ther elaborated on his constitutional view in that case, noting that the "right to privacy" on which the Court's opinion was based, was nowhere to be found in the Constitution, and, whatever its scope, had certainly never been thought to include a right to abortion. He continued:

> The fact that a majority of the States, reflecting, after all the majority sentiment in those States, have had restrictions on abortions for at least a century is a strong

---

[17] E.g. Michael Rappaport, *It's the O'Connor Court.* . . . 99 Nw. U. L. Rev. 369 (2004).
[18] 54 Tex. L. Rev. 693 (1976).
[19] 430 U.S. 762.
[20] 410 U.S. 113, 174.

indication, it seems to me, that the asserted right to an abortion is not "so rooted in the traditions and conscience of our people as to be ranked as fundamental."

It is ironic then that, as Professor Sunstein has pointed out,

> [I]n its first seventy five years, the Supreme Court struck down only two acts of Congress. In the eighteen years since Ronald Reagan nominated William H. Rehnquist as Chief Justice, the Court has invalidated more than three dozen. Under Rehnquist, the Court has compiled a record of judicial activism that is, in some ways, without parallel in the nation.[21]

Sometimes, as in all of the cases mentioned above, this activism has been over the resistance of Rehnquist and his fellow conservatives. Other times, as in the federalism cases and *Bush v. Gore*,[22] which effectively decided the 2000 election for the Republicans, it has been the conservatives taking the initiative. In the view of Professor Sunstein,

> *Bush v. Gore* was a far more radical intervention into political processes than anything dared by the Warren Court, and it . . . is merely the most visible of a long line of cases in which the Rehnquist Court has seized on ambiguous constitutional provisions to invalidate decisions of Congress and state governments. . . . (I)n limiting national authority to protect disadvantaged groups, and in protecting property rights, it has shown unmistakable sympathy for the pre–New Deal Constitution. This is a political program in legal dress. The harsh irony is that the program has been advanced especially aggressively by those (conservative) members of the Rehnquist Court who contend, and even appear to believe, that they are speaking neutrally for the Constitution.

In fairness to Rehnquist and his fellow conservatives, though, sometimes the goals of deference to the political branches and dedication to principles of strict construction and federalism may clash, as they did in *United States v. Lopez*.[23] There, the Court dealt with Congress's power to regulate commerce among the states in the context of the Gun-Free School Zones Act. This statute prohibited bringing guns near any school without any reference to whether the gun or the school was connected to interstate commerce. Holding that the Commerce Clause was limited to regulating commercial activity, not exercising the "police power" that was reserved to the states, the Court struck down the statute. Thus, principles of federalism and strict construction trumped deference to the legislative branch.

It is also true that Rehnquist has moderated his positions somewhat since he became Chief Justice. For example, in *Dickerson v. United States*, he abandoned his long quest to overrule *Miranda* and authored a majority opinion to uphold it, over an outraged dissent by Justice Scalia. However, this probably had more

---

[21] Cass R. Sunstein, *The Rehnquist Revolution*, New Republic, December 27, 2004, at 32.

[22] 531 U. S. 98 (2001).

[23] 514 U.S. 549 (1995).

to do with resistance to Congress's attempt to "overrule" *Miranda* than with any newfound fondness for the holding of that case, and he soon agreed with subsequent opinions that significantly limited *Miranda*'s impact.[24] Similarly, in *Nevada Dep't of Human Resources v. Hibbs*[25] he enhanced federal power over the states by authoring an opinion (over the dissents of Justices Scalia, Thomas, and Kennedy) holding that Congress could abrogate states' rights that would otherwise be protected by the Eleventh Amendment by acting under §5 of the Fourteenth Amendment. It cannot be known whether *Dickerson* and *Hibbs* represent Rehnquist's true beliefs, or efforts to limit the damage done by decisions with which he would have preferred to disagree. In any event, his opinions for the majority in both cases show an increased willingness to work toward consensus and compromise.

Nevertheless, as Professor Tushnet has put it, on the Rehnquist Court, "*everyone* has been a judicial activist."[26] Rehnquist, with his ambitious and frequently fulfilled goals of overruling key criminal procedure decisions, as well as *Roe v. Wade,* and of significantly limiting the power of Congress vis-à-vis the states is likewise deserving of that appellation. However, it is fair to say that his activism is generally more closely tied to the terms of the Constitution than are some of the decisions he has railed against.

As this book was going to press in September 2005, the Chief Justice died, and his former law clerk, John Roberts, was named to replace him. It remains to be seen how Rehnquist's legacy will fare in the Roberts Court, but it is unlikely to be diminished.

---

[24] *United States v. Patane,* 124 S. Ct. 2620 (2004) holding that the "fruit of the poisonous tree" doctrine does not apply to *Miranda* violations. He joined the dissent in *Missouri v. Seibert,* 124 S. Ct. 2601 (2004) where the majority excluded a confession obtained by police tactics designed to circumvent *Miranda.*

[25] 538 U.S. 721 (2003).

[26] Mark V. Tushnet, *On the Rehnquist Court, Everyone Has Been a Judicial Activist,* Chronicle Rev., November 26, 2004, at A10.

SECTION ONE

THE FIRST AMENDMENT

CHAPTER ONE

THE *HUSTLER*: JUSTICE REHNQUIST AND "THE FREEDOM OF SPEECH, OR OF THE PRESS"

Geoffrey R. Stone*

In his more than thirty years on the Supreme Court, William Rehnquist has participated in 259 decisions involving "the freedom of speech, or of the press."[1] Over the course of his tenure, the jurisprudence of the First Amendment has changed dramatically. When Justice Rehnquist first joined the Court, no one had yet heard of "content-based restrictions," "low" value speech, or "designated" public forums. The Internet did not exist, commercial speech was "unprotected," and money was not "speech." All that has changed, and more.

What are Justice Rehnquist's contributions to the evolution of First Amendment doctrine? To what extent, and in what circumstances, has he protected "the freedom of speech, or of the press"?

I

In the 259 speech or press cases in which Justice Rehnquist has participated, he rejected the First Amendment claim 80% of the time. In only 53 of the 259 cases did he vote to uphold the First Amendment claim. Standing alone, however, this tells us little. We need some base of comparison.

One base of comparison is how other Justices voted. In these 259 decisions, the other Justices (Blackmun, Brennan, Breyer, Burger, Douglas, Ginsburg, Kennedy, Marshall, O'Connor, Powell, Scalia, Souter, Stephens, Stewart, Thomas, and White) voted to uphold the First Amendment claim 53% of the time.[2] Thus, Rehnquist's colleagues on the Court were 2.6 times more likely than Justice Rehnquist to hold a law in violation of "the freedom of speech, or of the press."

---

* I thank my colleagues Ronald Collins, Cass Sunstein, and Eugene Volokh for their comments on an earlier draft, and Ambika Kumar for her splendid research assistance.
[1] As an obvious caveat, I should note that the counting and classification of decisions always involves an element of judgment and subjectivity. Another person undertaking the same exercise might come up with slightly different results.
[2] In the 259 cases in which Rehnquist participated, the other justices cast 1,118 votes to sustain the First Amendment claim and 986 votes to reject the First Amendment claim.

This suggests that, relative to his colleagues, Rehnquist was no friend of the First Amendment. But this only scratches the surface. Even the Supreme Court has easy cases, and these are best identified by unanimity. If all the Justices agree that a law is constitutional or unconstitutional, an individual Justice's vote does not tell us anything very interesting about his or her views.

Sixty-three of the 259 cases were decided by unanimous vote. If we exclude those "easy" decisions, we find that Justice Rehnquist voted to uphold the First Amendment claim in only 18 of the 196 nonunanimous decisions. In the "hard" cases, he rejected the First Amendment challenge 92% of the time.

How does this compare with his colleagues? In the 196 nonunanimous decisions, the other Justices voted to uphold the First Amendment challenge 55% of the time. Thus, in nonunanimous decisions the other Justices were six times more likely than Justice Rehnquist to find a law in violation of "the freedom of speech, or of the press."[3]

This may be misleading. Perhaps the "liberal" Justices, such as Brennan, Douglas, and Marshall, skewed the data. Before drawing any conclusions, we should compare Rehnquist's voting record with those of his more "conservative" colleagues, such as Burger, White, Scalia, and Thomas.

Rehnquist and Burger sat together on 165 cases involving "the freedom of speech, or of the press." Rehnquist voted to uphold the First Amendment claim in 30 of those cases. Burger voted to sustain the constitutional challenge in 54. Burger was thus 1.8 times more likely than Rehnquist to rule in favor of the First Amendment.[4]

In the 230 cases in which Rehnquist and White both participated, White voted to sustain the First Amendment claim in 88 cases, whereas Rehnquist voted to uphold it in only 46. White was therefore 1.9 times more likely than Rehnquist to support "the freedom of speech, or of the press."[5]

Scalia and Rehnquist sat together in 108 of these decisions. Scalia voted to uphold the First Amendment challenge in 49, Rehnquist in only 31. Scalia was thus 1.6 times more likely than Rehnquist to sustain a First Amendment claim.[6]

Finally, Thomas and Rehnquist participated together in 60 of these cases. Rehnquist voted to sustain the First Amendment claim in 23, Thomas in 35. Thomas was therefore 1.5 times more likely than Rehnquist to rule in favor of the First Amendment.[7]

---

[3] In the 196 nonunanimous decisions, the other justices cast 854 votes to sustain the First Amendment claim and 701 votes to reject the First Amendment claim.

[4] Rehnquist voted to sustain the First Amendment claim in 18.2% of these cases. Burger voted to sustain the First Amendment claim in 32.7% of these cases.

[5] Rehnquist voted to sustain the First Amendment claim in 20.0% of these cases. White voted to sustain the First Amendment claim in 38.3% of these cases.

[6] Rehnquist voted to sustain the First Amendment claim in 28.7% of these cases. Scalia voted to sustain the First Amendment claim in 45.4% of these cases.

[7] Rehnquist voted to sustain the First Amendment claim in 38.3% of these cases. Thomas voted to sustain the First Amendment claim in 58.3% of these cases.

The conclusion, then, is clear. During the course of his tenure, Justice Rehnquist has been, by an impressive margin, the member of the Supreme Court *least* likely to invalidate a law as violating "the freedom of speech, or of the press."

II

To understand Rehnquist's approach to the First Amendment, it is useful to divide these decisions into several categories. Thirty-nine of the 259 cases involved "the freedom of . . . the press." These decisions addressed such issues as whether the First Amendment guarantees a journalist–source privilege, the government may enjoin the publication of truthful information, the press has a First Amendment right of access to certain places or information, the government may regulate the media, and the press may be held liable for defamation or invasion of privacy.[8]

In the thirty-nine decisions involving "the freedom of . . . the press," Rehnquist voted only six times to sustain the constitutional claim, or 15% of the time. Other Justices voted to uphold the First Amendment claim 60% of the time. His colleagues were therefore four times more likely than he to sustain the claims of the press. If we exclude unanimous decisions, the contrast is even starker: All six cases in which Rehnquist supported "the freedom of . . . the press" were unanimous decisions. He rejected the constitutional claim in 100% of the nonunanimous decisions. Thus, in his more than thirty years on the Court, Rehnquist never *once* found a violation of "the freedom of . . . the press" when any other Justice disagreed with him.[9]

A second category involved sexually oriented expression. These forty-three decisions addressed such issues as obscenity, profanity, indecency, child pornography, public nudity, and adult entertainment.[10] In only five of these cases did

---

8 *See, e.g.,* Branzburg v. Hayes, 408 U.S. 665 (1972) (journalist's privilege); Gertz v. Robert Welch, Inc., 418 U.S. 323 (1974) (libel); Cox Broadcasting v. Cohn, 420 U.S. 469 (1975) (privacy); Houchins v. KQED, 438 U.S. 1 (1978) (access of press to prison); Richmond Newspapers v. Virginia, 448 U.S. 555 (1980) (access of public to criminal trial); Turner Broadcasting System, Inc. v. Federal Communications Commission, 512 U.S. 622 (1994) (regulation of cable).

9 The unanimous decisions were Miami Herald Publishing Company v. Tornillo, 418 U.S. 24 (1974) (right-of-reply statute); Nebraska Press Association v. Stuart, 427 U.S. 539 (1976) (gag order); Oklahoma Publishing Company v. District Court, 430 U.S. 308 (1977) (privacy); Landmark Communications, Inc. v. Virginia, 435 U.S. 829 (1978) (confidential information); Hustler Magazine v. Falwell, 485 U.S. 46 (1988) (intentional infliction of emotional distress); Masson v. New Yorker Magazine, 501 U.S. 496 (1991) (libel).

10 *See, e.g.,* Miller v. California, 413 U.S. 15 (1973) (obscenity); Federal Communications Commission v. Pacifica Foundation, 438 U.S. 726 (1978) (profanity); Renton v. Playtime Theatres, Inc., 475 U.S. 41 (1986) (zoning adult theaters); Barnes v. Glen Theatre, Inc., 501 U.S. 560 (1991) (nude dancing); Denver Area Educational Telecommunications Consortium, Inc. v. Federal Communications Commission, 518 U.S. 727 (1996) (cable); Ashcroft v. Free Speech Coalition, 535 U.S. 234 (2002) (virtual child pornography).

Rehnquist find a violation of the First Amendment.[11] He voted to uphold the First Amendment challenge in only 12% of these cases, whereas the other Justices voted to uphold the constitutional claim 55% of the time. Rehnquist's colleagues were therefore 4.6 times more likely than he to sustain the First Amendment challenge. If we focus on only nonunanimous decisions, the pattern is even clearer. All five of the cases in which Rehnquist voted to uphold the First Amendment claim were unanimous decisions. As in the free press area, he voted 100% of the time to reject the constitutional claim in nonunanimous decisions.

A third category concerned content-neutral restrictions on the time, place, or manner of speech. These thirty-four decisions dealt with such issues as whether individuals have a constitutional right to distribute leaflets at a state fair, whether they have a right to post signs on their front lawns, whether the First Amendment protects a right to picket in a residential neighborhood, and whether individuals may protest near abortion clinics.[12] Justice Rehnquist voted to sustain the First Amendment claim in only three of these thirty-four cases.[13] Other Justices voted to uphold the free speech claim 64% of the time, or 7.1 times more often than Rehnquist. Again, Rehnquist voted to uphold the First Amendment claim only when the Court was unanimous. There was not a single decision in this category in which he voted to invalidate a law when any other Justice voted to uphold it.

A fourth group of decisions involved persons in a "special" relationship with the government, such as prisoners, soldiers, students, and public employees.[14] In general, the Court has held that the government may restrict the First Amendment rights of such individuals to a greater degree than it may restrict the rights of the general public. Justice Rehnquist found a First Amendment violation in ten of these thirty-six cases, whereas other Justices upheld the constitutional

---

[11] See Jenkins v. Georgia, 418 U.S. 153 (1974) (obscenity); McKinney v. Alabama, 424 U.S. 669 (1976) (obscenity procedure); Fort Wayne Books v. Indiana, 489 U.S. 46 (1989) (obscenity procedure); Sable Communications of California v. Federal Communications Commission, 492 U.S. 115 (1989) (dial-a-porn); Reno v. American Civil Liberties Union, 521 U.S. 844 (1977) (Internet).

[12] See, e.g., Grayned v. City of Rockford, 408 U.S. 104 (1972) (noise near a school); Hynes v. City of Oradell, 425 U.S. 610 (1976) (door-to-door canvassing); Members of the City Council of Los Angeles v. Taxpayers for Vincent, 466 U.S. 789 (1984) (signs on public property); Roberts v. United States Jaycees, 468 U.S. 609 (1984) (antidiscrimination law); Forsyth County, Georgia v. The Nationalist Movement, 505 U.S. 123 (1992); Cohen v. Cowles Media Company, 501 U.S. 663 (1991) (confidentiality contract); Bartnicki v. Vopper, 532 U.S. 514 (2001) (wiretapping).

[13] United States v. Grace, 461 U.S. 171 (1983) (speech near Supreme Court); Board of Airport Commissioners v. Jews for Jesus, Inc., 482 U.S. 569 (1987) (rule banning all First Amendment activity in airports); City of Ladue v. Gilleo, 512 U.S. 43 (1994) (signs on front lawn).

[14] See, e.g., Papish v. Board of Curators of University of Missouri, 410 U.S. 667 (1973) (students); Broadrick v. Oklahoma, 413 U.S. 601 (1973) (employees); Parker v. Levy, 417 U.S. 733 (1974) (military); Elrod v. Burns, 427 U.S. 347 (1976) (employees); Jones v. North Carolina Prisoners' Union, 433 U.S. 119 (1977) (prisoners); Turner v. Safley, 482 U.S. 78 (1987) (prisoners); Bethel School District v. Fraser, 478 U.S. 675 (1986) (students).

claim 64% of the time – 2.3 times more often than Rehnquist. Moreover, seven of the ten cases in this category in which Rehnquist found a violation of "the freedom of speech, or of the press" were unanimous decisions.[15]

Another category involved "government speech," such as programs granting public funds to family planning clinics that agree not to inform their patients of the right to abortion, to lawyers in legal services organizations who agree not to challenge the constitutionality of certain federal laws, or to artists who agree not to violate general standards of "decency."[16] Justice Rehnquist voted to uphold every one of these programs, whereas his colleagues voted to invalidate them 38% of the time.

A final, "catchall" category includes a broad spectrum of decisions addressing such diverse issues as flag burning,[17] subject-matter restrictions,[18] cross burning,[19] hate crimes,[20] election regulations,[21] union speech,[22] copyright,[23] passport and immigration regulations,[24] and compelled expression.[25] Although these decisions have nothing distinctively in common, they reveal a similar pattern. In only eight of these fifty-two cases, or 15%, did Rehnquist vote to uphold the constitutional

---

[15] *See* Procunier v. Martinez, 416 U.S. 396 (1974) (prisoners) (unanimous); Madison Joint School District v. Wisconsin Employment Relations Commission, 429 U.S. 167 (1976) (employees) (unanimous); Givhan v. Western Line Consolidated School District, 439 U.S. 410 (1979) (employees) (unanimous); Chicago Teachers' Union Local No. 1 v. Hudson, 475 U.S. 292 (1986) (employees) (unanimous); Keller v. State Bar of California, 496 U.S. 1 (1990) (lawyer licensing) (unanimous); Rosenberger v. Rector and Visitors of the University of Virginia, 515 U.S. 819 (1995) (students) (not unanimous); O'Hare Truck Service, Inc. v. City of Northlake, 518 U.S. 712 (1996) (independent contractors) (not unanimous); Board of County Commissioners, Wabaunsee County, Kansas v. Umbehr, 518 U.S. 668 (1996) (independent contractors) (not unanimous); Board of Regents v. Southworth, 529 U.S. 217 (2000) (students) (unanimous); Shaw v. Murphy, 532 U.S. 223 (2001) (prisoners) (unanimous).

[16] *See, e.g.,* Regan v. Taxation with Representation, 461 U.S. 540 (1983) (tax benefit for veterans' organizations); Federal Communications Commission v. League of Women's Voters, 468 U.S. 364 (1984) (public broadcasting); Rust v. Sullivan, 500 U.S. 173 (1991) (family planning counseling); National Endowment for the Arts v. Finley, 524 U.S. 569 (1998) (arts funding); Legal Services Corporation v. Velazquez, 531 U.S. 533 (2001) (legal services); United States v. American Library Association, 539 U.S. 194 (2003) (Internet support for libraries).

[17] *See, e.g.,* Spence v. Washington, 418 U.S. 504 (1974); Texas v. Johnson, 491 U.S. 397 (1989); United States v. Eichman, 486 U.S. 310 (1990).

[18] *See, e.g.,* Police Department of Chicago v. Mosley, 408 U.S. 92 (1972); Lehman v. City of Shaker Heights, 418 U.S. 298 (1974); Carey v. Brown, 447 U.S. 455 (1980).

[19] *See, e.g.,* R.A.V. v. City of St. Paul, 505 U.S. 377 (1992); Virginia v. Black, 538 U.S. 343 (1993).

[20] *See, e.g.,* Wisconsin v. Mitchell, 508 U.S. 476 (1993).

[21] *See, e.g.,* Communist Party of Indiana v. Whitcomb, 414 U.S. 441 (1974); Tashjian v. Republican Party, 479 U.S. 208 (1987); McIntyre v. Ohio Elections Commission, 514 U.S. 334 (1995).

[22] *See, e.g.,* Old Dominion Branch No. 496 v. Austin, 418 U.S. 264 (1974); National Labor Relations Board v. Retail Store Employees Local 1001, 447 U.S. 607 (1980).

[23] *See, e.g.,* Eldred v. Ashcroft, 537 U.S. 186 (2003).

[24] *See, e.g.,* Kleindeist v. Mandel, 408 U.S. 753 (1972); Haig v. Agee, 453 U.S. 280 (1981).

[25] *See, e.g.,* Wooley v. Maynard, 430 U.S. 705 (1977); PruneYard Shopping Center v. Robins, 447 U.S. 74 (1980); Pacific Gas & Electric Co. v. Public Utilities Commission of California, 475 U.S. 1 (1986).

claim.[26] His colleagues voted to sustain the First Amendment claim 50% of the time. Moreover, Rehnquist voted to invalidate the challenged law in only two of the thirty-nine nonunanimous decisions. His colleagues, on the other hand, voted to invalidate these laws 49% of the time. Thus, in these "miscellaneous" nonunanimous decisions, the other Justices were almost ten times more likely than Rehnquist to vote to invalidate restrictions on "the freedom of speech, or of the press."

The cases in these six categories comprise 82% of the Court's decisions on "the freedom of speech, or of the press" during Justice Rehnquist's tenure to date. In these 211 decisions,[27] Rehnquist voted to uphold the First Amendment claim only 14% of the time, whereas his colleagues voted to uphold the constitutional challenge 55% of the time – nearly four times more often. Moreover, in only 5 of these 211 cases did Rehnquist vote to uphold a First Amendment claim when the Court was not unanimous in the result.[28] I will return to those few decisions later.

III

Were there *any* areas of First Amendment law in which Justice Rehnquist displayed more vigor in protecting "the freedom of speech, or of the press"? In fact, there were three such areas, and they constitute the remaining 18% of the Court's decisions. These reveal quite a bit about Rehnquist's understanding of the First Amendment.

First, Rehnquist voted to sustain the First Amendment claim in ten of the Court's twenty-seven decisions involving commercial speech.[29] He was 2.6 times

---

[26] See *Mosley,* 408 U.S. 92 (1972) (subject matter) (unanimous); *Whitcomb,* 414 U.S. 441 (1974) (elections) (unanimous); NAACP v. Claiborne Hardware, 458 U.S. 886 (1982) (boycott) (unanimous); Lowe v. Securities and Exchange Commission, 472 U.S. 181 (1985) (securities regulation) (unanimous); Dawson v. Delaware, 503 U.S. 159 (1992) (introduction of evidence of hate speech) (not unanimous); *R.A.V.,* 505 U.S. 377 (1992) (cross burning) (unanimous); Republican Party v. White, 536 U.S. 765 (2002) (elections) (not unanimous); *Black,* 538 U.S. 343 (2003) (cross burning) (unanimous).

[27] The number 212 is slightly inflated because a few cases fall into two categories. For example, *Finley,* 524 U.S. 569 (1998), falls into both the sexual expression and government subsidy categories, and *PruneYard,* 447 U.S. 74 (1980), falls into both the content-neutral and compelled speech categories.

[28] See *O'Hare Truck,* 518 U.S. 712 (1996); *Umbehr,* 518 U.S. 668 (1996); Boy Scouts of America v. Dale, 530 U.S. 640 (2000); *Dawson,* 503 U.S. 159 (1992); *White,* 536 U.S. 735 (2002).

[29] This is not to say that Justice Rehnquist was particularly "activist" in these cases relative to his colleagues. During Rehnquist's tenure, the Court decided twenty-seven cases involving commercial advertising. Justice Rehnquist voted to sustain the First Amendment claim in ten, or 37%, of these cases, whereas his colleagues voted to sustain the First Amendment claim almost twice as often, or 67.9% of the time. This was largely a temporal factor. Rehnquist was slow to accept the argument that commercial advertising deserved serious First Amendment protection. But once he accepted that proposition, he became quite assertive in applying the doctrine.

more likely to invalidate laws restricting commercial advertising than laws restricting political or artistic expression. Of Rehnquist's eighteen votes in nonunanimous decisions to hold a law in violation of "the freedom of speech, or of
the press," four involved regulations of commercial advertising.[30]

A second area in which Rehnquist took a more speech-protective approach involved campaign finance regulation. In these twelve cases, he was even more "activist" than his colleagues, voting to invalidate campaign finance legislation 67%
of the time. Other Justices voted to invalidate such laws 57% of the time. Of Rehnquist's eighteen votes in nonunanimous decisions to sustain a First Amendment
claim, seven involved laws regulating political expenditures.[31]

The third area in which Rehnquist was especially solicitous of "the freedom
of speech, or of the press" concerned laws limiting religious expression. In all of
these cases, Rehnquist voted to invalidate the challenged law. Of his eighteen
votes to hold restrictions of speech unconstitutional in nonunanimous decisions,
two were in cases involving religious expression.[32]

Thus, thirteen of the eighteen nonunanimous decisions in which Rehnquist
voted to hold a law violative of "the freedom of speech, or of the press" involved
commercial advertising, campaign expenditures, or religious speech. In nonunanimous decisions in these three areas, he voted to uphold the First Amendment challenge 44% of the time. In all other nonunanimous decisions, he voted
to uphold the First Amendment claim 3% of the time. Thus, in nonunanimous
decisions, Rehnquist was 14.7 times more likely to vote to invalidate a law restricting commercial advertising, campaign expenditures, or religious expression
than one involving any other aspect of "the freedom of speech, or of the press."[33]
A cynic might say that Rehnquist's First Amendment reads, "Congress shall make
no law abridging the freedom of speech of corporations, the wealthy, or the
church." Beyond that, I can discern no unifying theory.

---

[30] *See* Zauderer v. Office of Disciplinary Counsel, 471 U.S. 626 (1985); Glickman v. Wileman Brothers
& Elliott, Inc., 512 U.S. 1145 (1997); Edenfield v. Fane, 507 U.S. 761 (1993); United States v. United
Foods, 533 U.S. 405 (2003).

[31] Buckley v. Valeo, 424 U.S. 1 (1976); Citizens Against Rent Control v. Berkeley, 454 U.S. 290 (1981);
Federal Election Commission v. National Conservative Political Action Committee, 470 U.S. 480
(1985); Colorado Republican Federal Campaign Committee v. Federal Election Commission, 518
U.S. 604 (1996); California Democratic Party v. Jones, 530 U.S. 567 (2000); Federal Election Commission v. Colorado Republican Federal Campaign Committee, 533 U.S. 431 (2001); McConnell
v. Federal Election Campaign Commission, 540 U.S. 93 (2003).

[32] *See* Widmar v. Vincent, 454 U.S. 263 (1981) (not unanimous); Lamb's Chapel v. Center Moriches
Union Free School District, 508 U.S. 384 (1993) (unanimous); and *Rosenberger*, 515 U.S. 819 (1995)
(not unanimous).

[33] Ten of the forty-two decisions in these three areas were unanimous; in fourteen of the thirty-
two nonunanimous decisions, or 43.8%, Rehnquist voted to hold the challenged law unconstitutional. There were 162 nonunanimous decisions outside these three areas; in five of these, or
3.1%, Rehnquist voted to invalidate the challenged law.

IV

This brings me back to the five nonunanimous decisions in which Rehnquist voted to invalidate a law that did *not* involve commercial advertising, campaign expenditures, or religious expression. Four of these five cases were relatively minor decisions. In *Dawson v. Delaware*,[34] the Court held 8–1 that the government could not constitutionally admit evidence of a criminal defendant's political beliefs when those beliefs were irrelevant to the crime charged. Only Justice Thomas's rather idiosyncratic dissent prevented this clearly correct decision from being unanimous.

In the companion cases of *O'Hare Truck Service, Inc. v. City of Northlake*[35] and *Board of County Commissioners v. Umbehr*,[36] Rehnquist joined the Court in holding that independent contractors, like public employees, are protected against discharge in retaliation for their speech. Scalia and Thomas dissented, in clear disregard of settled precedent. And in *Republican Party of Minnesota v. White*,[37] Rehnquist joined Scalia, Thomas, O'Connor, and Kennedy in holding unconstitutional a state law prohibiting candidates for elective judicial office from announcing their views on any issue that might come before them as judges. The disagreement among the Justices was over a narrow question concerning the relationship between the "announce" clause and the concededly constitutional prohibition on "promising" certain results.

The only *important* nonunanimous decision outside the areas of commercial advertising, campaign expenditures, and religious expression in which Justice Rehnquist voted to uphold the First Amendment claim was *Boy Scouts of America v. Dale*.[38] This decision is significant, not only because of Rehnquist's vote, but also because he wrote the opinion of the Court. During Rehnquist's tenure to date, he has written twenty-seven majority opinions concerning "the freedom of speech, or of the press." In twenty-one of these decisions, or 78%, he rejected the First Amendment claim. In the six decisions in which his majority opinion upheld the claim, the Court was unanimous in all but one – *Dale*.[39]

In *Dale,* Justice Rehnquist, joined by Scalia, Thomas, O'Connor, and Kennedy, held that the First Amendment protects the right of the Boy Scouts to exclude gay scoutmasters. Although the case involved the freedom of expressive association, it is difficult to blink the reality that the decision was more about sexual orientation than the meaning of the First Amendment. This is evident if we compare Rehnquist's position in *Dale* with his votes in similar cases.

---

[34] 503 U.S. 159 (1992).
[35] 518 U.S. 712 (1996).
[36] 518 U.S. 668 (1996).
[37] 536 U.S. 735 (2002).
[38] 530 U.S. 640 (2000).
[39] The other five were *Hustler,* 485 U.S. 46 (1988); Butterworth v. Smith, 494 U.S. 624 (1990); *Keller,* 496 U.S. 1 (1990); *Dawson,* 503 U.S. 159 (1992); and *McKinney,* 424 U.S. 669 (1976).

The New Jersey public accommodations law invalidated in *Dale* prohibited private organizations from discriminating on the basis of race, sex, religion, or sexual orientation. Because the challenged law was not directed at speech, it was a familiar type of content-neutral restriction. Over the course of his service on the Court, Rehnquist has participated in seventy-nine decisions addressing content-neutral restrictions. In seventy-one of these cases, or 90%, he voted to uphold the restriction of speech.[40] Seven of the eight decisions in which he voted to hold the law invalid were unanimous.[41] Thus, over the course of more than thirty years, the *only* nonunanimous decision in which Rehnquist voted to invalidate a content-neutral restriction was *Dale.*

The singular nature of Rehnquist's position in *Dale* becomes even clearer if we consider the decision as part of a subset of content-neutral restrictions. Because the New Jersey law was not directed at First Amendment activity, but prohibited discrimination without regard to whether the discriminator was engaged in expression, it had only an "incidental" effect on speech. This is a critical factor in the Court's analysis. As a general rule, the Court invalidates laws under the First Amendment only if they are directed at expressive activity. Laws prohibiting leafleting in airports,[42] requiring newspapers to publish replies to their editorials,[43] forbidding homeowners from posting signs on their property,[44] or obliging shopping center owners to permit protesters to distribute pamphlets[45] illustrate content-neutral laws that directly target speech.

Other laws have only an incidental effect on speech. Examples include those prohibiting public urination, as applied to a person who urinates on the Pentagon to express his opposition to a war;[46] laws forbidding public nudity, as applied to a person who walks naked down Pennsylvania Avenue to protest contemporary moral values;[47] or those that impose taxes on an individual who then has less disposable income with which to support her favorite political candidates.

---

[40] Other justices voted to uphold these laws 48.4% of the time. This group of seventy-nine cases includes the thirty-four decisions discussed earlier as content-neutral time, place, or manner restrictions plus an additional forty-five decisions that dealt with content-neutral restrictions that did not regulate the time, place, or manner of expression. Examples of the latter cases would be *Broadrick,* 413 U.S. 601 (1973); Zacchini v. Scripps-Howard Broadcasting Co., 433 U.S. 562 (1977); Regan v. Time, Inc., 468 U.S. 490 (1981); Arkansas Writers' Project v. Ragland, 481 U.S. 221 (1987); *Barnes,* 501 U.S. 560 (1991); Leathers v. Medlock, 499 U.S. 439 (1991); *Bartnicki,* 532 U.S. 514 (2001); *Cohen,* 501 U.S. 663 (1991); and *Mitchell,* 508 U.S. 476 (1993).

[41] The seven unanimous decisions were *Grace,* 461 U.S. 171 (1983); Press-Enterprise Co. v. Superior Court, 464 U.S. 501 (1984); *Jews for Jesus,* 482 U.S. 569 (1987); Meyer v. Grant, 486 U.S. 414 (1988); *Ladue,* 512 U.S. 43 (1994); Hurley v. Irish-American Gay, Lesbian and Bisexual Group of Boston, 515 U.S. 557 (1995); *Southworth,* 529 U.S. 217 (2000).

[42] International Society of Krishna Consciousness v. Lee, 505 U.S. 672 (1992).

[43] *Miami Herald,* 418 U.S. 241 (1974).

[44] *Ladue,* 512 U.S. 43 (1994).

[45] *PruneYard,* 447 U.S. 74 (1980).

[46] *Cf.* United States v. O'Brien, 391 U.S. 367 (1968).

[47] *Cf. Barnes,* 501 U.S. 560 (1991).

Because almost every law can incidentally interfere with *someone's* preferred means of expression, the Court almost never invalidates laws on this basis. On the rare occasion when it does so, it is because the incidental impact of the law is extremely severe. In *NAACP v. Alabama*,[48] for example, the Court considered the constitutionality of an Alabama statute requiring all out-of-state organizations operating in Alabama to disclose the names of their Alabama members. The Court held that, in light of the tense circumstances of the civil rights movement in the South in the late 1950s, including a long history of instances in which the "revelation of the identity" of NAACP members had resulted in "economic reprisal, loss of employment, threat of physical coercion, and other manifestations of public hostility," the compelled disclosure of NAACP membership lists would inevitably "induce members to withdraw . . . and dissuade others from joining . . . because of fear of exposure."[49] In such circumstances, the Court held that the state's interest in knowing the names of the NAACP's members was not sufficiently weighty to justify the crippling effect that disclosure would have on First Amendment rights. The Court therefore held the law unconstitutional as applied to the NAACP.[50]

During his tenure, Justice Rehnquist has consistently rejected the idea that a law could be unconstitutional because of its incidental effect on First Amendment rights.[51] But in *Dale*, he failed even to acknowledge the issue. Given the result he reached, this was not surprising. Whatever else one might say about the Boy Scouts, it certainly is not a political organization analogous to the NAACP, and whatever else one might say about the effect of the New Jersey law on the Boy Scouts, it is not even remotely analogous to the impact of the Alabama law on the NAACP. Indeed, given the Court's consistent and generally well-founded reluctance to invalidate laws having only an incidental effect on speech, it seemed quite unlikely that the Court would invalidate the law in *Dale*, and nothing short of implausible that Rehnquist would vote to support that result – let alone write the opinion.

Moreover, in a series of decisions prior to *Dale*, Rehnquist consistently rejected First Amendment claims almost identical to those in *Dale* itself. In *Roberts v. U.S. Jaycees*,[52] for example, the Court upheld a Minnesota law, prohibiting dis-

---

[48] 357 U.S. 449 (1958).

[49] *Id.* at 462.

[50] Similarly, in Brown v. Socialist Workers '74 Campaign Committee, 459 U.S. 87 (1982), the Court held that the disclosure provisions of the Ohio campaign reporting law could not constitutionally be applied to the Socialist Workers Party, "a minor party which historically has been the object of harassment by government officials and private parties." *Id.* at 89.

[51] *See, e.g.*, Wayte v. United States, 470 U.S. 598 (1985) (selective service enforcement); United States v. Albertini, 477 U.S. 675 (1985) (access to military base); Acara v. Cloud Books, 478 U.S. 697 (1986) (zoning against prostitution); Board of Directors of Rotary International v. Rotary Club of Duarte, 481 U.S. 537 (1987) (antidiscrimination law); New York State Club Association, Inc. v. City of New York, 487 U.S. 1 (1988) (antidiscrimination law); Barnes v. Glen Theatre, Inc., 501 U.S. 560 (1991) (public nudty); City of Erie v. Pap's A.M., 529 U.S. 277 (2000) (public nudity).

[52] 468 U.S. 609 (1984).

crimination on the basis of sex, as applied to an organization whose objective was to provide young men with an opportunity for personal development and achievement. Although a significant part of the Jaycees' activities involved expression about political, social, economic, and cultural affairs, the Court unanimously held that the antidiscrimination law would not sufficiently impede the Jaycess' First Amendment activities to render the act unlawful as applied, particularly because it "does not aim at the suppression of speech."[53] With Justice Rehnquist's unvarying support, the Court unanimously reached similar results in a long line of other pre-*Dale* decisions.[54]

Dale was an easy case. The challenged law was not directed at speech. Although it had some incidental effect on the desire of the Boy Scouts to do as they pleased, the impact was unexceptional. *Dale* was much more like *Roberts* than like *NAACP v. Alabama.* In assessing Rehnquist's performance in *Dale,* it is enlightening to recall that *Dale* was the *only* important nonunanimous decision outside the areas of commercial advertising, campaign finance reform, and religious expression in which Rehnquist has *ever* voted to uphold a First Amendment claim. It is more than a little revealing, and more than a little unsettling, that Rehnquist suddenly discovered the power of the First Amendment in a case invalidating a law designed to protect gays and lesbians against discrimination.

V

What all this leads me to conclude is that Justice Rehnquist's record with respect to "the freedom of speech, or of the press" has been quite dismal. Not only has he been the Justice least likely to protect these freedoms, but his general "passivity" cannot be defended as principled, coherent, or even-handed. His inclination to sustain First Amendment claims *only* when they involve commercial advertising, campaign expenditures, religious expression, or the right of the Boy Scouts to exclude homosexuals belies any plausible theory of originalism, judicial restraint, or principled constitutional interpretation.

This is not to say, by the way, that Rehnquist was "wrong" to protect commercial advertising, campaign expenditures, or religious speech. It is certainly possible to articulate a reasonable theory of the First Amendment that protects such expression. But there is *no* coherent theory of the First Amendment – or of the Court's docket, precedents, or jurisprudence – that can possibly justify his willingness to protect those forms of expression at the same time that he has shown nothing short of indifference to almost every other claim to the protection of "the freedom of speech, or of the press."

[53] *Id.* at 623.

[54] *See Rotary,* 481 U.S. 537 (1987); *New York State Club Ass'n,* 487 U.S. 1 (1988). The Court has invalidated compelled association in circumstances in which the law directly (rather than incidentally) regulates expression and the affected organizations were political parties. *See Jones,* 530 U.S. 567 (2000) (holding that a state may not permit individuals who are not members of a political party to vote in that party's primary.)

Nonetheless, it would be inaccurate for me to leave the impression that in his more than thirty years on the Court Justice Rehnquist has not left *any* positive mark on the law of the First Amendment. To the contrary, in the 259 cases involving "the freedom of speech, or the press" in which he has participated, he did write one opinion that both embraced a strong free speech stance and will stand the test of time as a significant contribution to our First Amendment jurisprudence.

Perhaps ironically, in this opinion Justice Rehnquist held that the First Amendment protected the speech of Larry Flynt, the publisher of *Hustler* magazine. An issue of *Hustler* included a parody of the once-popular Campari ads that employed a not-so-subtle double entendre about one's "first time." The mock ad portrayed the Rev. Jerry Falwell as having lost his virginity in a drunken, incestuous rendezvous with his mother in an outhouse. Falwell sued Flynt for intentional infliction of emotional distress. Although conceding that the parody contained no false statement of fact that any reasonable person could believe to be true, the lower courts ruled that Falwell could recover damages for the intentional infliction of emotional distress because of the "outrageous" nature of the parody. The Supreme Court reversed in a unanimous opinion written by Justice Rehnquist.[55]

In the critical passage of this opinion, Rehnquist strung together a chain of quotations from seven noteworthy Supreme Court opinions, all written by other Justices. These quotations articulated central insights about "the freedom of speech, or of the press." For example: "The freedom to speak one's mind is not only an aspect of individual liberty – and thus a good unto itself – but also is essential to the common quest for truth and the vitality of society as a whole."[56] "One of the prerogatives of American citizenship is the right to criticize public men and measures."[57] In robust political debate, public figures and public officials will inevitably be subject to "vehement, caustic, and sometimes unpleasantly sharp attacks."[58] And, most famously, "when men have realized that time has upset many fighting faiths, they may come to believe even more than they believe the very foundations of their own conduct that the ultimate good is better reached by free trade in ideas – that the best test of truth is the power of the thought to get itself accepted in the competition of the market."[59] This is heady stuff for a Justice with Rehnquist's voting record in First Amendment cases, and it is no wonder he was unable to state any of these points in his own words.

Rehnquist next turned to Falwell's argument that the Court should distinguish Flynt's mock Campari ad from constitutionally protected speech because of its "outrageousness." Rehnquist rejected this contention, explaining that the concept

---

[55] *Hustler*, 485 U.S. 46 (1988).

[56] Bose Corp. v. Consumers Union of United States, Inc., 466 U.S. 485, 503–04 (1984).

[57] Baumgartner v. United States, 322 U.S. 665, 673–74 (1944).

[58] New York Times v. Sullivan, 376 U.S. 254, 270 (1964).

[59] Abrams v. United States, 250 U.S. 616, 630 (1919) (Holmes, J., dissenting).

of outrageousness "has an inherent subjectiveness about it which would allow a jury to impose liability on the basis of the jurors' tastes or views, or perhaps on the basis of the dislike of a particular expression."[60] Such a standard, he opined, would run "afoul of our longstanding refusal to allow damages to be awarded because the speech in question may have an adverse emotional impact on the audience."[61]

One might reasonably wonder why Justice Rehnquist waxed so eloquent about this "longstanding" principle in *Hustler.* After all, in case after case, both before and after this decision, he has shown no inclination to invoke this principle in other First Amendment contexts. In *Federal Communications Commission v. Pacifica Foundation,*[62] for example, he voted to uphold an FCC regulation of "indecent" language, even as applied to a political parody of such regulations. In *Young v. American Mini-Theatres,*[63] he voted to uphold a city zoning ordinance that dispersed movie theaters exhibiting movies that depicted "Specified Sexual Activities." And in *National Endowment for the Arts v. Finley,*[64] he voted to uphold a federal statute directing the NEA to take "general standards of decency" into account in awarding artistic grants. Although each of these cases is distinguishable from *Hustler,* in none of them, nor in any other decision, has Rehnquist expressed any concern about "inherent subjectiveness" or the risk that inherently subjective standards might be applied on the basis of the regulators' or jurors' "tastes or views, or perhaps on the basis of the dislike of a particular expression."

Rehnquist next turned to the history of political cartoons. Extolling the work of such distinguished satirists as Thomas Nast and Walt McDougal, Rehnquist observed that "our political discourse would have been considerably poorer without them."[65] He then went on at some length to describe the often cruel nature of such parody:[66]

> The appeal of the political cartoon or caricature is often based on exploitation of unfortunate physical traits or politically embarrassing events – an exploitation often calculated to injure the feelings of the subject of the portrayal. The art of the cartoonist is often not reasoned or evenhanded, but slashing and one-sided. One cartoonist expressed the nature of the art is these words: "The political cartoon is a weapon of attack, of scorn and ridicule and satire. . . ."

Against this background, Rehnquist concluded that "public figures and public officials may not recover for the tort of intentional infliction of emotional distress by reason" of the asserted "outrageousness" of a publication.[67]

Hustler is an important First Amendment decision that teaches an invaluable lesson, and in this opinion Rehnquist boldly defended a core free speech prin-

---

[60] 485 U.S., at 53.   [61] *Id.*
[62] 438 U.S. 726 (1978).   [63] 427 U.S. 50 (1976).
[64] 524 U.S. 569 (1998).   [65] 485 U.S., at 55.
[66] *Id.* at 54, quoting Long, *The Political Cartoon: Journalism's Strongest Weapon,* The Quill 56, 57 (Nov. 1962).
[67] *Id.* at 56.

ciple in an area far removed from the First Amendment questions that usually caught his fancy. Why? One explanation, of course, may be that this was simply an easy case. It was, after all, a unanimous decision. But, in fact, it seems easy only *after* the fact. When the case was pending, there was much speculation and uncertainty about the likely outcome. The lower courts had both held in favor of Falwell, and it seemed certain that Rehnquist would side with him as well. Indeed, as one commentator has noted, "[c]lose students of Rehnquist's writing counted him a sure vote for Falwell," and "after the opinion was released, First Amendment lawyers in Washington walked around shaking their heads in amazement – not because of the outcome, but because the decision was unanimous and Rehnquist [had written so strong an] opinion."[68] Certainly, the passion of Rehnquist's defense of the First Amendment in *Hustler* was strikingly out of tune with his general approach to the First Amendment. One suspects that something else must have been afoot. But what could it have been?

Professor Rodney Smolla has speculated that Justice Rehnquist was sympathetic to Flynt's position because he "likes to laugh." According to Smolla, Rehnquist likes to poke fun "at himself," is an inveterate practical joker, and could do an unforgettable imitation of Adolf Hitler. As Smolla put it, although "everything in William Rehnquist's judicial philosophy pointed toward a vote for Falwell, there was always the possibility that the *Hustler* ad [would appeal] to the joker in [Rehnquist] and that he [would treat] it as merely part of what a famous person must endure."[69]

That may seem pretty lame, but Smolla was actually on to something. In his book on the Rehnquist Court, David Savage sharpened the point. Savage observed that Rehnquist not only had a sense of humor, but "absolutely delighted in political cartoons," especially those that deflated "pompous politicians." Indeed, as far back as high school, Rehnquist had been known to mock "the self-important tone used by the eminent radio commentators of the day."[70] Completing the puzzle, in a marvelous bit of detection, Roger Newman recently took the trouble to consult William Rehnquist's high school yearbook, which briefly but tellingly noted, "The favorite pastime of Bill, in and out of school, is cartooning."[71]

And so, Justice Rehnquist's one great First Amendment opinion is a Rosebud. Of course, this is not a phenomenon unique to Rehnquist. Other Justices have been affected by their life experiences. Justice Stewart was thought to be sensitive to free press issues because of his years as a student journalist at Yale. Justice Blackmun's position on abortion was thought to be shaped by his work as house counsel for the Mayo Clinic. Justice Brennan's empathy for the labor movement

---

[68] David G. Savage, *Turning Right: The Making of the Rehnquist Supreme Court* 159, 162 (1992).
[69] Rodney A. Smolla, *Jerry Falwell v. Larry Flynt: The First Amendment on Trial* 253–54 (1988).
[70] Savage, *supra* note 68, at 160.
[71] Roger K. Newman, *Original Sin and Original Intent: Interpreting the Constitution* (April 1, 2004) (unpublished manuscript).

and distrust of the police grew in part out of his father's experiences as a labor organizer in Newark. And Justice Marshall's approach to constitutional law was surely shaped by his experience as an African American and by his work with the NAACP.

In the case of Justice Rehnquist, however, one might have hoped he would have drawn a somewhat broader lesson about the central meaning of the First Amendment than that it can be invoked in the interest of protecting cartoons. Had he done so, he might have left a more meaningful legacy in this area of the law.

CHAPTER TWO

LESS IS MORE: JUSTICE REHNQUIST, THE FREEDOM OF SPEECH, AND DEMOCRACY

Richard W. Garnett

I

With time or overuse, even the most spot-on insight can degrade to a tired cliché or shopworn truism. That said, Tocqueville was right: In the United States, sooner or later, almost every interesting or controversial question becomes a legal one.[1] What's more, a present-day Tocqueville might add, it seems that all of the *really* interesting or controversial problems are eventually packaged by creative litigants in free speech terms. As a result, the First Amendment's Free Speech Clause – "Congress shall make no law . . . abridging the freedom of speech" – now occupies much of the field of our public debates on matters of law, policy, and morality. This "free speech takeover" of public discourse has been one of the more striking and significant developments during William H. Rehnquist's long tenure on the Supreme Court.

Now, the point here is not merely to rehash the complaint that certain forms of once outcast, low-value expression – pornography, commercial advertising, defamation, and so on – have come to enjoy First Amendment protection.[2] The free speech takeover has been more dramatic, and more interesting, than just that. Today, in the courts of both law and public opinion, arguments about a huge range of human activities – from cutting-edge scientific research to legal aid work to beef promotion to foul-mouthed cheering at basketball games – are constructed using First Amendment premises, precedents, and jar-

---

[1] ALEXIS DE TOCQUEVILLE, DEMOCRACY IN AMERICA 257 (Harvey C. Mansfield & Delba Winthrop eds., 2000) (1835) ("There is almost no political question in the United States that is not resolved sooner or later into a judicial question."). *See also id.* at 93 ("There is . . . no political event in which [one] does not hear the authority of the judge invoked[.]").

[2] *See, e.g.,* Miller v. California, 413 U.S. 15 (1973) (nonobscene, sexually explicit expression is constitutionally protected speech); Virginia State Bd. of Pharmacy v. Virginia Citizens Consumer Council, Inc., 425 U.S. 748 (1976) (commercial advertising is protected by First Amendment); New York Times v. Sullivan, 376 U.S. 254 (1964) (reversing money damages award to a public official for defamatory falsehood relating to official conduct).

gon.[3] The Supreme Court's First Amendment doctrines have invited and also, in turn, been shaped by this tendency to transpose our conversations about things that matter into a free speech key.

It is fair to say that Chief Justice Rehnquist has resisted, or at least regretted, this tendency. (In Chapter 1, Professor Geoffrey Stone concludes that "[d]uring the course of his tenure, Justice Rehnquist has been, by an impressive margin, the member of the Supreme Court *least* likely to invalidate a law" on free speech grounds.)[4] For example, in 1976, when the Justices switched course and extended the First Amendment's protections to commercial advertising, he chided his colleagues for second-guessing duly enacted economic regulations, insisting that "in a democracy, the economic is subordinate to the political."[5] He highlighted what was, for him, a "troublesome" implication of this extension, namely, that it invited free speech claimants to seek constitutional review of "legislative determinations." Just a few years later, Rehnquist dissented from the Court's ruling striking down certain restrictions on election-related speech and spending by corporations, insisting that "a corporation is an artificial being, invisible, intangible, and existing only in contemplation of law" and, therefore, does not necessarily enjoy "the right of political expression."[6] And in *Texas v. Johnson*, the flag-burning case, he again insisted in dissent that flag burning should be regarded as "the equivalent of an inarticulate grunt or roar" rather than an "essential part of any exposition of ideas."[7]

But it would be a mistake to chalk up Justice Rehnquist's views in these and other free speech cases simply to an unyielding deference to legislative majorities, a law-and-order disposition, or midwestern reserve. Nor is it clear that, as Professor Stone charges, his record cannot be explained or justified in terms of any

---

[3] *See, e.g.,* Roy G. Spence, Jr., & Jennifer Weinzier, *First Amendment Protection of Experimentation,* 8 S. CAL. INTERDISC. L.J. 185 (1998); Legal Services Corp. v. Velazquez, 531 U.S. 533 (2001) (First Amendment protects government-funded legal aid attorneys' advocacy); Livestock Marketing Ass'n v. U.S. Dep't of Agriculture, 335 F.3d 711 (8th Cir. 2003) (considering First Amendment challenge to statutorily mandated assessments in beef promotion campaign); Howard M. Wasserman, *Cheers, Profanity, and Free Speech,* 31 J.C. & U.L. 377 (2005). *See generally, e.g.,* Frederick Schauer, *Must Speech Be Special?,* 78 NW. U. L. REV. 1284, 1288 (1983) ("[R]ecent developments have made First Amendment considerations applicable to issues that in the recent past were considered well without the boundaries of the First Amendment. Moreover, for every instance of judicial broadening of the First Amendment, there seem to be at least ten attempts in the academic literature to have the First Amendment swallow up one more segment of society or of governmental action.").

[4] Geoffrey R. Stone, The Hustler: *Justice Rehnquist and "The Freedom of Speech, or of the Press,"* Chapter 1 in the present volume, 13 (claiming also [12] that "relative to his colleagues, Justice Rehnquist was no friend of the First Amendment").

[5] *Virginia Pharmacy, supra* note 2 (Rehnquist, J., dissenting).

[6] First Nat'l Bank of Boston v. Bellotti, 435 U.S. 765 (1978) (Rehnquist, J., dissenting) (quoting Dartmouth College v. Woodward, 4 Wheat. 518 [1819]).

[7] Texas v. Johnson, 491 U.S. 397 (1989) (Rehnquist, J., dissenting).

"plausible" or "coherent theory of the First Amendment."[8] In fact, Rehnquist's decisions and disposition in First Amendment cases reveal an instructive appreciation for the fact that the expansion of constitutionalized free speech rights and the accompanying translation, or reduction, of so many policy questions to free speech problems have come at a cost.[9] Of course, it is almost *always* costly to recognize and protect constitutional and human rights; we do so anyway, not because rights are painless, but because we think it is *worth* the price – the inefficiencies, the offense, the occasional lost conviction, and so on – in order to signify and advance our commitments to human dignity and democratic government. Perhaps it is a bit tightfisted, then, for Rehnquist to drag his feet while the Court and the culture steadily push back the free speech frontier? After all, what could be wrong with more expression, more rights, more freedom?

Just this, Rehnquist might say: "Sometimes, more is less."[10] As the civic, social, and political territory controlled by the Free Speech Clause grows, the amount shrinks that is governed democratically by the people and their representatives or that is left under the direction of private persons, groups, and institutions. That is, one implication of the free speech takeover is that difficult policy decisions depend increasingly on judges' evaluation of the abstract weight or worthiness of the government's interests rather than on deliberation, compromise, and trial and error in the public and political arenas. Moreover, Rehnquist's reasonably consistent aversion to this result is of a piece with a theory of the First Amendment specifically, and of the Constitution generally, that is coherent, plausible, and normatively attractive.[11] This chapter is an effort to flesh out these claims by focusing on just a few of Chief Justice Rehnquist's free speech opinions.

II

When paying light-hearted tribute to the Court's nonblockbuster decisions, Chief Justice Rehnquist has been known to reference Thomas Gray's *Elegy Written in a Country Churchyard* to describe each term's sleeper cases as "flowers which are born to blush unseen and waste their sweetness on the desert air."[12] This chapter focuses primarily on Rehnquist's majority opinions in *Rust v. Sullivan*,[13] *International Society for Krishna Consciousness v. Lee*,[14] and *United States v. American*

---

[8] Stone, *supra* note 4, at 21.

[9] *See generally* MARY ANN GLENDON, RIGHTS TALK: THE IMPOVERISHMENT OF POLITICAL DISCOURSE (1991).

[10] *Cf.* Philip Hamburger, *More Is Less*, 90 VA. L. REV. 835 (2004). Professor Hamburger observes, with respect to the First Amendment's Free Exercise Clause, that "expanded definitions of rights" can result in "diminished access" to them.

[11] *See* William H. Rehnquist, *The Notion of a Living Constitution*, 54 TEX. L. REV. 693 (1976).

[12] *See* Jennifer Myers, *No Talk of Retirement at Circuit Meeting*, LEGAL TIMES, July 9, 2001, at 8.

[13] 500 U.S. 173 (1991).

[14] 505 U.S. 672 (1992). *See also* Lee v. International Society for Krishna Consciousness, 505 U.S. 830 (1992).

Library Association, Inc.,[15] three decisions that, while not exactly unseen blushing flowers, are also unlikely to fire up the pundits or take center stage in scholarly discussions of his work and legacy. As the foregoing observations suggest, however, they feature themes that go to the heart of Rehnquist's judicial philosophy and constitutional vision.

These cases involve the often hazy line between government speech and spending, on the one hand, and government-facilitated or -subsidized private speech, on the other. Indeed, some of the more difficult questions in contemporary First Amendment law sit at the intersection of the Supreme Court's public forum and government speech doctrines. It makes sense, then, to first set the stage, put the cases in context, and outline the basics.[16]

As Rehnquist once put it, "we start with first principles."[17] Accordingly, it is essential to remember that the First Amendment is a constraint on the acts and aims of federal government (extended to states via the Fourteenth). True, it expresses deep commitments and reflects fundamental values, but it does so by regulating government action: Again, "Congress shall make no law. . . ." It is important, then, to appreciate that governments act in all kinds of ways and in a variety of capacities. Public officials enact and enforce criminal statutes, run jails and courts, operate schools and hospitals, hire and fire millions of people, conduct medical research and assemble football teams, sponsor advertisements and monuments, manage parks and forests, build roads and office buildings, sort and deliver mail, collect taxes and disburse benefits, raise armies and fight wars.

As Rehnquist emphasized thirty years ago, the particular constraints the First Amendment imposes on government activities will vary, depending on the capacity – regulator, subsidizer, property manager, employer, and so forth – in which the government acts.[18] The Supreme Court's free speech doctrine makes it easier for government to, say, control protests in government buildings or to regulate what teachers say in the classrooms of public elementary schools than to prosecute newspaper publishers for hostile editorials. The rules that apply to an official's decision to fire a public employee for her outrageous or offensive comments are not the same as those that apply to an effort to criminalize such comments. And, generally speaking, these distinctions make sense: Some kinds of speech-affecting government action pose a greater threat to, or impose more severe burdens upon, the core of the "freedom of speech" than others do.[19]

---

[15] 539 U.S. 194 (2003).
[16] For a helpful overview of these doctrines, see EUGENE VOLOKH, THE FIRST AMENDMENT: PROBLEMS, CASES, AND POLICY ARGUMENTS (2001).
[17] United States v. Lopez, 514 U.S. 549 (1995).
[18] Buckley v. Valeo, 424 U.S. 1 (1976) (Rehnquist, J., concurring in part and dissenting in part) ("The limits imposed by the First and Fourteenth Amendments on governmental action may vary in their stringency depending on the capacity in which the government is acting.").
[19] *See generally, e.g.,* Robert C. Post, *Between Governance and Management: The History and Theory of the Public Forum,* 34 UCLA L. REV. 1713 (1987).

The Court's "public forum" doctrine is designed to address those situations where the government is acting in a managerial, rather than a regulatory, capacity, with respect to parks, government buildings, sidewalks, or even a public university's Student Activities Fund.[20] The basic idea here is fairly straightforward: "[I]t is . . . well settled that the government need not permit all forms of speech on property that it owns and controls," Chief Justice Rehnquist wrote in the *Krishna Consciousness* case. And "[w]hen the government is acting as a proprietor, managing its internal operations, rather than acting as a lawmaker . . . , its action will not be subjected to the heightened review to which its actions as a lawmaker may be subject." In other words, the freedom of speech means something different, and has different implications, in situations where the government is managing public property than when it is legislating and regulating more generally.

Things are complicated somewhat, though, by the fact that the permissibility of efforts to manage speech on public property depends in part on the classification of the specific property or "forum" at issue. Not all "state action" is the same, for First Amendment purposes, nor are all "public forums" the same: There are "traditional" public forums, "designated" or "limited" public forums, and "nonpublic" forums. In a nutshell, the more open the forum, the less proprietary or managerial leeway the government has. And so, in a case involving a challenge to an official's managerial decision about speech – for example, "no political or religious advertisements on the side of a city bus" – a lot can turn on the place of the forum at issue in the free speech pecking order.[21] Public parks and sidewalks are fairly easy to classify as traditional public forums because they have, in the Court's words, "immemorially been held in trust for the use of the public and, time out of mind, have been used for purposes of assembly, communicating thoughts between citizens, and discussing public questions."[22] But when the case involves a university bulletin board, specialty license plates, a televised candidate debate, or funding for the arts, it can be difficult to identify, let alone to classify, the forum.

Because, as was just noted, the principal work of the First Amendment is to constrain government action, protecting speech *by* the government is not, strictly speaking, the Free Speech Clause's concern.[23] Still, the government does, may, and must "speak" all the time. This speech includes more than speed-limit signs or pamphlets describing the National Parks. Governments also take stands and take sides; they both participate in and powerfully shape our conversations and

---

[20] *See* Rosenberger v. Rector and Visitors of the University of Virginia, 515 U.S. 819 (1995) (University's Student Activities Fund is a "metaphysical" designated public forum).

[21] *See* Children of the Rosary v. City of Phoenix, 154 F.3d 972 (9th Cir. 1998).

[22] Hague v. Committee for Industrial Organization, 307 U.S. 496 (1939).

[23] *Cf.* Columbia Broadcasting System, Inc. v. Democratic National Committee, 412 U.S. 94 (Stewart, J., concurring) ("The First Amendment protects the press *from* governmental interference; it confers no analogous protection *on* the government.").

commitments.[24] They oppose smoking, support recycling, celebrate democracy, commemorate fallen soldiers, urge people to help tsunami victims, and encourage family dinners.[25] Though some libertarian purists might regret it, there's no getting around the fact that governments are – by virtue of their speaking, subsidizing, facilitating, *and* regulating – influential players in the "marketplace of ideas" as well as in the economic markets.

The government speaks directly, through public officials, but also indirectly. It frequently does this by, in effect, subcontracting out its message to third parties, whose agreed-to job then becomes getting the government's word out into the marketplace of ideas. For instance, a struggling Rust Belt town might pay graphic designers and consultants to put out flashy promotional materials touting the town's until-now unappreciated status as "Gateway to" a slightly more attractive place. No First Amendment red flags should go up if the government, like any other advertising customer, insists on controlling the content of the speech produced by its more creative subcontractors. In other words, a government may, in a sense, regulate those through whom it speaks, precisely because it is the *government's* message that the government is funding. No one would think that an author was censoring a publisher if she demanded that it publish her words between the covers of what purports to be her book; similarly, it is not constitutionally suspect for the government to tell the advertising agency that is awarded the Smokey the Bear account that its task is to fight forest fires, not to campaign for drug legalization.[26]

Careful distinctions are required, however, between officials' efforts to control the government's *own* messages and attempts to regulate the expression and messages of others. This line drawing is harder than it might sound, in part because both kinds of state action will often take the form of public spending. When money exits the public treasury and – eventually – pays for expression, it is not always easy to tell whether the government is speaking, subcontracting, or subsidizing. Cash flow from government accounts tends to look the same, whether it is going to the budget of the Government Printing Office, which produced the widely read *9/11 Commission Report;* or paying an advertising agency to "get out the government's message" about smoking or reading to children; or supporting struggling artists; or keeping up the gazebo and bandstand at a public park. The government "speaks" by and through spending public money, but obviously, not

---

24 *See generally, e.g.,* Richard W. Garnett, *Assimilation, Toleration, and the State's Interest in the Development of Religious Doctrine,* 51 UCLA L. Rev. 1645 (2004).

25 For a fascinating discussion of the ways that governments and communities speak through public commemorations, *see* SANFORD LEVINSON, WRITTEN IN STONE: PUBLIC MONUMENTS IN CHANGING SOCIETIES (1998).

26 *See, e.g.,* National Endowment for the Arts v. Finley, 524 U.S. 569 (1998) (Souter, J., dissenting) ("[I]f the Food and Drug Administration launches an advertising campaign on the subject of smoking, it may condemn the habit without also having to show a cowboy taking a puff on the opposite page; and if the Secretary of Defense wishes to buy a portrait to decorate the Pentagon, he is free to prefer George Washington over George the Third.").

every expression-facilitating disbursal of public funds is or should be treated like "government speech."

To sum up: The key to the public forum doctrine is the idea that the *classification* of public property – from parks to Web sites to legal aid funding – determines the standards that constrain government efforts to regulate private expression on such property. The government has more leeway when managing its own speech-related affairs than when managing others'. In the government speech context, the central point is that government is permitted to participate in the marketplace of ideas, to have a point of view, and to advance a position. The challenge, then, lies in differentiating spending or actions that facilitate the government's own speech from those that create public forums or subsidize private expression. This distinction matters because, generally speaking, the government may "say" whatever it wants. It does not have to be "neutral" or "even-handed"; it can be as partisan and biased as it likes. "When the State is the speaker," the Court has made clear, "it may make content-based choices."[27] But again, this does not mean that government may regulate or otherwise control the expression of others – even on public property and even when that expression is supported by public money – merely to suit the government's purposes or preferences.

III

The just-mentioned forum classification problem was front and center in *International Society for Krishna Consciousness v. Lee.*[28] The Port Authority of New York and New Jersey had adopted a rule banning "the repetitive solicitation of money or distribution of literature" in parts of the terminals at the La Guardia, Kennedy, and Newark airports. Members of the society, however, complained that this rule hampered their ability to engage in *sankirtan,* a religious ritual that happened to involve precisely what the rule prohibited – namely, the solicitation of money for the Krishna Consciousness movement and the distribution of religious literature.

Everyone agreed that these activities were "speech" protected by the First Amendment. Accordingly, the task for the Justices was to clarify the content and implications of this protection, to identify those limits that the Free Speech Clause imposed on the Port Authority's ability to regulate such conduct, and then to determine whether those limits had been violated.

The first and fundamental step, then, was to classify the relevant public property – that is, the airport terminals. Again, as Rehnquist emphasized at the outset of his majority opinion, "the government need not permit all forms of speech on property that it owns and controls. . . . Where the government is acting as a

[27] *Rosenberger, supra* note 20.
[28] 505 U.S. 672 (1992).

proprietor . . . , rather than acting as lawmaker . . . , its actions will not be subjected to the heightened review to which its actions as a lawmaker may be subject." Instead, the height of the constitutional bar that the Port Authority's regulation had to clear depended on what *kind* of forum its airport terminals were. If the terminals were "traditional" public forums – that is, "property that has traditionally been available for public expression" – then the restrictions on *sankirtan*-type activities would be difficult to justify. Speech controls in "designated" public forums – "property that the State has opened up for expressive activity by part or all of the public" – also trigger fairly exacting (though not *quite* as exacting) judicial scrutiny.[29] Finally, with respect to other public properties, or "nonpublic" forums, the First Amendment imposes only a very deferential standard of "reasonableness" and viewpoint neutrality.

Rehnquist and his dissenting colleagues in *Krishna Consciousness* agreed on this framework. They disagreed, though, about how to apply it to the airport terminals (and also, at the next step in the analysis, about the reasonableness of the restrictions). For the Chief Justice, these public spaces are less like streets and parks – places that have, as a "principal purpose . . . the free exchange of ideas" – than they are like a municipal office building or other location with a specific, relatively narrow, nonspeech purpose. Airport terminals have not, in Justice Robert Jackson's words from a half-century before, "immemorially been held in trust for the use of the public" and have not, "time out of mind, . . . been used for purposes of assembly, communicating thoughts between citizens, and discussing public questions." Quite the contrary: "[A]irport terminals have only recently achieved their contemporary size and character." They have not "historically been made available for speech activity[,]" nor have they been "intentionally opened by their operators" for speech and solicitation. Airports, at the end of the day, "are commercial establishments funded by user fees and designed to make a regulated profit"; their purpose and traditional use is "the facilitation of passenger air travel, not the promotion of expression." And because the terminals qualify neither as traditional or designated public forums, the Port Authority's restrictions "need only satisfy a requirement of reasonableness," and they did.[30]

The *Krishna Consciousness* case illustrated the importance to First Amendment analysis of classifying the forum (if any) at issue. *Rust v. Sullivan*,[31] by contrast, highlights the significance of the lines between the government as regulator, the government as subsidizer, and the government as speaker. In *Rust*, the rule that

---

[29] "The necessities of confining a [designated] forum to the limited and legitimate purposes for which it was created may justify the State in reserving it for certain groups or for the discussion of certain topics." *Rosenberger, supra* note 20.

[30] The Court was badly and confusingly divided on the question whether the Port Authority's regulations of solicitation and literature distribution satisfied the relevant constitutional standards. A majority agreed that the ban on solicitation was permissible; but a different majority invalidated the leafleting prohibition.

[31] *Supra* note 13.

the government, when funding its own message, may regulate its speech sub-contractors in order to preserve that message, bumped up against the equally well established public forum principle that, even in the context of public property, the government's ability to leverage its control over the forum into control over private conversations and expression is limited by the First Amendment.

The dispute in *Rust* involved Title X of the Public Health Service Act of 1970. Title X provided, among other things, federal funding for family-planning services. The act also made it clear, though, that "none of the[se] funds . . . shall be used in programs where abortion is a method of family planning." In 1988, new regulations from the Department of Health and Human Services were put in place, to provide "clear and operational guidance" to funding recipients "about how to preserve the distinction between Title X programs and abortion as a method of family planning." In brief, the new regulations declared, *first,* that family-planning projects receiving federal funds "may not provide counseling concerning the use of abortion as a method of family planning" (the so-called gag rule); *second,* that such projects could not engage in activities that "encourage, promote or advocate abortion as a method of family planning" (e.g., pro-abortion rights lobbying or litigation); and *third,* that Title X projects must be organized so that they are "physically and financially separate," and have an "objective integrity and independence," from prohibited abortion-related activities.

Soon after these new regulations were announced, a group of doctors and Title X grantees challenged the rules' constitutional validity. They argued, among other things, that the constraints on grantees violated the First Amendment rights of Title X clients and providers by "impermissibly imposing viewpoint-discriminatory conditions on government subsidies."[32] The conditions were "viewpoint-discriminatory," the challengers contended, because "Title X continues to fund speech ancillary to pregnancy testing in a manner that is not even-handed with respect to views and information about abortion" and therefore "invidiously discriminates on the basis of viewpoint." Although "the Government may place certain conditions on the receipt of federal subsidies," nonetheless, the challengers argued, "it may not discriminate invidiously in such a way as to aim at the suppression of dangerous ideas."

Now, it should be highlighted here that the "viewpoint neutrality" invoked by the challengers in *Rust* has become perhaps the First Amendment's most fundamental, exceptionless norm. Even when regulating speech that is, categorically speaking, unprotected, such as obscenity, fighting words, or threats, the government remains bound by a rule – a metacommand – that it not discriminate against expression on the basis of the viewpoint the expression espouses.[33] In a

---

[32] This chapter does not discuss the claims having to do with the burdens allegedly imposed by the regulations on a woman's right to an abortion, or with the argument that they were invalid for being "arbitrary and capricious" implementations of Title X.

[33] *See, e.g.,* Virginia v. Black, 538 U.S. 343 (2003); R.A.V. v. City of St. Paul, 505 U.S. 377 (1992).

field where so much is, or seems to be, uncertain, this viewpoint neutrality requirement serves as a welcome fixed point. But again, when the government
speaks for itself, either directly or indirectly, it may say – pretty much– whatever
it wants; it does not have to eschew bias or strive for evenhandedness.[34] So, the
challenge in *Rust* was to decide whether, by attaching the no-abortion-counseling
conditions to its family-planning dollars, the government was acting (more or
less) in its capacity as regulator or public forum manager, in which case viewpoint discrimination would be a problem. Or was it acting in (something like)
its expressive capacity, in which case it may – like any other speaker – "discriminate" against viewpoints by advancing their opposite. As Rehnquist observed,
"[w]hen Congress established a National Endowment for Democracy to encourage other countries to adopt democratic principles, . . . it was not constitutionally required to encourage competing lines of political philosophy such as
communism and fascism."

Along the same lines, the Supreme Court had already held, in *Maher v. Roe*,[35]
that the government may "make a value judgment favoring childbirth over abortion, and . . . implement that judgment by the allocation of public funds." It may,
Rehnquist observed, "selectively fund a program to encourage certain activities
it believes to be in the public interest, without at the same time funding an alternative program which seeks to deal with the problem in another way." Should
it matter, though, that in the Title X context, the government's attempt to "encourage [or discourage] certain activities" takes the form of restrictions on third-
party speech?

In Rehnquist's view, it should not. The "challenged regulations," he insisted,
"implement the statutory prohibition by prohibiting counseling, referral, and the
provision of information regarding abortion as a method of family planning."
These rules are not designed to serve as restrictions on speech with which the
government disagrees, but merely "to ensure that the limits of the federal program are observed." Thus, doctors participating in a Title X funded program are
told that they may not engage in abortion counseling, referrals, and advocacy not
in order to suppress what the government might regard as offensive or "dangerous ideas," but because such services and expression "are outside the scope of the
federally funded program." After all, Rehnquist noted, the regulations "do not
force . . . Title X grantees [or their employees] to give up abortion-related speech;
they merely require that the grantee keep such activities distinct and separate
from Title X activities."

Of course, the government's prerogative to control the expressive content
of its own spending programs, even by constraining the government-funded

[34] The First Amendment's Establishment Clause, of course, limits the ability of government to speak
in a way that "endorses" religion or "sends a message to nonadherents that they are outsiders,
not full members of the political community[.]" *See, e.g.,* Elk Grove Unified School Dist. v. Newdow, 542 U.S. 1 (2004) (O'Connor, J., concurring in the judgment).

[35] 432 U.S. 464 (1977).

expression of its subcontractors, does not translate into full-blown regulatory authority over their *own* speech. Nor should this license be permitted to undermine the protections afforded by the First Amendment to private speakers in publicly subsidized public forums. Rehnquist clearly acknowledged as much, rejecting the notion that "funding by the government . . . is invariably sufficient to justify Government control over the content of expression. For example, this Court has recognized that the existence of a Government 'subsidy,' in the form of Government-owned property, does not justify the restriction of speech in areas that have been traditionally open to the public for expressive activity." However, the government's decision to fund non-abortion-related family-planning services – unlike, as we now know, its decision to fund student publications out of a university's Student Activities Fund, or to pay for lawyers to represent indigent clients – does not create a forum for the airing of a diverse array of private views and, accordingly, is not subject to the no-viewpoint-discrimination requirement.[36]

However – and notwithstanding Rehnquist's statement that Title X does not operate as, or create, a public forum – he nonetheless asserted in passing that, by choosing to promote conception and childbirth and declining to support or fund abortions, "the Government has not discriminated on the basis of viewpoint; it has merely chosen not to fund one activity to the exclusion of another." But this is not quite right. The government *did* pick one point of view or position over another and it *did*, in a sense, "discriminate" against the position it rejected. The point, though, is that the Constitution permits this. Justice Blackmun was not far off, then, complaining in dissent that "by refusing to fund those family-planning projects that advocate abortion because they advocate abortion, the Government has plainly targeted a particular viewpoint." The Chief Justice could have responded, though – and, implicitly, he did respond – by saying, "not 'targeted,' endorsed. And, the government is allowed to endorse the messages it likes when spending and speaking through public money. If you want a different message, elect a different government."

Next, fast-forward a decade to *United States v. American Library Association*.[37] That case concerned the federal Children's Internet Protection Act, under which "a public library may not receive federal assistance to provide Internet access unless it installs software to block images that constitute obscenity or child pornography, and to prevent minors from obtaining access to material that is harmful to them." In the association's view, this requirement was unconstitutional because it used public funds, including discounted Internet access and grants for acquiring relevant technology, to induce public libraries to violate their patrons' First Amendment rights. The association also claimed that, in effect, the act imposed a content-based restriction on access to a "designated public forum," namely, Internet access within a public library.

---

[36] *Velazquez, supra* note 3 (public funding for legal assistance to the poor through the Legal Services Corporation creates a public forum).
[37] 539 U.S. 194 (2003).

The question at the heart of the case, then, was, "what is a public library *doing* when it provides Internet access to its customers?" Is it opening a gate to a bustling, diverse forum for unfettered expression and conversation? Or is providing such access more like the everyday, pedestrian library practice of acquiring and shelving books for patrons' use (a practice that is, by and large, subject to only the most deferential constitutional review)?[38] By attaching conditions to its library-related spending, was the federal government censoring the expression of Internet speakers and library users? Or was it – as in, say, *Rust v. Sullivan* – merely defining the limits, and controlling the content, of the program it established for a specific purpose?

Writing – on this point – for a majority of the Court, Chief Justice Rehnquist insisted that "Internet access in public libraries is neither a 'traditional' nor a 'designated' public forum." After all, "this resource . . . did not exist until recently[,]" and the Court has "rejected the view that traditional public forum status extends beyond its historical confines," for instance, sidewalks, parks, and the like. Nor, in Rehnquist's view, had the government created a designated public forum by subsidizing libraries' Internet terminals. "To create such a forum," he emphasized, "the government must make an affirmative choice to open up its property for use as a public forum."

True, he conceded, public forum analysis is not limited to the government's physical properties; as in the *Rosenberger* case, it is possible for the government to create a designated public forum through a spending program aimed at subsidizing private speech. In *Rosenberger,* the University of Virginia had established such a forum by deciding to fund a range of student newspapers, that is, to "encourage a diversity of views from private speakers." Having done so, the university was required to adhere to the First Amendment standards governing such forums. In *American Library Association,* though, Rehnquist reasoned that the point of subsidized Internet access, like the point of buying and shelving books, is not to promote private expression, but to "facilitate research, learning, and recreational pursuits by furnishing materials of appropriate and requisite quality."[39]

The Chief Justice also rejected the claim that, by linking federal funds to the use of blocking software, Congress had imposed an "unconstitutional condition"

[38] Rehnquist noted that "the government has broad discretion to make content-based judgments in deciding what private speech to make available to the public," citing Arkansas Educ. Television Comm'n v. Forbes, 523 U.S. 666 (1998) (public forum principles do not generally apply to a public television station's editorial judgments), and *Finley, supra* note 26 (content-based considerations may be employed in the arts-funding process).

[39] As Chief Justice Rehnquist put it, "[a] public library does not acquire Internet terminals in order to create a public forum for Web publishers to express themselves, any more than it collects books in order to provide a public forum for the authors of the books to speak." Rehnquist observed that there might be good reasons to avoid entirely "import[ing]" the public forum doctrine into the Internet context, adding that "we are wary of the notion that a partial analogy in one context, for which we have developed doctrines, can compel a full range of decisions in such a new and changing area."

on the libraries that receive the subsidies by "requiring them . . . to surrender their First Amendment right to provide the public with access to constitutionally protected speech." In Rehnquist's view, however – and putting aside, for the sake of argument, the question whether public libraries have First Amendment rights – the funding and the conditions at issue here were like the ones addressed in *Rust v. Sullivan.* There, the Court had affirmed that "[w]ithin broad limits, when the Government appropriates public funds to establish a program it is entitled to define the limits of that program." And there, as in this case, by imposing requirements on those receiving federal funds – requirements that, in each case, arguably constrained the recipients' expression – Rehnquist concluded that the government was "simply insisting that public funds be spent for the purposes for which they were authorized." In both cases, it was not so much that the government was regulating the *recipients'* expression as protecting the integrity or content of its *own* message (if any) or program. As in *Rust,* the requirement that the recipients of government subsidies use blocking software "does not 'penalize' libraries that choose not to install such software. . . . Rather, [the act] simply reflects Congress' decision not to subsidize their doing so. To the extent that libraries wish to offer unfiltered access, they are free to so without federal assistance."

   Stepping back from these three cases, a few general points and themes are worth highlighting. It is fair to say, for example, that one does not detect in these opinions – and they are typical in this respect – any burning enthusiasm for increasing the scope of the First Amendment, either by expanding the notion of what counts as speech or by increased judicial sensitivity to possible burdens on that speech. For example, where the dissenters in *Rust* saw government-sponsored compulsion and suppression,[40] the Chief Justice saw free choice, offer and acceptance, and garden-variety politics. Recall also, in *American Library Association,* Rehnquist's reservations about importing public forum doctrine into the Internet context, and his refusal in *Krishna Consciousness* to accord much First Amendment significance to Justice Kennedy's claim that "[o]ne of the places left in our mobile society that is suitable for discourse is a metropolitan airport." That airports are "suitable for discourse" – assuming that they are – is not, Rehnquist might have responded, a reason to assign decisions about their management and operation to courts and First Amendment litigants.[41] More specifically, these opinions appear to confirm what was suggested at the outset of this chapter, namely, that Rehnquist has tried to avoid increasing the range of policy questions and political decisions that are subject to judicial review for compliance with the First Amendment. He has done this by refusing to classify public properties or

---

[40] Justice Blackmun complained, in dissent, that "[w]hile suppressing speech favorable to abortion with one hand, the Secretary compels antiabortion speech with the other." *Rust, supra* note 13.
[41] *Cf., e.g.,* United States Postal Service v. Council of Greenburgh Civic Associations, 453 U.S. 114 (1981) (Rehnquist, J.) (letterboxes approved by the United States Postal Service are not public forums merely because they serve as instrumentalities for the exchange of ideas).

funding programs as public forums to begin with (as in *Rust* and *American Library Association*) and also by guarding jealously the category of "traditional public forum" (as in *Krishna Consciousness*), where the most exacting constitutional scrutiny applies.

Consider, by way of additional illustration, Rehnquist's opinion in *PruneYard Shopping Center v. Robins*.[42] In that case, the Court considered whether a ruling of the California Supreme Court that California's own constitution recognizes and protects the freedom of speech in certain *privately* owned properties – including a shopping mall – violated federally protected property and free speech rights of these properties' owners. The California court, moved by the fact that "[a]s a result of advertising and the lure of a congenial environment, [thousands] of persons are induced to congregate daily" in shopping malls, proclaimed that "the California Constitution protects speech and petitioning, reasonably exercised, in shopping centers even when the centers are privately owned." In keeping with his goal of managing the reach of the First Amendment's purview, Rehnquist wrote both that the California court's interpretation of its own constitution's free speech guarantee did not abridge the mall owners' First Amendment freedoms, and that the First Amendment – unlike, apparently, the California Constitution – does not support the proposition that private property becomes, for constitutional purposes, a public forum simply because it is open to the public and even if, in current conditions, it plays a forumlike role for many people. Justice Marshall, in contrast, noted that "shopping centers had opened their centers to the public at large, effectively replacing the State with respect to such traditional First Amendment forums as streets, sidewalks, and parks." He observed that governments have made their trespass laws available to the centers' owners, "enabling them to exclude those who wished to engage in expressive activity on their premises," and warned that "[r]ights of free expression become illusory when a State has operated in such a way as to shut off effective channels of communication."[43]

More recently, Rehnquist exhibited a similar reluctance to use the public forum doctrine to expand the reach of the Free Speech Clause in *Locke v. Davey*.[44] The *Davey* case involved a challenge to a Washington law prohibiting state aid – in this case, a scholarship program for academically gifted students – to any postsecondary student pursuing a degree in theology. In the Supreme Court, the case was litigated and decided primarily on Religion Clause grounds.[45] The Court of Appeals for the Ninth Circuit, however, had borrowed heavily from the Justices' public forum precedents in concluding that Washington's decision to single out

---

[42] 447 U.S. 74 (1980).

[43] For a similar argument, see Justice Kennedy's concurring opinion in *Krishna Consciousness*, *supra* note 14.

[44] 540 U.S. 712 (2004).

[45] *See generally* Daniel O. Conkle, *Indirect Funding and the Establishment Clause: Rehnquist's Triumphant Vision of Neutrality and Private Choice*, Chapter 4 in the present volume.

scholarship eligible theology students for exclusion from the public benefit program was a form of viewpoint discrimination, and the scholarship program a kind of forum.[46] On review, though, Chief Justice Rehnquist wanted none of it: This was not a free speech case, he declared, and "[t]he scholarship program is not a forum for speech." Relying on his own opinion in *American Library Association*, he reasoned – or, perhaps, asserted – that the "purpose of the [scholarship program] is to assist students from low- and middle-income families with the cost of postsecondary education, not to encourage a diversity of views from private speakers." Thus, "[the] cases dealing with speech forums are simply inapplicable." Rehnquist then went on to conclude that Washington's restriction did not violate the First Amendment's Religion Clause.

It should be emphasized, in the interests of both fairness and understanding, that Rehnquist's evident reluctance in his public forum and government speech decisions to increase the reach of the Free Speech Clause should not be mistaken for a hostility to the clause, or to the freedom of speech itself. Contrary to the argument advanced in the previous chapter by Professor Stone, it is not obviously the case that Rehnquist's voting record in free speech cases – he has, clearly, over the years proved less likely than other Justices to endorse First Amendment challenges to state action – means that he is "no friend of the First Amendment."[47] It could mean, instead, that he is less likely than other Justices to second-guess other government actors' determinations, implicit or explicit, that the action in question is consistent with our free speech commitments. It could also reflect, as was mentioned earlier, a realization that sometimes, in constitutional law, "more is less," and that it might enhance the vigor with which the First Amendment can be applied to limit the conduct and contexts to which it applies.

IV

In a provocative analysis of the *Krishna Consciousness* case, published soon after the decision was announced, Professor Lillian BeVier suggested that the Court's public forum doctrine was in "disarray" and noted the "deep division among the Justices about the underlying purpose of public forum doctrine."[48] She suggested that two models – an "Enhancement" and a "Distortion" model – were competing "to supply the underlying premise of the public forum right." The Enhancement model, she wrote, "is concerned with how much speech takes place in society and with the overall quality of public debate. . . . It presupposes that the core mission of the First Amendment is to promote an idealized vision of the democratic process by promoting speech about public and, in particular, political issues." The less ambitious Distortion model, on the other hand, "portrays

---

[46] Davey v. Locke, 299 F.3d 748 (9th Cir. 2002), *rev'd*, 540 U.S. 712 (2004).
[47] Stone, *supra* note 4, at 12.
[48] BeVier, *Rehabilitating Public Forum Doctrine: In Defense of Categories,* 1992 Sup. Ct. Rev. 79.

the First Amendment as embodying nothing more than a set of constraints upon government actors. . . . According to the Distortion model, the essential task of First Amendment rules is to restrain government from deliberately manipulating the content or outcome of public debate."

Rehnquist's "categorical" approach, and his "relatively modest set of assumptions about the appropriate boundaries of the judicial task,"[49] place him squarely in the Distortion model camp. For the Chief Justice, Professor BeVier might have said, the aim is not to interpret, expand, and deploy the First Amendment in order to achieve the quality and quantity of constitutionally protected speech that is regarded as optimal by the Court's Justices. Or, as Rehnquist himself put it, thirty years ago: "It should not be easy for any one individual or group of individuals to impose by law their value judgments upon fellow citizens who may disagree with those judgments. Indeed, it should not be any easier just because the individual in question is a judge."[50] The goal, instead, should be to police vigorously government attempts to misuse its regulatory and managerial powers to stack the deck against disapproved viewpoints – and nothing in *Krishna Consciousness*, Rehnquist could argue, suggests a retreat from such policing – while minimizing the debate-skewing dangers associated with judicial review and preserving as much room as possible for politics, experimentation, and compromise.[51] After all, "however socially desirable the goals sought to be advanced . . . , advancing them through a freewheeling, non-elected judiciary is quite unacceptable in a democratic society."[52]

Professor BeVier's thesis explains a lot – at least, it does at first. At the same time, it must be conceded that some of Chief Justice Rehnquist's votes and opinions in recent First Amendment cases – cases often outside the public forum and government money contexts – might seem inconsistent with BeVier's claim that Rehnquist is working from a model that is skeptical of judicial review and deferential to politics. For example, Justice Rehnquist has substantially retreated from – if not abandoned entirely – his strong position against First Amendment protection for commercial advertising.[53] His vote and dissenting opinion in *McConnell v. Federal Election Commission*, the Court's recent decision regarding the so-called Bipartisan Campaign Reform Act of 2002, indicate a marked move away from his previous view that regulations of political speech by corporations are not the First Amendment's concern.[54] And his majority opinion in the *Boy Scouts*

---

[49] *Id.*

[50] Rehnquist, *supra* note 11.

[51] *See, e.g.,* James Weinstein, *Free Speech, Abortion Access, and the Problem of Judicial Viewpoint Discrimination,* 29 U.C. Davis L. Rev. 471 (1996).

[52] Rehnquist, *supra* note 11.

[53] *See generally* Earl M. Maltz, *"I Give Up!" William Rehnquist and Commercial Speech,* Chapter 3 in the present volume.

[54] *See generally* Richard H. Pildes, *The Constititutionalization of Democratic Politics,* 118 Harv. L. Rev. 28 (2004) (noting that Rehnquist had "abandoned his votes in nearly all the corporate political speech cases of the past twenty years").

case,[55] which concluded that the Scouts' First Amendment right of "expressive association" entitled it to fire an openly gay scoutmaster notwithstanding a state law prohibition on such discrimination, seems to embrace a notion of association as speech that is broader than Rehnquist might have been expected to believe.[56] What's going on?

One explanation, of course, is that Rehnquist's relatively narrow understanding of the Free Speech Clause's content and reach always had more to do with bringing about his preferred policy outcomes than with a principled commitment to democratic government or a deep-seated concern about the distorting effects on civil society of judicial review. But this explanation is both uncharitable and unsatisfactory. Fortunately, a better one is available.

At the outset of this chapter, it was suggested that Rehnquist's decisions in the public forum and government speech cases reflect his concern that as the civic, social, and political territory controlled by the Free Speech Clause grows, the amount shrinks that is governed democratically and experimentally by the people and their representatives, or that is left under the direction of private persons, groups, and institutions. In keeping with this concern, Rehnquist has tended to resist using the public forum doctrine to constitutionalize disputes about the management of public property and resources, a resistance that indicates a desire to protect the workings and structure of civil society from intrusive, and possibly distorting, First Amendment review. In his ambitious "retrospective on the Rehnquist Court," Professor John McGinnis contends that, in a number of areas, the Chief Justice has developed a jurisprudence "that "invigorates decentralization and the private ordering of social norms," in part by protecting the autonomy of mediating associations and institutions – like corporations, political parties, local governments, and the Scouts – "from the encroachments of more centralized power."[57] If this is right, then Rehnquist's recent decisions and votes in favor of Free Speech claimants can, and perhaps should, be seen not so much as a departure from his earlier rulings, but instead as an application of the same, overriding belief that the First Amendment should be understood and applied in a way that protects and values localism, pluralism, and politics, and that "permits . . . debate to continue, as it should in a democratic society."[58]

---

[55] Boy Scouts of America v. Dale, 530 U.S. 640 (2000) (concluding that the application of New Jersey's public accommodations law to require the Scouts to retain an openly gay scoutmaster violated the First Amendment right of expressive association).

[56] See, e.g., Jed Rubenfeld, The Anti-Antidiscrimination Agenda, 111 YALE L.J. 1141 (2002) ("[T]here can be no doubt that Boy Scouts displays, textually speaking, a most generous and expansive approach to constitutional meaning. The First Amendment does not make any reference to a 'freedom of association,' nor is that right referred to anywhere else in the Constitution.").

[57] John O. McGinnis, Reviving Tocqueville's America: The Rehnquist Court's Jurisprudence of Social Discovery, 90 CAL. L. REV. 485 (2002).

[58] Washington v. Glucksberg, 521 U.S. 702, 735 (1997).

CHAPTER THREE

"I GIVE UP!" WILLIAM REHNQUIST AND COMMERCIAL SPEECH

Earl M. Maltz*

The dispute over the constitutional status of commercial speech provides a fascinating case study of the evolution of the jurisprudence of Justice William Rehnquist. While not as politically charged as the Court's decisions to intervene aggressively in cases involving issues such as sex discrimination and abortion, in doctrinal terms the enhancement of constitutional scrutiny for government limitations on commercial speech during the Rehnquist era was no less dramatic. Initially, Rehnquist fought hard to limit the protections afforded to commercial speech. However, by the latter part of his long tenure on the Court, he had fully embraced the enhanced scrutiny and turned it to his own purposes. This shift reflected not only a change in Rehnquist's personal approach, but also the evolution of conservative constitutional jurisprudence more generally.

At the time that Rehnquist joined the Court in 1972, the decision in *Valentine v. Chrestensen*[1] was generally viewed as having established the rule that the First Amendment did not impose any significant restrictions on government regulation of purely commercial speech. Indeed, constitutional challenges to such restrictions were often not conceptualized in First Amendment terms at all. *Williamson v. Lee Optical of Oklahoma, Inc.*[2] is a classic example from the Warren era. *Williamson* was a constitutional challenge to a state prohibition on the advertisement of eyeglass frames. Viewing the claim in substantive due process terms, the Court unanimously rejected the challenge, applying the most lenient version of the rational basis test.

By the mid-1970s, however, two quite different developments combined to undermine the continued vitality of the *Valentine* principles. The first of these was a change in the political climate surrounding limitations on commercial speech. At the time they were adopted, regulations such as that challenged in *Williamson* were no doubt seen as serving the public interest by enhancing professionalism

* Much of Chapter 3 is drawn from *The Strange Career of Commercial Speech*, 6 Chapman L. Rev. 161 (2003).

[1] 316 U.S. 52 (1942).

[2] 348 U.S. 483 (1955).

and preventing inappropriate competition. By contrast, as the twentieth century progressed, *Williamson*-like regulations were increasingly viewed as devices by which special interests shielded themselves from the rigors of the marketplace, thereby depriving the public generally of the benefits of competition.

The second development was doctrinal. During the Warren era, the liberal Justices on the Court had developed an increasingly libertarian free speech jurisprudence.[3] In particular, these Justices evinced an increasing hostility to the exclusion of specific categories of speech from First Amendment protections. A blanket exception for commercial speech fit at best uneasily into this regime.

These themes came together in the Burger Court's watershed decision in *Virginia State Board of Pharmacy v. Virginia Citizens Consumer Council, Inc.*[4] In that case, the Court invalidated a state statute that prohibited pharmacists from advertising the prices that they would charge for prescription drugs. Speaking for the Court, Justice Harry A. Blackmun first observed that, in other contexts, the First Amendment had been held to protect speech that is sold for profit. The only question remaining, therefore, was whether *purely* commercial speech was entitled to First Amendment protection. In concluding that the First Amendment did protect the advertising in *Virginia Pharmacy,* Blackmun focused primarily on the interest of the consumer in receiving product information, declaring that "so long as we preserve a predominantly free enterprise economy, the allocation of our resources in large measure will be made through numerous private economic decisions. It is a matter of public interest that those decisions, in the aggregate, be intelligent and well informed. To this end, the free flow of commercial information is indispensable." He sounded a similar theme in rejecting the claim that the prohibition was necessary to preserve the professionalism of pharmacists and to protect the public from those who would offer inferior service at low prices:

> There is . . . an alternative to this highly paternalistic approach. That alternative is to assume that this information is not in itself harmful, that people will perceive their best interest if only they are well enough informed, and that the best means to that end is to open channels of communication rather than to close them. . . . The choice among these approaches is not ours to make or the Virginia Assembly's. It is precisely this kind of choice, between the dangers of suppressing information, and the danger of its misuse, that the First Amendment makes for us.

Rehnquist dissented alone from this conclusion. He conceded that, at least in a general sense, *Virginia Pharmacy* presented "a fairly typical First Amendment problem – that of balancing interests in individual free speech against public welfare determinations embodied in a legislative enactment." However, unlike the majority, he described the weight of the challenger's interest as "trivial" for constitutional purposes, largely because, in Rehnquist's view, First Amendment protections related primarily to speech that dealt with "public decisionmaking as to

---

[3] *See, e.g.,* New York Times Co. v. Sullivan, 376 U.S. 254 (1964).

[4] 425 U.S. 748 (1976).

political, social and other public issues, rather than the decision of a particular individual as to whether to purchase one or another brand of shampoo." By contrast, he contended that "the societal interest against the promotion of drug use for every ill, real or imaginary, [is] extremely strong." In addition, analogizing the decision in *Virginia Pharmacy* to the discredited economic substantive due process jurisprudence of the *Lochner* era, Rehnquist attacked the reasoning of the majority in language that echoed Oliver Wendell Holmes's famous statement that "[t]he Fourteenth Amendment does not enact Mr. Herbert Spencer's Social Statics," asserting that "there is . . . nothing in the United States Constitution which requires the [government] to hew to the teachings of Adam Smith in its legislative decisions regulating the pharmacy profession."

Rehnquist also warned of what he saw as the broad implications of *Virginia Pharmacy*. Anticipating the types of pharmaceutical advertisements that have since become so prevalent, he gave examples that he insisted would necessarily be constitutionally protected under the majority's approach:

> Pain getting you down? Insist that your physician prescribe Demerol. You pay a little more than for aspirin, but you get a lot more relief.
>
> Can't shake the flu? Get a prescription for Tetracycline from your doctor today.
>
> Don't spend another sleepless night. Ask your doctor to prescribe Seconal without delay.

Brushing aside the majority's claim that its decision covered only product advertising and not solicitations for service by professionals, Rehnquist also predicted that the principles enunciated in *Virginia Pharmacy* would soon be used to invalidate well-established limits on such solicitations. He asserted that "if the sole limitation on permissible state proscription of advertising is that it may not be false or misleading, surely the difference between pharmacists' advertising and lawyers' and doctors' advertising can only be one of degree and not of kind." He also noted that the Court's analysis would threaten the legality of restrictions on the advertising of harmful but legal commodities such as liquor and cigarettes. This assessment of the implications of the majority opinion ultimately proved entirely accurate.

The following year, the Court began a First Amendment assault on traditional limitations on attorney advertising in *Bates v. State Bar of Arizona*.[5] *Bates* was a challenge to a then-typical rule that prohibited attorneys from publicizing the fees that they charged for services. The challenge was mounted by a law firm that provided routine legal services to people of moderate income. The three most conservative members of the *Virginia Pharmacy* majority contended that the prohibition on advertising fees was constitutional, insisting that legal services could not be standardized in the same manner as pharmaceuticals, and that stringent limitations on advertising were justified as a means of preserving the professionalism of lawyers. However, speaking for the majority in *Bates*, Justice Blackmun

[5] 433 U.S. 350 (1977).

disagreed. Blackmun rejected the professionalism argument as anachronistic and argued that, with respect to the specific legal services at issue in *Bates,* a schedule of fees could provide accurate information to consumers. Moreover, while conceding that advertising could not provide members of the public with all the information needed to select a lawyer, Blackmun asserted that, in the post–*Virginia Pharmacy* era, "we view as dubious any justification that is based on the benefits of public ignorance."

Although on its facts dealing only with routine legal services, *Bates* was the precursor of a wide-ranging judicial assault on the rules that limited attorney advertising. Not surprisingly, Rehnquist consistently voted to uphold the existing rules against First Amendment attacks. He lamented that "once the Court took the first step down the 'slippery slope' in [*Virginia Pharmacy*] the possibility of understandable and workable differentiations between protected speech and unprotected speech in the field of advertising largely evaporated." This perspective continued to inform his approach to commercial problems for much of his career.

Initially, the efforts of the other members of the Court to provide "understandable and workable differentiations" in commercial speech cases did nothing to assuage Rehnquist's dissatisfaction. In 1980, a majority of the Justices united around a single formulation in *Central Hudson Gas and Electric Corp. v. Public Service Commission.*[6] *Central Hudson* was a challenge to a New York regulation that prohibited electric utilities from sponsoring advertising that "promot[es] the use of electricity." Speaking for the Court in holding the prohibition unconstitutional, Justice Lewis F. Powell also established a framework for the analysis of commercial speech problems more generally

> For commercial speech to come within th[e] protection [of the First Amendment] it at least must concern lawful activity and not be misleading. Next, we ask whether the asserted governmental interest is substantial. If both inquiries yield positive answers, we must determine whether the regulation directly advances the governmental interest served, and whether it is not more extensive than is necessary to serve that interest.

Predictably, Rehnquist stood alone in arguing that this test was too protective of commercial speech. His dissenting opinion reiterated the view that "the Court unlocked a Pandora's Box when it 'elevated' commercial speech . . . by according it First Amendment protection [in *Virginia Pharmacy*]." Rehnquist found the specific holding in *Central Hudson* particularly offensive, contending that the "New York order . . . is in my view more akin to economic regulation to which complete deference should be accorded by the Court" and that "by labeling economic regulation of business conduct as a restraint on 'free speech,' [the Court has] gone far to resurrect the discredited doctrine of cases such as *Lochner.*"

---

[6]   447 U.S. 557 (1980).

Notwithstanding his distaste for the *Central Hudson* test, Rehnquist was able to turn the test to his advantage in *Posadas de Puerto Rico Assoc. v. Tourism Co. of Puerto Rico.*[7] *Posadas* was a challenge to a Puerto Rico statute that prohibited local casinos from advertising their facilities to residents of Puerto Rico. In *Virginia Pharmacy,* Rehnquist had predicted that such challenges would succeed under the new regime, asserting that the First Amendment would be held to protect "active promotion of . . . products, the use of which it has previously been thought desirable to discourage." Nonetheless, in *Posadas,* he was able to muster a five-Justice majority that rejected the constitutional attack on the statute.

Speaking for the Court, Rehnquist began by conceding that the advertisements at issue were neither misleading nor fraudulent. Turning to the remaining steps of the *Central Hudson* analysis, he then cataloged the potential negative consequences of gambling, concluded that limiting the demand of local citizens served a "substantial" interest in preserving the health, safety, and welfare of the citizenry, and determined that the legislature reasonably believed that the prohibition on advertising was closely related to that interest. Rehnquist then rejected the contention that the legislature was constitutionally required to choose the less restrictive alternative of mounting a counteradvertising campaign, declaring that "we think it is up to the legislature to decide whether or not such a 'counter-speech' policy would be as effective in reducing the demand for casino gambling as a restriction on advertising." Thus, concluding that "the greater power to completely ban casino gambling necessarily includes the lesser power to ban advertising of casino gambling," Rehnquist concluded that the constitutional challenge was without merit.

Posadas was the first major victory in Rehnquist's campaign to limit the scope of First Amendment protection for commercial speech. At the time it was decided, the case seemed likely to have significant implications. By its terms, the reasoning in the case suggested that the state and federal governments would have wide-ranging authority to regulate the advertising of legal but undesirable products and activities. Rehnquist thus appeared to be on the verge of having the Court accept at least some of his views on the scope of state power to regulate commercial speech. However, *Posadas* proved to be an aberration; in later decisions dealing with analogous issues, the Court showed a general hostility to the challenged government regulations.

The process of eroding the authority of *Posadas* began in 1995, with the decision in *Rubin v. Coors Brewing Co.*[8] *Rubin* was a challenge to the constitutionality of a provision of the Federal Alcohol Administration Act that prohibited beer labels from displaying alcohol content. A unanimous Supreme Court held that this provision violated the First Amendment. In defending the statute, the federal government argued that the restriction was justified by the need to prevent beer manufacturers from engaging in "strength wars" – competing in the beer market

[7] 478 U.S. 328 (1986).
[8] 514 U.S. 476 (1995).

on the basis of the alcoholic content of their products. Such a competition, the government reasoned, would lead to an increase in alcoholism and its attendant social costs. Speaking for the Court, Justice Clarence Thomas conceded that this interest was sufficiently weighty to satisfy the second prong of the *Central Hudson* analysis. However, noting that the other aspects of the regulatory scheme allowed and in some cases required manufacturers to indicate the strength of alcoholic beverages, Thomas contended that "the irrationality of this unique and puzzling regulatory framework ensures that the labeling ban will fail to achieve [the purpose of curtailing strength wars]." Thomas also argued that the government could have adopted less intrusive means to achieve this goal. Thus, he concluded that the labeling ban failed to satisfy both the third and fourth prongs of *Central Hudson.*

Because (at least on its face) the holding in *Rubin* was based on the idiosyncracies of the Federal Alcohol Administration Act, Justice Thomas did not feel constrained to make more than a passing reference to the *Posadas* decision. However, the following year, *Posadas* met its demise in *44 Liquormart, Inc. v. Rhode Island.*[9] This case was a challenge to a pair of Rhode Island statutes that, taken together, essentially prohibited the advertising of the prices of alcoholic beverages. The state asserted that the limitations were justified as a means of limiting the demand for such beverages – an interest that the Court once again conceded was sufficiently weighty to satisfy the second prong of the *Central Hudson* analysis. Against this background, at least eight Justices agreed that *44 Liquormart* was analogous to *Posadas.* Nonetheless, overruling *Posadas,* the Justices unanimously held that the Rhode Island statute was unconstitutional. While disagreeing on the precise standard of review to be applied to the statute, all of the Justices concluded that the Court should not defer to the state's assertions that its regulation directly furthered the asserted interest and that the regulation was no more restrictive than necessary to serve that interest. Instead, the Justices conducted a more searching inquiry and determined that the ban on price advertising unduly restricted the First Amendment rights of the beer merchants.

In 2001, the principles underlying *44 Liquormart* were reiterated and strengthened in *Lorillard Tobacco Co. v. Reilly.*[10] In *Lorillard,* the Court was faced with a First Amendment challenge to Massachusetts regulations that prohibited all outdoor advertising of tobacco products within one thousand feet of any school or playground, and also point-of-sale advertising of such products placed lower than five feet off of the ground in any retail establishment located within a thousand feet of a school or playground. The majority opinion conceded that "'tobacco use, particularly among children and adolescents, poses perhaps the single most significant threat to public health in the United States,'" and also that there was clear evidence of a link between advertising and an increase in the use of tobacco products by young people. Thus, the majority concluded that the restrictions on out-

[9] 517 U.S. 484 (1996).
[10] 533 U.S. 525 (2001).

door advertisements at least passed muster under the third prong of the *Central Hudson* analysis. Nonetheless, a deeply divided Court struck down both regulations, with the majority observing that in some urban areas the regulations would ban virtually all outdoor advertisements of tobacco products and faulting the state Attorney General for failing to make a "careful calculation of the speech interests involved [in the advertising ban]."

This holding confirmed the fears expressed by the young Justice Rehnquist's *Virginia Pharmacy* dissent; the First Amendment had been interpreted to sharply limit government authority to restrict the advertising of socially undesirable products. However, by the year 2001, Rehnquist himself had come to see this development in a less nightmarish light.

On one level, the evolution of the law from *Virginia Pharmacy* through *Central Hudson* and *Posadas* to *44 Liquormart* and *Lorillard* is a fairly prosaic story. When the Court breaks new ground, as it did in *Virginia Pharmacy*, it is not unusual for there to be some hesitancies and even reversals of course before the doctrinal analysis takes on a firm, lasting structure. Moreover, in the interim between the decisions in *Posadas* and *Rubin*, six of the nine Justices had been replaced, including three of the five members of the *Posadas* majority. By its nature, such a dramatic alteration in the composition of the Court carries with it the possibility of significant doctrinal change.

However, these factors do not explain the actions of Chief Justice Rehnquist in the post-1995 cases. Beginning in 1995, when he concurred silently in the opinion of the Court in *Rubin*, Rehnquist abandoned his adamant opposition to First Amendment protection of commercial speech in favor of the view that the Court should act aggressively to limit government authority to regulate commercial advertising. Thus, in *44 Liquormart*, he joined a concurring opinion by Justice Sandra Day O'Connor – the only other Justice remaining from the *Posadas* majority – that observed that *Rubin* and other cases decided subsequently to *Posadas* rejected the deference shown by the Court in that case in favor of the *Central Hudson* requirement that the government "show that the speech requirement directly advances its interest and is narrowly tailored."[11] Subsequently, in 2001, Rehnquist provided a critical vote in support of the majority opinion in *Lorillard*.

Rehnquist's newfound affinity for the protection of commercial speech extends beyond the *Posadas–Lorillard* line of cases. For example, in *Glickman v. Wileman Bros. & Elliot, Inc.*[12] and *United States v. United Foods, Inc.*,[13] he concluded that the government could not compel producers of agricultural products to pay assessments that funded generic advertising of those products. Admittedly, Rehnquist is not as zealous in protecting commercial speech as some of his colleagues

---

[11] 44 Liquormart, 517 U.S. at 532 (O'Connor, J., concurring in the judgment).
[12] 521 U.S. 597 (1997).
[13] 533 U.S. 405 (2001).

on the Court.[14] Nonetheless, from a jurisprudential perspective, his approach to commercial speech cases has clearly changed dramatically since 1986.

How is one to explain this extraordinary volte-face? Certainly, Rehnquist himself has provided no explanation. Indeed, he has never written any opinion in a case in which he voted to strike down a government regulation of commercial speech. Justice O'Connor's opinion in *44 Liquormart*, which he joined, suggests that the doctrine of *stare decisis* influenced his thinking. But this explanation is entirely too facile; Rehnquist has never been one to be constrained by precedent on issues about which he has strong opinions.

In large measure, Rehnquist's newfound willingness to embrace strong First Amendment protections for commercial speech is best understood as reflecting changes in the political and jurisprudential context in which these cases were decided. During the period beginning with *Virginia Pharmacy* and ending with *Posadas,* liberal judges and commentators often extolled the virtues of judicial activism is support of values that they viewed as "fundamental," even if those values would have been foreign to those who were the Framers of the Constitution. By contrast, conservatives generally argued that nonoriginalist judicial activism was an illegitimate exercise of the Court's power. At the time, Rehnquist – who was viewed as being at best on the conservative edge of the American mainstream – was the leading judicial apostle of this belief. In a well-known 1976 law review article, he asserted that

[T]o the extent that it makes possible an individual's persuading one or more appointed federal judges to impose on other individuals a rule of conduct that the popularly elected branches of government would not have enacted and the voters have not and would not have embodied in the Constitution, [nonoriginalist review] is genuinely corrosive of the fundamental values of our democratic society.

Although Rehnquist's commitment to judicial deference was far from absolute, its impact on jurisprudence was apparent in his approach to issues such as commercial speech. It was this rejection of the activism of more liberal members of the Court that many commentators viewed as defining his place on the political spectrum.

The voting pattern of the Justices in the commercial speech cases decided between 1976 and 1986 reflected the link between political conservatism and jurisprudential deference in that period. In ordinary political terms one might not expect conservatives to be less sympathetic than liberals to the laissez-faire impulse that animated *Virginia Pharmacy* and its progeny. However, since, at the time a commitment to judicial deference was (at least in theory) a hallmark of conservative constitutional theory, it should not be surprising that Rehnquist himself – at that time viewed as the paradigmatic conservative jurist – would become the most consistent and vocal critic of the abandonment of *Valentine v. Chrestensen.*

---

[14] *See* Thompson v. Western States Medical Center, 122 S. Ct. 1497 (Rehnquist, C.J., joining dissenting opinion of Breyer, J.).

The same dynamic dictated that, in *Posadas,* Rehnquist would find his allies among the less liberal members of the Burger Court.

However, the association of conservative politics with judicial restraint was by no means inevitable. Instead, it was a contingent by-product of the specific political and jurisprudential climate of the Warren era.[15] Conservatives did not simply criticize the results of the Warren Court; instead, much of their criticism was couched in purely institutional terms. The institutional critique had a number of advantages. First, by emphasizing the institutional importance of restraint rather than the need for the advancement of conservative political values per se, conservatives could accuse their liberal allies of politicizing the Court – a charge that had a strong emotive impact and drew on the work of some of the leading academics of the day. Further, in the 1950s and 1960s, widespread conservative activism seemed unthinkable; more than a decade of Warren Court jurisprudence had created the strong impression that activism would inevitably be associated with liberal values. Against this background, distrust of judicial activism became ingrained in the conservative psyche. At the same time, liberal politicians and commentators also came to associate calls for judicial deference exclusively with conservative political views.

As late as 1987, the disposition of the nomination of Robert Bork to the Supreme Court reflected the degree to which advocacy of judicial deference had become associated with political conservatism. Bork was defeated because his opponents were successful in portraying him as "an extremist . . . who would use his position on the Court to advance a far right, radical judicial agenda."[16] The primary evidence offered to support this charge would not have supported claims that Bork would use a position on the Court to overturn left/center initiatives from other branches of government. Indeed, Bork had been outspoken in his opposition to the use of judicial power to invalidate economic legislation that might be anathema to conservatives. Instead the charge of "extremism" rested on the likelihood that Bork would be unwilling to interpose the Constitution against legislation that left/center forces found distasteful, most notably on matters dealing with contraception, abortion, and sex discrimination.[17] The subsequent nomination of Justice Anthony M. Kennedy was approved only because some of those who opposed Bork believed (correctly, as it turned out) that Kennedy might be more receptive to liberal arguments on these issues.[18] In neither case did liberal politicians take seriously the belief that the advocacy of deference might not necessarily be associated with conservative political views.

Even before the Bork debacle, however, judicial deference was beginning to lose its charm for some conservatives. Antonin Scalia was the first of a new breed

[15] The argument that follows is elaborated in much greater detail in Earl M. Maltz, *The Prospects for a Revival of Conservative Activism in Constitutional Jurisprudence,* 24 Ga. L. Rev. 629 (1990).

[16] S. Exec. Rep. No. 7, 100th Cong., 1st Sess. 210 (1987).

[17] *Id.* at 24–36, 45–49, 131–32.

[18] *See,* e.g., N.Y. Times, Dec. 20, 1987, at E18, col. 1; Wash. Post, Nov. 12, 1937, at A7, col. 1.

of more activist conservatives to join the Supreme Court. Scalia was appointed to succeed Rehnquist as an Associate Justice when Rehnquist ascended to the Chief Justiceship in 1986. He quickly replaced Rehnquist as the darling of conservatives and the bête noire of liberal commentators. Scalia was equally steeped in conservative political ideology and even more committed to a formal style of legal analysis then the newly appointed Chief Justice. However, although Scalia often extravagantly praises the concept of democracy in theory, in practice the idea of judicial deference per se has had fewer charms for Scalia than for Rehnquist. In 1991, Rehnquist and Scalia were joined on the Court by Clarence Thomas, an even more activist conservative.

The commercial speech cases exemplify the dominance of activist jurisprudence in the late Rehnquist era. Although differing at times on particulars, both liberal and conservative Justices have voted to invalidate a variety of limitations on professional advertising, as well as advertising of legal but undesirable products. Thomas and Scalia have been in the forefront of these efforts; Thomas has argued that commercial speech should be treated no differently than other speech for First Amendment purposes, and in *Lorillard*, Scalia joined an opinion suggesting that the *Central Hudson* test was insufficiently protective of truthful advertising. The conservatives have also spearheaded the effort to use the First Amendment to prevent the government from compelling contributions from producers to support generic product advertising.

Faced with the determination of both conservatives and liberals to expand the outer limits of First Amendment protection of commercial speech, Rehnquist apparently decided that resistance was futile. He abandoned the principled deference of his early commercial speech opinions in favor of what might be described as the "sauce for the gander" theory of constitutional adjudication. Put another way, if all of the other Justices on the Court – whatever their political stripe – were determined to deploy the First Amendment to protect their favored forms of product advertising, Rehnquist no longer saw any reason not to join the party.

More generally, the evolution of Rehnquist's approach to commercial speech reflects his position as an important transitional figure in the history of constitutional jurisprudence. After an era in which the most conservative philosophy among the Justices was the watered-down liberalism of Justices John Marshall Harlan and Potter Stewart, Rehnquist (and, to a lesser extent, Warren Burger) brought a truly conservative perspective to the Court for the first time in a generation. His jurisprudential philosophy was shaped by having lived in a period in which judicial activism favored *only* liberal causes. Thus, from the perspective of a political conservative in 1971, a general commitment to deference must have seemed to be the best that could be hoped for.

However, by the 1990s, there was clearly no possibility that liberals and conservatives might reach a judicial détente on the basis of a shared commitment to deference. With the more liberal members of the Court showing no signs of abandoning their activist posture, continued advocacy of judicial deference by conservatives could result only in constitutional jurisprudence becoming a permanent one-way ratchet, threatening conservative initiatives but leaving liberal actions of the other branches of government untouched. Against this background, it should be no surprise that conservative judges and commentators increasingly joined their liberal colleagues in embracing an activist role for the Court (although, of course, the areas in which they have advocated judicial intervention are often quite different). In such a context, a single judge who consistently deferred to the decisions of other branches of government could accomplish nothing except to see his own political preferences devalued. It was against the background of this reality that William Rehnquist changed his approach to the problem of commercial speech. The same reality will no doubt also shape the more general jurisprudence of conservative judges who serve on the Court in the future.

CHAPTER FOUR

INDIRECT FUNDING AND THE ESTABLISHMENT CLAUSE: REHNQUIST'S TRIUMPHANT VISION OF NEUTRALITY AND PRIVATE CHOICE

Daniel O. Conkle

The constitutional jurisprudence of Chief Justice Rehnquist is complex and multifaceted, but it is dominated by two related themes. First, Rehnquist has sought to limit the power of the national government and to enhance the power of the states. Second, he has been reluctant to adopt broad interpretations of the Bill of Rights. These themes are related because the Bill of Rights, as applied through the Fourteenth Amendment, acts to restrict the states and to constrain their ability to decide policy questions for themselves. To read the Bill of Rights narrowly, as Rehnquist has urged, limits the scope of these nationally imposed constitutional requirements and thereby enhances the power and discretion of the states.

These general themes inform Chief Justice Rehnquist's understanding of the First Amendment's Establishment Clause. By its terms, the Establishment Clause provides that "Congress shall make no law respecting an establishment of religion." Based on the well-settled doctrine of Fourteenth Amendment incorporation, this prohibition extends not only to the federal government, but also to the states.[1] According to Rehnquist, however, the Establishment Clause prohibition is quite limited, and it leaves the states with substantial leeway.

In important respects, Rehnquist's relaxed interpretation of the Establishment Clause has not prevailed, but instead has been expressed in dissenting opinions. In 2000, for example, Rehnquist dissented in *Santa Fe Independent School District v. Doe*.[2] In *Santa Fe*, the Supreme Court extended its strict prohibition on school-sponsored prayers in the public school context, ruling that the prohibition applied even to school-sponsored prayers that student volunteers, selected by their classmates, were to compose and offer at sporting events. Dissenting vehemently, Rehnquist wrote that the Court's opinion "bristles with hostility to all things religious in public life." More generally, in his far-reaching 1985 dissent in *Wallace v. Jaffree*,[3] Rehnquist argued that the Court's interpretation of the Estab-

[1] *See* Everson v. Board of Educ., 330 U.S. 1, 8, 14–15 (1947).
[2] 530 U.S. 290 (2000).
[3] 472 U.S. 38, 91–114 (1985) (Rehnquist, J., dissenting).

lishment Clause has been fundamentally flawed since the 1940s. Citing the original understanding of the clause, Rehnquist argued that it should not be read to preclude the government from promoting religion. Instead, he contended, the Establishment Clause permits the government to favor religion as long as it avoids discrimination among competing religious sects.[4] Notably, however, Rehnquist's dissenting opinion in *Wallace* was for himself alone, and his dissent in *Santa Fe* was joined only by Justices Scalia and Thomas.

Although his broad-brush attack on basic Establishment Clause doctrine has failed, Chief Justice Rehnquist has prevailed in one important area, that of public funding for religious schools and organizations. More precisely, Rehnquist has successfully championed a relaxed approach to the Establishment Clause in the particular context of voucher programs and other types of "indirect" funding. "Indirect" funding, for this purpose, is public funding that flows initially to individuals and that reaches religious schools or organizations only because the individual recipients, as a matter of private choice, elect to use it there. In this context, Rehnquist – acting within the framework of prevailing Establishment Clause tests and premises – has persuaded a majority of the Court that indirect funding programs should be upheld as long as they are "neutral." An indirect funding program is "neutral" and therefore constitutional as long as it permits funding for religious and nonreligious organizations alike, without targeting religious beneficiaries for special, advantageous treatment. Under this approach, the actual destination of the aid is beside the point, even if the bulk of the funding flows to religious organizations.

Rehnquist first suggested this approach in his majority opinion in *Mueller v. Allen*,[5] decided in 1983. Ten years later, in *Zobrest v. Catalina Foothills School District*,[6] he authored another majority opinion that relied heavily on the distinction between direct and indirect aid and on the importance of governmental neutrality and private choice. A decade after that, in *Zelman v. Simmons-Harris*,[7] Rehnquist's majority opinion solidified this approach and announced a doctrine that was very close to categorical. In *Zelman*, the Court not only approved a voucher program that included religious schools, but also suggested that neutral programs of indirect funding are almost invulnerable to constitutional challenge. Most recently, in 2004, Rehnquist authored yet another important opinion for the Court, in *Locke v. Davey*.[8] *Locke* ruled that the doctrine exemplified by *Mueller, Zobrest*, and *Zelman* is permissive, not mandatory. Thus, even though the states are permitted to include religious beneficiaries in neutral programs of indirect funding, they are not necessarily required to do so.

---

[4] *See generally* DEREK DAVIS, ORIGINAL INTENT: CHIEF JUSTICE REHNQUIST AND THE COURSE OF AMERICAN CHURCH/STATE RELATIONS (1991).

[5] 463 U.S. 388 (1983).

[6] 509 U.S. 1 (1993).

[7] 536 U.S. 639 (2002).

[8] 540 U.S. 712 (2004).

This chapter begins with an overview of contemporary Establishment Clause values and doctrinal tests, attempting to explain how and why, over Rehnquist's objection, the Supreme Court has developed its general approach to the clause. It then recounts the Court's public funding doctrine in the 1970s and 1980s and the more recent trend, supported by Rehnquist, to relax Establishment Clause restrictions even with respect to direct funding. The remainder of the chapter focuses on indirect funding, examining Rehnquist's critical role in this context and analyzing his opinions in *Mueller, Zobrest, Zelman,* and *Locke.* In so doing, the chapter explores the constitutional values that are at the heart of Rehnquist's (and the Court's) thinking in this area. This analysis reveals that, in the context of indirect funding, the general themes of Rehnquist's constitutional jurisprudence – themes favoring a narrow interpretation of the Bill of Rights and broad leeway for the states – are supported by reasonable interpretations of the more specific constitutional values that undergird the Establishment Clause. As a result, it is not surprising that Rehnquist has obtained majority support in this area. Although he has failed to reshape Establishment Clause doctrine from the ground up, he has prevailed in this important setting, permitting a more selective version of his constitutional vision to triumph.

I. THE GENERAL CONSTITUTIONAL LANDSCAPE

A. Establishment Clause Values

Although the Justices are loath to admit it, the Supreme Court's interpretations of the Establishment Clause have taken the Court well beyond the text and original understanding of the Constitution. In the jargon of constitutional theory, the Court's interpretive methodology has been "nonoriginalist." That is, the Court has interpreted the Establishment Clause in a manner reflecting not only American history, but more contemporary values as well. The Court's nonoriginalist decision making in this area, however, has not been purely subjective. Instead, the Court has been guided by its identification of a variety of broadly shared constitutional values – values deeply embedded in the political and cultural history of the United States, and values emerging and evolving over time. These various values are general in nature. They are sometimes complementary, but sometimes in tension. Their significance and relative weight in particular contexts is highly debatable, contributing to the Justices' frequent disagreements in Establishment Clause cases.

Elsewhere the author has recounted the origin and evolution of a set of constitutional values that inform contemporary Establishment Clause doctrine.[9]

---

[9] *See* DANIEL O. CONKLE, CONSTITUTIONAL LAW: THE RELIGION CLAUSES 28–48 (2003). As the book's title suggests, its discussion of constitutional values extends not only to the Establishment Clause, but also to the First Amendment's Free Exercise Clause, which precludes the government from "prohibiting the free exercise" of religion. *See also* Steven H. Shiffrin, *The Pluralistic*

Here, it suffices to highlight five Establishment Clause values that are especially relevant in the context of public funding for religious schools and organizations. First, the clause protects the value of religious equality, not only between and among competing religions and religious groups, but also between religion and irreligion. Second, the clause – like its First Amendment companion, the Free Exercise Clause – protects religious voluntarism, meaning the freedom of individuals to make religious (or irreligious) choices for themselves, free from governmental compulsion or improper influence. Third, and more broadly, the Establishment Clause calls for the government to respect the religious (or irreligious) identity of dissenting individuals, including dissenting taxpayers, by avoiding the promotion or endorsement of religious values that the dissenters do not share. Fourth, the clause seeks to further a religiously inclusive political community, a value that likewise may be threatened by the official promotion or endorsement of religion. Finally, the clause seeks to protect the autonomy of religious organizations, which may require at least some degree of institutional separation between church and state.

B. General Establishment Clause Tests and Their Operation in the Public Funding Context

These various constitutional values, taken together, have led the Supreme Court to conclude – over Chief Justice Rehnquist's objection – that the Establishment Clause not only forbids the government from favoring one religion over another, but also from promoting religion in general over irreligion. Thus, as far back as 1947, the Supreme Court declared in *Everson v. Board of Education* that the clause prohibits "laws which aid one religion, aid all religions, or prefer one religion over another."[10] Over time, the Court elaborated the meaning of this prohibition, and, in its 1971 decision in *Lemon v. Kurtzman,* it announced a general, three-pronged test for Establishment Clause cases. To survive judicial scrutiny under *Lemon,* a statute (or other governmental action) must satisfy each of three requirements: "First, the statute must have a secular legislative purpose; second, its principal or primary effect must be one that neither advances nor inhibits religion . . . ; finally, the statute must not foster 'an excessive governmental entanglement with religion.'"[11]

Chief Justice Rehnquist has harshly criticized the *Lemon* test, as have other Justices. But the Supreme Court continues to invoke it, albeit less consistently than in the 1970s and 1980s, and sometimes in modified form. In the Court's recent school prayer decision in *Santa Fe Independent School District v. Doe,* for example,

Foundations of the Religion Clauses, 90 CORNELL L. REV. 9 (2004) (agreeing that the religion clauses serve multiple values and offering a sophisticated account of the values underlying each clause).

[10] Everson v. Board of Educ., 330 U.S. 1, 15 (1947).

[11] Lemon v. Kurtzman, 403 U.S. 602, 612–13 (1971).

a six-Justice majority – much to Rehnquist's chagrin – cited the *Lemon* test and relied upon its first prong in finding a constitutional violation.[12] In the context of public funding, the Court has explicitly modified the *Lemon* test, but the test's basic principles remain intact. Thus, in its 1997 decision in *Agostini v. Felton,* the Court stated that it "continue[s] to ask whether the government acted with the purpose of advancing or inhibiting religion" and "continue[s] to explore whether the aid has the 'effect' of advancing or inhibiting religion."[13] The Court went on to declare, however, that it would no longer treat entanglement as a separate prong. Instead, this issue now is merely one aspect of the effect inquiry, a modification that serves to weaken, but not eliminate, the doctrinal significance of entanglement.

The *Lemon* test, as modified by *Agostini,* is the Supreme Court's primary Establishment Clause test in the context of public funding. The Court also relies to some extent on another doctrinal formulation, the endorsement test. First proposed in 1984 by Justice O'Connor,[14] the endorsement test has since been adopted and applied by the Court in a variety of Establishment Clause contexts. According to this test, the Court's inquiry into purpose and effect should focus on the symbolic nature of governmental action, and it should be designed to prevent governmental action concerning religion that constitutes a message of endorsement or disapproval. Under this reformulation of *Lemon,* the government violates the Establishment Clause if it intends to communicate a message that endorses or disapproves religion, or if, whatever the government's intention, its action has the effect of communicating such a message. The endorsement test is a separate analytical tool, but it is not inconsistent with the original *Lemon* test, and the Court often uses the two tests together. Not surprisingly, Chief Justice Rehnquist and other critics of *Lemon* would repudiate the endorsement test as well. Despite their opposition, however, the endorsement test is an important component of the Court's prevailing doctrine. In the funding context, it adds a symbolic inquiry that supplements and complements the more tangible focus of the *Lemon–Agostini* analysis.

The *Lemon–Agostini* and endorsement tests can be combined into a single, more unitary inquiry. Under the first prong of each test, the government cannot act with the purpose of advancing or endorsing religion, nor with the purpose of inhibiting or disapproving it. Instead, the government must have a secular purpose for its action. Second, even if the government has a secular purpose, its

---

[12] Santa Fe Indep. Sch. Dist. v. Doe, 530 U.S. 290, 314 (2000); *see id.* at 319–20 (Rehnquist, C.J., dissenting). In an even more recent case, Rehnquist urged the Court to reject the *Lemon* test in the context of governmental displays of the Ten Commandments. *See* Van Orden v. Perry, 125 S. Ct. 2854, 2860–61 (2005) (plurality opinion). But he could secure only four votes for his opinion, and, in a companion ruling, the Court explicitly reaffirmed and relied upon the purpose prong of *Lemon* to find a constitutional violation. *See* McCreary County v. American Civil Liberties Union, 125 S. Ct. 2722 (2005).

[13] Agostini v. Felton, 521 U.S. 203, 222–23 (1997).

[14] *See* Lynch v. Donnelly, 465 U.S. 668, 687–94 (1984) (O'Connor, J., concurring).

action cannot have the primary effect of advancing or endorsing religion, nor of inhibiting or disapproving it. This second prong, as modified in *Agostini,* includes a prohibition on excessive governmental entanglement with religion.

Taken together, the *Lemon–Agostini* and endorsement tests advance the five Establishment Clause values that were highlighted earlier. First and foremost, the Court's broad prohibition on deliberate or unintentional advancement/endorsement or inhibition/disapproval reflects the value of religious equality, not only between and among religions, but also between religion and irreligion. This prohibition also protects the second value, that of religious voluntarism. The government cannot promote religion or irreligion, but must instead permit individuals to make religious choices for themselves. Third, and more broadly, the endorsement test requires the government to respect the religious identity of individuals by avoiding the symbolic affront that can arise from governmental messages of endorsement or disapproval. The endorsement test also protects the fourth value, that of a religiously inclusive political community, by preventing governmental messages that treat religious dissenters as "outsiders, not full members of the political community."[15] Finally, the Court's prohibition on excessive entanglement serves, in part, as a device for ensuring the independence and autonomy of religious organizations.

With these values at work, the Supreme Court has invoked and applied the *Lemon–Agostini* and endorsement tests in evaluating a variety of funding programs. Virtually without exception, the first requirement of these tests, that of secular purpose, has been readily satisfied. This requirement forbids the government from acting with the purpose of advancing/endorsing or inhibiting/disapproving religion. It would be violated by a deliberately discriminatory program of benefits, such as a program that funded private education only at religious schools. But the challenged programs typically do not involve deliberate discrimination. Rather, they are general programs of aid that include both religious and nonreligious beneficiaries, without distinction. As a result, the Court's decisions in this area have hinged on the remaining portions of the doctrinal analysis, addressing effect and entanglement. Entanglement has sometimes been an issue, especially when a program of aid requires close governmental supervision. The bulk of the cases, however, have focused more generally on the question of effect (which, after *Agostini,* now embraces the entanglement issue as well). Thus, the critical question has been whether a program of funding has the impermissible effect of advancing/endorsing or inhibiting/disapproving religion.

II. PUBLIC FUNDING DOCTRINE IN THE 1970s AND 1980s[16]

In a series of cases decided during the 1970s and 1980s, the Supreme Court suggested that it would analyze public funding programs with an eye to various

---

[15] *Id.* at 688.

[16] This section is adapted from CONKLE, *supra* note 9, at 178–83.

considerations, generally under the rubric of the second prong of the *Lemon* test. Almost all of these cases involved aid to religious schools or their students or parents. The Court approved some programs, but, with Rehnquist invariably in dissent, it invalidated others. The Court's doctrine was muddled and depended on fine distinctions, but at least five considerations appeared to be playing significant roles.

First, the Supreme Court addressed the manner in which the aid was provided. The Court was more likely to invalidate aid that was provided directly to the religious schools, and it was less likely to invalidate aid that was targeted initially to individual students or parents and that reached the religious schools only indirectly, as a result of individual choice. A program that directly reimbursed religious schools for educational expenses, for example, was more likely to be invalidated than a program of educational tax deductions that extended to parents who chose to educate their children at such schools.[17] As we will see, this emphasis on the manner of funding – direct or indirect – has, under the leadership of Chief Justice Rehnquist, become a critical factor in contemporary doctrine. In the 1970s and 1980s, it was an important factor, but it did not appear to be as crucial as it plainly is today.

Second, the Court suggested that the quantity or percentage of aid reaching religious beneficiaries was a relevant consideration in evaluating the effect of a public funding program. Substantial benefits, or benefits that mainly assisted religious schools, were more likely to be invalidated.[18]

Third, the Court was more likely to invalidate funding programs that were designed to benefit elementary or secondary education, as opposed to higher education. Although most religious colleges and universities have strong secular components, the Court described elementary and secondary religious schools as "pervasively sectarian" – religious through and through. At the same time, the younger age of the students made them more susceptible to the religious training and instruction that they received. For these reasons, the Court believed that public aid reaching religious beneficiaries in the context of elementary or secondary education was more likely to be used – and used successfully – to advance religion, suggesting a constitutionally impermissible effect. Conversely, the Court was more likely to uphold funding programs that were directed to higher education, even if religious colleges and universities were included.[19]

Fourth, the Court considered the substance of the aid being provided, with the question being whether this particular type of aid might itself be used to inculcate religion, again suggesting an improper effect. For example, providing instructional materials and equipment for use in religious schools was more

---

[17] *Compare* Lemon v. Kurtzman, 403 U.S. 602, 621 (1971), *with* Mueller v. Allen, 463 U.S. 388, 399 (1983).

[18] *See, e.g.,* Committee for Public Educ. & Religious Liberty v. Nyquist, 413 U.S. 756 (1973).

[19] *See* Tilton v. Richardson, 403 U.S. 672 (1971); Hunt v. McNair, 413 U.S. 734 (1973); Roemer v. Board of Public Works, 426 U.S. 736 (1976).

problematic than providing textbooks on purely secular subjects, because the instructional materials and equipment could more readily be used for religious as well as secular education.[20] Aid that was clearly and effectively segregated to secular activities was more likely to be approved.

Fifth, the Court considered the extent to which a particular funding program might require continuing governmental involvement and monitoring. Using what was then the separate third prong of the *Lemon* test, the Court reasoned that this kind of continuing relationship might create a constitutionally impermissible entanglement of religion and government.

Two 1985 cases provide examples of the Supreme Court's reasoning in this period, and they also illustrate just how strictly the Court sometimes read the Establishment Clause. In *School District of Grand Rapids v. Ball*[21] and *Aguilar v. Felton,*[22] a deeply divided Court ruled that the Establishment Clause barred publicly paid teachers from providing secular, remedial education on the premises of elementary and secondary religious schools. The challenged programs extended to religious and nonreligious schools alike, and the Court found that they had the purpose of supporting secular education, thereby satisfying the first prong of *Lemon*. Utilizing some of the considerations just outlined, however, the Court concluded that the programs could not survive the remainder of the analysis.

In *Grand Rapids,* the Supreme Court found that the challenged programs had the primary effect of advancing religion and therefore violated the second prong of *Lemon*. The Court stated that the programs impermissibly advanced the "sectarian enterprise" of the religious schools because the aid was "direct and substantial." Addressing the substance of the aid, the Court reasoned that the publicly funded teachers might knowingly or unwittingly "conform their instruction to the environment in which they teach," thereby furthering the schools' religious mission. In part as a result, the Court also concluded that the impressionable children attending the schools might perceive a "symbolic union of church and state" reflecting an improper governmental endorsement of religion. In *Aguilar,* the challenged program was designed to mitigate the Establishment Clause vices that the Court identified in *Grand Rapids*. In particular, it included a system of governmental monitoring to ensure that the remedial classes and therefore the aid would remain entirely secular, both in reality and in perception. That very system of monitoring, however, led the Court to find an excessive governmental entanglement with religion, this in violation of *Lemon*'s third prong.

Then-Justice Rehnquist's dissenting opinion in *Aguilar* lamented the "Catch-22" that he believed the Court had created. His position has since prevailed, and

---

[20] *See* Meek v. Pittenger, 421 U.S. 349 (1975); Wolman v. Walter, 433 U.S. 229 (1977). This specific distinction has since been expressly rejected, with *Meek* and *Wolman* being overruled on this point. *See* Mitchell v. Helms, 530 U.S. 793, 808, 835 (2000) (plurality opinion); *id.* at 837 (O'Connor, J., concurring in the judgment).

[21] 473 U.S. 373 (1985).

[22] 473 U.S. 402 (1985).

Grand Rapids and *Aguilar* have been overruled. Indeed, in hindsight, *Grand Rapids* and *Aguilar* represent the end of a doctrinal era. They are the last Supreme Court decisions to follow the complex and sometimes strict approach of the 1970s and 1980s. Since then, Chief Justice Rehnquist and his judicial allies have ushered in a new doctrinal era.

III. DOCTRINAL RELAXATION CONCERNING DIRECT FUNDING

In the 1970s and 1980s, the Supreme Court frequently invalidated direct aid, especially aid that flowed directly to "pervasively sectarian" organizations, including elementary or secondary religious schools. *Grand Rapids* and *Aguilar* illustrate this pattern. More recently, however, the Court has relaxed its restrictive approach to direct funding and has overruled a number of its earlier decisions. This recent trend is exemplified by *Agostini v. Felton,*[23] decided in 1997. As discussed previously, *Agostini* modified the *Lemon* test as applied in the funding context, eliminating entanglement as a separate prong and incorporating the entanglement inquiry into the effect prong. Because the purpose prong is rarely at issue in funding cases, the critical question under the modified test is "whether the aid has the 'effect' of advancing or inhibiting religion." Answering this question in the case before it, the Court in *Agostini* approved the very same program of direct aid that it had invalidated twelve years earlier in *Aguilar*. Expressly overruling *Aguilar* and relevant portions of *Grand Rapids,* the Court declared that the Establishment Clause does not forbid publicly paid teachers from providing secular, remedial education on the premises of elementary and secondary religious schools. More generally, the Court indicated a new inclination to approve direct funding programs that are neutrally drawn. When "aid is allocated on the basis of neutral, secular criteria that neither favor nor disfavor religion, and is made available to both religious and secular beneficiaries on a nondiscriminatory basis," the Court wrote, "the aid is less likely to have the effect of advancing religion."

Agostini suggests that neutral programs of direct aid are "likely" to be upheld. There have been hints that the Court might go further, adopting an approach that would approve virtually any program of aid that is neutrally drawn to include religious and nonreligious organizations alike.[24] But the Court has not accepted that position. Instead, it appears that programs of direct aid, even if neutrally drawn, remain subject to four additional limitations. First, even after *Agostini,* a program of direct aid cannot involve an unconstitutionally "excessive" entanglement between the government and religious schools or organizations. Second, the Court continues to suggest that the amount of direct aid to religious schools or organizations – at least if "pervasively sectarian" – cannot be too substantial. Third, the Court has indicated that the substance of direct aid must be secular. More precisely, the aid must be segregated and confined to secular uses and can-

[23] 521 U.S. 203 (1997).
[24] *See* Mitchell v. Helms, 530 U.S. 793, 801–36 (2000) (plurality opinion).

not be diverted by its recipients to religious purposes. And fourth, the Court has suggested that direct money payments (as opposed to in-kind support) to "pervasively sectarian" religious schools and organizations might be problematic even if the grants are restricted to secular uses.[25]

These four limitations themselves are subject to important exceptions and qualifications, and, given the Court's inclination to approve neutral programs of funding, the limitations are likely to be construed in a relatively permissive fashion.[26] In any event, the Court's new approach to direct funding represents a substantial relaxation of the Establishment Clause. Not surprisingly, Chief Justice Rehnquist has welcomed and joined this doctrinal shift, and he is among a group of Justices who would go even further in approving direct aid and in easing or erasing the limitations that continue to exist. But Rehnquist has not played a prominent role in these developments.[27] The major opinions have been authored by other Justices.[28] Instead, Rehnquist has marshaled his arguments in the context of indirect aid, where he has led a majority of the Court to adopt an approach that is exceedingly relaxed and that, indeed, approximates a categorical rule that neutral programs of funding are constitutionally permissible.

IV. INDIRECT FUNDING: REHNQUIST'S SUCCESSFUL ADVOCACY OF A DISTINCTIVE AND HIGHLY PERMISSIVE APPROACH

Rehnquist joined the Supreme Court as an Associate Justice in 1972. During his first ten years, he had very limited influence on the Court's Establishment Clause decision making. He wrote a significant majority opinion concerning standing,[29] but his only opinions addressing the substance of the Establishment Clause were dissenting (or concurring and dissenting) opinions, invariably taking the Court to task for reading the clause too strictly. In 1980, for instance, Rehnquist denounced the Court's summary decision in *Stone v. Graham,* which struck down a Kentucky law requiring that the Ten Commandments be posted in public school classrooms.[30] And in 1982, he was the lone dissenter in *Larkin v. Grendel's Den, Inc.,* arguing that the Court was wrong to invalidate a Massachusetts statute giving churches the power to nullify applications for nearby liquor licenses.[31]

---

[25] For documentation and discussion of these four limitations, see CONKLE, *supra* note 9, at 192–95.

[26] *See id.* at 196–201.

[27] In the 1980s, Rehnquist did author an important majority opinion in the direct aid context, rejecting a facial challenge to a statute that included religious organizations as permissible grant recipients. *See* Bowen v. Kendrick, 487 U.S. 589 (1988).

[28] Justice O'Connor wrote the majority opinion in *Agostini.* In Mitchell v. Helms, 530 U.S. 793 (2000), Justice Thomas wrote a plurality opinion for four justices, advocating an even more lenient approach. Chief Justice Rehnquist silently joined each of these opinions.

[29] *See* Valley Forge Christian College v. Americans United for Separation of Church and State, 454 U.S. 464 (1982).

[30] *See* Stone v. Graham, 449 U.S. 39, 43–47 (1980) (Rehnquist, J., dissenting).

[31] *See* Larkin v. Grendel's Den, Inc., 459 U.S. 116, 127–30 (1982) (Rehnquist, J., dissenting).

In many respects, not much has changed since 1982. Rehnquist has never persuaded the Court to adopt his revisionist and minimalist interpretation of the
Establishment Clause, as articulated most fully in his 1985 dissenting opinion in
Wallace v. Jaffree.[32] By all indications, however, Rehnquist himself has never wavered from that view. Thus, throughout his tenure, he has voted to reject virtually every Establishment Clause challenge he has confronted. When a majority
of the Court has agreed, he typically has joined the majority opinion silently. If
a majority has found a violation, by contrast, Rehnquist almost always has dissented, often issuing his own opinion to protest the Court's decision.

In the particular context of indirect funding, however, 1983 marked the beginning of an active and influential role for Rehnquist. In that year, he wrote the majority opinion in *Mueller v. Allen*.[33] This was Rehnquist's first majority opinion
concerning the substance of the Establishment Clause, and, in hindsight, it was
the foundation upon which he built his limited but important Establishment
Clause legacy. In later years, using his authority as Chief Justice, Rehnquist assigned himself to write additional opinions concerning indirect aid. In those
opinions, he took a broad view of what he had written in *Mueller* and persuaded
the Court to conclude that neutral programs of indirect funding are virtually
immune from constitutional challenge.

A. *Mueller v. Allen*

In *Mueller,* the Supreme Court addressed a Minnesota state income tax deduction for tuition, textbooks, and transportation for children attending elementary
and secondary schools. Taxpayers could deduct up to $500 for every child in el-
ementary school and up to $700 for every child in secondary school, regardless
of whether the school was public or private and, if private, regardless of whether
the school was secular or religious. In actual operation, however, the deduction
worked disproportionately and overwhelmingly to the benefit of families with
children in religious schools. Public school students, of course, generally pay no
tuition, and they incurred the other eligible expenses to no more than a minimal
degree. And of the private school students paying tuition in Minnesota, some
95 percent attended religious schools. As a result, it appeared that more than 90
percent of the economic benefit of the deduction was flowing to families attending religious schools and thus, in a sense, to the religious schools themselves.

When *Mueller* was decided, Establishment Clause questions were governed by
the unmodified, three-part test of *Lemon v. Kurtzman;* neither the *Agostini* modification nor the endorsement test had yet been developed.[34] In public funding
cases, where the analysis hinged largely on effect and entanglement, the doctrinal
approach of the 1970s and 1980s was still in full flower.[35] Under this approach,

[32] 472 U.S. 38, 91–114 (1985) (Rehnquist, J., dissenting).
[33] 463 U.S. 388 (1983).   [34] *See supra* §I.B.   [35] *See supra* §II.

the Minnesota tax deduction seemed vulnerable. Although the lower courts in *Mueller* had approved it, other courts had invalidated similar deductions.

In the Supreme Court, the Justices were as divided as the lower courts, but a 5–4 majority voted to reject the Establishment Clause challenge. Writing for the Court, Justice Rehnquist did not advance his own, broadly revisionist interpretation of the clause. Instead, to retain his narrow majority, Rehnquist worked within the confines of *Lemon* and contended that the Court's decision was fully compatible with existing precedent. At the same time, he planted the seeds for an important doctrinal revision that would treat indirect aid as a distinctive, and broadly permissible, method of funding religious schools and organizations.

As in other funding cases, the first prong of *Lemon* was easily satisfied, a point that even the dissenters did not dispute. As Rehnquist explained, the tax deduction had a secular purpose, furthering public as well as private education by assisting parents with the cost of educational expenses. By its terms, the deduction did not discriminate between religious and nonreligious schools, and there was no persuasive evidence that it rested on the impermissible purpose of advancing the former over the latter. Rehnquist likewise found that the third prong of *Lemon,* precluding excessive entanglement, also was satisfied, and once again there was no disagreement from the dissenters. Thus, as in many funding cases, the difficult and dispositive question in *Mueller* was compliance with the second prong of *Lemon.* Given its actual operation, did the deduction have the principal or primary effect of advancing religion?

In his dissenting opinion for four Justices, Justice Marshall argued that it did. Citing factors of the sort that had been influential in previous decisions, he noted the disproportionate benefit to religious schools and argued that the deduction created an incentive for parents to send their children to such schools. He also emphasized that the economic benefit of the deduction, especially as to tuition, was in no way segregated and confined to secular uses. Instead, it extended without limitation to religious as well as secular education at religious schools. As Marshall noted, the Supreme Court had invalidated a similar tax benefit for parents in its 1973 decision in *Committee for Public Education v. Nyquist.*[36] Quoting *Nyquist* and *Lemon,* Marshall argued that "[i]ndirect assistance in the form of financial aid to parents for tuition payments is . . . impermissible because it is not 'subject to . . . restrictions' which '"guarantee the separation between secular and religious educational functions and . . . ensure that State financial aid supports only the former."'"

Writing for the majority, Rehnquist purported to leave *Nyquist* intact. He noted that the tax benefit in *Nyquist* was restricted by its terms to private education, thereby formally precluding any benefit at all for families attending public schools. He further argued that the benefit in *Nyquist,* although nominally a tax deduction, also had features of a tax credit, unlike the "genuine tax deduction"

---

[36] 413 U.S. 756 (1973).

at issue in *Mueller*. These distinctions arguably put form over substance, but they permitted Rehnquist to uphold the Minnesota deduction without overruling *Nyquist* or any other precedent.

More generally, Rehnquist utilized a multifaceted analysis, stating that the issue was "whether Minnesota's tax deduction bears greater resemblance to those types of assistance to parochial schools we have approved, or to those we have struck down." In concluding that the deduction did not have the impermissible effect of advancing religion, Rehnquist found that "several features" of the law were "particularly significant." Among other factors, he noted that the deduction was but one of many deductions available under Minnesota's tax laws; that state legislative judgments concerning tax law and policy are entitled to substantial deference; and that the deduction extended by its terms to all parents, including those whose children attended public schools.

Rehnquist then turned to the themes of neutrality and private choice that would become the critical points of analysis in indirect funding cases. "[A] program . . . that neutrally provides state assistance to a broad spectrum of citizens," he wrote, "is not readily subject to challenge under the Establishment Clause." "We also agree," he continued, "that, by channeling whatever assistance it may provide to parochial schools through individual parents, Minnesota has reduced the Establishment Clause objections to which its action is subject."

Without suggesting that these factors should be determinative, Rehnquist argued that the states should have considerably more leeway in the context of indirect as opposed to direct aid, as long as the states themselves remain neutral, at least formally, by avoiding the purposeful targeting of religion for special advantage. Rehnquist conceded that "financial assistance provided to parents ultimately has an economic effect comparable to that of aid given directly to the schools attended by their children," but he noted that "under Minnesota's arrangement public funds become available only as a result of numerous, private choices of individual parents." Rehnquist observed that "the means by which state assistance flows to private schools is of some importance," in part because indirect funding does not necessarily implicate *the state* in any advancement of religion that thereby results. Quoting earlier precedent[37] but anticipating the symbolic focus of the endorsement test, Rehnquist reasoned that "[w]here, as here, aid to parochial schools is available only as a result of decisions of individual parents no 'imprimatur of State approval' can be deemed to have been conferred on any particular religion, or on religion generally."

In the context of this "attenuated financial benefit, ultimately controlled by the private choices of individual parents," Rehnquist found it immaterial that, in application, the benefit redounded mainly to religious schools. "We would be loath to adopt a rule," he wrote, "grounding the constitutionality of a facially neutral law on annual reports reciting the extent to which various classes of private

---

[37] *See* Widmar v. Vincent, 454 U.S. 263, 274 (1981).

citizens claimed benefits under the law." In so ruling, Rehnquist largely abandoned, in the context of indirect funding, any inquiry into the percentage of aid
reaching religious beneficiaries. He also jettisoned, in this context, any requirement that the aid be segregated and confined to secular uses. Instead, as Justice
Marshall lamented in dissent, "For the first time, the Court has upheld financial
support for religious schools without any reason at all to assume that the support will be restricted to the secular functions of those schools and will not be
used to support religious instruction."

Three years after *Mueller,* the Supreme Court decided *Witters v. Washington
Department of Services for the Blind.*[38] In *Witters,* the Court unanimously upheld
the extension of vocational rehabilitation funding to a blind student who was attending a Christian college in preparation for a career as a pastor, missionary, or
youth director. Rehnquist had not yet become Chief Justice, and his predecessor,
Chief Justice Burger, assigned the opinion to none other than Justice Marshall.
In his majority opinion, Marshall mentioned *Mueller* only in passing and omitted it entirely from his substantive analysis. He also made a point of noting that
aid can have an impermissible effect under *Lemon* "even though it takes the form
of aid to students or parents." Marshall nonetheless relied in part on the themes
of neutrality, indirect funding, and private choice. Thus, he noted that the Washington funding program extended neutrally to students pursuing various careers
and that the aid was transmitted to particular colleges "only as a result of the genuinely independent and private choices of aid recipients." Marshall also emphasized, however, that even through this indirect route "no more than a minuscule
amount of the aid awarded" would be used for religious training. "[I]mportant-
ly," he wrote, "nothing in the record indicates that . . . any significant portion of
the aid expended under the Washington program as a whole will end up flowing
to religious education."

In a separate concurring opinion, Justice Powell, joined by Justice Rehnquist
and Chief Justice Burger, argued that Justice Marshall had seriously underesti-
mated the significance of *Mueller.* Relying on *Mueller,* Powell questioned Marshall's final point of analysis, and he argued that neutral programs of indirect
funding should be upheld even if most of the recipients used the aid for religious
purposes. In their own separate concurrences, Justices White and O'Connor indicated that they essentially agreed with Justice Powell on this point. Even so,
Marshall's narrowly drawn opinion for the Court in *Witters* temporarily clouded
the precedential weight of *Mueller.*

B. *Zobrest v. Catalina Foothills School District*

The next indirect funding case reached the Supreme Court in 1993. In *Zobrest
v. Catalina Foothills Schools District,*[39] Rehnquist, now Chief Justice, assigned

[38]   474 U.S. 481 (1986).
[39]   509 U.S. 1 (1993).

himself the majority opinion and wrote an opinion that reinvigorated and extended the reasoning of *Mueller*. In *Zobrest*, the Court ruled that governmental aid in the form of a sign-language interpreter could be extended to a deaf student attending a Roman Catholic high school. As in *Witters*, the program in *Zobrest* did not have the effect of disproportionately favoring religious institutions, not even indirectly, but Rehnquist did not rely on this factor. Instead, speaking for a five-Justice majority, he emphasized the neutrality of the program and the fact that the interpreter reached the premises of the religious school only as a result of private choice. Citing *Mueller* and *Witters* together, Rehnquist wrote that "government programs that neutrally provide benefits to a broad class of citizens defined without reference to religion are not readily subject to an Establishment Clause challenge just because sectarian institutions may also receive an attenuated financial benefit." Rehnquist treated *Mueller* as his leading precedent; noted that "the vast majority" of the tax deductions in *Mueller* went to families attending religious schools; cited Justice Powell's reliance on *Mueller* in his *Witters* concurrence; and asserted that *Mueller* and *Witters* were premised on "virtually identical reasoning."

"That same reasoning," Rehnquist continued, "applies with equal force here." He noted that the program neutrally provided interpreters to deaf students regardless of whether their school was public or private and, if private, regardless of whether it was secular or religious. He then explained how the program depended on private choice and thereby protected religious voluntarism even as it avoided any implication that the government was sponsoring or promoting religion:

> By according parents freedom to select a school of their choice, the statute ensures that a government-paid interpreter will be present in a sectarian school only as a result of the private decision of individual parents. In other words, because the [statute] creates no financial incentive for parents to choose a sectarian school, an interpreter's presence there cannot be attributed to state decisionmaking.

In a dissenting opinion, Justice Blackmun argued that the Establishment Clause forbids a public employee, even a translator, from participating in a student's religious education at a religious school. Citing *School District of Grand Rapids v. Ball*,[40] among other cases, Rehnquist conceded in his majority opinion that Blackmun might be right in the context of direct aid. But here, he emphasized, the primary beneficiaries were disabled children, regardless of their religion, and any benefit to religious schools from the services of an impartial translator was both "attenuated" and the product of private choice.

C. *Zelman v. Simmons-Harris*

Mueller, Witters, and *Zobrest* suggested that neutral programs of indirect funding were likely to be upheld, but the Supreme Court had yet to indicate how

---

[40] 473 U.S. 373 (1985).

broadly its approval might reach. Notably, it had not confronted the hotly contested question of whether school voucher programs, offering sizable amounts of public funding, could be extended to religious schools. More generally, it had not drawn a clear doctrinal line between direct and indirect funding. Four years after *Zobrest,* the Court's 1997 decision in *Agostini* indicated a new and more relaxed approach to neutral funding programs even in the context of direct aid.[41] As discussed earlier, however, the Court continued to recognize several Establishment Clause limitations in that context.[42] It remained to be seen whether some of those limitations, or variants of them, might apply also to indirect funding.

Five years after *Agostini,* and nearly a decade after *Zobrest,* the Supreme Court finally confronted these questions in its 2002 decision in *Zelman v. Simmons-Harris.*[43] At issue in *Zelman* was an Ohio voucher program for poor families residing in the Cleveland City School District. Cleveland's public schools were among the worst performing in the nation, and the voucher program was part of a broader initiative that included special state funding for community and magnet schools within the district. The challenged program itself included tutorial support for students choosing to remain in the public schools, but the primary feature of the program was its provision for vouchers.

Under the terms of the program, vouchers could be used at participating private schools, whether secular or religious, that were located within the Cleveland City School District. For the poorest families, the vouchers covered 90 percent of their total tuition. Participating schools were required to cap the annual tuition for these families at $2,500 per student, meaning a maximum voucher amount of $2,250 per student per year. If additional public funding was available, other eligible families could receive vouchers for 75 percent of their tuition costs, up to $1,875 per student per year, with no tuition cap required. The program also authorized participation by public schools in districts adjacent to the Cleveland district. Participating public schools were to receive annual supplemental state funding in the amount of $2,250 per voucher student. In fact, however, no adjacent public school district elected to participate in the program, and most of the participating private schools were religious. Indeed, statistics for a recent academic year showed that of more than 3,700 voucher students, 96 percent were attending religious schools.

As in *Zobrest,* Chief Justice Rehnquist took the opinion in *Zelman* for himself, and, as in *Mueller* and *Zobrest* alike, he found himself with a slender, five-Justice majority. Once again lacking support for his broadly revisionist interpretation of the Establishment Clause, Rehnquist worked within the Court's basic constitutional tests and policies. Yet he was able to persuade his majority that these basic tests and policies supported not only the constitutionality of the voucher program under review, but also a significant reinterpretation of the Court's analysis

[41] *See* Agostini v. Felton, 521 U.S. 203 (1997).
[42] *See supra* §III.
[43] 536 U.S. 639 (2002).

in public funding cases – a reinterpretation that, in reality, constituted an important doctrinal revision.

By the time of *Zelman,* the Court's general approach to public funding cases included *Agostini*'s modification of the *Lemon* test, which reduced the three-part test of *Lemon* to a two-pronged inquiry into purpose and effect, with entanglement subsumed within the effect prong. It also included the endorsement test, a supplemental constitutional standard focusing on the symbolic nature of the challenged governmental program.[44] Although Rehnquist has made it clear that he personally would prefer to abandon each of these tests, he relied upon them in *Zelman* even as he approved the voucher program and reformulated the Court's approach to public funding cases.

Addressing the *Lemon* test as modified in *Agostini,* Rehnquist readily concluded that the first prong of the test was satisfied. The challenged program did not discriminate by its terms between religious and nonreligious schools, and it concededly "was enacted for the valid secular purpose of providing educational assistance to poor children in a demonstrably failing public school system." As a result, Rehnquist continued, the critical question under *Agostini* was "whether the Ohio program nonetheless has the forbidden 'effect' of advancing or inhibiting religion." In answering this question, Rehnquist announced a two-track doctrine for public funding cases, with one track for direct funding programs and another, exceedingly lenient track for indirect funding programs that depend on private choice. Rehnquist rested this approach on his earlier opinions for the Court in *Mueller* and *Zobrest.* He also relied on *Witters,* interpreting that decision even more broadly than he had in *Zobrest.*

According to Rehnquist, the Court's decisions "have drawn a consistent distinction between government programs that provide aid directly to religious schools and programs of true private choice, in which government aid reaches religious schools only as a result of the genuine and independent choices of private individuals." Suggesting that direct aid raises different issues, Rehnquist relied on *Mueller, Witters,* and *Zobrest* in articulating a highly permissive approach to indirect funding. Not surprisingly, he invoked the same arguments about neutrality and private choice that he had used before. But he went beyond the earlier cases in suggesting that neutral programs of indirect funding are virtually immune from constitutional challenge.

As long as a program of indirect aid is neutrally drawn and is "a program of true private choice" that is not "skewed" to create incentives favoring the selection of religious schools, Rehnquist wrote, the program "is not readily subject to challenge under the Establishment Clause." He contended that the Court had never invalidated such a program, and he implied that it never would. Echoing and expanding upon earlier statements, Rehnquist suggested that neutral programs of private choice honor the constitutional value of religious voluntarism. He also

---

[44] *See supra* §I.B.

suggested that in the absence of improper "skewing" that favors or disfavors religious choices, neutral governmental programs in this context promote religious equality, not only between and among competing religions and religious groups, but also between religion and irreligion.

Rehnquist concluded that neutral programs of indirect funding should be found to withstand not only the "effect" inquiry under *Lemon–Agostini*, but also the endorsement test:

> A program that shares these features permits government aid to reach religious institutions only by way of the deliberate choices of numerous individual recipients. The incidental advancement of a religious mission, or the perceived endorsement of a religious message, is reasonably attributable to the individual recipient, not to the government, whose role ends with the disbursement of benefits.

"[W]e have repeatedly recognized," he continued, "that no reasonable observer would think a neutral program of private choice, where state aid reaches religious schools solely as a result of the numerous independent decisions of private individuals, carries with it the imprimatur of government endorsement." According to this reasoning, neutral programs of private choice satisfy the endorsement test, and, as a result, they neither disrespect the religious identity of citizens nor undermine the religious inclusiveness of the political community.

Utilizing this analysis in the case at hand, Rehnquist upheld the Ohio voucher program. He found that it was "neutral in all respects toward religion" and that it was not skewed to favor religious schools, especially when considered in light of the more general Ohio initiative of which it was a part. In the absence of such skewing, it was enough that families in Cleveland retained viable secular options and were not being coerced to choose religious schools. It mattered not that, in actual operation, the voucher program included no adjacent public schools and that an overwhelming majority of the vouchers were being used at religious schools. "The constitutionality of a neutral educational aid program," Rehnquist wrote, "simply does not turn on whether and why, in a particular area, at a particular time, most private schools are run by religious organizations, or most recipients choose to use the aid at a religious school." He emphasized the importance of doctrinal clarity and the weakness of statistical evaluations in assessing primary effect. He noted that although 96 percent of the Cleveland voucher students attended religious schools in one recent year, the percentage was only 78 percent in an earlier year, and the percentage would drop to under 20 percent if non-voucher-based public school options – including community schools, magnet schools, and traditional public schools with tutorial assistance – were added to the denominator.

As in *Mueller*, Rehnquist saw no need to formally overrule *Committee for Public Education v. Nyquist*,[45] although he appeared to limit *Nyquist* virtually to its

---

[45] 413 U.S. 756 (1973).

facts. He claimed that *Nyquist* was distinguishable from the Ohio program, in part because the Ohio program, properly understood, included public as well as private school options. Whether the existence of various public school options is essential to the validity of a voucher program remains to be seen, especially in light of Rehnquist's further statement that "we now hold that *Nyquist* does not govern neutral educational programs that, like the program here, offer aid directly to a broad class of individual recipients defined without regard to religion."[46] In any event, voucher programs typically will include public school options, and such options can be incorporated without difficulty.

Zelman signals the constitutionality of virtually any school voucher program that is crafted with minimal care. In addition, it strongly supports the constitutionality of noneducational "charitable choice" programs to the extent that they authorize social-service vouchers that recipients can use at the provider of their choice, whether or not the provider is a religious organization.[47] More broadly, Rehnquist's opinion in *Zelman* firmly establishes a two-track approach for public funding cases, with indirect funding subject to minimal constitutional scrutiny.

As discussed earlier, direct aid to religious schools or organizations, even through funding programs that are neutrally drawn, remains subject to various constitutional restrictions.[48] Under *Zelman*, by contrast, the constitutional touchstones for indirect aid are neutrality and private choice, and these conditions are easily met. Neutrality seems to depend entirely on the formal reach of the funding program, not its actual effect. Thus, a program satisfies this condition if it does not facially discriminate between religious and nonreligious beneficiaries or organizations, and if it is not "skewed" to favor the former over the latter. Moreover, these same formal features will typically support a finding of "true private choice" by providing viable secular as well as religious options. Unlike direct aid, indirect aid need not be confined to secular uses, and, indeed, the ultimate destination of the aid can be overwhelmingly religious. Likewise, the substantiality of the aid seems not to matter, and the indirect manner of funding is likely to defeat any claim of excessive entanglement. In terms of the *Lemon–Agostini* test, it seems that the effect inquiry – and with it any concern about entanglement – has almost disappeared from view. The government cannot deliberately discriminate in favor of religion, but that much is demanded by the first prong of the test, the requirement of secular purpose, a requirement that itself is readily satisfied.

---

[46] The various public school options, including community and magnet schools, may have been important to Justice O'Connor. Although she joined Rehnquist's majority opinion, O'Connor also wrote a separate concurring opinion, in part to support Rehnquist's conclusion that Cleveland parents had genuine secular options.

[47] For comprehensive analysis of "charitable choice" and related initiatives, see IRA C. LUPU & ROBERT W. TUTTLE, GOVERNMENT PARTNERSHIPS WITH FAITH-BASED SERVICE PROVIDERS: THE STATE OF THE LAW (2002), along with the authors' annual updates to this report.

[48] *See supra* § III.

V. DENOUEMENT: *LOCKE v. DAVEY*

Through his opinions in *Mueller, Zobrest,* and especially *Zelman,* Chief Justice Rehnquist, citing conventional constitutional tests and accepted constitutional values, in reality brought about a substantial revision in the Supreme Court's public funding doctrine, one that makes neutral programs of indirect funding all but immune from Establishment Clause challenge. After *Zelman,* the question was no longer whether the government is permitted to include religious organizations in such programs. Rather, the question was whether the government retains the constitutional option of *excluding* religious alternatives from otherwise general programs of indirect, voucher-based funding for privately provided education or social services. This question arises not under the Establishment Clause, but under the First Amendment's Free Exercise Clause, which precludes the government from "prohibiting the free exercise" of religion.

The Free Exercise Clause bars substantial and discriminatory burdens on the exercise of religion, and, on the basis of precedent, there was a strong argument that the exclusion of religious options from indirect funding programs would violate this prohibition. By precluding voucher recipients from choosing religious alternatives, the government arguably would be imposing a burden on religious decision making that would be constitutionally substantial under free exercise cases such as *Sherbert v. Verner.*[49] Likewise, the exclusion of religious options might be regarded as deliberate discrimination against the exercise of religion, triggering strict scrutiny and probable invalidation under the reasoning of *Church of the Lukumi Babalu Aye, Inc. v. City of Hialeah.*[50]

A variant of this question reached the Supreme Court in 2004, only two years after *Zelman.* In *Locke v. Davey,*[51] the Court considered a State of Washington program that provided merit- and income-based scholarships, ranging from about $1,000 to about $1,500 per year, to students at public and private colleges within the state. Students at religious colleges were not ineligible for that reason alone, but they were denied funding if they majored in devotional theology, as, for example, in preparation for careers in the ministry. To support this denial of funding, the state cited a state constitutional provision that mandated a stronger separation of church and state than that required by the Establishment Clause. Relying on the Free Exercise Clause, however, the Ninth Circuit Court of Appeals held that the First Amendment trumped the Washington Constitution and demanded an end to Washington's discriminatory exclusion.[52]

---

[49] 374 U.S. 398 (1963).

[50] 508 U.S. 520 (1993); *see also* McDaniel v. Paty, 435 U.S. 618 (1978). Even apart from the Free Exercise Clause, one could argue that the exclusion would violate the Free Speech Clause principle of "equal access" by discriminating against religious speech on the basis of its viewpoint. *See, e.g.,* Rosenberger v. Rector and Visitors of the Univ. of Va., 515 U.S. 819 (1995).

[51] 540 U.S. 712 (2004).

[52] *See* Davey v. Locke, 299 F.3d 748 (9th Cir. 2002), *rev'd,* 540 U.S. 712 (2004). The Court of Appeals relied on the Free Exercise Clause, but its opinion also included free speech, "equal access" reasoning.

To the surprise of many, the Supreme Court reversed the Ninth Circuit by a lopsided, 7–2 margin, with Chief Justice Rehnquist writing for the majority. Rehnquist reiterated the Establishment Clause doctrine of *Zelman* and noted that it clearly would permit the State of Washington, if it wished, to include devotional theology majors in this program of indirect funding. Even so, he wrote, the state had the discretion to make this policy decision for itself and could choose to deny funding without violating the Free Exercise Clause. In so ruling, Rehnquist parted company with Justices Scalia and Thomas, his fellow travelers in Establishment Clause cases, who argued vigorously in dissent that the state had improperly discriminated against religion.

Speaking for the majority, Rehnquist wrote that "'there is room for play in the joints'" between the Establishment and Free Exercise Clauses[53] and that states sometimes are free to promote antiestablishment policies that go beyond what the Establishment Clause demands. In this case, he concluded, the state's disfavor of religion was minimal and did not suggest hostility. Rather, "[t]he State has merely chosen not to fund a distinct category of instruction." According to Rehnquist, the state's decision tracked historical antiestablishment concerns about taxpayer-supported clergy, concerns that were reflected in a number of state constitutions. As a result, the state's exclusion of devotional theology majors did not violate the Free Exercise Clause.[54]

The scope of the Court's decision remains to be seen. If interpreted narrowly, *Locke* means only that, due to distinctive antiestablishment concerns, an indirect funding program may selectively exclude funding for the devotional religious work and training of clergy and other religious professionals. Under this interpretation, the Free Exercise Clause might still preclude, in other settings, the exclusion of religious options from otherwise general programs of indirect funding, such as voucher-based programs for education or social services. But Rehnquist's emphasis on "play in the joints" might suggest a broader interpretation of *Locke,* one that would give the states considerable leeway.[55]

Rehnquist himself might welcome a broad view of *Locke* and the constitutional discretion it accords to the states. In any event, his rejection of the free exercise argument confirms that his Establishment Clause emphasis on neutrality and private choice is part of a deeper constitutional vision that seeks to limit the reach of the Bill of Rights and thereby to enhance the prerogatives of the states. Neutrality and private choice, without more, would support the dissenters' position in *Locke,* not the position of Rehnquist and the majority. The challenged exclusion plainly was not neutral; it singled out religious vocations for distinctive disfavor.

---

[53] Rehnquist drew the quoted language from Walz v. Tax Comm'n, 397 U.S. 664, 669 (1970).

[54] The Court also rejected the challenger's free speech, "equal access" argument.

[55] For lower-court decisions interpreting *Locke* broadly and extending its reasoning to uphold state law exclusions of religious schools from voucher programs for elementary and secondary education, see Eulitt v. Maine, 386 F.3d 344 (1st Cir. 2004); Bush v. Holmes, 886 So. 2d 340 (Fla. Dist. Ct. App. 2004) (en banc; related question certified to Fla. S. Ct.).

And it did not honor the principle of private choice. Instead, Washington's discriminatory denial of scholarship funding created an obvious financial disincentive – a "financial penalty," in the words of Justice Scalia's dissent – for any student otherwise inclined to pursue a religious calling. For Chief Justice Rehnquist and his *Locke* majority, however, these realities were not enough to restrict the state's policy-making discretion.

VI. CHIEF JUSTICE REHNQUIST, CONSTITUTIONAL VALUES, AND THE ESTABLISHMENT CLAUSE

As evidenced by the Justices' 5–4 split in *Zelman*, the Supreme Court is narrowly divided concerning the proper approach to indirect funding for religious schools and organizations. This is hardly surprising. Although most of the Justices agree, in general terms, concerning the constitutional values that the Establishment Clause reflects, the specific meaning and relative weight of these values in particular settings is subject to reasonable debate. This is certainly true with respect to indirect funding.

As discussed at the outset of this chapter, a number of Establishment Clause values are relevant in this context. For the *Zelman* dissenters, these values require significant constitutional restrictions on indirect funding, even if the funding program is formally neutral and depends on private choice.[56] Many constitutional scholars agree,[57] and this position certainly is not unreasonable. At the same time, however, the much more relaxed approach that Chief Justice Rehnquist has championed likewise has scholarly support,[58] and it, too, reflects a reasonable consideration of constitutional values.[59] If his position were not reasonable in light of constitutional values that most of the Justices accept, Rehnquist would find himself languishing in dissent, just as he has in his more radical attempt to rewrite Establishment Clause doctrine from the ground up. To secure majority support in this particular context, Rehnquist has bracketed his distinctive

---

[56] *See, e.g.*, Zelman v. Simmons-Harris, 536 U.S. 639, 686–717 (2002) (Souter, J., dissenting).

[57] *See, e.g.*, Steven K. Green, *The Illusionary Aspect of "Private Choice" for Constitutional Analysis*, 38 WILLAMETTE L. REV. 549 (2002); Steven H. Shiffrin, *The First Amendment and the Socialization of Children: Compulsory Public Education and Vouchers*, 11 CORNELL J.L. & PUB. POL'Y 503, 541–50 (2002); Laura S. Underkuffler, *Vouchers and Beyond: The Individual as Causative Agent in Establishment Clause Jurisprudence*, 75 IND. L.J. 167 (2000).

[58] *See, e.g.*, Michael J. Perry, *What Does the Establishment Clause Forbid? Reflections on the Constitutionality of School Vouchers*, in SCHOOL CHOICE: THE MORAL DEBATE 231 (Alan Wolfe ed., 2003); Eugene Volokh, *Equal Treatment Is Not Establishment*, 13 NOTRE DAME J.L. ETHICS & PUB. POL'Y 341 (1999).

[59] For additional academic commentary on both sides of this debate, see *Commentary on School Vouchers and the Establishment Clause*, 31 CONN. L. REV. 803 (1999); *Symposium on Law and Religion*, 13 NOTRE DAME J.L. ETHICS & PUB. POL'Y 239 (1999). For a nuanced appraisal of the constitutional issues raised by vouchers in various contexts, see Ira C. Lupu & Robert Tuttle, *Sites of Redemption: A Wide-Angle Look at Government Vouchers and Sectarian Service Providers*, 28 J.L. & POL'Y 539 (2002).

general approach to the Establishment Clause and has advanced a reasonable interpretation of conventional constitutional tests and values – tests and values that honor the constitutional commitments of a broader range of Justices.

In *Mueller, Zobrest,* and *Zelman,* Rehnquist applied the Court's prevailing Establishment Clause tests: the tests of *Lemon v. Kurtzman* and *Agostini v. Felton,* as well as the endorsement test. These tests themselves reflect a range of contemporary Establishment Clause values, but Rehnquist also has discussed these values more directly. Indeed, his opinions have invoked, explicitly or implicitly, four of the five Establishment Clause values that are especially relevant in this context.

First, Rehnquist's approach to indirect funding relies heavily on the value of religious equality, not only between and among competing religions and religious groups, but also between religion and irreligion. According to Rehnquist, this value is well served by "neutral" funding programs, programs that avoid any deliberate discrimination or "skewing" that favors either one religion over others or religion in general over irreligion. Second, Rehnquist has emphasized the value of religious voluntarism. Programs of "true private choice," by definition, create no financial or other incentive favoring religious choices, but instead permit individuals to make these choices for themselves, free from governmental compulsion or influence.

The third relevant value requires the government to respect the religious (or irreligious) identity of dissenting individuals, including dissenting taxpayers, by avoiding the promotion of religious values that the dissenters do not share. Related to this third value is the fourth, the protection of a religiously inclusive political community, which likewise may be threatened by the official promotion of religion. These twin values are linked especially to the endorsement test, which Rehnquist discussed and found satisfied in *Zelman.* But Rehnquist also had anticipated and dismissed similar concerns in *Mueller,* long before the endorsement test, as such, had been formally adopted by the Court. In *Mueller* and *Zelman* alike, Rehnquist emphasized that indirect funding, by its very nature, does not carry a message of *governmental* endorsement of religion. Instead, any endorsement of religion is the product of independent private choices. Depending on their choices, individual recipients might be endorsing religion, but the government is not.

By contrast, one relevant Establishment Clause value is conspicuously absent from Rehnquist's analysis in this area: the autonomy of religious organizations to determine and control their religious and worldly missions for themselves. This value is implicated by governmental funding programs, including programs of indirect funding, when the government imposes conditions that participating organizations must follow. Under the school voucher program approved in *Zelman,* for instance, participating schools are barred from discriminating on the basis of religion. In his dissenting opinion in *Zelman,* Justice Souter argued that this "foot-in-the-door of religious regulation" threatened the autonomy of religious schools. He noted that the condition precludes religious schools from favoring members of their own religion over others – for example, Roman Catholics over Protestants, Jews, Muslims, or atheists – in the admission of students and, it would seem, even in the hiring of administrators and teachers. Likewise, this prohibition would appear to forbid religious schools from requiring students or teachers to participate in prayer or other religious exercises.

Over time, moreover, the strings attached to governmental funding might expand even as the participating organizations become more and more dependent on the government's financial support. Religious schools, for instance, might expand their facilities to accommodate an increasing number of voucher students, only to see the government impose new conditions on participation, perhaps in the form of curriculum regulations. Although the financial support is a carrot, not a stick, it might nonetheless induce religious organizations to modify and weaken their religious practices and requirements in response to the government's demands.[60] This prospect seriously threatens the autonomy of religious institutions, but, especially after *Locke,* they would face an uphill battle in challenging the constitutionality of funding conditions.[61] Due to differences in theology and mission, moreover, the adverse impact might be greater for some religions than others, meaning that the value of religious equality might also be impaired.

This concern about institutional autonomy may be the strongest argument against the Rehnquist approach to indirect funding. But there are potential answers to this concern, including the freedom of religious organizations to decline or withdraw from participation, as difficult as that might be. In any event, as Rehnquist himself has demonstrated, other Establishment Clause values can be understood to support the Rehnquist approach. On balance, it represents a resolution of this problem that, at a minimum, is credible and reasonable.

Through his opinions in *Mueller, Zobrest,* and *Zelman,* Chief Justice Rehnquist has successfully championed an Establishment Clause doctrine that makes indirect funding programs almost invulnerable to constitutional challenge. He has achieved this result by focusing on neutrality and private choice and by explaining his approach in terms of conventional constitutional tests and conventional constitutional values. As *Locke* makes clear, however, Rehnquist's Establishment Clause emphasis on neutrality and private choice does not extend to the Free

---

[60] *See* Daniel O. Conkle, *The Path of American Religious Liberty: From the Original Theology to Formal Neutrality and an Uncertain Future,* 75 IND. L.J. 1, 21–24 (2000); *see also* William P. Marshall, *Remembering the Values of Separatism and State Funding of Religious Organizations (Charitable Choice): To Aid Is Not Necessarily to Protect,* 18 J.L. & POL'Y 479 (2002); *see generally* Vincent Blasi, *School Vouchers and Religious Liberty: Seven Questions from Madison's* Memorial and Remonstrance, 87 CORNELL L. REV. 783 (2002) (evaluating this and related questions from the perspective of James Madison).

[61] *See* Douglas Laycock, *Theology Scholarships, the Pledge of Allegiance, and Religious Liberty: Avoiding the Extremes but Missing the Liberty,* 118 HARV. L. REV. 155, 195–200 (2004). For pre-*Locke* discussions, *see* Thomas C. Berg, *Vouchers and Religious Schools: The New Constitutional Questions,* 72 U. CIN. L. REV. 151, 208–20 (2003); Ira C. Lupu & Robert W. Tuttle, *Zelman's Future: Vouchers, Sectarian Providers, and the Next Round of Constitutional Battles,* 78 NOTRE DAME L. REV. 917, 972–82 (2003); Mark Tushnet, *Vouchers After Zelman,* 2002 S. CT. REV. 1, 22–29.

Exercise Clause. And even in the Establishment Clause context, his analysis of indirect funding may be largely strategic. In this distinct but important area, it has permitted partial fulfillment of a broader goal: a limited reading of the Establishment Clause, one that does not substantially constrain state policy making on matters affecting religion. In this light, Rehnquist's opinion in *Locke* is hardly surprising. Rather, it is part of the same fundamental vision: reading the Bill of Rights narrowly and thereby enhancing the power and discretion of the states.

CRIMINAL PROCEDURE

CHAPTER FIVE

THE FOURTH AMENDMENT: BE REASONABLE

Craig M. Bradley*

In a 1985 interview with the *New York Times*, (then) Justice Rehnquist described one of the achievements of the Burger Court, of which he had been a member for 13 years, as "call(ing) a halt to a number of the sweeping rulings (of) the Warren Court" in "the area of constitutional rights of accused criminal defendants."[1] But while Rehnquist was pleased with the overall trend of the Burger Court's criminal procedure decisions up to that point, the Court had not gone nearly as far as Rehnquist would have liked.

In more recent years, the Court has steered an even more moderate course. From the time the Court attained its current membership with Justice Breyer's arrival in 1994, through 2005, the Court has decided roughly equal numbers of cases involving police procedures for and against criminal defendants.[2]

But if the Court overall has been rather moderate, Chief Justice Rehnquist, with very rare exceptions, has consistently called for further limiting the rights of individuals vis-à-vis the state. This chapter examines the techniques employed by him and others to achieve this goal in that area of constitutional law in which, year in and year out, the Court has been the most active: the Fourth Amendment.[3] The Amendment provides:

> The right of the people to be secure in their persons, houses, papers and effects, against unreasonable searches and seizures, shall not be violated, and no Warrants shall issue but upon probable cause, supported by Oath or affirmation, and particularly describing the place to be searched, and the person or thing to be seized.

In a series of cases decided during the 1960s the Warren Court had greatly expanded the ability of criminal defendants to challenge their convictions on the

---

* Thanks to Jim Tomkovicz and Yale Kamisar for their thoughtful comments on an earlier draft of this chapter.

[1] John A. Jenkins, *The Partisan*, N.Y. Times Magazine, March 3, 1985, at 28.

[2] *See* Craig M. Bradley, *The Middle Class Fourth Amendment*, 6 Buff. Crim. L. Rev. 1123, 1132 fn. 36 (2003).

[3] For example, between 1979 and 1984 the Court decided thirty-five Fourth Amendment cases. Craig M. Bradley, *Two Models of the Fourth Amendment*, 83 Mich. L. Rev. 1468 (1985).

ground that evidence used against them had been obtained in violation of the Fourth Amendment. By far the most significant decision was *Mapp v. Ohio*,[4] decided in 1961. While the Supreme Court had made the states subject to the Fourth Amendment in 1949, they had specifically refused to apply the exclusionary rule to the states,[5] even though it had been applied to federal prosecutions since 1914.[6] Thus, unless a state had adopted its own exclusionary rule, evidence obtained by police in violation of the Fourth Amendment could nevertheless be used in the defendant's trial. This meant that police were basically free to disregard Fourth Amendment rules, such as the requirement that a warrant must be obtained to search someone's home, because there was no effective remedy for violation of the rules.

Recognizing this, the Supreme Court in *Mapp* declared that, without the exclusionary remedy to back it up, the Fourth Amendment would be "a form of words, valueless and undeserving of mention in a perpetual charter of inestimable human liberties. . . ." Accordingly, the Court held that evidence seized in violation of the Fourth Amendment could not be used in state criminal prosecutions. Further, the appointment of more liberal federal judges by the Kennedy/Johnson administrations from 1961 through 1968, as well as an expansion of the ability of federal courts to overturn state convictions occasioned by the 1963 case of *Fay v. Noia*[7] meant that, if the state courts didn't follow the Fourth Amendment and exclude evidence for its violation, the federal courts would force them to do so.

But what were the requirements of the Fourth Amendment? There was and is no code of police procedures at the federal level, as most countries have, that could simply be applied to the states. Furthermore, the Court's decisions on the subject prior to 1961 had been spotty and often contradictory.[8] Accordingly, it fell to the Warren Court, and to subsequent Courts, to follow up on *Mapp* with an extended series of cases delineating the scope of Fourth Amendment (as well as Fifth and Sixth Amendment) rights that the states were expected to enforce.

One principle of Fourth Amendment law was already in place: The Fourth Amendment ordinarily requires a warrant as a precondition of a reasonable search.[9] The origins of the so-called warrant requirement are murky since it is not contained in the Fourth Amendment itself, which requires only that searches be "reasonable" and then states the preconditions that a warrant must meet if it

---

[4] 367 U.S. 643.

[5] Wolf v. Colorado, 338 U.S. 25.

[6] Weeks v. United States, 232 U.S. 383 (1914).

[7] 372 U.S. 391.

[8] *See, e.g.,* Chimel v. California, 395 U.S. 752, 755–63 (1969), explaining the convoluted history of "search incident to arrest" doctrine.

[9] *E.g.,* Johnson v. United States, 333 U.S. 10, 14–15 (1948).

is used.[10] Nevertheless the "warrant requirement" was an established rule by 1961, albeit subject to many exceptions.[11]

In expounding the nature of the warrant requirement, the Warren Court defined those areas for which a warrant must be used to include apartments, hotel rooms, and business premises.[12] It struck down search warrants for not adequately setting forth "probable cause."[13] It ruled that the "fruits" of Fourth Amendment violations, such as a confession obtained from someone during an illegal search or arrest, must also be excluded from evidence.[14] It required a search warrant to "bug" a phone booth and other places in which a defendant might have an "expectation of privacy."[15] And it limited the scope of searches incident to arrest of someone at home to areas within the "immediate control" of the arrestee, rather than his whole house or apartment.[16]

At the same time, the Warren Court was also expanding and defining defendants' rights in other areas of criminal procedure, most notably requiring that counsel be appointed for indigent defendants who wanted one at all felony trials,[17] and that arrested suspects be given the famous *Miranda* warnings before they could be interrogated by police.[18]

Meanwhile, over at the Justice Department, Assistant Attorney General Rehnquist, who came in with the Nixon administration in 1969, along with his fellow conservatives, was stewing about this liberal court that, as Rehnquist was later to declare at his confirmation hearings, had swung the pendulum "too far toward the accused not by virtue of a fair reading of the Constitution" but rather "the personal philosophy of one or more of the Justices."[19]

Rehnquist was acutely aware of the issue because one of his jobs as head of the Office of Legal Counsel was to choose Justices for the Supreme Court who would reverse the trend, which Richard Nixon had complained of in his campaign, toward "weaken(ing) the peace forces as against the criminal forces in this

[10] *See, e.g.,* Akhil Amar, *Fourth Amendment First Principles,* 107 Harv. L. Rev. 757 (1994) for a discussion of the disconnect between the language of the Fourth Amendment and the Supreme Court's interpretation of it.

[11] As of 1985, I counted more than twenty exceptions to the search warrant "requirement." Bradley, *supra* note 3, at 1473.

[12] *See* cases cited in Wayne LaFave *et al., Criminal Procedure* §3.2, at 133 (3d ed. 2000).

[13] *E.g.,* Aguilar v. Texas 378 U.S. 108 (1964).

[14] Wong Sun v. United States, 371 U.S. 471 (1963).

[15] Katz v. United States, 389 U.S. 347 (1967).

[16] *Chimel, supra* note 6.

[17] Gideon v. Wainwright, 372 U.S. 335 (1963). This was extended to misdemeanor trials by the Burger Court in *Argersinger v. Hamlin,* 407 U.S. 25 (1972) but not to those trials which could not result in imprisonment. Scott v. Illinois, 440 U.S. 367 (1979). (See Chapter 7.)

[18] Miranda v. Arizona, 384 U.S. 436 (1966). For a brief history of the "criminal procedure revolution" *see* Craig Bradley, *The Failure of the Criminal Procedure Revolution* ch. 2 (1993).

[19] Senate Judiciary Committee, *Nominations of William H. Rehnquist and Lewis F. Powell, Jr.,* 92d Cong., 1st Sess.(1971), serial Y4.J89/2:R 26/2, 26–27.

country."[20] As it turned out, Nixon got to appoint four Justices, giving the Court a Republican majority by 1972 for the first time since the mid-1930s. First there were Burger and Blackmun. Then Nixon planned to appoint a southerner, an Arkansas bond lawyer named Hershel Friday, and a woman, Mildred Lillie, a California appellate court judge. These plans foundered on the rocks of American Bar Association disapproval, and another potential candidate, Senator Howard Baker, couldn't make up his mind. So, much to his surprise, the forty-seven-year-old Rehnquist, along with Lewis Powell of Virginia, found himself on the Supreme Court.[21]

Rehnquist was undoubtedly committed to reversing *Mapp v. Ohio* from the moment he joined the Court, but he didn't express this position in an opinion until 1979 in *California v. Minjares,* dissenting from the denial of a stay.[22] As discussed above, *Mapp* is the keystone to Fourth Amendment rights. If *Mapp* could be eliminated, the entire structure of federally protected rights against unreasonable searches would collapse because police would no longer have an incentive to follow the rules.[23]

There was nothing radical in Rehnquist's argument, which only Chief Justice Burger joined. He essentially repeated the points made by the *Mapp* dissenters, Justice Harlan, joined by Justices Frankfurter, Whittaker and, in part, Stewart.[24] That is, he said that it made no sense to give the defendant a windfall by excluding relevant and competent evidence from his case especially when, as in *Minjares,* the "violation" of his rights was in good faith or, arguably, not a violation at all. (In *Minjares* the officer, with probable cause to search a car, also searched a bag in the car without a warrant. The California Supreme Court had concluded that the bag search was a Fourth Amendment violation, and certiorari was denied. However, the Supreme Court, in a later case, concluded that such a search was legitimate.)[25]

Rehnquist further argued that the 1976 case of *Stone v. Powell,* by declaring that the exclusionary rule "is a judicially created remedy rather than a personal constitutional right,"[26] had removed the constitutional underpinnings of the exclusionary rule, making it ripe for overruling.[27] (He had taken a similar position about *Miranda* in a majority opinion in *Michigan v. Tucker* in 1974, trying to set the stage for *Miranda* to be overruled as well.) Finally, he pointed out that civil suits, which might have been an ineffective remedy for constitutional violations

---

[20] *See* Bradley, *supra* note 18, at 30.

[21] The story of Rehnquist's appointment is described in detail in John Dean, *The Rehnquist Choice* (2001).

[22] 443 U.S. 916 (1979).

[23] My experience as a prosecutor in Washington, D.C., confirmed my belief that the exclusionary rule is necessary for police compliance with Supreme Court criminal procedure rules.

[24] *Mapp, supra* note 4, at 872 *et seq.*

[25] California v. Acevedo, 500 U.S. 565 (1991).

[26] 428 U.S. 465, 495 n. 37 (1976).

[27] *Minjares, supra* note 22, at 924.

at the time of *Mapp,* had been beefed up by more recent Supreme Court decisions such that they would adequately deter police misconduct.[28]

Rehnquist's view is shared to an extent by all of the countries of Western Eu-
rope and Canada. The United States is unique in having mandatory exclusionary rule for Fourth Amendment violations, though most countries do exclude
evidence on a discretionary basis more often than Rehnquist would like.[29] In any
case, the majority of the Republican Court never came around to his view, being
comfortable with cabining the exclusionary rule in various ways rather than overruling it. This has forced Rehnquist to conduct a sort of career-long guerrilla
campaign against the exclusionary rule, and Fourth Amendment rights in general, seeking at every opportunity to limit them as much as possible, sometimes
winning and sometimes losing, but obdurately slogging on. In the process, he and
his fellow conservatives have developed what might be considered a manual of
techniques for limiting Fourth Amendment rights (or for "returning the Fourth
Amendment to its true meaning," as they might put it). There follows a discussion of how these various techniques have been employed.

I. LIMIT THE DEFINITION OF "SEARCH"

As noted, the Supreme Court did not begin in earnest the process of developing
a body of Fourth Amendment rules, to which the exclusionary rule would apply,
until after *Mapp* was decided in 1961. At the rate of between five and eight cases
a year, there were still many unanswered questions left to be taken up after Burger
took over as Chief Justice in 1970. In particular, the question of whether various
police activities constituted a "search," and hence qualified for Fourth Amendment protection, was a significant part of the Court's jurisprudence throughout the 1970s and 1980s. Although Rehnquist was not called upon to write any
majority opinions in this area, he consistently joined Court majorities that limited the scope of the Fourth Amendment.

Thus, the Court held that searches of open fields,[30] searches of trash left at the
curb,[31] and helicopter[32] and airplane surveillance[33] were not "searches" as far as
the Fourth Amendment was concerned, because they did not violate "reasonable
expectations of privacy." Consequently they need not be justified by probable
cause, much less a warrant. Likewise, use of a "pen register" to ascertain the tele-
phone numbers dialed by a suspect was not a search.[34] The Court reaffirmed an

---

[28] *Id.* at 925–26, citing Monroe v. Pape, 365 U.S. 167 (1961), and Monell v. New York Dep't of Social
Services, 436 U.S. 658 (1978).

[29] Craig Bradley (ed). *Criminal Procedure: A Worldwide Study* 405 (1999).

[30] Oliver v. United States, 466 U.S. 170 (1984). This repeated an old position first taken in *Hester
v. United States,* 265 U.S. 57 (1924).

[31] California v. Greenwood, 486 U.S. 35 (1988).

[32] Florida v. Riley, 488 U.S. 445 (1989).

[33] California v. Ciraolo, 476 U.S. 207 (1986).

[34] Smith v. Maryland, 442 U.S. 735

old rule that searches by private parties were not covered by the Fourth Amendment, and held further that police reopening a package previously opened by a private party did not amount to a Fourth Amendment search either.[35] Moreover, taking paint scrapings from the outside of an automobile,[36] or entering the automobile and removing papers from the dashboard to view the Vehicle Identification Number[37] were not deemed searches.

Finally, the "plain view doctrine," which had long held that police simply viewing, or hearing or smelling, something that any member of the public could sense was not a "search,"[38] was expanded in *Dow Chemical Co. v. United States*[39] to include the use of a high-resolution camera by EPA officials to photograph the petitioner's industrial plant, though the Court noted that the result might be different if a residence were involved. It was further applied to determine that use of a drug-detecting dog to sniff luggage at an airport, or of a car stopped for a traffic violation, was not a "search."[40]

None of these decisions was directly inconsistent with Warren Court holdings nor inherently unreasonable. But the consistent holding that various police activities, which could only be termed "searches" in common parlance, were not "searches" for the purposes of the Fourth Amendment caused many to wonder whether Fourth Amendment protections would eventually be whittled away to nothing.[41] For example, the "trash" case, *California v. Greenwood*,[42] led Justice Brennan in dissent to bemoan:

> [T]he Court paints a grim picture of our society. It depicts a society in which local authorities may . . . monitor (citizens) arbitrarily and without judicial oversight – a society that is not prepared to recognize as reasonable an individual's expectation of privacy in the most private of personal effects. . . .

However, these fears proved to be unfounded as this trend petered out in the 1990s, with no more holdings that put police investigative activities outside the bounds of the Fourth Amendment.[43] The trend was reversed by two important decisions in the 2000s, one of which, surprisingly, was authored by Rehnquist himself. In studying all of the Fourth Amendment cases decided during his thirty-odd years on the Court, this is the *only* nonunanimous case that I have found

---

[35] United States v. Jacobsen, 466 U.S. 109 (1984).

[36] Cardwell v. Lewis, 417 U.S. 583 (1974).

[37] New York v. Class, 475 U.S. 106 (1986).

[38] The "plain view doctrine" also includes the concept that the police may *seize* objects found in plain view of a policeman who has a right to be where he obtains that view. LaFave *et al., supra* note 12, at 135.

[39] 476 U.S. 227 (1986).

[40] United States v. Place, 462 U.S. 696 (1983). *Accord,* Illinois v. Caballes, 125 S. Ct. 824 (2005) (suspicionless dog sniff of car during traffic stop approved).

[41] *See, e.g.,* Silas Wasserstrom, *The Incredible Shrinking Fourth Amendment,* 21 Am. Crim. L. Rev. 257 (1984).

[42] *Supra* note 31.

[43] Except for the recent extension of the dog sniff case in *Caballes, supra* note 40, in 2005.

in which Rehnquist voted for the defendant on a Fourth Amendment issue.[44] (On the other side of the bench, Justices Brennan and Marshall voted for the government in Fourth Amendment cases only twice – including unanimous decisions – from 1972 until their retirements in the early 1990s).[45]

In *Bond v. United States*[46] the petitioner was riding on a bus that stopped at a permanent immigration checkpoint in Texas so that the immigration status of the passengers could be checked. However, the zealous Border Patrol agent also decided to see if he could discover any drugs. So he walked down the aisle squeezing the soft-sided luggage in the overhead storage space. When he got to Bond's bag, he felt a "brick-like" object.[47] He opened the bag with Bond's consent and found a "brick" of marijuana.

The issue was whether or not the initial manipulation of the bag was a "search." Rehnquist, writing for a seven-Justice majority, concluded that it was. The Court applied the standard test, derived from the Warren Court's *Katz* decision. It concluded that even though the defendant realized that "his bag may be handled" by passengers or bus personnel, he had a "reasonable expectation" that his bag would not be manipulated in an "exploratory manner" by police.[48]

As surprising as Rehnquist's being in the majority was that Breyer (joined by Scalia) wrote the dissent, citing newspaper articles about how people's bags are manhandled by fellow passengers all the time and arguing that the agent's intent didn't affect the defendant's expectation of privacy.[49] This was certainly not an unreasonable position, and one that Rehnquist would ordinarily have been expected to join.

One may speculate as to why Rehnquist abandoned his virtually invariable stance in this case. As a frequent traveler, he may not have liked the idea of the authorities being free to investigate one's bags, but since Supreme Court Justices usually travel by plane, where luggage inspections are routine, that does not seem a very satisfactory explanation. It may also be that, with a clear majority already lined up behind the defendant, he, as Chief Justice, diplomatically joined up, as he has indicated that the Chief Justice should in cases "not involving matters of high principle."[50] However, that belief has not moved him in other Fourth Amendment cases.

Rehnquist may have an overriding general philosophy of lack of sympathy toward defendant's claims of constitutional protection, but he doesn't necessarily

---

[44] For a discussion of some of the unanimous decisions favoring defendants which he joined, and why some of his dissents against defendant's rights were not "hard core," *see* Craig Bradley, *Criminal Procedure in the Rehnquist Court: Has the Rehnquistion Begun?* 63 Ind. L.J. 273, 287–90 (1987).

[45] Craig Bradley & Joseph Hoffmann, *Be Careful What You Ask for,* 76 Ind. L.J. 889, 929 (2001).

[46] 529 U.S. 334 (2000).

[47] *Id.* at 336.

[48] *Id.* at 339.

[49] *Id.* at 340–41.

[50] *Chief Justices I Never Knew,* 3 Hastings Const. L.Q. 637 (1976).

ask himself in each case how this case fits into that philosophy. He, in common with other judges, looks at the facts of the case and asks if the search seems reasonable or not under these facts – which, as Rehnquist has pointed out, is all that the Fourth Amendment requires.[51] To him, it almost invariably *does* seem reasonable, though in *Bond* it did not. Then he presents the legal reasoning to support his view. The way Supreme Court cases typically get written is that the Justice tells the law clerk how he voted and, if the case is assigned to that Justice to write, the law clerk then writes a first draft of the decision. The draft fits the holding in this case into the existing case law, attempting, in typical lawyer fashion, to explain how this case is consistent with previous cases (except in the rare case that the Court has determined to overrule a previous decision).

The point is that each decision is much more fact-driven than is generally recognized. A conclusion is reached based on the facts of the case, and the doctrine is then massaged to accommodate that result, rather than the decision being driven by previous doctrine, as the opinion claims, or by a desire to change the doctrine. Thus when a Justice writes an opinion that has the effect of, for example, limiting Fourth Amendment rights by holding that helicopter overflights are not Fourth Amendment searches, it's not necessarily that he or she set out to constrict Fourth Amendment rights. Rather, on the facts of the case, usually granted because of a conflict in the lower courts on this point, not requiring a warrant or probable cause for such overflights seems like the best result. Fourth Amendment rights get constricted incidentally. Indeed, it would be essentially impossible to get a majority of the Justices to agree, when the decision is made to hear a case, how they would specifically resolve it after argument, even though they may have a general sense of what the outcome will be at the time certiorari is granted.

The fact-specific nature of decisions is illustrated by how often, at least in the Fourth Amendment area, Justices, excluding Rehnquist, vote contrary to type. Thus, the generally liberal Breyer dissented from Rehnquist's decision in *Bond*. In the *Kyllo* case, discussed below, Scalia wrote an opinion for the defendant with the Court's most consistent liberal, Stevens, voting for the government. And, in *Atwater v. City of Lago Vista,*[52] the usually liberal Justice Souter authored a 5–4 decision holding that a "soccer mom" could be subjected to custodial arrest for a seatbelt violation.

Whatever Rehnquist's reasons, *Bond* is a significant case for holding that your knowing that *other* people could intrude on your privacy in some way does not necessarily mean that your expectation of privacy is lost with regard to the *police*. This could have important implications for apartment dwellers, for example, who might maintain an expectation of privacy vis-à-vis the police in the common areas of their building even though the other residents, and their guests, frequent those areas. Likewise, just because neighbors may cut through your yard,

---

[51] Robbins v. California, 453 U.S. 420, 438 (1981) (opinion of Rehnquist, J., dissenting).
[52] 532 U.S. 318 (2001).

it doesn't necessarily mean that the police are free to do so. However, since *Bond* itself involved a manipulation of the bag that *exceeded* what the public might be expected to do, the Court may not extend it this far.

In the other case calling a halt to the "not a search" trend, Rehnquist returned to his normal stance: against Fourth Amendment claims. In *Kyllo v. United States*,[53] a federal agent beamed a thermal-imaging machine at the petitioner's house to ascertain if it was emitting excess heat. The thermal image showed only how much heat was being emitted from a house relative to surrounding areas, nothing else about the activities inside. The excess heat from Kyllo's house suggested that he was growing large quantities of marijuana, using heat-producing halide lamps.

The government argued that it was simply enhancing "plain view" by using the machine, much like the use of binoculars or a dog sniff. Moreover, it was obtaining information only about the *exterior* of the house, that is. the "heat profile" that the machine detected. Consequently, this was not a "search," and neither probable cause nor a warrant were required. The Supreme Court disagreed in a 5–4 decision authored by Justice Scalia, whose libertarian tendencies occasionally trump his enthusiasm for tough law enforcement. The Court held that the heat was emanating from the interior of the house, and "obtaining by sense enhancing technology any information regarding the interior of the house that could not otherwise have been obtained without physical intrusion into a constitutionally protected area"[54] was a "search" and required a search warrant – at least as long as the device was not "in general public use."[55]

II. LIMIT THE WARRANT REQUIREMENT

The Supreme Court's favorite, and oft-repeated, Fourth Amendment maxim is that "[I]t is a cardinal principle that 'searches conducted outside the judicial process, without prior approval of a judge or magistrate, are *per se* unreasonable . . . subject only to a few specifically established and well delineated exceptions."[56] In fact, as I observed in 1985, "these exceptions are neither few nor well-delineated," as there were more than twenty at the time.[57] By 1991, as Justice Scalia noted, concurring in *California v. Acevedo*, at least two more had been added.[58]

Search warrants are a nuisance for the police, requiring them to commit their probable cause to writing and find a prosecutor to approve it and a judicial officer to sign it. This leaves them open to a good deal of second-guessing when the defense attorney examines these papers prior to the trial. Consequently, if the

[53] 553 U.S. 27 (2001).
[54] *Id.* at 34.
[55] *Id.* at 40.
[56] United States v. Ross, 456 U.S. 798, 825 (1982), quoting earlier cases.
[57] Bradley, *supra* note 3.
[58] 500 U.S. 565, 583.

government cannot convince a court that a given investigatory technique is not a "search," the next best technique is to exempt it from the warrant requirement.

In this exercise, the Burger and Rehnquist Courts were particularly helpful to the police, either creating or expanding many of the numerous exceptions mentioned above. Thus, though automobile searches had long been justified without a warrant,[59] Rehnquist significantly extended the automobile exception in 1973 in *Cady v. Dombrowski*.[60] Whereas previously the exception had been limited to cars "on the highway," based on their "mobility,"[61] *Cady* extended the exception to a wrecked car searched 2½ hours after it had been towed to a garage.[62] The Court has further made it clear that this warrant exception extended to containers found in vehicles even though they could have been seized and held pending a warrant.[63] Likewise, recreational vehicles – which, as "residences"of a sort, could have fallen outside the exception – were nevertheless held to be searchable on probable cause, without a warrant,[64] at least unless they were up on blocks at a trailer park. This was so despite the fact that police could ordinarily detain such a vehicle pending arrival of a warrant. Finally, just putting a suitcase in a car would deprive it of the warrant protection that it had while outside the car.[65]

Searches incident to arrest had also long been recognized as an exception to both the warrant and probable cause requirements (given the probable cause for the arrest itself). They had been limited by the Warren Court in *Chimel v. California*[66] to the person of the suspect and the "area within his immediate control . . . from within which he might gain possession of a weapon or destructible evidence."[67] Again the Burger Court, without changing the *Chimel* rule, expanded this exception to add to police power in *United States v. Robinson*,[68] written by Rehnquist in 1973.

Robinson was arrested in Washington, D.C., for driving with a revoked driver's license. Since he was to be taken into custody, the policeman thoroughly searched his person, disclosing a cigarette package in his coat pocket which, upon opening, was found to contain fourteen gelatin capsules of heroin. The court of appeals held that the heroin should be suppressed and that only a frisk of the individual for weapons was allowed for such a traffic offense, for which there was no evidence to be found. In other words, the evidentiary search allowed in *Chimel* would not apply where there was not any evidence to be searched for.

The Supreme Court rejected this argument, concluding that the arrest alone justified a full search of the arrestee, for both weapons and evidence, including opening the cigarette package, or, presumably, any other containers, found in his pocket. Rehnquist noted that since an arrest is based on probable cause, it was reasonable to allow a fuller search than the more limited weapons frisk allowed

[59] Carroll v. United States, 267 U.S. 132 (1925).
[61] *Id.* at 451, Opinion of Justice Brennan, dissenting.
[63] United States v. Ross, 456 U.S. 798 (1982).
[65] *Acevedo, supra* note 58.
[67] *Id.* at 763.

[60] 413 U.S. 433.
[62] *Id.* at 450.
[64] California v. Carney, 471 U.S., 386 (1985).
[66] 395 U.S. 792 (1969).
[68] 414 U.S. 218 (1973).

on mere "reasonable suspicion" of criminal activity by *Terry v. Ohio.*[69] He rejected the dissent's position that the reasonableness of such a search should depend
on the facts of each case, thus giving the police a clear, and permissive, rule to
follow in every case.[70] In *Robinson*, Rehnquist was able to grant the police a significant victory – and, in the process, slap down the ultraliberal D.C. Circuit, led
by Chief Judge David Bazelon, Chief Justice Burger's old nemesis from his days
on that court.

The Burger Court expanded searches incident to arrest further in *New York v.
Belton,*[71] in which it was held that a "search incident to arrest" of someone arrested from a car extended to the entire passenger compartment of the car, including closed containers in the back seat. This was a significant expansion of *Chimel*
since, once the person was removed from the car, the passenger compartment
and containers found therein were clearly no longer the "area within his immediate control" as *Chimel* had stipulated. In 2004, Rehnquist authored *Thornton
v. United States,*[72] expanding *Belton* to allow such searches even though the defendant had exited the car before the police arrived.

Another important exception to the warrant requirement is the "inventory
search." This is one of a large class of so-called special needs searches, which are
supposedly undertaken for purposes other than criminal investigation and require neither warrants nor probable cause. Some of these, such as drunk-driving
roadblocks[73] or drug testing of high school athletes,[74] do serve obvious societal
needs beyond ordinary criminal law enforcement. Inventory searches of im-
pounded vehicles and other possessions, by contrast, often seem more like a
backdoor way to permit police to conduct searches for criminal evidence without probable cause.

Nevertheless, the Supreme Court has approved both "inventory searches" of
cars, including opening any containers found in them, and of a backpack seized
from an arrestee,[75] despite the possibility of simply seizing these cars or containers and holding them unopened pending either the arrival of a search warrant
or the release of the property to its owner. (These cases were decided before the
possibility of such containers holding explosives was a serious issue). Rehnquist
wrote *Colorado v. Bertine*[76] upholding inventory searches of cars as long as they
were conducted according to "standardized criteria."[77] Obviously, if the Court
had been serious about a "warrant requirement," it would not have approved
these searches.

[69] 392 U.S. 1 (1968).
[70] 414 U.S. at 235.
[71] 453 U.S. 454 (1981).
[72] 124 S. Ct. 2127.
[73] *See* Michigan Dep't of State Police v. Sitz 496 U.S. 444 (1990).
[74] Vernonia School Dist. 47J v. Acton 515 U.S. 646 (1995).
[75] Illinois v. Lafayette, 462 U.S. 640 (1983).
[76] 479 U.S. 367 (1987).
[77] *Id.* at 373 n. 6.

Again, however, the 2000s have seen the Court calling a halt to the growth of these "special needs" searches. In *City of Indianapolis v. Edmond*,[78] the Court struck down a drug interdiction checkpoint because its primary purpose was to "uncover evidence of ordinary criminal wrongdoing"[79] rather than promoting traffic safety or some other "special need." Chief Justice Rehnquist, joined by Scalia and Thomas, dissented. Rehnquist pointed out that the intrusion on the motorist's privacy was exactly the same as that approved in other roadblock cases.

In *Ferguson v. City of Charleston*[80] the Court rejected a plan by a public hospital to try to protect fetuses from drug-abusing mothers by testing the pregnant women's urine without their consent and, if they tested positive, turning the results over to law enforcement officials. Even though the aim of the program was to protect babies, not to prosecute mothers, the Court felt that "the central . . . feature of the policy . . . was the use of law enforcement to coerce the patients into substance abuse treatment," and that was unacceptable without a warrant based on probable cause.[81] Rehnquist joined Scalia's dissent.

The bottom line of the Supreme Court's opinions in the Burger/Rehnquist years has been to exempt from the warrant requirement virtually all outdoor searches and seizures.[82] If arrests, searches incident to arrest, and automobile searches, including containers found in automobiles, can all be performed without warrants, what's left? There are only two narrow categories of outdoor search for which the warrant requirement is still in effect: searches of containers either not in transit or carried by hand by people whom police lack probable cause to arrest.[83] Thus, as to outdoor searches, Rehnquist's battle against the warrant requirement has largely been won.

When it comes to indoor searches, however, the Court has consistently enforced the warrant requirement, and not just as to homes but as to businesses, hotel rooms, phone booths, and so on.[84] This is a trend that Rehnquist, alone among his fellow Justices, has never joined, instead holding to the textualist view that the Fourth Amendment doesn't include a warrant requirement at all.[85] The *Kyllo* case, involving the use of a heat detector beamed at a house, has already been discussed, with Rehnquist's usual allies, Scalia and Thomas, voting for the defendant and requiring a warrant, while Rehnquist voted against the warrant requirement. In *United States v. Knotts*[86] the Court had held that police did not need a warrant to follow a car by means of an electronic "beeper." But in *United*

[78] 531 U.S. 32 (2000).
[79] *Id.* at 41.
[80] 532 U.S. 67 (2001).
[81] *Id.* at 80.
[82] *See* Craig Bradley, *The Court's "Two Model" Approach to the Fourth Amendment: Carpe Diem!*, 84 J. Crim. L. & Criminology 429 (1993) discussing this trend.
[83] United States v. Chadwick, 433 U.S. 1 (1977).
[84] *See* Bradley, *supra* note 82.
[85] *Robbins* dissent, *supra* note 51.
[86] 460 U.S. 276 (1983).

States v. Karo[87] it concluded that to monitor such a beeper when it was inside a house, even though it disclosed no more than the presence in the house of the drum of chemicals in which the beeper was concealed, a warrant was required. Rehnquist disagreed (along with O'Connor) that such monitoring constituted a "search" and hence argued that a warrant was not required.[88]

Likewise, *United States v. Watson*[89] had held that arrests outside the home could be made on probable cause without a warrant. But when it came to arresting a suspect at his home, *Payton v. New York*[90] required an arrest warrant plus "reason to believe that the suspect is within." White, Burger, and Rehnquist dissented. *United States v. Steagald* held that searching another person's home for a suspect required a search warrant.[91] Rehnquist, joined by White, dissented, referring to the "Court's ivory tower misconception of the realities of the apprehension of fugitives from justice. . . ." In a series of other cases, the Court has consistently upheld the warrant requirement for various intrusions into the home.[92] Though Rehnquist has not been the sole dissenter in any of these cases, he is the only Justice who has dissented in all of them.

In *Mincey v. Arizona*,[93] Rehnquist did join a unanimous opinion that there was no "homicide scene" exception to the search warrant requirement that allowed police unlimited access to the murder scene over a period several days. The proper course, the Court held, was to conduct a preliminary investigation at the time of the (warrantless) response to the homicide and then get a warrant if a more thorough subsequent search was required. Since this would ordinarily be easy to do, this decision imposed no great burden on police. Rehnquist nevertheless wrote separately to minimize the effect of the Court's holding by opining that much of the evidence used at trial had been properly seized during the initial warrantless entry.[94]

As illustrated by the fact the Rehnquist was never in sole dissent in these cases, none of the positions that he has taken is unreasonable. But his consistent rejection of claims of individual rights over more than thirty-three years shows much narrower concern for the property and privacy interests protected by the Fourth

---

[87] 468 U.S. 705 (1984).
[88] *Id.* at 722 (opinion of O'Connor, J., concurring in part and concurring in the judgment).
[89] 423 U.S. 411 (1976).
[90] 445 U.S. 573 (1980).
[91] 451 U.S. 204 (1981).
[92] *E.g.*, Welsh v. Wisconsin, 466 U.S. 740 (1984) (no "exigent circumstances" exception to the warrant requirement for minor offenses), White and Rehnquist dissented; Minnesota v. Olson, 495 U.S. 91 (1990) (exigent circumstances did not justify warrantless entry), Blackmun and Rehnquist dissented. *See also* Arizona v. Hicks, 480 U.S. 321 (1987) (picking up and examining stereo equipment in house during emergency entry is a "search" requiring probable cause – though not a warrant, since the police were already legitimately inside), Powell, Rehnquist, and O'Connor dissented.
[93] 437 U.S. 385 (1978).
[94] *Id.* at 406.

Amendment than has been exhibited by the sixteen other Justices with whom he
has shared the Supreme Court bench.

III. DILUTE THE CONTENT OF "PROBABLE CAUSE"

In general, once a police investigatory activity has been deemed a "search" it must
be based on probable cause, whether or not a warrant is required. ("Special
needs" searches, discussed above, and "frisks" – brief pat-downs for weapons –
are exceptions). Arrests, likewise, are Fourth Amendment "seizures" requiring
probable cause. Although one might suppose that "probable cause" means "more
probable than not," the Supreme Court, led by Rehnquist, has held that this is
not the case. In the 1983 case of *Illinois v. Gates*[95] the Court, per Rehnquist, dealt
with the meaning of probable cause in the context of search warrants.

The Warren Court case of *Spinelli v. United States*[96] had established a two-
pronged analysis of search warrants based on tips from confidential informants.
The police had to establish both the "basis of knowledge" (How does he know
what he claims?) and the "veracity" (Why should we believe him?) of the informant. Since the informant in *Gates* was an anonymous letter writer, completely
unknown to the police, there was no way to establish his or her "veracity," and
the Illinois Supreme Court ruled that the search warrant was no good, based on
Spinelli.[97] This despite the fact that the letter provided a lot of suspicious details,
many of which were corroborated by the police, such that most people would
have agreed that probable cause existed.

While it is not at all clear that *Spinelli* required such a slavish adherence to its
two-pronged analysis in a case such as this, the *Gates* Court overruled *Spinelli*
and held that, while both factors were still relevant, the evaluation of the search
warrant was to be more holistic – simply examining the "totality of the circumstances" to determine whether "there is a fair probability that . . . evidence of a
crime will be found in a particular place."[98] Moreover, "the duty of a reviewing
court is simply to ensure that the magistrate had a 'substantial basis for . . . concluding' that probable cause existed."[99] A "substantial basis" for a "fair probability" sounds like a lot less than "more probable than not."

Gates's more expansive definition of probable cause was to be largely super-
seded in warrant cases the following year when the Court held that, even if probable cause were lacking, evidence would not necessarily be excluded. This case,
United States v. Leon, is discussed in the next section. But *Gates*'s loosening of the
definition of probable cause would prove helpful to police in warrantless search
and arrest cases as well.

---

[95] 462 U.S. 213 (1983).   [96] 393 U.S. 410 (1969).
[97] 462 U.S. at 229.   [98] *Id.* at 238.
[99] *Id.* (citations omitted).

IV. LIMIT THE APPLICATION OF THE EXCLUSIONARY RULE

If the government cannot convince the courts that a given investigatory activity is not a search, that a warrant is not required, or that the warrant was based on probable cause, there is a fourth line of defense established by the 1984 case of *United States v. Leon*.[100] Prior to *Leon* it had been assumed by the Court that, if a Fourth Amendment violation were found, the evidence would automatically be excluded. *Leon* held that, if the police got a search warrant from a magistrate or other judicial officer and relied on it in good faith, then the evidence would *not* be excluded, even if the trial judge concluded that the warrant was not in fact based on probable cause. The Court reasoned that the police had done their job properly by submitting their evidence of probable cause to the magistrate. If the magistrate made a mistake as to whether probable cause existed, the blame should not be laid at the feet of the police, as long as they relied in reasonable good faith upon the magistrate's decision. The purpose of the exclusionary rule, to deter police misconduct, would not be well served by excluding evidence where the magistrate, not the police, had made the mistake. This was a 6–3 decision, with Rehnquist joining Justice White's majority opinion.

Leon was an important victory for police, making it difficult for defendants to suppress evidence in cases where the police had gotten a warrant, even if the warrant was defective. However, the worst fear of liberals has not been realized: that is, that the "good faith exception" to the exclusionary rule would be extended to all "good faith" mistakes by police, even in nonwarrant cases. This was essentially Rehnquist's position in *Minjares*. Since it would be difficult to establish *bad* faith, the effect would be largely to wipe out the exclusionary rule as an effective remedy against illegal searches. Instead, Rehnquist was able to extend *Leon* only modestly in his 1995 opinion in *Arizona v. Evans*.[101] In *Evans,* the defendant was arrested based on erroneous computer information that an arrest warrant had been issued for him. Marijuana was found during the search incident to the arrest. The Court held that since the erroneous information appeared to have been entered into the system by a court clerk, rather than by a police official, this was not a mistake of the police and, as in *Leon,* deterrence of police misconduct would not be served by excluding the evidence.

Since then, the Court had left *Leon* alone until a surprising 2004 decision, *Groh v. Ramirez*.[102] In *Groh*, federal agents had probable cause that Ramirez possessed illegal weapons, including grenades and grenade launchers. The agents prepared an affidavit that set forth their probable cause and properly described the place to be searched and the weapons to be seized. However, in the separate search warrant itself, which the agents had prepared for the magistrate's signature, the

[100] 468 U.S. 897 (1984).
[101] 514 U.S. 1 (1995).
[102] 124 S. Ct. 1284 (2004).

description of the weapons was omitted due to a clerical error, and the description of the house to be searched was repeated in the "property to be seized" section. Nobody noticed this omission, and the warrant was executed. As it happened, no evidence was found, but Ramirez brought a lawsuit under 42 U.S.C. §1983 based on a violation of his constitutional rights.

Despite the clerical nature of this error, and the fact that the magistrate was partly at fault for signing this defective warrant, the Court held, 5–4, that the "good faith exception" of *Leon* did not apply in this case. Rather, citing an exception in *Leon*, the Court held that this warrant was "so facially deficient . . . that the executing officers cannot reasonably presume it to be valid."[103] Consequently, the evidence, had they found any, should have been suppressed and Groh, as the leader of the search team, was not entitled to immunity from civil suit. Needless to say, Rehnquist was among the dissenters.

By finding that even negligent mistakes by police in warrant cases could lead to exclusion, the Court limited any tendency that the lower courts might have to read *Leon* expansively and put to rest any hope Rehnquist might have had of using *Leon* as a beachhead from which to further undercut the exclusionary rule.

Another important way that the Court has limited application of the exclusionary rule is to find it inapplicable to proceedings other than the criminal trial. Although the Warren Court held that the exclusionary rule would be applied in criminal forfeiture proceedings as well as at the defendant's trial,[104] the Burger and Rehnquist Courts have refused to extend its application any further. Thus, in a series of cases, they have found the exclusionary rule inapplicable in grand jury proceedings,[105] parole revocation proceedings,[106] deportation proceedings,[107] and civil forfeiture proceedings brought by the IRS.[108] The Court's view, consistently joined by Rehnquist, is that the cost of using the exclusionary rule in these ancillary proceedings exceeds the deterrence benefit.

Using similar reasoning, the Court has further held that, though evidence must be excluded from the prosecution's case-in-chief due to its wrongful obtainment by police, it may be used to impeach the defendant's testimony if he takes the stand[109] – though not, over Rehnquist's objection, to impeach defense witnesses.[110]

Finally, the Court has limited the extent of evidentiary exclusion by narrowly interpreting the "fruit of the poisonous tree" rule. The leading Warren Court case

---

[103] *Id.* at 1294, quoting *Leon*.
[104] One 1958 Plymouth Sedan v. Pennsylvania, 380 U.S. 693 (1965).
[105] United States v. Calandra, 414 U.S. 338 (1974).
[106] Pennsylvania Board of Probation and Parole v. Scott, 514 U.S. 357 (1998).
[107] I.N.S. v. Lopez-Mendoza, 468 U.S. 1032 (1984).
[108] United States v. Janis, 428 U.S. 433 (1976).
[109] Harris v. New York, 401 U.S. 222 (1971) (*Miranda* violations); United States v. Havens, 446 U.S. 620 (1980) (illegal searches).
[110] James v. Illinois, 493 U.S. 307 (1990).

on this subject is *Wong Sun v. United States*,[111] which held that, when police had illegally entered the suspect's residence and arrested him (the "poisonous tree"), not only physical evidence found there, but also the suspect's incriminating statement must be excluded as fruit of the illegal entry. However, the application of the rule depends on the nature of both the "poisonous tree" and the "fruit." In some of these cases, the poisonous tree is a confession obtained in violation of *Miranda* requirements. Those cases are discussed in detail in Chapter 6.

If the poisonous tree is an illegal search or arrest, the Court has been fairly tough, holding, for example, that a confession obtained after an illegal arrest, even if voluntary and preceded by *Miranda* warnings, must be excluded.[112] Rehnquist dissented, joining Justice Powell, who opined that such confessions should only be excluded when the Fourth Amendment violation is "flagrant."[113]

In *United States v. Ceccolini*,[114] Rehnquist limited the fruit of the poisonous tree doctrine, holding that the testimony of witnesses who were discovered as a result of an illegal search ordinarily could not be excluded as a fruit. Finally, the Court with Rehnquist's concurrence has held that evidence that is a fruit of a poisonous tree, but would have been "inevitably discovered" by a legal search, may also be used at the defendant's trial.[115]

V. ENHANCE THE "STOP AND FRISK" POWER

One way to avoid most of the strictures of the Fourth Amendment is for the police investigatory activity to be considered a "stop" and "frisk" rather than an "arrest" and "search." The authority of the police to detain people briefly when they have "reasonable suspicion" that "criminal activity is afoot" was established in the waning days of the Warren Court in the famous case of *Terry v. Ohio*.[116] *Terry* recognized that police will make such stops whatever the courts say, so it attempted to bring them under the auspices of the courts. Thus, it recognized that stops are "seizures" and frisks are "searches" within the meaning of the Fourth Amendment. But to subject these brief investigatory procedures to the warrant or even the probable cause requirements would be unworkable. Accordingly, the Court held that brief detentions for investigation, "stops," are permitted on the lesser standard of "reasonable suspicion," with frisks permitted if it is reasonably believed that the suspect is "armed and dangerous."

It fell to the Burger and Rehnquist Courts to flesh out this standard, and predictably, they did so in ways that generally favored police. In *United States v.*

---

[111] 371 U.S. 471 (1963).

[112] Brown v. Illinois, 422 U.S. 590 (1975).

[113] *Id.* at 606 (opinion of Powell, J., concurring in part).

[114] 435 U.S. 268 (1978).

[115] Nix v. Williams, 467 U.S. 431 (1984). *Nix* involved a body found as a result of an improperly obtained statement, rather than an illegal search. But the reasoning would apply equally to a Fourth Amendment violation.

[116] 391 U.S. 1 (1968).

Hensley,[117] the Court expanded the "stop" power to extend to past criminal behavior, not just criminal activity that is "afoot" as *Terry* had held. In *Florida v. Bostick,*[118] they held that, just because the defendant on a bus was not "free to go" (because he didn't want the bus to drive off without him) did not mean that he was "stopped" in the *Terry* sense. Consequently, reasonable suspicion was not needed to ask him some questions and to seek consent to search his luggage. Likewise, in *California v. Hodari D.,*[119] the Court held that merely chasing someone (who abandoned contraband during the chase) was not a "stop" requiring reasonable suspicion.

In other cases, the question has been whether the "stop" was sufficiently lengthy as to turn it into an arrest for which probable cause would have been required. The Court, over Rehnquist's objections, has been tougher on the police in these cases. For example, it held, in *Florida v. Royer,*[120] that taking an air traveler's ticket and removing him to a private room at the airport had turned a stop, for which DEA agents had reasonable suspicion, into an "arrest" for which they lacked probable cause. Likewise, detaining a suspect's luggage for an extended period of time awaiting a dog sniff was an "arrest," even though the dog sniff itself did not constitute a search.[121] On the other hand, when the defendants' own evasive activities caused the stop of two vehicles traveling in tandem to extend over a substantial period of time, the Court reasonably concluded that this would not turn a stop into an arrest.[122]

As for the frisk, in 1972, Rehnquist wrote *Adams v. Williams,*[123] in which the Court approved the frisk of a person regarding whom the policeman knew only that an informant had told him that a person in a car had narcotics and a gun. This was upheld despite the fact that possession of the gun was legal. Following *Adams,* the understandable desire of the courts to allow the police to protect themselves has led lower courts to be extremely permissive toward police in approving frisks for all sorts of crimes and in all sorts of circumstances.[124] However, in *Minnesota v. Dickerson,*[125] a Court majority, over Rehnquist's dissent, did hold that squeezing and manipulating a lump felt in the defendant's pocket exceeded the bounds of the weapons frisk authorized by *Terry.*

The Court has extended the reasoning of *Terry* to auto stops, holding, in *Delaware v. Prouse,*[126] that police could not stop individual cars at random but, like stops of people on the street, must have reasonable suspicion of either a crime or a traffic violation. Rehnquist was the sole dissenter, arguing that random stops should be permissible.[127]

---

[117] 469 U.S. 221(1985).   [118] 501 U.S. 429 (1991).
[119] 499 U.S. 621 (1991).   [120] 460 U.S. 491 (1983).
[121] United States v. Place 462 U.S. 696 (1983).   [122] United States v. Sharpe, 470 U.S. 675 (1985).
[123] 407 U.S. 143.
[124] *See* David Harris, *Frisking Every Suspect: The Withering of Terry,* 28 U.C. Davis L. Rev. 1 (1994).
[125] 508 U.S. 366 (1993).
[126] 440 U.S. 648 (1979).
[127] *Id.* at 665–66.

VI. ENCOURAGE CONSENT SEARCHES

There is a way in which police can avoid all of the pitfalls discussed above, and create what I have called a "black hole into which Fourth Amendment rights are swallowed up and disappear."[128] This is by getting the defendant to consent to the search in the first place. If the defendant consents, neither warrant nor probable cause is required. The leading case on this subject is a 1973 holding, *Schneckloth v. Bustamonte*,[129] a 6–3 decision written by Justice Stewart and joined by Rehnquist. *Schneckloth* considered the holding of the lower court that, before a valid consent could be obtained, the police must inform the defendant that he or she had a right *not* to consent. This arguably followed from the Court's 1964 holding in *Miranda v. Arizona* that interrogation must be preceded by a warning that the suspect need not answer questions.

The Court rejected the warning requirement. It held that consents must be "voluntary," that is, not induced by coercive behavior by police, but that suspects need not be warned of their right to refuse consent. The Court distinguished *Miranda,* arguing that involuntary confessions are inherently unreliable, whereas physical evidence obtained by a consented search is just as reliable as if it had been obtained by a search warrant.[130] This distinction is fallacious. The reliability of the evidence obtained has nothing to do with the voluntariness of the consent – whether it's a consent to search or to talk to the police. *Miranda*'s holding that a statement given in ignorance of one's rights is not truly voluntary[131] is equally applicable to consent searches.

The Court rejected another limitation on consent searches in *Florida v. Bostick*[132] (also discussed in Section V), where, in an opinion by Justice O'Connor, it held, by a 6–3 vote, that police need not have any "articulable suspicion" to approach somebody to ask for consent to search. Moreover, it was not relevant that the defendant, who was approached by police on a bus, was not "free to leave" when asked to consent. In this context, the Court held, the "appropriate inquiry is whether a reasonable person would feel free to decline the officers' requests or otherwise terminate the encounter."[133] A "reasonable person" the Court further adumbrated, means an *innocent* person.[134] But since the defendant, by definition, is *not* an innocent person, the Court is not considering whether the actual defendant in the case acted voluntarily or not. In 2002, the Court, in another 6–3 decision, reaffirmed these principles in *United States v. Drayton.*[135]

---

[128] Craig Bradley, *The Court's Curious Consent Search Doctrine,* 38 Trial 72 (Oct. 2002).

[129] 412 U.S. 218.

[130] *Id.* at 243–44.

[131] "For those unaware of the privilege, the warning is needed simply to make them aware of it – the threshold requirement for an intelligent decision as to its exercise." 384 U.S. 436, 468 (1966).

[132] 501 U.S. 429 (1991).

[133] *Id.* at 436.

[134] *Id.* at 437–38.

[135] 122 S. Ct. 2105.

Clearly, defendants in these cases, who are carrying incriminating evidence of various sorts, are not consenting to these searches "voluntarily" in any normal sense of the word. They are consenting either because they believe that they have no choice or that refusing consent would only arouse greater suspicion and the police would find a way to search anyway. But the Court evidently believes that, whatever the psychological pressure on these suspects to consent, it is enough that the police not use force or the threat of force to obtain this incriminating evidence. The consistent pattern of 6–3 votes over thirty years, moreover, shows that this is a doctrine that is unlikely to change. This is a major victory for Rehnquist and his fellow conservatives, since police routinely use consents to avoid Fourth Amendment limitations. In one case, *Ohio v. Robinette*, where Rehnquist wrote the majority opinion eschewing any "bright line" rules for determining the voluntariness of consents, it was disclosed that the sheriff's deputy involved in the case had alone requested 786 consents to search during traffic stops in the year of the defendant's arrest.[136]

VII. EMPLOY "STANDING" LIMITATIONS AGAINST DEFENDANTS

In contrast to consent search doctrine, where Rehnquist has generally played a supporting role, he has been a major player in creating another limitation on the defendant's ability to raise Fourth Amendment claims. This is the requirement of standing.

Standing is an old and sensible limitation of constitutional law. It holds that, because the Constitution limits the Court's jurisdiction to various "cases" or "controversies,"[137] only people who have "alleged . . . a personal stake in the outcome of the controversy" are entitled to litigate a case in federal court. "The plaintiff himself" must have "suffered 'some threatened or actual injury resulting from the putative illegal action.'"[138]

In a criminal prosecution, it might seem obvious that the defendant would have standing to litigate Fourth Amendment violations by the police, since he (or she) obviously has a "personal stake in the outcome of the controversy" and will suffer a criminal conviction as a result of the "putative illegal action." However, the Supreme Court has long recognized that "Fourth Amendment rights are personal rights which . . . may not be vicariously asserted."[139] Therefore, in order to bring a motion to suppress illegally obtained evidence, a defendant must show that *his* constitutional rights were violated by the search. If the police illegally search *A*'s house and find evidence incriminating *B*, then *B*, subject to an important exception discussed below, would lack standing and could not suppress the evidence.

[136] 519 U.S. 33, 40 (1996).
[137] U.S. Const., art. III, §2.
[138] *E.g.*, Warth v. Seldin, 422 U.S. 490, 498–99 (1975) (citations omitted).
[139] Alderman v. United States, 394 U.S. 165 (1969) (citations omitted).

This doctrine is inconsistent with the Court's oft-stated position that the purpose of the exclusionary rule is to deter police misconduct.[140] Standing limitations invite the police to violate Fourth Amendment rules when they are willing to sacrifice evidence against a property owner in order to obtain evidence against someone else. Maximum deterrence would be achieved by allowing the defendant to exclude evidence regardless of whose Fourth Amendment rights were violated. But the Warren Court reaffirmed the old standing limitations, holding that

> [We] are not convinced that the additional benefits of extending the exclusionary rule to other defendants would justify further encroachment upon the public interest in prosecuting those accused of crime and having them acquitted or convicted on the basis of all the evidence which exposes the truth.[141]

Still, the Warren Court had been generous in its determination of who had standing, holding that anyone "legitimately on the premises"[142] had standing to protest a search of those premises. Thus if *B* was a visitor in *A*'s house, or a passenger in *A*'s car, he would have standing to protest an illegal police search. In *Rakas v. Illinois*[143] the Court, per Rehnquist, significantly narrowed standing doctrine. *Rakas* held that passengers in an automobile lacked standing to protest a search of the vehicle because they had no "expectation of privacy" in the car. Only the driver and/or owner had standing to protest the search of the car.

Rehnquist expanded *Rakas* into another context in *Rawlings v. Kentucky*.[144] In *Rawlings*, as the police were arriving to search a house that the defendant and his girlfriend were visiting, the defendant dumped his narcotics into the girlfriend's purse. The defendant attempted to argue that the search of the purse was illegal, but the Court held that he lacked standing to protest the search of the purse. He had no more "reasonable expectation of privacy" in her purse than Rakas had in the car in which he was riding. The fact that Rawlings owned the drugs found did not give him standing to protest the search of the purse.

In a third case, Rehnquist was able to narrow standing somewhat more, but this time he could not get a majority to go as far as he wanted. In *Minnesota v. Carter*,[145] a policeman peering through the window of an apartment observed the defendant bagging cocaine for resale. It turned out that the defendant had paid the apartment's resident to use it for that purpose.

Without deciding whether the policeman's peering through the window was an illegal search, the Court held that a "business visitor" to a home, such as Carter, lacked standing to protest the illegal search of that home. Consequently, the cocaine would not be suppressed at Carter's trial.

---

[140] *See, e.g.,* United States v. Calandra, 414 U.S. 338 (1974).
[141] *Id.* at 174–75.
[142] Jones v. United States, 362 U.S. 257 (1960).
[143] 439 U.S. 128 (1978).
[144] 448 U.S. 98 (1980).
[145] 525 U.S. 83 (1998).

Carter left open an issue that affects many more people than the "business visitor" holding: whether a social guest, or a combined social and business guest, in a home has standing to protest an illegal search of the home. But though this issue was technically not decided in *Carter*, five Justices – including Kennedy, who joined the Rehnquist opinion – made it clear that, in their view, social visitors generally *did* have standing. Since, as was made apparent by his dissent (without opinion) in *Minnesota v. Olson*,[146] Rehnquist would have limited standing to the homeowner himself, not his visitors, overnight, social, or otherwise, the Court's current position on standing is considerably more generous than Rehnquist would like.

If these five Justices take a similar view as to "social guests" in a car, they will largely overrule *Rakas* and only slightly narrow the old Warren Court standing definition ("legitimately on the premises") to deny standing to purely business visitors. However, it is more likely that a majority will continue to apply *Rakas* to automobiles, which have consistently been held to afford their occupants reduced expectations of privacy compared to homes, while eventually holding that social guests to homes do have standing.

VIII. LIMIT POSTCONVICTION REMEDIES

Once the defendant has been convicted, he (or she) still has many ways to challenge the conviction, both in state and federal courts, including raising Fourth Amendment issues. Rehnquist has been in the vanguard of a movement to limit the defendant's postconviction access to federal courts, which is discussed in detail in Chapter 8. But one case, authored by Justice Powell and joined, of course, by Rehnquist, specifically deals with Fourth Amendment claims. In *Stone v. Powell*,[147] the Court held that Fourth Amendment claims would usually not be cognizable on federal habeas corpus. That is, if the defendant could not get the state courts to accept his Fourth Amendment arguments, he could not raise them in federal court, even if the police had clearly violated his Fourth Amendment rights, unless he didn't get a full and fair hearing in the state courts.

The reason was that

> The exclusionary rule (is) a judicially created means of effectuating the rights secured by the Fourth Amendment. . . . The primary justification for the exclusionary rule . . . is the deterrence of police misconduct that violates Fourth Amendment rights. Post-Mapp decisions have established that the rule is not a personal constitutional right. It is not calculated to redress the injury to the privacy of the victim of the search or seizure for any reparations come too late.[148]

Since the Court felt that the deterrent effect on police misconduct of recognizing exclusionary rule claims on federal habeas was not sufficient to justify the

[146] *Id.*
[147] 428 U.S. 465 (1976).
[148] *Id.* at 482–86 (citations omitted).

costs, in terms of new trials and increased litigation of these claims, it denied federal habeas review. Rehnquist in turn used *Stone*'s relegation of exclusionary claims to second-class status as one of the bases for his argument in *Minjares*, with which we began this chapter, that the exclusionary rule should be abandoned altogether.[149]

IX. MISCELLANEOUS TECHNIQUES

Related to the "not a search" cases is a Rehnquist decision that relies on other literal language of the Fourth Amendment: "The right of *the people*. . . ." While this phrase might seem to have no substantive content, Rehnquist used it as the basis of his opinion in *United States v. Verdugo-Urquidez*.[150] In this case, DEA agents, along with Mexican officials, conducted a warrantless search of the defendant's house in Mexico. Rehnquist, writing for a five-Justice majority, ruled that "the people" referred to in the Fourth Amendment "refers to a class of persons who are part of a national community or who have otherwise developed sufficient connection with this country to be considered part of that community."[151] Thus it did not apply when the person searched "was a citizen and resident of Mexico . . . and the place searched was located in Mexico."[152] Rehnquist went on to suggest in dictum that the Fourth Amendment also might not apply to searches of illegal aliens in the United States,[153] a suggestion that the Court has not endorsed in a holding.

In a related case, Rehnquist authored the majority opinion in *United States v. Alvarez-Machain*.[154] In this case, the defendant was kidnapped from his home in Mexico by DEA agents, and convicted in Texas of the murder of another DEA agent. The Supreme Court, by a 6–3 vote, rejected the claim that the federal courts lacked jurisdiction to try him because of an "unreasonable seizure." Rehnquist relied on the 1886 case *Ker v. Illinois*,[155] which held that "forcible abduction is no sufficient reason why the party should not answer when brought within the jurisdiction of the court. . . ."[156]

X. CONCLUSION

When it comes to the Fourth Amendment, the police have had no greater friend on the Supreme Court than William Rehnquist. It has been said that "a liberal is a conservative who's been indicted." To the extent that personal feelings and experiences underlie a Justice's attitudes about the law, the prospect of being stopped or searched by police would not seem to be a personal concern of Rehnquist's. Nor does he empathize with those people for whom it is a more realistic possibility. But though he has been strikingly consistent in voting to uphold the

---

[149] *Minjares, supra* note 22. [150] 494 U.S. 259 (1990).
[151] *Id.* at 265. [152] *Id.* at 274–75.
[153] *Id.* at 272. [154] 504 U.S. 655 (1992).
[155] 119 U.S. 436 (1886). [156] 504 U.S. at 661, quoting 119 U.S. at 444.

power of the police to search and arrest, this is hardly the "foolish consistency" that is the "hobgoblin of little minds."[157] More often than not, he has convinced a majority of his colleagues to go along with his conservative views and, even in dissent, invariably advances cogent and well-reasoned arguments. He is hardly the "extremist" that some branded him when he was nominated for Chief Justice.[158]

Rehnquist would deny the claim that his narrow view of Fourth Amendment rights is primarily based on a conservative political philosophy. Rather he points out that "it is often forgotten that nothing in the Fourth Amendment itself requires that searches be conducted pursuant to warrants. The terms of the Amendment simply mandate that the people be secure from unreasonable searches and seizures, and that any warrants which may issue shall only issue upon probable cause."[159] Each search must be assessed according to its reasonableness. Likewise, the Fourth Amendment includes no exclusionary rule. Thus, his narrow view of defendant's rights under the Fourth Amendment is based on the narrowness of the Amendment itself.

But to say that the Fourth Amendment, by its terms, requires only that searches be "reasonable" does not mean that "reasonableness" must be assessed anew in each case. As Rehnquist has often insisted, the basic function of criminal procedure jurisprudence is to make "rules" for police "in carrying out their work. . . ."[160] Rehnquist has joined Court holdings that searching open fields and curbside trash containers were not "searches," despite the fact that these activities would seem to fall under the literal terms of the Fourth Amendment, in order to give the police "clear rules" to follow. Just as it may be necessary to define the Fourth Amendment narrowly in order to give police direction as to when they may need probable cause or warrants, so, on other occasions, may it be necessary to read it broadly – to require search warrants to search dwellings or other places, even though the Amendment by its terms imposes no such requirement. And it may be necessary to exclude evidence in order to ensure that police abide by Fourth Amendment rules. There is certainly nothing in the Constitution that suggests that the Court may read the Bill of Rights only narrowly, to avoid undue interference with other branches of government, when a majority of the Court believes that it should be read broadly to effectuate its overarching goal of protecting individual liberty and private property.

As noted in the Introduction, Rehnquist joined the Court on a particularly propitious day, for that same day, the swearing in of Lewis Powell gave the Court a Republican majority, which it has never relinquished during Rehnquist's tenure. As this chapter shows, his numerous decisions in the Fourth Amendment area,

---

[157] "A foolish consistency is the hobgoblin of little minds, adored by little statesmen, philosophers and divines." Ralph Waldo Emerson, *Essays, First Series: Self-Reliance* (1841).

[158] *See* Bradley, *Rehnquisition, supra* note 44, summarizing comments about Rehnquist, including Senator Kennedy's statement that Rehnquist was an "extremist."

[159] Robbins v. California, 453 U.S. 420, 438 (1981) (opinion of Rehnquist, J., dissenting), citing T. Taylor, *Two Studies in Constitutional Interpretation* 23–24 (1969).

[160] *Minjares, supra* note 22, at 927.

as well as the many other opinions that he joined, have had a tremendous impact on the development of the law of criminal procedure , which was largely unformed when he joined the Court in 1972. Though no single Rehnquist opinion in this area stands out as particularly influential, the ability of criminal defendants to succeed in Fourth Amendment claims has been significantly circumscribed by Rehnquist's opinions and his votes.

Rehnquist would have gone considerably further in limiting the rights of defendants, but he has been checked by the defection, over the years, from the ranks of the conservatives of several of his Republican colleagues, notably Blackmun, Stevens, and Souter. Moreover, even his most dependable conservative allies, Scalia and Thomas, sometimes exhibit libertarian tendencies that cause them to support defendant's rights more often than Rehnquist does. Though this may have led to frustration on Rehnquist's part in individual cases, the overall trend of the Court's Fourth Amendment work in recent years has been relatively balanced – a trend for which Rehnquist, as Chief Justice, should be proud.

CHAPTER SIX

DICKERSON v. UNITED STATES: THE CASE THAT DISAPPOINTED MIRANDA'S CRITICS – AND THEN ITS SUPPORTERS

Yale Kamisar*

INTRODUCTION

It is difficult, if not impossible, to discuss *Dickerson*[1] intelligently without discussing *Miranda*,[2] whose constitutional status *Dickerson* reaffirmed (or, one might say, resuscitated). It is also difficult, if not impossible, to discuss the *Dickerson* case intelligently without discussing cases the Court has handed down in the five years since *Dickerson* was decided. The hard truth is that in those five years the reaffirmation of *Miranda*'s constitutional status has become less and less meaningful.

In this chapter I focus on the Court's characterization of statements elicited in violation of the *Miranda* warnings as not *actually* "coerced" or "compelled" but obtained *merely* in violation of *Miranda*'s "prophylactic rules." This terminology has plagued the *Miranda* doctrine and puzzled and provoked many commentators since then-Justice Rehnquist utilized this label to describe and to diminish *Miranda* – and he was the first Justice ever to do so – thirty-two years ago.

At that time, Justice Rehnquist observed for the Court: "[T]he police conduct at issue here did not abridge respondent's constitutional privilege against self-incrimination, but departed only from the prophylactic standards later laid down by the Court in *Miranda* to safeguard the privilege."[3]

Rehnquist's opinion for a 7–2 majority in *Dickerson* calls *Miranda* "a constitutional decision of this Court,"[4] a case that "announced a constitutional rule that

---

* I am grateful to Craig Bradley for his helpful suggestions.

[1] Dickerson v. United States, 530 U.S. 428 (2000).

[2] Miranda v. Arizona, 384 U.S. 436 (1966).

[3] Michigan v. Tucker, 417 U.S. 433, 445–46 (1974). Justice Rehnquist was not the first Justice to describe the *Miranda* rules as "prophylactic" (Justice Powell was) but the first to use this terminology to disparage *Miranda*. In *Michigan v. Payne*, 412 U.S. 47, 53 (1973), in the course of explaining and defending a presumption designed to protect against indicative sentencing when a defendant is retried, Powell spoke *approvingly* of *Miranda*. He considered the rule protecting against vindictive sentencing "analogous to *Miranda*."

[4] 530 U.S. at 432.

Congress may not supersede legislatively,"[5] and one that "laid down 'concrete constitutional guidelines for law enforcement agencies and courts to follow.'"[6] But the "prophylactic" language has not disappeared. Indeed, since *Dickerson* was decided the Chief Justice has joined two plurality opinions that refer to the *Miranda* rules as "a prophylactic employed to protect against violations of the Self-Incrimination Clause"[7] and as "prophylactic rules designed to safeguard the core constitutional right protected by the Self-Incrimination Clause."[8]

REHNQUIST'S VIEWS ON THE WARREN COURT'S CRIMINAL PROCEDURE CASES BEFORE ASCENDING TO THE SUPREME COURT

Mark Tushnet, the author of a new book on the Rehnquist Court (and of Chapter 9 in the present volume), informs us that Rehnquist kept in mind "the constitutional theories of Robert Jackson, the Supreme Court justice for whom he had clerked,"[9] and that "to understand Rehnquist, it helps to understand Jackson."[10] If so, this helps explain why Rehnquist did not welcome the Warren Court's "revolution" in American criminal procedure.

In a famous 1944 confession case, *Ashcraft v. Tennessee*,[11] a majority of the Court concluded that thirty-six hours of continuous relay interrogation was "inherently coercive." It is hard to believe that anybody would disagree with that conclusion *today*.[12] Yet when *Ashcraft* was decided, Justice Jackson wrote a powerful dissent, severely criticizing the majority for departing from the traditional "due process"–"totality of the circumstances"–"voluntariness" test.[13]

Five years later, in another coerced confession case, *Watts v. Indiana*,[14] concurring Justice Jackson warned that the Bill of Rights, as interpreted by the Supreme Court up to that time, had imposed "the maximum restrictions upon the power of organized society over the individual that are compatible with the maintenance of organized society itself" – good reason for not indulging in any further expansive interpretation of them.[15]

---

[5] *Id.* at 444.

[6] *Id.* at 435 (quoting from *Miranda*).

[7] United States v. Patane, 124 S. Ct. 2620, 2626 (2004) (Thomas, J., joined by Rehnquist, C. J., & Scalia, J.).

[8] Chavez v. Martinez, 538 U.S. 760, 770 (2003) (Thomas, J., joined by Rehnquist, C. J., O'Connor, J., & Scalia, J.).

[9] MARK TUSHNET, A COURT DIVIDED: THE REHNQUIST COURT AND THE FUTURE OF CONSTITUTIONAL LAW 9 (2005).

[10] *Id.* at 14.

[11] 322 U.S. 143.

[12] *Cf.* Scalia, J., dissenting in *Minnick v. Mississippi*, 498 U.S. 146, 164 (1990), suggesting that the Court might adopt a bright-line rule "marking out the situations in which knowledge or voluntariness cannot possibly be established – for example, a rule excluding confessions obtained after five hours of continuous interrogation."

[13] *See* 322 U.S. at 164–67. Justices Roberts and Frankfurter joined Jackson's dissent.

[14] 338 U.S. 49 (1949).

[15] *Id.* at 61.

Justice Jackson's 1949 observation about the Bill of Rights imposing the maximum restrictions on organized society allowable is worth dwelling on. I have
little doubt that many shared Jackson's view *at the time*.[16] But looking back on
it more than a half-century later, Jackson's comment seems astonishing.

Jackson's observation was made more than a decade before the Warren Court's
"revolution" in criminal procedure got underway. Although the right to counsel
has aptly been called "the most pervasive" right of an accused, "for it affects his
ability to assert any other rights he may have,"[17] 1949 was a time when the U.S.
Constitution, as then interpreted, did not entitle indigent defendants, in noncapital state criminal prosecutions, to appointed counsel.[18] Thus, in some states
whose own laws or court rules did not provide for appointed counsel, indigent
persons charged with such serious crimes as manslaughter and armed robbery
had to fend for themselves. The year 1949 was also a time when there were no
constitutional constraints on pretrial identification (indeed, there was no constitutional restrictions on one-person lineups)[19] – even though mistaken identification has probably been the single greatest cause of conviction of the innocent.[20]

Moreover, 1949 was a time when many state courts, and the U.S. Supreme
Court as well, were upholding the admissibility of confessions obtained under
conditions that would jolt many of us today.[21] It was also a time when state courts
were free to admit illegally seized evidence – and most of them did so.[22]

Mark Tushnet also tells us that although Rehnquist harbored no hatred or
disdain for African Americans, he was "simply indifferent" to their situation and
"placed the claims of the civil rights movement in a framework of constitutional theory shaped by his experience as Jackson's law clerk."[23] Nor did his views
change. Years later, as an important player in Goldwater's effort to transform the
Republican Party, Rehnquist was of the view, Tushnet tells us, "that advocates of
civil rights were going too far, trampling on other important constitutional values
in their misguided effort to cleanse the United States of racism."[24]

---

[16] When I started teaching law in 1957, I had the distinct impression that a goodly number of my
colleagues and many of my students agreed with Jackson.

[17] Walter V. Schaefer, *Federalism and State Criminal Procedure*, 70 HARV. L. REV. 1, 8 (1956).

[18] The Supreme Counsel did not construe the Sixth and Fourteenth Amendments as requiring indigent defendants who could not afford a lawyer to be provided with appointed counsel in noncapital state prosecutions until 1963. *See* Gideon v. Wainwright, 372 U.S. 335.

[19] The Supreme Court did not begin to address the problem of lineups and other pretrial identi-
fications until 1967, when it decided a trilogy of cases: *United States v. Wade*, 388 U.S. 218; *Gilbert
v. California*, 388 U.S. 263; and *Stovall v. Denno*, 388 U.S. 293.

[20] *See* Francis A. Allen, *The Judicial Quest for Penal Justice: The Warren Court and the Criminal Cases*,
1974 U. ILL. L.F. 518, 541–42.

[21] *See, e.g.*, Stroble v. California, 343 U.S. 181 (1952).

[22] In 1949, thirty-one states admitted evidence seized in violation of the protection against unreasonable search and seizure, including California, Massachusetts, New York, Ohio, and Pennsylvania. *See* Wolf v. Colorado, 338 U.S. 25, 29, 38 (1949), *overruled*, Mapp v. Ohio 367 U.S. 643
(1961).

[23] TUSHNET, *supra* note 9, at 23.

[24] *Id.*

This is another reason why Rehnquist was unlikely to be impressed by – or even see the need for – the Warren Court's criminal procedure revolution. As Dean Kenneth Pye observed as the Warren Court era was coming to an end:

> The Court's concern with criminal procedure can be understood only in the context of the struggle for civil rights. . . . Concern with civil rights almost inevitably required attention to the rights of defendants in criminal cases. It is hard to conceive of a Court that would accept the challenge of guaranteeing the rights of Negroes and other disadvantaged groups to equality before the law and at the same time do nothing to ameliorate the invidious discrimination between rich and poor which existed in the criminal process. . . .
>
> If the Court's espousal of equality before the law was to be credible, it required not only that the poor Negro be permitted to vote and to attend a school with whites, but also that he and other disadvantaged individuals be able to exercise, as well as possess, the same rights as the affluent white when suspected of crime.[25]

So far I have been largely speculating about why Rehnquist was probably discontented with *Miranda* and other Warren Court criminal cases before he himself was appointed to the Supreme Court. But there is more direct – and quite powerful – evidence of Rehnquist's displeasure with the so-called criminal procedure revolution: a memorandum he wrote when he worked for the Nixon administration.

On April 1, 1969, when he had been Assistant Attorney General in charge of the Office of Legal Counsel for fewer than ninety days, Rehnquist sent a nineteen-page memorandum to John Dean (of Watergate fame), who was then the Associate Deputy Attorney General. The memorandum charged that "there is reason to believe that the Supreme Court has failed to hold true the balance between the right of society to convict the guilty and the obligation of society to safeguard the accused."[26] Therefore, recommended Rehnquist, "the President [should] appoint a Commission to review these decisions, to determine whether the overriding public interest in law enforcement . . . requires a constitutional amendment."[27]

Although Rehnquist's memorandum complained about other matters – such as the ban on comments about a defendant's refusal to take the stand in his or her own defense, the search and seizure exclusionary rule, and the sharp increase in habeas corpus petitions[28] – its heaviest fire was directed at *Miranda:*

---

[25] A. Kenneth Pye, *The Warren Court and Criminal Procedure*, 67 MICH. L. REV. 249, 256 (1968).

[26] Memorandum from William H. Rehnquist to John W. Dean, III, re: Constitutional Decisions Relating to Criminal Law, April 1, 1969, Summary of Memorandum, p. 2. The memorandum was marked "administratively confidential," which, according to Dean, "kept it locked up for many years." JOHN W. DEAN, THE REHNQUIST CHOICE 268 (2001). I am indebted to Professor Thomas Y. Davies of the University of Tennessee College of Law for calling this memorandum to my attention and providing me with a copy (which he obtained from the National Archives).

[27] *Id.*

[28] *See id.* at 6, 8–9, 12–14.

The past decade has witnessed a dramatic change in the interpretation given by the Supreme Court of the United States to the constitutional rights of criminal defendants. Limitations both drastic and novel have been placed on the use by both the state and federal governments of pre-trial statements of the defendants. . . .[29]

The impact of Miranda and its progeny on the practices of law enforcement officials is far-reaching.

The Court is now committed to the proposition that relevant, competent, uncoerced statements of the defendant will not be admissible at his trial unless an elaborate set of warnings be given which is very likely to have the effect of preventing a defendant from making any statement at all. As Mr. Justice Jackson observed in *Watts v. Indiana* [a confession case discussed in the text at note 14 *supra*]:

"Any lawyer worth his salt will tell the suspect in no uncertain terms to make no statement under any circumstances."[30]

The Rehnquist memorandum then made an argument that other critics of the Warren Court's criminal cases, and *Miranda* particularly, have made:[31]

The Court, believing that the poor, disadvantaged criminal defendant should be made just as aware of the risk of incriminating himself as the rich, well-counseled criminal defendant, has undoubtedly put an additional hurdle in the way of convicting the guilty.[32]

I find two things especially interesting about the Rehnquist memorandum:

First of all, Rehnquist *never mentions* a provision of Title II of the Omnibus Crime Control and Safe Streets Act of 1968 (usually called § 3501 because of its designation under Title 18 of the United States Code) that purports to abolish *Miranda* and to make the pre-*Miranda* "voluntariness" rule the sole test for the admissibility of confessions in federal prosecutions. This strikes me as astonishing.

How could the Assistant Attorney General in charge of the Office of Legal Counsel write a good-sized memorandum spelling out the need for a commission to consider repealing or greatly modifying *Miranda* by constitutional amendment without making any reference to a recently enacted federal law purporting to overturn *Miranda*? Rehnquist was too good a lawyer, and the nineteen-page document he authored too carefully written, for him to miss a ten-month-old statute that had an important bearing on the subject of his memorandum.

---

[29] *Id.* at 1.

[30] *Id.* at 5. In the *Miranda* context, the quotation from Justice Jackson is somewhat misleading. A suspect can waive his *Miranda* rights and agree to talk to the police *without ever consulting* with an attorney – and, as every student of police interrogation agrees today, the great majority of suspects do waive their right to counsel, as well as their right to remain silent. As Justice O'Connor emphasized in Moran v. Burbine, 475 U.S. 412, 426 (1986), *Miranda* rejected the argument – what the *Burbine* Court called "the more extreme position" – that the actual presence of a lawyer is necessary to dispel the coercion inherent in custodial interrogation.

[31] *See, e.g.,* Gerald M. Caplan, *Questioning Miranda,* 38 VAND. L. REV. 1417, 1471–73 (1985).

[32] Rehnquist memorandum, *supra* note 26, at 5.

(Moreover, presumably some of the bright lawyers in his office must have contributed to, or at least seen, a draft of the memorandum.)

One cannot help wondering whether Rehnquist ignored §3501 because he thought it was obviously unconstitutional. It would hardly be surprising if he did.

Only *a few days* before Rehnquist finished writing the memorandum, the Supreme Court had reversed a conviction because "the use of these admissions obtained in the absence of the required warnings was a flat violation of the Self-Incrimination Clause of the Fifth Amendment as construed in *Miranda*."[33] No member of the Court seemed troubled by this language. Indeed, Justice Harlan, one of the *Miranda* dissenters, concurred in the result "purely out of respect for *stare decisis*."[34]

This brings me to the other interesting thing about the Rehnquist memorandum. No doubt is expressed about *Miranda*'s constitutional status. Nowhere are the *Miranda* rules described as "prophylactic" or "procedural" rules or "protective" of the Self-Incrimination Clause. When he discussed *Miranda* in April 1969, Rehnquist told us that although "[t]here was no evidence of physical coercion [in *Miranda* and its three companion cases], nor were the cases examples of unusual psychological pressure having been brought to bear in the interrogation process," the Court "held that the statements elicited from each of the defendants violated the Fifth Amendment's privilege against self-incrimination."[35]

This, too, is hardly surprising. The *Miranda* opinion itself never called the warnings "prophylactic" or "not themselves rights protected by the Constitution."[36] Nor did any of the three Justices who wrote separate dissenting opinions.[37] Justice White wrote the angriest and most-quoted dissent, but he called the *Miranda* holding a "reinterpretation of the Fifth amendment"[38] and, although he disagreed, he saw nothing "illegitimate" or improper about it. Indeed, he called *Miranda* the "mak[ing] [of] new law and new public policy in much the same way [the Court has gone about] interpreting other great clauses of the Constitution."[39]

A year later, in an address he gave at the annual meeting of the Conference of Chief Justices – an address that has never received the attention I think it deserves – Justice White made clear that, as much as he disagreed with the result

---

[33] *Orozco v. Texas*, 394 U.S. 324 (1969). *Orozco* was decided on March 25, 1969; Rehnquist's memorandum is dated April 1969.

[34] *Id.* at 328.

[35] Rehnquist memorandum, *supra* note 26, at 4–5.

[36] This is how the Court, speaking through Justice Rehnquist, characterized the *Miranda* rules in *Michigan v. Tucker*, 417 U.S. at 444.

[37] In *Miranda*, 384 U.S. at 544, Justice White did say that "the Court's *per se* approach may not be justified on the ground that it provides a 'bright line,'" but he did not suggest that there was anything "illegitimate" or improper about a per se approach or a rule that provides a "bright line."

[38] 384 U.S. at 531.

[39] *Id.* at 531.

in *Miranda*, he considered the decision a straightforward interpretation of the privilege against self-incrimination:

> Is the arrested suspect, alone with the police in the station house, being "compelled" to incriminate himself when he is interrogated without proper warnings? Reasonable men may differ about the answer to that question, but the question itself is a perfectly straightforward one under the Fifth Amendment and little different in kind from many others which arise under the Constitution and which must be decided by the courts. . . . The answer lies in the purpose and history of the self-incrimination clause and in our accumulated experience.
>
>   . . . In terms of the function which the Court was performing, I see little difference between *Miranda* and the several other decisions, some old, some new, which have construed the Fifth Amendment in a manner in which it has never been construed before, or as in the case of *Miranda*, contrary to previous decisions of the Court and of other courts as well.[40]

THE DEPARTMENT OF JUSTICE MEMORANDUM AND JUSTICE REHNQUIST'S OPINION IN *MICHIGAN v. TUCKER*

At the time Rehnquist sent his memorandum to John Dean, it may fairly be said that there was a wide consensus that *Miranda* was a straightforward interpretation of the Fifth Amendment's privilege against self-incrimination and that a confession elicited in violation of the *Miranda* rules was one obtained in violation of the Constitution. A short time later, however, that consensus came to an end.

In June 1969, with the authorization of the head of the Department of Justice, Attorney General John Mitchell, a memorandum "consistent with President Nixon's frequent criticism of Warren Court decisions on interrogation and related aspects of police procedure"[41] was sent to all United States Attorneys. It explained why "the failure to give the warnings required by *Miranda* will not necessarily require exclusion of a resulting confession."[42]

The DOJ memorandum made the best case – indeed, the only tenable case – ever made up to that point for the constitutionality of § 3501. It foreshadowed the reasoning in later Supreme Court opinions disparaging *Miranda*. I have in mind such cases as *Michigan v. Tucker*[43] (which allowed the testimony of a witness whose identity had been discovered as a result of questioning the defendant without giving him a complete set of warnings); *New York v. Quarles*[44] (another Rehnquist opinion, which recognized a "public safety" exception to the need for the

---

[40] Justice Byron R. White, *Recent Developments in Criminal Law*, Address Before the Nineteenth Annual Meeting of the Conference of Chief Justices (Aug. 3, 1967), in COUNCIL OF STATE GOVERNMENTS, PROCEEDINGS OF THE NINETEENTH ANNUAL MEETING OF THE CONFERENCE OF CHIEF JUSTICES (1967).

[41] OTIS H. STEPHENS, JR., THE SUPREME COURT AND CONFESSIONS OF GUILT 164 (1973).

[42] Memorandum from the Department of Justice to the United States Attorneys (June 11, 1969), 5 CRIM. L. REP. (BNA) 2350 (1969).

[43] 417 U.S. at 433 (1974).

[44] 467 U.S. 649 (1984).

Miranda warnings and thus held admissible both the suspect's statement, "the gun is over there," and the gun found as the result of the statement); and *Oregon v. Elstad*[45] (an O'Connor opinion, where the fact that the police had obtained a statement from the defendant when they questioned him without giving him the required *Miranda* warnings did not bar the admissibility of a later statement obtained at another place when, this time, the police did comply with *Miranda*).

The reasoning in the DOJ memorandum was quite similar to the reasoning of Justice Rehnquist's opinion in *Tucker,* an opinion that, in turn, greatly influenced the way later cases viewed *Miranda*. Indeed, looking back on the memorandum more than three decades later, it seems to have provided a road map for those who wanted to read *Miranda* as narrowly as possible.

Who wrote the 1969 Justice Department memorandum? Will Wilson, the Assistant Attorney General in charge of the Criminal Division, signed the communication to "United States Attorneys," notifying them that "[t]he attached memorandum sets forth the Department's position in respect to implementing" §3501 and another provision of the Crime Control and Safe Streets Act of 1968 concerning the admissibility of eyewitness testimony.[46] But who actually wrote "the attached memorandum"?

The memorandum was described as Attorney General Mitchell's memorandum, but surely Mitchell did not write this memorandum by himself, if he contributed to it at all. The memorandum skillfully dissected both the *Miranda* opinion and the text of §3501. The writing had a certain talmudic quality to it.

Assistant Attorney General Wilson may have had a hand in writing the memorandum. What about Assistant Attorney General Rehnquist? Given his position and his earlier memo disparaging *Miranda*, he seems an obvious choice.

Although Rehnquist had not mentioned §3501 in his memorandum, there might be a connection between Rehnquist's memo and the Justice Department's memorandum a short time later defending the constitutionality of §3501. At the time he rejected Rehnquist's proposal,[47] Attorney General Mitchell might have asked himself: Why do we need a constitutional amendment to deal with *Miranda* when we already have a federal statute on the books that purports to overturn that case? Surely the lawyers in the Office of Legal Counsel can make a credible argument that the statute is constitutional.

Whether or not Rehnquist contributed to the DOJ memorandum, he must have known about it and studied it when it was sent to all United States Attorneys and published in its entirety in the *Criminal Law Reporter*. After all, he *was* the head of the Office of Legal Counsel. Whether or not he had a hand in writing it, he must have remembered it when he wrote his first opinion of the Court in

---

[45] 470 U.S. 298 (1985).
[46] *See* DOJ memorandum, *supra* note 42, at 2350. Wilson's communication to United States Attorneys also contained a brief summary of the arguments in the attached memorandum.
[47] According to John Dean, Mitchell had a negative reaction to Rehnquist's proposal because he doubted whether the Nixon Administration could control a constitutional commission. *See* DEAN, *supra* note 26, at 268.

a *Miranda* case, the aforementioned *Michigan v. Tucker*. I don't think it can be denied that the arguments Justice Rehnquist makes in *Tucker* are quite similar to those made five years earlier in the DOJ memorandum.

The 1969 memorandum emphasized (as Justice Rehnquist was to do in *Tucker*)[48] that the *Miranda* Court itself had recognized that the Constitution does not require adherence to "*any particular* solution for the inherent compulsion of the interrogation process,"[49] only compliance with "*some* 'system' to safeguard against [the] inherently compulsive circumstances" that jeopardize the privilege.[50] Therefore, continued the DOJ memorandum, the *Miranda* warnings "are not themselves constitutional absolutes."[51]

Five years later, in *Tucker*, Justice Rehnquist was to point out that the *Miranda* Court had observed that it could not say that "the Constitution necessarily requires adherence to *any particular solution* for the inherent compulsion of the interrogation process."[52] Therefore, concluded Justice Rehnquist, the *Miranda* Court itself had recognized that the *Miranda* safeguards "are not themselves rights protected by the Constitution."[53]

All this is quite misleading. The *Miranda* warnings are not "constitutional absolutes" or "not themselves rights protected by the Constitution" in the sense that *another* set of procedural safeguards, *another* system to protect against the inherently compulsive circumstances of custodial interrogation, *might* constitute a suitable substitute. Unfortunately, however, §3501 did not provide a suitable substitute. Chief Justice Rehnquist was to make this very point a quarter-century later in *Dickerson* when he wrote the opinion of the Court invalidating §3501: When it had enacted the statutory provision known as §3501, pointed out the Chief Justice, Congress had "intended . . . to overrule *Miranda*" and simply replace it with the old "totality-of-the-circumstances"–"voluntariness" test[54] – one that the *Miranda* Court had found woefully inadequate.

The author of the majority opinion in *Tucker* overlooked some key language in the *Miranda* opinion:

> We encourage Congress and the States to continue their laudable search for increasingly effective ways of protecting the rights of the individual while promoting efficient enforcement of our criminal law. *However, unless we are shown other procedures which are at least as effective* in apprising accused persons of their right of silence and in assuring a continuous opportunity to exercise it, *the following safeguards* [the *Miranda* warnings] *must be observed.*[55]

> . . .

[48] *See Tucker*, 417 U.S. at 444.
[49] DOJ memorandum, *supra* note 42, at 2351 (emphasis added).
[50] *Id.* (emphasis in the original).
[51] *Id.* at 2351–52.
[52] *Tucker*, 417 U.S. at 444, quoting *Miranda*, 384 U.S. at 467 (emphasis added).
[53] *Id.*
[54] *See* 530 U.S. at 436–37.
[55] *Id.* at 467 (emphasis added).

It is also urged upon us that we withhold decision on this issue until state legislative bodies and advisory groups have had an opportunity to deal with these problems by rule making. We have already pointed out that the Constitution does not require any specific code of procedures for protecting the privilege against self-incrimination during custodial interrogation . . . *so long as they are fully as effective as those described above* [the *Miranda* warnings] *in informing accused persons of their right of silence and in affording a continuous opportunity to exercise it.*[56]

. . .

We turn now [to the facts of the cases before us] to consider the application to these cases of *the constitutional principles discussed above.* In each instance, we have concluded that statements were obtained from the defendant under circumstances that did not meet *constitutional standards for protection of the privilege.*[57]

In this respect, the 1969 DOJ memorandum – although it is a piece of advocacy straining to make "a legitimate constitutional argument" in favor of § 3501[58] – is more balanced than Justice Rehnquist's majority opinion in *Tucker*. Unlike Justice Rehnquist's opinion, the DOJ memorandum does recognize that, although various alternatives to the method spelled out by Chief Justice Warren for dispelling the inherent coercion of the custodial interrogation are potentially available, "the [*Miranda*] Court stated, *until* such 'potential alternatives for protecting the privilege' are devised by Congress and the states [384 U.S. at 467], a person must be warned [in accordance with *Miranda*] prior to any in-custody questioning."[59]

As Geoffrey Stone described it many years ago, in what I consider the classic critique of *Tucker*, Rehnquist's reading of *Miranda* in 1974 constituted nothing less than a "rewriting" of that famous case.[60] That is a strong word, but I don't think it is an exaggeration.

Although the *Tucker* opinion certainly suggested otherwise, absent any suitable substitute (and there was none in *Tucker* or any of the other post-*Miranda* cases), the *Miranda* warnings *are required* to dispel the compelling pressures inherent in custodial interrogation. Absent an equally effective alternative, the police *must* give an individual about to be subjected to custodial questioning the *Miranda* warnings if the privilege is not to be violated.

To respond directly to the DOJ memorandum and Justice Rehnquist's opinion in *Tucker*, absent another equally effective protective device, there is no gap

---

[56] *Id.* at 490 (emphasis added).
[57] *Id.* at 491 (emphasis added).
[58] At one point (2361), the DOJ memorandum states: "The area where we believe the statute [§ 3501] can be effective and where a legitimate constitutional argument can be made is where a voluntary confession is obtained after a less than perfect warning or a less than conclusive waiver. . . ."
[59] *Id.* (emphasis added).
[60] In *The* Miranda *Doctrine in the Burger Court*, 1977 SUP. CT. REV. 99, Professor Stone analyzed the first eleven cases involving *Miranda* decided by the Supreme Court since Warren Burger became Chief Justice. The subheading for Stone's ten-and-a-half-page analysis of *Tucker* was "*Miranda* Rewritten." *See id.* at 115.

between a violation of the *Miranda* warnings and a violation of the privilege –
in the context of custodial interrogation the privilege and the *Miranda* warnings
are inseparable. The *Miranda* warnings cannot be breached without breaching
the privilege as well.

Absent an adequate alternative, the *Miranda* warnings are not "*suggested*" safeguards (as both the DOJ memorandum and the *Tucker* Court called them).[61] Nor
are they "*recommended* procedural safeguards*" (as the *Tucker* Court characterized then at one point).[62] Neither are they "protective *guidelines*" (as *Tucker* characterized them at another point).[63]

One may disagree strongly with the conclusions the *Miranda* Court reached.
One may even think the *Miranda* Court's interpretation of the Fifth Amendment
was preposterous. Nevertheless, according to *Miranda*, absent a suitable substitute, the warnings are "an absolute prerequisite to interrogation";[64] they are safeguards *required by the Constitution* to prevent the privilege from being violated.

In short, as Professor Stone expressed it, "the conclusion that a violation of
Miranda is not a violation of the privilege is flatly inconsistent with the Court's
declaration in *Miranda* that '[t]he requirement of warnings and waiver of rights
is a fundamental with respect to the Fifth Amendment privilege.'"[65]

Tucker did not only rewrite *Miranda* by driving a wedge between the privilege
and the *Miranda* warnings. It also rewrote *Miranda* by badly blurring the distinction between the privilege against self-incrimination and the "voluntariness"
doctrine (the prevailing test for the admissibility of confessions before *Miranda*
applied the privilege to custodial interrogation).[66] Thus it seemed to miss the
main point of *Miranda*, which was to extend the Fifth Amendment's concept of
"compulsion" to include statements obtained in ignorance of one's constitutional
rights.

THE APPARENT DECONSTITUTIONALIZATION OF *MIRANDA*

From the point of view of the prosecution, *Tucker* was just about the most appealing case imaginable. The defendant had been questioned and had confessed before *Miranda* was decided. Thus, *Miranda* was just barely applicable.[67] Moreover,
the police had only failed to give the defendant one of the four *Miranda* warnings
– the advice that he would be provided counsel if he could not afford to hire a

---

[61] DOJ memorandum, *supra* note 42, at 2352; 417 U.S. at 444.
[62] 417 U.S. at 443 (emphasis added).
[63] *Id.* (emphasis added).
[64] 384 U.S. at 471.
[65] Stone, *supra* note 60, at 119, quoting *Miranda*, 384 U.S. at 476.
[66] *See* Justice Rehnquist's discussion of the pre-*Miranda* test in *Tucker*, 417 U.S. at 441–43.
[67] In Johnson v. New Jersey, 384 U.S. 719 (1966), the Court ruled that *Miranda* affected only those
cases in which *the trial* began after that decision was handed down. This was a mistake. The Court
probably should have held that *Miranda* affected only those confessions obtained by *police questioning* conducted after the date of the decision.

lawyer himself. No police officer could be faulted for such an omission at that time – two months before the *Miranda* case was decided.

At one point, Justice Rehnquist informed us that he considered these facts "significant" to the decision in *Tucker*.[68] However, he seemed to forget all about these facts in subsequent cases.

Although, again speaking for the Court, Justice Rehnquist relied heavily on *Tucker* in *New York v. Quarles* (the case that established a "public safety" exception to *Miranda*)[69] and made sure to quote *Tucker*'s language to the effect that "[t]he prophylactic *Miranda* warnings . . . are 'not themselves rights protected by the Constitution but [are] instead measures to insure that the right against compulsory self-incrimination [is] protected,'"[70] he did not mention any of the unusual facts in *Tucker*. Nor, a year later, did Justice O'Connor do so when, in *Oregon v. Elstad*,[71] she, too, chanted the *Tucker* mantra that "[t]he prophylactic *Miranda* warnings are 'not themselves rights protected by the Constitution.'"[72]

In *Elstad*, a 6–3 majority speaking through Justice O'Connor declined to apply the "fruit of the poisonous tree" doctrine to a "second confession" (one immediately preceded by the *Miranda* warnings) following a confession obtained an hour earlier without giving the defendant the required warnings. Although Justice O'Connor relied heavily on Justice Rehnquist's opinions in *Tucker* and *Quarles*, she seemed to be even more emphatic about *Miranda*'s subconstitutional status than he was.

The *Elstad* Court chided the state court for having "misconstrued" the protections afforded by *Miranda* by assuming that "a failure to administer *Miranda* warnings necessarily breeds the same consequences as police infringement of a constitutional right, so that evidence uncovered following an unwarned statement must be suppressed as 'fruit of the poisonous tree.'"[73] There is, Justice O'Connor emphasized, "a vast difference between the direct consequences flowing from coercion of a confession by physical violence [and] the uncertain consequences of disclosure of a 'guilty secret' freely given in response to an unwarned but noncoercive question, as in this case."[74] At one point, she described a person whose *Miranda* rights had been violated as someone "who has suffered no identifiable constitutional harm."[75]

Justice O'Connor also observed:

Respondent's ["fruit of the poisonous tree" argument] assumes the existence of a constitutional violation. . . . But as we explained in *Quarles* and *Tucker*, a procedural

---

[68] 417 U.S. at 447.   [69] 467 U.S. 649 (1984).

[70] *Id.* at 654.   [71] 470 U.S. 298 (1985).

[72] *Id.* at 305.   [73] *Id.* at 304.

[74] *Id.* at 312.

[75] *See id.* At 307: "[Under *Miranda*], unwarned statements that are otherwise voluntary within the meaning of the Fifth Amendment must nevertheless be excluded. . . . Thus, in the individual case, *Miranda*'s preventive medicine provides a remedy even to the defendant who has suffered no identifiable constitutional harm."

Miranda violation differs in significant respect from violations of the Fourth Amendment, which have traditionally mandated a broad application of the "fruits" doctrine. . . .

The *Miranda* exclusionary rule . . . serves the Fifth Amendment and sweeps more broadly than the Fifth Amendment itself. It may be triggered even in the absence of a Fifth Amendment violation. . . .[76]

If errors are made by law enforcement officers in administering the prophylactic *Miranda* procedures, they should not breed the same irremediable consequences as police infringement of the Fifth Amendment itself.[77]

Although *Elstad* can be read fairly narrowly,[78] the majority opinion seems to say – it certainly can plausibly be read as saying – that a violation of *Miranda* is not a violation of a *real* constitutional right, but only of a procedural safeguard or prophylactic rule designed to protect a constitutional right. Therefore, unlike evidence derived from an unreasonable search or a coerced confession (in the traditional due process sense) – which *are* real constitutional violations – it is not entitled to, or worthy of, the "fruit of the poisonous tree" doctrine.

When § 3501 was enacted, few, if any, had taken it seriously. One of the nation's leading constitutional law scholars, and one whose criticism of the bill containing the anti-*Miranda* section "was especially weighty" because he was "unsympathetic with the *Miranda* decision,"[79] concluded that offensive as § 3501 was, it did not justify a veto of the bill because it was so likely to be held "constitutionally ineffective" that

[n]o responsible trial judge would jeopardize a criminal conviction by following the statute in his rulings on admissibility, nor would a sensible prosecutor even seek a ruling in these terms since it would certainly invite reversal.[80]

A decade and a half later, however, the Burger Court's characterization of *Miranda* and its comments about the case gave reason to believe that § 3501 might survive constitutional attack after all.

It had all started with *Tucker*, a case whose facts read like a law professor's exam question, a case where the police could hardly have been expected to anticipate all the *Miranda* warnings, a case that never would have arisen if the Court had thought through its retroactivity jurisprudence.[81] Then came *Quarles* and *Elstad*.

---

[76] *Id.* at 305–06.

[77] *Id.* at 309.

[78] At the very end of her opinion, *id.* at 318, Justice O'Connor states: "We hold today that a suspect who has once responded to unwarned yet uncoercive questioning is not thereby disabled from waiving his rights and confessing after he has been given the requisite *Miranda* warnings."

[79] CHARLES ALAN WRIGHT, FEDERAL PRACTICE AND PROCEDURE: CRIMINAL § 76 at 187 n. 30 (3d ed. 1999).

[80] Herbert Wechsler, *Letter to the Editor: Legislating Crime Control*, N.Y. TIMES, June 16, 1968, at B19.

[81] A year after *Miranda*, the Court seemed to realize its mistake. It applied the new rules governing lineups announced in *United States v. Wade*, 388 U.S. 218 (1967), to identification procedures (not trials) conducted after the date *Wade* was handed down. *See* Stovall v. Denno, 388 U.S. 293 (1967).

When the Warren Court's revolution in criminal procedure was at its height, Judge Henry Friendly complained about what he called "the domino method of constitutional adjudication" – a method that made a case that was extremely appealing from the defendant's perspective the occasion for a general expansion of the rights of the accused.[82] (Friendly thought the Court should handle the extremely appealing case on an individualized basis.)

During the Burger Court era, however, it became the turn of the defense-minded to complain about the Court's use of a very sympathetic case from the prosecution's perspective (and it is hard to think of a better example than *Tucker*) as the occasion to contract the rights of the accused or to throw some dirt on landmark decisions like *Miranda*. Moreover, the defense-minded couldn't help wondering whether some day the domino effect of *Tucker, Quarles,* and *Elstad* would end with the overruling of *Miranda*.

FROM *TUCKER* TO *DICKERSON* – AND BACK AGAIN

In 1999, despite the fact that the Justice Department had instructed the United States Attorney's office not to rely on §3501, a panel of the U.S. Court of Appeals for the Fourth Circuit in *United States v. Dickerson*[83] held that a confession was admissible under that statutory provision. In sustaining the constitutionality of §3501, the Fourth Circuit relied heavily on the fact that the post–Warren Court had "consistently (and repeatedly) ... referred to the [*Miranda*] warnings as 'prophylactic' ... and 'not themselves rights protected by the Constitution.'"[84] Indeed, the Fourth Circuit went so far as to say that §3501 had been "enacted at the invitation of the Supreme Court."[85]

When the *Dickerson* case reached the Supreme Court, the Department of Justice refused to defend the constitutionality of §3501. Instead, during the oral arguments in the Supreme Court, Solicitor General Seth Waxman attacked the reasoning of *Tucker* and its progeny early and often. Again and again, he explained how *Miranda* is a constitutional decision even though the *Miranda* warnings are not constitutionally required. The warnings, he pointed out, would not be constitutionally required if Congress or a state legislature were to come up with a suitable substitute (perhaps a videotape system, time limits, or questioning by magistrates). In the absence of an effective alternative, however, emphasized the Solicitor General, the warnings *are* required.[86]

To the surprise of some (including myself), Justice O'Connor, author of the majority opinion in *Elstad*, joined a 7–2 majority opinion "conclud[ing] that

---

[82] *See* Henry J. Friendly, *The Bill of Rights as a Code of Criminal Procedure*, 53 CAL. L.REV. 929, 950, 954–55 and n. 135 (1965).

[83] 166 F.3d 667 (4th Cir. 1999), *overruled*, 530 U.S. 428 (2000).

[84] *Id.* at 689.

[85] *Id.* at 672. *See also id.* at 688–89.

[86] Transcript of Oral Arguments in *Dickerson*, 6–8.

Miranda announced a constitutional rule that Congress may not supersede leg-islatively."[87] To the surprise of many (especially myself), Chief Justice Rehnquist, author of the *Tucker* and *Quarles* opinions, wrote the opinion of the Court.

The Chief Justice put on a remarkable display of nimble backpedaling.

What about the reasoning in *Tucker* and *Quarles* and what Rehnquist had said about *Miranda* in those cases? In *Dickerson*, Rehnquist dismissed his *Tucker* and *Quarles* opinions in one sentence:

> Relying on the fact that we have created several exceptions to *Miranda*'s warnings requirement and that we have repeatedly referred to the *Miranda* warnings as "pro-phylactic" [citing *Quarles*] and "not themselves rights protected by the Constitution" [citing *Tucker*], the Court of Appeals concluded that the protections announced in *Miranda* are not constitutionally required.
>
> We disagree with the Court of Appeals conclusion, although we concede that there is some language in some of our opinions that supports the view taken by that court.[88]

I doubt that any Justice in Supreme Court history has dismissed his own ma-jority opinions more summarily or nonchalantly.

In *Tucker*, Rehnquist maintained that the fact that the *Miranda* Court stated that it would not say that "'the Constitution necessarily requires adherence to any particular solution for the inherent compulsion of the interrogation process as it is presently conducted'"[89] was proof that "[t]he [*Miranda*] Court recognized that these procedural rights were not themselves protected by the Constitution."[90] But in *Dickerson* the fact that the *Miranda* Court invited the Congress to con-sider equally effective alternatives to the *Miranda* warnings somehow *cut the oth-er way:* "Additional support for our conclusion that *Miranda* is constitutionally based is found in the *Miranda* Court's invitation for legislative action to protect the constitutional right against coerced self-incrimination."[91]

Some portions of Chief Justice Rehnquist's *Dickerson* opinion read as if he had read the *Miranda* opinion closely – or thought about it intently – for the first time.

In *Tucker*, as Professor Stone has pointed out, "[t]*he only evidence* Mr. Justice Rehnquist offered to support his conclusion [that a violation of *Miranda* is not a violation of the privilege] was the Court's statement in *Miranda* that the Con-stitution does not necessarily require 'adherence to any particular solution' to the problem of custodial interrogation."[92] In *Tucker*, he failed to mention that the

---

[87] 530 U.S. at 444.

[88] *Id.* at 437–38.

[89] *Tucker*, 417 U.S. at 444, quoting *Miranda*, 384 U.S. at 467.

[90] 417 U.S. at 444.

[91] 530 U.S. at 440. As pointed out earlier, the *Dickerson* Court should have referred to the consti-tutional right against *compelled* self-incrimination; "coercion" is a term of art used when the Court is applying the traditional due process test.

[92] Stone, *supra* note 60, at 119 (emphasis added).

Miranda Court had made it clear that "any particular solution" *other than* the *Miranda* warnings had to be *at least as effective* as the *Miranda* warnings. Chief Justice Rehnquist did not make that mistake in *Dickerson*: "[The *Miranda* Court] opined that the Constitution would not preclude legislative solutions that differed from the prescribed *Miranda* warnings but which were '*at least as effective* in apprising accused persons of their right of silence and in assuring a continuous opportunity to exercise it.'"[93]

Are we supposed to believe that when Justice Rehnquist wrote his opinion in *Tucker* he was unaware that the *Miranda* opinion had stated that *unless* alternatives were devised by the legislature that were *fully as effective as the warnings* the fourfold warnings *were* constitutionally required? The *Miranda* Court issued the caveat that any alternatives to the warnings had to be "fully as effective" or "at least as effective" as the warnings were in apprising custodial suspects of their right of silence and ensuring a continuous opportunity to exercise that right as many as five times![94]

In *Dickerson*, Chief Justice Rehnquist points out that the *Miranda* opinion "is replete with statements indicating that the majority thought it was announcing a constitutional rule."[95] "Indeed," he continues, "the Court's ultimate conclusion was that the unwarned confessions obtained in the four cases before the Court in *Miranda* 'were obtained from the defendant under circumstances that did not meet constitutional standards for protection of the privilege.'"[96]

Are we supposed to believe that Justice Rehnquist did not know the *Miranda* opinion contained the language referred to above when he told us in *Tucker* that the *Miranda* Court itself "recognized that these procedural safeguards [the *Miranda* warnings] were not themselves rights protected by the Constitution"?[97]

In *Dickerson*, Chief Justice Rehnquist told us that "first and foremost of the factors on the other side – that *Miranda* is a constitutional decision – is that both *Miranda* and two of its companion cases applied the rule to proceedings in state courts – to wit, Arizona, California, and New York."[98] Since the Supreme Court has no supervisory authority over state courts, reasoned Rehnquist, the *Miranda* Court must have announced a constitutional rule.[99]

"*First and foremost* of the factors . . . that *Miranda* is a constitutional decision"? If so, why didn't Justice Rehnquist take this into account when he wrote about *Miranda*'s constitutional status (or lack of it) in *Tucker* and *Quarles*? Justice Douglas made the same point Justice Rehnquist was to make many years later when Douglas dissented in *Tucker*.[100] Justice Stevens also made the same point when he dissented in *Elstad*.[101] Are we supposed to believe that in the 1970s and

---

[93] 530 U.S. at 440, quoting *Miranda*, 384 U.S. at 467 (emphasis added).
[94] *See* 384 U.S. at 444, 467, 476, 478, and 490.
[95] 530 U.S. at 439.
[96] *Id.* at 439–40.
[97] 417 U.S. at 444.
[98] 530 U.S. at 438.
[99] *See id.* at 437–48.
[100] *See* 417 U.S. at 462.
[101] *See* 470 U.S. at 370–71.

1980s Justice Rehnquist didn't realize the significance of the fact that *Miranda*'s full name was *Miranda v. Arizona*?

Why did Chief Justice Rehnquist, who could hardly be called a friend of *Miranda,* come to its rescue?[102]

The Chief Justice might have regarded *Dickerson* as an occasion for the Court to maintain its power against Congress.[103] But that doesn't explain the unwillingness of Rehnquists and six other Justices "to overrule *Miranda* ourselves."[104]

Was the Chief Justice concerned that the "overruling" of *Miranda* would have wiped out more than three decades of confession jurisprudence – and almost sixty cases? Was this worth doing when the police had come to learn to live fairly comfortably with *Miranda*?[105] The Chief Justice must have been aware that the police obtain waiver of rights in the "overwhelming majority" of cases and that once they do "*Miranda* offers very little protection."[106]

Then there is my favorite reason why Chief Justice Rehnquist and six of his colleagues voted the way that they did: Overruling *Miranda* after all these years would have caused enormous confusion.[107]

The due process–voluntariness–totality of the circumstances test had become "increasingly meticulous through the years."[108] One week after *Miranda,* in the course of declining to apply that case retroactively, but only to trials begun after the decision was announced, Chief Justice Warren had pointed out that the traditional "voluntariness" test "*now takes specific account* of the failure to advise the accused of his privilege against self-incrimination or to allow him access to outside assistance."[109]

If *Miranda* had been overturned in *Dickerson,* it would have been extremely difficult for a police officer to know how to respond when (a) a suspect *not warned* of her rights *had asserted* what she thought were her rights, or (b) *had*

---

[102] Of course, there is always the possibility that he would not have voted this way if the Court had been split 4–4 and he could have cast the pivotal vote. He might have voted in favor of *Miranda* so that he could have assigned the opinion to himself, rather than let someone like Justice Stevens write the opinion of the Court. But I shall proceed on the premise that Chief Justice Rehnquist would have voted the way he did regardless of how his colleagues were voting.

[103] *See* Craig Bradley, *Behind the Dickerson Decision,* 36 TRIAL 80 (Oct. 2000); Michael C. Dorf & Barry Freedman, *Shared Constitutional Interpretation,* 2001 SUP. CT. REV. 61, 72.

[104] 530 U.S. at 444.

[105] According to Professor Richard A. Leo – a close student of police interrogation and confessions, and a leading commentator on the subject: "Once feared to be the equivalent of sand in the machinery of criminal justice, *Miranda* has now become a standard part of the machine." *Questioning the Relevance of* Miranda *in the Twenty-First Century,* 99 MICH. L. REV. 1000, 1027 (2001).

[106] *Id. See also* William J. Stuntz, Miranda*'s Mistake,* 99 MICH. L. REV. 975, 977 (2001).

[107] *See* Yale Kamisar, Miranda *Thirty-Five Years Later: A Close Look at the Majority and Dissenting Opinions in* Dickerson, 33 ARIZ. ST. L.J. 387, 388–90 (2001).

[108] Johnson v. New Jersey, 384 U.S. 719, 730 (1966). Consider, too, *Miranda,* 384 U.S. at 508 (Harlan, J., dissenting) ("synopses of the cases [applying the pre-*Miranda* voluntariness test] would serve little use because the overall gauge has been steadily changing, usually in the direction of restricting admissibility.")

[109] *Id.* (emphasis added). *See also id.* at 731: "[P]ast decisions treated the failure to warn accused persons of their rights, or the failure to grant them access to outside assistance, as factors tending to prove the involuntariness of the resulting confession."

asked the police whether she had a right to remain silent or (c) whether the police had *a right* to get answers from her or (d) whether she could meet with a lawyer before answering any questions or (e) whether the officer would *prevent her* from trying to contact a lawyer.

If the Court had wiped out *Miranda* – after the police had worked with and relied on that landmark case for more than three decades – I venture to say the situation in the "interview room" would have been close to chaotic.

Although it finally said "good riddance" to a thirty-eight-year-old statutory provision that purported to "overrule" *Miranda,* the *Dickerson* Court left a number of questions unanswered. It is hard to improve on Professor Donald Dripps's comment:

> Once the Court granted [certiorari in *Dickerson*], court-watchers knew the hour had come. At long last the Court would have to either repudiate *Miranda,* repudiate the prophylactic-rule cases, or offer some ingenious reconciliation of the two lines of precedent. The Supreme Court of the United States, however, doesn't "have to" do anything, as the decision in *Dickerson* once again reminds us.[110]

Logically, *Dickerson* undermines the holdings in the prophylactic-rule cases, especially *Elstad,* which repeatedly emphasized that *Miranda* was a subconstitutional rule. But the Chief Justice did not repudiate any of the prophylactic-rule cases. Indeed, he labored hard to avoid doing so.[111] Yet he did not approve of the reasoning in those cases either. How could he?

Rehnquist's one attempt to explain *Elstad* in light of *Dickerson* – and most commentators agree that it was an extremely feeble attempt[112] – was to say:

> Our decision in that case [*Elstad*] – refusing to apply the traditional "fruits" doctrine developed in Fourth Amendment cases – does not prove that *Miranda* is a nonconstitutional decision, but simply recognizes the fact that unreasonable searches under the Fourth Amendment are different from unwarned interrogation under the Fifth Amendment.[113]

---

[110] Donald A. Dripps, *Constitutional Theory for Criminal Procedure:* Dickerson, Miranda, *and the Continuing Quest for Broad-but-Shallow,* 43 Wm. & Mary L. Rev. 1, 33 (2001).

[111] *See id.* at 62.

[112] Indeed, Professor Susan Klein commented, with considerable justification, that the Chief Justice's attempt to explain why the "poisonous tree" doctrine developed in search and seizure cases doesn't apply to *Miranda* violations "comes dangerously close to being a non sequitur." Susan R. Klein, *Identifying and (Re)Formulating Prophylactic Rules, Safe Harbors, and Incidental Rights in Constitutional Criminal Procedure,* 99 Mich. L. Rev. 1030, 1073 (2001).

The fact that the Chief Justice's attempt to reconcile *Elstad* with the "constitutionalized" *Miranda* doctrine was inadequate does not mean, however, that no tenable explanations exist. As David Strauss has suggested, one might have said that although *Miranda* strikes the best balance of advantages and disadvantages in the circumstances presented, a different balance might be best in the *Elstad* circumstances. As Professor Strauss observed, "The fact that the Court refined the balance it struck in *Miranda,* when cases presenting different circumstances arose, has no bearing on the constitutional status or legitimacy of that decision." David A. Strauss, Miranda, *The Constitution, and Congress,* 99 Mich. L. Rev. 958, 969 (2001).

[113] 530 U.S. at 441.

But *why* is a statement obtained in violation of the *Miranda* rules "different from" evidence obtained in violation of the Fourth Amendment? As far as the "fruit of the poisonous tree" doctrine is concerned, *there is nothing inherently different* between a coerced statement or one obtained in violation of the privilege on the one hand and a violation of the Fourth Amendment on the other.

Last year Chief Justice Rehnquist joined a plurality opinion by Justice Thomas that recognized that "the physical fruit of actually coerced statements" must be excluded.[114] In the same case, Deputy Solicitor General Michael Dreeben conceded that if, in response to a grand jury subpoena, a person under threat of contempt of court revealed the existence of a gun, the weapon, as well as the statement itself, would have to be excluded – because where the core privilege against self-incrimination is violated, *the derivative use*, as well as the direct use, of compelled utterances is prohibited.[115]

The only difference the *Elstad* Court recognized was one between a violation of the Constitution and a violation of a rule or set of rules *lacking constitutional status*, notably *Miranda*. But didn't *Dickerson* change that?

If, as the *Dickerson* Court seems to have told us, in the absence of an equally effective alternative procedure (and nobody claims there was an effective alternative in *Elstad* or *Dickerson*), the *Miranda* warnings *are constitutionally required* – are "constitutional standards for protection of the privilege" – then a breach of the warnings *does amount to* a breach of the Constitution – and the distinction the *Elstad* Court repeatedly made is no longer valid.

This point did not escape dissenting Justice Scalia: Unless one agrees with the *Elstad* Court that "*Miranda* violations are not constitutional violations,"[116] it would be hard to explain why the "fruits" doctrine applies to the fruits of illegal searches but not to the fruits of *Miranda* violations "since it is *not* clear on the face of the Fourth Amendment that evidence obtained in violation of that guarantee must be excluded from trial, whereas it *is* clear on the face of the Fifth Amendment that unconstitutionally compelled confessions cannot be used."[117]

Nevertheless, a recent *Miranda* "poisoned fruit" case, *United States v. Patane*,[118] leaves little doubt that *Elstad* has survived *Dickerson* completely unscathed.

The *Patane* case arose as follows: Without administering a complete set of *Mi-

---

[114] United States v. Patane, 124 S. Ct. 2620, 2630 (2004).

[115] Transcript of Oral Argument at 15, United States v. Patane.

[116] 530 U.S. at 455 (Scalia, J., dissenting).

[117] *Id. See also* Dripps, *supra* note 110, at 35: "The Chief Justice must know . . . that the Fifth Amendment exclusionary rule for fruits under *Kastigar* [*v. United States*, 406 U.S. 441 (1972)] is *more* strict, not more lax, than the Fourth Amendment exclusionary rule. The difference between the Fourth and Fifth Amendment exclusionary rules cut against, not in favor of, reconciling *Elstad* with *Miranda, Dickerson*, and *Kastigar*."

As Professor Dripps points out elsewhere in his article, see *id.* at 31, *Kastigar* makes it quite clear that immunity for testimony compelled by formal process before a grand jury would not be constitutional if evidence derived from compelled testimony were admissible.

[118] 124 S. Ct. 2620 (2004).

randa warnings, a detective questioned defendant Patane about the location of a Glock pistol he was supposed to own. Patane responded that the weapon was on a shelf in his bedroom. This admission led almost immediately to the seizure of the weapon where the defendant said it was. The prosecution conceded that Patane's statement was inadmissible, but argued that the physical fruit of the failure to comply with *Miranda* – the pistol itself – should be admitted. A unanimous panel of the Tenth Circuit disagreed, concluding that "*Miranda*'s deterrent purpose would not be vindicated meaningfully by suppression only of Patane's statement."[119]

The government relied on both *Tucker* and *Elstad,* but Judge Ebel, who wrote the Tenth Circuit opinion, thought that neither case was still good law: Both *Tucker* and *Elstad* "were predicated upon the premise that the *Miranda* rule was a prophylactic rule, rather than a constitutional rule" whereas the "poisonous tree" doctrine "requires suppression only of the fruits of *unconstitutional* conduct." However, continued Judge Ebel, "the premise upon which *Tucker* and *Elstad* relied was fundamentally altered in *Dickerson.* [That case] undermined the logic underlying *Tucker* and *Elstad*."[120]

Those of you who have come with me this far know that I think Judge Ebel's reading of *Dickerson* is a plausible, sensible one – indeed a perfectly logical one. Unfortunately, I don't have any votes on the Supreme Court – and five people who do disagreed.

There was no opinion of the Court. Justice Thomas announced the judgment of the Court and delivered the three-Justice plurality opinion he'd written. The Court was able to reverse the Tenth Circuit only because Justice Kennedy, joined by Justice O'Connor, concurred in the judgment.

The fact that Justice Scalia joined Thomas's plurality opinion is not surprising. The fact that the Chief Justice did is. In a post-*Dickerson* confession case, the two dissenters in *Dickerson* and the author of the majority opinion in *Dickerson* make strange bedfellows.

At no time in *Dickerson* did Chief Justice Rehnquist contrast the prophylactic rules of *Miranda* with the "actual Self-Incrimination Clause." Nor, in *Dickerson,* did he ever contrast *Miranda* violations with a "core" violation of the Self-Incrimination Clause itself. Indeed, at no time in *Dickerson* did Rehnquist call the *Miranda* rules "prophylactic."[121]

However, in his *Patane* plurality opinion, Justice Thomas repeatedly characterizes the *Miranda* rules as "prophylactic"[122] and repeatedly refers to "the core protection afforded by the Self-Incrimination Clause,"[123] "the core privilege against

---

[119] Patane v. United States, 304 F.3d 1013, 1029 (10th Cir. 2002) (Ebel, J.,), *rev'd,* 124 S. Ct. 2620 (2004).

[120] *Id.* at 1019.

[121] In *Dickerson* the Chief Justice did note that earlier cases had characterized the *Miranda* rules as "prophylactic."

[122] *See* 124 S. Ct. at 2626, 2627, 2630.

[123] *Id.* at 2626.

self-incrimination"[124] protected by prophylactic rules, "the actual right against compelled self-incrimination"[125] and "actual violations of the Due Process Clause or the Self-Incrimination Clause."[126]

Justice Thomas also tells us, in language very similar to that used in *Elstad,* that because prophylactic rules such as the *Miranda* rule "necessarily sweep beyond the actual protections of the Self-Incrimination Clause, any further extension of these rules must be justified by its necessity for the protection of the actual right against compelled self-incrimination."[127]

To be sure, Justice Thomas wrote for only three Justices. But *Miranda* supporters will gain little comfort from Justice Kennedy's concurring opinion.

Although Kennedy did not, as Thomas had done, contrast *Miranda*'s "prophylactic rules" with the "core privilege" or "actual right against compelled self-incrimination," he did not seem at all troubled by the fact that the plurality had reiterated the old *Tucker–Quarles–Elstad* rhetoric about *Miranda* four years after *Dickerson.* Nor did Kennedy give any indication that he thought *Dickerson* had any bearing on the case.

Justice Kennedy did mention *Dickerson* once – but only to say that he "agree[d] with the plurality that *Dickerson* did *not* undermine [such cases as *Elstad* and *Quarles*] and, in fact, cited [those cases] in support."[128] (In support of what? Surely not *Dickerson*'s holding that *Miranda* is a constitutional decision.)

Not only did Justice Kennedy fail to question the soundness of *Elstad*'s reasoning in light of *Dickerson,* he actually praised *Elstad.* The result in cases like *Elstad,* he told us, cases upholding the admissibility of evidence obtained "following an unwarned interrogation," was "based in large part on our recognition that the concerns underlying the *Miranda* rule must be accommodated to other objectives of the criminal justice system."[129]

Have I overlooked the companion case to the *Patane* case, *Missouri v. Seibert?*[130] I think not. In *Seibert,* a 5–4 majority did uphold the suppression of a so-called second confession, one obtained after the police had deliberately used a two-stage interrogation technique designed to undermine the *Miranda* warning. But Justice Souter, who wrote a four-Justice plurality opinion, never relied on *Dickerson.* His opinion is written just as if *Dickerson* had never been decided. Nor did Souter ever question the continued validity of *Elstad.* Indeed, at one point he treated *Elstad* with some reverence. In the course of rejecting Ms. Seibert's argument that her confession should be excluded under the "poisonous tree" doctrine developed in *Wong Sun v. United States,*[131] Justice Souter reminded the defendant that *Elstad* had "rejected the *Wong Sun* fruits doctrine for analyzing the admissibility of a subsequent warned confession following 'an initial failure to administer the warnings required by *Miranda.*'"[132]

---

[124] *Id.* at 2627.
[127] *Id.* at 2627.
[130] 124 S. Ct. 2601 (2004).

[125] *Id.*
[128] *Id.* at 2631 (emphasis added).
[131] 371 U.S. 471 (1963).

[126] *Id.* at 2529.
[129] *Id.*
[132] *Id.* at 2610 n. 4.

The *Seibert* facts were easy to distinguish from *Elstad*'s, and Justice Souter did so. The failure to advise Mr. Elstad of his *Miranda* rights the first time seemed inadvertent. At one point Justice O'Connor called it an "oversight."[133] This was a far cry from *Seibert*.

As I have observed elsewhere, the decision in *Seibert* turns on its extreme facts and would have turned on these same facts even if *Dickerson* had never been written:

> The officer involved had "resort[ed] to an interrogation technique he had been taught." At the first questioning session he had made "a 'conscious decision' to with-hold *Miranda* warnings" and after obtaining incriminating statements, had called a short recess (twenty minutes) before resuming the questioning. At the outset of the second session the officer did advise the suspect of her rights, and did obtain a waiver, but he then confronted the suspect with the statements she had made during the first session (when she had not been warned of her rights). Not surprisingly, the suspect confessed again. The new statement was "'largely a repeat of information . . . obtained' prior to the warnings."
>
> The failure to comply with *Miranda* was so deliberate and so flagrant that an 8–1 or 7–2 ruling in favor of the defense would not have been surprising. The fact that the vote on these extreme facts was 5–4 and that the derivative evidence was held inadmissible only because of Justice Kennedy's somewhat grudging concurring opinion is significant evidence of the low state to which *Miranda* has fallen.[134]

It should be noted that although he concurred in the *Seibert* judgment, Justice Kennedy took no more cognizance of *Dickerson* than he had when he concurred in the result in *Patane*. And in *Seibert*, too, he had nice things to say about *Elstad*. That case, he maintained, "was correct in its reasoning and its result. *Elstad* reflects a balanced and pragmatic approach to enforcement of the *Miranda* warning."[135] And he left no doubt that in the typical "second confession" case he would admit the evidence.[136]

A final word about Justice Thomas's plurality opinion in *Patane*. At one point, he discusses and quotes from a number of cases that have read *Miranda* narrowly and/or established exceptions to it. Then, in case we haven't quite grasped his message, he tells us: "Finally, nothing in *Dickerson*, including its characterization of *Miranda* as announcing a constitutional rule, changes any of these observations."[137]

Why not? Aside from invalidating § 3501, did *Dickerson* accomplish *anything*? A majority of the Court seems to think not. Indeed, *Patane* and *Seibert* leave us

---

[133] *Elstad*, 470 U.S. at 316.
[134] Yale Kamisar, *Postscript: Another Look at* Patane *and* Seibert, *the 2004* Miranda *"Poisoned Fruit" Cases*, 2 OHIO ST. J. CRIM. L. 97, 108 (2004).
[135] 124 S. Ct. at 2615.
[136] *See id.* at 2616.
[137] *Id.* at 2628.

wondering whether *any* member of the Court believes that *Dickerson* affected *Tucker, Quarles,* or *Elstad* – or, for that matter, *any* of the nearly sixty confession cases the Court has handed down since *Miranda* was decided. To borrow a line from Justice Roberts, *Dickerson* seems to be a decision good for "this day and train only."[138]

It is not too surprising that only four years after *Dickerson* was decided Justice Thomas would more or less shrug off that case. After all, Thomas did join Justice Scalia's long, forceful dissent in *Dickerson*. What is quite surprising, however, is that the Chief Justice, the author of the majority opinion in *Dickerson, would join* Thomas's plurality opinion in *Patane*.

It is hard to believe that any Justice could write an opinion of the Court "reject[ing] the core premises of *Miranda*,"[139] and establishing the groundwork for its overruling,[140] only to come to its rescue a quarter-century later. It is also hard to believe that any Justice could write an opinion of the Court advancing almost every argument conceivable for why *Miranda* must be said to have announced a constitutional rule only to concur four years later in an opinion written by a colleague neither impressed by, nor even interested in, what that Justice had to say four years earlier. It is doubly astonishing when we are talking about *the same Justice.*

Despite the fact that he wrote the opinion of the Court in *Dickerson,* Chief Justice Rehnquist's majority opinions in *Tucker* and *Quarles* make him the Justice who has probably contributed more to the depreciation of *Miranda* than any other member of the Court. Those opinions drove a wedge between the *Miranda* rules and the privilege against self-incrimination. There was reason to believe that *Dickerson* had removed that wedge. But it is hard to miss *Patane*'s message that the wedge is still there – or has been reinserted.

Moreover, because he wrote the majority opinions in *Tucker* and *Quarles,* then flip-flopped in *Dickerson* and then flip-flopped again in *Patane,* the Chief Justice has probably contributed more to the confusion over *Miranda* than any other member of the Court.

[138] Smith v. Allwright, 321 U.S. 649, 669 (1944) (Roberts, J., dissenting).
[139] Stone, *supra* note 60, at 118.
[140] *See id.* at 123.

CHAPTER SEVEN

AGAINST THE TIDE: REHNQUIST'S EFFORTS TO CURTAIL EXPANSION OF THE RIGHT TO COUNSEL

James J. Tomkovicz[*]

I. INTRODUCTION

"The right to counsel has historically been an evolving concept."[1] This chapter discusses William Rehnquist's distinctive roles in that evolutionary process. Rehnquist's vision has had enormous impact on the *scope* of the right to counsel at trial and on appeal. More specifically, his opinions have halted the previously steady, some might say relentless, expansion of indigent defendants' entitlements to government-funded attorneys. At the *trial* level, the Chief Justice's opinions in *Scott v. Illinois* and *Nichols v. United States* imposed and maintained a significant limitation upon the entitlement to appointed assistance. At the *appellate* stage, his opinion in *Ross v. Moffitt* rebuffed an effort to broaden indigents' entitlements to appointed counsel to assist their quests to overturn convictions. In contrast, Rehnquist's unapologetic assault on the legitimacy of the right to retained or appointed *pretrial* assistance against government efforts to secure confessions has not gained favor with his colleagues. His only noteworthy influence is an opinion in *Texas v. Cobb,* which prevented further growth of the pretrial entitlement.

II. THE ENTITLEMENT TO COUNSEL'S ASSISTANCE AT, AFTER, AND BEFORE TRIAL

A. The Scope of the Right to Appointed Counsel at Trial

An appreciation of Chief Justice Rehnquist's significant role in the evolution of the right to counsel requires some understanding of the centuries of history that predate his arrival. Because Rehnquist's contributions are the concern here, the historical sketch will be minimal, providing the highlights essential for context.[2]

---

[*] I am very grateful to Jennifer Donovan, Kevin Morgan, and Thomas O'Brien for their exceptional research assistance.

[1] Argersinger v. Hamlin, 407 U.S. 25, 44 (1972) (Burger, C. J., concurring in the result).

[2] For a more complete history of the evolution of the right to the assistance of counsel, see JAMES J. TOMKOVICZ, THE RIGHT TO THE ASSISTANCE OF COUNSEL: A REFERENCE GUIDE TO THE CONSTITUTION 1–43 (2002).

1. *The Evolution of the Right to the Assistance of Counsel before Rehnquist's Arrival*

British common law granted the accused an exceedingly limited entitlement to defense counsel. Those accused of misdemeanors and trespass could retain representation, while those accused of serious crimes – felonies and treason – were prohibited from employing lawyers.[3] This rule was transplanted to the colonies, but suffered serious erosion during the years preceding the American Revolution and the adoption of the United States Constitution. Before the arrival of the Bill of Rights in 1791, all but one of the thirteen colonies had abandoned the restrictive common-law approach and – by constitution, statute, or common-law rule – had recognized a broader right to retain legal assistance. A number of the statutory enactments had even created entitlements to state-provided counsel.[4]

As originally ratified, the U.S Constitution contained no right to the assistance of counsel. In 1791, however, the Bill of Rights was adopted. Among the rights included was the Sixth Amendment guarantee that "[i]n all criminal prosecutions, the accused shall enjoy the right . . . to have the Assistance of Counsel for his defence." Two significant limitations upon the reach of this right merit mention. First, the Sixth Amendment promise of counsel applied only in *federal* prosecutions.[5] Consequently, our Constitution, as initially amended, provided *no* right to counsel in *state* prosecutions. Second, the apparent intent of the Sixth Amendment's drafters was to constitutionalize a right to *retained* legal assistance. There is no textual or historical evidence that the provision was meant to encompass a guarantee of appointed, government-funded assistance for indigent defendants.[6] Despite these limitations, the adoption of the Sixth Amendment was a central event in the history of the right to counsel.

The next major development was the 1868 adoption of the Fourteenth Amendment, a provision that prohibited *states* from depriving "any person" of "life, liberty, or property without due process of law." Although this guarantee did not specify the rights that were essential components of due process and made no explicit reference to a right to legal assistance, it would prove to be a critical foundation for dramatic leaps forward in the evolution of the right to counsel. Over time, the Supreme Court concluded that every Sixth Amendment right, including counsel, was essential to fundamental fairness and, thus, a part of the due process states had to afford.

The first two important steps in the American evolution of the right to counsel were these constitutional amendments. The next four would be Supreme Court interpretations of those amendments. All four opinions addressed indigents' constitutional entitlements to appointed assistance.

---

[3] For a description of the original common-law rule and an account of its evolution in England, see *id.* at 2–9.

[4] For a fuller account of the development of the right to counsel in the colonies, see *id.* at 9–14.

[5] *See* Barron v. Baltimore, 32 U.S. 243 (1833).

[6] *See* TOMKOVICZ, *supra* note 2, at 20.

Sixty-four years after the adoption of the Fourteenth Amendment, in a landmark ruling in *Powell v. Alabama*,[7] the Court concluded that indigent defendants had a constitutional entitlement to appointed counsel for their trials in *state* courts. The *Powell* opinion spoke in general terms about an accused's need for counsel to ensure a fair opportunity to be heard, present a defense, and prevent unjust conviction. It was possible, therefore, to interpret the case as a recognition of a broad due process entitlement to appointed assistance for every indigent state defendant accused of a serious offense. Nonetheless, the Court carefully confined its holding to the facts of *Powell*, mandating appointment only in "capital case[s]" involving defendants who are "incapable of making [their] own defense because of ignorance, feeblemindedness, illiteracy or the like." Consequently, the right to state-funded assistance defined by *Powell* was exceedingly narrow. In future cases, the Court would decide whether, and how much, that right would evolve. In doing so, it would have to reckon with *Powell*'s expansive reasoning.[8]

Six years later, in 1938, the Court decided *Johnson v. Zerbst*,[9] a *federal* prosecution that implicated the express Sixth Amendment guarantee of counsel. With little fanfare, the Court concluded that the Bill of Rights did, in fact, encompass a right for indigents to have counsel furnished by the government. The Court paid no attention to the likely original intent of the drafters of the Bill of Rights. Instead, calling counsel one of the "essential barriers against arbitrary and unjust deprivation of human rights," the Court held that federal courts do not have "the power and authority to deprive an accused of his life or liberty unless he has or waives the assistance of counsel." A federal court lacks jurisdiction unless it provides counsel for an indigent. The *Zerbst* rule was clearly not confined to cases involving special circumstances, but instead encompassed a categorical entitlement to appointed counsel that extended, at a minimum, to *all* prosecutions for serious federal offenses.[10]

Four years after *Zerbst*, the Court revisited the due process entitlement to appointed assistance in state proceedings. In *Betts v. Brady*,[11] the Court rejected a claim that the failure to appoint counsel for a defendant accused of a felony was a denial of due process, concluding that in the particular circumstances of the case counsel was not essential to ensure a fundamentally fair trial. The *Betts* Court refused to recognize a due process entitlement to counsel as generous as that discovered in the Sixth Amendment, but did acknowledge that the right to appointed assistance in state court was broader than that specified in *Powell*'s narrow holding. After *Betts*, states were constitutionally obligated to provide assistance whenever the particular circumstances – the complexities of the case, the abilities

---

[7]   287 U.S. 45 (1932).
[8]   For a more complete discussion of *Powell v. Alabama*, see TOMKOVICZ, *supra* note 2, at 22–25.
[9]   304 U.S. 458 (1938).
[10]   For more details about *Zerbst*, see TOMKOVICZ, *supra* note 2, at 25–27.
[11]   316 U.S. 455 (1942).

of the accused, and the risks posed by the charges – rendered counsel essential for a fundamentally fair trial.[12]

The final pre-Rehnquist evolutionary step occurred in one of the most celebrated decisions of the Warren Court – a critical component of the 1960s revolution in criminal procedure. In *Gideon v. Wainwright*,[13] decided in 1963, the Court overruled *Betts* and held that a state defendant need not demonstrate special circumstances. Because "lawyers in criminal courts are necessities, not luxuries," and because counsel is always "fundamental and essential to fair trials," every indigent has an entitlement to counsel. Case-by-case determinations of need are inappropriate because it is "an obvious truth" that "in our adversary system of criminal justice, *any* person haled into court, who is too poor to hire a lawyer, cannot be assured a fair trial unless counsel is provided for him" (emphasis added). According to *Gideon*, the Fourteenth Amendment does mandate a general entitlement to appointed assistance identical to that provided by the Sixth Amendment.[14]

2. Rehnquist's Views Regarding the Indigent's Right to Appointed Assistance
a. Argersinger v. Hamlin: *Initial Insights*

In 1972, William Rehnquist's first year as a Supreme Court Justice, a case testing the meaning and scope of *Gideon* arrived. *Argersinger v. Hamlin*[15] involved a claim that Florida was required to appoint counsel to assist an indigent defend against a *petty misdemeanor* charge that was punishable by a six-month jail sentence, a $1,000 fine, or both. The defendant had been convicted and sentenced to ninety days in jail. Although *Gideon*'s reasoning suggested no limits on the right to appointed assistance,[16] its holding was technically limited to felony-grade offenses.[17] Consequently, it was uncertain whether the entitlement to appointed counsel extended to any or all accused of misdemeanors.[18]

A unanimous Court held that the petitioner was entitled to state-funded assistance. Six Justices joined a majority opinion that *assumed* an entitlement to counsel for all serious misdemeanors and decided that *at least* for petty misdemeanor prosecutions that *result* in sentences of imprisonment, appointed counsel is constitutionally required. The majority believed that the logic of *Powell* and *Gideon* applied to any trial involving a deprivation of liberty and concluded that

[12] For a more complete exploration of *Betts*, see TOMKOVICZ, *supra* note 2, at 27–30.
[13] 372 U.S. 335 (1963).
[14] For more discussion of *Gideon*, see TOMKOVICZ, *supra* note 2, at 32–34. For a colorful, insightful, and thorough account of the background and development of the Court's monumental decision, see ANTHONY LEWIS, GIDEON'S TRUMPET (1964).
[15] 407 U.S. 25 (1972).
[16] *See id.*, 407 U.S. at 31, 32.
[17] *See Gideon*, 372 U.S. at 351 (Harlan, J., concurring). The Court has recognized that *Gideon* does extend an unqualified, categorical right to appointed counsel in *all* felony prosecutions. *See* Nichols v. United States, 511 U.S. 738, 743 n. 9 (1994).
[18] *See Argersinger*, 407 U.S. at 44–45 n. 1 (Powell, J., concurring in the result).

in petty cases counsel "may well be necessary for a fair trial." The majority was unconvinced that the questions in petty offense trials that result in imprisonment are "any less complex than" the questions in serious offense trials. Moreover, the majority was concerned that the large volume of misdemeanor prosecutions could "create an obsession for speedy dispositions" no matter how unfair the results, and that defendants might be prejudiced by the "'assembly-line justice'" spawned by the extant, systemic pressures. The Court put aside the question of what the Constitution required "where the loss of liberty is not involved" and held that unless assistance is waived, "no person may be imprisoned for any offense, whether classified as petty, misdemeanor, or felony, unless he was represented by counsel at his trial."

Justice Rehnquist joined a lengthy concurrence in the result authored by Justice Powell, an opinion that provides significant insights into Rehnquist's initial thinking about the breadth of the right to counsel. At the outset, Powell asserted that the right to appointed assistance had to reach *all serious misdemeanor* prosecutions – that is, all cases in which the authorized punishment triggers a right to jury trial. He then observed that some accused of petty misdemeanors were also entitled to assistance. Rejecting the majority's rigid holding, Powell declared that due process demands flexible, case-by-case determinations of whether "counsel is necessary to assure a fair trial." Counsel must be furnished if, but only if, the complexity of the case, the seriousness of likely consequences – both the sentence and collateral consequences[19] – and the "individual factors peculiar to each case," including the defendant's abilities and disabilities and the attitude of the community, make legal assistance "essential to a fair trial."

The right to counsel described by Justice Powell was in one respect broader than the right defined by the majority – it extended to some defendants not sentenced to imprisonment. In his view, excessive emphasis on imprisonment could "derogate from the need for counsel" in trials that did not result in imprisonment. For the most part, however, the Powell scheme was more constraining. It would not have extended assistance to all who suffer incarceration. More important, his approach was substantially more restrictive than the entitlement he believed to be the inevitable offspring of *Argersinger*. An undeniable and significant motivation for the concurrence Justice Rehnquist joined was a genuine concern that *Argersinger*'s logic "foreshadow[ed] the adoption of a broad[er]" entitlement in all petty offense prosecutions.[20]

---

[19] Powell and Rehnquist expressed specific concern with the stigma of a conviction, with the loss of a license, and with such civil disabilities as public office forfeiture, disqualification for a profession, and a loss of pension rights. *Id.* at 48, n. 11 (Powell, J., concurring in the result).

[20] Justice Powell conceded that he was "strongly drawn to the ideal of extending the right to counsel," observed that "[m]any petty offenses . . . present complex . . . issues that may not be fairly tried if the defendant is not assisted by counsel," and concluded that "counsel [would] often [be] essential to a fair trial" under the case-by-case approach described in his concurrence. *Id.* at 47, 49 (Powell, J., concurring in the result).

According to the concurrence, a serious flaw in the actual imprisonment cri-
terion is that it forces judges to make pretrial decisions about whether to "forgo"
the discretion to impose and "abandon" the responsibility to consider legislatively
authorized sentences of imprisonment. Undesirable consequences could include
erosion of "the concept that justice requires . . . personalized decision[s]," judicial overruling of "legislative determination[s] as to the appropriate range of
punishment," and "unfair and unequal treatment" or "arbitrary and discriminatory" results.

The concurrers were intensely concerned with the *costs* resulting from the
Argersinger rule and from the extension to *all* petty offenses that would surely
follow. In their opinion, due process does not require states to provide counsel
when "the costs of assistance . . . exceed the benefits." Unless counsel is essential
to ensure fundamental fairness, states should not be forced to sustain the unforeseeable, but potentially steep, costs of providing counsel for indigent defendants
– costs that include the compensation for defense lawyers, the expenses of additional prosecutorial and courtroom time, and increases in systemic delays,
congestion, and backlogs. Moreover, because the majority's categorical approach
"may seriously overtax the capabilities" of states to furnish competent counsel,
it could ultimately prevent communities from enforcing their laws.

b. Scott v. Illinois: *Charting a Different Course*

Scott v. Illinois[21] presented Justice Rehnquist with his first chance to write a majority opinion concerning the scope of the right to assistance at trial. He made
the most of the opportunity, crafting an opinion that had a major – surely his
most significant – impact on right to counsel jurisprudence.

Scott involved an indigent accused of shoplifting, an offense with potential penalties of "a $500 fine or one year in jail, or both." The state did not provide ap-
pointed counsel. A judge convicted Scott and fined him fifty dollars. The Illinois
Supreme Court rejected the contention that *Argersinger* required the appointment of counsel whenever imprisonment was an *authorized* punishment for an
offense, refusing to extend that decision beyond cases where imprisonment is
imposed.

A bare majority of five Justices, including Rehnquist, held "that the Sixth and
Fourteenth Amendments . . . require *only* that no indigent criminal defendant
be sentenced to imprisonment unless the State has afforded him the right to
the assistance of appointed counsel for his defense" (emphasis added). Put otherwise, for charges below felony grade, the right to appointed counsel extends
only to those who are actually sentenced to some period of incarceration.[22] Be-

---

[21] 440 U.S. 367 (1979).

[22] *See* Glover v. United States, 531 U.S. 198, 203 (2001) (stating that "any amount of actual jail time
has Sixth Amendment significance"). Because the right to counsel for felony charges does not
depend on imprisonment, the distinction between felonies and misdemeanors is important. It
seems likely that the *constitutional* dividing line corresponds to the distinction commonly made
by state law – *i.e.*, that crimes punishable by one year in jail or less are misdemeanors, whereas
those with potential imprisonment longer than one year are felonies.

cause Scott had received only a fine, he had no entitlement to a state-funded lawyer.[23]

Rehnquist's opinion focused first on whether *Argersinger* had already resolved the issue before the Court. The question was whether the *Argersinger* Court had restrictively held that states had to provide assistance *only* when jail time results from a misdemeanor conviction *or* had instead left open the question of appointed counsel in misdemeanor cases not entailing imprisonment. Despite ambiguity, Justice Rehnquist declared that *Argersinger* had circumscribed the right to appointed assistance. Moreover, Rehnquist concluded that even if the question had not been resolved, actual imprisonment was an appropriate determinant of the reach of appointed counsel.

Rehnquist first posited doubt that the Bill of Rights had been intended to guarantee more than a right to retain legal assistance. He then found in the "number of separate opinions" in the appointed counsel precedents – *Powell, Gideon,* and *Argersinger* – a suggestion "that constitutional line drawing becomes more difficult as the reach of the Constitution is extended further." He noted, in addition, that "the process of incorporation creates special difficulties, for the state and federal contexts are often different and application of the same principle may have ramifications distinct in degree and kind." From these premises, Rehnquist derived an important principle of "constitutional adjudication" – that the Court was "less willing to extrapolate an already extended line when . . . its precise limits and their ramifications are" somewhat unclear.

According to Rehnquist, the Sixth Amendment's text, which grants a right to counsel "[i]n all criminal prosecutions," could not be dispositive because the right to appointed assistance was itself a "depart[ure] from the literal meaning of" that guarantee. The promise of counsel for *all* prosecutions was an entitlement to retain assistance. The scope of the extended guarantee of appointed assistance – a right not specified by the terms of the Sixth Amendment – could not be dictated by words defining the narrower right to recruit counsel. History, also, could not resolve the issue because the pre–Sixth Amendment common law had extended a *less generous* right to counsel to those accused of felonies than that granted to those facing misdemeanor charges.

To this point, Justice Rehnquist had provided virtually no affirmative reasons for extending the right to appointed counsel to trials resulting in jail sentences but not to other misdemeanor prosecutions. In two final paragraphs he explained that the entitlement must extend to those sentenced to jail because "incarceration is so severe a sanction that it should not be imposed as a result of a criminal trial unless an indigent defendant [has] been offered appointed counsel." In his view, "actual imprisonment is a penalty different in kind from fines or the

---

[23] Four dissenters believed that Scott had a due process entitlement to appointed assistance. Three would have extended the right to every offense for which imprisonment is an authorized penalty. *See Scott,* 440 U.S. at 382 (Brennan, J., dissenting). One thought that the entitlement reaches all serious misdemeanors and petty misdemeanors that lead to jail sentences. *See id.* at 389–90 (Blackmun, J., dissenting).

mere threat of imprisonment." When a deprivation of liberty is involved, the state must sustain the costs of providing counsel. On the other hand, expansion of the entitlement to state-funded assistance beyond cases of actual imprisonment would engender "confusion" and would burden the states with "unpredictable, but necessarily substantial, costs." When the consequences for a convicted misdemeanant are markedly less severe, the confusion and costs resulting from a broader guarantee justify the conclusion that states have no obligation to furnish assistance.

Scott is a remarkable, historically significant decision. The majority's decision to limit the promise of counsel ended centuries of evolutionary expansion. For the first time, the Court concluded that the scope of trial assistance would grow no further. Led by Rehnquist, a majority announced that the right to state-funded counsel had reached its apogee in *Argersinger* and that for nonfelony cases the *only* indigents entitled to assistance are those sentenced to "actual imprisonment."

Scott proved that William Rehnquist was willing to stand against a powerful historical tide. It evinced a willingness to rethink and, in large measure, to abandon views he had once endorsed. In *Argersinger,* Rehnquist had endorsed an extension of appointed counsel to all serious misdemeanors.[24] In *Scott,* however, he concluded that appointed assistance does not reach serious misdemeanor prosecutions without jail sentences.[25] In *Argersinger,* Rehnquist had supported flexible, case-by-case assessments of the need for counsel to ensure fair trials. In *Scott,* he eschewed that approach, adopting a very different, rigid, bright-line standard.[26]

The opinion Rehnquist had joined in *Argersinger* had sought to cabin the right to counsel, but had also acknowledged the central significance of legal representation in our adversary system and the need for legal assistance to ensure fair misdemeanor trials. In those respects, the Powell concurrence was consistent with the animating spirit of *Gideon* and other landmarks. In dramatic contrast, Rehnquist's opinion in *Scott* makes no mention of the vital role lawyers play in ensuring fair trials for those who lack the abilities to defend themselves. The opinion simply does not engage with the critical premise underlying *Powell, Zerbst,* and *Gideon* – that is, that lawyers are indispensable to fair trials and just results.[27]

In addition, in *Argersinger* Rehnquist had joined Justice Powell's strong crit-

[24] The *Argersinger* majority seems to have assumed that appointed counsel reached all serious misdemeanor cases no matter what the actual punishment. See *Scott,* 440 U.S. at 379–80 (Brennan, J., dissenting). Thus, on this point, the *Argersinger* Court was apparently unanimous. In *Scott,* therefore, Justice Rehnquist did not merely halt the expansion of the right to state-provided lawyers, he *withdrew* protection that had been recognized seven years earlier.

[25] In *Argersinger,* Rehnquist agreed with the assertion "that an indigent [must have] a right to appointed counsel in all cases in which there is a due process right to a jury trial," or "the right to trial by jury [would] become[] meaningless." *Argersinger,* 407 U.S. at 46 (Powell, J., concurring in the judgment). The scenario he found intolerable was made a realistic possibility by *Scott.*

[26] He even managed to garner Justice Powell's essential, though exceedingly grudging, support. See *Scott,* 440 U.S. at 374 (Powell, J., concurring).

[27] See *id.* at 375–79 (Brennan, J., dissenting).

icisms of the constitutional dividing line announced in *Scott*. Powell had asserted that the "actual imprisonment" line was too broad because it extended assistance to some with no need and too narrow because it denied some who need
counsel and could suffer serious collateral consequences; that it was not mandated by the Fourteenth Amendment; that it would impose unnecessary costs on
states; and that it would force judges to make sentencing decisions before trial,
would undermine the notion of personalized guilt and sentencing decisions,
would prompt judges to overrule legislative punishment ranges, and could engender equal protection problems. Although the *Scott* dissenters voiced many of
these same criticisms,[28] Justice Rehnquist gave not the slightest hint of why he
no longer found them persuasive.

A noteworthy similarity between Rehnquist's positions in *Argersinger* and *Scott*
is the palpable concern with excessive expansion of the right to assistance and
with the variety of unforeseeable, but probably substantial, costs that could en-
sue. While he did not explore those costs in detail, Rehnquist made it clear that
the cost factor was a critical justification for his refusal to go a single step beyond
"actual imprisonment." The potent influence of federalism was apparent in these
cases, just as it would be in his future right to counsel opinions.

In adopting the "actual imprisonment" standard, Justice Rehnquist prevented
the growth of appointed assistance that Justice Powell had predicted and feared.
The *Argersinger* concurrence was an admonition against riding the historical tide
to its logical conclusion – a sweeping entitlement for every criminal defendant.
In *Scott*, a Rehnquist-led Court heeded that admonition and held back that tide.[29]

c. Nichols v. United States: *Resisting the Erosion of* Scott

The most significant issue to arise under *Scott* reached the Court just one year
later. In *Baldasar v. Illinois*,[30] the question was whether an uncounseled misdemeanor conviction that was valid because no actual imprisonment resulted could
subsequently be used to *enhance* punishment for another offense. A deeply divided Court gave what would prove to be a virtually indecipherable answer.

After a trial in which he was not afforded counsel, Baldasar was convicted of
misdemeanor theft, an offense punishable by up to one year of imprisonment
and a fine of $1,000. According to *Scott*, the conviction was valid because the
judge had imposed a $159 fine. Six months later, Baldasar was again charged with
misdemeanor theft. Under a state enhancement statute, a prior conviction for
the same offense could elevate the new charge to a felony punishable by one to
three years in prison. At trial, the government introduced evidence of Baldasar's

---

[28] *See id.* at 382–84 (Brennan, J., dissenting).
[29] *Scott* has been criticized by commentators. *See, e.g.,* B. Mitchell Simpson III, *A Fair Trial: Are
      Indigents Charged With Misdemeanors Entitled to Court Appointed Counsel?* 5 Roger Williams U.
      L. Rev. 417 (2000); Lawrence Herman & Charles A. Thompson, Scott v. Illinois *and the Right to
      Counsel: A Decision in Search of a Doctrine?* 17 Am. Crim. L. Rev. 71 (1979).
[30] 446 U.S. 223 (1980).

prior conviction, the jury found him guilty of felony theft, and he was sentenced to prison for one to three years.

In a *per curiam* opinion that contained no reasoning and was joined by only five Justices, the Court held that it had been constitutionally impermissible to use the uncounseled conviction in this manner. The reasons for this ruling were spelled out in three separate opinions, none of which attracted majority support. Four Justices thought that the constitutional logic forbidding actual imprisonment for an uncounseled conviction also forbade an *increased* loss of liberty for a subsequent offense when that increase was clearly based on – and would not have been possible without – the uncounseled conviction. Justice Blackmun's critical fifth vote for the result was based on his refusal to accept *Scott*. Because he still maintained that the right to assistance extended to all serious misdemeanor trials, he deemed Baldasar's initial conviction *invalid*.

Three Justices, including Justice Rehnquist, joined Justice Powell's dissenting accusation that the majority had "undermine[d] the rationale of *Scott* . . . and le[ft] no coherent rationale in its place." According to the dissent, the use of valid, uncounseled convictions to enhance sentences for subsequent offenses was entirely consistent with *Scott*'s logic. The *Scott* rule precluded actual imprisonment *for* an uncounseled conviction but did not ban increases in jail terms *for* other offenses.

The Court's split over the enhancement question engendered fourteen years of confusion.[31] Lower courts and scholarly commentators debated and disagreed over the meaning of *Baldasar* and the constitutional permissibility of relying on uncounseled convictions for sentence enhancement.[32] The Court finally reconsidered the issue in *Nichols v. United States*.[33] This time a majority agreed on both a result and rationale. Chief Justice Rehnquist authored an opinion designed to end the confusion and to preserve *Scott*'s objectives.

Nichols was a federal prosecution for a felony narcotics offense. In 1990, the defendant "pleaded guilty to conspiracy to possess cocaine with intent to distribute." During sentencing under the Federal Sentencing Guidelines, his 1983 uncounseled misdemeanor conviction for driving under the influence[34] added one "criminal history point." Without that point, the range of possible sentences would have been 168–210 months, but with that point the range was 188–235 months. The district judge imposed the maximum allowed, "a term 25 months longer than if the misdemeanor conviction had not been considered." The Court of Appeals affirmed.

The Supreme Court agreed with the lower courts. In a terse concluding paragraph, the Chief Justice's opinion professed continued adherence to *Scott*, ex-

---

[31] *See* Nichols v. United States, 511 U.S. 738, 738 (1994).

[32] For a discussion of the lower courts' divergent interpretations of *Baldasar*, see Ralph Ruebner et al., *Shaking the Foundation of Gideon: A Critique of Nichols in Overruling* Baldasar v. Illinois, 25 Hofstra L. Rev. 507, 525–34 (1996).

[33] 511 U.S. 738 (1994).

[34] Because Nichols was fined $250 for this offense and received no jail sentence, the failure to provide counsel was constitutional.

pressly overruled *Baldasar,* then held in clear and unequivocal terms that under the Sixth and Fourteenth Amendments "an uncounseled misdemeanor conviction, valid under *Scott* because no prison term was imposed, is also valid when used to enhance punishment at a subsequent conviction." As in *Scott,* Rehnquist explained his reasoning with exceptional economy.

The Chief Justice began with a cursory statement of *Scott*'s holding and *Argersinger*'s reasoning. He then described *Baldasar,* announcing that an effort to pinpoint the Court's precise holding would not be "useful." At that point, he began to lay a foundation for the constitutionality of enhancement use. He observed that *Scott*'s actual imprisonment line was based, in part, on the fact that prior appointed counsel decisions "had already expanded the language of the Sixth Amendment well beyond its obvious meaning." After declaring allegiance to *Scott*'s holding, Rehnquist announced that the *Baldasar* dissenters had correctly discerned the "logical consequence" of that holding — that is, that an initially valid uncounseled conviction "may be relied upon to enhance the sentence for a subsequent offense, even though that sentence entails imprisonment." The "logic" that led to this "consequence" consisted of two relatively simple premises.

The first premise was that the only outcome forbidden by the *Scott* rule is imprisonment *for* an offense that is the basis of an uncounseled conviction. "Enhancement statutes" do not alter penalties for prior convictions, but, instead, "'penaliz[e only] the last offense committed.'" Consequently, the use of an uncounseled conviction to augment a sentence for a distinct offense cannot run afoul of *Scott.*

The second premise was that the use of a valid, uncounseled misdemeanor conviction for enhancement purposes comports "with the traditional understanding of the sentence process." In fixing appropriate sentences, judges have traditionally and properly taken into account "prior convictions" and even criminal conduct that has *not* been the subject of a conviction. Without offending due process, the trial judge could have increased Nichols's sentence on the basis of proof by a mere preponderance of the evidence that he had engaged in the conduct underlying his DUI conviction. Surely, then, it had to be "constitutionally permissible to consider a prior uncounseled misdemeanor conviction based on the same conduct" – a conviction that had required proof "*beyond a reasonable doubt*" (emphasis added). In Rehnquist's view, a ban on enhancement use would have been logically irreconcilable with long-standing sentencing practices already given a constitutional imprimatur. A system that allows increases in liberty deprivations based on findings that unlawful conduct had more likely than not occurred cannot sensibly forbid reliance on a finding that it was much more likely that the same conduct had occurred.[35]

---

[35] As in *Scott,* only five Justices, including Rehnquist, joined the majority opinion. Justice Souter agreed with the result, but refused to join the majority opinion because of language that might be seen as approving a "sentencing scheme that *automatically requires enhancement.*" *Nichols,* 511 U.S. at 754 (Souter, J., concurring in the judgment) (emphasis added).

Three dissenters asserted that the *Nichols* majority's position was "neither compelled by *Scott* nor faithful to the concern for reliability that lies at the heart of our Sixth Amendment cases since *Gideon*." In their view, "a conviction that is invalid for imposing a [prison] sentence for [an] offense itself remains invalid for increasing the term of imprisonment imposed for a subsequent conviction." Fidelity to *Scott* requires a holding "that an uncounseled misdemeanor conviction *never* can form the basis for a term of imprisonment."[36]

In *Nichols,* as in *Scott,* Rehnquist made a significant, if controversial, contribution to right to counsel jurisprudence, making it clear that the entitlement to appointed assistance extends to misdemeanor trials *only* when they yield convictions punished by imprisonment. Indigents have no constitutional entitlement to counsel as a safeguard against delayed consequences – even if those consequences include substantial deprivations of liberty that could not be imposed but for an uncounseled conviction. If a misdemeanor conviction is valid initially, it is valid for *all* future purposes no matter what the impact on an accused's freedom. The Chief Justice spoke unequivocally and with a breadth unquestionably designed to foreclose the possibility of any limits upon the utility of *Scott*-valid convictions.[37] Moreover, the jurisprudential approaches in *Scott* and *Nichols* have distinct similarities. Once again, Rehnquist did not address the vital importance of counsel in our adversary system or the landmark decisions that had developed that theme. He explained his reasoning with noteworthy brevity, and found guidance in the principle that hesitance and caution must inform interpretations of a right that has already grown "well beyond its obvious meaning." As before, he did not respond to the accusations leveled by his dissenting colleagues.

Restrictions upon the usefulness of uncounseled convictions in later proceedings would have dramatically diminished states' freedom to deny appointed counsel. Fears of thwarting recidivism and enhancement provisions and concern that criminal history would have to be ignored and that repeat offenders might avoid appropriately severe sentences would surely induce precautionary appointments in cases where no immediate jail time was contemplated. *Scott*'s practical advantages would diminish, perhaps disappear. In *Nichols,* the Chief Justice defended *Scott* and preserved those advantages, resisting the tide of right to counsel expansion once again. At the *Nichols* crossroads, Rehnquist rejected a call to turn back, intrepidly leading a majority down the trail he had blazed in *Scott*.

d. Alabama v. Shelton: *A Setback for Rehnquist's Vision*

In *Alabama v. Shelton,*[38] the Court's most recent skirmish over the scope of the right to appointed counsel, an interpretation of *Scott* favored by the Chief Justice

---

[36] *Id.* at 754, 757, 762 (Blackmun, J., dissenting).

[37] The overruling of *Baldasar,* the reasoning of the majority opinion, and the language of the *Nichols* "holding" leave no doubt that the *Nichols* majority meant to approve schemes that involve "automatic" enhancement based on uncounseled misdemeanors.

[38] 535 U.S. 654 (2002).

suffered a slim defeat. Following a conviction for assault, a trial judge had sentenced the defendant to thirty days in jail and had immediately suspended that sentence, placing him on probation for two years.

A five-Justice majority explicitly acknowledged that "reliability" is the concern underlying *Scott* – that is, that uncounseled convictions are insufficiently reliable to justify deprivations of freedom. The majority then held that the Sixth Amendment, as interpreted by *Argersinger* and *Scott,* forbids not only the *activation* of but also the *imposition of a suspended prison sentence* for an uncounseled conviction.[39] The Court thereby extended the guarantee of appointed counsel to indigents who are not faced with the prospect of an immediate liberty loss for an uncounseled conviction.

Three Justices, including Rehnquist, joined Justice Scalia's dissent.[40] The dissenters accused the majority of "ignor[ing]" *Argersinger* and *Scott* and "extending" appointed counsel to misdemeanors involving only a "threat of imprisonment." In their view, imposition of a suspended prison sentence alone does not trigger a right to assistance because it effects no deprivation of "personal liberty." There is no entitlement to counsel *unless* a state seeks to require a defendant to serve a suspended jail sentence. According to the dissent, *Scott* had halted the expansion of the right to counsel for good reason. The majority's holding illegitimately restricted states' freedom to experiment, ignored *Scott*'s concern with "the practical consequences" of expanding appointed counsel, and would "impose[ ] a large, new burden on" most states.

It is uncertain whether *Shelton* constitutes a significant limitation of the *Scott* rule and of the freedom it accords states to avoid the many costs involved in appointing counsel for indigents accused of misdemeanors. To the extent that states feel a need for the option of suspended jail sentences in misdemeanor cases, their freedom has been severely restricted by *Shelton.* The decision is surely a setback, and perhaps a substantial one, for the Chief Justice's limiting vision of appointed counsel and for the goals advanced by his opinions in *Scott* and *Nichols.*

B. The Scope of the Right to Appointed Counsel on Appeal

1. *The Law Prior to Rehnquist's Arrival:* Douglas v. California

At common law, "appellate review" of criminal convictions was "'limited' and 'rarely used.'"[41] In this country, prior to the late nineteenth century, the criminal process in both state and federal courts ordinarily ended with the trial.[42] Conse-

---

[39] The Court did not rule out the possibility of probation unattached to a prison sentence. Moreover, it suggested that a suspended prison sentence and probation *might* be acceptable *if* activation of the sentence required a complete retrial or some other process that ensured reliability. Discussion of these ambiguities is beyond the scope of this chapter.

[40] *Shelton,* 535 U.S. at 674 (Scalia, J., dissenting).

[41] Martinez v. Court of Appeal of California, 528 U.S. 152, 159 (2000).

[42] *Id.* at 159.

quently, the law pertaining to counsel's assistance on appeal has a relatively short history. Today, although they are not constitutionally obligated to do so,[43] the federal government and all the states grant statutory rights to appeal convictions. Naturally, this dramatic expansion of the criminal process has generated questions concerning the entitlement to counsel on appeal.

In 1963, on the same day that the Court decided *Gideon v. Wainwright,* it also decided *Douglas v. California,*[44] a case in which an indigent claimed that California had a constitutional obligation to provide appointed appellate counsel. A majority agreed, holding that indigents have an entitlement to state-funded assistance for first appeals granted by states as a matter of right. Rejecting a contention that states should be free to make case-by-case determinations of the need for or usefulness of counsel, the Court announced a constitutional obligation to furnish assistance to every indigent appellant who wants it.

Unlike *Gideon, Douglas* has no roots in the Sixth Amendment or in the Fourteenth Amendment's "incorporation" of that provision. The Sixth Amendment guarantee of counsel – retained or appointed – extends *only* to trials and has no application to appeals.[45] Instead, the right to state-compensated appellate assistance is grounded in the Fourteenth Amendment's Due Process and Equal Protection Clauses.[46]

2. Ross v. Moffitt: *A Rehnquist-Led Refusal to Expand Appointed Appellate Assistance*

The holding in *Douglas* was limited to initial appeals granted by states as a matter of right. Just two years after Justice Rehnquist was appointed, the Court granted review in *Ross v. Moffitt.*[47] The question was whether *Douglas* "should be extended to require [appointed] counsel for discretionary state appeals and for applications for [Supreme Court] review." In an opinion authored by Rehnquist, a six-Justice majority held that the indigent appellants in *Moffitt* had no constitutional entitlement to appointed counsel for either discretionary review process.

Rehnquist's reasoning bears unsurprising similarities to the premises he employed to halt the expansion of trial counsel. He observed that the Court was being asked to "extend" *Douglas,* a decision that had "departed somewhat from the limited doctrine of" prior cases involving indigents' rights on appeal by undertaking "an examination of whether an indigent's access to the appellate system was adequate." The suggestion, once again, was that the Court should be reluctant to expand already stretched constitutional guarantees.

In Rehnquist's view, neither the Equal Protection Clause nor the Due Process Clause alone "provides an entirely satisfactory basis for" *Douglas*'s holding. Due

---

[43] *See* Evitts v. Lucey, 469 U.S. 387 (1985) (citing McKane v. Durston, 153 U.S. 684, 687 [1894]).
[44] 372 U.S. 353 (1963).
[45] *Martinez,* 528 U.S. at 159–60.
[46] *See* Ross v. Moffitt, 417 U.S. 600, 608–09 (1974); *see also Evitts,* 469 U.S. 387 (1985).
[47] 417 U.S. 600 (1974).

process focuses upon "fairness between the State and the individual," while equal protection "emphasizes disparity in treatment by a State between classes of individuals whose situations are arguably indistinguishable."

In addressing the relevance of the promise of due process at the discretionary review stage, Rehnquist first noted that the differences between trial and appeal are "significant." When the state seeks to overcome the presumption of innocence at trial, fairness can be guaranteed only if counsel is provided. When an accused initiates an effort to reverse a conviction on appeal, however, a lawyer serves "not as a shield," but instead "as a sword." States must conduct trials if they wish to secure convictions, but they do not have to "provide any appeal at all." If a state furnishes an appellate process, it treats indigent defendants unfairly – in violation of due process – "only" by singling them out and denying them "meaningful access to the appellate system because of their poverty." According to Rehnquist, "equal protection analysis" is a "more profitabl[e]" vehicle for making that determination.

Turning to the equal protection guarantee, Rehnquist sounded an antiexpansionist theme. He warned that all rights tended "'to declare themselves absolute to their logical extreme,'"[48] and announced that the principles of prior decisions impose "obvious limits" upon "equal protection analysis." More specifically, equal protection "'does not require absolute equality or precisely equal advantages.'"[49] An appellate process complies with the command of equal protection if it is "'free of unreasoned distinctions'" and affords "an adequate opportunity to present . . . claims fairly within the adversary system."[50] Procedures are impermissible only if they leave indigents "'entirely cut off from any appeal at all'"[51] or afford them "merely a 'meaningless ritual.'"[52]

Rehnquist discerned two reasons why equal protection principles did not require North Carolina to furnish appointed assistance for discretionary appeals. First, the North Carolina system did not deny "meaningful access" because it guaranteed every convicted defendant a right to a first appeal and provided appointed counsel for indigents. As a result, before discretionary review was sought, a lawyer had presented the indigent's claims and an appellate court had considered them. When the discretionary review stage was reached, the indigent had a trial record, an appellate brief, and often had an opinion from the intermediate appellate court. When supplemented by the defendant's *pro se* submissions, these documents furnished an adequate foundation for deciding whether discretionary review is appropriate.

In addition, the question at the discretionary review stage was not whether the guilt determination was correct. Review was to be granted only in a case of

---

[48] Quoting Hudson County Water Co. v. McCarter, 209 U.S. 349, 354 (1908).
[49] Quoting San Antonio Independent School District v. Rodriguez, 411 U.S. 1, 24 (1973).
[50] Quoting Rinaldi v. Yeager, 384 U.S. 305, 310 (1966).
[51] Quoting Lane v. Brown, 372 U.S. 477, 481 (1963).
[52] Quoting Douglas v. California, 372 U.S. 353, 358 (1963).

"'significant public interest,'" a case involving "'legal principles of major significance,'" or a case entailing "conflict" between the lower court's decision and a
state Supreme Court ruling. Counsel's organization and presentation of claims
in the initial appeal should enable the reviewing court to determine whether the
"legislative standards" that govern discretionary review were satisfied. Rehnquist
acknowledged that a lawyer could be "helpful," but deemed the "relative hand-
icap" to be insufficient to justify a right to appointed assistance. A refusal to furnish counsel does not offend equal protection because there is no duty "to du-
plicate the legal arsenal" available to those who can afford counsel. The state's
obligation is only to provide indigents with "an adequate opportunity to present
[their] claims fairly."[53]

In concluding, Rehnquist returned to a favorite theme – respect for states' freedom to make public policy choices and to protect themselves from the burdensome costs of appointed counsel. The intent of his opinion was not "to discourage" states from furnishing counsel for all appellate processes. Instead, his object
was merely to make it clear that the Constitution leaves them free to choose appointed counsel policy beyond first appeals and to decide whether they can afford to spend funds on a right to counsel that is broader than that mandated by
the Fourteenth Amendment.

Three Justices dissented, contending that the "concepts of fairness and equality" underlying *Douglas* dictated a similar right to counsel for discretionary review because the right to seek such review is "substantial" and because "a lawyer
can be of significant assistance" at the discretionary review stage.

In sum, as in *Scott,* the Rehnquist-led *Moffitt* majority rejected a right to
counsel claim because the principles underlying the already-recognized right to
appellate assistance did not mandate further extension *and* because the consequence of expansion might well be costly impositions on states' freedom to administer their criminal justice systems.[54]

C. The Scope of the Right to Pretrial Assistance of Counsel

The Chief Justice has been content to halt further expansion of the rights to appointed counsel at trial and on appeal. His opinions do not evince a particularly favorable attitude toward *Gideon* and *Douglas,* the landmarks sought to be extended in *Scott* and *Moffitt,* and may well intimate a belief that those opinions
were unjustifiably generous interpretations of Sixth and Fourteenth Amendment

---

[53] According to Rehnquist, there was even more reason to reject the contention that states had the
obligation to provide counsel for purposes of seeking a writ of certiorari from the United States
Supreme Court.

[54] *See also* Pennsylvania v. Finley, 481 U.S. 551 (1987) (Rehnquist majority opinion holding that there
is no right to appointed counsel for state postconviction proceedings), and Murray v. Giarratano,
492 U.S. 1 (1989) (Rehnquist plurality opinion concluding that even in capital cases states need
not provide appointed counsel for indigents seeking state postconviction relief).

rights. Nonetheless, he has expressed no explicit desire to overturn *Gideon* or *Douglas*.[55]

The same is not true with regard to the right to *pretrial* assistance first recognized in *Massiah v. United States*,[56] another Warren Court landmark. Rehnquist's initial hostility toward the *Massiah* entitlement to assistance ripened later into an unqualified assault on that doctrine's legitimacy. In contrast to his views regarding appointed counsel at trial and on appeal, however, the Chief Justice's views regarding *Massiah* have found little favor with his colleagues. He has managed to solidify one noteworthy limit on the scope of *Massiah*, but the core entitlement has survived his attacks.[57]

1. *The Origin and Content of the* Massiah *Right to Counsel*

Massiah v. United States, a lesser-known landmark of the Warren Court criminal procedure revolution, held that an accused has a Sixth Amendment right to the assistance of counsel when the government "deliberately elicits" incriminating statements after indictment. The decision was pathbreaking. It extended the right to counsel to an informal, extrajudicial pretrial encounter with a surreptitious government agent – that is, a confrontation in which the accused was unaware that he was dealing with a government operative. To the contention that counsel would impede the discovery of additional criminality, the majority pointedly responded that the Sixth Amendment does not forbid further investigative efforts, even efforts designed to elicit information from an accused. The right to counsel merely prevents the government from *using* deliberately elicited postindictment statements *against* an accused.

Three Justices strenuously objected to the *Massiah* majority's interpretation of the Sixth Amendment.[58] They perceived no "interference with [the] right to counsel," for there was no disturbance of, or spying upon, meetings with counsel, no obstruction of preparation for trial, no contact between government attorney and the accused, and no risk of "coercion." Moreover, the introduction of counsel into such encounters would erect unwarranted barriers to undercover investigations, and the exclusion of admissions secured without counsel would deprive factfinders of information that could aid ascertainment of the "truth." The dissenters believed that the due process ban on "involuntary" statements provided adequate constitutional protection against government efforts to secure inculpatory admissions.

---

[55] *But see Evitts,* 469 U.S. at 406 (1985) (Rehnquist, J., dissenting) (asserting that there is no due process right to effective assistance of appellate counsel).

[56] 377 U.S. 201 (1964).

[57] In some respects, *Massiah* has flourished during Rehnquist's tenure. *See, e.g.,* Maine v. Moulton, 474 U.S. 159 (1985); United States v. Henry, 447 U.S. 264 (1980). The Court recently *unanimously* reaffirmed that *Massiah* provides protection against more than official "interrogation." *See* Fellers v. United States, 540 U.S. 519 (2004). The unanimity of *Fellers* suggests the possibility that Rehnquist has given up his battle against the *Massiah* right and resigned himself to its endurance.

[58] 377 U.S. 201, 207 (1964) (White, J., dissenting).

The Supreme Court's decision in *Miranda v. Arizona*,[59] just two years later, cast doubt over the constitutional vitality of the *Massiah* doctrine. Some thought it might have been a false start that had been supplanted by *Miranda*. In the Supreme Court, *Massiah* lay virtually dormant for more than a decade.

2. *Rehnquist's Hostility Toward the* Massiah *Right to Counsel*
a. *An Initial Glimpse: The* Brewer v. Williams *Dissents*
The first intimations of Justice Rehnquist's attitude toward the *Massiah* doctrine appeared in a case that proved that the *Massiah* right was alive, well, and a source of independent constitutional shelter. In *Brewer v. Williams*,[60] a five-Justice majority held that the Sixth Amendment right against deliberate elicitation applied to a known police officer's "interrogation" of an accused. The majority rejected a claim of waiver because the record contained insufficient evidence of an actual "relinquishment" of counsel's assistance. Of the four remaining Justices, all but Rehnquist wrote dissents. Rehnquist joined two of those opinions.

The first was written by Justice White. After explaining why he believed a waiver of assistance had been proven, he asserted that conduct such as that engaged in by the officer in *Williams* posed no "risk of injury to society" and was not the sort of investigative effort that "should be deterred." The officer's behavior "did not, and was not likely to, jeopardize the fairness of the [defendant's] trial or in any way risk the conviction of an innocent man – the risk against which the Sixth Amendment guarantee of . . . counsel is designed to protect." He had, in fact, done nothing "'wrong'" or "'unconstitutional.'"

Rehnquist also joined Justice Blackmun's dissenting contention that no interrogation had occurred and that without interrogation there was no Sixth Amendment bar to the accused's statements. According to Blackmun, the Court's conclusion that *Massiah* governs "whenever police engage in any conduct with the subjective desire to obtain information" was "far too broad."

Rehnquist's endorsement of these two opinions provided powerful evidence that he viewed the *Massiah* entitlement to counsel as an illegitimate pretrial extension of the Sixth Amendment that constrained perfectly proper law enforcement activities posing no threats to the values underlying the right to counsel.

b. *A Clearer Picture: Rehnquist's Frontal Assault on* Massiah
Just three years later, Justice Rehnquist fully and clearly explained his belief that *Massiah* was fundamentally illegitimate. In a lengthy dissent in *United States v. Henry*,[61] he adopted a stance more hostile to *Massiah* than that of any other Justice.

Henry involved a situation more like *Massiah* than *Williams*. After Henry was indicted for bank robbery and while he was incarcerated pending trial, a fellow inmate working for the government had conversations with him and elicited inculpatory remarks. Six Justices decided that the cellmate's efforts triggered the

[59] 384 U.S. 436 (1966).   [60] 430 U.S. 387 (1977).   [61] 447 U.S. 264 (1980).

Massiah entitlement, that *Williams* had not limited the right to cases of actual "interrogation," and that Henry's statements could not be used at his trial. According to Chief Justice Burger's majority opinion, the government had run afoul of the Sixth Amendment "[b]y intentionally creating a situation likely to induce Henry to make incriminating statements without the assistance of counsel."

Rehnquist felt compelled to pen his own dissent this time, crafting a scathing indictment of the majority's conclusions and of the *Massiah* doctrine. He complained that the "exclusion" of Henry's admissions had "no relationship whatsoever to the[ir] reliability" and was based on a "prophylactic" interpretation of the Sixth Amendment that "entirely ignore[d] the doctrinal foundation of" the right to counsel. He then charged that *Massiah* needed to be reexamined because it constituted "a substantial departure from the traditional concerns that underlie the Sixth Amendment guarantee."

Rehnquist found the results in both *Henry* and *Massiah* to be irreconcilable "with the traditional notions of the role of an attorney." The government had not prevented consultation with counsel, had not disturbed or spied upon meetings with counsel, and had not obstructed preparation for trial. More important, the objectives of the Sixth Amendment are to ensure that laypersons have help "in arguing the law and in coping with intricate legal procedure, and to minimize the imbalance" between defendants and legally trained prosecutors. In determining whether there is an entitlement to counsel at any stage of the criminal process, it is imperative to acknowledge "the traditional role of an attorney as legal expert and strategist."

Rehnquist asserted that both *Henry* and *Massiah* "are fundamentally inconsistent with traditional notions of the role of the attorney that underlie the Sixth Amendment right to counsel." Those decisions extend a right to assistance to situations in which the risks against which the right to counsel is designed to protect are nonexistent. Because the accused faces no legal questions or procedures and is not confronted by an expert, legally trained prosecutor,[62] the encounter is not one that calls for the "special skill or knowledge" or the "legal expertise" of a lawyer. Statements elicited from the defendant by state agents are not the product of any "'unfair advantage.'"

According to Rehnquist, counsel "offer[s] advice and assistance in the preparation of a defense and . . . serve[s] as a spokesman for the accused in technical legal proceedings." Neither the Constitution nor history suggest "that an accused has a right to have his attorney serve as a sort of guru" in encounters with the government. Consequently, when the government induces an accused to freely disclose his guilt, there is simply no constitutionally defensible role for counsel. Moreover, efforts to elicit voluntary inculpatory admissions are not the sort of police misconduct that must be deterred by the exclusion of evidence.

[62] *See Henry,* 447 U.S. at 300–01 (Rehnquist, J., dissenting) (asserting that counsel is not "necessary . . . to enable [the accused] to cope with unfamiliar legal proceedings, or to counterbalance the expertise of the professional prosecutor").

With his *Henry* dissent, Rehnquist became the Court's leading critic of the pre-trial right to counsel recognized in *Massiah*.[63] The *Williams* dissents he had joined had indicated antipathy toward the doctrine, but in *Henry* Rehnquist found his own voice and used it to launch a potent attack on *Massiah*. Many of the themes Rehnquist sounded can be traced to Justice White's original *Massiah* dissent. Both Justices argued that in the situations governed by *Massiah* the government neither interferes with nor impedes counsel's efforts to assist the accused, and that those situations harbor none of the risks counsel is designed to combat. Rehnquist resurrected the themes, making them very much his own. Moreover, he went beyond the case White had built, laying a foundation for his assault with a detailed vision of the limited role counsel plays in our adversary system. While perhaps not surprising, it is at least noteworthy that the thoroughly developed logic of Rehnquist's *Henry* dissent is the antithesis of the relatively sketchy reasoning found in his majority opinions in *Scott, Nichols,* and *Moffitt*.

c. Rehnquist's Impact on the Massiah Doctrine: Solidifying a Significant Constraint

The Chief Justice's arguments against *Massiah*'s validity have not persuaded other members of the Court. In the twenty-five years since *Henry,* no Justice has endorsed his view. Rehnquist has had one opportunity, however, to author an opinion that confirmed and reinforced an important limitation on *Massiah*'s scope.

In *Texas v. Cobb*,[64] a considerable time after the defendant had been indicted for burglarizing a home, officers elicited a confession that he had killed a woman and child who had lived in the burglarized home. He was then charged with capital murder and convicted. The question before the Supreme Court was whether *Massiah*'s interpretation of the Sixth Amendment rendered use of the confession at trial improper.

In an opinion for a bare five-Justice majority, the Chief Justice observed that the Court had already deemed the *Massiah* right to be "offense specific" – that is, applicable *only* to formally charged offenses. Some courts, however, like the appellate court in *Cobb,* had discerned "an exception for crimes that are 'factually related' to a charged offense." The Rehnquist-led majority rejected this exception, reaffirming the "offense specific" restriction on the right to pretrial assistance.

The defense had argued that such a constraint on the reach of *Massiah*'s protection would "prove 'disastrous' to . . . constitutional rights and" would give police "license to conduct unwanted and uncounseled interrogations." Rehnquist

---

[63] Although Justices Blackmun and White also dissented in *Henry,* they conceded that *Massiah* itself was "not out of line with the Court's prior right-to-counsel cases." *Henry,* 447 U.S. at 281–82 (Blackmun, J., dissenting). In *Massiah,* Justice White had argued that the Court's Sixth Amendment extension was unfounded. By the time *Henry* was decided, however, Justice Rehnquist alone challenged the doctrine's legitimacy.

[64] 532 U.S. 162 (2001).

found no reason to fear this "parade of horribles" and noted that suspects retained the protection afforded by *Miranda*. He then turned to the societal interests at stake, emphasizing how "critical" it is for officers to be able to talk to all witnesses, including those charged with other offenses, and how essential uncoerced admissions of guilt are to effective law enforcement.

Rehnquist declared it "clear" that the entitlement to assistance "attaches only to charged offenses." He conceded that the term "offense" does encompass a small number of offenses beyond those statutory crimes that are the subject of a formal accusation. Specifically, the right to counsel attaches to other crimes that qualify as "the same offense" for purposes of the Fifth Amendment guarantee against double jeopardy – such as the lesser included offense of simple assault when assault with a deadly weapon or assault with intent to rob has been formally charged. For most uncharged offenses, however, no matter how closely related they are *in fact* to a charged offense, the government is free to elicit voluntary admissions without the impediment of counsel.

The effect of *Cobb* was to tightly confine the *Massiah* right to those offenses that are the subject of a formal accusation and a small number of offenses with very close statutory relationships to those charged.[65] By mustering a majority for this strict limitation on pretrial assistance, the Chief Justice prevented expansion of a Sixth Amendment entitlement that he believes to be fundamentally flawed. Moreover, he ensured that law enforcement would have an avenue for circumventing *Massiah*'s guarantee of counsel in some, perhaps many, cases. In cases involving multiple crimes, if charges are filed only for one minor offense, officers are free to elicit information for most, if not all, other offenses.

In Rehnquist's view, the hindrances to investigation and proof resulting from *Massiah* are constitutionally indefensible and injurious to society's efforts to protect itself against lawbreakers. Although abandonment of *Massiah* would be preferable, his fellow Justices are unwilling to take that route. Minimizing the scope of the pretrial entitlement is a fallback position – an acceptable second choice. *Cobb*'s refusal to recognize a right to assistance for offenses closely linked in fact to formally charged offenses was a partial, but significant, victory for Rehnquist's intense hostility toward the *Massiah* doctrine and its gratuitous obstruction of legitimate efforts to combat crime.[66]

---

[65] According to the "same offense" standard Rehnquist borrowed from double jeopardy law, the only offenses that are the same as a charged offense – and, thus, within the scope of right to counsel protection – are those whose statutory definitions include *every* element found in the charged offense or those whose statutory elements are *all* included within the definition of the charged offense. Two offenses are *not* the same if each has a single element not found in the other. *See* United States v. Dixon, 509 U.S. 688, 696 (1993).

[66] The Chief Justice has authored one other opinion that diminishes the impact of *Massiah*. *See* Michigan v. Harvey, 494 U.S. 344 (1990) (holding that statements obtained in violation of the Michigan v. Jackson, 475 U.S. 625 (1986), branch of *Massiah* doctrine may be used to impeach a testifying accused).

III. REFLECTIONS ON REHNQUIST'S RIGHT TO COUNSEL JURISPRUDENCE AND OPINIONS: PRINCIPLES, PREMISES, AND PATTERNS

A brief overview of the Chief Justice's right to counsel jurisprudence is in order. The discussion that follows identifies some of the recurrent themes in Rehnquist's right to counsel opinions.

A. A Genuinely Conservative Conception of the Right to the Assistance of Counsel

A conclusion that the Chief Justice has a "conservative" vision is hardly earth-shaking or novel. In this part, I highlight and explain the specific facets of his Sixth Amendment opinions that have prompted me to so describe his conception of the entitlement to a lawyer's assistance.

One clear indicator of Rehnquist's conservatism toward counsel is the fact that no Justice advocated a narrower entitlement than the Chief Justice in any of the cases discussed here.[67] In response to his opinions in *Scott, Nichols, Moffitt,* and *Cobb,* dissenters complained that he had defined the constitutional entitlement to assistance too restrictively. The dissents Rehnquist authored in *Henry* and joined in *Baldasar, Shelton,* and *Williams* and the concurrence he joined in *Argersinger* all evinced concern that the right to counsel had been interpreted too broadly. The Chief Justice's opinions and votes furnish ample evidence that no other Justice has a less generous vision of the right to counsel than he does.

Powerful evidence of the Chief Justice's constrained and constraining conception of the right to counsel can also be found in the words and phrases he neglects (or refuses) to employ. Supreme Court Justices have long sung the praises of the right to counsel in radiant terms. Counsel has repeatedly been described as the *most fundamental* of constitutional rights granted to the accused, a right *essential* to fundamental fairness in our adversarial system of justice, a right *necessary* for the enjoyment of other vital guarantees.[68] Rehnquist's opinions display a notable and stark absence of such descriptions. Of course, the Chief Justice's right to counsel opinions have all been designed to deny expansion (or to over-

---

[67] The same is true in other right to counsel opinions not discussed here. *See, e.g.,* Lockhart v. Fretwell, 506 U.S. 364 (1993) (majority opinion restricting ineffective assistance doctrine); Herring v. New York, 422 U.S. 853, 865 (1975) (Rehnquist, J., dissenting) (contending that majority had construed right to counsel too broadly).

[68] *See, e.g.,* Kimmelman v. Morrison, 477 U.S. 365, 377 (1986) (asserting that "it is through counsel that the accused secures his other rights"); United States v. Cronic, 466 U.S. 648, 654 (1984) (declaring that counsel is the "'most pervasive'" of the accused's constitutional rights); *Gideon,* 372 U.S. at 344 (1963) (stating that counsel is "fundamental and essential to fair trials"); *Zerbst,* 304 U.S. at 462 (1938) (observing that counsel is "necessary to insure fundamental human rights of life and liberty").

throw previous extension) of the counsel guarantee. It would be odd if his conclusions had been *supported* by the recurrent premises that have justified the right's considerable growth. On the other hand, it is hardly unheard-of for limiting opinions to acknowledge and reiterate the principles in landmark rulings being limited and to explain how the present restriction is consistent with them. In the Sixth Amendment realm, one might expect *some* effort to address the themes so often relied on to justify expansion of the counsel guarantee. Rehnquist's consistent failures even to acknowledge the effusive characterizations integral to the Sixth Amendment precedents he has confronted speak volumes about his abiding conservatism regarding the promise of counsel.

A recurrent premise in the Chief Justice's opinions is hostility to expansive interpretations of Sixth and Fourteenth Amendment rights. The first hint of this tendency appeared in *Argersinger,* when he joined an opinion motivated in part by a concern that the evolutionary trajectory pointed toward recognition of a right to appointed counsel for *all* petty offenses. When the opportunity to prevent that outcome presented itself in *Scott,* Rehnquist observed that the Court had already "departed from" the Sixth Amendment's "literal meaning" and had expanded the right to counsel beyond that intended by the Framers. His refusal to go further was based, in large measure, upon a central tenet of the Rehnquistian creed – that the Court must hesitate "to extrapolate an already extended line." In *Nichols,* Rehnquist's rejection of an attempt to limit the utility of uncounseled convictions rested on the premise that pre-*Scott* opinions "had already expanded the" guarantee of counsel "well beyond its obvious meaning." And in *Moffitt,* the case for confining appointed counsel to first appeals as a matter of right was built in part on an accusation that *Douglas* had broadened the doctrine of earlier cases involving appellate entitlements for indigents and in part on an admonition that rights have a dangerous "tendency . . . 'to declare themselves to their logical extreme.'" Finally, in his *Henry* dissent, Rehnquist deemed the *Massiah* doctrine "a substantial departure from . . . traditional [Sixth Amendment] concerns" and suggested that its grant of pretrial counsel was an indefensible expansion of the constitutional entitlement.

As already noted, it is uncertain whether the Chief Justice believes that the landmark rulings regarding appointed assistance predating his arrival were, like *Massiah,* constitutionally illegitimate extensions of the right to counsel. He indicated that *Zerbst, Gideon,* and *Douglas* were "departures," but did not advocate overturning any of those decisions. What is clear is that Rehnquist believes that these landmarks went to the brink, stretching the Constitution to the breaking point, and that any further extension of appointed assistance would be irresponsible. In *Henry,* the Chief Justice went one step further, accusing the Warren Court of recognizing an entitlement when defendants have no legitimate needs and lawyers have no legitimate roles. Throughout, Rehnquist has evinced a consistently and distinctively antiexpansionist attitude toward a constitutional right with a long expansionist history.

Rehnquist's conservatism comes through as well in his limited conception of the roles lawyers play, in his narrow understanding of the objectives of guaranteeing legal assistance, and in his implicit beliefs about the impacts lawyers have on trials and appeals. In his *Henry* dissent, he made clear his commitment to a "traditional" understanding "of the role of the attorney." Counsel's sole functions are to furnish the "legal expertise," the "special skill[,] and [the] knowledge" that the layperson lacks, enabling an accused to cope with *legal* questions, *legal* procedures, and the *legal* training of the prosecutor. The Constitution contemplates no entitlement to "a guru" – a ubiquitous, multipurpose mentor to guard against unwise or disadvantageous decisions and prevent the adversary from inducing her client to aid its efforts to convict.[69] In the absence of legal questions or an opponent with legal expertise, the Constitution leaves the accused to her or his own devices.

Rehnquist agrees with other members of the Court that the aim of the Sixth and Fourteenth Amendment rights to counsel is to ensure a "fair trial."[70] His conception of the fairness counsel is designed to ensure, however, is somewhat constrained.[71] The Chief Justice believes that counsel's main objective is to ensure the *reliability* of outcomes, guarding against conviction of the innocent.[72] He concedes that counsel also serves to safeguard other constitutional rights – that is, to ensure that an accused can take advantage of the basic procedural entitlements specified in the Bill of Rights.[73] In Rehnquist's view, however, counsel does not have independent significance as a "process" right.[74] Assurances of equalization in the adversarial process and of a fair chance to contest a criminal accusation are not themselves essential components of the fair process counsel provides.[75] This limited (and limiting) understanding of the fair trial interests

---

[69] Although the Court has not explained the constitutional rationales for the *Massiah* right to assistance, that pretrial guarantee is defensible only if it is rooted in a conception of the roles and functions of counsel broader than the Chief Justice's. For an explanation of the functions of counsel that might provide a rational justification for the *Massiah* entitlement, see James J. Tomkovicz, *An Adversary System Defense of the Right to Counsel Against Informants: Truth, Fair Play, and the* Massiah *Doctrine*, 22 U.C. DAVIS L. REV. 1, 39–62 (1988).

[70] *See Fretwell*, 506 U.S. at 368–69 (1993).

[71] Rehnquist is not unique in this respect. This understanding of counsel is shared by most, if not all, of his fellow Justices. *See* Strickland v. Washington, 466 U.S. 668, 684 (1984).

[72] *See* Brewer v. Williams, 430 U.S. 387, 437 (1977) (White, J., dissenting) (observing that the Sixth Amendment guarantee of counsel "is designed to protect" against the "risk [of] conviction of an innocent man").

[73] *See Fretwell*, 506 U.S. at 372.

[74] For a description of the view that counsel is itself a process right, see *Strickland*, 466 U.S. at 711 (Marshall, J., dissenting); *see also* TOMKOVICZ, *supra* note 2, at xxiv, 168–69.

[75] Those who envision a broader role for counsel in ensuring fairness contend that counsel sometimes serves a fair process function that may not promote accurate outcomes (or may even impede them) and may not be tied to the enjoyment of any other right. *See* Tomkovicz, *supra* note 69, at 47–52.

furthered by counsel informs many, if not most, of Rehnquist's right to counsel opinions.[76]

Scott v. Illinois is probably the Chief Justice's most significant right to counsel opinion. The holding of that case – that unimprisoned misdemeanor defendants have no right to appointed counsel – cannot be explained by the Chief Justice's constrictive conception of counsel's role in ensuring fairness. The end of appointed trial counsel's expansion declared by *Scott* must rest on another premise. A likely, though unexpressed, possibility is a belief that lawyers have a limited impact on the reliability of trials – at least those involving misdemeanor charges.[77] Every person subject to a criminal conviction and punishment is undoubtedly entitled to a fair process – that is, one that accords procedural protections that safeguard against an erroneous stigma and deprivation. The conclusion that the Constitution does not require appointed counsel unless imprisonment is imposed must rest, at least in part, on a belief that counsel's absence does not diminish the reliability of the process too seriously.[78] If fair outcomes and fair processes are possible without a lawyer's participation, then the salutary effects of counsel must be of limited magnitude.

One last facet of Justice Rehnquist's conservatism regarding counsel merits mention. Both *Gideon* and *Douglas* were prompted, in part, by a desire to ensure "equality" between those who could afford to retain assistance and those who could not.[79] *Scott,* the decision that muted *Gideon*'s trumpet, made no mention of the equality concern. Rehnquist's opinion paid no heed to the inevitable disparity between misdemeanor defendants with funds and those who were indigent. In *Moffitt,* Rehnquist's response to the claim that equal protection requires appointed counsel for discretionary appeals was that the Constitution does not mandate absolute equality. Although the process afforded unaided indigents was not identical, it was good enough to satisfy the Fourteenth Amendment's concern

[76] The Chief Justice's attack on the *Massiah* right is clearly founded on this narrow view of counsel's purposes. *See also Fretwell,* 506 U.S. at 372 (1993) (concluding that an accused is denied effective assistance only when an attorney's performance either "renders the result of [a] trial unreliable or [a] proceeding fundamentally unfair" – that is, only when a lawyer's inadequacy "deprive[s] the defendant of [a] substantive or procedural right to which the law entitles him").

[77] The holding in *Moffitt* would also seem to rest, at least in part, on the notion that counsel's effect on the outcome of discretionary appeals is limited. *See* Ross v. Moffitt, 417 U.S. 600, 615 (1974) (noting that the appellant already has entitlements that afford adequate access to the discretionary review process).

[78] This premise is undeniably inconsistent with the fundamental tenets that informed the opinions that expanded indigents' rights to appointed assistance at trial and on appeal – *Powell, Zerbst, Gideon, Argersinger,* and *Douglas.*

[79] *See Gideon,* 372 U.S. at 344 (1963) (stressing the long-standing and "noble ideal" that "every defendant stands equal before the law"); *Douglas,* 372 U.S. at 355 (1963) (asserting that "there can be no equal justice where the kind of an appeal a man enjoys 'depends on the amount of money he has'").

with equal treatment. Whether focusing on the issue or not, the Chief Justice has accorded equality a very "conservative" role in right to counsel cases.

B. An Abiding Concern with States' Interests

Chief Justice Rehnquist's right to counsel jurisprudence is marked by a distinctive pattern of balancing in which states' interests typically outweigh the interests of defendants. One need not read between the lines. His opinions express a genuine disdain for constitutional interpretations that impose heavy financial burdens, infringe on freedom to administer criminal justice systems, or impede efforts to investigate and prosecute crime efficiently. According to the Chief Justice, states' interests are weighty and at times even sufficient to counterbalance the incremental gains in fairness counsel might produce.

In *Scott*, Rehnquist refused to extend the appointed counsel line beyond actual imprisonment in part because of the "unpredictable, but necessarily substantial costs" that would be imposed on states.[80] In *Shelton*, he joined a dissent that bemoaned the "large, new burden" that the majority's holding placed on states' shoulders.[81] In *Moffitt*, Rehnquist asserted that the Constitution leaves states free to decide whether "other claims for public funds . . . preclude" free counsel at the discretionary appeal stage.[82]

Dissenters in *Scott* and *Nichols* argued that the costs of providing counsel are not relevant to the constitutional analysis.[83] Rehnquist did not respond with an explanation of why states' interests are a legitimate variable in the Sixth Amendment equation. It seems fair to say that in the Chief Justice's jurisprudence costs of various sorts are germane because fundamental fairness is a relative construct that depends not only on the likelihood of inaccuracy and the consequences of error, but also on the "price" of enhancing the quality of a process.[84]

IV. CONCLUSIONS

In a series of opinions over a more than thirty-year span, William Rehnquist has pursued a consistent, narrowing vision of the right to the assistance of counsel. His conservative understanding of the scope and importance of the constitutional entitlement to legal assistance has stemmed a powerful evolutionary tide that,

[80]   440 U.S. 367, 373 (1979).

[81]   535 U.S. 654, 679–80 (2002).

[82]   417 U.S. 600, 618 (1974).

[83]   *See Scott*, 440 U.S. at 384 (Brennan, J., dissenting); *Nichols*, 511 U.S. at 764 (1994) (Blackmun, J., dissenting).

[84]   Rehnquist's attitude stands in contrast to that evident in landmark right to counsel precedents. *Gideon*'s extension of appointed assistance to *all* state defendants charged with serious offenses undoubtedly imposed substantial costs on the states, costs that the majority ignored. While extending appointed counsel to misdemeanors entailing imprisonment, the *Argersinger* majority quickly dismissed the argument "that the Nation's legal resources" might be "insufficient to implement" its holding. *Argersinger*, 407 U.S. at 37 n. 7 (1972).

prior to his arrival, had led to ever more expansive rights to appointed *trial* counsel. It has halted the further growth of the relatively young entitlement to appointed counsel on *appeal.* And it has resisted extension of a right to *pretrial* assistance that Rehnquist finds constitutionally indefensible.

Always backed very slim majorities, Rehnquist has repeatedly taken controversial positions regarding the Sixth and Fourteenth Amendment rights to counsel, positions that have provoked powerful dissent. His reasoning has typically been terse and minimalist, explained with noteworthy brevity and economy and devoid of the stirring rhetoric characteristic of earlier right to counsel opinions. In form, his holdings have usually delineated relatively clear and stark bright lines that generate few issues and ambiguities. Moreover, the Chief Justice has refined the art of not engaging with naysayers. His opinions march to their own beat, refusing to respond to criticisms and accusations leveled by dissenters.

Chief Justice Rehnquist's understanding of the constitutional right to counsel has had an undeniably dramatic impact on the Court's interpretations of the criminal defendant's entitlement to a lawyer's assistance. For better or worse, Rehnquist has led a quiet, determined resistance to a potent historical tide and has succeeded in halting the growth of a constitutional right that seemed destined to expand to its logical limits. His profound influence in this realm will surely be felt for many years to come.

CHAPTER EIGHT

NARROWING HABEAS CORPUS

Joseph L. Hoffmann

Federal habeas corpus is a relatively obscure and often complicated legal procedure that provides state prisoners the opportunity to challenge the constitutionality of their criminal convictions in federal court. Over the past half-century,
federal habeas frequently has served as the battleground for disputes over federalism and the death penalty. Supporters of federal habeas see it as a key protection
for federal constitutional rights, ensuring that final decisions about those rights
will be made by federal judges instead of possibly less sympathetic state judges.
Opponents view it as a device for obstructing justice, especially in capital cases,
permitting inmates to engage in endless and protracted federal litigation over
legal technicalities that have little to do with the merits of their convictions.

In the 1960s, the Supreme Court, led by Justice William J. Brennan – a cham-
pion of federal power at the expense of the states – greatly expanded the availability and scope of federal habeas corpus review of state criminal convictions as
part of a broader agenda to elevate federal criminal procedure law over state law.
This expansion of federal habeas shifted the balance of power between federal
and state courts sharply in favor of the federal courts. And it ultimately led, by
the late 1970s, to severe limitations on the ability of the states to enforce their
capital punishment laws.

During his long career on the Court, Chief Justice William H. Rehnquist has
played a central role in reversing the Brennan-engineered expansion of federal
habeas corpus. In almost every aspect of federal habeas law, Rehnquist – a staunch
believer in the prerogatives of the states vis-à-vis the federal government, as well
as in the inherent right of society to punish criminals as it sees fit – consistently
has advocated for a far narrower federal habeas remedy than the one Brennan
envisioned in the 1960s.

Today, it is clearly Rehnquist's view of federal habeas corpus that has prevailed.
Rehnquist has written many of the leading federal habeas opinions, and his thinking about habeas has influenced many others. In the few areas where he has failed
to win a Court majority for restructuring federal habeas, Congress has stepped
in and largely completed the task for him. As a consequence, federal habeas law

today largely reflects the Rehnquistian vision of strictly limited federal court review of state criminal convictions.

A HABEAS PRIMER

The common-law writ of habeas corpus – often called the "Great Writ" – is of ancient origin, dating back to Magna Carta.[1] Throughout its long history, it has served as a bulwark for individual liberty, providing judges with the legal authority to investigate and remedy unjust executive detentions. This accounts for its special status in the text of the Constitution, which provides: "The Privilege of the Writ of Habeas Corpus shall not be suspended, unless when in Cases of Rebellion or Invasion the public Safety may require it."[2]

The common-law writ operates in the following manner: When an imprisoned person wishes to complain about the legality of his detention, he may file a petition for a writ of habeas corpus with a judge who possesses jurisdiction over the prisoner's custodian (hence the name, *habeas corpus*, Latin for "you have the body"). The judge may then order the production in court of the prisoner for the purpose of inquiring into the reasons for the detention. If the detention is found to be arbitrary, illegal, or otherwise without appropriate justification, the judge may issue the writ and order the release of the prisoner.

One of the traditional defenses to the common-law writ is that the prisoner is being detained pursuant to a facially valid judgment of criminal conviction entered by a court. This is presumed to be an appropriate reason for the detention, at least so long as the court that convicted the prisoner had proper jurisdiction to do so. Thus, the common-law writ has never been of significant value to convicted persons.

In addition to the common-law version of habeas corpus, however, there is also a statutory form of the writ, enacted in 1867 to protect Reconstruction-era federal officials and newly freed slaves from abuses of state criminal justice.[3] The 1867 act, for the first time, extended the protection of habeas corpus to persons who were imprisoned by the states because they had been convicted of crimes in state court, allowing them to seek judicial relief from federal courts.

---

[1] The history of habeas corpus has been the subject of numerous books and articles, including W. Church, *A Treatise on the Writ of Habeas Corpus* (1893); William F. Duker, *A Constitutional History of Habeas Corpus* (1981); Daniel J. Meador, *Habeas Corpus and Magna Carta – Dualism of Power and Liberty* (1996); Paul M. Bator, *Finality in Criminal Law and Federal Habeas Corpus for State Prisoners*, 76 Harv. L. Rev. 441 (1963); Eric M. Freedman, *The Suspension Clause in the Ratification Debates*, 44 Buff. L. Rev. 451 (1996); and Dallin H. Oaks, *Legal History in the High Court – Habeas Corpus*, 64 Mich. L. Rev. 451 (1966).

[2] U.S. Constitution, art. I, §9, cl. 2.

[3] An earlier statutory form of habeas corpus for federal prisoners was part of the original Judiciary Act of 1789. Because relatively few crimes were then, or are now, federal crimes, this earlier form of habeas corpus – codified today at 28 U.S.C. §2255 – is much less important in practice than the one described in the text, and will not be a major subject of this chapter.

The new, statutory form of habeas corpus – the core of which is codified to-day at 28 U.S.C. §2254, and which henceforth we will call federal habeas corpus, federal habeas, or simply habeas – operates as a so-called collateral attack on the underlying state criminal conviction (as opposed to a "direct appeal" of the con-viction). The state prisoner who files a petition in federal court for a writ of ha-beas corpus under §2254 can raise any issue of federal constitutional law that he alleges to be implicated by his case.[4] The federal court has the authority to review such issues, subject to the procedural rules of habeas, and to grant relief if the conviction involves a constitutional violation. Relief generally consists of an order to release the prisoner, unless the state elects to retry him within a cer-tain period of time.

HABEAS AND FEDERALISM

The story of federal habeas corpus is closely intertwined with the story of feder-alism. Beginning with its enactment in 1867, the scope of federal habeas has con-sistently expanded during periods when the federal government sought to assert greater control over the states, and has consistently contracted during periods when state power was in relative ascendancy.

As noted above, federal habeas was born in the crucible of the post–Civil War Reconstruction era. At the time, the Reconstruction Congress was concerned that the Southern states might try to misuse their criminal justice systems to punish either the newly freed slaves or anyone else who might try to protect them. The U.S. Supreme Court clearly did not have enough time, and – because it still was dominated by antebellum appointees – also may not have had the inclination, to police the states. Congress therefore enacted the Habeas Corpus Act of 1867,[5] empowering the lower federal courts to intervene on behalf of any person con-victed in state court whose federal rights may have been violated.

Almost immediately, this new form of federal habeas corpus for state pris-oners became one of the front lines in the never-ending American war of fed-eralism. Shortly after the enactment of the 1867 act, a Mississippi editor who was detained by federal military authorities for publishing "incendiary and libellous" articles filed a petition for a writ of habeas corpus on the ground that the Recon-struction Acts (which implemented military rule in the South) were unconsti-tutional. The lower federal court initially denied habeas relief, but the Supreme Court, over vigorous objection by government lawyers, held that it possessed appellate jurisdiction under the 1867 act to review the denial.[6] Congress, fearing that the Court might invalidate Reconstruction, hastily passed a new statute de-

---

[4] Section 2254 also allows habeas petitions to be based on alleged violations of federal statutes or treaties, although these rarely arise because there are few federal statutes or treaties that purport to govern state criminal cases.

[5] Act of Feb. 5, 1867, ch. 28, §1, 14 Stat. 385.

[6] *Ex parte* McCardle, 73 U.S. (6 Wall.) 318 (1868).

priving the Court of appellate jurisdiction over habeas cases.[7] In April 1868, the Court gave effect to the new statute and dismissed the appeal.[8]

The Supreme Court's appellate jurisdiction over habeas cases was not restored by Congress until March 1885.[9] At that point, Congress obviously was no longer concerned about Court interference with Reconstruction; instead, by 1885, Congress had become worried about what it viewed as needless interference by lower federal courts with state criminal cases, and felt that the Supreme Court could be trusted to use its restored appellate review powers to prevent such interference.[10] The very first case decided by the Court under the new statute vindicated Congress's trust, giving birth to the rule of exhaustion – still followed today – which provides that federal habeas review of state criminal convictions generally should not occur until after the state courts have had the chance to complete their handling of the case.[11]

During the next sixty-eight years, federal habeas played a relatively minor role in the American criminal justice system.[12] There are two prevailing theories for why this was so.[13] The first is that the rules of federal habeas, for most of that time, did not permit federal court review of anything but the legality of the state court's jurisdiction to enter the criminal conviction. If the state court had proper jurisdiction, then no further inquiry into the constitutionality of the conviction was allowed. The second theory is that, even if the federal habeas rules may have permitted a broader inquiry into alleged constitutional violations, there simply was not much constitutional law for the habeas courts to apply; during that period, the constitutional standard of "due process" was vaguely defined and easily satisfied. Hence the federal courts, sitting in habeas, may have had the legal authority to act, but had very few legal grounds upon which to do so.

The situation began to change in 1953, when the Court decided, in *Brown v. Allen*,[14] that (1) all federal constitutional issues (and not merely jurisdictional ones) are cognizable in federal habeas; (2) federal habeas courts are not bound by prior state court adjudication of federal issues; and (3) the denial of discretionary certiorari review by the Court does not preclude later federal habeas review. The situation changed even more dramatically during the 1960s. Led by Justice Brennan, an unabashed devotee of expansive federal constitutional criminal

---

[7] Act of March 27, 1868, ch. 34, 15 Stat. 44.

[8] *Ex parte* McCardle, 74 U.S. (7 Wall.) 506 (1869).

[9] Act of March 3, 1885, ch. 353, 23 Stat. 437.

[10] *See* H.R. Rep. No. 730, 48th Cong., 1st Sess. (1884).

[11] *Ex parte* Royall, 117 U.S. 241 (1886).

[12] The most notable exception was the case of *Moore v. Dempsey*, 261 U.S. 86 (1923), in which habeas relief was granted to African-American defendants whose convictions were tainted by the presence of an angry mob outside the courthouse. *But see* Frank v. Mangum, 237 U.S. 309 (1915), denying habeas relief on an almost identical claim made by a Jewish defendant.

[13] The first view was perhaps best expressed by Paul M. Bator, *supra* note 1. The second view is most closely associated with Justice Brennan, *see* Fay v. Noia, 372 U.S. 391 (1963), and Gary Peller, *In Defense of Federal Habeas Corpus Relitigation*, 16 Harv. C.R.–C.L. L. Rev. 579 (1982).

[14] Brown v. Allen, 344 U.S. 443 (1953).

procedure rights, the Court began to develop the well-known body of case law that eventually came to be known as the "criminal procedure revolution." Among the Court's many innovations were such landmark decisions as *Gideon v. Wainwright*,[15] *Mapp v. Ohio*,[16] *Miranda v. Arizona*,[17] and *Duncan v. Louisiana*.[18] These decisions completely transformed the way that the states handled their criminal cases, requiring them to provide appointed counsel to indigents, exclude illegally seized evidence, warn suspects about their rights during custodial interrogations, grant jury trials in all but the most minor cases, and comply with a host of additional new federal constitutional requirements.

These new Supreme Court decisions, which trumped long-standing and less protective state law rules of criminal procedure, were often unpopular with both the American people (who saw them as coddling criminals) and state officials (who saw them as unwarranted intrusions into areas of traditional state power). Among those who disagreed with many of the Court's edicts were many state judges. And at least some state judges resisted the Court's edicts, applying them grudgingly or not at all.

The Court soon realized that it needed to find a way to police these recalcitrant state courts. The situation partially resembled the one that prevailed during Reconstruction times – during the 1960s, the Court clearly had the inclination to supervise the state courts, but just as in the days of Reconstruction, it lacked the capacity to do so.

The Court, once again led by Justice Brennan, turned in the 1960s to the same remedy that had been created by Congress in the 1860s – federal habeas corpus. Concurrently with *Gideon, Mapp, Miranda,* and *Duncan,* the Court also rendered a series of less-famous but equally momentous decisions – most notably *Fay v. Noia*,[19] *Townsend v. Sain*,[20] *Sanders v. United States*,[21] and *Linkletter v. Walker*.[22] These cases collectively established that federal habeas courts (1) could review federal claims that had been rejected in the state courts for failure to comply with valid state procedural rules, so long as the defendant did not "deliberately bypass" the state courts; (2) could relitigate issues of both fact and law previously determined in the state courts; (3) could review federal claims in successive habeas petitions, so long as the failure to raise the claim in a prior petition was not in "bad faith"; and (4) could grant habeas relief based on newly decided case law that did not even exist at the time of the original state criminal trial, so long as the Court did not hold such new case law to be "nonretroactive." The net effect was a dramatic expansion of the scope of federal habeas, thereby empowering the lower federal courts to carry the load of ensuring state court compliance with the Court's new constitutional criminal procedure cases.

---

[15] Gideon v. Wainwright, 372 U.S. 335 (1963).
[16] Mapp v. Ohio, 367 U.S. 643 (1961).
[17] Miranda v. Arizona, 384 U.S. 436 (1966).
[18] Duncan v. Louisiana, 391 U.S. 145 (1968).
[19] *Noia,* 372 U.S. at 391.
[20] Townsend v. Sain, 372 U.S. 293 (1963).
[21] Sanders v. United States, 373 U.S. 1 (1963).
[22] Linkletter v. Walker, 381 U.S. 618 (1965).

Within a relatively short time, the Supreme Court won the war of federalism in two important respects.[23] The Court's constitutional criminal procedure decisions replaced state law criminal procedure rules with a new federal version that provided much greater protection for those accused of crimes. And the Court's habeas decisions enabled the lower federal courts, sitting in habeas, to review and reverse virtually any state court decision that did not conform to the spirit as well as the letter of the Court's new constitutional criminal procedure law. By the end of the 1960s, state criminal justice was regulated largely by federal constitutional law, and the ultimate enforcement of those regulations rested primarily with the federal courts.

HABEAS AND THE DEATH PENALTY

The Supreme Court's expansion of federal habeas corpus in the 1960s coincided with a historic decline in public support for capital punishment. Throughout the decade, public opinion polls showed ever-narrowing majorities in favor of the death penalty, and many elected officials chose not to implement the sanction, producing a de facto national moratorium on executions that began in 1967.

Against this background, in 1972, the Supreme Court decided *Furman v. Georgia*,[24] invalidating all then-existing capital punishment statutes. Although *Furman* produced nine separate opinions, the bottom line was that a five-Justice majority of the Court found the death penalty – at least as it was administered under those existing statutes – to be applied in an arbitrary, and sometimes discriminatory, manner, thus violating the Eighth Amendment's prohibition on "cruel and unusual punishment."[25]

Many observers believed that the end was near for the American death penalty. Justice Brennan's opinion in *Furman*, for example, expressed the view that the death penalty "has been almost totally rejected by contemporary society. . . . The progressive decline in, and the current rarity of, the infliction of death demonstrate that our society seriously questions the appropriateness of this punishment today. . . . Rejection could hardly be more complete without becoming absolute."[26]

Such assessments of American public opinion proved woefully inaccurate. Almost immediately after *Furman*, public opinion began to swing back in favor of capital punishment, and state legislatures began to enact new death penalty statutes designed to cure the various ills that had led to the *Furman* decision. These legislatures were emboldened by the fact that only two of the *Furman* Justices – Brennan and Marshall – took the absolute position that the death penalty

---

[23] *See* Joseph L. Hoffmann & William J. Stuntz, *Habeas After the Revolution*, 1993 Sup. Ct. Rev. 65.

[24] Furman v. Georgia, 408 U.S. 238 (1972).

[25] "Excessive bail shall not be required, nor excessive fines imposed, nor cruel and unusual punishments inflicted." U.S. Const., amend. VIII.

[26] *Furman*, 408 U.S. at 295, 299–300 (Brennan, J., concurring in the judgment).

itself was "cruel and unusual punishment." The others in the *Furman* major-ity[27] held open the possibility that new death penalty statutes might pass con-stitutional muster.

Four years after *Furman,* in *Gregg v. Georgia* and its companion cases,[28] the Court vindicated the legislatures of Georgia, Florida, and Texas by upholding their new capital punishment statutes. Before long, more than two-thirds of the states adopted new statutes based on those approved by the Court in *Gregg.* The death penalty was back, and with a vengeance.

The battle over capital punishment, however, did not end. Opponents of the death penalty continued to litigate individual cases, arguing that although the death penalty itself may not be "cruel and unusual punishment," its application still might violate the Constitution.

In 1978, just two years after *Gregg,* the Supreme Court decided *Lockett v. Ohio,*[29] the first in what would become an extensive series of cases defining an entirely new set of constitutional criminal procedure requirements specifically for cap-ital cases. Starting with *Lockett,* the Court held that death penalty cases are dif-ferent from other, run-of-the-mill criminal cases, and thus demand special pro-cedural rules designed to ensure higher levels of fairness and accuracy. The Court found justification for this approach in the Eighth Amendment, concluding that the death penalty is "cruel and unusual punishment" *unless* it is administered pursuant to more reliable procedures than apply to normal criminal cases. These new procedural rules for capital cases collectively became known as "super due process."[30]

One possibly unintended consequence of the Court's new growth industry in "super due process" rules, however, was that the states quickly became frustrated in their efforts to carry out the death penalty. Every year, throughout the late 1970s and early 1980s, the Court handed down many rulings establishing new consti-tutional criminal procedure requirements for capital cases. And every year, most of these new requirements were applied to all of the capital cases that had been previously tried in the state courts – meaning that, every year, dozens if not hun-dreds of such cases were reversed and sent back for new trials or new capital sen-tencing hearings.[31]

---

[27] The other concurring Justices in *Furman* were Douglas (who primarily felt the death penalty was being administered in a discriminatory manner), Stewart (who primarily felt that it was administered in an arbitrary manner), and White (who primarily felt that it was administered too rarely, and thus could serve no useful purpose).

[28] Gregg v. Georgia, 428 U.S. 153 (1976); Jurek v. Texas, 428 U.S. 262 (1976); and Proffitt v. Florida, 428 U.S. 242 (1976). In two other cases – Roberts v. Louisiana, 428 U.S. 325 (1976), and Wood-son v. North Carolina, 428 U.S. 280 (1976) – the Court struck down death penalty statutes, be-cause they sought to make the death penalty mandatory for certain crimes.

[29] Lockett v. Ohio, 438 U.S. 586 (1978).

[30] *See* Robert M. Cover, *Violence and the Word,* 95 Yale L.J. 1601 (1986); Robert Weisberg, *Deregu-lating Death,* 1983 Sup. Ct. Rev. 305; Margaret J. Radin, *Cruel Punishment and Respect for Per-sons: Super Due Process for Death,* 53 S. Cal. L. Rev. 1143 (1980).

[31] *See* Joseph L. Hoffmann, *Is Innocence Sufficient? An Essay on the U.S. Supreme Court's Continuing Problems with Federal Habeas Corpus and the Death Penalty,* 68 Ind. L.J. 817 (1993).

The bulk of these "super due process" reversals were ordered by federal habeas courts. Although every state provides the right to appeal criminal convictions in a state appellate court, and although such appeals necessarily include the right to raise federal constitutional issues, the right to appeal in state court is limited by strict time constraints. In general, a convicted person has a limited time after the date of conviction – maybe six months, or one year – to file an appeal. Thus, any person whose conviction occurred more than a year before the date of a new Supreme Court constitutional criminal procedure ruling could not benefit from that ruling on appeal, because it simply came too late.

Federal habeas, on the other hand, traditionally has no time limits. Moreover, traditionally there are no limits on the number of federal habeas petitions that can be filed to challenge a particular criminal conviction. So, through the late 1970s and 1980s, whenever the Court handed down a new "super due process" ruling, death row inmates flooded the federal courts with habeas petitions seeking the benefit of the new ruling. And federal habeas courts usually provided such relief, overturning hundreds of state death sentences.

After *Gregg*, therefore, federal habeas became closely intertwined not only with federalism but also with the death penalty. This relationship can be seen clearly in federal habeas corpus statistics. In noncapital state criminal cases, federal habeas corpus petitions – which are rarely filed in the first place – succeed only 3.2 percent of the time.[32] But in capital cases, where multiple habeas petitions are virtually universal, the habeas success rate is more than 45 percent – and, during the late 1970s and early 1980s, was even higher.[33] Throughout the modern, post-*Gregg* era of the death penalty, federal habeas has served as the legal arena within which almost all of the important conflicts have been fought. And, over time, most of the Justices have allowed their views about the proper scope of federal habeas corpus to be colored by their views about the death penalty: those who favor capital punishment have sought to restrict federal habeas, while those who oppose capital punishment (or are ambivalent about it) have sought to preserve broad federal habeas authority.

REHNQUIST'S VIEWS ON HABEAS AND FEDERALISM

Justice Rehnquist joined the Supreme Court in 1972, the same year *Furman* was decided. By then, the bulk of the Court's "criminal procedure revolution," led by Justice Brennan, had already taken place. The corresponding expansion of federal habeas corpus, likewise orchestrated by Brennan, also was largely complete. The impact of these twin developments on the administration of capital punishment in the states, however, was yet to be seen. Only after *Gregg*, in 1976, would that impact gradually become apparent.

[32] *See* Daniel J. Meltzer, *Habeas Corpus Jurisdiction: The Limits of Models*, 66 S. Cal. L. Rev. 2507, 2524 (1993).

[33] *See* Brief Amici Curiae of Benjamin Civiletti *et al.* in Support of Respondent in *Wright v. West*, No. 91-542, 505 U.S. 277 (1992) (filed Mar. 4, 1992), at App. B.

Nevertheless, in 1977, even before the first real effects of federal habeas on capital punishment could be felt, Rehnquist wrote the single most important habeas decision of his career, and one of the most important in history – *Wainwright v. Sykes*.[34] In *Sykes*, Rehnquist took down one of the central pillars of Brennan's 1960s habeas expansion, *Fay v. Noia*. The doctrinal significance of *Sykes* is discussed in a later section ("Habeas and Procedural Default"). For present purposes, however, what is important is the narrow view of federal habeas corpus reflected in Rehnquist's majority opinion in *Sykes*. Rehnquist's vision of federal habeas, as expressed in *Sykes*, became the leading theoretical and doctrinal counterpoint to Brennan's vision, as outlined in *Fay v. Noia*.

Rehnquist's *Sykes* majority opinion set the stage for almost everything else that would follow in the dismantling of Brennan's broad vision of federal habeas. In *Sykes*, Rehnquist laid out four key issues that he saw as central to defining the proper scope of federal habeas corpus:

1. What types of federal claim may a federal habeas court properly consider?
2. Where a federal claim is cognizable by a federal habeas court, to what extent must that court defer to a resolution of the claim in prior state proceedings?
3. To what extent must the petitioner who seeks federal habeas exhaust state remedies before resorting to the federal court?
4. In what instances will an adequate and independent state ground bar consideration of otherwise cognizable federal issues on federal habeas review?[35]

Only the fourth of these issues actually was involved in *Sykes;* but Rehnquist's *Sykes* opinion left little doubt as to where he stood on the other three issues. Influenced by a strong states' rights view of federalism, Rehnquist's answers to the above questions were relatively straightforward and clear:

1. Federal habeas should be available only for truly fundamental federal constitutional claims, and other less important claims should be excluded from habeas.
2. Federal habeas courts generally should defer to prior state court adjudications.
3. Federal habeas petitioners should be required to exhaust their federal claims in state court before seeking relief from a habeas court.
4. Any adequate and independent state law ground for the prior state court decision (such as the state law procedural default involved in *Sykes* itself) should operate as a bar to subsequent federal habeas review.

Over time, each of these four issues would be addressed, either by the Court or by Congress. And, with the exception of the first issue (as is discussed in the section "The One Unfinished Battle"), each would be resolved decisively in favor

---

[34] Wainwright v. Sykes, 433 U.S. 72 (1977).
[35] *Id.* at 78–79.

of Rehnquist's view that federal habeas is an exceptional remedy to be applied judiciously, and with proper deference to state courts.

REHNQUIST'S VIEWS ON HABEAS AND THE DEATH PENALTY

A few years after *Wainwright v. Sykes,* Rehnquist – increasingly frustrated by the Court's apparent reluctance to dismantle some of Brennan's remaining federal habeas expansions, and by the corresponding impact of habeas on the administration of capital punishment in the states – lashed out, in a series of three remarkable individual opinions (including two dissents from the denial of certiorari, and one in-chambers opinion denying a request for a stay of execution). These three opinions represent Rehnquist's manifesto on federal habeas and the death penalty. Together with the *Sykes* majority opinion, they sound the major themes that have continued to influence Rehnquist's views on federal habeas throughout his career.

The first of the three individual opinions came in the case of John Spenkelink, the first inmate executed under a post-*Gregg* death penalty statute who did not voluntarily give up his legal challenges to his sentence. In *Spenkelink v. Wainwright,*[36] Rehnquist wrote to explain his denial of a request for a stay of execution. He first cataloged the many stages of judicial review that already had been provided to Spenkelink, and then concluded:

> Throughout these many hearings, appeals, and applications, there has been virtually no dispute that substantial evidence supported the jury's verdict that appellant was guilty of first-degree murder, or that the Florida state trial judge had ample basis for following the jury's recommendation that the death penalty be imposed. . . .
>
> Applicant has had not merely one day in court. He has had many, many days in court. It has been the conclusion of the Supreme Court of Florida that the death sentence was imposed in accordance with the requirements of Florida law as well as those of the United States Constitution, and it has been the conclusion of the United States District Court . . . and the [United States] Court of Appeals . . . that there was no federal constitutional error in the process by which applicant was sentenced to death. Three times this Court has refused to review the determinations of these state and federal courts. I do not believe that the claim presented in the present application would be any more successful that the claims presented in the preceding three petitions for certiorari. The application for stay of execution . . . is accordingly denied.[37]

The second opinion, in *Estelle v. Jurek,*[38] involved the same death row inmate who had been the losing petitioner in the 1976 Supreme Court case upholding the new Texas death penalty statute. In 1980, Jurek managed to obtain federal

---

[36] Spenkelink v. Wainwright, 442 U.S. 1301 (1979) (in-chambers opinion of Rehnquist, J., Circuit Justice, denying stay of execution).

[37] *Id.* at 6, 11–12.

[38] Estelle v. Jurek, 450 U.S. 1014 (1981) (Rehnquist, J., dissenting from denial of certiorari).

habeas relief from the United States Court of Appeals for the Fifth Circuit on the ground that, although his oral confession and first written confession were voluntary, his second written confession – which had been found voluntary by the Texas state courts – was involuntary and thus inadmissible. Rehnquist dissented from the Supreme Court's denial of certiorari to review the Fifth Circuit's decision:

> What is particularly troubling about this case is that I have no doubt that the decision below was colored by the fact that this is a capital punishment case. The severity of a defendant's punishment, however, simply has no bearing on whether a particular confession is voluntary or on the extent to which federal habeas courts should defer to state-court findings. . . .
>
> By overturning Jurek's conviction on the basis of a procedural nicety, the decision below not only renders Texas' death penalty statute an ineffective deterrent, it also frustrates society's compelling interest in having its constitutionally valid laws swiftly and surely carried out. A potential murderer will know that even if he is convicted and sentenced to death, he will very likely not be put to death. If he litigates the case long enough, the odds favor his finding some court which will accept a legal theory previously rejected by other courts.[39]

The third, and perhaps most remarkable, opinion came in the case of *Coleman v. Balkcom*.[40] This time, the lower federal courts denied habeas relief. Coleman, a death row inmate, petitioned the Supreme Court for certiorari review, and the Court denied certiorari. Rehnquist nevertheless dissented – on the novel ground that the Court should cut off the seemingly endless chain of federal habeas litigation by granting certiorari review, and then denying all of Coleman's federal claims on the merits, thereby requiring the swift dismissal of any future habeas petitions. Rehnquist wrote:

> It seems to me that we have thus reached a stalemate in the administration of federal constitutional law. Although this Court has determined that capital punishment statutes do not violate the Constitution, . . . and although 30-odd States have enacted such statutes, apparently in the belief that they constitute sound social policy, the existence of the death penalty in this country is virtually an illusion. . . . Of the hundred of prisoners condemned to die who languish on the various "death rows," few of them appear to face any imminent prospect of their sentence being executed. . . .
>
> As Justice Jackson stated in *Stein v. New York* . . . : "The petitioners have had fair trial and fair review. The people of the State are also entitled to due process of law." . . .
>
> I believe we have in our judicial decisions focused so much on controlling the government that we have lost sight of the equally important objective of enabling the government to control the governed. When our systems of administering criminal justice cannot provide security to our people in the streets or in their homes, we are rapidly approaching the state of savagery. . . . In the Nation's Capital, law enforcement authorities cannot protect the lives of employees of this very Court who

---

[39] *Id.* at 1019–21.
[40] Coleman v. Balkcom, 451 U.S. 949, 956 (1981) (Rehnquist, J., dissenting from denial of certiorari).

live four blocks from the building in which we sit and deliberate the constitutionality of capital punishment.[41]

Rehnquist proceeded to argue that the Court should grant certiorari, allow full
briefing and oral argument, and then dispose of all of Coleman's federal claims:

> Thus the jurisdiction of the federal courts over petitioner's sentence of death would
> be at an end, and unless the appropriate state officials commuted petitioner's sen-
> tence, it would presumably be carried out. In any event, the decision would then be
> in the hands of the State which had initially imposed the death penalty, not in the
> hands of the federal courts.[42]

Although Rehnquist could not carry a Court to do so in *Coleman,* his idea
reemerged more than a decade later, in connection with California's first post-
Furman execution. The inmate, Robert Alton Harris, in the last days leading up
to his scheduled execution, managed to obtain a series of stays of execution from
the lower federal courts. On April 21, 1992, the Court vacated stays of execution
that had been entered by the Ninth Circuit on the previous day,[43] only to have
that court immediately issue another stay of execution. Within hours, in response
to the new stay, the Court – by a 7–2 vote, with only Justices Blackmun and Stevens dissenting – handed down the following extraordinary order:

> The application to vacate the stay of execution . . . is granted, and it is ordered that
> the order staying the execution entered by the United States Court of Appeals for
> the Ninth Circuit . . . is vacated. No further stays of Robert Alton Harris' execution
> shall be entered by the federal courts except upon order of this Court.[44]

The order in *Harris* exceeded even Rehnquist's suggestion in *Coleman,* because
it foreclosed further lower-court federal habeas litigation not only of claims that
had already been made by Harris, but also of future claims not yet made. Harris
was executed on the same day as the Court's order.

Given both the content and the tone of his individual opinions in *Spenkelink,
Jurek,* and *Coleman,* it is not surprising that Rehnquist would spend the rest of
his career looking for opportunities to cut back on federal habeas corpus. The remainder of this chapter examines how Rehnquist's positions on federal habeas –
partly through decisions of the Court, and partly through Congressional action
– ultimately became the prevailing law.

HABEAS JURISDICTION

One issue that has been of interest to Rehnquist for more than thirty years is the
territorial jurisdiction of the habeas court. Does a habeas petition always have to

---

[41] *Id.* at 957–58, 960, 962.
[42] *Id.* at 964.
[43] Gomez v. U.S. District Court for the Northern District of California, 503 U.S. 653 (1992).
[44] Vasquez v. Harris, 503 U.S. 1000 (1992).

be filed in the federal court for the particular district within which the prisoner is confined? And does that court also have to possess territorial jurisdiction over the person who is in charge of the prisoner's confinement?

In two of Rehnquist's earliest habeas opinions, he took the strong position that habeas courts must possess territorial jurisdiction over both the prisoner and the person in charge of the imprisonment. In both cases, however, Rehnquist was on the losing side, and wrote in dissent.

In *Braden v. 30th Judicial Circuit Court of Kentucky*,[45] the Court majority, per Justice Brennan, ruled that a prisoner confined in Alabama, but wanted for trial in Kentucky, could file a habeas petition in the federal court in Kentucky to challenge the Kentucky indictment on constitutional grounds. Based on considerations of litigation convenience and the broad remedial purposes of habeas, the Court held that habeas courts do not always have to possess territorial jurisdiction over the prisoner, but instead must possess territorial jurisdiction only over the person responsible for the allegedly unconstitutional confinement.

In *Strait v. Laird*,[46] the Court concluded that a military reservist living in California could file a habeas petition in the federal court there to challenge an adverse decision about his term of duty that was made at a military record-keeping center in Indiana. The Court noted that almost all of the petitioner's contacts with the military had occurred in California, and that it would "entail needless expense and inconvenience"[47] for him to have to file his habeas petition in Indiana. Strangely, the Court ultimately held that "[t]he concepts of 'custody' and 'custodian' are sufficiently broad to allow us to say that the commanding officer in Indiana, operating through officers in California in processing petitioner's claim, is in California for the limited purpose of habeas jurisdiction."[48]

The net effect of *Braden* and *Strait* was to expand habeas jurisdiction beyond its traditional (and strict) territorial limits. Although the two cases were rarely applied, they symbolized Brennan's commitment to providing individuals with virtually unlimited opportunities to challenge governmental action. But Rehnquist did not agree, and he proved willing to bide his time. In June 2004, Rehnquist finally carried a Court majority to interpret both *Braden* and *Strait* narrowly in the case of *Rumsfeld v. Padilla*.[49] Jose Padilla, a U.S. citizen, was arrested in Chicago on a warrant issued by the U.S. District Court for the Southern District of New York, and was later transferred to military custody at the Navy brig at Charleston, South Carolina, on allegations that he was an "enemy combatant" who plotted to set off a "dirty bomb" as a terrorist attack against the United States. The military detention was authorized by a presidential order, and was implemented at the behest of Secretary of Defense Donald Rumsfeld, who (according

---

[45] Braden v. 30th Judicial Circuit Court of Kentucky, 410 U.S. 484 (1973).
[46] Strait v. Laird, 406 U.S. 341 (1972).
[47] *Id.* at 345.
[48] *Id.* at 345–46.
[49] Rumsfeld v. Padilla, 124 S. Ct. 2711 (2004).

to the lower court) exercised the "legal reality of control" over Padilla and was personally involved in ordering his detention. Padilla filed a habeas petition[50] against Secretary Rumsfeld[51] in the Southern District of New York, which held that it possessed nonterritorial "long-arm" jurisdiction over Rumsfeld based on New York law. The district court therefore denied the government's motion to dismiss the habeas petition on jurisdictional grounds, and the denial was affirmed by the Second Circuit.

The Supreme Court, by 5–4, with the majority opinion written by Rehnquist, held that Padilla's habeas petition should have been dismissed for lack of jurisdiction. According to the Court, for more than a hundred years "the [habeas] default rule is that the proper respondent is the warden of the facility where the prisoner is being held, not . . . some other remote supervisory official."[52] And habeas petitions generally must be filed in the district where the prisoner is being held:

> This rule, derived from the terms of the habeas statute, serves the important purpose of preventing forum shopping by habeas petitioners. Without it, a prisoner could name a high-level supervisory official as respondent and then sue that person wherever he is amenable to long-arm jurisdiction. The result would be rampant forum shopping, district courts with overlapping jurisdiction, and the very inconvenience, expense, and embarrassment Congress sought to avoid when it added the jurisdictional limitation years ago.[53]

As for *Braden* and *Strait*, Rehnquist's *Padilla* opinion characterized them as narrow "exceptions" to the general rule, applicable only to those rare situations when a habeas petition seeks to challenge something other than the petitioner's "present custody." And Rehnquist flatly rejected the suggestion that the broad remedial purposes of habeas could be used as a basis to dance around the territorial jurisdiction requirement, explaining that "it is surely just as necessary in important cases as in unimportant ones that courts take care not to exceed their 'respective jurisdictions' established by Congress."[54]

Thus, Rehnquist may have lost two early battles in *Braden* and *Strait,* but he won the war in *Padilla.* As a result of *Padilla,* in the vast majority of cases, the traditional habeas rule of strict territorial jurisdiction applies – meaning that petitions must name as the defendant the person who is in direct control of the habeas petitioner's custody, rather than some "remote supervisory official." And such petitions must be filed in the federal district court where the habeas petitioner is presently confined, rather than in some more "convenient" location.

---

[50] Because there was no criminal conviction in the *Padilla* case, the petition was filed under the current version of the old common-law writ of habeas corpus, now codified at 28 U.S.C. § 2241. But the jurisdictional issue remains the same, regardless of the particular statutory or common-law version of habeas corpus involved in the case.

[51] Padilla also named President George W. Bush and Melanie Marr, the Commander of the Navy brig, as defendants, but both were dismissed from the case before it reached the Court.

[52] *Padilla,* 124 S. Ct., at 2718.

[53] *Id.* at 2724–25.

[54] *Id.* at 2727.

HABEAS AND THE RIGHT TO APPOINTED COUNSEL

Another issue that has interested Rehnquist for many years is the right to appointed counsel, and other forms of legal assistance, for habeas petitioners. In 1974, in the case of *Ross v. Moffitt*,[55] Rehnquist, writing for the Court, held that indigent persons convicted of crimes, and whose convictions already have been upheld on a first appeal as of right, are not constitutionally entitled to appointed counsel for purposes of seeking further discretionary appellate review in the state courts or certiorari review in the Court. The ruling was based primarily on functional differences between direct appeal, on the one hand, and discretionary forms of posttrial review on the other. But Rehnquist's opinion also reflected his long-standing view that due process does not limit the power of the government to impose conditions when it chooses to give an individual something to which he or she is not constitutionally entitled in the first place. In *Ross v. Moffitt*, Rehnquist explained that since discretionary review is a matter of legislative grace, those who seek such review should not be heard to complain about the terms under which they must do so. In other words, one who avails himself of the government's largesse in permitting discretionary review must take the "bitter with the sweet."[56]

In 1977, Rehnquist sharply dissented from the Court's holding in *Bounds v. Smith*[57] that habeas petitioners have a fundamental constitutional "right of access to the courts," which requires that they at least be provided with access to legal materials such as those found in a law library. Despite this minor defeat, however, Rehnquist was able to hold the line in a subsequent series of cases that involved whether the new "right of access" might support a claim for appointed counsel, or some related form of legal assistance, in state or federal habeas.

For example, in *Pennsylvania v. Finley*,[58] the state provided an appointed lawyer for state postconviction review as a matter of legislative grace, and the defendant then argued that his appointed lawyer had a constitutional duty to press his desired claims, even if the lawyer found them meritless. The Court, per Rehnquist, disagreed. According to the majority, the reasoning in *Ross v. Moffitt* applies "with even more force" to postconviction review, because such review "is even further removed from the criminal trial than is discretionary direct review."[59] And the fact that the state chose to provide an appointed lawyer did not render the lawyer's performance subject to constitutional supervision, because "the Con-

---

[55] Ross v. Moffitt, 417 U.S. 600 (1974). This case is also discussed in Chapter 7 of the present volume (§B.2).

[56] The phrase "bitter with the sweet" was used by Rehnquist in another opinion written during the same term as Ross v. Moffitt. *See* Arnett v. Kennedy, 416 U.S. 134, 154 (1974) (plurality opinion of Rehnquist, J.).

[57] Bounds v. Smith, 430 U.S. 817 (1977).

[58] Pennsylvania v. Finley, 481 U.S. 551 (1987).

[59] *Id.* at 556–57.

stitution does not put the State to the difficult choice between affording no counsel whatsoever or following the strict procedural rules"[60] that apply to constitutionally mandated trial or appellate counsel – in short, once again, the defendant must take the "bitter with the sweet."

Furthermore, in *Murray v. Giarratano*,[61] Rehnquist – in a plurality opinion – rejected a claim that the "right of access" recognized in *Bounds v. Smith* could support a request by death row inmates for appointed counsel to handle their federal habeas cases. Rehnquist wrote that "[t]here is no inconsistency whatever between the holding of *Bounds* and the holding in *Finley*. . . . [W]e now hold that *Finley* applies to those inmates under sentence of death as well as to other inmates, and that holding necessarily imposes limits on *Bounds*."[62]

In the end, the decision in *Ross v. Moffitt* still remains good law, and serves as the basis for those subsequent Court decisions that reject a constitutional right to appointed counsel in state postconviction proceedings and federal habeas corpus cases. Today, some federal and state statutes provide a limited right to appointed counsel in at least some habeas cases (such as those filed by death row inmates); but wherever they do, Rehnquist's "bitter with the sweet" position continues to limit the extent to which defendants later can complain about the manner in which such legal assistance is provided.

HABEAS AND PROCEDURAL DEFAULT

As noted previously, perhaps the most important single habeas opinion of Rehnquist's career – and certainly the one with the greatest impact on habeas practice – was the 1977 majority opinion in *Wainwright v. Sykes*.[63] The issue in *Sykes* was the same one that had been decided by the Court more than a decade earlier, namely, should a federal habeas petitioner be allowed to seek habeas relief on a federal constitutional claim that was previously denied in state court, not on the merits, but instead on the basis of an "adequate and independent" state procedural ground? Or should such a "procedural default" under state law serve as a bar to federal habeas relief?

In *Fay v. Noia*,[64] Justice Brennan wrote the majority opinion rejecting the general application of the procedural default doctrine in federal habeas. According to Brennan, the broad remedial purpose of federal habeas – and especially its key role in ensuring that state courts vindicate the federal constitutional rights of criminal defendants – required that federal habeas relief remain available, even to petitioners who failed to comply with applicable state procedural rules. The only exception, according to Brennan, was for petitioners who "deliberate[ly] bypass[ed]" the state courts; where the petitioner himself (as opposed to his lawyer) made a knowing and voluntary decision to "deliberate[ly] bypass" the state

---

[60] *Id.* at 559.
[62] *Id.* at 12.
[64] *Noia*, 372 U.S. 391 (1963).
[61] Murray v. Giarratano, 492 U.S. 1 (1989).
[63] *Sykes*, 433 U.S. 72.

courts, then federal habeas relief could – but, even in such a case, did not have to[65] – be denied. In *Fay v. Noia* itself, the petitioner's lawyer forfeited the right to litigate the relevant federal issue on direct appeal by failing to file a timely notice of appeal; because no "deliberate bypass" had occurred, however, the Court held that federal habeas relief was not barred.

In *Wainwright v. Sykes,* Sykes's lawyer failed to object at trial to the admission of inculpatory statements Sykes had made to the police. Sykes was convicted of murder, and on direct appeal, his lawyer again failed to raise any challenge to the admissibility of his statements. Sykes then sought to raise such a challenge, based on alleged *Miranda* violations, in a federal habeas corpus petition.

Rehnquist's majority opinion opened with a review of the history of federal habeas law, mostly for the purpose of "illustrat[ing] this Court's historic willingness to overturn or modify its earlier views of the scope of the writ, even where the statutory language authorizing judicial action has remained unchanged."[66] Having thus "explained" why *stare decisis* would not bind the Court, Rehnquist went directly after Brennan's *Fay v. Noia* holding:

> [I]t is a well-established principle of federalism that a state decision resting on an adequate foundation of state substantive law is immune from review in the federal courts. . . . The area of controversy . . . has concerned the reviewability of federal claims which the state court has declined to pass on because not presented in the manner prescribed by its procedural rules. . . .[67]

Rehnquist cited two recent Supreme Court cases in which the petitioners had failed to complain about alleged grand jury discrimination before trial, in violation of applicable court rules, and then tried to litigate the issue in federal habeas.[68] The Court held these claims to be procedurally defaulted, and thus barred from federal habeas review, unless the petitioners could make a sufficient showing of "cause" and "prejudice" for their default.

According to Rehnquist, the "crux" of the *Sykes* case was whether the same procedural default rule – a rule clearly inconsistent with the "deliberate bypass" test of *Fay v. Noia* – also should apply to the waiver of an alleged *Miranda* violation by failure to make a contemporaneous objection at trial. Rehnquist's answer was a resounding "yes":

> The contemporaneous-objection rule . . . deserves greater respect than *Fay* gives it, both for the fact that it is employed by a coordinate jurisdiction within the federal system and for the many interests which it serves in its own right. . . .

---

[65] Under *Noia,* the habeas court retained the discretion to reach the merits of the federal constitutional issue, even in the case of "deliberate bypass," where necessary in order to serve the ends of justice.

[66] *Sykes,* 433 U.S. at 81.

[67] *Id.* at 81–82.

[68] *See* Davis v. United States, 411 U.S. 233 (1973); Francis v. Henderson, 425 U.S. 536 (1976).

We believe the adoption of the . . . rule in this situation will have the salutary effect of making the state trial on the merits the "main event," so to speak, rather than a "tryout on the road" for what will later be the determinative federal habeas hearing.[69]

Without attempting to define the precise contours of the "cause" and "prejudice" exceptions to the procedural default doctrine, Rehnquist concluded that the petitioner – who offered "no explanation whatever" for his failure to object at trial, and who was proven guilty by substantial evidence beyond the challenged inculpatory statement – could not possibly meet the test. Rehnquist also rejected *Fay v. Noia*'s stance that habeas petitioners generally should not be held responsible for the errors of their defense lawyers.

Since *Sykes,* the meaning of "cause" has been held to include "novel" legal claims,[70] claims that could not be made at trial due to the state's concealment of evidence,[71] and claims that were not raised in state court due to the defense lawyer's constitutional ineffectiveness.[72] "Prejudice" has been held to mean that the defendant must have had a "substantial likelihood" of prevailing if the constitutional error had not occurred.[73] If both standards are met, a federal habeas petitioner can pursue habeas relief on a federal claim that was procedurally defaulted in state court. Otherwise, however, even in cases where the default resulted from defense lawyer errors falling short of constitutional ineffectiveness, for the most part the petitioner is simply out of luck, subject only to the narrow "fundamental miscarriage of justice" exception discussed in the next section of this chapter.

Whereas *Fay v. Noia* contained Brennan's most eloquent, heartfelt, and rhapsodic endorsement of federal habeas corpus as a remedy for the deprivation of federal constitutional rights, *Wainwright v. Sykes* represented Rehnquist's vigorous counterattack of states' rights federalism. *Sykes* overruled *Fay v. Noia* in all but its narrowest possible construction, namely, the application of the "deliberate bypass" rule to the specific facts of the particular case there before the Court. The emasculated, case- and fact-specific version of *Fay v. Noia* survived for fourteen more years, until the Court delivered the final blow in *Coleman v. Thompson,*[74] holding that the *Sykes* "cause" and "prejudice" standard applied even to the failure to file a timely notice of appeal in a capital case. Today, thanks to Rehnquist, *Fay v. Noia* is long dead, while *Wainwright v. Sykes* lives on as a key limitation on federal habeas corpus review of state convictions.

[69] *Id.* at 88, 90.
[70] *See* Reed v. Ross, 468 U.S. 1 (1984).
[71] *See* Amadeo v. Zant, 486 U.S. 214 (1988).
[72] *See* Murray v. Carrier, 477 U.S. 478 (1986).
[73] *See* United States v. Frady, 456 U.S. 152 (1982).
[74] Coleman v. Thompson, 501 U.S. 722 (1991).

HABEAS AND THE ROLE OF INNOCENCE

In a famous 1970 law review article, Judge Henry Friendly asked, "Is Innocence Irrelevant?"[75] By this, he meant to pose the basic question whether the petitioner's factual guilt or innocence should have any bearing on the availability of federal habeas corpus relief. For most of its long history, habeas has known no such "innocence" limitation. In two important respects, however, the Court has established meaningful, though secondary, relationships between factual innocence and the scope of federal habeas corpus. Rehnquist opinions lie at the heart of both these relationships.

The first important role that factual innocence plays in federal habeas corpus involves the "fundamental miscarriage of justice" exception to the aforementioned *Sykes* procedural default doctrine. In a series of cases in the 1980s,[76] the Court acknowledged that, in relatively rare cases of substantive injustice, federal habeas courts should retain the authority to overlook a procedural default (or other procedural barrier to federal habeas relief) and reach the merits of the petitioner's federal claim. This exception helps to ensure that habeas continues to fulfill its historic mission of protecting against fundamentally unjust incarcerations.

The "fundamental miscarriage of justice" exception consistently has been defined in terms of "actual innocence." Adopting language from Judge Friendly's article, the Court required that, in order to avoid a procedural barrier to federal habeas relief, the petitioner must "show a fair probability that, in light of all the evidence, including that alleged to have been illegally admitted [and evidence that could have, but was not, produced and admitted], . . . the trier of the facts would have entertained a reasonable doubt of his guilt."[77] The Court has similarly stated that the exception applies "where a constitutional violation has probably resulted in the conviction of one who is actually innocent."[78] Given the narrowness of the exception, it is perhaps not terribly surprising that Rehnquist joined every one of the opinions that originally created and defined it.

Application of the "actual innocence" standard has proven especially complicated and controversial in the special context of death sentencing. What, exactly, does it mean to say that a petitioner is "actually innocent" of the death penalty? Does it mean that he might not have received that punishment, absent the alleged constitutional error? Or that he is not legally eligible for the death

---

[75] Henry J. Friendly, *Is Innocence Irrelevant? Collateral Attack on Criminal Judgments*, 38 U. Chi. L. Rev. 142 (1970).

[76] *See Carrier*, 477 U.S. 478 (recognizing "fundamental miscarriage of justice" exception to *Sykes* procedural default doctrine); Smith v. Murray, 477 U.S. 527 (1986) (same); Kuhlmann v. Wilson, 477 U.S. 436 (1986) (recognizing exception to "successive petition" procedural barrier to habeas relief); McCleskey v. Zant, 499 U.S. 467 (1991) (recognizing exception to "abuse of the writ" procedural barrier to habeas relief).

[77] *Kuhlmann*, 477 U.S. at 455 n. 17, quoting from Friendly, *supra* note 73, at 160.

[78] *Carrier*, 477 U.S. at 496.

penalty? Or, perhaps, that he must show that he is "actually innocent" of the crime?

In *Sawyer v. Whitley*,[79] Rehnquist wrote the majority opinion addressing this thorny issue, and resolved it by choosing the middle path out of the three described above:

> The phrase "innocent of death" is not a natural usage of those words, but we must strive to construct an analog to the simpler situation represented by the case of a noncapital defendant. . . . [T]o make it workable it must be subject to determination by relatively objective standards. . . .
>
> We agree with [several lower federal courts] that the "actual innocence" requirement must focus on those elements that render a defendant eligible for the death penalty. . . . We must determine if petitioner has shown by clear and convincing evidence that but for constitutional error, no reasonable juror would find him eligible for the death penalty. . . .[80]

Notable in *Sawyer* was the fact that Rehnquist chose "clear and convincing evidence" to describe the burden of proof that a habeas petitioner must meet in seeking to qualify for the "fundamental miscarriage of justice" exception. This language did not appear in any of the prior cases applying the exception, and may have signified an effort by Rehnquist to further narrow it.

If so, the effort ultimately succeeded only in part. A couple of years later, a different Court – with Rehnquist in dissent – distinguished capital cases involving a challenge solely to the imposition of the death sentence (as in *Sawyer*) from capital cases involving a claim of factual innocence. In *Schlup v. Delo*,[81] Justice Stevens, writing for the Court, held that the standard of *Murray v. Carrier* – which was whether the alleged constitutional error "probably" resulted in the conviction of an innocent person – should govern such a claim, rather than *Sawyer's* "clear and convincing evidence" standard. *Schlup v. Delo* essentially created two different burdens of proof for the application of the "fundamental miscarriage of justice" exception to capital cases: one standard for claims going to factual innocence, and another, tougher one for claims focusing on the legality of the death sentence.

The second important role for innocence in federal habeas corpus is as a potential stand-alone claim for habeas relief, unattached to a claim of constitutional criminal procedure error at trial. In *Herrera v. Collins*,[82] the petitioner, a Texas death row inmate, made just such a "naked" innocence claim; he admitted that his capital trial was procedurally sound, but claimed, based on allegedly newly discovered evidence, that the jury simply made a mistake and convicted the wrong man. Under Texas law, the new evidence came too late, and could not be

---

[79] Sawyer v. Whitley, 505 U.S. 333 (1992).
[80] *Id.* at 341, 347–48.
[81] Schlup v. Delo, 513 U.S. 298 (1995).
[82] Herrera v. Collins, 506 U.S. 390 (1993).

the basis for an appeal or motion for new trial. Herrera therefore argued that he should be entitled to federal habeas corpus relief, on the ground that it would be unconstitutional to execute an innocent man.

The Court, in a controversial decision, rejected Herrera's request for habeas relief. The majority opinion, written by Rehnquist, assumed "for the sake of argument in deciding this case" – but did not decide – that a "truly persuasive demonstration of 'actual innocence' made after trial would render the execution of a defendant unconstitutional."[83] Noting the "very disruptive effect" that such claims would have on state criminal justice, and the "enormous burden" that they would place on the states to retry such cases based on "often stale evidence," the Court concluded that "the threshold showing for such an assumed right would necessarily be extraordinarily high."[84] Under such a standard, Herrera's new evidence fell far short of what would be required. And in the course of rejecting Herrera's claim, Rehnquist emphasized that executive clemency, and not federal habeas corpus, is the traditional and preferred remedy for *Herrera*-type claims of "naked innocence" made after a conviction already has become final.

The Court has not returned to the subject of "naked innocence" claims since *Herrera*. In that case, however, six Justices – White, O'Connor, and Kennedy in concurrence,[85] and Blackmun, Stevens, and Souter in dissent – seemed to agree that the execution of an innocent man would, indeed, violate the Constitution. Thus, in a proper case, it seems clear that Rehnquist's cautious approach to the constitutional question posed in *Herrera* probably would be supplanted by a constitutional holding. Nevertheless, it is a mark of Rehnquist's influence on federal habeas that *Herrera* remains good law, and that the question whether executing an innocent man would be unconstitutional continues to be reserved for another day.

HABEAS AND HARMLESS ERROR

Rehnquist was the author of the majority opinion in *Brecht v. Abrahamson*,[86] the leading decision on the subject of harmless error in federal habeas corpus. Harmless error is a doctrine that allows courts to preserve criminal convictions even in the face of constitutional error, so long as the court is convinced, under the applicable standard, that the error did not make a difference in the outcome of the case. If the harmless error standard favors the criminal defendant, then most

---

[83] *Id.* at 417.

[84] Ibid.

[85] O'Connor's concurring opinion, 506 U.S. at 419, bears special mention. In it, she essentially argued that, although the execution of an innocent man would be a terrible thing, it may never happen, because the American criminal justice system (including the possibilities of clemency and pardon) contains so many procedural safeguards. In view of recent developments, especially with respect to DNA and the exoneration of numerous death row inmates in Illinois, O'Connor's *Herrera* concurrence now seems almost pitifully naive.

[86] Brecht v. Abrahamson, 507 U.S. 619 (1993).

constitutional errors will lead to reversals of the underlying convictions; if, on the other hand, the standard is relatively pro-prosecution, then at least some convictions, even if constitutionally erroneous, need not be reversed.

In *Brecht*, Rehnquist adopted a standard for harmless error in federal habeas that was decidedly pro-prosecution,[87] especially as compared with the corresponding standard on direct appeal. The latter standard, first established in *Chapman v. California*,[88] is whether the error was harmless "beyond a reasonable doubt"; the prosecution must carry the burden of proving, to the satisfaction of the appellate court, that the *Chapman* standard is met. The *Brecht* standard, by contrast, is whether the error "had substantial and injurious effect or influence in determining the jury's verdict";[89] moreover, it is the federal habeas petitioner, not the prosecutor, who must prove such an effect in order to obtain habeas relief. The net result is that, if the state courts do not act to remedy a federal constitutional violation on direct appeal (and assuming, as is highly likely, that the Supreme Court does not grant certiorari), then the pro-prosecution habeas harmless error standard of *Brecht* will tend to ensure that the conviction will be sustained, notwithstanding the presence of constitutional error. *Brecht* thus manages to achieve, through indirection, an outcome perfectly consistent with Rehnquist's narrow view of the proper scope of the federal habeas corpus remedy.

HABEAS RETROACTIVITY

One of the primary reasons for the significant impact of federal habeas corpus on state death penalty administration during the late 1970s and 1980s was the fact that most new Supreme Court "super due process" decisions were applied retroactively to past capital cases. Death row inmates therefore were able to use such new decisions to obtain federal habeas relief, even in cases where the original trial occurred many years earlier.

In a landmark 1989 case, *Teague v. Lane*,[90] the Court took a major step to remedy this problem. The lead opinion in *Teague* was written by Justice O'Connor, but she was not able to garner a majority for her position. It remained for Rehn-

---

[87] The Court's holding in *Brecht* was specifically limited to so-called *trial errors*, or errors that occur "during the presentation of the case to the jury," 507 U.S. at 629. But this category of error includes "most constitutional errors," *see* Arizona v. Fulminante, 499 U.S. 279, 307–08 (1991), and thus it seems appropriate to refer to *Brecht* as establishing a general "harmless error" standard for federal habeas corpus. One example of a *nontrial error* would be denial of the defendant's right to appointed counsel under *Gideon;* in such a case, harmless error analysis does not even apply, and reversal is automatic. Such nontrial errors, however, are understandably rare.

[88] Chapman v. California, 386 U.S. 18 (1967).

[89] *Brecht,* 507 U.S. at 637.

[90] Teague v. Lane, 489 U.S. 288 (1989) (plurality opinion).

quist, in the follow-up case of *Butler v. McKellar*,[91] to do so – and in the process, he even managed to extend the rule that was first adopted in *Teague*.[92]

The intellectual origins of both *Teague* and *Butler* dated back to Justice John Harlan's view, in the 1960s, that new Court decisions generally should apply retroactively to all cases still pending on direct appellate review,[93] but generally should not apply retroactively to cases in federal habeas. Harlan's retroactivity approach was based on the notion that the main goal of federal habeas is not to do justice in individual cases, but instead to deter state court misapplications of the federal constitution. The overriding purpose of federal habeas is to ensure that state courts "toe the constitutional mark"; in order to fulfill this purpose, "the habeas court need only apply the constitutional standards that prevailed at the time the original [state] proceedings took place."[94] According to Harlan's view, there is no good reason to apply "new law" retroactively to federal habeas cases, because in such cases, the state courts (which presumably didn't know, at the time they acted, that the "new law" was on its way) did nothing wrong that needs to be deterred.

According to Harlan's view, as interpreted by O'Connor in *Teague*, only two exceptions could justify the retroactive application of new law to federal habeas cases: (1) new law that places "certain kinds of primary, private individual conduct beyond the power of the criminal law-making authority to proscribe,"[95] and (2) new law that declares a "watershed rule[] of criminal procedure" without which "the likelihood of an accurate conviction is seriously diminished."[96] O'Connor opined that it was "unlikely" that many such "watershed rules" still remained to be declared by the Court.[97]

Teague can be a very confusing decision. One key is to remember that, given the Court's basic holding of nonretroactive application of "new law" to federal habeas cases, it is usually very bad for habeas petitioners if a new decision handed down by the Court is characterized as "new law." Habeas petitioners want new Court decisions to be characterized as "old law," because then they have at least a chance to rely upon them in their habeas petitions.[98]

---

[91] Butler v. McKellar, 494 U.S. 407 (1990).

[92] For general discussions of *Teague, Butler,* and the habeas retroactivity issue, see Joseph L. Hoffmann, *The Supreme Court's New Vision of Federal Habeas Corpus for State Prisoners,* 1989 Sup. Ct. Rev. 165; Hoffmann & Stuntz, *supra* note 23.

[93] This half of Harlan's view was adopted by the Court in Griffith v. Kentucky, 479 U.S. 314 (1987).

[94] Desist v. United States, 394 U.S. 244, 256–57 (1969) (Harlan, J., dissenting).

[95] Mackey v. United States, 401 U.S. 667, 692 (1971) (Harlan, J., concurring in the judgments in part and dissenting in part).

[96] *Teague,* 489 U.S. at 311 (plurality opinion).

[97] *Id.* at 312–13 (plurality opinion).

[98] Of course, even reliance on "old law" will be unavailing if the habeas petitioner runs afoul of some other procedural barrier to habeas relief. A good example would be the procedural default doctrine of *Sykes.* If the habeas petition relies on "old law," then the petitioner's defense lawyer should have known enough to raise and litigate the issue properly at trial. Failure to do so, in the case of "old law," will give rise to procedural default; then it is up to the petitioner to show either "cause" and "prejudice," or a "fundamental miscarriage of justice," in order to get around the *Sykes* barrier. Still, this is usually better than trying to rely on "new law," which – under *Teague* – is simply unavailable in federal habeas.

Enter *Butler v. McKellar*. In *Butler*, Rehnquist pulled together a majority for the general nonretroactivity rule announced by O'Connor in *Teague*. Moreover, Rehnquist managed to subtly, but effectively, redefine the meaning of "new law" in a way that made *Teague*'s impact on federal habeas cases even more significant than it already was. According to Rehnquist, "new law" is any decision that "breaks new ground or imposes a new obligation on the States or the Federal Government." Quoting directly from *Teague*, he explained that this means that the result "was not dictated by precedent existing at the time the defendant's conviction became final."[99] Rehnquist then proceeded to make matters even worse for habeas petitioners:

> The "new rule" principle therefore validates reasonable, good-faith interpretations of existing precedents made by state courts even though they are shown to be contrary to later decisions.[100]

After Rehnquist's turn of a phrase in *Butler*, almost every new decision made by the Court will be characterized as "new law," for habeas retroactivity purposes, because the Court rarely bothers to take a case for review unless it can be said that the underlying federal constitutional issue is one on which lower courts, acting in "reasonable good faith," could disagree. In short, after *Butler*, there just isn't much room left for anything the Court does to be characterized as "old law." As a result, habeas petitioners rarely will be able to take advantage of Supreme Court decisions rendered after their direct appeal is concluded.

HABEAS STANDARDS OF REVIEW AND THE AEDPA OF 1996

One of the most important issues in habeas, identified as such by Rehnquist in *Sykes*, is the appropriate standard of review for a federal habeas court reviewing a state criminal conviction. Should the federal court defer to prior state court adjudication of factual, legal, or mixed fact-and-law issues? Or should the federal court decide such issues on its own, de novo, in order to ensure that federal constitutional rights are vindicated?

As for factual issues, the appropriate standard of review has been clear since before Rehnquist even joined the Court. In *Townsend v. Sain*,[101] one of the 1963 "trilogy" cases, Justice Brennan held that federal habeas courts can relitigate most factual issues that previously had been decided in the state courts. Congress did not agree, however, and in 1966 – just three years later – the federal habeas statute was amended to make factual findings by state courts binding on federal habeas courts, unless the case fits one of eight narrow statutory exceptions. After the 1966 amendments, it became clear that federal habeas courts, in most instances, were obliged to defer to state court fact-finding.

---

[99] *Butler*, 494 U.S. at 412 (quoting *Teague*, 489 U.S. at 301).
[100] *Id.* at 414. *Leon*, cited in *Butler*, was the case establishing a limited "good faith" exception to the Fourth Amendment's exclusionary rule.
[101] Townsend v. Sain, 372 U.S. 293 (1963).

As for legal issues, the traditional view – dating back to 1953 and *Brown v. Allen*[102] – was that federal habeas courts were not required to defer to prior state court adjudication. This view prevailed until the *Teague* decision in 1989. Although *Teague* was styled as a habeas retroactivity case, it also can be seen as a standard-of-review case. Under *Teague*, and especially in light of Rehnquist's gloss on the "new law" issue in *Butler*, federal habeas courts are not allowed to reverse state court adjudications of federal law issues unless the state court's legal ruling was "unreasonable." This roughly approximates a rule of deference to prior state court adjudication of legal issues.

As for mixed issues of fact and law, such as the voluntariness of a confession or guilty plea, the Court considered the appropriate standard of review in the 1992 case of *Wright v. West*.[103] In that case, Virginia argued that – since deference was statutorily mandated for factual issues, and judicially mandated under *Teague* for legal issues – mixed issues of fact and law must be subject to a similar rule of deference. Rehnquist agreed with Virginia, but a majority of the Court did not, although no majority opinion was generated.

In 1996, just four years after *Wright v. West*, Congress passed the first wholesale revision of the federal habeas corpus statute since its original enactment in 1867. The Antiterrorism and Effective Death Penalty Act of 1996[104] (AEDPA) made numerous changes to federal habeas, the most important of which was the adoption of new set of standards of review for federal habeas.

Under the AEDPA's new standards, federal habeas courts must defer to prior state court factual findings even more strongly than they did under the 1966 statutory amendments: "[A] determination of a factual issue made by a State court shall be presumed to be correct. The applicant shall have the burden of rebutting the presumption of correctness by clear and convincing evidence."[105]

As for both legal and mixed fact-and-law issues, the AEDPA sets the following new standards:

> (d) An application for a writ of habeas corpus . . . shall not be granted with respect to any claim that was adjudicated on the merits in State court proceedings unless the adjudication of the claim –
>   (1) resulted in a decision that was contrary to, or involved an unreasonable application of, clearly established Federal law, as determined by the Supreme Court of the United States. . . .[106]

For legal issues, the AEDPA provides that habeas courts cannot reverse the prior ruling of a state court unless that ruling was contrary to federal law that,

---

[102] *Brown*, 344 U.S. 443.
[103] Wright v. West, 505 U.S. 278 (1992).
[104] Pub. L. 104-132, 110 Stat. 1214 (1996). The very title of the act seems eerily reminiscent of Rehnquist's view, as expressed in *Coleman v. Balkcom*, that federal habeas needed to be transformed in order to make the death penalty more "effective."
[105] *See* 28 U.S.C. §2254(e).
[106] *See* 28 U.S.C. §2254(d).

"as determined by the Supreme Court," not by lower federal courts, was "clearly established." This may not be exactly the same thing as deference to prior state court adjudication, but it comes pretty close.

For mixed law-and-fact issues, the AEDPA requires deference to "reasonable" state court applications of federal law – which the Court has construed as requiring more than the simple conclusion that the state court was "wrong."[107] The AEDPA thus overturns the Court's decision in *Wright v. West*, adopting essentially the same deferential standard of review that Rehnquist voted for in that case.[108]

In addition to the new standards of review, the AEDPA also makes other substantial changes. For example, the AEDPA creates, for the first time, a strict time limit for the filing of a federal habeas petition – generally, one year from the time the underlying state conviction became final.[109] The AEDPA also imposes strict limits on the filing of new federal habeas petitions raising issues that were, or could have been, included in a prior petition, with extremely narrow exceptions for (1) new claims that rely on "new law" made retroactive by the Court, and (2) new claims based on facts that could not reasonably have been discovered before, and that would essentially prove the petitioner's innocence.[110] Finally, although the AEDPA does not explicitly mention procedural default, the Court has held that it preserves the preexisting *Sykes* procedural default doctrine.[111]

The AEDPA completed the rewrite of federal habeas corpus begun by Rehnquist in the 1970s. What Rehnquist could not achieve in the Court – primarily, a deferential habeas standard of review for mixed fact-and-law issues – he ultimately received from Congress. With the new, strict time limits on the filing of federal habeas petitions, and the much more severe restrictions on second and successive petitions, the AEDPA gave Rehnquist almost everything he could possibly have asked for.

THE ONE UNFINISHED BATTLE:
COGNIZABLE CONSTITUTIONAL ISSUES IN HABEAS

In his thirty-plus-year tenure, there is only one major federal habeas issue on which Rehnquist has not largely prevailed. In *Stone v. Powell*,[112] decided in 1976, Rehnquist joined Justice Powell's majority opinion holding that Fourth Amendment issues generally are not cognizable in federal habeas corpus, because the deterrent purpose of the Fourth Amendment exclusionary rule would not be served by applying that rule to federal habeas cases. At the time, many observers believed

[107] *See* Terry Williams v. Taylor, 529 U.S. 362 (2000) (opinion of O'Connor, J., for the Court).
[108] *Id.*
[109] *See* 28 U.S.C. §2244(d).
[110] *See* 28 U.S.C. §2244(b).
[111] *See* Bousley v. United States, 523 U.S. 614 (1998), another Rehnquist majority opinion, holding that the *Sykes* doctrine continues to apply after the AEDPA.
[112] Stone v. Powell, 428 U.S. 465 (1976).

that *Stone v. Powell* would be only the tip of the iceberg, and that the Court eventually would add other federal constitutional claims to the list of constitutional issues not cognizable in federal habeas. In *Sykes*, Rehnquist clearly alluded to the cognizability issue, noting that the issue of cognizability of alleged *Miranda* violations in federal habeas was not raised by the parties and thus would have to wait for another day.

The expected *Stone v. Powell* revolution, however, never materialized. The closest the Court came to extending *Stone v. Powell* was in *Withrow v. Williams*,[113] where a narrow majority of the Court – with Rehnquist in dissent – held that alleged *Miranda* violations are, indeed, cognizable in federal habeas, even in the absence of an underlying voluntariness problem with the petitioner's confession. Over the years, the Court also rejected extending *Stone v. Powell* to insufficiency-of-the-evidence claims,[114] claims of ineffective assistance of counsel based on the failure to suppress illegally seized evidence,[115] and to claims of racial discrimination in the selection of a grand jury foreman.[116]

Perhaps the most that can be said about the habeas cognizability issue is that, having gotten virtually everything he could have wanted in almost every other respect – and more – Rehnquist may not feel that he has lost very much by virtue of his failure to extend the rule of *Stone v. Powell*. And it is always possible that, sooner or later, Rehnquist's view may prevail even on this issue.

CONCLUSION

In the late-twentieth-century war of federalism, a considerable portion of which was waged on the battlefield of federal habeas corpus, there were two great opposing warriors. Justice William J. Brennan fought for broad federal habeas corpus review of state criminal cases, unfettered by time limits or other procedural barriers to relief, and open to de novo relitigation of every kind of issue that might affect the adjudication of federal constitutional rights. Chief Justice William H. Rehnquist, on the other hand, fought for narrow federal habeas, in order to free the states to carry out their desired penal policies (especially the death penalty), and in order to show the state courts the kind of respect properly due to them, as an equal partner in federalism.

Although it may seem unkind to say so, Rehnquist ultimately vanquished Brennan on almost every front. From territorial jurisdiction, to the right to appointed counsel, to procedural default, to innocence, to harmless error, to habeas retroactivity, to the appropriate habeas standard of review, Rehnquist eventually routed Brennan at every turn. As a result, very little remains today of the grand edifice of federal habeas law that was constructed by Brennan during the 1960s

---

[113] Withrow v. Williams, 507 U.S. 680 (1993).
[114] *See* Jackson v. Virginia, 443 U.S. 307 (1979).
[115] *See* Kimmelman v. Morrison, 477 U.S. 365 (1986).
[116] *See* Rose v. Mitchell, 443 U.S. 545 (1979).

and early 1970s. Only on the lone issue of cognizability have Brennan and his judicial legatees managed to hold the line, limiting the damage to the singular *Stone v. Powell* exclusion of Fourth Amendment exclusionary rule cases from federal habeas.

Today, especially in light of the AEDPA's recent revisions of the federal habeas corpus statute, federal habeas no longer poses a serious threat to the administration of state criminal justice, nor to the death penalty in the states. This change reflects the fact that the original motivation for the great expansion of habeas jurisdiction in the 1960s – forcing the states to conform to new federal constitutional rules of criminal procedure – is no longer a pressing problem.

This does not mean, however, that Rehnquist's hoped-for efficiency in the administration of the death penalty has come to pass. There are actually fewer executions per year today than there were in the 1990s. But this is no longer the fault of federal habeas. Today, the primary barriers to implementation of the death penalty are political, not legal. Fears about executing the innocent, and concerns about the high costs of capital litigation, have dramatically shifted the political landscape to the point where few politicians see much gain in advocating publicly for executions. State governors and attorneys general, from Connecticut to California and almost every place in between, have read the tea leaves and decided not to push most capital cases vigorously toward their eventual endgame. Rehnquist might disagree with these state officials, as a matter of policy, but he surely would agree that the important decisions should be left almost entirely up to them, and not handed over to federal habeas courts. In this regard, Rehnquist's legacy – the transformation of federal habeas based on his vision – is secure.

SECTION THREE

THE STRUCTURE OF GOVERNMENT

CHAPTER NINE

WILLIAM REHNQUIST'S FEDERALISM

Mark Tushnet

"We start with first principles."[1] This, the first sentence in Chief Justice Rehnquist's analysis for the Court of the constitutional question presented in *United States v. Lopez,* is a simple and direct assertion, yet one that seems to open up large possibilities for a reconstruction of the constitutional law of federalism. First principles, though, are not enough to support such a reconstruction. Second- and even third-order principles are necessary for the courts to have standards by which to evaluate whether congressional legislation is consistent with some coherent vision of federalism. (Second-order principles help courts determine whether a particular statute violates the first principle by showing how the values promoted by the first principles generate specific outcomes; third-order principles define the boundaries of the role the courts play in enforcing federalism.) Rehnquist and his colleagues in the majority in *Lopez* and related cases knew that federalism was important – that it somehow mattered that, as the second sentence in the *Lopez* analysis put it, "[t]he Constitution creates a Federal Government of enumerated powers." Exactly how it mattered, though, remained unclear.

Rehnquist contributed to the unclarity in two ways. His opinions frequently deploy an interesting rhetorical move: They assert that it is unnecessary to specify second-order principles because *any* such principle would support the conclusion that the statute at issue is unconstitutional. In addition, the *Lopez* opinion catalogs the constitutionally permissible bases for national action in a way that looks like a specification of second-order principles, but is actually only a simulacrum of them: The catalog does not describe the ways in which outcomes are connected to underlying principles.

As Justice Anthony Kennedy once put it, in a metaphor that shared some of the difficulties of Rehnquist's formulations, the Constitution's Framers created a federalism that "split the atom of sovereignty."[2] Federalism organizes a nation's people in two ways, once in a national constituency and once in a number

---

[1] United States v. Lopez, 514 U.S. 549 (1995).
[2] U.S. Term Limits v. Thornton, 514 U.S. 779 (1995) (Kennedy, J., concurring).

of state-level constituencies. Ideally, a federal system advances a complex set of values. It lodges in the national government sufficient power to address the challenges the nation faces as judged by the people organized nationwide. Simultaneously, it ensures that the people organized in their different state-level constituencies retain enough power to achieve the goals that *they* seek, without regard to what their cocitizens organized in other states want; enough power to be truly self-governing with respect to matters decided on the state level; and enough power to generate innovative policies that people in other states and perhaps eventually the people organized as a nation might choose to emulate. The Constitution enacts these values of federalism in its first principles.

The constitutional law of federalism has several branches. One, at issue in *Lopez,* involves cases asking whether the national government has the power to enact legislation that seems to serve national goals but also seems to impair some of the reasons we have for having state and local governments. During Rehnquist's tenure most of those cases raised questions about the reach of Congress's power to regulate "Commerce . . . among the several States" (known less formally as the Commerce Clause). A second involves cases where state legislation seems to have some adverse impact on the achievement of national goals. Nearly all of those cases implicate the Commerce Clause as well, with the courts asking whether a state law interferes with interstate commerce in a manner prohibited by the Constitution itself and without regard to whether Congress has dealt with the problem. Constitutional scholars describe these cases as involving the "dormant" Commerce Clause. A third branch of federalism doctrine deals with the interpretation of national statutes that might preclude state regulation of some subject. These cases involve what is called the preemption of state law by national statutes. Although preemption cases sometimes articulate and apply presumptions about federalism itself, they typically turn more importantly on the details of specific statutes, making it difficult to extract larger themes from the decisions. This chapter focuses on the first two branches of federalism doctrine, to which Rehnquist made important contributions.

Transforming the values and first principles of federalism into legal doctrine by means of second- and third-order principles has proven extraordinarily difficult. The central problem is that such principles are inevitably inaccurate proxies for federalism's values: For example, a doctrine that does a good job of capturing the value of allowing the people organized in their state constituencies to pursue the particular policies they prefer might undermine the ability of the nation's people to achieve the policy outcomes *they* believe necessary for the nation as a whole. The history of federalism doctrine in the Supreme Court has been one of recurrent efforts to specify second- and third-order principles that do a good enough job of advancing federalism's values, followed by decisions reflecting the Justices' judgment that the principles that once seemed to do a good enough job, actually (in their view) did not. Rehnquist's rhetorical strategy of refraining from specifying second- and third-order principles eliminates the prospect of direct repudiation by some later Court, but it leaves him open to the charge of substituting an intuition or feeling for a *legal* account of federalism in the United States, which in turn makes later repudiation possible.

Rehnquist's reference to first principles but not second-order ones was a variant of that rhetorical strategy. Its more common form was to observe that there was no need to specify second-order principles, because whatever such principles there were would certainly be satisfied in the case at hand. In a 1985 dissent, for example, Rehnquist wrote: "I do not think it incumbent on those of us in dissent to spell out further the fine points of a principle that will, I am confident, in time again command the support of a majority of this Court."[3] This lack of concern for second-order principles characterized his jurisprudence of federalism. The effect was to leave the precise contours of Rehnquist's federalism quite ill-defined. William Rehnquist's federalism was more an impulse or intuition than a constitutional structure or even a vision of such a structure.

Rehnquist seemed to envision a new constitutional law around federalism from the start of his tenure on the Court. In 1975 he wrote a lone dissent from the majority's decision rejecting the state of Ohio's challenge to the imposition of a wage freeze on its employees.[4] The majority relied on an earlier decision finding it constitutionally permissible for Congress to require that states comply with the federal Fair Labor Standards Act.[5] The theory of that decision, as elaborated by later ones, was that Congress had the power to require state governments to comply with national laws applicable to a large class of corporations and employers: Because state governments were not singled out for adverse treatment, the Court held, they had no constitutional immunity from regulation. Rehnquist's dissent culminated with the proposition that Congress could not regulate "the traditional governmental activities of a State."

That proposition received brief vindication a year later when the Court overruled the cases on which the Court had relied in the wage freeze case and held that Congress could not require state governments to comply with the requirements of the federal Fair Labor Standards Act – minimum wage and maximum hour regulations – for state employees engaged in traditional governmental functions.[6] That victory was short-lived, and for a reason Rehnquist discerned in his 1975 dissent. As he put it then, the distinction between traditional governmental activities and novel ones "would undoubtedly present gray areas to be marked out on a case-by-case basis." Such decisions would provide the second-order principles necessary for coherent doctrine. But, he contended, he had no need to identify any second-order principle in the wage freeze case because Congress had included essentially all state employees within the freeze.

---

[3] Garcia v. San Antonio Metropolitan Transit Auth., 469 U.S. 528 (1985) (Rehnquist, J., dissenting).

[4] Fry v. United States, 421 U.S. 542 (1975).

[5] Maryland v. Wirtz, 392 U.S. 183 (1968).

[6] National League of Cities v. Usery, 426 U.S. 833 (1976).

After 1976 the Court grappled with the "gray areas" associated with the "traditional governmental functions" test. Just under a decade later a majority concluded that the test was unworkable in practice, and found no judicially enforceable principle barring Congress from imposing wage and hour regulations on state governments as it did on private employers.[7] Dissenting from that decision, Rehnquist observed that other dissenters offered principles that were not precisely identical to each other, nor the same as the test articulated in the 1976 decision. But, he wrote, no matter which approach was taken, the older decision should be affirmed. Again, he felt no need to identify second-order principles.

The Court twice enforced a somewhat different principle from the one toward which Rehnquist gestured. It held that the national government could not "commandeer" the legislative or executive resources of state governments to implement national policies. It could not direct states to adopt laws dealing with the disposal of the low-level nuclear waste that comes from hospitals (and watches).[8] Nor could it require state law enforcement officials to check the backgrounds of gun purchasers in the period before a national system of such checks was developed.[9]

The anticommandeering principle focuses directly on preserving the institutions of state and local government. In contrast, Rehnquist's concern in the wage freeze case was that limiting the wages a state government paid to its employees might impair its ability to implement whatever substantive policies the state's people wanted to pursue. In that sense the anticommandeering principle is more directly responsive to concerns that expansive exercises of the national government's power transform state and local governments into mere units for administering national law. Yet, along a different dimension, the anticommandeering principle was significantly narrower than Rehnquist's initial efforts to protect state autonomy. It did target national legislation that directly interfered with the decision-making process that is the heart of the operation of state governments. Yet, as the Court observed in finding commandeering unconstitutional, that technique was a recent development, rarely used. National legislation imposing the same regulatory requirements on state governments as are placed on corporations and other nongovernmental actors – of which the wage freeze was an example – is far more prevalent than commandeering. The actual displacement of the choices made by a state's voters is quite substantial when the national government's power to regulate state governments forces those governments to comply with mandates that the state's voters have not themselves placed on their governments.

In 1975 Rehnquist quoted a century-old decision describing the states as "indestructible." Federal statutes that commandeer the states are like an acid that erodes the structures that make them states. The infrequency of commandeer-

---

[7] *Garcia, supra* note 3.
[8] New York v. United States, 488 U.S. 1041 (1992).
[9] Printz v. United States, 521 U.S. 98 (1997).

ing, though, meant that the erosion was small. Subjecting state governments to substantive regulation, like the wage and hour laws, eats away at state autonomy more subtly, like the effects of air pollution on old buildings. Put most grossly, a state that must spend its money complying with federal mandates can pursue fewer distinctive state initiatives – the meat and potatoes that make having autonomous state governments valuable. Rehnquist agreed with decisions limiting the *remedies* available when state governments failed to comply with national mandates, which does slow the rate of erosion. But, as long as the national government's requirements are enforceable at all, states are not "indestructible" in the sense Rehnquist hoped them to be.

The anticommandeering cases aimed at preserving the *structures* of state decision making, but dealt with only a handful of national laws affecting state governments. Rehnquist was unable to persuade his colleagues that his position in the wage freeze case was right. As a result, Congress retains essentially unlimited power to force state governments to comply with national mandates, at least those imposed equally on governments and others alike. Congress, that is, can prescribe the *substance* of what state governments do as they carry out their ordinary operations.

There was a final strategy for protecting federalism as Rehnquist understood it. That strategy was to limit to *scope* of national power, identifying some areas into which the national government could not enter and thereby leaving the power to regulate those areas to the states. The Court adopted that strategy in two important decisions, with the majority's opinions expressed by Rehnquist.

Alfonso Lopez was the lucky beneficiary of the Court's first decision in decades holding that Congress had exceeded its power under the Commerce Clause. In 1990, prodded by Wisconsin Senator Herbert Kohl, Congress enacted the Gun-Free School Zones Act, which made it a federal crime for a person to possess a gun near a school. Lopez, who appears to have been basically a good kid who got caught up in gang violence, took forty dollars from a friend to deliver a handgun at school to another student who planned to use it in a gang war. The local prosecutor charged Lopez under a state law carrying a potential prison sentence of two to ten years. A day later the federal prosecutor in San Antonio filed charges against Lopez under the Gun-Free School Zones Act, and the state prosecutor dropped the state charges. Eventually Lopez was convicted in federal court, and received a six-month sentence. (After the Supreme Court held the federal statute unconstitutional, Lopez enlisted in the Marines and apparently stayed out of trouble.)

The need for a *federal* law against guns near schools was hardly obvious. As Justice Kennedy pointed out when the case reached the Supreme Court, forty states already had laws against gun possession near schools, and state and local lawmakers were experimenting with other ways of controlling gun violence at schools. The Constitution, though, does not require that Congress have really good reasons for enacting statutes. All it requires is that the statute fall within one of the powers of Congress listed or, as the Court put it, enumerated in the Constitution. Starting in 1824 the Supreme Court tried to work out the scope of the Commerce Clause. By the 1940s, the Court seemed to have settled on doctrines that swept nearly everything imaginable into the clause's reach. The reasons for this development were both negative and positive. From the beginning the Justices knew that there had to be *some* limits on the clause; as Chief Justice John Marshall put it, an "enumeration presupposes something not enumerated." Working out those limits proved to be surprisingly difficult. The pattern was embarrassingly clear: The Justices would define a limit on Congress's power to regulate interstate commerce in one case, only to discover in a case arising only a few years later that the test seemed to bar Congress from regulating something that then seemed plainly within any reasonable definition of "Commerce among the several States." And, as the national economy became increasingly integrated, so many activities were obviously interstate in character that it became hard to understand what could possibly lie outside the scope of that congressional power.

Lopez gave Rehnquist the chance to reassert the proposition that our federal system required that Congress's powers be limited. The fact that the only apparent reason for enacting the Gun-Free School Zones Act was that it gave members of Congress the opportunity to claim credit for doing something about the problem of violence in schools made the case a particularly attractive vehicle for doing so. Saying that Congress lacked the power to enact the statute would not directly weaken any important national policy, and could send a message to Congress to take more seriously its obligation to link its statutes to an enumerated power.

The difficulty in the case, though, was the same that had bedeviled the Court in the past – devising a second-order doctrine that identified sensible limits on Congress's power. Rehnquist's opinion provided a *tour d'horizon* of constitutional history. Synthesizing the prior cases, Rehnquist identified "three broad categories of activity that Congress may regulate under its commerce power." It could "regulate the use of the channels of interstate commerce," which included the power to prohibit the interstate transportation of goods, and it could "protect the instrumentalities of interstate commerce." Neither category, he wrote, was implicated in the Lopez case. What about the third category? As Rehnquist interpreted the precedents, Congress could regulate "those activities that substantially affect interstate commerce." And, in determining whether Congress was dealing with such an activity, the courts would look to whether individual acts, which one by one might not have large effects, might nonetheless have a substantial effect when taken all together.

The three categories look as if they might supply second-order principles, but they do not. Consider the regulation of the use of the channels of interstate commerce. Rehnquist did not repudiate decisions seeming to allow Congress to use a "jurisdictional hook" to activity that actually crossed state lines. For example, the national Child Support Recovery Act makes it a federal crime for a person to fail to pay required child support to a child in another state or to travel from one state to another in order to avoid paying child support, and another statute makes it a federal crime to cross state lines with intent to commit a crime of violence against one's spouse. In *Lopez* Rehnquist suggested that Congress could exercise its power to regulate interstate commerce without constitutional impediment by including such a "jurisdictional hook" – a requirement that, on a case-by-case basis, prosecutors show that something (like the gun Lopez possessed) crossed a state line.

And so Congress did, in a way showing that the first category is not really connected to any important first principle. The opinion says that the Gun-Free School Zones act could not be justified as an "attempt to prohibit the interstate transportation of a commodity through the channels of commerce." Congress enacted a statute making it a federal crime for a person to possess, near a school, a gun that had traveled in interstate commerce. Although no cases appear to have been brought under that revised statute, it does not take an extremely clever lawyer to explain why the jurisdictional hook should matter: Congress wanted to deter the interstate transportation of guns and believed that enough guns so transported ended up near schools that making it a crime to possess such a gun near a school would reduce the amount of interstate transportation of guns. But, in terms of any of federalism's values, the reenacted statute makes *Lopez* entirely pointless.

Lopez focused on the third category, that dealing with regulation of activities that, in the aggregate, had a substantial effect on interstate commerce. What was the aggregate effect of the possession of guns near schools? Justice Stephen Breyer's dissent mounted a strong case that it was entirely reasonable for Congress to conclude that the widespread possession of guns at schools had substantial *economic* effects. Students fearing outbreaks of violence might skip classes, and certainly would be diverted from their studies by fear and efforts to protect themselves from violence. But, Rehnquist wrote, Breyer's demonstration of the economic effects of gun possession near schools, even if accurate, was irrelevant. For, in the third category, all the precedents established was that Congress could rely on the aggregated economic effects of *economic* activity or enterprise, or, as the opinion also put it, "commercial" activity.

The next step was to justify this doctrinal formulation. The answer is *not* that commercial activities affect commerce though noncommercial ones do not, nor that the reason for giving Congress the power to regulate interstate commerce was to ensure that such commerce be protected. Breyer later made the point well: Under the Court's approach, Congress could regulate the discharge of pollutants from power plant smokestacks because pollution had bad consequences for the national economy, but it could not regulate the discharge of those very same pollutants from house chimneys – even if *more* pollution came from chimneys than from smokestacks. That is, the Court acknowledged that what mattered was not the underlying activity itself – the activity that was subject of congressional regulation – but rather the effects of that activity on interstate commerce. The distinction between commercial and noncommercial activities ended up having no connection to federalism's values.

The justification for Rehnquist's applying the commercial–noncommercial distinction, it turned out, lay in what two scholars have called the "non-infinity" principle.[10] The argument connecting possession of guns near schools to economic effects would, if accepted, mean that there was no "activity by an individual that Congress is without power to regulate." All noncommercial activities might, in the aggregate, affect the national economy – violent crime generally, or family law, or education. As Rehnquist said, at Breyer's level of generality, even child rearing could be described as commercial. Congress might conclude that children whose parents divorced and then shared custody would not spend as much time studying as children with one parent having primary custody, would not learn as much, and would not become as productive when they entered the workforce – so, on Breyer's theory, Congress could enact a statute prohibiting joint custody arrangements. And, indeed, Rehnquist observed pointedly that Breyer was "unable to identify any activity that the States may regulate but Congress may not." Yet, the "first principle" required that there be *some* such activity.

Rehnquist acknowledged that the line between commercial and noncommercial activities might be hard to draw. Legal scholars dealing with the case have wondered whether ordinary robbery should be treated as a commercial activity – a forced "exchange" of something valuable.[11] Rehnquist's rhetorical trope came into play once more, in his statement introducing his conclusion: "These are not precise formulations, and in the nature of things they cannot be. But we think they point the way to a correct decision in this case."

Rehnquist's next excursion into the area added little to an explanation of *why* federalism required the Court to invalidate a national statute. *United States v. Morrison* involved a provision in the national Violence Against Women Act (VAWA) allowing victims of gender-motivated assaults to sue their attackers in federal court.[12] VAWA included a number of relatively uncontroversial provisions, providing funds for programs aimed at supporting victims of gender-motivated violence and more, but Rehnquist had opposed enactment of the civil remedy provision as the legislation moved through Congress, saying that the provision would "involve the federal courts in a whole host of domestic relations disputes."[13]

Christy Brzonkala's case, though, was hardly a domestic relations dispute. Brzonkala alleged that she had been raped by two members of the football team at Virginia Polytechnic Institute – allegations that the defendant Antonio Morri-

---

[10] Glenn H. Reynolds & Brannon P. Denning, *Lower Court Readings of Lopez, or What If the Supreme Court Held a Constitutional Revolution and Nobody Came?*, 2000 WIS. L. REV. 369 (2000).

[11] Allan Ides, *Economic Activity as a Proxy for Federalism: Intuition and Reason in* United States v. Morrison, 18 CONST. COMMENT. 563 (2001).

[12] 529 U.S. 598 (2000).

[13] Quoted in Judith Resnik, *The Programmatic Judiciary: Lobbying, Judging, and Invalidating the Violence Against Women Act*, 74 S. CAL. L. REV. 269 (2000).

son and James Crawford vigorously disputed. Neither side ended up establishing the facts in court, because Brzonkala filed a suit in federal court, invoking VAWA's civil remedy provision, and the Supreme Court threw the case out because the Commerce Clause did not give Congress the power to enact it.

Unsurprisingly, Rehnquist's opinion relied heavily on the analysis he had developed in *Lopez*. Brzonkala (and the federal government, which appeared in the case to defend the statute's constitutionality) argued that gender-motivated assaults on women had a substantial economic impact, deterring women from taking some jobs, from traveling to unfamiliar venues, and the like. But, Rehnquist said, even were that true, it would be irrelevant. *Lopez* established that the Commerce Clause provided a basis for enacting legislation dealing with activities that, in the aggregate, had a substantial effect on interstate commerce only if the underlying activities were economic in nature themselves. No one contended that a rape is an economic activity, and so the statute was unconstitutional: "Gender-motivated crimes of violence are not, in any sense of the phrase, economic activity."

Once more Rehnquist relied on the non-infinity principle: "[Brzonkala's] reasoning would allow Congress to regulate any crime as long as the nationwide, aggregated impact of that crime has substantial effects on employment, production, transit, or consumption." Even more, that reason could "be applied equally as well to family law and other areas of traditional state regulation since the aggregate effect of marriage, divorce, and childrearing on the national economy is undoubtedly significant."

Rehnquist's opinion in *Morrison* again left unclear precisely what the "first principles" of federalism do. *Lopez* and *Morrison* gesture in the direction of what some scholars call an "enclave" theory of federalism – that there are some subjects, such as family law, education, and the regulation of ordinary crime, to which national power does not extend. But gestures are all the cases could make. Both experience and contemporary practice show that it is exceptionally difficult – if not impossible – to identify protected enclaves of authority left entirely to the states. National income support policy, for example, deals in some detail with relations among mothers, fathers, and their children; for several decades Presidents have made improvement in the education provided in public elementary and secondary schools a focus of legislative proposals. Statutes mentioned earlier in this chapter dealing with child support and domestic violence use jurisdictional hooks to avoid constitutional problems, but in so doing make it impossible to sustain an enclave theory of federalism.

Often the statutes embodying national policies affecting family law or education policy rest on congressional powers other than the power to regulate interstate commerce. In particular, Congress has often relied on its power to provide funds to state and local institutions on condition that those institutions comply with national mandates. But, to think that there is some enclave protected from federal intrusion when Congress exercises it power to regulate interstate commerce but not protected when Congress uses its spending power is to strain at a gnat while swallowing a camel. The "first principle" that simultaneously licenses Congress to intrude substantially on state-based decisions about family law and educational policy when it spends money but prohibits it from intruding even in a small way when it purports to regulate directly is difficult to discern. There may be one, but Rehnquist's opinions do not give it enough flesh – or, to revert to my earlier formulation, do not offer appropriate second- and third-order principles – for us to know exactly what his federalism is all about.

The absence of second- and third-order principles leaves large openings for Congress to get away with almost as much today as before *Lopez* and *Morrison*. Justice Breyer's dissent in *Morrison* pointed out another loophole. In *Lopez* Rehnquist, again to preserve established precedent, observed that the Gun-Free School Zones Act was "not an essential part of a larger regulation of economic activity, in which the regulatory scheme could be undercut unless the intrastate activity were regulated." So, Breyer asked, could Congress authorize victims of gender-motivated violence to sue in federal court if that provision were part of a larger "Safe Transport" or "Workplace Safety" statute with provisions dealing with the provision of safe equipment, protection against collapsing walls, and the like? Again, perhaps not, but only if we had some second-order principle, not identified by Rehnquist, to flesh out the first principles of federalism.[14]

We can accept the first principle that the national government is one of enumerated powers, the related principle that having vibrant state and local governments promotes important national values of self-government and efficiency, and even the principle that overly aggressive exercises of national power can deprive state and local governments of their vitality – yet still think that something more is needed to convert those principles into legal mandates the courts can enforce. Rehnquist's reliance on first principles alone, and the trope of saying that the statute at issue goes too far no matter what second-order principles we might develop, fail to provide what is needed, and therefore fail to explain why the Court's federalism decisions make *legal* sense.

The constitutional law of federalism has a second component, dealing with the dormant Commerce Clause. This component, as described earlier, involves the power of the courts to invalidate state regulations that adversely affect interstate commerce even when Congress has done nothing to indicate its disapproval of the regulations. Here Rehnquist did provide substantial guidance – albeit mostly in dissent. The reason, I believe, is that in this branch of federalism doctrine the primary issue is not whether the national government or, instead, state governments have the power to regulate some subject, but rather whether courts can do so without guidance from Congress. So, in this branch Rehnquist's sense that

---

[14] Rehnquist dissented when six Justices used this loophole to uphold a federal statute prohibiting the use of homegrown marijuana for medical purposes, under a doctor's supervision, in a state where such use was legal under state law. Gonzales v. Raich, 125 S. Ct. 2195 (2005).

limiting national power is important was supplemented by a more developed acount, often residing in the background of the opinions rather than on their surface, of why judicial activism – action by the courts overriding legislative decisions that do not contravene obvious constitutional prohibitions – is undesirable.

Dormant Commerce Clause doctrine has two elements. The first is easily described: A state cannot enforce a regulation that discriminates between commercial activity that originates within the state and activity that originates outside it, unless the differential treatment is justified by something intrinsic to the place of origin (as it rarely is), and even then, only if the state is pursuing some truly important purpose. Impermissible discrimination can take the form of imposing a cost on out-of-state activity while insulating in-state activity from the same cost, or of giving in-state activity a benefit not available to out-of-state activity. The heartland of this element consists of legislation that expressly treats in-state and out-of-state activity differently; on its periphery are cases in which the courts are willing to infer an intent to discriminate from the fact that the regulations, though not explicitly using geographical terms, seem to be "gerrymandered" so as to distinguish quite precisely between in-state and out-of-state activity. On the far periphery are extremely controversial cases in which there is such a large disparity between the impact of the regulation on in-state and out-of-state activity that it seems fair to describe the regulations as discriminatory even though they do not use geographical terms, and even though the courts are not willing to infer an intent to discriminate from the extreme disparity alone.

The second element of dormant Commerce Clause doctrine deals with regulations that are said to place excessive burdens on interstate commerce even as they treat in-state and out-of-state commerce exactly the same. The stated doctrine is that regulations that impose significant burdens on interstate commerce – that is, that significantly increase the costs of operating a business across state lines – are unconstitutional unless there is some strong justification in local policy for them. In practice, though, the Supreme Court's test is substantially more generous to the states. In one version, regulations are unconstitutional if they impose quite substantial burdens – that is, if the cost increases are quite high – without a reasonably strong justification. In another version, toward which the Rehnquist Court moved, regulations are unconstitutional only if they impose substantial burdens on interstate commerce while providing no more than an extremely small local benefit.

Rehnquist criticized both the "no discrimination" doctrine and the "burden on commerce" doctrine. Statistics are revealing. According to one count made in 1999, at that point Rehnquist had voted to uphold state regulations against dormant Commerce Clause challenges in 79 percent (42 out of 53) of the cases presenting the issue.[15] No one else on the Court came close to that figure, with

---

[15] Christopher R. Drahozal, *Preserving the American Common Market: State and Local Governments in the United States Supreme Court*, 7 SUP. CT. ECON. REV. 233 (1999).

Warren Burger's 53 percent and Antonin Scalia's 50 percent being the only competitors even within hailing distance. Notably, these are votes to support states'
rights to *regulate*. Some critics of the Rehnquist Court's decisions on the scope
of Congress's powers treated them as fundamentally pro-business, apparently on
the theory that groups seeking to regulate business benefit from constitutional
rules that give Congress wide power – and therefore give those groups the ability
to win once and for all by securing national legislation, rather than having to fight
one battle after another in state after state. Whatever might be said about the
accuracy of that account of those decisions, Rehnquist's position in the dormant
Commerce Clause cases is about state power to regulate business. It cannot plausibly be attributed to pro-business sympathy. His votes are *federalism* votes pure
and simple.

Rehnquist objected when the Court invalidated an Iowa regulation limiting to
sixty feet the length of trucks that could be used on the interstate highways in the
state.[16] Neighboring states allowed sixty-five-foot "double" trailers – trucks with
two linked trailers behind the cab – which, trucking companies said, were a more
efficient method of shipping certain loads. A fractured majority struck Iowa's
regulation down in part because Iowa's ban stopped trucking companies from
routing their trucks through the state and thereby increased their operating costs
substantially without, in the majority Justices' view, significant offsetting safety
benefits to drivers on Iowa roads. The state argued that "doubles" took longer to
pass and generated more spray on wet roads, obstructing other drivers' vision
more than shorter trucks did, and had a greater tendency to "jackknife" than did
trucks with a single trailer. But, the Justices concluded, these safety risks were
offset by some safety benefits doubles had. In addition, some of the Justices sus-
pected that Iowa's regulation was *designed* to exclude out-of-state trucking: The
ban did not apply to transportation into and out of certain cities on the state's
borders, and in vetoing a proposal to allow sixty-five-foot trucks on the state's
roads its governor noted that the revision "would benefit only a few Iowa-based
companies while providing a great advantage for out-of-state trucking firms and
competitors at the expense of our Iowa citizens."

Rehnquist objected to what might be called the trucking companies' "slice and
dice" tactics. No doubt, he argued, it was hard to show that sixty-five-foot trucks
were riskier than sixty-foot trucks, but the same would be true about efforts to
show that seventy-foot trucks were riskier than sixty-five-foot ones. His colleagues' analysis, he suggested, could lead, step by step, to finding it unconstitutional for a state to ban hundred-foot trucks – triples or even quadruples – on
its roads. That, Rehnquist suggested, was simply absurd. In his view, all the Constitution required was that state regulations have some minimal relationship to
advancing safety – that they be, in the jargon of constitutional law, "rationally
related" to safety. Rehnquist argued that it was obvious, first, that truck-length
regulations were, as a class, related to safety, and second, that Iowa's reasons for

[16] Kassel v. Consolidated Freightways Corp., 450 U.S. 662 (1981).

limiting truck lengths to sixty feet – its concerns about passing times on wet roads, and about jackknifing – were rational.

Rehnquist premised his detailed arguments about Iowa's regulations on a broader argument. Despite some suggestions in the language of the Court's precedents, he said, the courts' task was not to "directly compare safety benefits to commerce costs and strike down the legislation if the latter can be said in some vague sense to 'outweigh' the former," or in the case at hand, "to balance [the] incremental safety benefits" of the longer length requirement "against the burden on interstate commerce." A few years later Scalia offered a criticism of this sort of balancing as well. It was, Scalia said, conceptually impossible: "It is . . . like judging whether a particular line is longer than a particular rock is heavy."[17] Rehnquist's expressed concern was different. Balancing safety against commerce "would . . . arrogate to this Court functions of forming public policy, functions which, in the absence of congressional action, were left by the Framers of the Constitution to state legislatures."[18] This element of dormant Commerce Clause doctrine threatened to make the courts activists with respect to state legislation, and thereby to interfere with the sound operation of our federal system.

Was there *any* judicial role in the area? After all, Congress certainly had the power to respond to real interferences with the flow of commerce across state lines. Indeed, a few years after the Court struck down Iowa's truck-length regulations, Congress enacted a statute embodying a compromise between trucking interests and state governments, in which longer truck lengths were traded off for higher taxes on gasoline, the proceeds of which were to be used for road repair.[19] Some thought there might still be some place for an independent judicial role because, as Justice Robert Jackson put it, there were some regulations that were "too petty" to capture the attention of a Congress with many, more important items on its agenda and yet did indeed interfere with interstate commerce.[20]

For Rehnquist, courts did have some role, but only in connection with the first, antidiscrimination element of dormant Commerce Clause doctrine. In cases involving asserted burdens on interstate commerce, the courts were to ask only whether "the asserted safety justification, although rational, is merely a pretext for discrimination against interstate commerce."[21] His colleagues thought that there might be discrimination in Iowa's border-cities exception and in the governor's veto statement. Rehnquist thought not: The exception was quite narrow, and affected in-state and out-of-state shippers equally, and he could not see how any discriminatory motivation for vetoing *other* legislation might somehow infect the truck-length statute that remained on the books because of the veto.

[17] Bendix Autolite Corp. v. Midwesco Enterprises, Inc., 486 U.S. 888 (1988) (Scalia, J., concurring).
[18] 450 U.S. at 691 (Rehnquist, J., dissenting).
[19] For a description of the compromise, see GEOFFREY STONE ET AL., CONSTITUTIONAL LAW 273 (5th ed. 2005).
[20] Duckworth v. Arkansas, 314 U.S. 390 (1941) (Jackson, J., concurring in the result).
[21] 450 U.S. at 692 (Rehnquist, J., dissenting).

Rehnquist's opinion in the Iowa truck-length case shows both that he acknowledged the proper role of the courts in striking down state regulations that discriminated against interstate commerce, and that he was more skeptical than his colleagues about invalidating regulations as discriminatory. The Court's modern cases often involve statutes that are expressly discriminatory – that, in terms, do something about commerce originating out-of-state differently from what they do for exactly the same thing originating inside the state. Even here Rehnquist was often willing to allow the regulating state to go its own way.

Probably the most dramatic example is *Philadelphia v. New Jersey*, which involved New Jersey's prohibition on the importation of garbage generated outside the state.[22] New Jersey defended its regulation as an environmental protection measure. New Jersey's sanitary landfills for disposing of garbage were of course limited, and the state feared that making them available to garbage generated outside the state would make the local landfills unavailable for garbage generated inside the state – as, indeed, it would. The Court struck New Jersey's regulation down, finding the discrimination impermissible. After all, the landfills in *every* state were limited, and garbage disposal was a national problem from which New Jersey could not insulate itself.

Rehnquist dissented. For him, the state faced a serious problem. Obviously, New Jersey residents were going to generate garbage, but disposing of it in a manner that did not threaten health and safety was difficult. New Jersey's local landfills provided the route for doing so. Requiring that New Jersey's landfills be available for trash generated in Pennsylvania would "multiply[ ] the health and safety problems which would result if it [were allowed to deal] only with such wastes generated within the State." In this argument, Rehnquist implicitly asked why New Jersey's residents should have to bear the burdens of Pennsylvania's irresponsibility in generating too much solid waste: "The physical fact of life that New Jersey must somehow dispose of its own noxious items does not mean that it must serve as a depository for those of every other State."

Still, there was no question that the New Jersey regulation was discriminatory: People who generated garbage in New Jersey could buy access to New Jersey landfills, but people who generated garbage elsewhere could not. Rehnquist did not question the general proposition that discriminatory regulations were highly suspect. Instead, he relied on old cases involving quarantine laws. Those cases allowed states to exclude infected cows or meat or rags, the latter of which certainly looks a lot like the trash at issue in *Philadelphia v. New Jersey*. The majority said that the quarantine cases allowed states to ban importation of materials whose "very movement risked contagion." Rehnquist replied that the asserted difference between materials that posed a threat while they were moving and materials that posed a threat once they stopped moving was "pointless." More important than this assimilation of the policies at stake in the quarantine cases to the garbage

[22]   437 U.S. 617 (1978).

problem, I think, was the fact that those precedents were simply there, available for Rehnquist to rely on.[23] I find some modest resonance between this approach – relying simply on precedents without defending them – and Rehnquist's lack of interest in specifying second-order principles in the cases involving the scope of Congress's power under the Commerce Clause. There is an important difference, though: One can provide a full-bore defense of a state's power to choose whatever policies it wants in the dormant Commerce Clause context without offering second-order principles because in the background lies Congress's undoubted power to supplant the state's choices with its own.

Rehnquist addressed another aspect of the problem of discrimination in his dissent in *West Lynn Creamery v. Healy*.[24] One of the foundation cases of the modern law of the dormant Commerce Clause observed that discriminatory legislation was particularly troubling because the adversely affected groups, outside the state, were not able to influence the legislative process inside the state: "[W]hen the regulation is of such a character that its burden falls principally upon those without the state, legislative action is not likely to be subjected to those political restraints which are normally exerted on legislation where it affects adversely some interests within the state."[25] This analysis suggests that the constitutionality of state legislation might depend on the results of an inquiry into how interest group politics plays itself out in state legislatures.

Healy involved a Massachusetts scheme to provide financial support to the states' milk producers. The scheme had two components: a tax imposed on all milk dealers in the state (whether they bought their milk inside or outside Massachusetts), and a subsidy tax to Massachusetts milk producers funded by that tax. Everyone agreed that the tax standing alone was nondiscriminatory, and that the subsidy, had it come from the state's general revenues, would be constitutionally permissible. The Court held, though, that combining the dedicated tax with the subsidy was unconstitutional. Among its reasons was an interest group analysis: Local milk producers might have opposed the tax standing alone, but their opposition was bought off by the subsidy they received. Scholars have also suggested that subsidies from general tax funds attract more political attention, and opposition from consumers, than subsidies from dedicated funds. Rehnquist observed that the interest group analysis was actually entirely indeterminate. After all, the state's milk drinkers would oppose the tax under any circumstances, because it increased the cost of milk, as would the state's milk dealers, who had to pay the tax (and so who would face lower demand for milk).

Behind this specific observation lay a broader concern about relying on interest group analysis. Such analysis "may serve many useful purposes, but serving

---

[23] *See also* Hughes v. Oklahoma, 441 U.S. 322 (1979), in which Rehnquist's dissent similarly relied on an old decision that the majority overruled in the course of invalidating Oklahoma's ban on the export of minnows taken from the state's streams.

[24] 512 U.S. 186 (1994).

[25] South Carolina Highway Dept. v. Barnwell Bros., Inc., 303 U.S. 177 (1938).

as the basis for interpreting the dormant Commerce Clause is not one of them."
A full-scale interest group analysis is almost certainly beyond the capacity of the
courts.[26] What should courts do? In the end, Rehnquist suggested, formalism
was the best course. The ban on discriminatory legislation could itself be administered in an entirely formal manner – through the separation of tax and subsidy – and, perhaps most important, the formality of adhering to precedents
would give the states the latitude Rehnquist believed they should have.

   Rehnquist's opinion in the Iowa truck-length case had another important
theme, echoing the implicit observations about Pennsylvania's irresponsibility
in *Philadelphia v. New Jersey*. Rehnquist pointed out that in a federal system one
state's regulations necessarily had some effects on activities outside the state,
and that the constitutional law of federalism had to ensure a *coordinated* solution rather than a solution that imposed one state's rules on another. The theme
emerged in Rehnquist's discussion of his colleagues' observation that Iowa's rules
were out of step with those in neighboring states, which was precisely why trucking companies had to route around Iowa. Invalidating Iowa's rule, he said, effectively meant "[f]orcing Iowa to yield to the policy choices of neighboring States,"
which, he continued, "pervert[ed] the primary purpose of the Commerce Clause,
that of vesting power to regulate interstate commerce in Congress, where all the
States are represented."[27]

   The Commerce Clause, then, provided a mechanism of coordinating state regulations through congressional – *legislative* – action, but it gave little role for the
courts. In Rehnquist's view, though, there was another constitutional provision
directly responsive to the need for coordination under which the courts did have
at least some role, albeit a limited one. This was the Privileges and Immunities
Clause contained in Article IV: "The Citizens of each State shall be entitled to
all Privileges and Immunities of Citizens in the several States." By its terms, of
course, this *is* a nondiscrimination provision. However, Rehnquist wrote in one
of his opinions dealing with the clause, its purpose is to promote interstate harmony, not interstate commerce. The clause, in his view, had an important but
limited role in ensuring interstate coordination.

   The first case involved what was at heart an affirmative action program in
Camden, New Jersey.[28] The city adopted an ordinance requiring that at least 40
percent of the employees of contractors working on city construction projects
be residents of the city. A recent Supreme Court decision held that such an ordinance did not violate the dormant Commerce Clause because the city was acting
as a "market participant," deciding to whom it would give it contracts, rather than
a "market regulator," imposing requirements on everyone in a particular market.[29]

---

[26] For an attempt to illustrate the complexities, see STONE ET AL., *supra* note 18, at 238–39.
[27] 450 U.S. at 699 (Rehnquist, J., dissenting).
[28] Building Trades & Construction Council v. Mayor and City Council of Camden, 465 U.S. 208 (1984).
[29] White v. Massachusetts Council of Construction Employers, Inc., 460 U.S. 204 (1983).

Still, the Court held in a Rehnquist opinion, the Privileges and Immunities Clause did apply. Under that clause, New Jersey and Camden had to provide the same privileges to "an out-of-state citizen who ventures into New Jersey . . . as the New Jersey resident residing in Camden."

The question then was whether employment on city projects was one of the "privileges" covered by the clause. According to Rehnquist, precedent indicated that such privileges were those that were "'fundamental' to the promotion of interstate harmony." Employment generally was such a privilege – so that, for example, the Privileges and Immunities Clause as well as the dormant Commerce Clause would bar Camden from requiring that all grocery store employees be local residents – but *public* employment was not. What then of employment on city construction projects? Were such workers in effect "working for the city"? Rehnquist concluded that they were not, given the purposes of the Privileges and Immunities Clause. The city had to justify its discrimination against out-of-state citizens employed by employers building public works.

Here Rehnquist's concern that state and local governments have a wide range of choices available to them came into play. "The fact that Camden is expending its own funds . . . is certainly a factor – perhaps the crucial factor – to be considered in evaluating" whether the discrimination is justified. Similarly, Rehnquist described sympathetically the city's aims in enacting the ordinance as a means of halting the city's economic decline. In the end, the Court sent the case back to the state courts for another round of litigation.

Rehnquist demonstrated his expansive understanding of the permissible goals a state could pursue by discriminating against out-of-state citizens when he dissented from a decision finding it unconstitutional for New Hampshire to give licenses to practice law only to state residents.[30] Rehnquist began by invoking the obverse of the "first principle" he invoked in *Lopez:* With respect to *state* authority, "[t]he assumption from the beginning was that the various States' laws need not, and would not, be the same; the lawmakers of each State might endorse different philosophies and would have to respond to differing interests of their constituents, based on the various factors that were of inherently local character." For Rehnquist, the important role lawyers played in a state's public life – as legislators, judges, and, most important, civic leaders – was a completely adequate justification for restricting the privilege of practicing law to state residents:

> [T]he State . . . might conclude that those citizens trained in the law are likely to bring their useful expertise to other important functions that benefit from such expertise and are of interest to state governments – such as trusteeships, or directorships of corporations or charitable organizations, or school board positions, or merely the role of the interested citizen at a town meeting.

This is clearly a rather loose standard, and it was predicated, once more, on an underlying concern about the judicial role. Rehnquist's defense of the state's

---

[30] Supreme Court of New Hampshire v. Piper, 470 U.S. 274 (1985).

policy choice was quite conditional. It was, he wrote, "entitled to believe and hope that its lawyers will provide the various unique services mentioned above, just as it is entitled to believe that the residency requirement is the appropriate way to that end."

Rehnquist's opinions in cases involving the dormant Commerce Clause and the Privileges and Immunities Clause defend a robust role for states in policy making. So do his opinions in the cases involving Congress's power to regulate interstate commerce. Note, though, an important contrast between the two sets of cases. In the former, all that Rehnquist needed to do was to hold that states had a domain of choice to select whatever policies they preferred, with which the courts should not interfere. He did not have to describe the contours of that domain, because they were determined negatively: The courts should not displace state policy choices wherever Congress had refrained from exercising its undoubted power to regulate interstate commerce. In this set of cases, then, Rehnquist did not have to identify the values of federalism and explain why they supported particular judicial outcomes. His interest in federalism converged with a concern about judicial displacement of (state) legislative choices.

The cases involving congressional power under the Commerce Clause, though, did require an identification of the ways in which particular statutes impaired the values of federalism, and to that extent diverged from the concern about judicial "activism." Rehnquist's refusal to spell out second- and third-order doctrines left his federalism unanchored to anything that could be fairly described as an account of constitutional federalism. In the dormant Commerce Clause cases, believing that states were important without explaining why was truly sufficient to generate judicial doctrine. In the cases dealing with the reach of Congress's powers, such a belief certainly motivated Rehnquist's opinions, but it was insufficient to generate doctrine.

William Rehnquist's federalism was less than a constitutional doctrine or even, I think, a vision; it was instead an intuition that led him to particular results for which his opinions did not provide elaborated defenses. The difficulty with intuitions in constitutional law is that, alone, they rarely provide the basis for stable doctrine. The Court might develop a robust constitutional law of federalism and of limitations on Congress's powers in the next decades. But, I believe, although that constitutional law might have its origins in Court decisions during Rehnquist's tenure, it will not be William Rehnquist's federalism – because, in the end, we actually know rather little about what William Rehnquist's federalism is.

CHAPTER TEN

FEDERALISM AND THE SPENDING POWER FROM
DOLE TO *BIRMINGHAM BOARD OF EDUCATION*

Lynn A. Baker*

In 2005, it is uncontroversial that *South Dakota v. Dole*[1] is a significant part of
the Rehnquist legacy. But the importance of the case was far less clear when it
was before the Court in 1987. In that world of 1987, in which the "front door" of
the commerce power seemed to be perpetually open, there was little reason to
be concerned with the extent to which the "back door" of the spending power
should or could be kept closed.[2] And it is reasonable to assume that the Court
would not even have granted certiorari in *Dole* if it had not involved the issue of
the extent of state powers to regulate liquor under the Twenty-first Amendment:
The Eighth Circuit had not invalidated the challenged legislation;[3] and South
Dakota's petition for a writ of certiorari did not present the question of whether
the challenged legislation fell within Congress's power under the Spending Clause
to impose conditions upon grants of federal funds.

The "federalist revival" that began with the Court's 1992 decision in *New York
v. United States*[4] and its 1995 decision in *United States v. Lopez*[5] focused new attention on Congress's spending power and on *Dole*. That the Court had never
held a federal statute to fail scrutiny under *Dole* caused me (and others) to suggest that *Dole* offered Congress a seemingly easy end run around any restrictions
the Constitution might impose on its ability to regulate the states.[6] Ironically,
Chief Justice Rehnquist had authored both the majority opinion in *Lopez* and

---

* I thank Mitch Berman and Larry Sager for insightful conversations on issues raised herein, Craig
  Bradley and Stacy Jacobs for valuable comments on early drafts, Lynn Blais for invaluable help
  reading Justice Blackmun's handwritten notes, and Claire Morris for excellent research assistance.
[1] 483 U.S. 203 (1987).
[2] This is Professor Albert Rosenthal's wonderful metaphor. *See* Albert J. Rosenthal, *Conditional
Federal Spending and the Constitution*, 39 Stan. L. Rev. 1103, 1131 (1987).
[3] 791 F.2d 628 (8th Cir. 1986).
[4] 505 U.S. 144 (1992).
[5] 514 U.S. 549 (1995).
[6] *See, e.g.*, Lynn A. Baker, *Conditional Federal Spending after* Lopez, 95 Colum. L. Rev. 1911, 1914
(1995); Lynn A. Baker & Mitchell N. Berman, *Getting Off the Dole: Why the Court Should Abandon Its Spending Doctrine, and How a Too-Clever Congress Could Provoke It To Do So*, 78 Ind.
L.J. 459, 460 (2003); and sources cited *id.* at 460 n. 6, and 499 nn. 204, 205.

the majority opinion in *Dole* that threatened to render *Lopez* (and the rest of the federalist revival) moot.

In this chapter, I discuss Chief Justice Rehnquist's legacy for federalism with particular reference to the spending power. Parts I and II describe his opinion in *Dole* and trace the apparent origins of the five-prong test that he set out there and that the Court has never suggested altering. In Part III, I briefly discuss the dissenting opinion in *Davis v. Monroe County School Board*[7] that Justice Kennedy authored and that Chief Justice Rehnquist (along with Justices Scalia and Thomas) joined. This 1999 opinion is noteworthy because it was the first time since *Dole* itself that Rehnquist (or any other member of the Court) would have held a federal statute to violate *Dole*.

Part IV describes the decision of the Supreme Court of Washington in *Guillen v. Pierce County*,[8] which was the first decision in which any state or federal court had found a federal statute to exceed Congress's spending power under *Dole*. I then in Part V discuss the puzzling, subsequent decision of the U.S. Supreme Court in that case,[9] in which Chief Justice Rehnquist (and the rest of the "States' Rights Five" – Justices Kennedy, O'Connor, Scalia, and Thomas) seemed aggressively to avoid reaching the spending power issue even though the challenged statute arguably presented a relatively easy case for invalidation under both the Spending Clause and the Commerce Clause.

The chapter concludes with the tentative thesis (Part VI) that *Guillen* can be reconciled with Rehnquist's other spending power and Commerce Clause decisions, including the 2005 dissent in *Jackson v. Birmingham Board of Education*,[10] if one acknowledges that what drives his jurisprudence in both areas is a (sometimes) unstated inquiry into whether the congressional statute would regulate an area "where States historically have been sovereign,"[11] or whether it instead involves a traditional and appropriate federal function. That is, Chief Justice Rehnquist's legacy in the area of federalism and the spending power (Part VII) may be a quiet, and to date only partially successful, revival of the doctrine he set forth in 1976 in *National League of Cities v. Usery*[12] and that the Court, over his dissent, declared "unsound in principle and unworkable in practice" in 1985 in *Garcia v. San Antonio Metropolitan Transit Authority*.[13]

I. *SOUTH DAKOTA v. DOLE* IN 1986–87

At issue in *Dole* was a federal statute that conditioned states' receipt of a portion of federal highway funds on the state's adoption of a minimum drinking age of

---

[7] 526 U.S. 629, 654 (1999) (Kennedy, J., dissenting).
[8] 31 P.3d 628 (Wash. 2001).
[9] Pierce County v. Guillen, 537 U.S. 129 (2003).
[10] 125 S. Ct. 1497 (2005).
[11] *Lopez*, 514 U.S. at 564; *see also* National League of Cities v. Usery, 426 U.S. 833, 849 (1976) (whether the congressional enactment would "interfere with traditional aspects of state sovereignty").
[12] 426 U.S. 833 (1976).
[13] 469 U.S. 528, 546 (1985).

twenty-one.[14] The State of South Dakota, which permitted persons as young as nineteen to purchase certain alcoholic beverages, sought a declaratory judgment that the statute violated the Twenty-first Amendment to the U.S. Constitution and exceeded Congress's spending power.

The Twenty-first Amendment provides, in relevant part, that "The transportation or importation into any State . . . for delivery or use therein of intoxicating liquors, in violation of the laws thereof, is hereby prohibited." Congress's spending power derives from Article I, Section 8 of the Constitution, which empowers Congress to "lay and collect Taxes, Duties, Imposts, and Excises, to pay the Debts and provide for the common Defense and general Welfare of the United States."

Writing for the *Dole* majority, Rehnquist began by noting that there was no need for the Court to decide the Twenty-first Amendment claim. Observing that "[h]ere, Congress has acted indirectly under its spending power to encourage uniformity in the States' drinking ages," the Court went on to hold the legislation "within constitutional bounds *even if Congress may not regulate drinking ages directly*."[15]

Because a state always has "'the "simple expedient" of not yielding to what she [considers] federal coercion,'" the *Dole* Court concluded that the "Tenth Amendment limitation on congressional regulation of state affairs [does] not concomitantly limit the range of conditions legitimately placed on federal grants." At the same time, the Court was clear that "[t]he spending power is of course not unlimited . . . but is instead subject to several general restrictions articulated in our cases." Ultimately, however, none of the four stated restrictions was portrayed as having much "bite."

Thus, the first restriction articulated in *Dole*, that "the exercise of the spending power must be in pursuit of 'the general welfare,'" is subject to the caveat that "courts should defer substantially to the judgment of Congress" when applying this standard. Indeed, the Court acknowledged that the required level of deference is so great that it has "questioned whether 'general welfare' is a judicially enforceable restriction at all."[16] Second, the Court affirmed that Congress must state any conditions on the states' receipt of federal funds "'unambiguously[,] . . . enabl[ing] the States to exercise their choice knowingly, cognizant of the consequences of their participation.'"[17] But it could cite only one instance in which it had found that an enactment did not meet this requirement.[18]

Third, the *Dole* Court noted that "conditions on federal grants might be illegitimate if they are unrelated 'to the federal interest in particular national projects

---

[14] 483 U.S. 203 (1987).

[15] *Id.* at 206 (emphasis added).

[16] *Id.* at 207 n. 2 (citing Buckley v. Valeo, 424 U.S. 1, 90–91 [1976] [*per curiam*]).

[17] *Id.* at 207 (quoting Pennhurst State Sch. & Hosp. v. Halderman, 451 U.S. 1, 17 [1981]).

[18] *Id.* Moreover, the import of the Court's holding in that instance was not to require Congress to continue providing funds to a state that had failed to comply with an ambiguously worded condition on those funds, but to deny relief to a third-party beneficiary of the funds who alleged that the state of Pennsylvania had failed to comply with the federal condition that the Court ultimately found to be impermissibly ambiguous. *Pennhurst*, 451 U.S. at 27–28.

or programs,'" but added that this restriction was merely "suggested (without sig-nificant elaboration)" by prior cases.[19] Indeed, the Court could cite no instance in which it had invalidated a conditional grant of federal money to the states on this ground.[20] Fourth, the Court concluded that "other constitutional provisions may provide an independent bar to the conditional grant of federal funds." That is, Congress may not use its powers under the Spending Clause "to induce the States to engage in activities that would themselves be unconstitutional," such as "a grant of federal funds conditioned on invidiously discriminatory state action or the infliction of cruel and unusual punishment."[21] But again, the Court could cite no case in which it had invalidated a conditional grant to the states on this basis.[22]

In addition to these four restrictions, the *Dole* Court read the Spending Clause to impose limits on Congress's ability to "coerce" the states in ways that it could not directly mandate under its other Article I powers. "[I]n some circumstances," the Court observed, "the financial inducement offered by Congress might be so coercive as to pass the point at which 'pressure turns into compulsion.'"[23] The Court concluded that a threatened loss to states of 5 percent of their otherwise obtainable allotment of federal highway funds did not pass this critical point, but did not suggest what percentage of these (or any other) funds might do so.

II. THE ORIGINS OF THE *DOLE* TEST

Since deciding *Dole* in 1987, neither Rehnquist nor the Court has ever wavered in their apparent commitment to the doctrinal test set out there. Given the lon-gevity and ultimate importance of the test, one might imagine that great thought and effort lay behind it. A close review of the historical record, however, suggests that Chief Justice Rehnquist crafted the test casually, and did not consider the case an especially important one, doctrinally or otherwise, at the time it came before the Court.

The papers of Justice Blackmun include his handwritten notes of the Court's internal conference on *Dole* three days after oral argument. Those notes indicate that Rehnquist voted to uphold the challenged legislation at the conference and said the following:

---

[19] *Id.* at 207 (quoting Massachusetts v. United States, 435 U.S. 444, 461 [1978] [plurality opinion]).
[20] *See id.* at 207–08. The *Dole* Court cited *Massachusetts v. United States*, 435 U.S. 444, 461 (1978) (plurality opinion), and *Ivanhoe Irrigation Dist. v. McCracken*, 357 U.S. 275, 295 (1958). But the Court had not invalidated a condition on federal funds in either case.
[21] *Id.* at 210.
[22] *See id.* at 208. The Court cited three cases, but in none of them had it invalidated a conditional grant of federal money to the states on this ground. *See* Lawrence County v. Lead-Deadwood Sch. Dist., 469 U.S. 256, 269–70 (1985); *Buckley*, 424 U.S. at 91 (*per curiam*); King v. Smith, 392 U.S. 309, 333 and n. 34 (1968).
[23] *Id.* (citing Steward Machine Co. v. Davis, 301 U.S. 548, 590 [1937]).

Avoid metaphysical abstractions

US grants can be restricted

Not much more here and Congress can do this

Exemplifying Rehnquist's view that the case did not merit heavy intellectual lifting, his opinion occupies only eight pages in the *U.S. Reports*,[24] and largely tracks that of the U.S. Court of Appeals for the Eighth Circuit.[25]

The first prong of Rehnquist's test – the "general welfare" prong – was also the first mentioned by the Eighth Circuit. Interestingly, however, the circuit court sought to give substance and bite to that prong by distinguishing "the well-being of the nation as a whole" from "the well-being of a particular region or locality." Rehnquist, in contrast, not only did not elaborate in this way, but went on to indicate that the prong was essentially a throwaway in light of the level of deference to be paid Congress's judgment in this area.

Rehnquist's "relatedness" prong echoed that of the Eighth Circuit, though the latter stated that the conditions must be "reasonably related to the national interest" whereas Rehnquist's requirement was softer: Conditions "might be illegitimate if they are unrelated 'to the federal interest in particular national projects or programs.'"

The requirement of no "independent constitutional bar" was stated in comparable language by the Eighth Circuit and Rehnquist, with the latter elaborating that this prong of the test "stands for the unexceptionable proposition that the power may not be used to induce the States to engage in activities that would themselves be unconstitutional."

Rehnquist's opinion further tracked that of the Eighth Circuit in its observations (1) that Congress's power under the Spending Clause is not limited by its other broad legislative powers; (2) that Congress's spending power is not unlimited; and (3) that the Tenth Amendment is not violated when the conditions on federal funds "implicate areas that Congress could not directly regulate under its other legislative powers."

In several noteworthy respects, however, Rehnquist's opinion deviated from that of the Eight Circuit. The requirement that conditions on the states' receipt of federal funds be stated "unambiguously" has proven to be Rehnquist's most important addition to the test set out in the Eighth Circuit's opinion. It is not surprising that Rehnquist was concerned to include such a requirement since he had authored the Court's 1981 opinion in *Pennhurst v. Halderman* in which the conditional-spending-as-contract analogy was first spelled out in some detail.[26]

In addition, the Solicitor General's brief for the Respondent[27] in *Dole* reminded the Court of the *Pennhurst* precedent: "[A]t least with respect to grants to a state,

---

[24] 483 U.S. at 205–12.

[25] 791 F.2d 628 (8th Cir. 1986).

[26] 451 U.S. at 17–18.

[27] Available on Westlaw at 1987 WL 880322.

'if Congress intends to impose a condition on the grant of federal moneys, it must do so unambiguously' (Pennhurst State School v. Halderman, 451 U.S. 1, 17 (1981) (footnote omitted)." This mention came only in a footnote, however, the Solicitor General having taken the view that this "requirement needs no discussion here . . . because there can be no claim that the condition imposed . . . is in any way unclear."

Later in his brief, the Solicitor General reiterated *Pennhurst*'s contract analogy and further suggested that it logically mandated a coercion inquiry:

> The Court has characterized legislation enacted pursuant to the Spending Clause as "much in the nature of a contract; in return for federal funds, the States agree to comply with federally imposed conditions. The legitimacy of Congress' power to legislate under the spending power thus rests on whether the State voluntarily and knowingly accepts the terms of the 'contract'" (Pennhurst State School v. Halderman, 451 U.S. at 17). *The contract analogy confirms that the relevant inquiry under the Tenth Amendment is whether the state has a genuine option of declining the grant and the condition* – the Tenth Amendment can be violated only if Congress has exercised the Spending Power in a manner that precludes the state from making that choice.[28]

The Eighth Circuit opinion acknowledged the potential role of coercion, but essentially dismissed it with the observation that if a state finds the conditions distasteful, "the state has available to it the simple expedient of refusing to yield to what it urges is 'federal coercion.'"[29] Rehnquist, in contrast, repeated that quotation from the Court's 1947 decision in *Oklahoma v. Civil Service Commission*,[30] but went on to observe – citing only *Steward Machine Co. v. Davis*,[31] in which the Court sustained the challenged legislation – that "[o]ur decisions have recognized that in some circumstances the financial inducement offered by Congress might be so coercive as to pass the point at which 'pressure' turns into compulsion."

There are two other noteworthy respects in which Rehnquist's *Dole* decision differed from that of the Eighth Circuit. First, he omitted the Eighth Circuit's observation, citing *Buckley v. Valeo*,[32] that the necessary and proper clause is part of the source of the breadth of Congress's spending power: The spending power "when viewed in conjunction with the necessary and proper clause, is quite expansive, and without question includes the authority to attach conditions to the receipt and further expenditure of federal funds." Rehnquist cited *Buckley*, but for the somewhat different proposition that the Constitution's "general welfare" constraint on the spending power is of questionable justiciability.

---

[28] Emphasis added.
[29] 791 F.2d 628, 634 (8th Cir. 1986) (quoting Oklahoma v. Civil Service Commission, 330 U.S. 127, 143–44 [1947]).
[30] 330 U.S. 127 (1947).
[31] 301 U.S. 548 (1937).
[32] 424 U.S. 1 (1976) (*per curiam*).

Second, and surely of greatest importance, Rehnquist declined to subscribe to the Eighth Circuit's larger vision of federalism. The Court, with Rehnquist, Burger, O'Connor, and Powell dissenting, had decided *Garcia v. San Antonio Metropolitan Transit Authority*[33] the year before the Eighth Circuit decided *Dole*. In its discussion of the Tenth Amendment's limitations on the spending power, the Eighth Circuit quoted the *Garcia* majority's claim that "The political process ensures that laws that unduly burden the states will not be promulgated" and, like the majority in *Garcia*, concluded that "'[i]n the factual setting of [this] case[] the internal safeguards of the political process have performed as intended.'" Given that Rehnquist had authored the decision in *National League of Cities*[34] that the *Garcia* majority explicitly overruled, and given that Rehnquist promised in his *Garcia* dissent that his view would "in time again command the support of a majority of this Court," his failure to mention *Garcia* in his opinion in *Dole* is not surprising.

III. *DAVIS v. MONROE COUNTY BOARD OF EDUCATION*

Between 1987, when the Rehnquist Court decided *Dole*,[35] and 1999, when the Court decided *Davis v. Monroe County Board of Education*,[36] there was reason to wonder whether the test set forth in *Dole* imposed any meaningful restrictions on Congress's power under the Spending Clause. As was noted in Part I above, at the time *Dole* was decided Rehnquist could give no examples of a case in which challenged legislation would have been invalidated under even one of the five prongs of the *Dole* test. And as of 1999, no Justice had suggested that any federal statute should fail to pass muster under *Dole*.

Insofar as *Dole* was decided on the heels of *Garcia*,[37] there was also reason to wonder whether it even mattered if Congress's spending power was de facto unlimited. If, after *Garcia*, the Tenth Amendment was to be a nonjusticiable truism, and if the Commerce Clause was to continue to be interpreted to authorize Congress to regulate the states directly in virtually any way it chose, the contours of the spending power would be of scant concern. But by 1999, the Court had decided *New York*[38] and *Lopez*,[39] and discussion of conditional federal spending therefore had become meaningful.

The question presented in *Davis*[40] was whether a private damages action may lie against a school board under Title IX of the Education Amendments of 1972 ("Title IX") in cases of student-on-student harassment. A bare majority of the court held that Title IX was enacted pursuant to Congress's spending power and that it met the requirements set forth in *Dole*. Writing for the majority, Justice O'Connor acknowledged that "the scope of liability in private damages actions

---

[33] 469 U.S. 532 (1985).   [34] 426 U.S. 833 (1976).
[35] 483 U.S. 203 (1987).   [36] 526 U.S. 629 (1999).
[37] 469 U.S. 532 (1985).   [38] 505 U.S. 144 (1992).
[39] 514 U.S. 549 (1995).   [40] 526 U.S. 629 (1999).

under Title IX is circumscribed by *Pennhurst*'s requirement that funding recipients have notice of their potential liability," and she went on to conclude that "the regulatory scheme surrounding Title IX has long provided funding recipients with notice that they may be liable for their failure to respond to the discriminatory acts of certain nonagents." She observed that the Court had previously determined "that sexual harassment is a form of discrimination for Title IX purposes and that Title IX proscribes harassment with sufficient clarity to satisfy *Pennhurst*'s notice requirement and serve as a basis for a damages action."

Chief Justice Rehnquist joined the dissent authored by Justice Kennedy (which was joined also by Justices Scalia and Thomas). The dissenters observed that "there is no established body of federal or state law on which courts may draw in defining the student conduct that qualifies as Title IX gender discrimination" and asserted that the majority had failed "to provide any workable definition of actionable peer harassment." The dissenters termed the clear notice (*Pennhurst*) prong of the *Dole* test a "vital safeguard for the federal balance" and contended that it was "eviscerate[d]" by the majority, that the majority's was a "watered-down version of the Spending Clause clear-statement rule."

The dissenters concluded that schools "cannot be held liable for peer sexual harassment because Title IX does not give them clear and unambiguous notice that they are liable in damages for failure to remedy discrimination by their students." En route the dissenters asserted that "[w]ithout doubt, the scope of potential damages liability is one of the most significant factors a school would consider in deciding whether to receive federal funds," and they offered the following context-specific elaboration on *Dole*'s "clear notice" prong:

> the Court must not imply a private cause of action for damages unless it can demonstrate that the congressional purpose to create the implied cause of action is so manifest that the State, when accepting federal funds, had clear notice of the terms and conditions of its monetary liability.

The *Davis* dissent heartened those (including myself) who had feared that the *Dole* test had no bite and that the spending power would provide Congress an eternally available means of circumventing those limitations on its other Article I powers that the Court has recognized. But it was still only a dissent and, as of 1999, no state or federal court had yet held a federal statute invalid under *Dole*. That would change in 2001.

IV. *GUILLEN V. PIERCE COUNTY* IN THE WASHINGTON SUPREME COURT

In 2001, the Supreme Court of Washington became the first state or federal court to use the *Dole* doctrine to strike down a federal statute as exceeding Congress's spending power.[41] Indeed, *Guillen v. Pierce County* was the first case in which any court had struck down a federal statute on purely Spending Clause grounds.

---

[41] Guillen v. Pierce County, 31 P.3d 628 (Wash. 2001).

Guillen involved various constitutional challenges to a federal statute, 23 U.S.C. § 409, as amended in 1995 ("§ 409"), that, in relevant part, regulates the rules of evidence to be applied in state court proceedings involving causes of action brought solely under state law. These regulations – which protect from discovery and introduction into evidence certain accident reports and highway safety data compiled and held by city and county governments – are included among the conditions that attach to the states' receipt of certain federal highway safety monies.

The statute became the focus of litigation when the families of two Washington State motorists involved in traffic accidents requested accident reports and other materials and data held by county agencies related to the traffic history of the sites of their accidents. The family members sought the information in order to pursue tort claims that the relevant city and county governments were negligent in their maintenance and operation of the intersections at which the accidents occurred. Pierce County refused to provide the requested reports and data, relying on § 409, which states in relevant part:

> Notwithstanding any other provision of law, reports, surveys, schedules, lists, or data compiled or collected for the purpose of identifying, evaluating, or planning the safety enhancement of potential accident sites . . . , pursuant to section[] . . . 152 of this title or for the purpose of developing any highway safety construction improvement project which may be implemented utilizing Federal-aid highway funds shall not be subject to discovery or admitted into evidence in a Federal or State court proceeding or considered for other purposes in any action for damages arising from any occurrence at a location mentioned or addressed in such reports, surveys, schedules, lists, or data.

Because the accident reports and other materials that the plaintiffs sought had been collected by the relevant county as part of an application to the state of Washington for federal hazard elimination funds under § 152, the county argued that they were privileged under § 409.

The question for the Washington Supreme Court was whether the collecting of certain reports and other materials for this statutorily specified purpose rendered them privileged even if those reports and other materials had been compiled for other purposes, such as routine law enforcement. The Washington Supreme Court held that they were. Less happily for Pierce County, the Court went on to hold that when construed so broadly the § 409 privilege exceeded Congress's powers under both the Commerce Clause and the Spending Clause.

The Washington Supreme Court reasoned that § 409 was not a valid exercise of Congress's commerce power because such an expansive privilege "cannot reasonably be characterized as an 'integral part' of the Federal-aid highway system's regulation."[42] The court also concluded that the privilege did not meet *Dole*'s requirement that any condition attached to the receipt of federal funds be related to the spending program:

---

[42] *Guillen*, 31 P.3d at 654 (quoting Hodel v. Indiana, 452 U.S. 314, 328 n. 17 [1981]).

We find that no valid federal interest in the operation of the federal safety enhancement program is reasonably served by barring the admissibility and discovery in
state court of accident reports and other traffic and accident materials and "raw
data" that were originally prepared for routine state and local purposes, simply because they are "collected," . . . *among other reasons,* pursuant to a federal statute for
federal purposes.[43]

The court therefore held § 409, as amended, to exceed Congress's spending power.

Lastly, relying heavily on its construal of recent Rehnquist Court federalism
decisions as displaying a "fundamental respect for state sovereignty," the court
reasoned that § 409 "cannot be characterized as a valid exercise of any power constitutionally delegated to the federal government." Simply stated, Congress lacks
"power to intrude upon the exercise of state sovereignty in so fundamental an
area of the law as the determination by state and local courts of the discoverabil-
ity and admissibility of state and local materials and data relating to traffic and
accidents on state and local roads."

Three justices of the Washington Supreme Court disagreed with the majority's
interpretation of § 409. As these concurring justices read the privilege, an individual report originally compiled for an ordinary state or local law enforcement
purpose was not covered by § 409 merely because it was later collected, along with
other reports or data, for the purpose of applying for a share of the state's federal safety improvement funds.

V. *GUILLEN* IN THE U.S. SUPREME COURT

Because the Washington Supreme Court had held a federal statute unconstitutional, there was no question that the U.S. Supreme Court would grant certiorari
in the case. And for those interested in the spending power (and federalism), the
case was positively bursting with possibilities. Most obviously, the case offered
Chief Justice Rehnquist and the rest of the "States Rights' Five" an opportunity
that they would not likely soon again have to significantly narrow the one remaining, and potentially eviscerative, loophole that existing spending doctrine
provides to the Rehnquist Court's important project of restoring a meaningful
balance between the state and federal spheres.

No matter how narrowly the Court might read Congress's powers under the
Commerce Clause[44] and Section 5 of the Fourteenth Amendment,[45] and no matter how absolute a prohibition the Court might impose on Congress's "commandeering" of state and local officials,[46] the states will be at the mercy of Congress

---

[43] *Id.* at 651 (emphasis in original).

[44] *See, e.g.,* United States v. Morrison, 529 U.S. 598 (2000); *Lopez,* 514 U.S. 549.

[45] *See, e.g.,* Board of Trustees of the Univ. of Ala. v. Garrett, 531 U.S. 356 (2000); *Morrison,* 529
    U.S. 598; Kimel v. Fla. Bd. of Regents, 528 U.S. 62 (2000); City of Boerne v. Flores, 521 U.S. 507
    (1997).

[46] *See, e.g.,* Printz v. United States, 521 U.S. 898 (1997); *New York,* 505 U.S. 144. But see Reno v. Con-
    don, 528 U.S. 141 (2000).

so long as there are no meaningful limits on its spending power.[47] In this context, *Guillen* presented Chief Justice Rehnquist a range of potentially alluring opportunities. He could have used the case to affirm that the doctrine set forth in *Dole* does in fact have "bite," and that the spending power does not provide Congress an eternally available means of circumventing those limitations on Congress's other Article I powers that the Court has recognized. Or he could have used the case to strengthen, to add further "bite" to, the *Dole* doctrine. Or, perhaps most intriguingly, he could have used the case to revisit the question, noted in *Dole*, of whether the Constitution's "general welfare" restriction on Congress's spending power is a judicially enforceable restriction at all.[48]

It seemed clear that the statute at issue could not be sustained under existing Commerce Clause doctrine. Hornbook law holds that, after *Lopez*, the Commerce Clause allows Congress to regulate "three types of activities":[49] the channels of interstate commerce; the instrumentalities of interstate commerce; and intrastate economic activities that, in the aggregate, substantially affect interstate commerce. But § 409 does not regulate instrumentalities or channels, in the sense that these are not the things upon which the statute operates. Rather, § 409 is, at best, a regulation of state court procedure arguably adopted for the purpose of protecting instrumentalities and channels of interstate commerce.

Even insofar as Commerce Clause precedent permits Congress to regulate some things other than instrumentalities and channels when the aim is to protect instrumentalities or channels, that precedent is not indifferent to what those other things, matters, or subjects of regulation are. To the contrary, numerous opinions authored by Rehnquist and others of the States' Rights Five have strongly suggested that the Constitution imposes special constraints upon federal legislation that intrudes upon integral areas of historical state sovereignty.[50] Thus, the fact that § 409 proceeds by the specific means of regulating the rules of evidence to be applied in state court proceedings involving causes of action brought solely under state law would seem to be a matter of constitutional concern.

It seemed equally clear that the challenged statute exceeded Congress's spending power insofar as it unambiguously violated *Dole*'s "clear notice" requirement for constitutionally permissible conditions on federal funds. Under this prong of

---

[47] Today, the major constitutional constraint on Congress's spending power is the Establishment Clause of the First Amendment. *See, e.g.,* Flast v. Cohen, 392 U.S. 83, 105 (1968) (holding that "the Establishment Clause of the First Amendment does specifically limit the taxing and spending power conferred by Art. I, § 8").

[48] *Dole*, 483 U.S. at 207 n. 2.

[49] Erwin Chemerinsky, *Constitutional Law: Principles and Policies* 261 (2d ed. 2002). *See Lopez*, 514 U.S. at 558 ("[W]e have identified three broad categories of activity that Congress may regulate under its commerce power.").

[50] Then-Justice Rehnquist's plurality opinion in *Usery*, 426 U.S. at 852 (invalidating federal legislation because it "operate[s] to directly displace the States' freedom to structure integral operations in areas of traditional governmental functions"), is the most obvious point of reference, especially given his and Justice O'Connor's refusal to accept the legitimacy of *Usery*'s subsequent overruling in *Garcia*. *See Garcia*, 469 U.S. at 580 (Rehnquist, J., dissenting); *id.* at 589 (O'Connor, J., dissenting). *See also infra* note 72 and accompanying text.

the *Dole* test, any conditions on the states' receipt of federal funds must be stated "'unambiguously[,] . . . enabl[ing] the States to exercise their choice knowingly, cognizant of the consequences of their participation.'"[51] The text of § 409, however, contains at least four significant ambiguities of the sort that surely would have precluded states and their political subdivisions from knowing with any certainty the terms of their "contract" with the federal government.[52] The most noteworthy of these ambiguities is the one that divided the Washington Supreme Court, as described above: Can a local government shield from discovery and introduction into evidence all preexisting, highway-related reports and data simply by collecting them for the purposes specified in § 409?

The justices of the Washington Supreme Court were not alone in finding the text of § 409 ambiguous in this regard. The fifteen additional courts that that have discussed this aspect of § 409 have been divided in their interpretations, with ten courts reading this aspect of § 409 broadly as the *Guillen* majority did,[53] and five courts reading the text more narrowly, essentially as the *Guillen* concurrence did.[54] In the words of one federal district court, "Section 409 has engendered some confusion in the courts, thanks to its unwieldy language and the absence of any significant legislative history."[55]

The extent of the ambiguity in § 409 is further underscored by the fact that the U.S. Supreme Court found it necessary to "determine the statute's proper scope" before it could address the constitutional questions raised. Indeed, as the Court noted, the Petitioner, Respondents, and the United States as intervenor each proposed a different interpretation of § 409 in their briefs, with the Court ultimately adopting the government's interpretation of the statute.

In many contexts, the Court has the option – indeed the self-imposed obligation – to construe an ambiguous statute to avoid a "constitutionally doubtful" construction where possible.[56] Under the Court's spending power doctrine as set forth in *Dole*, however, the mere existence of the ambiguity is constitutionally de-

---

[51] *Dole*, 483 U.S. at 207 (quoting *Pennhurst*, 451 U.S. at 17).
[52] *See* Amicus Brief of Law Professors Lynn A. Baker and Mitchell N. Berman in Support of Respondents, Pierce County v. Guillen, 537 U.S. 129 (2003), available on Westlaw at 2002 WL 1964091.
[53] *See* Powers v. CSX Transportation, 177 F. Supp. 2d 1276, 1280 (S.D. Ala. 2001); National Railroad Passenger Corp. v. Transwood, Inc., 2001 WL 986868 *1, *2 (E.D. La. 2001); Isbell v. Arizona, 9 P.3d 322, 324 (Ariz. 2000) (en banc); Dowell v. Louisiana, 750 So. 2d 498, 501 (La. App. 2000); Sevario v. Louisiana, 752 So. 2d 221, 230 (La. App. 1999); Palacios v. Louisiana and Delta Railroad, Inc., 740 So. 2d 95, 101–02 (La. 1999); Coniker v. New York, 695 N.Y.S.2d 492, 495, 496 (N.Y. Ct. Claims 1999); Fry v. Southern Pacific Trans. Co., 715 So. 2d 632, 637 (La. App. 1998); Hardenstein v. Cook Construction, 691 So. 2d 177, 182 (La. App. 1997); Reichert v. Louisiana, 694 So. 2d 193, 200 (La. 1997).
[54] *See* Werner v. IA Construction Corp., 51 Pa. D. & C. 4th 509, 513 (2001); Irion v. Louisiana, 760 So. 2d 1220, 1226 (La. App. 2000); Guillen v. Pierce County, 982 P.2d 123, 129 (Wash. App. 1999); *Ex parte* Alabama Dep't of Trans., 757 So. 2d 371, 374 (Ala. 1999); Palacios v. Louisiana & Delta Railroad, Inc., 682 So. 2d 806, 810 (La. App. 1997).
[55] Powers v. CSX Transportation, Inc., 177 F. Supp. 2d 1276, 1277 (S.D. Ala. 2001).
[56] *See, e.g.*, Jones v. United States, 529 U.S. 848, 851, 857 (2000); Edward J. DeBartolo Corp. v. Florida Gulf Coast Building & Constr. Trades Council, 485 U.S. 568, 575 (1988); United States *ex rel.* Attorney General v. Delaware & Hudson Co., 213 U.S. 366, 408 (1909).

terminative – and fatal. This is not only because such legislation is "in the nature of a contract,"[57] but also because "the clear-notice safeguard of our Spending Clause jurisprudence" is a "vital safeguard for the federal balance."[58] As Justice Kennedy, joined by Chief Justice Rehnquist and Justices Scalia and Thomas, wrote in their dissent in *Davis,* "Only if states receive clear notice of the conditions attached to federal funds can they guard against excessive federal intrusion into state affairs and be vigilant in policing the boundaries of federal power."[59]

Given its various textual ambiguities and the extensive disagreement as to its meaning and scope among the many judges nationwide who have studied § 409, it seemed inevitable, particularly in light of the *Davis* dissent, that the *Guillen* Court would hold that the provision violated *Dole*'s clear notice requirement.

VI. SOLVING THE PUZZLE OF *GUILLEN*?

In light of the above, it would seem that *Guillen* presented a relatively easy – and important – case of a statute that exceeded Congress's powers under both the Spending Clause and the Commerce Clause. In fact the entire Court did find the case easy, but not in the way the preceding analysis predicts. In a brief, fifteen-page opinion, released ten short weeks after oral argument in the case, the Court unanimously concluded that the statute at issue was a valid exercise of Congress's commerce power.[60] The Court therefore never reached the spending power issue.

The Commerce Clause analysis in Justice Thomas's opinion comprises a mere seven sentences and proceeds as a straightforward syllogism. First, quoting *Lopez,* "under the Commerce Clause, Congress 'is empowered to regulate and protect the instrumentalities of interstate commerce, . . . even though the threat may come only from intrastate activities.'" Second, the statute at issue "can be viewed as legislation aimed at improving safety in the channels of commerce and increasing protection for the instrumentalities of interstate commerce." Therefore, the legislation "fall[s] within Congress' Commerce Clause power."

This is a highly questionable and conclusory Commerce Clause analysis, made further remarkable by its failure to acknowledge at any point that the statute at issue in fact regulates the rules of evidence to be employed in state court proceedings. From the Court's opinion, one might have imagined that the statute instead regulated highways.

Why was Chief Justice Rehnquist (and the rest of the States' Rights Five) willing to resolve the case through a dubious Commerce Clause analysis that is seemingly inconsistent with the Court's own precedent?[61] Why did Rehnquist (and the

---

[57] *Davis,* 526 U.S. at 640 (1999); *see also id.* at 655 (Kennedy, J., dissenting).
[58] *Id.*   [59] *Id.*
[60] 537 U.S. 129 (2003).
[61] For a thoughtful discussion of this question that proposes a different answer, see Mitchell N. Berman, Guillen *and Gullibility: Piercing the Surface of Commerce Clause Doctrine,* 89 Iowa L. Rev. 1487, 1533 (2004) (concluding that "*Guillen* issued not from attention to the Court's own Commerce Clause doctrine but rather from sensitivity to the Court's understanding of Commerce Clause meaning").

rest of the States' Rights Five) forgo this rare opportunity to strengthen or re-affirm the significance of existing spending power doctrine, which is so central to any meaningful "federalist revival"?

There are not many data points to connect, but I believe that the decision in *Guillen* can be reconciled with Rehnquist's opinions in *Lopez*[62] and *Morrison*,[63] as well as with the opinions that he authored and joined, respectively, in the three cases to date in which any member of the Court has held that a federal statute exceeded Congress's spending power: *South Dakota v. Dole*,[64] *Davis v. Monroe County Board of Education*,[65] and *Jackson v. Birmingham Board of Education*.[66] My quite preliminary thesis is that Rehnquist's fundamental focus in both the spending power and Commerce Clause cases has been on whether the regulated area at issue is one in which the States "historically have been sovereign"[67] or is instead a traditional and appropriate federal function.

By the time the Court decided *Guillen,* Rehnquist was on record in *Davis*[68] as having been willing to invalidate a federal statute under the doctrine set out in *Dole.* It therefore seems unlikely that he was aggressively avoiding reaching the spending power issue in *Guillen.* It seems more likely, notwithstanding my own contrary analysis, that Rehnquist in fact believed that the statute at issue in *Guillen* should be sustained under *Dole.* There was therefore no pressing need for him to reach the spending power issue in that case.

Why is it plausible that Rehnquist would not have applied the *Dole* doctrine in *Guillen* as I applied it above? My larger thesis is that Rehnquist's inquiry would in fact, if implicitly, have focused on whether the core regulatory activity at issue was a "traditional" and appropriate area of federal rather than state regulatory concern.

To see how this (undertheorized and incompletely articulated) inquiry may have been deployed in the past, consider the dissenting opinion in *Davis.*[69] The question presented, recall, was whether a private damages action may lie against a school board under Title IX in cases of student-on-student harassment. In a dissent authored by Justice Kennedy, Rehnquist, Scalia, and Thomas would have held the challenged provision to be invalid. Although their explicit contention was that the challenged condition on federal funds did not pass muster under the "clear notice" prong of the *Dole* test, the core of these Justices' concern was that the statute, ultimately, was about the federal regulation of local schools. Consider the following excerpt from that dissent:

> . . . The Nation's schoolchildren will learn their first lessons about federalism in classrooms where the Federal Government is the ever-present regulator. The Federal Government will have insinuated itself not only into one of the most traditional areas of state concern but also into one of the most sensitive areas of human affairs.

---

[62] 514 U.S. 549 (1995).
[64] 483 U.S. 203 (1987).
[66] 125 S. Ct. 1497 (2005).
[68] 526 U.S. at 654 (Kennedy, J., dissenting).

[63] 529 U.S. 598 (2000).
[65] 526 U.S. 629 (1999).
[67] *Lopez,* 514 U.S. at 564.
[69] *Id.*

This federal control of the discipline of our Nation's schoolchildren is contrary to our traditions and inconsistent with the sensible administration of our schools. . . .

The majority opinion, authored by Justice O'Connor, in contrast, portrays the case as being about certain antidiscrimination regulations contained in Title IX. And such regulations, at least since the Civil War, generally have been considered to be an appropriate area of federal concern. If Rehnquist had shared her view that the case was "about" a traditional area of state concern, my thesis predicts that he also would have shared O'Connor's view that the challenged condition on federal funds passed muster under *Dole*.

Similarly, consider the 2005 case of *Jackson v. Birmingham Board of Education*.[70] The question before the Court was whether the acknowledged private right of action for sex discrimination under Title IX extends to claims of retaliation. Justice O'Connor, again writing for the majority, held that Title IX does encompass such claims "where the funding recipient retaliates against an individual because he has complained about sex discrimination." Justice Thomas, writing for the dissenters including Chief Justice Rehnquist, in contrast, contended that a "claim of retaliation is not a claim of discrimination on the basis of sex." Thus, for the dissenters the case was not about sex discrimination nor, therefore, was it about an appropriate area of federal concern. Predictably, they went on to find that an implied right of action under Title IX for retaliation claims would violate *Dole*'s clear notice requirement, while the majority held that Title IX "supplied sufficient notice to the Board that it could not retaliate against Jackson after he complained of discrimination against the girls' basketball team."

Now reconsider *Guillen*.[71] The text of the opinion makes clear that the unanimous court in that case considered the statutory provision at issue to be about the regulation of highway safety. Although the challenged provision itself was a regulation of the rules of evidence to be applied in state court proceedings involving causes of action brought under state law, the regulation was indeed limited to evidence related to highway safety. Highways are generally considered to be a regulatory area of traditional and appropriate federal concern. It would therefore be consistent with my thesis for Rehnquist to have concluded that the challenged provision did not exceed Congress's spending power.

If my thesis is persuasive thus far, the question remains of why Rehnquist and the Court did not simply decide *Guillen* on spending power grounds rather than on the basis of a seemingly distorted Commerce Clause analysis. One possibility is that Rehnquist did not consider the Commerce Clause analysis in *Guillen* to be any significant distortion of existing precedent.

Recall that Thomas wrote for the Court in *Guillen* that *Lopez* interpreted the Commerce Clause to permit Congress "to regulate and protect the instrumentalities of interstate commerce . . . even though the threat may come only from

---

[70] 125 S. Ct. 1497 (2005).
[71] 537 U.S. 129 (2003).

intrastate activities." And the Court explicitly interpreted the regulation at issue in *Guillen* to be "aimed at . . . increasing protection for the instrumentalities of interstate commerce." Thus, perhaps *Guillen was* an easy case under the Commerce Clause?

The problem, however, is that neither *Lopez* nor the precedents upon which it relies remotely establish that Congress is authorized under the Commerce Clause to regulate just *anything* – including state court judicial proceedings – so long as it is "aimed at" protecting the instrumentalities of interstate commerce. Why did Rehnquist in *Guillen* apparently ignore this distinction?

One plausible answer, I believe, has at its core an appreciation that Rehnquist's Commerce Clause jurisprudence, like his spending power jurisprudence, is driven by a (sometimes) unstated inquiry into whether the congressional enactment seeks to regulate an area "where States historically have been sovereign,"[72] or whether it instead involves an appropriate and traditional federal function.

In support of this thesis one might recall that subjects of traditional state regulation was an unambiguous focus of Rehnquist's opinions for the majority in both *Lopez* and *Morrison*. In both cases, Rehnquist was explicit that federal power should not extend to "areas such as criminal law enforcement or education where States historically have been sovereign."[73] And in each case Rehnquist, writing for the majority, held that Congress had exceeded its power under the Commerce Clause because it deemed the regulatory area at issue in fact to be one of traditional state concern. The Gun-Free School Zones Act at issue in *Lopez* was quite reasonably understood by the majority to involve both criminal law enforcement and education, two of the areas in which it contended that states historically had been sovereign. And in *Morrison*, which involved the civil remedy provision of the Violence Against Women Act, Rehnquist, writing for the majority, observed:

> . . . The Constitution requires a distinction between what is truly national and what is truly local. . . . The regulation and punishment of intrastate violence that is not directed at the instrumentalities, channels, or goods involved in interstate commerce has always been the province of the States. . . . Indeed, we can think of no better example of the police power, which the Founders denied the National Government and reposed in the States, than the suppression of violent crime and vindication of its victims.

In *Guillen*,[74] although the statutory provision regulates state court rules of evidence, it does so only with regard to evidence related to highway safety. Thus, this provision, and the sense in which the case is "about" an appropriate federal function (i.e., the regulation of highway safety), seems markedly different from a hypothetical analogous statutory provision that might regulate state court rules of evidence more broadly (i.e., in areas including, but not limited to, highway

---

[72] *Lopez*, 514 U.S. at 564.
[73] *Id.; Morrison*, 529 U.S. at 613.
[74] 537 U.S. 129 (2003).

safety). Once *Guillen* is understood in this way, its Commerce Clause analysis seems quite consistent with the above conception of both *Lopez* and *Morrison* in which the notion of "areas in which States historically have been sovereign" serves as a pivotal, if incompletely theorized, decisional principle.

Further, once *Guillen* is understood in this way, there seems to be no reason for the Court instead to decide the case on spending power grounds. The Commerce Clause analysis was seemingly simple and straightforward. A Spending Clause analysis, in contrast, would inevitably be lengthier and potentially more complex, while posing awkward questions under *Dole*'s "clear notice" prong.

VII. REHNQUIST'S LEGACY FOR THE SPENDING POWER (AND FEDERALISM)

If there is merit to the above analysis, there is also a certain irony. The inquiry into notions of "traditional" and "appropriate" areas of state and federal regulatory concern, after all, is precisely the sort of inquiry that a majority of the Court in 1985 in *Garcia*[75] declared a failure, and that Chief Justice Rehnquist in dissent promised would "in time again command the support of a majority of this Court."

Future spending power (and Commerce Clause) decisions will reveal the extent to which the very preliminary positive theory that I have sketched here accurately portrays Rehnquist's legacy in this area. No less important, future decisions will also tell us whether Rehnquist's apparent second attempt at a *National League of Cities*[76] type of doctrine is in any significant way an improvement on the first.

[75] 469 U.S. 532 (1985).
[76] 426 U.S. 833 (1976).

CHAPTER ELEVEN

THE INDEPENDENT COUNSEL CASE: A TALE OF TWO CONSERVATIVES

Daniel A. Farber

I. INTRODUCTION

Chief Justice Rehnquist may be most remembered for his impact on the law in the areas of federalism and individual rights. Yet he also authored one of the most important separation of powers decisions of the twentieth century, *Morrison v. Olson*.[1] In that case, a nearly unanimous Supreme Court upheld the constitutionality of the Independent Counsel statute, confirming in broad terms the ability of Congress to control the appointment and removal of Executive Branch officials.

In retrospect, the case is particularly interesting because the lone dissenter was Justice Antonin Scalia. In an era when judicial positions were often thought to be dictated by ideology, *Morrison* reveals a deep jurisprudential gulf between two Justices who were generally classified with the conservative wing of the Court. Thus, *Morrison* warns against overly simplistic categorization of the Justices, while also demonstrating some of the cleavages within conservative constitutional thinking.

Although in sympathy on many issues, Scalia and Rehnquist subscribed to different visions of the separation of powers. Debates over separation of powers are dominated by two camps: *functionalists* who think that the structure of government should be flexible, and *formalists* who demand rigid demarcations among the three branches of government. Rehnquist and Scalia belonged to different camps on this issue. Scalia was (and still is) a fervent formalist. Rehnquist was a committed functionalist, not only in *Morrison* but in his other important ruling on the separation of powers, the Iranian Hostages case.[2] In this, Rehnquist may have been influenced by his clerkship for Justice Robert H. Jackson, who is quot-

---

[1] 487 U.S. 654 (1988).

[2] Dames & Moore v. Regan, 453 U.S. 654 (1981). On the formalist and functionalist approaches to separation of powers, see Gary Lawson, *The Rise and Rise of the Administrative State,* 107 Harv. L. Rev. 1231 (1994); Gerhardt Casper, *An Essay in Separation of Powers: Some Early Versions and Practices,* 30 Wm. & Mary L. Rev. 211 (1989); Peter Strauss, *Formal and Functional Approaches to Separation of Powers Questions – A Foolish Inconsistency?,* 72 Cornell L. Rev. 488 (1987).

ed in both opinions. Regardless of his motivations, however, Rehnquist's opinion in *Morrison* was among the greatest victories for the functionalists in the past century. Functionalists favor a flexible view of separation of powers, placing a lot of emphasis on checks and balances, whereas formalists want sharp boundaries between the powers of the President and Congress.

To understand what was at stake in *Morrison*, we must begin with some background on the Independent Counsel statute and the *Morrison* litigation. A careful analysis of Rehnquist's and Scalia's opinions is then in order. The context of *Morrison* includes not only the past of the Independent Counsel statute but what was to turn out to be its future: the Starr investigation and Clinton impeachment, followed by Congress's abandonment of the statute. We close by asking whether the verdict of history favors Rehnquist's or Scalia's view of the Office of Independent Counsel.

II. BACKGROUND

Morrison was about the use of independent counsels (or "ICs" for short). This issue cannot be understood outside its historical context or without an understanding of the terms of the Independent Counsel statute. We begin, then, with some background.

A. Precursors to the Independent Counsel Statute

Throughout the twentieth century, the use of independent prosecutors was associated with periods of political scandal. During the Teapot Dome scandal, Congress appropriated funds for a special counsel, to be appointed with the advice and consent of the Senate. A special prosecutor was appointed, with subsequent appointment of a future Supreme Court Justice (Owen Roberts) as his assistant. The upshot was a series of prosecutions of high-level government officials.[3]

Almost three decades later, a special prosecutor was appointed to investigate corruption during the Truman administration. The Attorney General almost immediately fired the special prosecutor when he requested access to the Attorney General's files and diary; in turn, President Truman immediately fired the Attorney General. Various government officials were later indicted and convicted after the Eisenhower administration continued the investigation.

By far the most important use of a special prosecutor, however, took place during the Nixon administration in connection with the Watergate scandal. The Watergate scandal had begun on June 17, 1972, with a break-in at Democratic National Headquarters by agents of CREEP (the Campaign to Re-Elect the President). As congressional investigations continued, former White House Counsel John Dean implicated President Nixon in a cover-up. After one Attorney General

---

[3] The information in this paragraph and the following two is drawn from *In re* Olson, 818 F.2d 34, 39–41 (D.C. Cir. 1987).

voluntarily resigned on the basis of his conflict of interest, his successor established a special prosecutor's office, and Nixon appointed Archibald Cox, an eminent Harvard law professor, to the position. In March 1974 a grand jury indicted seven defendants, including a former Attorney General (John Mitchell) and
key White House staff. The President himself was named as an unindicted co-
conspirator.

When Cox refused to back off from demands that Nixon turn over incriminating tapes of White House conversations, Nixon ordered Attorney General Elliott
Richardson to fire him. Richardson refused to do so and resigned, as did the Deputy Attorney General, William Ruckelshaus. Finally, Solicitor General Robert H.
Bork fired Cox. Within a few days, however, Nixon announced that a new special
prosecutor would be named. The President continued to argue that executive
privilege should apply to the tapes, making them immune from subpoena.

The dispute about the tapes reached the Supreme Court in *United States v.
Nixon*.[4] The case is best known for its holding that the President did indeed have
to turn over the tapes, a ruling that led inexorably to his resignation shortly thereafter. But in order to reach the merits of the dispute, the Court first had to determine that it had a genuine case in front of it. The President claimed that he had
the right to remove the special prosecutor at any time, making the special prosecutor his agent. Hence, he argued, there was no real case because one of the
parties to the litigation was actually under the control of the other. The Court
rejected this argument on the ground that a federal regulation prevented the dismissal of the prosecutor without charge; this regulation might be withdrawn by
the President, but so long as it was in effect, the special prosecutor had a separate
legal existence and was not simply a subordinate of the President. Reliance on the
regulation seemed a little contrived, although the Court's ruling can be defended
on the realistic ground that the litigation before it was as genuine and adversarial
as any it would ever see. In any event, along with the firing of Cox, the Court's
ruling confirmed the importance of protecting special prosecutors from removal
by the President. It also helped confirm the legitimacy of the office as a safeguard
against government officials who were corrupt or otherwise running amok.

B. The Independent Counsel Statute

The Independent Counsel statute was one of the legacies of Watergate. It was part
of the Ethics in Government Act, first passed in 1978 and subsequently amended. The statute defined a limited category of targets for investigation by the IC,
primarily consisting of cabinet-level officials and high-ranking members of the
White House staff. When the Attorney General received credible allegations about
illegality by these individuals, he was given ninety days to determine whether
there are "reasonable grounds to believe that further investigation or prosecution
is warranted." The Attorney General would then report on this investigation to

[4] 418 U.S. 683 (1974).

a court called the Special Division (consisting of three federal judges appointed by the Chief Justice). If the Attorney General did find grounds for further investigation, the Special Division would appoint an independent counsel. The Special Division would also define the IC's "prosecutorial jurisdiction."[5]

Within the limits of that jurisdiction, the IC exercised the full powers of the Justice Department. This included supervising grand jury proceedings, conducting investigations, and trying cases. Although the IC was free from any direct supervision by the Justice Department, the statute required the IC "except where not possible" to "comply with the written or other established policies of the Department of Justice respecting enforcement of the criminal laws." Moreover, under some circumstances, the IC could be removed by the Attorney General:

> An independent counsel . . . may be removed from office, other than by impeachment and conviction, only by the personal action of the Attorney General and only for good cause, physical disability, mental incapacity, or any other condition that substantially impairs the performance of such independent counsel's duties.

Finally, the IC was required to inform the House of Representatives of "substantial and credible information . . . that may constitute grounds for an impeachment." This provision took on historic importance years after *Morrison,* when Kenneth Starr reported to the House on possible grounds for impeaching President Clinton in connection with the Monica Lewinsky matter.

Before turning to the constitutional issues, it is well to observe that this scheme contrasts starkly with the usual arrangements for federal law enforcement. Most law enforcement is in the hands of U.S. Attorneys with jurisdiction over specific localities. U.S. Attorneys are appointed by the President and serve at his (or her) will. These U.S. Attorneys are also subject to some degree of oversight by the Department of Justice in Washington; that department reports to the Attorney General, who in turns reports to the President. Thus, unlike the IC, these prosecutors and their staffs are anything but legally "independent" from the President, though how much practical presidential control exists is variable. It's not surprising that believers in the need for a strong presidency found the IC statute constitutionally suspect because of its dramatic restriction of presidential authority over prosecutors.

III. THE CONSTITUTIONAL BASES FOR PRESIDENTIAL AUTHORITY

The debate in *Morrison* involved the meaning and boundaries of executive power. To understand that debate, we must begin with an examination of the text of the Constitution.

Article II of the Constitution is devoted to the presidency. It begins by saying that the "executive Power" is vested in the President, but it does not define that term. Almost half of Article II is devoted to the mechanics of the office: election

[5] These provisions were contained in 18 U.S.C. §§591–99, first enacted as P.L. 95-521.

procedures, qualifications for office, salary, and so forth. The first section of Article II ends with the oath of office, calling upon the President to "preserve, protect and defend the Constitution of the United States." The next two sections of Article II combined are about half as long and contain a laundry list of presidential powers, most notably the commander-in-chief power and the duty to "take Care that the laws be faithfully executed." Also listed are the power to make treaties and appoint key officials (with Senate approval), to issue pardons, to give the State of the Union address, to receive ambassadors, and to demand the opinions of cabinet officers in writing. Lest these powers be unchecked, Article II closes with a section establishing procedures for impeachment. That's about it: You could read the whole of Article II aloud in about two minutes.

How did the Framers envision the presidency? Robert H. Jackson, one of the great Supreme Court Justices of the mid-twentieth century and a former Attorney General under FDR, once summarized the historical record as follows: "Just what our forefathers did envision, or would have envisioned had they foreseen modern conditions, must be divined from materials almost as enigmatic as the dreams Joseph was called upon to interpret for Pharaoh." Justice Jackson added that "a century and a half" – now over two centuries – "of partisan debate and scholarly speculation yields no net result but only supplies more or less apt quotations from respected sources on each side of any question."[6]

The Framers may have known that they had left these questions less than wholly resolved. Indeed, in *Federalist* 39, Madison himself had said that "[e]xperience has instructed us that no skill in the science of government has yet been able to discriminate and define, with sufficient certainty, its three great provinces – the legislative, executive, and judiciary." Instead, Madison said, these boundary lines would have to be fixed over time, in the practical operation of the government.

Whatever else may be said about the meaning of Article II, it has not suffered from a lack of vigorous debate. One key question has been the significance of the clause vesting the executive power in the President. Is this Vesting Clause merely descriptive, or is it an independent source of presidential authority, and if so, of how much? Advocates of the "unitary executive" (i.e., the concentration of all executive power in the hands of the President) believe that the Vesting Clause is a source of power – indeed, the primary source of presidential power. They also contend that independent administrative agencies and special prosecutors are unconstitutional efforts to remove parts of that power from the President, and that the President has sweeping authority independent of Congress. According to the more enthusiastic advocates of the unitary executive, "the textual case" for their theory "is as free of ambiguity as the textual case that the President must be at least thirty-five years old."[7] In the contemporary setting, the "unitary executive" is the foremost example of the formalist approach to separation of powers.

---

[6] Youngstown Sheet and Tube Co. v. Sawyer (The Steel Seizure Case), 343 U.S. 579, 634–35 (1952).
[7] Steven G. Calabresi & Saikrishna B. Prakash, *The President's Power to Execute the Laws*, 104 Yale L.J. 541, 559, 578 (1994).

The central implication of this theory is that the President needs absolute control over all administrative activities. The theory also lends itself to the view that the President's authority is encompassed within a sweeping conception of the "executive power" with which he or she is vested. It is easier to argue that a power is of the kind traditionally exercised by the British Crown (and hence "executive") than to tie it to the small list of more specific powers in Article II.

This theory has not gone unchallenged. Critics retort that there was no well-understood bundle of executive powers that could simply be conveyed by the Vesting Clause. They also insist that the subtle differences of phrasing between the Vesting Clauses for the various branches simply escaped any notice at the time. What the evidence does *not* allow, says one critic, "is an assertion that the cryptic phrase 'executive power' refers to a clear, eighteenth-century baseline that just happens to dovetail with the modern formalist conception of that same term."[8]

Enough has been said here to give the flavor of this debate, though not a full sense of its intricacies. Clearly, the constitutional issues regarding the IC would be approached quite differently by formalist advocates of the unitary executive and their functionalist opponents. For advocates of the unitary executive, the question in *Morrison* was whether the President could be deprived of full control of a core executive function. Their theory of executive power dictates a negative answer to this question. For those with more functionalist understandings of executive power, the analysis was necessarily more complicated, but the Watergate experience strongly indicated the need for independent counsels to maintain governmental integrity. Much of the argument involved details of constitutional text, original understanding, and often obscure Supreme Court precedents (many a century old or more). But judges' reading of these materials would inevitably be highly colored by their overall approach to executive power.

IV. THE *MORRISON* RULING

The Supreme Court's ruling in *Morrison* was the culmination of extensive litigation in the lower courts. We begin with a look at the background of the case, before turning to a detailed analysis of Chief Justice Rehnquist's opinion and Justice Scalia's impassioned dissent. The conflict between executive "unitarians" and functionalists was a major theme throughout the litigation, from the court of appeals through the Supreme Court.

---

[8] Flaherty, *Most Dangerous Branch*, 105 Yale L.J. *1725, 1790* (1996) ("no such generally understood bundle existed"), 1792 ("cryptic phrase"); Calabresi & Prakash, *supra* note 7, at 629 ("meaningless"); Lawrence Lessig & Cass Sunstein, *The President and the Administration,* 94 Colum. L. Rev. 1 (1994) (distinguishing between Executive departments and other administrators); A. Michael Froomkin, *Still Naked After All These Words,* 88 Nw. U. L. Rev. 1420 (1994) (critiquing Calabresi's views).

A. The Dispute

The *Morrison* case had its origins in a controversy over, of all things, hazardous waste cleanup. In 1982, as part of an investigation of charges that the Reagan administration was shortchanging environmental enforcement, two House subcommittees requested the Environmental Protection Agency (EPA) to provide internal documents relating to cleanup efforts. The two subcommittees ultimately issued subpoenas for the documents. After considerable fussing and some litigation, a deal was finally worked out regarding the documents. As a spinoff from that dispute, a subcommittee opened an investigation of the Justice Department's role in the dispute. At the hearings, the committee heard testimony from Assistant Attorney General Theodore Olson. The subcommittee found evidence of serious wrongdoing and concluded that Olson had been involved in misleading Congress. The subcommittee asked the Attorney General to request an independent prosecutor.[9]

After a preliminary investigation, the Attorney General requested the appointment of an independent prosecutor for Olson but not for two other Justice Department figures whom the subcommittee had named. Specifically, the Attorney General asked for independent counsel to investigate whether Olson's testimony regarding the document delivery issue violated any criminal laws. The request specifically named two criminal statutes, one dealing with obstruction of congressional investigations and the other prohibiting false statements on any matter within the jurisdiction of a government agency.[10] The ultimate choice as IC was Alexia Morrison.

Olson vigorously attacked the constitutionality of the Independent Counsel statute. His first two efforts were unsuccessful. He first attacked the statute before the Special Division, the D.C. Circuit panel of senior judges charged with appointing independent counsels. Although the panel contained at least one fairly conservative judge, George MacKinnon, the Special Division unanimously rejected the constitutional claim.[11]

Olson's next attempt was before the district court judge in charge of his case. Here, too, he was unsuccessful. The district judge was quite unimpressed with the argument that the Independent Counsel statute violated the separation of powers. Instead, he stressed that "[t]he Supreme Court has admonished the lower courts that, in matters involving the separation of powers, a pragmatic, flexible approach must control, and that separation of powers questions must be resolved 'according to common sense and the inherent necessities of the governmental coordination.'"[12] In these first two opinions, functionalism reigned.

---

[9] *In re* Sealed Case, 838 F.2d 476, 478 (D.C. Cir. 1988).

[10] *In re* Theodore Olsen, 818 F.2d 34, 37 (D.C. Cir. 1097) (charges against Olson); *In re* Sealed Case, 838 F.2d at 7–8 (appointment of independent counsel).

[11] *In re* Theodore Olson, 818 F.2d 34 (D.C. Cir. 1987).

[12] *In re* Sealed Case, 665 F. Supp. 56, 60 (D.D.C. 1987).

Olson's third effort, this time before the D.C. Circuit's active judges, was more successful. The majority opinion by Judge Silberman (joined by Judge Williams) established the framework for the arguments later made before the Supreme Court. Silberman's lengthy opinion discussed three major issues: (1) whether the method for appointing the IC was constitutional; (2) whether the method for removal of an errant IC was constitutional; and (3) whether the statute as a whole was consistent with the separation of powers. His answer to all three questions was a resounding "no."

To understand the challenge to the IC's appointment, we need to return to Article II of the Constitution. The Appointments Clause of Article II, section 2, provides that the President

> shall nominate, and by and with the Advice and Consent of the Senate, shall appoint Ambassadors, other public Ministers and Consuls, Judges of the Supreme Court, and all other Officers of the United States whose Appointments are not herein otherwise provided for, and which shall be established by Law; but the Congress may by Law invest the Appointment of such inferior Officers, as they think proper, in the President alone, in the Courts of Law, or in the Heads of Departments.

The IC was not appointed by the President but rather by federal judges. The question, then, was the scope of Congress's power to assign the appointments power to "the Courts of Law." At this point, the arguments become convoluted and technical. There were two main subissues. The first was whether the IC was an "inferior officer" whose appointment Congress could invest elsewhere than with the President. The second was whether, assuming the IC was an inferior officer, Congress's power to control the appointment of inferior officers was limited to reassigning the appointing authority to someone within the same branch as the position to be filled, or whether Congress could cross the lines between two different branches of government. That is, as here, could Congress designate the courts of law to appoint an executive officer?

Judge Silberman's answers were that the IC was emphatically not an "inferior officer," and that in any event, Congress could only redirect the power of appointing executive officers within the Executive Branch itself, not to the judiciary. Judge Silberman considered the IC too free of supervision to be considered an inferior officer, and in any case thought that "[i]t strains belief that . . . the Framers would insert a clause into the Constitution that would allow Congress, the branch most feared by the Framers, to abrogate the President's power to appoint Executive Branch officers."[13]

Judge Silberman was equally staunch in his holding on removal of the IC. The Constitution actually says nothing about presidential power to remove subordinates. As we will see later, the Supreme Court had previously constructed a constitutional right of presidential removal in a series of somewhat unsteady rulings.

---

[13] *In re* Sealed Case, 838 F.2d at 482.

Judge Silberman was relatively untroubled by the niceties of this doctrinal evolution: "the Act further trenches on the concept of a unitary executive and departs
from separation of powers doctrine by substantially limiting the President's ability to remove or supervise the independent counsel."

As to the overall separation of powers issue, Judge Silberman's view was sim-
plicity itself: "The constitutional scheme is as simple as it is complete – Congress
passes the criminal law in the first instance, the President enforces the law, and
individual cases are tried before a neutral judiciary involved in neither the creation nor the execution of that law." Indeed, the "Framers provided for a unitary
executive to ensure that the branch wielding the power to enforce the law would
be accountable to the people."[14] So the unconstitutionality of the IC was patent.

Indeed, for a staunch believer in the unitary executive, it is hard to see how the
case could come out any other way. If criminal enforcement is not "executing the
law," and therefore part of the "executive power," then what is? And if it is within
the executive power, then the unitary executive theory means that only people
appointed by and accountable to the President can exercise that power. So, *obviously* the President had to be able to appoint and remove all federal prosecutors.

Notably, there was a lengthy dissent from Judge Ruth Bader Ginsburg, herself
later to be appointed to the Supreme Court. Her dissent stressed the extent to
which the IC remained subject to executive authority:

> The Ethics Act effects only a limited incursion into executive territory. The Attorney
> General makes two important decisions at the outset: whether there is sufficient
> information to conduct a preliminary investigation and, after undertaking such an
> investigation, whether there are reasonable grounds to believe further investigation
> or prosecution warranted. The Attorney General alone has the power to remove an
> independent counsel, albeit he must have cause to do so. Most significantly, the At-
> torney General's application for independent counsel sets boundaries for the assign-
> ment given to independent counsel. In short, the Attorney General exercises very
> significant authority at the crucial junctures in the process of establishing an office
> of independent counsel.

All in all, Ginsburg said, the statute is a "carefully considered congressional jour-
ney into the sometimes arcane realm of the separation of powers doctrine.
. . . It is a measure faithful to the eighteenth century blueprint, yet fitting for our
time."

Inevitably, the case then went to the Supreme Court. In oral argument, Independent Counsel Morrison stressed the broad discretion of the Attorney General in connection with the IC. For example, regarding the decision to appoint
an IC, she said that the "statute leaves the matter entirely within his discretion."
She also maintained that the IC must follow Justice Department policies except
in very narrow situations, such as when the DOJ policies "require specific reporting up a particular chain of command of events . . . that is clearly committed to
the discretion of the independent counsel under the statute." She also told the

[14] *Id.* at 488.

Court that in the "majority of investigations to date," the result had been to clear the name of the individual.

In contrast, the Solicitor General portrayed the statute as stripping the President of a "purely Executive function" and placing that function "in one almost wholly untethered to the President." He also warned of the dangers of vesting executive appointments in the judiciary: "[T]he appropriate thing to do is simply to recognize and to maintain the integrity of each of the branches, and not countenance a system which would allow the Executive Branch to be shattered into a thousand small offices, each of whom would be appointed by the courts of law."[15]

B. The Majority Opinion

The opinion of the Court was announced two months after oral argument. Chief Justice Rehnquist's opinion for the Court came down squarely on the side of the independent counsel. His handling of the three major issues requires careful study.[16]

1. Appointment of the IC

The constitutionality of the procedure for appointing the IC had absorbed considerable attention in the D.C. Circuit. The Supreme Court found the issue much more straightforward. Chief Justice Rehnquist began by observing that the "line between 'inferior' and 'principal' officers is one that is far from clear, and the Framers provided little guidance into where it should be drawn." However, the Court found several reasons to conclude that the IC "clearly falls on the 'inferior officer' side of that line." First, the IC was subject to removal by the Attorney General for good cause. Second, the IC had limited duties, which did not include any general power to formulate policy for the Executive Branch. Indeed, the statute specifically required the IC to follow existing government policy where possible. Third, the IC's jurisdiction was limited by the scope of the grant by the Special Division, and lasted only so long as that task is incomplete.

After confirming the consistency of this conclusion with the Court's sparse precedents on the Appointments Clause, the Court turned to the question of whether Congress could place the appointment of even an inferior executive officer outside the Executive Branch. The Court began with the language of the clause, which "[o]n its face . . . admits of no limitation on interbranch appointments." Indeed, "the inclusion of 'as they think proper' seems clearly to give Congress significant discretion to determine whether it is 'proper' to vest the appointment of, for example, executive officials in the 'courts of Law.' Nor did the Court

---

[15] The transcript of oral argument is available at 1988 U.S. Trans Lexis 70 (April 26, 1988).

[16] The opinion also devotes considerable attention to another issue, whether the duties assigned to the Special Division are compatible with Article III. The Court may have had some concern that if it exercised too much discretion or played too active a role, the Special Division might have created an appearance that the judiciary was targeting the president. In any event, the constitutional difficulties were narrow and in my view not very serious.

find basis in the history of the clause for a blanket rule against interbranch appointments.

The Solicitor General had warned at oral argument about the danger of allowing Congress to divide the Executive Branch into small fragments, placing appointive power for each fragment in the judiciary and thereby crippling the presidency. The Court did not believe that it was opening the door to runaway fragmentation. Rather, the Court saw two implied limitations. First, separation of powers concerns would "arise if such provisions for appointment had the potential to impair the constitutional functions assigned to one of the branches." Second, a prior decision had suggested that vesting appointment power in the courts "would be improper if there was some 'incongruity' between the functions normally performed by the courts and the performance of their duty to appoint." But the Court found no such incongruity in having a judge appoint an attorney to exercise prosecutorial functions.

2. Limitations on Removal of the IC

Unlike its fairly brisk discussion of the appointment issue, the Court focused more closely on the question of removal. The debate had been framed by two prior decisions of the Court. One decision by Chief Justice Taft had struck down a statute giving Congress control over the removal of postmasters. The opinion contained some broad language about the President's power to remove executive officers, though the issue before the Court had been narrower (whether Senate permission could be required as a condition of presidential removal). A later decision from the New Deal era had upheld a limitation on the President's power to remove FTC commissioners, reading Taft's opinion narrowly and finding it inapplicable because of the quasi-judicial and quasi-legislative nature of some of the FTC's activities.

The Court might well have interpreted Taft's opinion as creating a general rule of removability by the President, with the FTC case as an exception. Having done so, it would have been only a small step to recognize the IC as another exception because of the compelling need to ensure integrity in government. This would have resulted in a narrow opinion upholding the IC. The Court did not follow that path, however. Instead, it read the Taft opinion narrowly, as holding only that Congress cannot be involved in the removal process. The rest of the Taft opinion was reduced to dictum, which the Court approved only to the extent of saying that there are "some 'purely executive' officials who must be removable by the President at will if he is to be able to accomplish his constitutional role." The FTC case was then recast in broader terms:

> We undoubtedly did rely on the terms "quasi-legislative" and "quasi-judicial" to distinguish the officials involved [in the previous cases], but our present considered view is that the determination of whether the Constitution allows Congress to impose a "good cause" type restriction on the President's power to remove an official cannot be made to turn on whether or not that official is classified as "purely ex-

ecutive." The analysis contained in our removal cases is designed not to define rigid categories of those officials who may or may not be removed at will by the President, but to ensure that Congress does not interfere with the President's exercise of the "executive power" and his constitutionally appointed duty to "take care that the laws be faithfully executed" under Article II.

Thus, rather than characterizing the FTC case as an exception to a rule of removability by the President created by the Taft opinion, the Court flipped the relationship: The Taft opinion was an exception from a general principle that Congress may reasonably restrict the President's removal power. This was a more generous reading of congressional power than the Court might have used to uphold the IC.

The Court squarely rejected the dissent's reading of the Vesting Clause – the core of the unitary executive theory – as requiring that "every officer of the United States exercising any part of that [executive] power must serve at the pleasure of the President and be removable by him at will." This "rigid demarcation," which would be "applicable to tens of thousands of holders of offices neither known nor foreseen by the Framers – depends upon an extrapolation from general constitutional language which we think is more than the text will bear."

Thus, according to Rehnquist, the crucial question was not the executive or mixed nature of an official's function, but "whether the removal restrictions are of such a nature that they impede the President's ability to perform his constitutional duty, and the functions of the officials in question must be analyzed in that light." Considering the functions of the IC, the Court could not "say that the imposition of a 'good cause' standard for removal by itself unduly trammels on executive authority." "Nor," the Court said, "do we think that the 'good cause' removal provision at issue here impermissibly burdens the President's power to control or supervise the independent counsel" as an executive officer. The Attorney General's power to remove the IC for good cause provided "ample authority to assure that the counsel is competently performing his or her statutory responsibilities in a manner that comports with the provisions of the Act."

The primary effect of *Morrison* was to weaken executive office claims by allowing restrictions on presidential removal even for purely executive officers. On the other hand, the Court's balancing test might sometimes work in the President's favor – even if an official is considered quasi-judicial or quasi-legislative in function, a restriction on presidential removal might still conceivably be an undue burden on the President's ability to perform his own executive functions.

3. *The IC and the Separation of Power*
The Court then turned to the broader question of whether the statute "taken as a whole, violates the principle of separation of powers by unduly interfering with the role of the Executive Branch." The Court began by noting that, unlike some previous cases, the case did not involve an effort to vest additional legal powers

in Congress itself, nor could it be considered a judicial usurpation of "properly executive functions," given the very limited powers of the Special Division. Nor did the Court find that the statute undermine the powers of the Executive Branch impermissibly. Here, the Court relied on the Attorney General's power of removal for good cause, the unreviewable discretion of the Attorney General in determining whether to ask for the appointment of an IC, and the general requirement that the IC follow Justice Department policy.

Two things are notable about the Court's general discussion of separation of powers. First, it is quite cursory, as if the Court found little more to say once it had dealt with the more specific challenges to the statute. The general implications of the separation of powers got less attention than the more specific discussion of the removal power. Second, the Court might well have taken a different tack. It could have acknowledged that the IC statute was in some ways an incursion on executive power but then justified the statute because of the lessons of Watergate and the compelling need to ensure governmental integrity. But the opinion as a whole says little about the exceptional justifications for the statute. Instead, it simply fails to find enough of a burden on the Executive Branch to raise constitutional concerns. In contrast, the IC's brief had included a subsection entitled "Any Impact on Executive Branch Powers is Justified by an Overriding Need to Promote an Objective Within the Constitutional Authority of Congress."

The scope of the Court's holding can be seen by considering its potential applications. Nothing in the Court's opinion would prevent Congress from utilizing the IC model in a much broader range of prosecutions where the justification for doing so might be much weaker. Indeed, it could use the model more broadly whenever judicial appointment of an executive officer did not seem "incongruous." Moreover, in terms of the removal power, Congress seems to have broad leeway to limit the President's power to remove officials at will, particularly if those officials were not directly appointed by the President. All of this is resolutely functionalist, and by the same token anathema to true believers in the unitary executive. Though the Court had shown some resistance to accepting the unitary executive in the late Burger Court, *Morrison* was the decisive precedent to reject that approach.

C. The Dissent

Justice Scalia dissented alone. A few examples will provide the flavor of the dissent's rhetoric:

- "Frequently an issue of this sort will come before the Court clad, so to speak, in sheep's clothing. . . . But this wolf comes as a wolf."
- "If to describe this case is not to decide it, the concept of a government of separate and coordinate powers no longer has meaning."
- The majority opinion "effects a revolution in our constitutional jurisprudence."

- "Once we depart from the text of the Constitution, just where short of that [a parliamentary system] do we stop? The most amazing feature of the Court's opinion is that it does not even purport to give an answer."
- "Evidently, the governing standard is to be what might be called the un-fettered wisdom of a majority of this Court, revealed to an obedient people on a case-by-case basis. This is not only not the government of laws that the Constitution established; it is not a government of laws at all."
- "Worse than what it has done, however, is the manner in which it has done it. . . . Today's decision on the basic issue of fragmentation of executive power is ungoverned by rule, and hence ungoverned by law."

Even for a judge who has often displayed a taste for hyperbole, the rhetorical heat of Justice Scalia's opinion seems remarkable. It was even more remarkable given that the target was Chief Justice Rehnquist, who was at that time Scalia's only real ally on the Supreme Court. (Justice Thomas had not yet been appointed.) But Scalia's ire is understandable: He had become closely identified with an aggressive approach to the separation of powers, including hostility to the existence of independent agencies like the FCC and the SEC, whose members cannot be readily removed by the President. *Morrison* was the death knell for his campaign. Moreover, having served in the Executive Branch more recently than any of the other Justices, he may have identified more emotionally with the fear of political abuse of the statute. Finally, he was clearly irate about Rehnquist's judicial methodology, which favored flexible balancing approaches over the kinds of rigid rule in which Scalia delights. In any event, given that it was Rehnquist whom he was accusing of betraying the basic commitments of the U.S. Constitution, the rhetoric was less than persuasive.

Despite their ideological affinities, *Morrison* reveals two deep fissures between Scalia and Rehnquist. As a number of the quotes indicate, Justice Scalia was especially unhappy that Rehnquist had failed to provide a bright-line rule governing executive power. Chief Justice Rehnquist seemed quite comfortable, however, with legal tests based on such elastic concepts as "incongruity" and "impermissible burden." This basic difference in jurisprudential perspectives separated Rehnquist from a younger generation of conservatives such as Scalia and Judge Frank Easterbrook of the U.S. Court of Appeals for the Seventh Circuit. It was this second group of conservatives who, in turn, were the fundamental influences on the lawyers who developed the Justice Department's constitutional views under the two Bush administrations; these lawyers never regarded Rehnquist as their jurisprudential model.

The second fissure relates to the unitary executive theory. Rehnquist's opinion for the Court is a direct repudiation of that theory. But for Scalia, it was central to the architecture of the Constitution. Indeed, it was confirmed not only by the constitutional text but by every source of political wisdom. Under the majority's approach, he said in his closing passage, the "law is, by definition, precisely what the majority thinks, taking all things into account, it *ought* to be." But Scalia modestly preferred to rely on higher sources of guidance: "I prefer to rely upon the judgment of the wise men who constructed our system, and of the people who approved it, and of two centuries of history that have shown it to be sound. Like it or not, that judgment says, quite plainly, that '[t]he executive Power shall be vested in a President of the United States.'" And, lest there be any doubt on that score, Scalia had already made it plain earlier that when the Constitution vests the executive power in the President, "this does not mean *some of* the executive power, but *all of* the executive power."

V. DID HISTORY PROVE REHNQUIST WRONG?

Rehnquist's approach can be called pragmatic while Scalia's might be considered formalist, but in some sense Scalia was also making a pragmatic argument. (And by the same token, Rehnquist could be seen as making formalist one, since his interpretation seemed to cleave more closely to the constitutional text – this is an illustration of how labels like "pragmatist" and "formalist" can be slippery.) Scalia contended that application of the IC statute would inevitably be political, that the statute would be a tool for political opponents of the President in Congress, and that the "context of this statute is acrid with the smell of threatened impeachment." The Starr investigation into Bill Clinton and the ensuing impeachment effort made these remarks seem prescient to some, and these events may be seen as calling into question the soundness of Rehnquist's opinion upholding the IC statute.

Indeed, similar concerns led Congress to repudiate the IC statute. In congressional hearings in 1999, a series of distinguished witnesses called the statute a complete disaster. Attorney General Janet Reno testified that the statute was "structurally flawed and that those flaws cannot be corrected within our constitutional framework." In a rare moment of solidarity with the Clinton administration, Ken Starr also denounced the statute. By general consensus, the statute was allowed to die.[17]

Despite this consensus, it may be hasty to conclude that the whole concept of independent counsel was wrong. We might yet have another Watergate-type crisis in which we will deeply rue the lack of an Independent Counsel statute. It is also possible that the statute could have been mended rather than eliminated. Assume, however, that the critics were right about the wisdom of the statute: What are the implications of this adverse judgment about the statute for the validity of Rehnquist's constitutional analysis?

A simple answer – a bit too simple – is that Rehnquist never said the statute was *wise*, he only said that it was *constitutional*. Rehnquist might well have writ-

---

[17] Ken Gormley, *Monica Lewinsky, Impeachment, and the Death of the Independent Counsel Law: What Congress Can Salvage from the Wreckage – A Minimalist View*, 60 Md. L. Rev. 97 (2001).

ten a much more vulnerable opinion – one upholding the statute on the basis of the compelling need to provide an independent counsel to maintain government integrity. If he had done so, and if the statute in fact caused much more harm than good, the foundation of his analysis would have crumbled. But the actual opinion carefully steers away from endorsing the benefits of the statute; perhaps Rehnquist himself had his doubts on that score. So if the statute turned out to be a mistake, Rehnquist's argument nowhere assumed otherwise.

Still, later developments do raise three questions about the analysis in *Morrison*. First, the opinion largely accepts the Independent Counsel's claims about the limitations of the office in terms of the Attorney General's discretion and the controlling effect of Justice Department policies. A careful examination of the Starr investigation might raise some doubts about the strength of these legal restraints, on which the *Morrison* Court had relied in concluding that the IC was an inferior officer. Perhaps, as the statute was ultimately construed in the Clinton era, the IC was too much of a free agent to be considered an inferior officer. Yet the problem may not have been with the IC law as such, but with the behavior of the particular individuals involved in the Clinton investigation. Perhaps the Court's understanding of the law was correct and either Starr misunderstood the limits on his decisions or Reno failed to make effective use of her powers. A close look at the history of the Starr investigation, however, is beyond the scope of this chapter.

Second, in determining that the statute did not as a whole offend the separation of powers, Rehnquist may have focused too much on limitations of presidential prerogatives and not enough on the ability of IC investigations to undermine the President politically. As in *Clinton v. Jones*,[18] where a similar argument was made unsuccessfully, the claim would be that the statute impaired the President's effectiveness rather than invading specific executive prerogatives. It is not at all clear, however, that the ability of a statute to result in political embarrassment to the President should count as a decisive argument against its constitutionality.

Third, these later events might cause one to question Rehnquist's general approach. The opinion assumes that the courts are in a position to make accurate judgments about sensitive issues: the extent of practical independence enjoyed by a particular officer, such as the IC, and about the likelihood of impairing the operation of the Executive Branch. The Court's judgment on these matters in *Morrison* may have been flawed, at least in hindsight. This might argue in favor of a more categorical approach to these issues, of the kind proposed by Scalia. Yet Scalia's approach carries a heavy price in limiting the flexibility of Congress to deal with evolving problems in government, and in potentially making the President too autocratic a figure in the operation of government.

---

[18] 520 U.S. 681 (1997). *Clinton v. Jones* held that a sitting president is subject to civil litigation on allegations of private misconduct.

Indeed, later events can be seen as casting just as much doubt on Scalia's approach as on Rehnquist's. Scalia's opinion is permeated by distrust of Congress. For example, consider the following passage from his dissent:

> If the removal of a prosecutor, the virtual embodiment of the power to "take care that the laws be faithfully executed," can be restricted, what officer's removal cannot? This is an open invitation for Congress to experiment. What about a special Assistant Secretary of State, with responsibility for one very narrow area of foreign policy [who could] be removed only pursuant to certain carefully designed restrictions? ... Or a special Assistant Secretary of Defense for Procurement? The possibilities are endless, and the Court does not understand what the separation of powers, what "[a]mbition ... counter[ing] ambition," is all about, if it does not expect Congress to try them.

Yet, far from using the IC statute as a model for other laws, Congress eventually concluded that the statute was a bad idea and eliminated the IC. Scalia's opinion may have been prescient on some questions, but its confident prediction of future congressional overreaching proved utterly unfounded. Congress apparently saw no reason to insulate other officials from presidential control, when those officials were performing traditional Executive Branch functions with no countervailing need for the kind of independence from the President that occasioned the need for a special prosecutor.

As Rehnquist's opinion pointed out, the IC statute did not involve any transfer of authority from the Executive Branch to Congress. Congress had no authority over the IC or his or her appointment. The current view, at least, is that the IC statute was a failed experiment. But to experiment is always to risk failure. When Congress has provided innovative structures for other branches without attempting to provide its own members with additional legal powers or tampering with the specific lawmaking procedures provided by Article I, should it have the power to undertake this kind of experiment?[19]

The ultimate issue is whether Congress can be entrusted with the power to engage in such experiments. At least when its own powers are not directly at issue and the language of the Constitution is not directly thwarted, should Congress have leeway to try modifications of government structure in response to what it considers pressing needs? Rehnquist was willing to trust Congress with the power to engage in such experiments within limits. Scalia was sure that such power would be abused. On this particular issue, the verdict of history seems to be in Rehnquist's favor, for Congress has not been eager to exploit the leeway given by the *Morrison* decision.

[19] For cases involving these exceptions, see Clinton v. City of New York, 524 U.S. 417 (1998) ("line-item veto" statute struck down as violation of detailed lawmaking procedures of Article I); Metropolitan Washington Airports Authority v. Citizens for Abatement of Aircraft Noise, Inc., 501 U.S. 252 (1991) (Congress improperly aggrandized its own powers by requiring that members of Congress be included on an airport commission).

If questions can still be raised about the validity of Rehnquist's analysis in *Morrison*, no one can doubt the historic significance of the ruling. For lawyers, it is a major statement of constitutional doctrine. It definitively halted a trend in prior Burger Court opinions toward an aggressively formalist view of the separation of powers. Those prior opinions had led some observers to believe that a threat to the existence of independent agencies like the SEC could be on the horizon, though the Court had never gone so far as to embrace that view. Since *Morrison*, however, the Court has never shown any sign of challenging the basic structure of the modern administrative state.

But more than that, *Morrison* was a key step in the post-Watergate history of the presidency, a step that helped lead in turn to the impeachment of another President. *Morrison* occupies a pivotal point between the Nixon and Clinton impeachment efforts. The evolution of the presidency in the late twentieth century cannot be understood apart from the Independent Counsel statute and the Court's decision upholding that statute. When the full history of the Rehnquist Court is written, *Morrison* will be one of the key opinions of that era.

CHAPTER TWELVE

THE BATTLE OVER STATE IMMUNITY

William P. Marshall

Chisholm v. Georgia[1] holds a special place in constitutional history. In *Chisholm*, the United States Supreme Court held that states were not entitled to the protections of sovereign immunity – a doctrine providing that sovereign entities could not be sued by individual citizens without their consent. Decided on February 19, 1793, *Chisholm* was the first major opinion issued by the U.S. Supreme Court,[2] and is also notable in that it was the first decision to lead to the passage of a constitutional amendment designed to overturn a Supreme Court decision.[3] Equally important, *Chisholm* was additionally the first salvo in a constitutional battle over state sovereign immunity that has continued throughout American legal history.

Justice Rehnquist was appointed to the Court some one hundred and seventy-eight years after *Chisholm* was decided.[4] Despite his late entry into the fray, however, few would disagree that his contributions to state sovereign immunity doctrine have been enormously significant. He has written the most important state immunity decisions of the past thirty years, and his influence has been apparent even in the cases he did not author. When one also considers that there has been an unprecedented volume of state immunity decisions during his tenure, it becomes no exaggeration to claim that Rehnquist has been the most influential Justice in this field in constitutional history. Certainly no other Justice has framed and guided the law in this area so completely.

The significance of Justice Rehnquist's accomplishments in state immunity jurisprudence is considerable. The state immunity issue is not only the nation's longest-running judicial controversy, it is also, as a substantive matter, one of the

---

[1] 2 U.S. (2 Dall.) 419 (1793).

[2] JOHN V. ORTH, THE JUDICIAL POWER OF THE UNITED STATES: THE ELEVENTH AMENDMENT IN AMERICAN HISTORY 12 (1987).

[3] U.S. Const., amend. XI. Supreme Court decisions have been overturned by constitutional amendment in only three other instances: The Fourteenth Amendment overturned the decision of *Dred Scott v. Sanford*, 60 U.S. 393, 19 How. 393 (1856), the Sixteenth Amendment overturned the decision of *Pollock v. Farmers' Loan & Trust Co.*, 157 U.S. 429 (1895), and the Twenty-sixth Amendment overturned the decision of *Oregon v. Mitchell*, 400 U.S. 112 (1970).

[4] Justice William H. Rehnquist joined the Supreme Court as an Associate Justice in 1972.

most central issues in American constitutional law. Indeed, the reason why the
state immunity debate continues to retain its vibrancy is that the underlying policies on both sides are so fundamental to our constitutional identity. On one side
are the principles that rights create remedies and that, in a democracy, no entities, including the states, should be above the law.[5] On the other are the concerns
for respecting the autonomy and authority of states in a federal system.[6] And
while it may be true that, unlike in the 1790s, state immunity from suit is no
longer thought of as necessary for a state's fiscal survival,[7] the issue's overarching significance remains intact.[8] After all, inherent in the immunity issue are not
only concerns of state identity but also the limits of federal judicial and legislative power.

That Justice Rehnquist has achieved historical preeminence on such a fundamental constitutional issue, moreover, is only half the story. The other half concerns the tactical skill that he used to achieve this dominance. At the time Justice
Rehnquist joined the Court, the Court's commitment to enforcing state immunity doctrine was under siege from a number of doctrinal directions. Justice
Rehnquist, however, took the reigns and reversed course. Writing for a Court
majority in two important cases early in his tenure, *Edelman v. Jordan*[9] and *Fitzpatrick v. Bitzer,*[10] Rehnquist successfully turned back the then-existing challenges
to state immunity while creating an intellectual foundation from which state
immunity could be solidified and expanded in the future. Then, in a later set of
cases, he saw that vision realized. The story of Justice Rehnquist and state immunity is thus the story of how one Justice can forge a body of law in his own image. Whether one agrees with Rehnquist's immunity jurisprudence or not, his
legacy, vision, and skill in this area must be acknowledged and respected.

This chapter focuses on Justice Rehnquist's state immunity jurisprudence.
Part I provides the necessary background, reviewing the development of the law
of state immunity from *Chisholm* to the critical *Edelman v. Jordan* decision. Part
II discusses his landmark opinions in *Edelman* and *Fitzpatrick,* focusing specifically on how these cases effectively turned back the multiple challenges to state
immunity that existed at the time Rehnquist joined the Court. Part III traces the
state immunity decisions after *Edelman* and *Fitzpatrick* and demonstrates how

[5] Marbury v. Madison, 5 U.S. (1 Cranch) 137, 166 (1803); *see* Erwin Chemerinsky, *Against Sovereign Immunity*, 53 STAN. L. REV. 1201 (2001).

[6] Fed. Maritime Comm'n v. S. Carolina Ports Auth., 535 U.S. 743, 1874 (2002) ("[T]he preeminent purpose of [state immunity] is to accord States the dignity that is consistent with their status as sovereign entities.").

[7] As Professor Chemerinsky states, "[t]he consensus among historians is that the States were particularly concerned about the *Chisholm* decision because they feared suits against them to collect unpaid Revolutionary War debts." ERWIN CHEMERINSKY, FEDERAL JURISDICTION 402
(4th ed. 2003). *See also* ORTH, *supra* note 2, at 7–8.

[8] *See* Henry Paul Monaghan, *The Sovereign Immunity "Exception,"* 110 HARV. L. REV. 102, 103, 132
(1996).

[9] 415 U.S. 651 (1974).

[10] 427 U.S. 445 (1976).

those two cases effectively framed the future development of state immunity doctrine. Part IV discusses two possible wrong turns made by Justice Rehnquist in subsequent cases when he joined efforts to expand the scope of immunity outside of his original framework. Part V offers a brief conclusion and assessment.

One early definitional point is in order. The right of a state to be immune from lawsuits brought against it is sometimes referred to in the literature as "sovereign immunity" and at other times referred to as the state's "Eleventh Amendment immunity." Both terms are controversial. The term "sovereign immunity" derives from the common-law principle that a sovereign cannot be sued without its consent.[11] In the American constitutional debate, however, the question of whether state immunity is merely a common-law doctrine or is constitutionally compelled is highly contested.[12] The use of the term "sovereign immunity" is thus problematic because it appears to weigh in on one side of this issue. "Eleventh Amendment immunity," in turn, refers to the constitutional provision enacted in response to *Chisholm* that provides limitations on the susceptibility of states to suit in federal court.[13] Court cases, however, have long suggested that the scope of state immunity is not derived solely from the Eleventh Amendment and is broader than what is explicitly stated in the text.[14] Indeed, one recent case holds that such immunity applies in state courts – despite the fact the Eleventh Amendment speaks only to suits brought in federal court.[15] Characterizing state immunity only as Eleventh Amendment immunity is therefore at best incomplete. This chapter, accordingly, in order to avoid the definitional minefields, will refer to the rights of states to be immune from lawsuits simply as the issue of "state immunity."

I. BACKGROUND

A. *Chisholm* and the Enactment of the Eleventh Amendment

The facts of *Chisholm* itself are simple enough. In *Chisholm*, an executor of a South Carolina estate sued Georgia for monies owed for supplies provided to the state by the decedent during the Revolutionary War. Original jurisdiction was

---

[11] *See* Seminole Tribe of Florida v. Florida, 517 U.S. 44, 103–04 (1996) (Souter, J., dissenting). The doctrine of sovereign immunity has been part of the common law since at least the twelfth century, during which time it was clear that the king could not be sued in his own name. Although often said to derive from the principle that the king can do no wrong, the concept may be better understood not as a claim to sovereign infallibility, but as standing for the practical proposition that one cannot enforce a right against the state unless the state agrees to such enforcement. MELVYN R. DURCHSLAG, STATE SOVEREIGN IMMUNITY 3 (2002).
[12] *Seminole Tribe*, 517 U.S. at 100 (Souter, J., dissenting).
[13] U.S. Const., amend. XI.
[14] Hans v. Louisiana, 134 U.S. 1 (1890).
[15] Alden v. Maine, 527 U.S. 706 (1999).

sought before the United States Supreme Court.[16] The state, claiming that it was entitled to the defense of sovereign immunity, did not appear in the action. The Supreme Court, in a 4–1 decision, rejected the sovereign immunity claim.

The reaction to *Chisholm* was hostile and immediate.[17] The states, believing that the decision was an affront to their sovereignty and a threat to their treasuries, were outraged by the decision. (One of the houses of the Georgia legislature even went so far as to pass a bill that required that any federal marshal attempting to enforce the *Chisholm* judgment would "suffer death, without benefit of the clergy, by being hanged.")[18]

Congress as well quickly mobilized, and resolutions to overturn the decision by constitutional amendment were hastily proposed.[19] A final version of what is now the Eleventh Amendment soon passed Congress by a wide, bipartisan majority in both houses, and was subsequently ratified by the states.[20] The Amendment provides that the "[t]he Judicial power of the United States shall not be construed to extend to any suit in law or equity, commenced or prosecuted against one of the United States by Citizens of another State, or by Citizens or Subjects of any Foreign State."[21]

The passage of the Eleventh Amendment, however, did not end the state immunity controversy. Perhaps because it was passed in haste, its text was woefully incomplete in resolving numerous immunity issues. The text, for example, did not address suits against a state by the state's *own* citizens; shed no light as to whether a suit against a state officer would be construed as a suit against the state; and, in citing only the federal judicial power, left ambiguous whether its limitations also extended to congressional action. These, and other questions, kept courts involved in state immunity issues for the next two centuries.

B. *Hans v. Louisiana* and State Immunity in the Nineteenth Century

Two important cases regarding state immunity were decided in the first part of the nineteenth century. In *Cohens v. Virginia*,[22] Chief Justice Marshall, writing for the Court, held that an appeal prosecuted by a state court defendant against a state in the United States Supreme Court did not implicate the state's immunity defense. As he explained, such an appeal could "with no propriety, we think, be

---

[16] Because a state was a party to the action, the case could be filed originally in the Supreme Court under Article III, §2.

[17] *E.g.*, William A. Fletcher, *A Historical Interpretation of the Eleventh Amendment: A Narrow Construction of an Affirmative Grant of Jurisdiction Rather than a Prohibition Against Jurisdiction*, 35 STAN. L. REV 1033, 1058 (1983).

[18] *See* CLYDE E. JACOBS, THE ELEVENTH AMENDMENT AND SOVEREIGN IMMUNITY 57 (1972) (quoting the *Augusta Chronicle*, Nov. 23, 1793); Doyle Mathis, Chisholm v. Georgia: *Background and Settlement*, 54 J. AM. HIST. 19, 26 (1967).

[19] *See Seminole Tribe*, 517 U.S. at 108 (Souter, J., dissenting.)

[20] For a description of this history, *see* ORTH, *supra* note 2, at 20–21.

[21] U.S. Const., amend XI.

[22] 19 U.S. (6 Wheat.) 264 (1821).

denominated a suit commenced or prosecuted against the State whose judgment is so far re-examined."[23] Two separate concerns were critical to Marshall's reasoning. First, the appeal did not seek any affirmative relief against the state but sought only to reverse the state court judgment.[24] Second, the availability of appeal to the U.S. Supreme Court from a state court judgment was necessary to preserve federal law.[25]

The second case was *Osborn v. Bank of the United States*.[26] In *Osborn*, the Bank of the United States sued state officers to recover monies seized from a bank office in their execution of an unconstitutional tax. Holding that the action was one against the officers and not the state (even though "the direct interest of the state in the suit, as brought, is admitted")[27] the Court, again in an opinion written by Chief Justice Marshall, found that state immunity was not violated. Suits against state officers would not automatically trigger the state's immunity defense.[28]

Both *Cohens* and *Osborn* raised themes that have echoed throughout state immunity jurisprudence. As *Cohens* suggested, the availability of state immunity was to depend in part on the type of relief sought. As *Osborn* foreshadowed, immunity could also be contingent on the nature and identity of the party sued.

Undoubtedly, however, the most important immunity case of the nineteenth century was *Hans v. Louisiana*.[29] In some ways, the facts of *Hans* paralleled those in *Chisholm*. In *Hans*, as in *Chisholm*, a creditor sued the state in federal court to collect money damages for unpaid debts (this time from bonds issued during Reconstruction). There were, however, two significant differences. First, the action in *Hans* was based on a constitutional issue: The creditor claimed that the state's failure to pay violated the Constitution's Contract Clause.[30] Second, the creditor in *Hans* was an in-state citizen suing his home state. *Chisholm*, on the other hand, was based upon a common-law claim brought by an out-of-state citizen.

One might have thought these differences significant. Immunizing the state against the Contract Clause claim would have effectively left the plaintiff's constitutional rights without a remedy and would, accordingly, subvert the ideal of the Constitution as the supreme law of the land.[31] Additionally, the Eleventh

---

[23] *Id.* at 410.   [24] *Id.*

[25] *Id.* at 415.   [26] 22 U.S. (6 Wheat.) 738 (1824).

[27] *Id.* at 846.

[28] *Osborn*'s implication that state immunity could be avoided merely by the expedience of suing a state officer rather than the state itself was later explicitly rejected in cases where the state was construed as the real party in interest. *See In re* Ayers, 123 U.S. 443 (1887). At the same time, as *Osborn* suggested, state immunity would not bar suits for damages against state officials in their individual capacity. Scheuer v. Rhodes, 416 U.S. 232 (1974) (holding that suits against a governor are not barred by state immunity). The line between permissible suits for damages against state officers and those barred on grounds that the state is the real party in interest has proved difficult to draw. *See* David Currie, *Sovereign Immunity and Suits Against Government Officers*, 1984 SUP. CT. REV. 149 (1997).

[29] 134 U.S. 1 (1890).

[30] U.S. Const., art. I, §10

[31] *Cf.* Marbury v. Madison, 5 U.S. (1 Cranch) 137 (1803) (holding that the granting of rights necessarily implies the presence of a remedy for their violation).

Amendment explicitly addressed only state immunity from actions brought by out-of-staters. There was no textual basis immunizing the state from actions brought by in-staters as well.

The Court in *Hans* found the state immune nevertheless. First, the Court reasoned that strict adherence to the text would lead to the anomalous result that in-staters would be able to sue the state whereas out-of-staters would be precluded.[32] Such a conclusion would not be supported by any intelligible policy. Second, the Court explained that no explicit textual basis for its holding was necessary because the Eleventh Amendment embodied a constitutionally based principle of sovereign immunity that predated the Amendment. *Chisholm* had simply overlooked this fundamental principle. As the Court stated, "the cognizance of suits and actions unknown to the law, and forbidden by the law, was not contemplated by the Constitution when establishing the judicial power of the United States ... [and] [t]he suability of a State without its consent was a thing unknown to the law."[33]

C. *Ex parte Young* and the Foundations of Current Doctrine

Left alone, the *Hans* decision would have been devastating for the protection of constitutional rights. If the state could not be sued, plaintiffs would be unable to bring challenges to the constitutionality of state statutes. They would either have to violate a provision and wait for the state to bring an action against them, risking civil or criminal liability, or they would have to leave a potentially unconstitutional statute unchallenged. The availability of the direct action against the state, in short, was necessary to the effective enforcement of constitutional norms.

Against this background, the Court in the early twentieth century decided *Ex parte Young*.[34] *Young* involved the type of case that *Hans* conceivably precluded. The case was a federal court action challenging the constitutionality of a Minnesota statute regulating railroad rates. The plaintiffs in the case formally sued Edward Young, the state attorney general, rather than the state itself. This step, while necessary to circumvent the immunity defense, was not alone sufficient. The Court, qualifying Chief Justice Marshall's opinion in *Osborn,* had held in previous cases that even where state officers were sued in name, the action would still be considered as one against the state in circumstances where the state was effectively the real party in interest.[35]

What was significant to the *Young* Court, however, was the type of relief the plaintiffs sought. Unlike *Hans* (or *Chisholm* for that matter), which was a suit for damages, the relief sought in *Young* was injunctive. This proved to be critical. In a ruling that has strained the credulity of law students ever since, the Court held that when a state official is sued on constitutional grounds for injunctive or prospective relief, he was "stripped of his official or representative character and is subjected in his person to the consequences of his individual conduct."[36]

[32] *Hans,* 134 U.S. at 10.   [33] *Id.* at 15–16.   [34] 209 U.S. 123 (1908).
[35] *In re* Ayers, 123 U.S. 443 (1887).   [36] *Young,* 209 U.S. at 160.

For state immunity purposes, in short, he was no longer representing the state but was acting on his own.

As a practical matter, of course, this notion of "stripped" authority is nonsense. The plaintiffs were suing Young to prohibit him from enforcing a state statute, and if he had no official status, he would have had no authority to enforce the law in the first place. If the "stripped" language were taken literally, then, the plaintiffs' suit would be useless. But the *Ex parte Young* "fiction," as it has subsequently become known,[37] made sense from the policy perspective, discussed above, as necessary for upholding the Constitution. As one scholar has argued, "the doctrine of *Ex parte Young* seems indispensable to the establishment of constitutional government and the rule of law."[38]

Importantly, *Young* did not purport to overturn *Hans*, and it left the latter's specific bar on actions for damages (retrospective relief) intact. To be sure, the boundaries of the decision remained unclear. Where, after all, was the line between retrospective and prospective relief to be drawn? But *Hans*'s essential holding barring suits against the state for money damages remained.

The viability and scope of *Hans*'s prohibition on suits for retrospective relief, however, continued to be attacked from other directions in the years after *Young*. In *Parden v. Terminal Railroad*,[39] for example, the question was presented as to whether Alabama was immune from damage suits brought under the Federal Employees' Liability Act (FELA) for its actions in operating an interstate railway. In an important opinion, the Court rejected the state's immunity defense. First, the Court indicated that Alabama could be found liable under a doctrine of "constructive consent," whereby a state could be deemed to have waived its immunity by virtue of its participation in a particular activity.[40] Because Alabama knew FELA had been enacted at the time it began its railroad operation, it could be seen as constructively consenting to suit for FELA violations arising out of that operation.[41] Second, the Court indicated that Congress, in passing FELA, had intended that a state could be found liable for its violations and, in so doing, had overruled the state's immunity. Thus *Parden* implicitly suggested that Congress had the power to abrogate the state's immunity, an issue that up to then had not been decided. (The problem with reading too much into *Parden*, however, was that it combined its discussion of its constructive consent and abrogation theories; so it was difficult to determine upon which of the two grounds the Court relied.)[42]

---

[37] *E.g., Idaho v. Coeur d'Alene Tribe*, 521 U.S. 261, 272 (1997).

[38] CHEMERINSKY, *supra* note 7, at 421 (quoting CHARLES ALAN WRIGHT, LAW OF FEDERAL COURTS 292 [4th ed. 1983]).

[39] 377 U.S. 184 (1964).

[40] *Parden* itself relied heavily on Petty v. Tennessee–Missouri Bridge Comm., 359 U.S. 275 (1959), which held that the state had waived its immunity by entering into a congressionally approved interstate compact that by its terms provided that the Commission could sue and be sued.

[41] *See* CHEMERINSKY, *supra* note 7, at 441.

[42] RICHARD H. FALLON, DANIEL J. MELTZER, & DAVID L SHAPIRO, HART AND WECHSLER'S THE FEDERAL COURTS AND THE FEDERAL SYSTEM 1035 (5th ed. 2003).

In addition, on another front, a number of cases had begun to expand the scope of permissible prospective relief to include remedies such as the awarding of benefits wrongfully withheld. In *Shapiro v. Thompson*,[43] for example, the Court affirmed the lower court's decision ordering the retroactive payments of welfare benefits that had been denied on the basis of an unconstitutional eligibility provision. The Court, however, did not explain this development in immunity law. Indeed, it had yet to articulate a rationale underlying the retroactive–prospective distinction or even define the differences between the two.

Finally, in a case decided shortly after Justice Rehnquist was appointed to the Court, another challenge to state immunity was forming, reflected in the dissent of Justice Brennan. The case in question was *Employees of the Department of Public Health and Welfare v. The Department of Health and Welfare*.[44] At issue in the case was whether the state could be sued by its health care employees for money damages for failing to meet the overtime pay requirements of the Fair Labor Standards Act (FLSA). Taking their cues from *Parden*, the plaintiffs raised both the constructive consent and abrogation arguments. They contended that the state waived its immunity to FLSA actions by providing health care services and that Congress had intended to make the state liable when it passed the FLSA. The Court, in an opinion joined by Justice Rehnquist, rejected both arguments.[45] The Court dismissed the constructive waiver claim by noting that, unlike the operation of a railroad as in *Parden*, the state's provision of health care services was a nonproprietary, traditional government function. Accordingly, the fact that the state offered such basic governmental services could not be viewed as a waiver of its immunity.[46] The Court then rejected the plaintiff's abrogation contention, holding that if Congress wanted to subject states to liability in their provision of basic governmental services, its intent to do so must be expressed in the statutory language.[47]

Other than indicating that *Parden* was not going to be applied liberally, the majority opinion in the *Employees* case broke no new ground in the state immunity debate. The same cannot be said, however, of Justice's Brennan's dissent.[48] Brennan's opinion set forth what has become known as the "diversity theory" of the Eleventh Amendment. According to this theory, states enjoy immunity only in a very limited category of cases (those based on the federal courts' diversity jurisdiction) in which states are sued by out-of-state citizens based on state law. The states are not immune, however, in any cases in which they are sued for violations of federal law. As such, the decisions in *Hans* and *Employees*, according to Brennan, were wrong and should be overturned.

---

[43] 394 U.S. 618 (1969).
[44] 411 U.S. 279 (1973).
[45] *Id.* Justice Douglas wrote the majority opinion.
[46] *Id.* at 285.
[47] *Id.* at 287.
[48] *Employees,* 411 U.S. at 299. (Brennan, J., dissenting).

D. Summary

This then was the state of the law in 1974, two years after Justice Rehnquist assumed office. Suits for retrospective relief, such as the damage action in *Hans,* were barred. Suits for prospective relief against the state, on the other hand, could be maintained as long as brought in name against state officers, and suits for retrospective relief against state officers were also permissible as long as the state was not seen as the real party in interest. The prospective–retrospective line, however, had begun to be interpreted to allow more types of claim for relief to proceed. Additionally, the Court had adopted a doctrine of constructive consent that would waive state immunity in circumstances where the state was acting outside of its traditional governmental role, and had also suggested that immunity could be waived when Congress explicitly so decided. Finally, Justice Brennan was laying the groundwork for a full-scale assault on state immunity that would limit its application to the rare instances when out-of-state citizens sued the state for violations of state law.

II. *EDELMAN* AND *FITZPATRICK* – LAYING THE FOUNDATIONS

A. *Edelman v. Jordan*

If the majority opinion in *Employees* cannot be characterized as a landmark decision, the same cannot be said about the Court's next foray into state immunity law, *Edelman v. Jordan.*[49] In *Edelman,* the plaintiff, proceeding individually and as a class representative, sued a number of state and local welfare officials for administering the federal–state program of Aid to the Aged, Blind, or Disabled (AABD) in a manner inconsistent with federal regulations and the Fourteenth Amendment.[50] The plaintiff claimed that the defendants were not processing benefits applications in a timely fashion, with the result that eligible applicants did not begin receiving their benefits until months after the law required. The plaintiff sought declaratory and injunctive relief requiring the state to comply with federal time limits and a permanent injunction ordering the state "to award to the entire class of plaintiffs all AABD benefits wrongfully withheld."[51]

The lower court held for the plaintiff, offering two separate grounds for decision. First, it held that the relief sought was prospective and therefore permissible under *Ex parte Young.*[52] Second, it held that the state constructively consented to be sued by its participation in the AABD program.[53]

Justice Rehnquist wrote the opinion for the Court reversing the decision. Although he agreed with the court below that the plaintiff's action seeking to order the state to comply with the federal regulations in the future was permissible (a

[49] 415 U.S. 651 (1974).
[50] *Id.*
[51] *Id.* at 655.
[52] 209 U.S. 123 (1908).
[53] *See Edelman,* 415 U.S. at 652.

matter uncontested by the state on appeal), he held that the claim to award benefits wrongfully withheld was barred by state immunity.[54]

Edelman's significance in state immunity jurisprudence is apparent in a number of respects. First, the case set the precedent that "retrospective relief" was to be defined in a state-protective manner. Second, it signaled the beginning of the end of the doctrine of constructive consent. Third, it entrenched the prospective–retrospective relief distinction created by the juxtaposition of *Hans* and *Young* into the modern case law. Each of these developments merits separate discussion.

1. *Retrospective Relief*

Essential to Justice Rehnquist's decision in *Edelman* was his conclusion that the plaintiff's claim for benefits, wrongfully withheld because of the state's untimely processing, constituted the type of retrospective relief prohibited by *Hans*. The appellate court had characterized the relief in question as "equitable restitution" rather than damages and therefore outside of *Hans*'s ambit, but Rehnquist was not persuaded.[55] For him, the key to the retrospective–prospective distinction was whether the payments accruing to the plaintiff would be funded from the state treasury. It was not in the formality of how the relief was characterized.

Focusing on the effect of a lawsuit on state treasuries, however, was potentially problematic for the retrospective–prospective relief distinction. As Justice Rehnquist acknowledged, prospective relief could also, and frequently did, have an enormous impact on state treasuries. Even in *Young* itself, Rehnquist noted, the striking down of the Minnesota railroad rate regulation had fiscal impact.[56] Nevertheless, Rehnquist argued, the retrospective–prospective distinction made sense. First, he reasoned the financial impact on the state of ordering prospective relief was not the same as with retrospective relief:

> [W]e cannot agree that such a financial impact is the same where a federal court applies *Ex parte Young* to grant prospective declaratory and injunctive relief, as opposed to an order of retroactive payments as was made in the instant case. . . . This argument neglects the fact that where the State has a definable allocation to be used in the payment of public aid benefits, and pursues a certain course of action such as the processing of applications within certain time periods as did Illinois here, the subsequent ordering by a federal court of retroactive payments to correct delays in such processing will invariably mean there is less money available for payments for the continuing obligations of the public aid system.[57]

In the case of prospective relief, in short, the state could adjust its fiscal plans to account for whatever future expenditures demanded. The granting of retrospective relief, on the other hand, was a direct invasion of the state treasury and a disruption of the state's settled fiscal expectations.[58]

---

[54] *Id.* at 678.

[55] Jordan v. Weaver, 472 F.2d 985, 993 (7th Cir. 1973).

[56] *Edelman*, 415 U.S. at 668.

[57] *Id.* at 666, n. 11.

[58] *Id.* at 668.

Second, according to Rehnquist, the distinction was mandated by *Young*. Even
if prospective relief meant that "[s]tate officials, in order to shape their official
conduct to the mandate of the Court's decrees, would more likely have to spend
money from the state treasury than if they had been left free to pursue their previous course of conduct . . . [s]uch an ancillary effect on the state treasury is a
permissible and often an inevitable consequence of the principle announced in
Ex parte Young."[59] Retrospective relief, on the other hand, "requires payment of
state funds, not as a necessary consequence of compliance in the future with a
substantive federal-question determination, but as a form of compensation."[60]
Retrospective relief, therefore, was not required by the *Young* decision.

Rehnquist's *Edelman* opinion thus offered a coherent (albeit certainly debatable) explanation for the prospective–retrospective relief dichotomy and, on that
account alone, might be considered significant.[61] But the decision did more than
offer an intellectual foundation for a counterintuitive thesis; it also had real doctrinal effect. As noted above, in *Shapiro v. Thompson* and other cases, the Court
had affirmed decisions granting the plaintiffs the same type of relief of benefits
wrongfully withheld that were sought in *Edelman*.[62] Justice Rehnquist's opinion,
however, expressly "disapprove[d] the holdings in those cases."[63]

2. *Constructive Consent*
Edelman also made new law with respect to the doctrine of constructive consent.
Recall that the appellate court had held that by participating in the AABD program, the state had constructively agreed to be sued for violations of that program. In so holding, the appellate court was navigating the waters between *Parden* and *Employees*, the former holding constructive consent existed by virtue of
the state's operation of an interstate railway after the passage of the FMLA, and
the latter holding that the state did not constructively consent to FLSA suits merely by hiring employees to administer basic governmental services. The appellate
court followed *Parden*. While providing financial benefits to the blind and disabled under the AABD could be characterized as part a state's provision of basic
services, the state, as in *Parden*, had entered into the program fully knowing its
applicable rules and regulations.[64] It was not like the FLSA, which came into being long after the state had begun to hire and set wages for its employees. Justice
Rehnquist, however, reversed. That a state voluntarily participated in a federal
program was not enough to support the contention that the state had thereby

---

[59] *Id.*
[60] *Id.*
[61] For a cogent defense of the prospective–retrospective distinction *see* Roderick M. Hills, *The Eleventh Amendment as Curb on Bureaucratic Power*, 53 STAN. L. REV. 1225 (2001).
[62] *Shapiro*, 394 U.S. 618 (1969); State Dept. of Health and Rehab. Serv. v. Zarate, 407 U.S. 918 (1972); Sterrett v. Mothers' & Children's Rights Org., 409 U.S. 809 (1972); Wyman v. Bowens, 397 U.S. 49 (1970).
[63] *Edelman*, 415 U.S. at 652.
[64] *Jordan*, 472 F.2d at 995.

agreed to be sued for retrospective relief for violating the program's strictures. As Rehnquist explained, "[c]onstructive consent is not a doctrine commonly associated with the surrender of constitutional rights."[65]

Edelman did not, by this holding, formally overrule *Parden*. The latter could still be distinguished on grounds that in operating a railroad, the state was acting under its proprietary interests and not in its government capacity.[66] But the force of Rehnquist's "surrender of constitutional rights" rhetoric, as was to become clear in subsequent cases, could not so easily be confined.

3. *Entrenching Hans and Young*

Edelman was not only significant for changing some key aspects of state immunity law; it was also important for what it preserved. As we have already noted, the *Hans* and *Young* opinions uneasily coexisted. *Young's* approval of prospective relief, for example, was defended as necessary to enforce constitutional rights. But this rationale was not sufficient to distinguish *Hans*. The *Hans* decision left the plaintiff's Contract Clause rights wholly unenforceable.

Similarly, the rationale for *Hans* did not distinguish *Young*. *Hans* was defended on the grounds of protecting state treasuries, but state treasuries were also threatened by the prospective relief allowed in *Young*. Each case, therefore, cast doubt on the validity of the other. Justice Rehnquist's effort to provide an intelligible explanation reconciling the two cases thus shored up the foundations of both.

This would prove significant. As we shall see, Justice Brennan, proceeding from his *Employees* dissent and with strong academic support, was eventually able to garner three other votes in favor of overturning *Hans*.[67] If *Young* had been perceived as also supporting overrule, that may have been enough to tip the balance.

B. *Fitzpatrick v. Bitzer*

The one state immunity issue left relatively untouched by the *Edelman* decision was the question of whether Congress had the power to abrogate the state's immunity. In *Edelman* itself the Court did not reach this issue because it decided that there was no indication in the governing statutes that Congress had intended to abrogate the state's immunity for administering its welfare provisions improperly. The Court faced the issue directly two years later, however, in *Fitzpatrick v. Bitzer*.[68]

In *Fitzpatrick*, male employees of the State of Connecticut sued the state under Title VII of the 1964 Civil Rights Act alleging that the state retirement program

---

[65] *Edelman*, 415 U.S. at 673.

[66] *See Employees*, 411 U.S. at 282.

[67] *See* Atascadero State Hosp. v. Scanlon, 473 U.S. 234 (1985); Welch v. Texas Dept. of Highways & Pub. Trans., 483 U.S. 468 (1987).

[68] 427 U.S. 445 (1976).

discriminated against them on the basis of sex. The plaintiffs sought both injunctive relief and retroactive retirement benefits as compensation for any losses caused by the state's discrimination. The lower courts allowed the claim for prospective relief but dismissed the claim for benefits on grounds that it constituted the recovery of money damages from the state treasury and was therefore impermissible under *Edelman*.

Again Justice Rehnquist wrote the opinion but this time the decision went against the state. State immunity did not apply, claimed Rehnquist, because Title VII was passed pursuant to Section 5 of the Fourteenth Amendment, the provision that granted to Congress the power to enforce the guarantees of the Fourteenth Amendment by "appropriate legislation."[69] According to Rehnquist, this was significant because the prohibitions of the Fourteenth Amendment were directed to the states and were therefore appropriate limitations on state sovereignty. Measures enacted to enforce those prohibitions, accordingly, were permissible even if they overrode state immunity. As Rehnquist explained:

> [W]e think that the Eleventh Amendment, and the principle of state sovereignty which it embodies are necessarily limited by the enforcement provisions of §5 of the Fourteenth Amendment. In that section Congress is expressly granted authority to enforce "by appropriate legislation" the substantive provisions of the Fourteenth Amendment, which themselves embody significant limitations on state authority. When Congress acts pursuant to §5, not only is it exercising legislative authority that is plenary within the terms of the constitutional grant, it is exercising that authority under one section of a constitutional Amendment whose other sections by their own terms embody limitations on state authority. We think that Congress may, in determining what is "appropriate legislation" for the purpose of enforcing the provisions of the Fourteenth Amendment, provide for private suits against States or state officials which are constitutionally impermissible in other contexts.[70]

Fitzpatrick was the first case to hold definitively that Congress had the power to abrogate state immunity. That Justice Rehnquist wrote the decision might initially be seen as surprising, given that his *Edelman* opinion had already made clear that he was more committed to protecting state immunity than weakening it. But the rationale Rehnquist pursued in *Fitzpatrick* was illuminating. By tying Congress's power to abrogate state immunity to Congress's purportedly extraordinary powers under Section 5, Rehnquist inherently suggested that Congress does not have the power, outside of its Section 5 authority, to accomplish the same result. *Fitzpatrick* thus implicitly rejected the assertion left open in *Parden* and *Employees* that Congress has the power to abrogate state immunity under the Commerce Clause.[71]

---

[69] U.S. Const., amend. XIV, §5.

[70] *Fitzpatrick*, 427 U.S. at 456.

[71] Rehnquist's strategy did not go unnoticed. Both Justices Stevens and Justice Brennan did not join the majority opinion in part because they believed that Title VII's authorization of suit against the states for monetary relief could also be supported under the Commerce Clause. *See Fitzpatrick*, 427 U.S. at 457–60 (Brennan, J., concurring) (Stevens, J., concurring).

As such, *Fitzpatrick* may be accurately viewed as a decision designed more to protect state immunity than to limit it, because Congressional power under the Commerce Clause is far broader than its power under Section 5. Congress, after all, regulates under the Commerce Clause everything from the environment, to labor, to product safety, to antitrust. Its powers under Section 5, however, are limited only to enforcing constitutional rights. The conclusion that the commerce power would not be enough to abrogate state immunity then would be of far more practical significance than would allowing a relatively limited number of Section 5 claims to proceed against the state. Indeed, it did not take long for it to become apparent that *Fitzpatrick* was not going to lead to liberal results even on its own terms. One year later in *Quern v. Jordan*,[72] Justice Rehnquist held that suits brought under 42 U.S.C. § 1983 did not override state immunity because there was no clear indication that § 1983 had been passed pursuant to Section 5 and was intended to apply to the states.[73] And years later the Court indicated that Congress's Section 5 powers were not to be broadly construed in any event. Thus, even when Congress explicitly attempted to override state immunity by acting pursuant to its Section 5 powers, its efforts were turned back on grounds that, immunity issues aside, Section 5 didn't authorize Congress to legislate in a particular substantive area.[74] *Fitzpatrick*, in short, did not signal a retreat from Rehnquist's efforts to expand state immunity in *Edelman;* rather it was part of its advancement.[75]

III. AMBITIONS REALIZED: THE CASES AFTER *EDELMAN* AND *FITZPATRICK*

Edelman and *Fitzpatrick* certainly were not the last words in the state immunity debate. They did, however, serve to effectively guide state immunity's doctrinal development. Indeed what is remarkable is how closely subsequent cases stayed within the parameters of the *Edelman* and *Fitzpatrick* decisions – even, interestingly enough, in cases where Justice Rehnquist himself attempted to move the jurisprudence in new directions. This is not to say that the course of doctrinal development flowed smoothly. Some aspects of state immunity law, as the remainder of this section shows, took longer to achieve than others. But it is fair to state that by late in his tenure on the Court, the ambitions Rehnquist set forth in *Edelman* and *Fitzpatrick* had been effectively realized.

---

[72] 440 U.S. 332 (1979).

[73] Section 1983 is the basic civil rights law that creates an action in federal court against those acting under color of state law who violate the Constitution or federal laws.

[74] *See* Board of Trustees of the University of Alabama v. Garrett, 531 U.S. 356 (2001); Kimel v. Florida Bd. of Regents, 528 U.S. 62 (2000). In a notable exception to this trend, however, Justice Rehnquist authored Nevada Dept. of Human Resources v. Hibbs, 538 U.S. 721 (2003) (upholding Congress's power under § 5 to hold states liable for damages for violations of the Family and Medical Leave Act).

[75] Additional evidence that Justice Rehnquist himself intended that the reach of his *Fitzpatrick* opinion was to be limited comes from his dissent *Hutto v. Finney*, 437 U.S. 678 (1978). In that case, Rehnquist argued that § 5 did not authorize the awarding of attorney's fees against the state to a prevailing plaintiff pursuant to 42 U.S.C. § 1988. *Id.*

A. The Demise of Constructive Consent

After *Edelman,* the doctrine announced in the *Parden* case – that states could be deemed to have waived their immunity by engaging in certain activities – continued to exist for a time in name only. In *Florida Department of Health and Rehabilitative Services v. Florida Nursing Home Association,*[76] the Court held that the state had not consented to be sued by agreeing to participate and be bound by the requirements of the federal Medicaid Act, and in *Atascadero State Hospital v. Scanlon,*[77] the Court similarly ruled that the state had not constructively waived its immunity by receiving federal funds under the federal Rehabilitation Act.

The formal internment of the constructive consent doctrine came in two later stages. The first was in *Welch v. Texas Department of Highways & Public Transportation.*[78] The facts in *Welch* closely paralleled those in *Parden.* While *Parden* had involved a suit by a state employee working for a state-owned railroad, *Welch* was a suit by a state employee working for a state-owned ferry. *Parden* thus could not be distinguished in *Welch,* as it had in other cases, on the grounds that the state activity in question involved traditional government services.[79] In both cases the state was acting in a proprietary rather than governmental capacity. Nevertheless, the Court upheld the state's immunity. Collapsing the question of whether the state constructively waived its immunity with the issue of whether Congress intended to abrogate the state's immunity, the Court held that before a state will be deemed to have waived its immunity, Congressional intent to subject the state to suit must be expressed in a clear statement. The Court then overruled *Parden* to the "extent it is inconsistent with the requirement that an abrogation of [the state's] immunity by Congress must be expressed in unmistakably clear language."[80]

The final blow to *Parden* came in *College Savings Bank v. Florida Prepaid Postsecondary Education Expense Board.*[81] In that case, the savings bank plaintiff sued the state under federal law for making false statements about the bank's products in its interstate marketing of its own state-operated tuition prepayment program. The plaintiff's contention that the state should not be immune from such actions was supported by two factors. First, like *Parden* itself, the state's activity in question was not a core state function. Rather the state was acting, in the words of the plaintiff, as a "market participant," competing with the bank for the same customers. Second, the statute under which the plaintiff sued clearly expressed Congress's intent to subject the state to liability. The Court, however, was unmoved. As it stated:

> *Parden*-style waivers are simply unheard of in the context of other constitutionally protected privileges. As we said in *Edelman,* "constructive consent is not a doctrine

---

[76] 450 U.S. 147 (1981).   [77] 473 U.S. 234 (1985).
[78] 483 U.S. 468 (1987).   [79] *See e.g., Employees,* 411 U.S. 279.
[80] *Welch,* 483 U.S. at 478.   [81] 572 U.S. 666 (1999).

commonly associated with the surrender of constitutional rights." . . . The classic description of an effective waiver of a constitutional right is the "intentional relinquishment or abandonment of a known right or privilege." . . . We see no reason why the rule should be different with respect to state sovereign immunity.[82]

Accordingly, the Court concluded, "[w]hatever may remain of our decision in *Parden* is expressly overruled."[83]

To be sure, Justice Rehnquist did not write the *College Savings* opinion. That task belonged to Justice Scalia. But, as the *College Savings* opinion's heavy reliance on *Edelman* establishes, the theoretical underpinnings for the decision were the work of Justice Rehnquist.

B. The Fight to Save *Hans*

In his *Employees* dissent, Justice Brennan powerfully wrote that:

> [I]n a nation whose ultimate sovereign is the people and not government, a doctrine premised upon kingship – or, as has been suggested, "on the logical and practical ground that there can be no legal right as against the authority that makes the law on which the right depends," . . . – is indefensible "if it represents, as the Court has more than once intimated, an unfortunate excrescence of a political and legal order which no longer enlists support. . . ."[84]

Also noting that "the trend since *Hans* was decided in 1890 has been against enforcement of governmental immunity except when clearly required by explicit textual prohibitions, as in the Eleventh Amendment,"[85] Brennan contended that *Hans* should be overruled.

Although in a minority of one at the time he wrote his *Employees* dissent, Justice Brennan was eventually able to attract others to his cause. In part, this may have been because, as Brennan's opinion indicates, enforcing state immunity may have seemed out of place with the times. The notions that governmental entities are above the law and aggrieved parties are not able to vindicate their rights are relatively alien to democratic jurisprudence. Also it may have been due in part to the fact that state immunity and the Eleventh Amendment had begun to attract important academic attention and much of this scholarly effort questioned whether *Hans* was correctly decided.[86] In any event, by the time of the *Atascadero*

---

82 *Id.* at 681.

83 *Id.* at 680.

84 *Employees,* 411 U.S. at 311 (Brennan, J., dissenting) (citation and quotation omitted).

85 *Id.* at 323.

86 *See, e.g.,* John E. Nowak, *The Scope of Congressional Power to Create Causes of Action Against State Governments and the History of the Eleventh and Fourteenth Amendments,* 75 COLUM. L. REV. 1413 (1975); Laurence H. Tribe, *Intergovernmental Immunities in Litigation, Taxation, and Regulation: Separation of Powers Issues in Controversies About Federalism,* 89 Harv. L. Rev. 682 (1976); John J. Gibbons, *The Eleventh Amendment and State Sovereign Immunity: A Reinterpretation,* 83 COLUM. L. REV. 1889 (1983); Fletcher, *supra* note 17.

decision in 1985, Brennan could count on three other Justices who supported the position that *Hans* should be overturned.[87]

Thanks to *Edelman*, however, the viability of *Hans* also had greater resonance. To begin with, *Edelman*'s successful reconciliation of *Hans* and *Young* undoubtedly helped protect the *Hans* decision. If *Young* had been perceived as inconsistent with *Hans*, the foundations of the latter decision would have been seriously eroded. Moreover, there was now a long line of cases affirming *Hans* that had explicitly considered and rejected the attacks mounted against the case.[88] *Stare decisis* was now firmly on the side of the *Hans* decision.[89] The issue came to a head in 1986 when, in *Welch*, the majority, citing *stare decisis* as one of its main concerns, was once again able to turn back an attempt to overturn *Hans*:

> Today, for the fourth time in little more than two years four Members of the Court urge that we overrule *Hans v. Louisiana* and the long line of cases that has followed it. The rule of law depends in large part on adherence to the doctrine of *stare decisis*. Indeed, the doctrine is a natural evolution from the very nature of our institutions. It follows that any departure from the doctrine of *stare decisis* demands special justification. . . . Despite these time-honored principles, the dissenters – on the basis of ambiguous historical evidence – would flatly overrule a number of major decisions of the Court, and cast doubt on others. Once again, the dissenters have placed in issue the fundamental nature of our federal system.[90]

The forces Rehnquist set in motion in his early tenure had again prevailed.

C. The Battle over Congressional Power to Abrogate State Immunity

The longest and most sustained battle over state immunity after *Edelman* and *Fitzpatrick* concerned the question of whether Congress had the power to abrogate the state's immunity. As it turned out, the abrogation issue was to provide Rehnquist with his hardest-earned victory. Indeed, for a time, Rehnquist was on the losing end of this issue.

Fitzpatrick established that Congress had the power to abrogate state immunity when acting pursuant to Section 5 of the Fourteenth Amendment. The abrogation issue, however, remained open with respect to other Congressional powers such as the Commerce Clause. As discussed above, the question had substantial practical significance given that Congress's power under the Commerce Clause covers virtually all federal economic, social, and environmental legislation, whereas its power under Section 5 is limited to enforcing constitutional guarantees.

---

[87] *See Atascadero*, 472 U.S. at 301–02 (Brennan, Marshall, Blackmun, and Stevens, JJ., dissenting).

[88] *E.g.*, Florida Dept. of State v. Treasure Salvors, Inc., 458 U.S. 670 (1982); Quern v. Jordan, 440 U.S. 332 (1979); Hutto v. Finney, 437 U.S. 678 (1978); Edelman v. Jordan, 415 U.S. 651, 662–63 (1974); Employees v. Missouri Dept. of Public Health and Welfare, 411 U.S. 279, 280 (1973).

[89] *See* William P. Marshall, *The Diversity Theory of the Eleventh Amendment: A Critical Evaluation*, 102 Harv. L. Rev. 1372 (1989).

[90] *Welch*, 483 U.S. at 478–9 (citations and quotations omitted).

The abrogation issue was also significant from a theoretical perspective. The question of whether Congress has the general power to abrogate the state's immunity touched a number of constitutional themes. These included whether the states were so sufficiently represented in Congress that they did not need protection from federal legislative power; whether the state immunity embodied in the Eleventh Amendment was only a limit on federal judicial power; whether state immunity itself was only a common law doctrine that could be overridden by statute; and whether state immunity meant immunity only from the state's own law and would therefore not apply to actions based upon federal statutory law.[91]

For more than fifteen years, beginning with the *Employees* case, the Court had played a game of cat and mouse with this question in order to avoid reaching the constitutional issue. Every time the question arose, the Court construed the statute under which the suit against the state was brought as being insufficiently clear in expressing that Congress had intended that the state be liable for violating that particular statute's provisions. To be sure, the Court explained this statutory construction gambit on grounds that constitutional concerns demanded that Congress express its intention "unmistakably clear in the language of the statute" in order to waive the state's immunity.[92] But the manner by which the Court enforced this "clear statement" requirement was particularly stringent. For example, in *Welch,* the Court held that the Jones Act,[93] which provides an action for *any* injured seamen, failed to constitute an "unmistakably clear expression" that it was intended to apply to seamen employed by the state.[94] Similarly, in *Atascadero,* the Court found that §504 of the Rehabilitation Act of 1973,[95] which provides remedies for "any recipient of Federal assistance," did not contain the unmistakable language necessary to negate the state's immunity, though the obvious target for those remedies would be the state entities administering the program.[96]

In one sense, this delay game advanced the interests of those, such as Justice Rehnquist, who believed that Congress did not have the power under the Commerce Clause to waive state immunity. Earlier cases such as *Parden* and *Employees* appeared to assume that such power existed, and there was thus some advantage in delaying the ultimate decision on the abrogation question until those particular precedents had been weakened. But there was also some risk. The clear statement requirement appeared to presume the existence of the Congressional power.[97] Otherwise, why would a clear statement be necessary?

[91] For an effective synopsis of the many theoretical issues underlying the abrogation debate *see* DURCHSLAG, *supra* note 11, at 113–15 (2002).

[92] *Atascadero,* 473 U.S. at 242.

[93] 46 U.S.C. §688(a).

[94] 483 U.S. 468 (1987).

[95] 29 U.S.C. §794.

[96] 473 U.S. 234 (1985).

[97] *See Atascadero,* 473 U.S. at 238; and Green v. Mansour, 474 U.S. 64, 68 (1985) ("States may not be sued in federal court . . . unless Congress, pursuant to a valid exercise of power, unequivocally expresses its intent to abrogate the immunity").

Eventually, the Court reached the abrogation issue in the case of *Pennsylvania v. Union Gas*.[98] The *Union Gas* litigation arose when the United States sued Union Gas, the operator of a coal gasification plant, to recoup the costs the federal government spent in cleaning up an environmental hazard. Union Gas, in turn, filed a third-party claim against Pennsylvania under CERCLA,[99] an environmental protection statute, alleging that the state was obligated to reimburse the company for its share of the cleanup costs owed to the United States because the state was an owner-operator of the hazardous waste site and because its flood control efforts had negligently caused or contributed to the environmental damage.[100] In a 5–4 decision, the Court found the language of CERCLA sufficiently clear to subject the state to suit under the clear statement requirement.[101] The Court then reached the constitutional issue and, in a different 5–4 alignment, ruled that Congress had the power to abrogate the state's immunity under its commerce power.[102] Because only four Justices could agree on why Congress had this power, however, the opinion was just a plurality decision.

Justice Brennan wrote the plurality opinion relying primarily on three separate points. First, he argued that previous cases assumed that Congress enjoyed such power.[103] Second, he relied on *Fitzpatrick* for the proposition that the Commerce Clause, like Section 5, imposed a limit on state sovereignty. As Brennan stated:

> In *Fitzpatrick v. Bitzer,* we held that Congress may subject States to suits for money damages in federal court when legislating under §5 of the Fourteenth Amendment. . . . *Fitzpatrick*'s rationale is straightforward: "When Congress acts pursuant to §5, not only is it exercising legislative authority that is plenary within the terms of the constitutional grant, it is exercising that authority under one section of a constitutional Amendment whose other sections by their own terms embody limitations on state authority." . . . Like the Fourteenth Amendment, the Commerce Clause with one hand gives power to Congress while, with the other, it takes power away from the States.[104]

Third, Brennan raised the "plan of the convention" theory that he had also advanced in this *Atascadero* dissent.[105] Under this theory, the states, by joining the

[98] 491 U.S. 1 (1989).

[99] 42 U.S.C. §9601 *et seq.*

[100] A *third-party claim* is an action by a defendant (the third-party plaintiff) against another party (the third-party defendant) claiming that latter is liable to it for all or part of the plaintiff's claim against the original defendant (the third-party plaintiff). *See* FED. R. CIV. P. 14(a).

[101] 42 U.S.C. §9607(d)(2) (1982 ed., Supp. IV).

[102] Justice Scalia joined the majority in holding that Congress had clearly intended to subject the state to suits under CERCLA but dissented from the portion of the opinion holding that the Court had the power to abrogate the state's immunity. Justice White, in turn, dissented from the Court's opinion holding that Congress had waived the state's immunity in CERCLA but concurred in the plurality's conclusion that Congress had the power to abrogate the state's immunity if it so chose.

[103] *Union Gas,* 491 U.S. at 14. In making this assertion Justice Brennan cited *Welch,* 483 U.S. 468 at 475–76, and n. 5; County of Oneida v. Oneida Indian Nation of New York, 470 U.S. 226, 252 (1985).

[104] *Union Gas,* 491 U.S. at 15–16.

[105] *Atascadero,* 473 U.S. at 275–76.

Union and adopting the Constitution, tacitly agreed to be bound by the terms of the constitutional compact. Accordingly, because the states gave Congress the authority to regulate commerce, they thereby relinquished their immunity in circumstances when Congress, acting pursuant to the Commerce power, found it necessary to render them liable. Under this plan of the convention theory, "[t]he States held liable under such a congressional enactment are thus not 'unconsenting'; they gave their consent all at once, in ratifying the Constitution containing the Commerce Clause, rather than on a case-by-case basis."[106]

The salient problem, as noted above, however, was that Brennan's opinion did not command a majority. Although Justice White stated that he believed Congress had the power to abrogate the state's immunity, he neither joined the plurality opinion nor offered reasons of his own. Rather, he cryptically wrote only that in finding that Congress has the power to abrogate state immunity, "I concur in Justice Brennan's conclusion, but not his reasoning."[107]

Union Gas was thus rife for second-guessing, and the Court did just that in *Seminole Tribe of Florida v. Florida.*[108] The specific question in *Seminole Tribe* was whether Congress had the power to abrogate the state's immunity when acting pursuant to the Indian Commerce Clause,[109] a parallel provision to the Interstate Commerce Clause at issue in *Union Gas.* After quickly dismissing any notion that the distinction between the Indian and Interstate Commerce powers was constitutionally significant with respect to the abrogation issue,[110] the Court revisited the exact issue it had faced in *Union Gas:* Does Congress have the power under the Commerce Clause to abrogate the states' immunity? This time, however, unlike in *Union Gas,* the Court answered the question in the negative. *Union Gas* was overruled.

Justice Rehnquist wrote the decision. He quickly dismissed Brennan's reliance in *Union Gas* on cases that assumed Congress had the power to abrogate the state's immunity. Those cases, Rehnquist pointed out, merely assumed the Congress had the requisite power to waive state immunity purely for the sake of argument.[111] He also dismissed the stronger version of this argument; that is, that the cases imposing the clear statement requirement necessarily implied that Congress had the power to abrogate.[112] Rehnquist responded that the clear statement cases should be understood only as the Court's adherence to the long-standing principle that it should avoid deciding constitutional questions when possible and not as shedding light on the merits of the constitutional issue itself.[113]

Rehnquist then countered Brennan's other main arguments by referencing his (Rehnquist's) own previous work. *Fitzpatrick,* Rehnquist explained, could hardly

---

[106] *Union Gas,* 491 U.S. at 20.
[107] *Id.* at 45.
[108] 517 U.S. 44 (1996).
[109] U.S. Const., art I, § 8, cl. 3.
[110] *Seminole Tribe,* 517 U.S. at 63.
[111] *Id.* at 61.
[112] This argument was raised by Justice Stevens in his *Seminole Tribe* dissent. *Id.* at 76.
[113] *Id.* at 71 n. 15.

be construed as authority for the proposition that Congress had the power to abrogate state immunity under the Commerce Clause. Rather, the scope of the decision was explicitly limited to Congressional enforcement of the Reconstruction Amendments. As Rehnquist stated: "*Fitzpatrick* was based upon a rationale wholly inapplicable to the Interstate Commerce Clause, viz., that the Fourteenth Amendment, adopted well after the adoption of the Eleventh Amendment and the ratification of the Constitution, operated to alter the pre-existing balance between state and federal power achieved by Article III and the Eleventh Amendment."[114]

Similarly, according to Rehnquist, Brennan's plan of the convention theory was repudiated by the Court's commitment (established in *Edelman* and later cases) to the continued viability of *Hans*. As Rehnquist maintained, the *Union Gas* plurality opinion, although purportedly not questioning *Hans*'s validity, would effectively overrule it.[115] This was so on two counts. First, as a practical matter, as Justice Scalia had argued in his *Union Gas* dissent, "[i]f *Hans* means only that federal-question suits for money damages against the States cannot be brought in federal court unless Congress clearly says so, it means nothing at all."[116] Second, although Rehnquist was not explicit on this point, the plan of the convention argument, could not, in any event, be limited in a manner that would not impugn the continued viability of *Hans*. If the states, by entering into the constitutional compact, had agreed to be subject to the strictures of that document, this would necessarily mean that they consented to be governed by the Contract Clause, the provision under which the suit in *Hans* was brought, as well as under the Commerce Clause. *Hans* was therefore not distinguishable. To uphold Congress's power to abrogate then would be to reverse this decision and a long line of precedents affirming its results. Again, Rehnquist's work in *Edelman* shoring up the *Hans* decision had proved to have enduring effect.

IV. WRONG TURNS

Although most state immunity law has followed from Justice Rehnquist's *Edelman* and *Fitzpatrick* decisions, the same can not always be said of Rehnquist's own efforts. Indeed, in two significant instances, Rehnquist tried to move state immunity law away from the framework that he originally created – succeeding in one of these efforts and failing in the other. Both deserve mention.

A. *Pennhurst State School and Hospital v. Halderman*

The first of these cases was *Pennhurst State School and Hospital v. Halderman*,[117] a class action challenging the conditions at a state institution for the mentally retarded. The plaintiffs sued for prospective relief seeking to require the defendants

[114] *Id.* at 65.   [115] *Id.* at 64.
[116] *Id.* (quoting *Union Gas*, 491 U.S. at 36).   [117] 465 U.S. 89 (1984).

to improve the conditions at the facility. The plaintiffs based their claim on a number of federal constitutional and statutory provisions and also upon a state statutory provision.

The case went to the Supreme Court twice. The first time the Court reviewed the decision of the appellate court holding that the plaintiffs were entitled to relief under a federal statute, the Developmentally Disabled Assistance and Bill of Rights Act.[118] The Court reversed, finding that the act did not create any judicially enforceable rights, and remanded the case to the lower court to consider the plaintiffs' other federal and state law claims.[119] Accepting this invitation, the lower court ruled that the state had violated state law and the plaintiffs were entitled to injunctive relief on that basis.[120] The Supreme Court, in a 5–4 decision authored by Justice Powell and joined by Justice Rehnquist, reversed again. Ignoring substantial precedent to the contrary and apparently unconcerned that it was reversing the appellate court for doing exactly what the Court itself in *Pennhurst I* had instructed it to do, the Court held that the Eleventh Amendment barred all actions against the state based on state law, including those for prospective relief.[121] The Court distinguished *Young* on grounds that the decision in that case was based on a "fiction" intended to preserve the supremacy of federal law, a policy that was not implicated when the claim against the state was based on state law.[122] Accordingly, there was no need to extend the *Ex parte Young* fiction to state law claims. Moreover, the Court concluded, "it is difficult to think of a greater intrusion on state sovereignty than when a federal court instructs state officials on how to conform their conduct to state law."[123]

Whatever may be the merits of *Pennhurst II* on its own terms, it was not consistent with *Edelman*. To begin with, it conceded what *Edelman* avoided – that a suit for prospective relief brought against a state officer is really a suit against the state. The significance of this concession is enormous because it means that all claims, whether prospective or retrospective, fully implicate the state's constitutionally based immunity protections.[124] It thus implicitly suggests that *Young* (and *Edelman*'s endorsement of that decision) must be wrong for failing to protect that interest.

The *Pennhurst II* Court's response to this point was to claim that *Young* nevertheless survives because of the necessity of protecting federal law. But retrospective claims may *also* be necessary to protect the supremacy of federal law,

---

[118] 42 U.S.C. §6010.

[119] Pennhurst State School and Hospital v. Halderman, 451 U.S. 1 (1981) (*Pennhurst I*).

[120] 673 F.2d 647 (3d Cir., 1982) (en banc).

[121] Although the claims in *Halderman* were brought nominally against state officials, the Court construed the case as being one in which the real party in interest was the state. *Halderman*, 465 U.S. at 101.

[122] *Id.* at 105.

[123] *Id.* at 106.

[124] MARTIN REDISH & SUZANNA SHERRY, CASES, COMMENTS, QUESTIONS ON FEDERAL COURTS (5th ed. 2002).

particularly in cases where there is no injunctive relief available. Thus, if the exigencies of protecting federal law are so compelling as to override the state's immunity in suits for prospective relief, they should also be sufficiently compelling to override the state's immunity in suits for retrospective relief. If so, then *Hans* is wrong (as is *Edelman's* endorsement of that decision). *Pennhurst II* cannot have it both ways.

Edelman, of course, had previously answered this dilemma. The prospective–retrospective distinction could be supported by the concern with protecting state treasuries from the peculiarly invasive form of retrospective relief. *Pennhurst II,* however, by abandoning that relief distinction, took *Edelman's* central concern for protecting state treasuries out of the equation. As such, it left no basis for the reconciliation of *Hans* and *Young* that was at the heart of the *Edelman* decision. The logic of *Pennhurst II,* then, is that the logic of *Edelman* is wrong.

Undermining *Edelman* by weakening the prospective–retrospective distinction, moreover, was not the only way that *Pennhurst II* harmed Justice Rehnquist's immunity jurisprudence. The latter *Pennhurst* Court also undercut the authority of *stare decisis* in state immunity cases by overruling a series of cases in which claims against the states based upon state law were allowed to proceed. As it turned out, this consequence of *Pennhurst II* was almost immediate. In *Atascadero,* decided one year later, Justice Stevens, who had previously voted to affirm *Hans* and *Edelman,* switched his position on grounds that if the *Pennhurst II* majority had no respect for *stare decisis,* then he need not as well. As he wrote:

> the Court has not felt constrained by stare decisis in its expansion of the protective mantle of sovereign immunity – having repudiated at least 28 cases in its decision in *Pennhurst State School and Hospital v. Halderman* – and additional study has made it abundantly clear that not only *Edelman,* but *Hans v. Louisiana,* as well, can properly be characterized as egregiously incorrect. I am now persuaded that a fresh examination of the Court's Eleventh Amendment jurisprudence will produce benefits that far outweigh the consequences of further unraveling the doctrine of *stare decisis* in this area of the law.[125]

The weakening of *stare decisis* in this area, moreover, may have had significance beyond the switch of one Justice's vote. Much of the precedential strength of *Edelman* was based on its adherence to *stare decisis.* Rather than overruling either *Hans* or *Young, Edelman* chose to work within their boundaries. The Court's decision in *Pennhurst II* to abandon *stare decisis* constraints in this area thus opened up the precedents that *Edelman* so carefully protected, including *Edelman* itself, to renewed scrutiny.[126]

---

[125] *Atascadero,* 473 U.S. at 304.
[126] *See Seminole Tribe,* 517 U.S. at 103–04 (1996) (Souter, J., dissenting) (arguing in favor of reconceptualizing *Hans* as solely a common-law case); *Coeur d'Alene Tribe,* 521 U.S. 261 (1997) (reexamining the decision in *Young*).

B. *Idaho v. Coeur d'Alene Tribe of Idaho*

The second instance where Justice Rehnquist significantly deviated from his initial state immunity jurisprudence was *Idaho v. Coeur d'Alene Tribe of Idaho*.[127] *Coeur d'Alene* involved a suit by the Coeur d'Alene Tribe claiming that certain submerged lands belonged to the tribe and not the state. The lower court, relying on *Ex parte Young,* ruled that state immunity did not bar the tribe's claim for injunctive and declaratory relief that, if awarded, would prevent the state from interfering with the tribe's ownership rights.[128]

The Supreme Court reversed. Writing for a five-person Court majority that included Chief Justice Rehnquist, Justice Kennedy held that the state was immune from the type of relief sought in the case.[129] This holding in itself, however, was not that dramatic a development in state immunity jurisprudence. The Court had previously ruled that actions against the state to quiet title were barred by state immunity,[130] and the relief sought in *Coeur d'Alene,* by prohibiting the state to exercise its rights of ownership, was "the functional equivalent" of such an action.[131] Moreover, the holding was also supported by the fact that state control over submerged lands under navigable waters had historically been considered a particularly integral and fundamental attribute of its sovereignty. As such, Justice Kennedy explained, relief against the state that interferes with such an essential sovereign prerogative is "as fully as intrusive as almost any conceivable retroactive levy upon funds in its Treasury."[132] Kennedy's conclusion, therefore, that "[u]nder these particular and special circumstances, we find the *Young* exception inapplicable"[133] might therefore be seen as a relatively modest decision standing only for some sort of public lands' exception to *Young*'s requirements.

Another part of Justice Kennedy's opinion, however, joined only by Chief Justice Rehnquist, was not so limited. Specifically, Kennedy and Rehnquist argued for what would amount to a general reworking of the *Young* formulation. Under their approach, the availability of prospective relief under *Young* would be decided on a case-by-case basis, analyzing such factors as "whether a state forum is available to hear the dispute, what particular federal right the suit implicates,

---

[127] 521 U.S. 261 (1997).

[128] Coeur d'Alene Tribe of Idaho v. Idaho, 42 F.3d 1244 (1994).

[129] *Coeur d'Alene Tribe,* 521 U.S. 261 (1997).

[130] Florida Dept. of State v. Treasure Salvors, Inc., 458 U.S. 670 (1982). Indeed, it would be difficult to consider an action to quiet title as only against a state officer given that the remedy of removing title would have to be executed against the state. See DURCHSLAG, *supra* note 11, at 82.

[131] *Id.* at 281. As Kennedy further explained, such relief, if awarded would "diminish, even extinguish, the State's control over a vast reach of land and waters long deemed by the State to be an integral part of its territory." *Id.* at 282.

[132] *Id.* at 287. But see Vicki C. Jackson, Coeur d'Alene, *Federal Courts and the Supremacy of Federal Law: The Competing Paradigms of Chief Justices Marshall and Rehnquist,* 15 CONST. COMMENT. 301, 312 (1998) (arguing that such "intrusiveness" does not distinguish the relief sought in *Coeur d'Alene* from other types of prospective relief).

[133] 521 U.S. at 287.

and whether 'special factors counse[l] hesitation' in the exercise of jurisdiction."[134]

Because it suggests that mere balancing is all that is required under *Young* and that a plaintiff's access to a federal forum is only a factor to be considered by a court in exercising its discretion, the *Coeur d'Alene* opinion considerably softened the proposition previously endorsed by Justice Rehnquist that *Young* "gives life to the Supremacy Clause."[135] After all, previous cases had indicated that part of protecting the life of the Supremacy Clause included protecting the availability of access to a federal forum. Even in *Pennhurst II*, for example, the Court had characterized *Young* as "necessary to permit *federal courts* to vindicate federal rights."[136] *Coeur d'Alene*, like *Pennhurst II*, then also undercut Justice Rehnquist's claim to the mantle of *stare decisis*. Ironically, however, this falling baton was picked up by other members of the Court. The seven Justices disagreeing with this part of the Kennedy–Rehnquist opinion rested much of their argument on the strength of Rehnquist's *Edelman* opinion. As Justice O'Connor stated, "*Edelman* is consistently cited for the proposition that prospective injunctive relief is available in a *Young* suit."[137] By the time of *Coeur d'Alene*, in short, *Edelman's* prospective–retrospective dichotomy was so entrenched that it no longer needed its own author.

V. CONCLUDING ASSESSMENT

In the early 1970s, when Justice Rehnquist joined the Court, state immunity was a fading doctrine. Things quickly changed. Under his stewardship, state immunity was revitalized and became an increasingly important factor in the ongoing constitutional debates over federalism and the limits of federal legislative and judicial power. If, as one writer has noted, Justice Rehnquist had as one of his primary missions the goal of reinvigorating the role of states in the constitutional structure, he surely accomplished that goal in his state immunity jurisprudence.[138]

Justice Rehnquist's success in this area is also a testament to his skills as a judicial craftsman and tactician. His early state immunity decisions were masterful both in turning back then-existing efforts threatening state immunity's long-term viability and in anticipating and protecting against the possible directions of future attacks. Moreover, in bringing together the seemingly irreconcilable precedents of *Hans* and *Young* while grounding his approach in the concern for protecting state treasuries that had been at center stage in the most critical moments of the state immunity debate,[139] he was able to forge a stable foundation for his

[134] 521 U.S. 261, 291 (1997) (O'Connor, J., concurring) (describing the Kennedy–Rehnquist approach).
[135] *Green*, 474 U.S. 64, 68 (1985).
[136] 465 U.S. at 105, citing *Young*, 209 U.S. at 160 (emphasis added).
[137] *Id.* at 294. *See also id.* at 476–77 (Souter, J., dissenting).
[138] H. Jefferson Powell, *The Compleat Jeffersonian: Justice Rehnquist and Federalism*, 91 YALE L.J. 1317, 1320 (1982).
[139] Recall that both *Chisholm* and *Hans* involved claims against the state for outstanding debts.

doctrinal approach, based solidly on constitutional history and long-term precedent, that could withstand the test of time. Only in later years, when in *Pennhurst II* and *Coeur d'Alene* he attempted to expand state immunity doctrine beyond his initial parameters, did he undercut the power of his original vision.

This is not to say that the path Justice Rehnquist chose to follow in the state immunity cases was obvious or self-evident. The attacks on sovereign immunity raised by Justice Brennan and others are supported by powerful concerns, including the principles that constitutional and statutory rights should be redressable and that no entity is above the law. But abandoning constitutional commitments established in history, text, and precedent can also be jurisprudentially troublesome. As David Currie has argued, although state immunity "is an unattractive doctrine that does not belong in an enlightened constitution . . . it is a part of ours."[140] Justice Rehnquist's state immunity jurisprudence recognized this central point.

[140] Currie, *supra* note 28, at 168.

CHAPTER THIRTEEN

TRANSCENDING THE ROUTINE: METHODOLOGY AND CONSTITUTIONAL VALUES IN CHIEF JUSTICE REHNQUIST'S STATUTORY CASES

Philip P. Frickey

When asked why he wanted to be Vice President of the United States in 1976, Robert Dole responded that it was "inside work with no heavy lifting."[1] Much the same can be said for the attractions of the work of a Supreme Court Justice in the unexceptional case that slides below public view. Most of these cases concern statutory interpretation. They amount to a vast wasteland of decisions involving such subjects as federal taxation, bankruptcy, social security, and pension regulation. The opinions often include laborious examination of often impenetrable statutory text, of mountains of legislative history, and of confusing attempts by lower-court judges and administrative agencies to exercise their frontline responsibility to make sense out of statutory fog.

William Rehnquist has shown an appreciation, even a touch of whimsy, for this routine. In a complicated environmental law case, for example, he wrote that the Environmental Protection Agency's interpretation of the Clean Air Act "was 'correct,' to the extent that it can be said with complete assurance that any particular interpretation of a complex statute such as this is the 'correct' one."[2] Yet, he has emphasized, the burdensomeness of decisions such as this does not justify complete judicial deference to the administrative agency charged with implementing a statute. In dissenting from the denial of certiorari in another environmental case, Justice Rehnquist wrote: "The fact that the requirements of the Clean Air Act Amendments virtually swim before one's eyes is not a rational basis, under these circumstances, for refusing to exercise our discretionary jurisdiction." "Admittedly," he continued, "it would be easier to decide a case turning on common-law principles of property or contract, and more interesting to decide a case involving competing fundamental principles of constitutional law."[3]

Justice Rehnquist has done more than his share of complex statutory cases, and as Chief Justice he has even inflicted a number of them on himself. A recent

---

[1] *See* N.Y. Times, Oct. 16, 1976, at 8 (transcript of vice-presidential debate).
[2] Train v. NRDC, 421 U.S. 60, 87 (1975).
[3] United States Steel Corp. v. EPA, 444 U.S. 1035, 1038–39 (1980) (Rehnquist, J., dissenting from denial of certiorari).

example is a case interesting only because of its Flintstonian title, *Bedroc Ltd. v. United States*,[4] raising the question whether sand and gravel are "valuable minerals" for purposes of §8 of the Pittman Underground Water Act of 1919. Like this case, many of the less scintillating matters on the Court's docket involve the western United States, with its vast federal public lands and environmentally regulated areas. Presumably because of his western heritage, Justice Rehnquist has taken on the burden of writing many of these decisions, and he has often found ways to make them more interesting. Illustratively, in a case involving the transcontinental railroad land grant statutes and later laws regulating public lands,[5] he wrote eloquently about the history of this region, in a manner that makes the reader "almost feel the wagon train moving you West."[6] Cases involving federal Indian law – governed by a complex mix of Indian treaties, federal statutes, executive orders, judicial decisions, and agency actions – have particularly interested him, for they have provided an opportunity to discuss the beauty of out-of-the-way places. The Wind River Indian Reservation in Wyoming, the reader learns, "straddles the Wind River, with its remarkable canyon, and lies in a mile-high basin at the foot of the Wind River Mountains, whose rugged, glaciated peaks and ridges form a portion of the Continental Divide."[7] In another Indian law case, we are told that Pyramid Lake in Nevada is "'widely considered the most beautiful desert lake in North America.'"[8] Indian law also gave Rehnquist a vehicle for discussing colorful figures of western lore, such as Judge Isaac Parker, better known as "Hanging Judge Parker."[9]

Beyond the precise holdings in the numerous statutory decisions he has written, Justice Rehnquist has two primary legacies in these cases. The first concerns the methodology of statutory interpretation. Before Antonin Scalia came to the Supreme Court in 1986, Rehnquist was the primary voice for a constrained approach to statutory construction that purports to render interpretation less vulnerable to the political ideology of judges. The second legacy concerns his extensive reliance upon certain constitutional values in shaping the meaning of statutes. These two contributions are the subjects of this chapter.

I. THE METHOD OF STATUTORY INTERPRETATION

To oversimplify, there are three basic possibilities for developing a theory of statutory interpretation: textualism, intentionalism, and purposivism.[10] *Textualism*

---

[4] 541 U.S. 176 (2004).

[5] Leo Sheep Co. v. United States, 440 U.S. 668 (1979).

[6] William N. Eskridge, Jr., Philip P. Frickey, & Elizabeth Garrett, *Cases and Materials on Legislation: Statutes and the Creation of Public Policy* 945 (3d ed. 2001).

[7] United States v. Mazurie, 419 U.S. 544, 546 (1975).

[8] Nevada v. United States, 463 U.S. 110, 114 (1983).

[9] *See* Oliphant v. Suquamish Indian Tribe, 435 U.S. 191, 200 and n. 10 (1978). *See also* William H. Rehnquist, *Isaac Parker, Bill Sikes and the Rule of Law*, 6 U. Ark. Little Rock L. Rev. 485 (1983).

[10] *See* William N. Eskridge, Jr., Philip P. Frickey, & Elizabeth Garrett, *Legislation and Statutory Interpretation* 211–47 (2000).

posits that courts should stick to the ordinary meaning of statutory text – though sometimes it is highly ambiguous, at other times it might seem poorly drafted, and in some contexts it might produce an absurd or odd result unlikely to have been anticipated and intended by the enacting legislature. In light of these potential problems with statutory text, courts could instead seek to follow, through *intentionalism*, the probable intent of the enacting legislature – though often such intent is not evident, and in any event it may be fictional to think that bicameral, multimember bodies had a shared, discernible inclination on a question emerging years later in litigation. Finally, in part because of these limitations arising from textual and intentional interpretation, it might be better, via *purposivism*, for judges to treat statutes as purposive, flexible instruments to be interpreted to produce reasonable policy outcomes – though liberating judicial discretion in this way may seem undemocratic and an invitation to the imposition of personal judicial values.

Implementing the rule of law such that judicial practices are consistent across time often involves deductive reasoning from a superior source of law. Nothing in the federal Constitution or the state constitutions, however, explicitly commands that one of these approaches to statutory interpretation be followed to the exclusion of others. Another way judicial consistency is achieved over time is the doctrine of precedent, or *stare decisis,* which presumes that later courts will adhere to the holdings of earlier decisions. The doctrine of precedent is not much help in resolving a methodological problem, however, because the doctrine entrenches only the holding – for example, certain activity done by the defendant violated a criminal statute – and not the rationale undergirding the holding – for instance, that the legislative history demonstrated that the enacting legislature probably intended to outlaw that conduct. Thus, the fact that some older case adhered to one of these interpretive approaches does not preclude a later court from taking a different one.

Of course, in practical affairs there is often no "top–down" authority commanding that people act in a certain way, but often people do reach a consensus on how to act. Unfortunately, in no small part due to the problems identified above with each theory, no consensus has emerged in the practice of statutory interpretation, either. Thus, even though statutory interpretation is probably the most common judicial activity in United States courts, American judges have never worked out a settled method of doing it.[11]

Indeed, in Justice Rehnquist's three decades on the Court, a variety of battles over statutory interpretation methodology have occurred in the context of deciding important cases. At least until recently, when he has often deferred to Justice Scalia's text-based approach, Justice Rehnquist was the most consistent ad-

---

[11] "The hard truth of the matter is that American courts have no intelligible, generally accepted, and consistently applied theory of statutory interpretation." Henry M. Hart, Jr., & Albert M. Sacks, *The Legal Process: Some Problems in the Making and Application of Law* 1169 (William N. Eskridge, Jr., & Philip P. Frickey eds., 1994).

herent of the view that statutory meaning must be grounded in the probable intent of the enacting legislature. Two of his opinions provide particularly clear examples of his approach.

Griffin v. Oceanic Contractors[12] was an odd case. The straightforward wording of a federal statute seemingly required that, for every day an employer fails to pay a seaworker an amount owed, the worker is entitled to a penalty equal to twice the amount withheld. On the facts of the case, this amounted to a recovery of over $300,000 for wrongful withholding of only $412.50. Justice Rehnquist's majority opinion upheld this seeming windfall. Rehnquist's rationale was not that the ordinary meaning of the statutory text was to be followed for its own (textualist) sake, however. Instead, consistent with his intentionalist perspective, Rehnquist treated the statutory text as the best evidence of original legislative intent and continued by considering whether the legislative history supported his presumptive conclusion. Justice Rehnquist was little concerned about the disproportionality between the amount withheld and the amount recovered. It was left to Justice Stevens, in dissent, to make the purposive counterargument that the disproportionality was dysfunctional and indicated a strong reason to prefer an interpretation that produced a more limited recovery.

Justice Rehnquist did not prevail in every analogous case pitting original legislative intent against more expansive judicial considerations of purpose and policy, however. One of the most important decisions of this sort is *United Steelworkers v. Weber*.[13] *Weber* concerned whether a private employer could provide a preference to racial minorities to make up for their gross lack of representation in its workforce. The significant disparity concerning the minority workforce created a fear that racial minorities could prevail in a lawsuit against the employer for violating Title VII of the 1964 Civil Rights Act, which has been interpreted to prohibit the use of employment practices that have a demonstrable exclusionary impact upon the employment of racial minorities.[14] But Title VII has also been interpreted to forbid intentional disadvantaging of nonminorities in employment.[15] The employer found itself in a Catch-22: Failing to correct the massive underrepresentation of racial minorities provided a basis for suit by them, but correcting the disparity by overtly advantaging racial minorities promised a suit by disadvantaged whites. Sure enough, when the employer and its union gave preference to racial minorities in a new apprenticeship program designed to help correct the underrepresentation, a disappointed white employee sued.

The Court in *Weber* divided along ideological and methodological grounds. Justice Rehnquist contended that the Court's role was to serve as the faithful agent of the enacting Congress. He read the statutory text as creating a strong indication that all intentional disadvantaging on the basis of race was prohibited, and

[12] 458 U.S. 564 (1982).
[13] 443 U.S. 193 (1979).
[14] *See* Griggs v. Duke Power Co., 401 U.S. 424 (1971) .
[15] *See* McDonald v. Santa Fe Trail Transp. Co., 427 U.S. 273 (1976).

took that textual understanding as the best evidence of original legislative intent. He also engaged in a long examination of the legislative history of the statute, quoting numerous congressional sources for the proposition that color-blind employment decisions were mandated by Title VII. Only Chief Justice Burger joined Rehnquist in this effort, however.

The majority opinion, by Justice Brennan, considered it appropriate to deviate from ordinary statutory meaning when it was necessary to avoid violating the purpose of the statute. Here, Brennan concluded, the 1964 Congress had been animated by the goal of opening employment opportunities to historically disadvantaged persons. Reading the statute as commanding color blindness, rather than authorizing narrowly tailored programs overtly designed to promote employment opportunities for racial minorities, would be inconsistent with Title VII's fundamental purpose. "It would be ironic, indeed," Brennan maintained, if the nation's first statute designed to attack long patterns of racial injustice in employment prohibited all private efforts "to abolish traditional patterns of racial segregation and hierarchy." Justice Rehnquist responded by accusing the majority of Orwellian revisionism in light of his numerous quotations from the comments of Title VII's supporters that, he contended, demonstrated that color blindness was what they had in mind.[16]

The debate between adhering to apparent original legislative intent and supplementing that source of statutory meaning with broader considerations of purpose and policy has been a long-standing one. One of the many aspects of partial consensus in public law arising out of the New Deal consolidation of governmental control in like-minded hands was a sense that statutory meaning was governed by the wishes of the enacting legislature.[17] Not long afterward, however, a postwar understanding emerged under which the legal system was presumed to work best if all law, including statutes, was understood as embodying purposive instruments serving functional, productive outcomes.[18] The product of a legal education in the immediate postwar period, William Rehnquist must have been exposed to both perspectives. Unsurprisingly, his basic orientation preferring legislative rather than judicial settlement of controversial issues[19] favored a narrower method of statutory interpretation purporting to follow historical evidence rather than to liberate judges to work out "better" solutions on a case-by-case basis.

In this postwar era, the argument for taking statutory text seriously for its own sake was not much on the table. It seemed the product of old-fashioned, un-

---

[16] A somewhat similar example is Bob Jones University v. United States, 461 U.S. 574 (1983), in which, over Justice Rehnquist's intentionalist dissent, the Court upheld the change of policy by the Internal Revenue Service such that racially discriminatory private schools no longer qualified as tax-exempt organizations.

[17] See United States v. American Trucking Ass'n, 310 U.S. 534 (1940).

[18] Hart & Sacks, *supra* note 11, embodied this approach.

[19] See Thomas W. Merrill, *Chief Justice Rehnquist, Pluralist Theory, and the Interpretation of Statutes,* 25 Rutgers L.J. 621 (1994).

sophisticated understandings of textual meaning that often appeared to force a finding of one "plain meaning" even when a consideration of the background and legislative history of the statute indicated that it was not designed to have that effect.[20] Moreover, the old plain meaning mentality really amounted to just an occasional rule of exclusion of the consideration of legislative history when the statutory text was so clear that it must be understood as the conclusive meaning of what the legislature had intended. In this sense, even the old plain meaning rule was a method of targeting original legislative intent. It would not have seemed much of a stretch to move to the approach that even a "plain meaning" was just excellent evidence of legislative intent, subject to (the probably rare) impeachment of that meaning by extremely clear legislative history to the contrary.

Intentionalism in statutory interpretation has been in decline, however, since the arrival of Justice Scalia in 1986.[21] According to Scalia, legislative intent is an oxymoron. The meaning of a statute should be governed by the ordinary meaning of its text, perhaps occasionally supplemented by long-standing canons of statutory interpretation, not by fragmentary comments found in disparate congressional materials. The goal for Scalia is a kind of objective determination of what Congress would have understood the statute to mean based on the text Congress had chosen, not a supposedly more subjective, historiographical inquiry.

In recent years, the Court's citation of legislative history has declined sharply, just as its use of dictionaries has skyrocketed.[22] Nonetheless, it would be wrong to conclude that Scalian textualism has come to dominate the Supreme Court. Even though Justice Rehnquist and Justice O'Connor (another long-standing intentionalist) often sign on to Scalia opinions, only Justice Thomas routinely goes along with Scalia's absolute exclusionary rule on legislative history. That Scalia sometimes produces majority opinions that are starkly textualist is probably the product of patterns of small-group interactions, whereby Justices often join opinions that reach the results that they believe are correct but do so by rationales on which there is not a consensus.[23] Without such "incompletely theorized agreements" resulting in judicial opinions, a nine-member Court that is fragmented ideologically and methodologically would find it exceedingly difficult to issue many majority opinions at all.

---

[20] A notorious example of this largely repudiated approach is Caminetti v. United States, 242 U.S. 470 (1917), finding a violation of the federal Mann Act, based on literal statutory meaning, when a man took a woman to whom he was not married across state lines for sexual purposes, whereas the legislative history indicated that the statute was aimed at a smaller target (i.e., prostitution and the like).

[21] Justice Scalia has elaborated on his approach in Antonin Scalia, *Common-Law Courts in a Civil-Law System: The Role of United States Federal Courts in Interpreting the Constitution and Laws*, in Antonin Scalia, *A Matter of Interpretation* (Amy Guttmann ed., 1997). For an overview, see William N. Eskridge, Jr., *The New Textualism*, 37 UCLA L. Rev. 621 (1990).

[22] *See* Eskridge *et al., supra* note 6, at 768–72.

[23] *See* Craig M. Bradley, The Uncertainty Principle in the Supreme Court, 1986 Duke L.J. 1; Thomas W. Merrill, *Textualism and the Future of the Chevron Doctrine*, 72 Wash. U. L.Q. 351 (1994).

Indeed, although no Justice has vigorously defended intentionalism in recent years, it remains a mainstay of Supreme Court practice. A relatively recent, very prominent example is FDA v. Brown & Williamson Tobacco Co.[24] Justice O'Connor, writing for a bare five-member majority that included Chief Justice Rehnquist, concluded that the Food and Drug Administration did not have the authority to regulate tobacco as a "drug," despite the fact that the relevant statutory text strongly supported that interpretation. The strongest arguments that Justice O'Connor articulated were that the enacting Congress would not have considered tobacco a drug, that the FDA itself had assumed for many years it lacked this authority, that Congress had adopted tobacco regulatory schemes rooted in the assumption that the FDA had no such authority, and that Congress had had many opportunities to amend the Food and Drug Act explicitly to authorize FDA regulation of tobacco and yet had nonetheless never done so. That Justices Scalia and Thomas provided two of the crucial votes for this bare majority is telling in at least two ways. The first is that, at least in this critical case, intentionalism drove the crucial votes of Rehnquist and O'Connor, and Rehnquist assigned the opinion to O'Connor with presumed full knowledge that she would write the opinion that way. The second is that even Scalia and Thomas are apparently not so firmly wedded to methodological textualism.

Hence the more things change – the rise of the new textualism – the more they remain the same – the lack of a working consensus on the Supreme Court about the method of statutory interpretation. One topic for continuing scrutiny is the division among the more conservative Justices between textualism and intentionalism. With the likelihood that several new Justices will appear on the scene in the near future, textualism may finally reach an ascendancy. A whole generation of young, engaged conservative lawyers has been trained in the methodology of Justice Scalia, not of Chief Justice Rehnquist. Textualism is the new thing; intentionalism is the old-fashioned, insufficiently theoretical and rigorous, method to be abandoned.[25]

If that happens, one of Chief Justice Rehnquist's possible legacies will have been lost – in my view, regrettably. Consider how Thomas Merrill contrasts the potentially deferential nature of intentionalism with the remarkably self-confident qualities of textualism:

> Intentionalism mandates an "archeological" excavation of the past, producing opinions written in the style of the dry archivist sifting through countless documents in search of the tell-tale smoking gun of congressional intent. Textualism, in contrast, seems to transform statutory interpretation into a kind of exercise in judicial ingenuity. The textualist judge treats questions of interpretation like a puzzle to which it is assumed there is one right answer. The task is to assemble the various pieces of linguistic data, dictionary definitions, and canons into the best (most coherent, most explanatory) account of the meaning of the statute. This exercise places a great pre-

---

[24] 529 U.S. 120 (2000).
[25] See Philip P. Frickey, *Interpretive-Regime Change*, 38.5 Loy. (L.A.) L. Rev. (2005).

mium on cleverness. In one case the outcome turns on the placement of a comma, in another on the inconsistency between a comma and rules of grammar, in a third on the conflict between quotation marks and the language of the text. One day arguments must be advanced in support of broad dictionary definitions; the next day in support of narrow dictionary definitions. New canons of construction and clear statement rules must be invented and old ones reinterpreted. This active, creative approach to interpretation is subtly incompatible with an attitude of deference toward other institutions – including Congress. . . .[26]

Recall that Rehnquist has taken no special joy in puzzling through complex statutory issues and that, in many instances, he admits that no crystal-clear resolution emerges.[27] He has engaged in no strong assumptions about the coherence of positive law and legislative history. On these understandings, statutory interpretation is messy and conflictual, a duty rather than a pleasure. The interpreter ought to remain humble in the task of combating the human tendency for statutory words to swim before the eyes. In contrast, the textualist takes delight in demonstrating how, far from swimming chaotically, the words cohere into a tidy package of meaning. By assuming that statutory interpretation is a word puzzle with a clear answer evident if only all others would bow to revealed analysis, textualism has a whiff of arrogance and is oddly decoupled from human institutions. Intentionalism at least purports to deal with what real people attempted to achieve in grappling with social problems at a particular point in human history. Conservative jurists, like anyone else, ought to recognize that law draws some of its legitimacy by rooting itself in the human condition.[28]

II. CONSTITUTIONAL VALUES IN STATUTORY INTERPRETATION

Canons of statutory interpretation purport to provide rules of thumb, if not rules of law, about how statutes should be interpreted. They come in three basic categories.[29] One set involves presumed textual meaning: presumptions that words are used in their common meaning unless a technical usage is evident, that words maintain the same meaning throughout their various statutory usages, that the expression of a few exclusions cuts against finding implied, unwritten exclusions, and so on. These textual canons are relatively uncontroversial, but also have only modest force to them. Another set of canons involves referential meaning – incorporation of sources of statutory meaning from other sources. For example, canons attempt to identify the degree of judicial deference that should be paid to the interpretations of a statute by the administrative agency charged with implementing it, to the meanings words were accorded by the common law, to the

---

[26] Merrill, *supra* note 23, at 372 (footnotes omitted).

[27] *See* text at notes 1–3, *supra*.

[28] *See* Robert C. Post, *The Supreme Court, 2002 Term – Foreword: Fashioning the Legal Constitution: Culture, Courts, and Law,* 117 Harv. L. Rev. 4 (2003).

[29] *See* Eskridge *et al., supra* note 10, at 249–75, 287–383.

understandings of private industry with respect to long-standing statutory regimes regulating it, and so on. This part of this chapter concerns the third set of canons, those that involve public values imported from outside the statute being interpreted. These values may come from the common law, from other statutes, from the federal Constitution, or simply from long-standing judicial impressions of good public policy. My focus here is on Justice Rehnquist's importation of constitutional values into statutory interpretation.

There are two common ways to achieve this melding of statutory and constitutional interpretation: one general, the other more specific. First, there is a long-standing canon that counsels that an interpretation that raises a serious doubt about the constitutionality of a statute should be rejected if another, plausible interpretation is available that avoids raising a serious constitutional question.[30] Second, the Supreme Court has sometimes implemented identified constitutional values by crafting specific canons to protect them. In this way, the Court has taken the general constitutional avoidance canon and refined it in a few specific circumstances.[31] Frequently, these canons protect constitutional values that, for a variety of reasons, are problematic to protect by ordinary judicial review.[32]

It is especially this second category of constitutionally inspired canons of statutory interpretation that constitute a portion of the legacy of Justice Rehnquist. The constitutional values that animate his most important opinions are structural in nature, concerning federalism (the division of authority between the federal and state governments) and the separation of powers (the allocation of responsibilities among the three federal branches of government).

A. Federalism

Justice Rehnquist has consistently sought to enforce the constitutional value of federalism – the notion that the federal government has limited authority to intrude upon the appropriate domain of state governmental powers. Justice Rehnquist's most famous opinions in this respect have argued for the constitutional invalidation of federal statutes that, in his view, invade the domain of the states. In other instances, however, the Court has moved from the constitutional level to the subconstitutional level: It has not invalidated the statute as unconstitutional, but instead used interpretive techniques to limit the intrusive force of federal statutes into state authority. Indeed, in three important series of cases, the values Justice Rehnquist first articulated as constitutionally rooted have influenced the interpretation of federal statutes.

---

[30] See, e.g., id. at 348–54.

[31] See, e.g., William N. Eskridge, Jr., & Philip P. Frickey, *Quasi-Constitutional Law: Clear Statement Rules as Constitutional Lawmaking*, 45 Vand. L. Rev. 593 (1992).

[32] See Philip P. Frickey, *Getting from Joe to Gene (McCarthy): The Avoidance Canon, Legal Process Theory, and Narrowing Statutory Interpretation in the Early Warren Court*, 93 Cal. L. Rev. 397 (2005).

The first set of cases concerns the extent to which Congress's authority to regulate "commerce among the states"[33] allows the regulation of local activity with some economic impact. In 1995, Chief Justice Rehnquist wrote the majority opinion in *United States v. Lopez*,[34] holding that Congress did not have the authority to prohibit possession of a gun within a thousand feet of a school. Rehnquist viewed the economic impact that might result from violence in and around schools as too remote from commerce to implicate congressional authority to regulate commerce among the states. Rehnquist later transformed the constitutional value in *Lopez* into a narrowing canon of statutory interpretation.

Solid Waste Agency v. Corps of Engineers[35] was a complicated case concerning a determination that the proposed filling of part of an abandoned sand and gravel pit in which water collects required a permit from the Corps of Engineers under the federal Clean Water Act. The conclusion was that the pit involved "navigable waters," the term triggering the permit requirement, because migratory birds used the ponds as habitat. This determination seems quite odd – it would seem impossible to navigate a vessel in the pit – except for the fact that the statute defines "navigable waters" as "waters of the United States." The Corps interpreted these two terms – ordinarily nonsynonymous, but here defined by Congress as synonyms – to include natural ponds "the use, degradation or destruction of which could affect interstate or foreign commerce. . . ." The Corps further elaborated that isolated waters used as habitat by migratory birds – as was the case at the pit in question – qualified under this definition.

For a narrow majority of the Court, Chief Justice Rehnquist held that the Corps was wrong to assert its permit jurisdiction over the isolated pit. He found it constitutionally questionable whether Congress's commerce power could be stretched that far. Without a clear statement in the statute by Congress authorizing the agency to take this action, he held that it lacked the authority to impinge upon "the States' traditional and primary power over land and water use."

In a second series of cases, Justice Rehnquist attempted to prevent Congress from using its commerce power to regulate core functions of state and local governments. He was successful in cobbling together a narrow majority for this proposition in *National League of Cities v. Usery*,[36] but nine years later the Court overruled that decision in *Garcia v. San Antonio Metropolitan Transit Authority*,[37] again by the narrowest of votes. Rehnquist vociferously dissented, positing that in time the new case would be abandoned and the law returned to *National League of Cities*. At this writing, a partial reversion of this kind has occurred as a matter of constitutional law. In *New York v. United States*[38] and in *Printz v. United States*,[39] the Rehnquist Court held that Congress could not commandeer either a state legislature or state executive officials to carry out a federal program. Beyond these

---

[33] U.S. Const., art. I, §8, cl. 3: Congress shall have authority "to regulate commerce with foreign nations, and among the several states, and with the Indian tribes."

[34] 514 U.S. 549 (1995).   [35] 531 U.S. 159 (2001).

[36] 426 U.S. 833 (1976).   [37] 469 U.S. 528 (1985).

[38] 505 U.S. 144 (1992).   [39] 521 U.S. 898 (1997).

cases, steps have been taken in the direction of reviving *National League of Cities* as a matter of statutory rather than constitutional interpretation. Just six years after *Garcia* was decided, a majority of the Court that included the Chief Justice, in an opinion by Justice O'Connor, held that the Court would presume that federal statutes do not regulate core state functions unless the statute contains an unmistakably clear expression of congressional intent to the contrary.[40]

A third set of cases involved congressional efforts to use a carrot rather than a stick to attain state compliance with federal objectives. In *Pennhurst State School and Hospital v. Halderman*,[41] Justice Rehnquist's majority opinion concluded that a federal statute providing financial assistance to the states for care and treatment of the developmentally disabled did not create rights enforceable against the participating states. The statute's listing of "rights" – to appropriate treatment in the least restrictive environment – was merely hortatory, Rehnquist concluded. To reach this result, he created a strong canon of statutory interpretation to protect states against inadvertent agreement to strings attached to federal money. Unless Congress has spoken unambiguously so that the state can be said to have made an informed choice, the conditions are not binding. One important factor in *Pennhurst* was that the purported rights were so indeterminate that it seemed unlikely that states would have knowingly agreed to subjecting themselves to suit in federal court for allegedly violating them. When the strings attached to federal money are clear, when they have a rational connection to the state program receiving the benefit, and when the state is under no strong coercion to accept the money, however, Justice Rehnquist has found no constitutional infirmity preventing Congress from attaining state compliance with federal goals in this matter.[42] In essence, Rehnquist has clearly preferred federal carrots to sticks, on a contractual rather than a coercive model of federalism.

B. Separation of Powers

Just as Justice Rehnquist has attempted to preserve the states as at least somewhat autonomous sovereigns, he has sought to protect the autonomy of the federal Executive Branch to exercise important functions. In a case involving great political importance, Justice Rehnquist wrote the opinion upholding the Executive Branch's actions in settling the Iran hostage crisis.[43] The American side of this agreement was implemented by executive orders by President Carter and President Reagan. The settlement disadvantaged American businesses that were creditors of Iran by preventing the enforcement of judgments issued by U.S. courts against Iran and shifting the claims to a U.S.–Iran Claims Tribunal. Congress was not asked to ratify these arrangements by the passage of a statute or by Senate

---

[40] Gregory v. Ashcroft, 501 U.S. 452 (1991).
[41] 451 U.S. 1 (1981).
[42] *See* South Dakota v. Dole, 483 U.S. 203 (1987).
[43] Dames & Moore v. Regan, 453 U.S. 654 (1981).

ratification of a treaty. Moreover, Congress had passed earlier statutes that authorized the Executive to settle foreign disputes on certain terms, and the Carter–Reagan approach was arguably not consistent with this delegated authority. Nonetheless, finding that nothing the Presidents had done was squarely inconsistent with congressionally adopted law, Rehnquist held that the Executive Branch had significant discretion in the circumstances to negotiate a solution to the crisis.

In a later case, the majority opinion by Justice Rehnquist reinforced the theme that Congress will not be presumed to have intruded upon traditional executive functions. In *Japan Whaling Association v. American Cetacean Society,*[44] statutes passed by Congress could easily have been understood as requiring the Executive Branch to evaluate whether Japan's whaling practices were consistent with international agreements and, if not, to refer the matter to an international body. Yet the Court held that Congress had not been sufficiently explicit in attempting to direct executive action in an area in which the President might want to negotiate a bilateral agreement with Japan to resolve the matter. Like in the federalism cases, *Japan Whaling* amounted to imposing a clear statement requirement upon Congress before the Court would assume Congress had intended to intervene in core executive functions.

In addition to policing whether Congress has interfered with executive functions, Justice Rehnquist had sought to limit the congressional capacity to delegate legislative authority to the Executive Branch. In effect, this strategy is an attempt to prevent Congress from shifting its legislative, policy-making responsibilities to the Executive. In two instances, he dissented from opinions that, in his view, did not sufficiently cabin congressional delegations of wide-ranging, vague authority to the Executive.[45] Ultimately, again like in the federalism cases, the Rehnquist Court resolved this matter by transforming his constitutional concern into a canon of statutory interpretation: Such vast delegations of lawmaking authority to the Executive Branch would be interpreted narrowly to avoid having invested the executive with policy-making power better left in the hands of Congress.[46]

III. CONCLUSION

Justice Rehnquist is not, at heart, a legal theorist. Unlike Justices Scalia and Breyer,[47] for example, the methodology of statutory interpretation is not something that stirs him to write legal scholarship or to debate fine points in separate opinions. Instead, his focus has been the concrete, case-by-case practice of statutory

---

[44]   478 U.S. 221 (1986).
[45]   *See* Justice Rehnquist's dissents in American Textile Mfrs. Inst., Inc. v. Donovan (1981); Industrial Union Dep't, AFL–CIO v. American Petroleum Institute, 448 U.S. 607 (1980).
[46]   *See* Whitman v. American Trucking Ass'ns, Inc., 531 U.S. 457 (2001).
[47]   *See* Stephen Breyer, *On the Uses of Legislative History in Interpreting Statutes*, 65 S. Cal. L. Rev. 845 (1992).

interpretation. His grounded implementation of intentionalism and constitutionally informed canons has the potential of being an important legacy of his time on the Court.

One question raised not only by Justice Rehnquist's work, but by all judicial decision making, is whether methodology makes a difference. Do judges reach decisions deductively through a methodology, or do they use methodology simply to mask decisions reached by other ways (intuition, politics, whatever)? Mark Tushnet has said that Justice Rehnquist's voting record is best explained as implementing the preferences of the Republican Party.[48] Tom Merrill has responded that Justice Rehnquist's opinions justifying his votes in statutory cases travel a methodologically defensible path based on a version of pluralist theory that assumes legislatures often reach good results, that courts are not well-equipped or even authorized to displace legislative policy judgments, and that local decisions should be preferred to national ones.[49] I mean no disrespect to either distinguished scholar, or to Justice Rehnquist, by suggesting that both Tushnet and Merrill may be correct. A nonpurposive originalism, informed by structural constitutional law, is more likely to limit the domain of federal statutes to matters that were relatively clearly resolved by the enacting Congress and that involve matters of truly national scope. This sort of weight on the scales favoring deregulation to regulation, and local to national regulation, is consistent with a conservative interest in limiting the reach of the federal government. The constitutionally informed canons of interpretation deployed by Rehnquist keep federal regulatory intrusion upon state sovereignty in greater check, promoting the agenda of federalism. The canons also give greater breathing room to executive autonomy, which further limits what conservatives would often consider unnecessary congressional meddling. To be sure, the methods promote identifiable political agendas. But the methods were also well established in statutory interpretation methodology long before Rehnquist came to the Supreme Court – he did not invent them to implement the platform of the Republican Party.

In the final analysis, it is the relatively rare statutory case that involves a major ideological controversy. Much more common are questions the importance of which does not transcend the parties and persons similarly situated to them. Whether sand and gravel are "valuable minerals" under some old federal statute is a question only a lawyer could love, and even most of them won't. Justice Rehnquist has done more than his share of the routine work of the Supreme Court with good cheer, few complaints, and an admirable humility. This is a legacy that the Republican Party – and everyone else – ought to remember when new Justices are nominated and subjected to Senate confirmation hearings.

---

[48] Mark V. Tushnet, *A Republican Chief Justice*, 88 Mich. L. Rev. 1326 (1990).

[49] *See* Merrill, *supra* note 19.

CHAPTER FOURTEEN

REHNQUIST AND FEDERALISM:
AN EMPIRICAL PERSPECTIVE

Ruth Colker and Kevin M. Scott*

Commentators generally agree that the Supreme Court has spurred a "federalism revolution" during Chief Justice William Rehnquist's tenure.[1] Nonetheless, the term "federalism revolution" is unclear, in part, because the early federalists offered little commentary on the proper judicial role under federalism. Arguably, this uncertainty continues today.

Broadly speaking, we can think of federalism as reflecting a respect for the relationship between state and federal government. Under federalism principles, Congress should be hesitant to interfere with state sovereignty. Similarly, the states should respect Congress's authority and not take actions that would jeopardize our national interests. Historically, the federalists sought a *greater* role for the federal government than had existed under the Articles of Confederation. Today, by contrast, we often think of the federalists as seeking a more restrained role for Congress as compared with the states.

But what is the role of the judiciary in this arrangement? Is a federalist inherently a restraintist, believing in a limited role for the judiciary? What is the role of the state judiciary as compared to the federal judiciary? The early federalists were restraintists and did not envision a broad role for the judiciary in maintaining the proper federalism balance. Today, by contrast, some might argue that the Court is more generally activist, and that even the federalists consider the judiciary to have a significant role in maintaining what it considers to be the proper allocation of power between the federal and state governments.

Finally, how does the ratification of the Fourteenth Amendment affect federalism? The early federalists could not have anticipated the ratification of the

* We thank Ohio State University for providing Professor Colker with a Distinguished Scholar Award, which we were able to use to fund this research. We also thank the law students who helped code the cases that became the basis for this project: Reid Caryer, Nathan DeDino, John Deeds, Michelle Evans, Kerry Hodak, Matthew Kear, Lee Ann Rabe, and Sabrina Riggs.
[1] *See generally* Ruth Colker & James J. Brudney, *Dissing Congress*, 100 MICH. L. REV. 80 (2001); A. Christopher Bryant & Timothy J. Simeone, *Remanding to Congress: The Supreme Court's New "On the Record" Constitutional Review of Federal Statutes*, 86 CORNELL L. REV. 328 (2001); William W. Buzbee, *Legislative Record Review*, 54 STAN. L. REV. 87 (2001).

Fourteenth Amendment, with its direct limitations on state action and allocation of greater power to Congress. We can only speculate as to how they might have modified their version of federalism had they known of the ratification of the Fourteenth Amendment.

Chief Justice Rehnquist has been a strong proponent of federalism. He has repeatedly invoked federalism principles – first in dissent, and then in majority opinions. As reflected in his opinions, Rehnquist's version of federalism appears to be more restraintist than the version propounded by Justice Antonin Scalia. Rehnquist also appears to consider the Fourteenth Amendment to create an important source of increased power for Congress in regulating the states.

In this chapter, we use both qualitative and quantitative tools to understand more fully Rehnquist's version of federalism. Using qualitative analysis, we argue that his version of federalism is different both from the one propounded by the early federalists and from that of Justice Scalia. Then, using quantitative analysis, we ask whether Rehnquist's decisions are consistent with the federalism model that he propounds in his opinions.

I. THREE VERSIONS OF FEDERALISM

A. The Classical View of Federalism

Today, federalism is often considered to be a states' rights perspective, but the antifederalists had the strongest states' rights perspective in the eighteenth century. James Madison sought to create a *balanced* system of government whereby both the federal government and the states had an appropriate scope of power. To him, "the federal constitution forms a happy combination in this respect; the great and aggregate interests being referred to the national, the local, and particular to the state legislatures."[2]

Madison emphasized that the proposed government would be a *federal,* not a *national* government. The federal character was achieved through the selection of the Senate and the selection of the President. Each state would receive the same number of Senators, and those Senators would be chosen by the state legislatures. The presidential election would use a winner-take-all method of counting electoral votes on a state-by-state basis. Madison believed that these rules would protect the states. "Thus, each of the principal branches of the federal government will owe its existence more or less to the favor of the state governments, and must consequently feel a dependence, which is much more likely to beget a disposition too obsequious, than too overbearing toward them."[3]

In general, the Framers did not emphasize the importance of the judicial role in protecting the constitutional design. Alexander Hamilton gave the most consideration to the proper role of the judiciary. Hamilton understood that the ju-

---

[2] *Federalist* No. 10 at 22.
[3] *Federalist* No. 45 at 100.

diciary, in some sense, is beholden to the other branches of government because it cannot enforce its rulings. Hence, some might call it the "weakest of the three departments of power."[4] Yet the independence of the judiciary was an essential aspect of the proposed new government. "[T]here is no liberty, if the power of judging be not separated from the legislative and executive powers." He then delineated the role of the courts in the proposed system of government:

> The complete independence of the courts of justice is peculiarly essential in a limited Constitution. . . . Limitations . . . can be preserved in practice no other way than through the medium of the courts of justice; whose duty it must be to declare all acts contrary to the manifest tenor of the Constitution void. Without this, all the reservations of particular rights or privileges would amount to nothing.

Hamilton does not specify whether this judicial role should be a broad or narrow one but his recognition that the judiciary is the weakest branch might suggest that he thought the judiciary should use its powers sparingly to maintain its integrity.

More modern writers also contemplated the judicial role under federalism. James Thayer and Herbert Wechsler have played a central role in the development of a judicial role for federalists, arguing for a restrained judicial role. Thayer defended the position that courts should only declare laws unconstitutional "when those who have the right to make laws have not merely made a mistake, but have made a very clear one, – so clear that it is not open to rational question."[5] Nonetheless, he considered it important for courts to have the power to declare laws unconstitutional. Otherwise, the Constitution "is reduced to nothing."

Although Thayer argued for judicial restraint, he suggested that the Supreme Court should be sensitive to whether a case is being appealed from a state or federal court. In this context, he makes two important points. First, he emphasizes the importance of the Supremacy Clause.

> If a State legislature passes a law which is impeached in the due course of litigation before the national courts, as being in conflict with the supreme law of the land, those courts may have to ask themselves a question different from that which would be applicable if the enactments were those of a co-ordinate department. . . . The judiciary now speaks as representing a paramount constitution and government, whose duty it is, in all its departments, to allow to that constitution nothing less than its just and true interpretation; and have fixed this, to guard against any inroads from without.

Second, and related, Thayer postulates that judges should be generally deferential to the views of a coordinate branch of government. Hence, state court judges would be deferential to the views of the state legislature and be disinclined to invalidate their legislation as violative of the Constitution. By emphasizing

---

[4] *Federalist* No. 78 at 143.
[5] James B. Thayer, *The Origin and Scope of the American Doctrine of Constitutional Law,* 7 HARV. L. REV. 129, 144 (1893).

the importance of deferring to the views of a coordinate branch of government, Thayer implied that a federal judge need *not* defer to the views of the state legislature, particularly when the state's highest court has validated those legislative acts. One might argue, then, that a federalist judge would be less deferential to a state court's review of state action than similar review by a federal court.

One must be careful not to overstate Thayer's view about the federal courts' relationship to state government. Thayer's view is predicated on the assumption that it will be extremely rare for state government to violate the Constitution, because his work predates use of the Fourteenth Amendment as a vehicle for incorporation. From his perspective, states had broad authority to enact legislation. The only meaningful limitation on the states would be the Supremacy Clause – when Congress had the power to preempt a field, chose to preempt the field, and the states did not honor those limitations. Thayer would therefore have expected that courts would rarely deal with situations in which the states had arguably violated the Constitution. But in instances in which the states may have violated the Supremacy Clause, he did not consider it likely that the state courts would vigorously enforce that constitutional principle. Hence, the federal courts would play an important role in protecting the federal government's prerogatives.

Herbert Wechsler also did not consider courts to have a central role in the maintenance of a federal system.

> [T]he national political process in the United States – and especially the role of the states in the composition and selection of the central government – is intrinsically well adapted to retarding or restraining new intrusions by the center on the domain of the states. . . . Federal intervention as against the states is thus primarily a matter for congressional determination in our system as it stands.[6]

Like Thayer, Wechsler envisioned the function of the courts in a federal system to be preservation of the Supremacy Clause, but this did not mean that he envisioned the courts as actively engaged in the policy-making process – that was to be left to the elected branches. According to Wechsler, "while the Court has an important function in [pre-emption], the crucial point is that its judgments here are subject to reversal by Congress, which can consent to action by the states that otherwise would be invalidated. . . . The Court makes the decisive judgment only when – and to the extent that – Congress has not laid down the resolving rule." On the other hand, Wechsler saw a fundamentally different role for the courts in protecting individual rights:

> In this latter area of the constitutional protection of the individual against the government, both federal and state, subordination of the Court to Congress would defeat the purpose of judicial mediation. For this is where the political processes cannot be relied upon to introduce their own correctives – except to the limited extent that individuals or small minorities may find a champion in some important faction.

---

[6] Herbert Wechsler, *Political Safeguards of Federalism: The Role of the States in the Composition and Selection of the National Government*, 54 COLUM. L. REV. 543, 558 (1954).

The classical version of federalism and the Thayer–Wechsler version are only modestly different. Both versions are restraintist while recognizing a legitimate federal judicial role in protecting the Supremacy Clause. The important difference is that Wechsler envisions a somewhat active role for the courts in the protection of individual rights, because he takes account of the Fourteenth Amendment in the development of his views.

B. Federalism since the 1970s: The Demise of Wechsler

Although the early federalists appear to have advocated a restrained role for the judiciary, a more activist version of federalism began to emerge in the 1970s and 1980s. Some political scientists have argued that this development was not a genuine reflection of federalist principles; instead, it was an example of the Supreme Court imposing its ideological preferences on Congress.[7] Within legal circles, a genuine federalism explanation is offered, with commentators suggesting that the Court has grown weary of Congress dramatically overstepping its proper authority.[8] We have entered the federalism versus political ideology debate in previous work but leave that issue to the side for the purposes of this chapter.[9]

The modern federalist position on the Tenth Amendment is reflected in Justice Powell's dissenting opinion in *Garcia v. San Antonio Metropolitan Transit Authority*.[10] Justice Powell argued for a vigorous judicial role to protect the states when Congress violates the Tenth Amendment by overreaching in its use of the Commerce Clause, stating: "Professor Wechsler, whose seminal article in 1954 proposed the view adopted by the Court today, predicated his argument on assumptions that simply do not accord with current reality." To Powell, the growth of the federal government had obviated the position advocated by Wechsler and his predecessors. Justice Powell also disagreed with Wechsler's premise that members of Congress, because they are elected from states, would protect state sovereignty. Instead, he posited that they would have a national, not local, perspective. The modern federalist position has therefore evolved from one of judicial restraint to one of active judicial enforcement of the principles of state sovereignty.[11]

---

[7] *See generally* Sue Davis, *Rehnquist and State Courts: Federalism Revisited*, 45 WEST. POL. Q. 772 (1992); Harold J. Spaeth, *Justice Sandra Day O'Connor: An Assessment*, in AN ESSENTIAL SAFE-GUARD: ESSAYS ON THE UNITED STATES SUPREME COURT AND ITS JUSTICES 94–95 (D. Grier Stephenson, Jr., ed., 1991); JEFFREY A. SEGAL & HAROLD J. SPAETH, THE SUPREME COURT AND THE ATTITUDINAL MODEL REVISITED (2002).

[8] *See, e.g.*, Robert F. Nagel, *The Future of Federalism*, 46 CASE W. RES. L. REV. 643 (1996); John C. Yoo, *The Judicial Safeguards of Federalism*, 70 S. CAL. L. REV. 1311 (1997).

[9] *See* Ruth Colker & Kevin M. Scott, *Dissing States?: Invalidation of State Action During the Rehnquist Era*, 88 VA. L. REV. 1301 (2002).

[10] 469 U.S. 528 (1984).

[11] *See* Lynn A. Baker, *Putting the Safeguards Back into the Political Safeguards of Federalism*, 46 VILL. L. REV. 951, 952 (2001) (arguing that "federal courts have a role in safeguarding state sovereignty that is as legitimate and essential as that generally acknowledged to be both necessary and constitutionally mandated for the protection of individual rights.").

Justice Scalia has been the bluntest proponent of action by the Court in defense of federalism. He has said:

> My Court is fond of saying that acts of Congress come to the Court with the presumption of constitutionality. That presumption reflects Congress's status as a coequal branch of government with its own responsibilities to the Constitution. But if Congress is going to take the attitude that it will do anything it can get away with and let the Supreme Court worry about the Constitution . . . then perhaps that presumption is unwarranted.[12]

This runs contrary to the assertions of some early federalists like Thayer and Wechsler. Thayer, in particular, argued that the Court should presume the constitutionality of Congress's conduct and strike such legislation only where there is "no room for reasonable doubt." Scalia criticized Congress's recent practice of creating expedited procedures for the courts to assess the constitutionality of legislation. Scalia argued that by doing so, Congress is flouting its unconstitutional conduct by readily acknowledging that it may have passed unconstitutional legislation.

This second version of federalism is less restraintist than the view offered by the early federalists. In addition, it appears to be more protective of states' interests. We would therefore expect that if this model explained the voting behavior of a federalist jurist, that voting behavior would be consistent with the views expressed by states in amicus briefs.

C. Rehnquist's Federalism

Although Rehnquist played an early and active role in pushing the Court to adopt a more activist posture with respect to enforcing federalist principles, his version of federalism does not appear to be as activist as the one propounded by Scalia because, like Wechsler and Thayer, Rehnquist seems to envision a role for the Court in the protection of individual rights even when congressional protection of individual rights seems to trounce state's rights.

Associate Justice Rehnquist played an early role in the articulation of a strong role for the federal courts in protecting federalism in his dissent in *Fry v. United States*,[13] three years after joining the Court. In 1975, he was the lone Justice to articulate this perspective. The issue in *Fry* was the constitutionality of the Economic Stabilization Act of 1970, which authorized the President to issue orders and regulations to stabilize wages and salaries at levels not lower than those prevailing on May 25, 1970. Not only did this statute apply to the workforce generally, but it was understood to apply to the conduct of state government. Hence,

---

[12] Antonin Scalia, Telecommunications Law and Policy Symposium (Apr. 18, 2000). (Transcribed from a videotape loaned by the *Law Review* of Michigan State University – Detroit College of Law.)

[13] 421 U.S. 542 (1975).

two state employees brought suit to invalidate the statute so that they could receive a salary increase that the state of Ohio had approved. The state employees challenged the statute under the Tenth Amendment as improperly interfering with state sovereignty.

The majority upheld the constitutionality of the Economic Stabilization Act, relying on the Court's holding in *Maryland v. Wirtz*[14] that the Fair Labor Standards Act could constitutionally be applied to schools and hospitals run by states. (Justices Douglas and Stewart dissented, arguing that the Tenth Amendment protected state sovereignty from such regulation, given the excessive cost that would accompany enforcement of the FLSA.) Justice Stewart joined the majority in *Fry;* Justice Douglas would have dismissed the writ as improvidently granted. Hence, in dissent, Justice Rehnquist was alone in extending Douglas and Stewart's dissent in *Wirtz* to *Fry.*

Justice Rehnquist had not been on the Court when *Wirtz* was decided, so *Fry* was his first opportunity to convey his view of federalism and the judicial role. Building on the Court's decision in *Hans v. Louisiana,*[15] in which it relied on the "pre-understanding" of the Eleventh Amendment to protect a state from litigation, Rehnquist argued that many aspects of state sovereignty are protected "quite apart from the provisions of the Tenth Amendment."

> Both Amendments [the Tenth and Eleventh] are simply examples of the understanding of those who drafted and ratified the Constitution that the States were sovereign in many respects, and that although their legislative authority could be superseded by Congress in many areas where Congress was competent to act, Congress was nonetheless not free to deal with a State as if it were just another individual or business enterprise subject to regulation.

Having articulated an activist role for the judiciary in safeguarding federalism, Rehnquist still had a challenging set of facts to assess, because the wage and salary ceilings were put into place as part of national emergency legislation. One might argue under the early federalist model that the states should defer to Congress in times of national emergency, and so the legislation should be upheld as constitutional. Rehnquist did not offer much scrutiny of the facts. He simply concluded: "nor do I believe that the showing of national emergency made here is sufficient to make this case one in which congressional authority may be derived from sources other than the Commerce Clause." He did acknowledge, however, that the Fourteenth and Fifteenth Amendments, as a general matter, can provide the authority for Congress to "impose significant restrictions on what would otherwise be thought state prerogatives." No Fourteenth or Fifteenth Amendment argument, however, was available in this case. Rehnquist therefore argued that *Wirtz* should be overruled but that *South Carolina v. Katzenbach,*[16] upholding the Voting Rights Act, could still be understood to be valid precedent.

---

[14] 392 U.S. 183 (1968).   [15] 134 U.S. 1 (1890).   [16] 388 U.S. 301 (1966).

Rehnquist recognized that he was calling for the overturning of precedent, which is inconsistent with the notion of *stare decisis*. In order to justify that step, he subscribed to a weak version of *stare decisis:* "important decisions of constitutional law are not subject to the same command of *stare decisis* as are decisions of statutory questions."[17] This weak version of *stare decisis* would be quite inconsistent with the tenor of Thayer's judicially cautious federalism. Rehnquist justified this weak version of *stare decisis* in the federalism context: "Surely there can be no more fundamental constitutional question than that of the intention of the Framers of the Constitution as to how authority should be allocated between the National and State Governments."

Rehnquist made two important contributions to the development of a federalism jurisprudence in *Fry*. First, he carved out an activist judicial role, even if that role required the overturning of precedent. Second, he recognized the power of Congress to regulate states and intrude on their sovereignty under the Fourteenth and Fifteenth Amendments, but not under the Commerce Clause. In 1975, he was alone in taking this view.

Within a year, Rehnquist commanded a 5–4 majority of support for his federalism views as articulated in *National League of Cities v. Usery*.[18] Justice Blackmun filed the pivotal concurrence to give Rehnquist a five-vote majority. (Ironically, Robert H. Bork defended the federal statute as Solicitor General.) The issue in *Usery* was essentially the issue in *Wirtz* – the constitutionality of Congress applying the Fair Labor Standards Act to state employees. Only two members of the Court had dissented from the conclusion in 1968. Now, however, a majority of the Court was willing to strike down the FLSA as applied to the states because it resulted in the "forced relinquishment of important governmental activities." Not only did the FLSA impose substantial costs on state and local government, but it "displaces state policies regarding the manner in which they will structure delivery of those governmental services which their citizens require."

Although the decision had far-reaching implications in reversing the recent decision in *Wirtz*, the *Usery* decision had cautious elements. First, Rehnquist was careful to note that the decision applied only to Congress's use of the Commerce Clause. He left open the possibility that Congress might regulate the states and "affect integral operations" under the spending power or Section 5 of the Fourteenth Amendment. Second, Rehnquist distinguished rather than overruled *Fry*. In contrast to the FLSA, he found that the Economic Stabilization Act, at issue in *Fry*, was a limited, temporary, national measure that reduced the pressures upon state budgets rather than increased them. Thus, Rehnquist left open the possibility that Congress, in the future, could use its emergency powers to enact legislation that might intrude upon state sovereignty. Nonetheless, he made no attempt to distinguish *Wirtz*: He directly overruled that precedent, implicitly relying on his view expressed in *Fry* that constitutional decisions are entitled to less weight as *stare decisis*.

[17] 421 U.S. at 559.   [18] 426 U.S. 833 (1976).

Rehnquist reiterated the moderate aspects of his federalism in *Fitzpatrick v. Bitzer.*[19] With no dissenters, Rehnquist again wrote the opinion of the Court. The issue in this case was the authority of Congress to permit monetary damage awards against the states in suits brought under Title VII of the Civil Rights Act of 1964. The Court upheld this congressional authority, finding that Congress's powers under Section 5 of the Fourteenth Amendment necessarily limited the principle of state sovereignty embodied in the Constitution. *Fitzpatrick* therefore continued the line of reasoning that Rehnquist had acknowledged in *Fry* – that cases involving Congress's authority under Section 5 present different problems than cases involving Congress's Commerce Clause authority.

Although Rehnquist still adhered to the view that Congress's Section 5 authority is broader than its Commerce Clause authority, with respect to regulating state action, his decision in *Rome v. United States*[20] suggested that he had moderated his views on the extent of Congress's authority under Section 5.

The issue in *Rome* was the constitutionality of the Voting Rights Act of 1965, as applied to Rome, Georgia. In 1965, the city of Rome made a number of changes to its electoral scheme; under §5 of the Voting Rights Act, these changes required preclearance. Yet §5 of the act required that the Attorney General may preclear a voting change only if it "does not have the purpose and will not have the effect of denying or abridging the right to vote on account of race or color."[21] The city claimed that §5 was unconstitutional, because Congress does not have authority under the Fourteenth Amendment to ban practices that are discriminatory in effect but lack discriminatory intent.

In a 6–3 decision, the majority upheld Congress's use of its Fourteenth Amendment authority to create the preclearance rules. Justice Rehnquist dissented, issuing an opinion that was joined by Justice Stewart. (Stewart, of course, had dissented from the majority's holding in *Wirtz* and had a long-standing concern for federalism.) Echoing his strong dissent in *Fry,* Rehnquist castigated the Court for abandoning its proper judicial role:

> While the presumption of constitutionality is due to any act of a coordinate branch of the Federal Government or of one of the States, it is this Court which is ultimately responsible for deciding challenges to the exercise of power by those entities. Marbury v. Madison, 1 Cranch 137 (1803); United States v. Nixon, 418 U.S. 683 (1974). Today's decision is nothing less than a total abdication of that authority, rather than an exercise of the deference due to a coordinate branch of the government.

The difference in tone between *Rome* and *Usery* is striking. In *Usery,* Justice Rehnquist was willing to revisit his own dissenting opinion in *Fry* and suggest limiting principles to a far-reaching decision. In *Rome,* he came close to Scalia's view of abandoning deference to a coordinate branch of government altogether. The difference in tone, however, can easily be attributed to the different role of

---

[19] 427 U.S. 445 (1976).   [20] 446 U.S. 156 (1980).   [21] 42 U.S.C. §1973c.

these decisions. *Usery* was a majority decision for the Court in which Rehnquist was trying to keep together a flimsy five-vote majority (which disappeared in less than a decade in *Garcia v. San Antonio Metropolitan Transit Authority.*)[22] In *Rome,* Rehnquist was writing freely in dissent, trying only to maintain the vote of one of his long-standing federalist compatriots. It is not surprising that his language in dissent would be more extreme – although it probably hints to his future path, where he often joins other federalists in striking down federal legislation, even legislation enacted pursuant to Congress's Section 5 authority.

Rehnquist's opinions lend support to two different models of federalism. When he writes in dissent, he sometimes sounds more like a proponent of the activist Scalia model of federalism than of the early restraintist model of federalism. But when he writes the opinion of the Court, he sounds more restraintist and more deferential to Congress's powers under the Fourteenth Amendment. Which model best describes his opinions from a quantitative perspective? Does Rehnquist's model of federalism have restraintist elements? Is he more deferential to Congress when it has invoked its powers under the Fourteenth Amendment?

II. HYPOTHESES

Although we have identified three different models of federalism, there are some elements common to each of these versions. Under these common elements, we posit that a judge who adheres to federalism would do the following:

- First, demonstrate greater respect for the decisions of state courts than of federal courts.[23]
- Second, respect the articulated wishes of the states, as demonstrated by amicus briefs submitted by the states.
- Third, treat states more as an equal to the federal government than a non-federalist would. (This is not to say that federalists would treat states as equals to the federal government; but they should be less willing than non-federalists to invalidate state action.)
- Fourth, observe some notion of judicial restraint. (Federalists should be more restrained than nonfederalists, even if there is a range of restrained behavior among the federalists.)
- Fifth, not hesitate to favor the federal government over the states when the Supremacy Clause is at issue.

Additionally, these behaviors should be observable regardless of the ideological implications of a vote to validate or invalidate action. We do not expect ideology to fail to explain the votes of Justices who have articulated a special interest in preserving the federalist structure, but we do expect an independent effect

---

[22] 469 U.S. 528 (1985).
[23] Although Thayer might reject this hypothesis, it does appear to be central to modern federalism as discussed by Sue Davis. *See infra* note 24.

for the hypothesized behaviors once we have accounted for the ideological implications of each case.

Finally, there may be different views of federalism articulated by current members of the Court. Chief Justice Rehnquist has suggested that there is a special place for the rights of the individual and that the courts might be part of the scheme of protection of those rights. This position, articulated first by Thayer and later by Wechsler, may manifest itself in the voting record of Chief Justice Rehnquist, but it may not emerge in the voting behavior of Justice Scalia, who has not articulated a similar commitment.

III. RESEARCH DESIGN

Very little quantitative analysis of judicial adherence to doctrine has occurred in either political science or legal literature. The advantage of such an approach is that it permits us to ascertain the degree to which the Justices' votes match the language they craft in their opinions. Several political scientists have attempted similar analyses of legal doctrines, but few have carefully tested an interest in federalism as a guiding judicial principle.[24] For this analysis, we collected data on any case decided by the Supreme Court where the constitutionality of a state action was considered during the 1986–2002 terms. Details of the research design, including a discussion of how the ideology of the underlying state action was measured, are discussed in the Appendix.[25] Additionally, each case was coded for the issue area covered by the Court, and we included independent variables to measure cases that covered individual rights and raised Supremacy Clause issues. Because the dependent variable is dichotomous (the Justice votes to invalidate or validate the government action under review), probit is an appropriate statistical tool, as we discuss in the Appendix. We present the results as the predicted probability that a Justice will vote to invalidate a state action.

Turning to our first hypothesis, we suggest that a federalist will be sensitive to the decisions rendered by state courts, particularly when state courts uphold choices made by the other branches of state government.

Table 1 reflects the predicted probability that Rehnquist will vote to affirm the lower-court decision. Chief Justice Rehnquist votes to affirm state courts more often when they validate state action than when they invalidate state action. And when the lower court has validated state action, he votes to affirm state courts

---

[24] Robert M. Howard & Jeffrey A. Segal, *A Preference for Deference? The Supreme Court and Judicial Review*, 57 POL. RES. Q. 131 (2004); Robert M. Howard & Jeffrey A. Segal, *An Original Look at Originalism*, 36 LAW & SOC'Y REV. 113 (2002). *See also* Sue Davis, *Rehnquist and State Courts: Federalism Revisited*, 45 WEST. POL. Q. 774 (1992).

[25] For a discussion of the role of these organizations, see J. Mitchell Pickerill & Cornell W. Clayton, *The Rehnquist Court and the Political Dynamics of Federalism*, 2 PERSPECT. POL. 233, 239 (2004). These two variables were, on average, negative. If states or state organizations file amicus curiae briefs, they generally do so to urge the Court to uphold a state action.

TABLE 1. *Predicted probability of Rehnquist voting to affirm by lower-court treatment*

	Probability of vote to affirm lower court	
Lower-court decision	Federal	State
Invalidated state action	18.67%	**12.24%**
Validated state action	**62.38%**	**75.92%**

Note: Boldface indicate statistical significance.

more frequently than he does federal courts.[26] Sue Davis argues for this view of federalism in her assessment of then–Associate Justice Rehnquist's votes on reviews of criminal convictions, concluding that a commitment to state autonomy means allowing state courts to be the final arbiters of state policy.[27] We observe this pattern of greater deference to state court than federal court decisions, but only when a lower court has validated the state action.

A federalist should also be sensitive to the articulated wishes of the states, expressed by the states themselves in amicus briefs, or by organizations that represent several state governments or government officials. In any given case, the Justices may not be familiar with the sentiments of the states as a group: Massachusetts (or Texas) may be pursuing a policy that many of the other states find odious, so a federalist may not know where the weight of state interests lie. However, if states themselves or the organizations that represent them weigh in on the case in the form of amicus curiae briefs, then the Justices have a better sense of the collective wishes of the states. We argue that the more states that favor invalidation of a state action, the more a federalist Justice should be willing to vote to invalidate the state action (and the reverse would also be true). But we find that amicus participation by state governments or by state government organizations does not correlate with the voting behavior of Chief Justice Rehnquist (Table 2).

A change in the number of states or state organizations signing briefs has no effect on the predicted probability of Chief Justice Rehnquist voting to invalidate the government action. On average, 4.7 states sign briefs to favor validation of state action. Increasing that number by one standard deviation (16.6 states favor-

---

[26] The difference in rate of affirmance when the lower court *invalidated* state action is not statistically significant. All of the other differences in predicted probabilities in Table 1 are statistically significant. For all of the tables, the baseline predicted probability is calculated based on a case that was invalidated by a lower state court, was a conservative state action, did not involve individual rights or premption, and had the average number of net amici for states (–6.07, or 6.07 states favoring validation) and state organizations (–0.54, or 0.54 organizations favoring validation). That baseline is 9.02% predicted probability of a vote to invalidate. Differences that are statistically significantly different from that value are marked by boldfaced cell entries.

[27] Sue Davis, *supra* note 24. Davis argues that Rehnquist rejects this respect for state courts in favor of ideology (reversing decisions that overturn convictions and affirming those that uphold convictions). Our results demonstrate that there appears to be some deference to state courts even after ideology has been taken into account.

TABLE 2. *Predicted probability of vote for invalidation, states and intergovernmental lobby as amicus*

Number of signers on briefs	States	State orgs.
Above average favoring invalidation	12.68%	11.72%
Average	12.24%	12.24%
Above average favoring validation	11.82%	12.78%

TABLE 3. *Predicted probability of Rehnquist and Stevens voting to invalidate government action by type of government*

Type of action under review	Justice	
	Rehnquist	Stevens
State	12.24%	71.47%
Federal	9.41%	**49.47%**

Note: Boldface indicate statistical significance.

ing validation) has no statistically significant impact on the likelihood of Chief Justice Rehnquist voting to validate the government action (the reverse being true as well). The effect of the intergovernmental lobby also lacks statistical significance: If anything, it is in the direction opposite of the one we predicted. It appears that the efforts of states and of organizations that represent their interests are wasted, at least insofar as Chief Justice Rehnquist is concerned.

We also hypothesize that federalists will be more deferential to the states than their brethren who reject the label of federalist. This suggests that there is no absolute standard by which a federalist can be judged, but rather that the Justices' behavior can be explained only in relation to one another. For comparison to Chief Justice Rehnquist, we turn to Justice Stevens, primarily because they have both served over the entire 1986–2002 period under analysis here. If we expand our regression to include review of both state and federal actions (and retain the same independent variables), it becomes clear that Justice Stevens approaches state statutes with a more critical eye than he does federal statutes. The same cannot be said, however, for Chief Justice Rehnquist (Table 3).

Justice Stevens is more than 20% more likely to vote to invalidate an action taken by a state government than one taken by the federal government, even after consideration of the ideological direction of the underlying action (though that is assumed to be conservative for these models) and of the treatment by the lower courts. Chief Justice Rehnquist appears nominally more likely to invalidate state than federal action, but the difference is not statistically significant (whereas it is for Justice Stevens). These results suggest that Rehnquist comes closer to treating state governments as equal to the federal government than does Justice Stevens.

Ruth Colker and Kevin M. Scott

TABLE 4. *Predicted invalidation rate by Justice, conservative and liberal state action*

Justice	Ideology of state action		
	Conservative	Liberal	Absolute difference
Rehnquist	12.24%	28.53%	16.29%
Scalia	12.86%	33.25%	20.39%
Thomas	10.03%	31.99%	21.96%
O'Connor	21.83%	37.73%	15.90%
Kennedy	22.89%	33.97%	11.08%
Ginsburg	80.66%	39.31%	41.35%
Souter	57.92%	28.29%	29.63%
Breyer	64.50%	33.01%	31.49%
Stevens	71.47%	32.74%	38.73%

Like respect for state versus federal action, judicial restraint can be understood only in a comparative context. To determine if Chief Justice Rehnquist and other Justices who claim to be federalists refrain from invalidating state action more often than their colleagues, we calculated overall invalidation rates for each of the nine current Justices, and then assessed the rate at which they invalidated liberal and conservative actions taken by the states (Table 4).

Chief Justice Rehnquist seems to qualify as a practitioner of judicial restraint, if only by relative terms. While he certainly invalidates liberal state actions at a much greater rate than he invalidates conservative state action, the difference in his predicted invalidation rates for liberal and conservative state actions (16.29%) is smaller than every other Justice except Justices Kennedy and O'Connor. Notably, the predicted difference is also much smaller than that of the more liberal Justices.[28] Justice Rehnquist's predicted invalidation rate is also the lowest of the current nine Justices on the Court. If judicial restraint can be read as a reluctance to interfere with the policy decisions made by officials of the other branches, then Rehnquist, at least in relative terms, appears to demonstrate some evidence of restraintist behavior. As reflected in the writings of Rehnquist and Scalia, we also see that Scalia has a less restraintist perspective than Rehnquist, although he is more restrained than the nonfederalists. Our data therefore support the view that federalists are comparatively restrained even if they differ among themselves in the degree to which they are restrained.

When looking at votes that assess the constitutionality of *federal* action, we find that the overall rates do not change significantly; but the difference between rates of invalidation for liberal and conservative government action are considerably greater (Table 5).

[28] Other quantitative analyses have suggested that the liberal Justices appear to be more ideological than the conservative Justices. *See* Robert M. Howard & Jeffrey A. Segal, *A Preference for Deference? The Supreme Court and Judicial Review*, 57 POL. RES. Q. 131 (2004).

TABLE 5. *Invalidation rate by Justice, conservative and liberal federal action*

Justice	Ideology of federal action		
	Conservative	Liberal	Absolute difference
Rehnquist	9.41%	23.57%	14.16%
Scalia	9.32%	26.71%	17.39%
Thomas	17.59%	45.25%	27.66%
O'Connor	9.91%	20.58%	10.67%
Kennedy	15.68%	24.87%	9.19%
Ginsburg	81.25%	40.15%	41.10%
Souter	54.60%	25.50%	29.10%
Breyer	51.3%	21.80%	29.50%
Stevens	49.47%	15.20%	34.27%

TABLE 6. *Predicted probability of Rehnquist voting to invalidate state action, supremacy clause cases*

State action	Rehnquist
Preemption not issue	12.24%
Preemption is the issue	**45.97%**

Note: Boldface indicate statistical significance.

The liberal–conservative difference for Chief Justice Rehnquist is 14.16% for federal actions, compared to 16.29% for state actions. He does therefore appear to engage in some form of judicial restraint, but an ideological component exists to his decisions to validate or invalidate government actions.

When a claim about the use of the Supremacy Clause is raised, we hypothesize that a federalist will be more likely to strike state action out of a desire to preserve the proper place of the federal and state government. Calculating the predicted probability for cases where federal preemption of state law is an issue, we find that Chief Justice Rehnquist is much more likely to strike the state action than when preemption claims have not been raised (Table 6).

When the Court chooses to decide a case on Supremacy Clause grounds, Chief Justice Rehnquist becomes far more critical of state actions. In cases in the baseline category, the invocation of a Supremacy Clause claim makes Rehnquist nearly four times more likely to vote to invalidate the state action under review. Most of the clearest articulations of federalist doctrine have acknowledged that the preservation of a federal system of government requires that the states and the federal government each respect the other's spheres of authority. Our analysis here clearly suggests that Rehnquist is not reluctant to use the authority of the Supreme Court to police those boundaries when necessary.

TABLE 7. *Predicted probability of Rehnquist and Scalia voting to invalidate, individual rights cases*

	Justice	
State action	Rehnquist	Scalia
Does not involve indiv. rights	12.24%	12.86%
Involves indiv. rights	15.54%	15.28%

Finally, one might expect that Chief Justice Rehnquist would be more protective of individual rights than is Justice Scalia, because he envisions a bigger role for Congress's right to enforce the Fourteenth Amendment under its Section 5 powers. These different views play out when one evaluates their votes cast in cases where the validity of state action is at issue.[29] The results for Rehnquist and Scalia are comparable, as reflected in Table 7. They are both somewhat more likely to invalidate state action when cases involve individual rights, but the difference is not statistically significant.

Finally, we note that the patterns that we have observed here generally transcend voting strictly related to ideology. In the most absolute sense, a conservative Justice motivated solely by ideology would strike liberal state actions and uphold conservative state actions. We find evidence of ideological behavior in Chief Justice Rehnquist's votes: He is significantly more likely to strike liberal state actions than conservative state actions, as demonstrated in Table 8.

But ideology is not the sole determinant of Rehnquist's voting behavior. As demonstrated above, he is also sensitive to whether the case involves the issue of preemption; which government, state or federal, is acting; what lower court handled the case; and what decision the lower court reached. Were Chief Justice Rehnquist motivated only by ideology, we would not expect any other factor to be a significant predictor of his votes.

IV. CONCLUSION

Overall, we find general support for the proposition that Chief Justice Rehnquist behaves according to the dictates of federalism. He demonstrates more respect for state courts than for federal courts, especially when state courts validate state action. Rehnquist's vision of federalism appears to equate to that articulated by Sue Davis – respect for the decisions of state courts, particularly when the state court affirms state action.

Chief Justice Rehnquist does not seem particularly solicitous of the requests made by the states or by intergovernmental lobbyists as amici curiae. Our results suggest that amicus briefs by state actors have no significant effect on his voting

---

[29] Cases dealing with individual rights are those dealing with First Amendment freedoms, equal protection claims, procedural due process, substantive due process, and §1983 damage suits.

TABLE 8. *Predicted probability of Rehnquist voting to invalidate, by ideology of state action*

State action	Rehnquist
Conservative	**12.24%**
Liberal	**28.53%**

Note: Boldface indicate statistical significance.

behavior. Because of the increased proliferation of amicus briefs in recent years, this may be an important finding. One explanation for this lack of effect is that the authors of amicus briefs do not typically target Rehnquist, as they consider his vote to be predictable. Instead, they may be targeting the perceived "swing Justice" such as Justice O'Connor. We expect to explore this issue further in future research.

Nonetheless, Chief Justice Rehnquist does fulfill the other criteria we outline for a federalist: treating the states on a more equal basis to the federal government than do nonfederalists, exercising what appears to be judicial restraint, and respecting the proper role of the federal and state governments when the Supremacy Clause is invoked.

Our empirical results suggest that the more restrained version of Rehnquist's federalism that appears in his opinions for the Court better reflect his federalism than his dissents. His recent opinion in *Nevada Department of Human Resources v. Hibbs*,[30] in which he wrote the opinion for the Court upholding the constitutionality of the Family and Medical Leave Act, is consistent with this restrained version of Rehnquist's federalism. Despite his purported concern for the Fourteenth Amendment as an important contributor to our system of government, we could find no evidence that Rehnquist has incorporated its ratification into his version of federalism in his individual-rights decisions decided under that Amendment's Section 1.[31] Like the federalism of Scalia, Rehnquist's federalism does not seem to be sensitive to the importance of the Fourteenth Amendment in our federalist system.

One of our most interesting findings was that Rehnquist's voting behavior can be explained, in part, by the ideology of the underlying state action. This result is certainly not surprising to social scientists who think that judicial voting behavior can be explained entirely by politics. But, maybe surprisingly, we found that Rehnquist's ideology may be *less* of an influence in his voting than that of many of the Courts' liberals in theirs. This finding also would benefit from further research but may be affected by the Court's role in defining its own docket, as well as the difficulty in applying the labels "conservative" or "liberal."

---

[30] 538 U.S. 721 (2003).
[31] *Hibbs* was decided under §5, not §1, of the Fourteenth Amendment: §5 cases involve the scope of Congress' power; §1 cases involve the question of whether states violated the due process or equal protection rights of individuals.

Whether government action is liberal or conservative appears to be a factor influencing whether the Court accepts certiorari in a particular case. In our database, the Supreme Court reviewed (i.e., granted certiorari) in 455 instances of conservative government action and only 153 liberal government actions. The large number of conservative government actions under review is attributable, in large part, to the substantial number of criminal law cases reviewed by the Court. Of the 455 conservative governmental actions, 209 involved criminal law cases.

Empirical analysis, however, has its limitations. We were not able to use empirical tools to see if Chief Justice Rehnquist tended to be more deferential to Congress when that body invoked its authority under Section 5 of the Fourteenth Amendment than under the Commerce Clause or spending power. The large number of criminal law cases may have skewed our analysis. (Of the 608 cases in the database, 230 involved criminal law.) We did run our analysis, however, without the criminal law cases, and the results did not change significantly. Nonetheless, a more refined analysis of the criminal law category would be useful, given its large contribution to the database. Finally, the amicus brief results deserve further qualitative analysis. It may be obvious from reading the opinions of Chief Justice Rehnquist, or another Justice, that a particular brief helped influence a result even if that influence cannot be demonstrated through empirical research. A combination of qualitative and quantitative analysis may thus be more appropriate in considering the influence of amicus briefs on the voting behavior of a Justice.

Despite these limitations, our work can contribute to the research on the legacy of Chief Justice Rehnquist. We are able to confirm that federalism, as opposed to purely "politics," predicts his voting behavior over time. We are also able to describe the judicial role that is consistent with Rehnquist's federalism: deference to state courts, concern about protecting federal preemption, and a comparatively restrained judicial role with some influence from political ideology. Although the Rehnquist Court may be well known for its "federalism revolution," Rehnquist himself appears to have helped move the Court in that direction through a relatively cautious judicial approach.

APPENDIX: METHODOLOGY

Data were collected on any Supreme Court decision in the 1986–2002 terms that considered the constitutionality of a state or federal action. The data were drawn from the Supreme Court Database created by Harold Spaeth and archived by the S. Sidney Ulmer Project at the University of Kentucky.[32] The cases were then coded for several attributes, including the primary issue considered in the case,

---

[32] *At* http://www.as.uky.edu/polisci/ulmerproject/databases.htm.

the number of amicus briefs, and the types and number of groups and individuals that signed on to briefs urging the Court to validate or invalidate the government action under review. Information on the amicus briefs was retrieved from the LEXIS Supreme Court briefs collection. If the LEXIS copies of the briefs had incomplete information, student assistants looked at the microfiche copy of the brief to get the total number of signers for each brief. Cases were coded for how the lower court treated the government action under review (if it was a federal or state court; if the lower court validated or invalidated the state action). Intergovernmental organizations include groups like the National Conference of State Legislatures and the National Governors Association.

Each case was also coded to reflect the ideology of the underlying government action. In cases raising claims of civil rights or civil liberties, government actions that favored the person accused of a crime, favored the civil rights or civil liberties claimant, favored affirmative action, or favored neutrality in religion cases were coded as liberal. In cases raising economic claims, government actions that were pro-union, pro-environmental protection, and pro-underdog were coded as liberal. The determination of the ideology of the underlying government action also relied on these definitions, derived from the Supreme Court database: A government action was coded as liberal if it was invalidated and the Court decision was considered conservative (in the Supreme Court database), *or* if the government action was validated and the Court decision was coded as liberal. The underlying government action was considered conservative if the government action was invalidated and the Court decision was considered liberal (in the Supreme Court database), *or* if the government action was validated and the Court decision was coded as conservative.

To calculate the predicted probabilities for the other Justices in Tables 3–5 and 7, models were run for each of the other eight Justices currently sitting on the Supreme Court. Because the dependent variable is dichotomous – a Justice votes either to invalidate the case or *not* to invalidate (i.e., to validate) the government action – the appropriate statistical technique is *probit,* a maximum-likelihood estimator. Probit coefficients are not particularly meaningful on their own merits, so one way to bring meaning to them is to look at predicted probabilities of a vote to invalidate given a particular case profile. The baseline profile we use in the analyses in this chapter is a case that reviews a *state* government action (as opposed to a federal one); was invalidated by a state court before it came to the Supreme Court; had *no* participation by the Solicitor General as an amicus; had the average number of states supporting invalidation (i.e., −4.70 states, or 4.7 states favoring *validation*); and had the average number of intergovernmental lobby organizations (i.e., −0.39, or 0.39 groups favoring *validation*) as amici. In addition, the baseline case did *not* involve individual rights or preemption. Perhaps most important, the baseline case is a review of a government action that is *conservative.*

TABLE 9. *Full probit model for Chief Justice Rehnquist's votes*

Federal action	−0.1532
	(0.1636)
Lower court – federal court validated	0.8474**
	(0.2298)
Lower court – state court validated	0.4590*
	(0.2085)
Lower court – federal court invalidated	0.2727
	(0.2205)
Solicitor General amicus favoring validation	−0.4575**
	(0.1610)
Solicitor General amicus favoring invalidation	0.4491*
	(0.2198)
Net number of states favoring invalidation	0.0018
	(0.0053)
State government organizations favoring invalidation	−0.0145
	(0.0330)
Ideology of challenged government action	0.5959**
	(0.1291)
Issue in case is individual rights	0.1495
	(0.1245)
Issue in case is preemption	1.0573**
	(0.2394)
Constant	−1.1602**
	(.1993)

Note: Number of observations = 604. S.E. in parentheses.
* = coefficients significant at the .05 level (two-tailed test).
** = coefficients significant at the .01 level.

The full probit model for Chief Justice Rehnquist's votes is shown in Table 9, with standard errors in parentheses.

THE SCOPE OF FOURTEENTH
AMENDMENT RIGHTS

CHAPTER FIFTEEN

ABORTION: A MIXED AND UNSETTLED LEGACY

Dawn Johnsen

INTRODUCTION

The best-known Supreme Court decision from William Rehnquist's time on the Court – and certainly one of the decisions about which the public cares most deeply – came very early in his tenure. Just one year after joining the Court, Rehnquist dissented in *Roe v. Wade*.[1] In that 1973 landmark decision, the Court recognized the fundamental right of a woman to choose to terminate a pregnancy. Rehnquist was one of two Justices who would have upheld the Texas statute that made it a felony to perform an abortion, on the ground that women do not possess a constitutionally protected right to be free of governmental control over their childbearing decisions. Throughout his decades on the Court, Rehnquist stood firm in his opposition to *Roe* and consistently called upon the Court to overrule it.

Viewed in one light, Rehnquist's legacy with regard to abortion seems a tale of failure – a failure all the more notable because it followed close on the heels of almost certain victory. Just when it seemed that new judicial appointments finally had given Rehnquist enough votes to overrule *Roe,* the Court startled the nation by reaffirming what it characterized as *Roe*'s "essential holding." The Court's 1992 *Planned Parenthood v. Casey* decision upheld the right of a woman to be free from undue governmental burdens in making the ultimate decision whether or not to have a previability abortion.[2] Rehnquist found himself again in strong, and unexpected, dissent.

Abortion unquestionably would be featured front and center in any evaluation of the legacy of Justices Harry Blackmun or Sandra Day O'Connor. They – not Rehnquist – are the Justices whose views most obviously have influenced the current state of abortion doctrine. Blackmun authored the majority opinion in *Roe,* and over the next two decades he successfully retained substantial constitutional safeguards for abortion against what seemed like overwhelming attack, from within and outside the Court. O'Connor, meanwhile, fashioned a compromise

---

[1] 410 U.S. 113 (1973).   [2] 505 U.S. 833 (1992).

position in the form of a new "undue burden" test that averted a complete over-ruling of *Roe,* but was sharply criticized by both sides.[3]

Rehnquist's relative failure on abortion, moreover, contrasts with his remark-able success in moving from dissent to majority on some other important issues. With the critical help of like-minded Justices appointed by Presidents Ronald Reagan and George H. W. Bush, Rehnquist has proven to be exceptionally able at shaping the direction of constitutional doctrine and at promoting what began as his dissenting positions. In perhaps the most striking example, in the 1990s the Court began to diminish Congress's legislative authority and to expand state sovereignty in ways Rehnquist had advocated in dissent beginning in the 1970s – in ways, moreover, at odds with the Court's approach of the previous half-century.[4] As longtime *New York Times* Supreme Court reporter Linda Green-house observed, "Any survey of Chief Justice Rehnquist's . . . career on the Court will yield two immediate observations: the consistency of his views, and his suc-cess over time in translating those views into majority opinions."[5] Rehnquist's views on abortion have remained characteristically consistent, but he has proven uncharacteristically ineffective in promoting those views.

The legacy of a Chief Justice, of course, encompasses not only those issues on which his (or her) views successfully shaped doctrine, but also important issues on which he (or she) repeatedly attempted but failed to move the Court. Rehn-quist's overall constitutional legacy closely (and not coincidentally) parallels that of the President who elevated him to Chief Justice: Ronald Reagan. In an inter-view in 2000, a dozen years after Reagan left office, his Attorney General, Edwin Meese III, was asked what he considered to be the Reagan administration's great-est legal successes and failures. Meese cited as a great success changes in constitu-tional doctrine on "the allocation of power and authority between the national government on the one hand and the States on the other." Meese's choice for most disappointing loss: "The failure to persuade the Court to date to overrule *Roe v. Wade.*"[6]

Notwithstanding Meese's (and Rehnquist's) disappointment, Rehnquist's lega-cy on abortion is not one of complete failure, but of mixed and unsettled results. In the almost two decades between *Roe* and *Casey,* the Court invalidated many abortion restrictions but upheld others. Rehnquist cast critical votes, for example, to uphold the exclusion of abortion from the publicly funded medical services

---

[3] Justice O'Connor first announced a version of the undue burden test in dissent in City of Akron v. Akron Center for Reproductive Health, Inc., 462 U.S. 416 (1983), and she continued to apply it in her separate opinions until a significantly changed version of the test became the control-ling standard of review in *Casey.*

[4] *See* Dawn E. Johnsen, *Ronald Reagan and the Rehnquist Court on Congressional Power: Presi-dential Influences on Constitutional Change,* 78 IND. L.J. 363 (2003).

[5] Linda Greenhouse, *The Last Days of the Rehnquist Court: The Rewards of Patience and Power,* 45 ARIZ. L. REV. 251 (2003).

[6] Edwin Meese III, *Reagan's Legal Revolutionary,* 3 GREEN BAG 2D 193 (2000).

provided to poor women, and later to uphold a ban on the performance of even privately funded abortions in public facilities.[7] *Casey* allowed even greater governmental restriction of women's abortion decisions. The Court claimed adherence to *Roe*, but in fact substantially diminished protection, from the most rights-protective "strict scrutiny" standard of judicial review to an untested but intentionally less protective "undue burden" standard. The surprise – and for many people, relief – occasioned by *Casey*'s eloquent reaffirmation that the government may not outlaw abortion obscured the ways in which *Casey* did "overrule" *Roe*. Rehnquist detailed them in his separate opinion in *Casey*, where he wrote: "*Roe* continues to exist, but only in the way a storefront on a western movie set exists: a mere facade to give the illusion of reality." *Casey* rejected much of *Roe*'s reasoning, upheld restrictions indistinguishable from those that the Court previously had held unconstitutional, and, in the process, overruled substantial portions of protective abortion decisions from the 1980s (just as Rehnquist had urged at the time in dissent).[8]

Rehnquist, though, was not satisfied with what he described as *Casey*'s gutting of *Roe*. Along with three other Justices, he complained at length that the Court had not torn down the remaining facade. For Rehnquist, the problem was not the resulting basic legality or availability of abortion services. His efforts to overrule *Roe* were not primarily about abortion per se, and certainly not about what motivates the antiabortion social movement: the protection of embryonic and fetal life. *Casey*, in fact, was more sympathetic to the antiabortion movement's stated basis for opposition to *Roe* than to Rehnquist's position in his *Roe* and subsequent dissents. The Court premised its new undue burden test on a recognition of the government's legitimate interest in protecting life as of the earliest stages of pregnancy. The test is quite malleable and, in the hands of a Court so inclined, could allow for drastic reductions in the availability of abortion services: Various state restrictions, newly constitutional under *Casey*, could combine with antiabortion violence, clinic blockades, and dramatically reduced numbers of abortion providers to make in-state abortions unavailable for many women. *Roe* already holds little practical meaning for a woman who lacks the money to pay for an abortion and also for the costs of traveling several hundred miles to the nearest abortion provider – a trip that state-mandated waiting periods sometimes force women to make twice. Significantly, *Roe*'s effect was not to increase substantially the overall abortion rate, but to allow women far greater access to legal and safe abortion services within their own state (and, of course, to eliminate virtually all dangerous, illegal abortions).[9]

---

[7] Harris v. McRae, 448 U.S. 297 (1980); Webster v. Reproductive Health Services, 492 U.S. 490 (1989).

[8] The Court in *Casey*, 505 U.S. 833, overruled in part *Akron*, 462 U.S. 416, and Thornburgh v. American College of Obstetricians & Gynecologists, 476 U.S. 747 (1986).

[9] Willard Cates, Jr., David A. Grimes, & Kenneth F. Schulz, *The Public Health Impact of Legal Abortion: 30 Years Later*, 35 PERSPECT. SEX. REPROD. HEALTH 25 (Jan.–Feb. 2003).

Rehnquist's objective, however, has not been to reduce abortion rates through governmental restrictions, but to leave the government – in particular the states – free to regulate abortion however they desire, without careful judicial review. Rehnquist's *Roe* dissent was an early and important effort in a career-long series of battles to limit judicial protection for individual rights not enumerated with great specificity in the constitutional text. In *Roe* and elsewhere, Rehnquist aggressively promoted his narrow vision of substantive due process doctrine – that is, those fundamental rights substantively protected under the Fourteenth Amendment's guarantee of liberty. In the process, he has engaged the Court on some of the most fundamental questions of constitutional law: the institutional role of the federal courts in our system of separated powers, the extent of state authority and sovereignty in our system of federalism, and the appropriate interpretive methodology for giving meaning to the Constitution's relatively undefined terms, including liberty. With regard to these broader questions, Rehnquist assumed leadership in closely fought battles and closely divided decisions involving not only abortion, but also the right to control the circumstances of one's own death and the right to engage in consensual sexual activity.[10]

Rehnquist has made some progress on the Court, as well as in the political and public opinion arenas, since his two-Justice dissent in *Roe*. He has remained, though, far from victory – farther, in fact, than when he became Chief Justice in 1986. If, one year after he became Chief, the Senate had confirmed Reagan's nomination of Robert H. Bork to the Supreme Court, instead of Reagan's subsequent choice of Anthony Kennedy, the Court almost certainly would have overruled *Roe* in *Casey* (and possibly earlier). Instead, Kennedy and O'Connor, the two critical Justices "in the middle," made clear in their *Casey* joint opinion (along with Justice David Souter) that, whatever disagreements they might have with *Roe*, they did not agree with Rehnquist's approach to overruling *Roe*.

Rehnquist also may have exerted another, more subtle influence on *Casey*'s erosion of *Roe*, one that worked against his desired outcome on *Roe*. *Casey* is notable for its remarkably strong view of judicial supremacy. The O'Connor–Kennedy–Souter joint opinion cited the preservation of the Court's interpretive supremacy and reputation among its reasons for not overruling *Roe*. In other contexts, Rehnquist famously promoted a similarly strong view of judicial supremacy that bordered on judicial exclusivity and intolerance for challenges to the Court's expressed interpretations. He thus can be seen as having contributed to the *Casey* Court's conception of judicial supremacy, even though he vehemently disagreed with its application.

No one can know whether the *Casey* compromise will hold or how a future Court will apply it. Even if the Court continues to reject Rehnquist's particular rationale for opposition to *Roe*, other potential grounds exist. *Roe* unquestionably remains a target for overruling. All that is possible is an interim assessment

---

[10] Washington v. Glucksberg, 521 U.S. 702 (1997); Lawrence v. Texas, 539 U.S. 558 (2003).

of Rehnquist's impact on abortion and substantive due process doctrine to date. Rehnquist's legacy will continue to unfold well into the twenty-first century.

ROE V. WADE AND *DOE V. BOLTON*

The Supreme Court held in *Roe* that the right to choose whether or not to terminate a pregnancy is a fundamental constitutional right protected from state interference by the Fourteenth Amendment's guarantee of liberty, under the doctrine known as substantive due process. To safeguard that fundamental right, which the Court characterized as a right to privacy, the courts would subject any government interference to strict scrutiny, which is the most protective of all standards of judicial review.[11] The *Roe* Court applied strict scrutiny to invalidate a Texas statute that criminalized abortion in all cases except when necessary to save the life of the pregnant woman. The 1854 Texas law, which the Court described as typical of the majority of states that had not revisited their abortion statutes for approximately a century, imposed a penalty of two to five years imprisonment for the performance of an abortion, or five years to life in some cases where the fetus was viable. In *Roe*'s important but often-ignored companion case, *Doe v. Bolton,* the Court invalidated some provisions of a 1968 Georgia law that had "a modern cast."[12] Georgia's abortion law had been "liberalized" to remove criminal penalties in highly limited circumstances: All abortions had to be performed in hospitals, and could be performed only for women who were Georgia residents and who had first secured the approval of three physicians and a hospital committee charged with determining whether the woman's situation fell within very narrow permissible reasons, including some cases of rape, severe and permanent health or life risks, and serious fetal abnormalities. The performance of a noncompliant abortion was punishable by one to ten years imprisonment.

Notwithstanding the tremendous controversy it engendered, the *Roe* Court was not closely divided: Seven Justices comprised the solid majority. Only Justices Rehnquist and Byron White dissented and would have upheld both the nineteenth-century criminal ban and the more modern abortion restrictions. Nor did the Court split along partisan lines. In fact, it was as bipartisan a decision as theoretically possible. A Republican president, Richard Nixon, had appointed Blackmun, the author of *Roe,* and two other Justices in the majority, whereas dissenter White had been appointed by President John F. Kennedy, a Democrat.

The *Roe* majority began with a review of the legality of abortion, starting in ancient times and civilizations and continuing throughout the course of United States history. The Court concluded that "a woman enjoyed a substantially broader right to terminate a pregnancy" from the time the Constitution was ratified throughout most of the nineteenth century "than she does in most States today." The Court then reviewed the support for liberalizing state abortion laws from

---

[11] *See generally* Jed Rubenfeld, *The Right of Privacy,* 102 HARV. L. REV. 737 (1989).

[12] 410 U.S. 179 (1973).

the leading medical, health, and legal professional associations. Against this background, the Court turned to the Fourteenth Amendment and held that its reference to "person" includes only those who have been born and therefore does not protect an embryo's or fetus's right to life. Most famously, the Court held that "a woman's decision whether or not to terminate a pregnancy" falls within what it described as a "fundamental" right of privacy "founded in the Fourteenth Amendment's concept of personal liberty and restrictions upon state action." The Court cited for support its prior decisions recognizing that liberty extended to private and personal decisions regarding marriage, procreation, contraception, family relationships, and child rearing.[13] It also discussed the harm imposed on women by the criminalization of abortion and the resulting forced childbearing.

Because the Court found decisions about abortion to be a fundamental right of individual women, abortion restrictions triggered strict scrutiny and could stand only if necessary to promote a compelling governmental interest. In evaluating whether a state possesses any such interest, the Court considered what it described as "important and legitimate" interests that Texas and Georgia offered to justify abortion restrictions: the potential life of the fetus and the health of the pregnant woman. The Court found these interests become sufficiently "compelling" to support abortion restrictions at different stages of pregnancy; hence its adoption of a trimester system for evaluating the constitutionality of abortion restrictions. A state's interest in the potential life of the fetus is greater at later stages of pregnancy than at conception and becomes compelling at the point of fetal viability, the point at which the fetus is capable of living outside of the woman (approximately twenty-four to twenty-eight weeks, or the end of the second trimester). A state therefore may go so far as to criminalize abortion after viability, as long as the prohibition includes an exception allowing postviability abortions when continuing a pregnancy would threaten the woman's health or life. The Court also drew a line between the first and second trimesters, finding that a state's interest in ensuring the safety of abortion services supported regulations designed to protect women's health after the first trimester.

REHNQUIST'S DISSENT AND OTHER APPROACHES TO OVERRULING *ROE*

The degree to which Rehnquist succeeded in advancing his dissenting position and the state of his legacy on abortion can be evaluated best against the backdrop of the range of possible bases for disagreement with the *Roe* majority. The Court could take at least four distinct approaches to overruling *Roe* and *Doe*, each with different practical and doctrinal implications.

---

[13] *E.g.*, Meyer v. Nebraska, 262 U.S. 390 (1923); Skinner v. Oklahoma, 316 U.S. 535 (1942); Griswold v. Connecticut, 381 U.S. 479 (1965); Loving v. Virginia, 388 U.S. 1 (1967); Eisenstadt v. Baird, 405 U.S. 438 (1972).

Approach 1. Constitutional Fetal Personhood

The Court could overrule *Roe* by recognizing legal rights or status for embryos and fetuses developing within pregnant women. As the *Roe* Court noted, "[t]he pregnant woman cannot be isolated in her privacy. She carries an embryo and, later, a fetus. . . ." The embryo and fetus, of course, serve as the overwhelming focus of intense, sometimes even violent, opposition to *Roe* and abortion from outside the Court. Overruling *Roe* on these grounds would not necessarily undermine liberty-based rights unrelated to pregnancy termination and also would not necessarily deny that abortion restrictions pose high costs to women's liberty – though any right possessed by the pregnant woman would be deemed outweighed by conflicting fetal rights.

Two distinct approaches to overruling *Roe* focus on the embryo and fetus. The more extreme of the two – an approach so extreme that no Justice ever has adopted it – would include the embryo or fetus within the meaning of "person" in the Fourteenth Amendment's guarantee that no state shall "deprive any person of life . . . without due process of law."[14] The state of Texas argued in *Roe* in favor of constitutional fetal personhood, but not a single Justice in that case or in any subsequent case thus far has agreed. If the Court were to hold that the fetus is a "person" with constitutional rights and protections, the Constitution almost certainly would require – not just permit – the prohibition of abortion in order to protect the constitutional right to life of the fetus. The only permissible exception likely would be extremely rare cases in which continuing a pregnancy would endanger a woman's life: A constitutional right to life of the embryo or fetus would prevail even when pregnancy resulted from rape or incest or the woman's health (but not life) was gravely threatened by the pregnancy. A woman also could suffer additional liberty infringements – limits on work or other activities – in the name of the well-being of the embryo or fetus developing within her, which would be deemed a distinct legal entity, a constitutional "person," but physically remain very much a part of a woman.[15]

Not even Rehnquist or the current Court's two other harshest critics of *Roe*, Justices Antonin Scalia and Clarence Thomas, have adopted this position. All Justices who have endorsed overruling *Roe* instead have urged that the Constitution is silent on the issue of abortion and leaves resolution of whether abortion should be legal to the states (and, by implication, Congress). Strong forces outside the judiciary, though, do seek to establish constitutional fetal personhood and a fetal right to life that would criminalize abortion nationwide, if necessary through a Human Life Amendment to the Constitution. Such advocates have included not only leading antiabortion organizations but also the Republican Party, Presidents

---

[14] U.S. Const., amend. XIV, §1; *see also* U.S. Const., amend. V (protection of life applicable to the federal government).

[15] *See generally* Dawn Johnsen, *Shared Interests: Promoting Healthy Births Without Sacrificing Women's Liberty*, 43 HASTINGS L.J. 569 (1992).

Ronald Reagan, George H. W. Bush, and George W. Bush, and many members of Congress.

Approach 2. State Interest in Potential Life

The second of the fetus-centered approaches to overruling *Roe* would not go as far as finding the fetus to be a person as a constitutional matter. Instead, the Court would allow the government (state or federal) to establish fetal personhood, or other fetal rights or protections inconsistent with abortion, by statute. Under the bifurcated strict scrutiny analysis of *Roe* (and cases involving claimed infringements of other constitutional rights), the Court first considers whether the government's challenged action interferes with a fundamental right and then whether the government possesses an interest sufficiently compelling to justify the infringement. The Court theoretically could view the choice of whether to continue or terminate a pregnancy as a fundamental right, yet hold that an asserted governmental interest in protecting the fetus outweighs that right. This approach would reject *Roe*'s (and *Casey*'s) viability distinction and Justice John Paul Stevens's observation in another case that "[a]s a secular matter, there is an obvious difference between the state interest in protecting the freshly fertilized egg and the state interest in protecting a 9-month-gestated, fully sentient fetus on the eve of birth." Several Justices have dissented on the grounds that they believe the government's interest does not so vary. Thomas in *Stenberg v. Carhart*,[16] Scalia in several opinions, and White in his dissents in *Roe* and subsequent cases, all have unambiguously written that they view the government's interest in fetal life as strong enough to support outlawing abortion from the outset of pregnancy. If the Court were to adopt this position, a compelling interest in the protection of embryonic life also could support governmental restrictions aimed at women outside the context of abortion, including bans on some methods of contraception that may act postfertilization and restrictions on the activities of women with desired pregnancies when the government deems those activities potentially harmful to fetal development.

Approach 3. No Fundamental Right

Rehnquist's calls to overrule *Roe* were not premised on the strength of the government's interest in embryonic and fetal life. His extensive abortion opinions say remarkably little about the embryo and fetus – less than any other dissenting Justice. His *Roe* dissent, for example, never mentions the fetus and makes no response to the majority's discussion of the weight of the government's interest in potential life. Of the Justices who have called for an express overruling of *Roe*, Rehnquist seemed the least concerned with whether the states actually would use that authority to prohibit abortion. (Rehnquist, though, did join several other

[16] 530 U.S. 914 (2000).

Justices' dissents that relied upon the government's interest in protecting potential fetal life; on abortion, as on other issues, he was willing to join opinions that
reached his desired results by very different reasoning.)

Rehnquist's disagreement with *Roe* and its progeny instead has fallen within a
third rationale for overruling *Roe:* Governmental restrictions on abortion do not
implicate any constitutional right that warrants special judicial protection. That
is, in declaring that the courts appropriately protect personal decisions about
abortion from legislative infringement, the *Roe* Court misconceived the nature
of women's liberty at stake and hence, too, the level of judicial protection from
governmental interference. Scalia and Thomas share this view with Rehnquist.

Variations on this approach would entail substantial differences in the impact
on other liberty-based privacy rights that the Court has declared fundamental.
The Court could overrule the entire line of liberty-based privacy rights; it could
distinguish *Roe* and leave the nonabortion privacy cases intact (on the ground
that the presence of a developing embryo or fetus is relevant to the existence of
the right itself and not only the strength of the government's countervailing interest); or it could take a position somewhere along the continuum between these
points. All variations have in common that restrictive abortion laws, even bans,
would not interfere with any fundamental liberty right deserving of strict judicial scrutiny and therefore would trigger only the most minimal level of judicial
review, known as rational basis review. Virtually all abortion restrictions would
be found rationally related to a legitimate governmental interest and therefore
enforceable. Rehnquist, for example, found that the Texas statute in *Roe* satisfied
rational basis review because it contained an exception for those rare cases in
which continuing a pregnancy would endanger a woman's life.

The Department of Justice, under Reagan's Attorney General Meese, called for
a particularly extreme version of this "no fundamental right" approach in a 1988
report, little known at the time, entitled *Guidelines on Constitutional Litigation.*
The report directed all government litigators to promote the Reagan administration's preferred interpretive methodology, commonly called "originalism":
"[C]onstitutional language should be construed as it was publicly understood
at the time of its drafting and ratification and government attorneys should advance constitutional arguments based only on this 'original meaning.'"[17] The report highlighted the "so-called 'right to privacy' cases" as "examples of judicial
creation of rights not reasonably found in the Constitution" under an originalist
methodology. It cited for support the writings of Judge Robert H. Bork, Reagan's
failed Supreme Court nominee and perhaps the most well-known of modern
originalists. Chapters on separate substantive issues closed with lists of Supreme
Court cases the Department of Justice had targeted for overruling. The targeting
of *Roe* comes as no surprise, given Reagan's public calls for the Court to overrule

---

[17] OFFICE OF LEGAL POLICY, U.S. DEP'T OF JUSTICE, GUIDELINES ON CONSTITUTIONAL LITI-
GATION (1988).

it. Startling, though, is the express condemnation of pre-*Roe* cases such as *Griswold v. Connecticut,* which invalidated a Connecticut law that criminalized the use of contraception including by married couples, and *Skinner v. Oklahoma,* which invalidated an Oklahoma law that ordered the forced sterilization of individuals convicted of three violations of certain laws, including inveterate chicken thieves but not white-collar embezzlers.[18] An overruling of *Roe* thus premised on a rejection of the fundamental liberty cases that preceded *Roe* would allow governmental interference not only with abortion, but also with the use of contraception, sterilization, marriage, and child rearing.

Rehnquist's basis for dissent changed little over the decades: No fundamental right warranted judicial invalidation, or even close scrutiny, of state legislatures' policy choices regarding abortion regulation. He consistently characterized women's ability to make personal decisions about whether to continue or terminate pregnancies as mere liberty interests – as opposed to fundamental rights – that the government may restrict with minimal judicial review and maximum judicial deference. Like the Reagan–Meese Department of Justice report, Rehnquist's *Roe* dissent had a strong originalist focus. He derided the Court for creating "a right that was apparently completely unknown to the drafters of the [Fourteenth] Amendment," listed thirty-six state or territorial laws that limited abortion in 1868, and concluded "the drafters did not intend to have the Fourteenth Amendment withdraw from the States the power to legislate with respect to this matter." He went on to cite continued abortion restrictions in most states as counter to a conclusion that a right to choose abortion is "so rooted in the traditions and conscience of our people as to be ranked as fundamental." Rehnquist did not directly discuss *Griswold, Skinner,* or any of the cases upon which the *Roe* majority relied, but his reasoning almost certainly would have led him to find no fundamental privacy right in those cases as well.

Subsequent to *Roe,* Rehnquist subtly shifted away from an originalist methodology, but the results for abortion restrictions and *Roe* remained unchanged. This shift is discussed throughout the remaining sections of this chapter. Briefly, Rehnquist relied less heavily on the Framers' intent and specific practices at the time of the Fourteenth Amendment's ratification. He continued to adopt a very narrow view of fundamental rights not specifically enumerated in the constitutional text, one that left little room for the courts to protect rights that the state legislatures did not already recognize and respect, but not so narrow as to be frozen in time in 1868. In *Casey* he also made what was for him a relatively rare mention of the fetus as a grounds for distinguishing *Griswold* and *Skinner.* In *Casey* as in *Roe,* however, Rehnquist's primary concern did not seem to be the restriction of abortion in particular, but more generally to limit the scope of liberty that the courts would protect from state infringement and to safeguard states' authority to do as they chose. Abortion, at bottom, was about Rehnquist's vision of fed-

[18] *Skinner,* 316 U.S. 535; *Griswold,* 381 U.S. 479.

eralism and the institutional role of the Court. Rehnquist described this vision early in his judicial career in a 1976 lecture entitled *The Notion of a Living Constitution*, where he cautioned against judicial protection of unenumerated rights. He argued that under some conceptions, a "living Constitution, in the last analysis, is a formula for an end run around popular government."[19]

Rehnquist similarly opposed what he viewed as the inappropriate judicial creation of unenumerated rights to constrain the states in other contexts, including cases involving asserted rights to engage in consensual sexual activity and to end one's life when terminally ill. One notable exception deserves mention, because it cannot easily be reconciled with his other judicial opinions. In *Boy Scouts of America v. Dale*, Rehnquist, writing for five Justices on a closely divided Court, found that the Boy Scouts had a constitutional "expressive association" right to exclude a gay assistant scoutmaster despite a New Jersey state law that prohibited such discrimination on the basis of sexual orientation – and notwithstanding that the Constitution does not enumerate such a right of "expressive association."[20] Rehnquist deviated here from his typical insistence on strong deference to the choices of elected representatives and instead recognized an unenumerated right that included the right to discriminate in contravention of state law protections.

Approach 4. Reduced Judicial Protection

Finally, the Court could overrule *Roe* in ways less transparent, direct, and complete than a finding that women possess no judicially protected rights or that fetuses or the government possess overriding rights or interests. The Court instead could devise a new framework for evaluating governmental interference with private abortion decisions that would retain some semblance of protection, at least from absolute criminal bans, but allow for numerous onerous abortion restrictions that in practice could make legal abortion services far less available, more expensive, and more dangerous. Rehnquist, for example, described the undue burden standard that the Court adopted in *Casey* as a rejection of much of *Roe*. Whether and to what extent *Casey*, or any change in abortion doctrine, should be viewed as an overruling of *Roe* depends largely on its applications and practical effects.

FROM *ROE* TO *WEBSTER:* REHNQUIST GAINS SUPPORT

Roe v. Wade of course did not quell public debate or political activity regarding abortion. Opposition raged and the political parties polarized. Opponents of *Roe* enacted hundreds of abortion restrictions, elected antichoice politicians who

---

[19] William H. Rehnquist, *The Notion of a Living Constitution,* 54 TEX. L. REV. 693 (1976).
[20] 530 U.S. 640 (2000).

would support and expand such restrictions, picketed and blockaded abortion clinics, and a few even resorted to violence and murder. Antiabortion activists – and more generally social conservatives – increasingly dominated the Republican Party, which committed to working toward overruling *Roe* through the appointment of judges who share that commitment. The Democratic Party, though less unified on this issue, to a far greater degree has supported the preservation of women's reproductive liberty. Pro-choice Americans understandably have relied upon judicial protection, and reproductive choice has been a less salient political issue to them than to those who would like to see abortion made illegal.

Post-*Roe* legislative activity focused on enacting various abortion restrictions, overwhelmingly at the state level. Some state laws sought to empower private individuals to do what *Roe* said the government could not do directly, such as by requiring women to obtain the consent of husbands or parents before having an abortion. Other laws targeted abortion providers and sought to decrease the availability of services, for example by limiting the type of facility in which abortions could be performed and the advertising of abortion services. Still others targeted women through their physicians and sought to discourage women from having abortions, including by requiring physicians to give their patients information and fetal development pictures designed to discourage abortion, and then requiring women to reconsider having an abortion during a mandatory waiting period. And still other laws sought to prohibit or mandate the use of certain abortion methods or standards, rather than allow the physician and woman to choose the method according to the woman's health needs and other circumstances.[21]

From 1973 until President Reagan took office in 1981 and began appointing Supreme Court Justices, Rehnquist and White continued to be the only two Justices who advocated overruling *Roe,* as well as the Justices most supportive of governmental power to restrict abortion through measures short of bans. The Court ruled many such state restrictions unconstitutional in the 1970s and 1980s, including husband consent requirements, mandatory waiting periods, and hospitalization requirements unrelated to women's health needs.[22] Rehnquist and White, though, attracted sufficient support to uphold, as consistent with *Roe,* two types of restriction that many *Roe* supporters strongly opposed: laws that prohibited underage girls from obtaining abortions without first obtaining parental consent (or a court order allowing them to bypass the consent require-

---

[21] NARAL Pro-Choice America has published fourteen editions of a state-by-state survey of abortion legislation. *See, e.g.,* NATIONAL ABORTION RIGHTS ACTION LEAGUE, WHO DECIDES? A STATE-BY-STATE REVIEW OF ABORTION RIGHTS (1st ed. 1989); NARAL PRO-CHOICE AMERICA, WHO DECIDES? THE STATUS OF WOMEN'S REPRODUCTIVE RIGHTS IN THE UNITED STATES (14th ed. 2005), *available at* http://www.prochoiceamerica.org/whodecides.

[22] *See, e.g.,* Planned Parenthood v. Danforth, 428 U.S. 52 (1976); Colautti v. Franklin, 439 U.S. 379 (1979); *Akron,* 462 U.S. 416; Planned Parenthood v. Ashcroft, 462 U.S. 476 (1983); *Thornburgh,* 476 U.S. 747.

ment)[23] and federal and state prohibitions on the use of public funds for abortions.[24]

Rehnquist saw his minority position steadily improve as Reagan made each of his three Supreme Court appointments. Reagan's first appointment to the Court, O'Connor, brought to three the number of Justices who disagreed with the *Roe* Court. She authored dissents in 1983 (joined by Rehnquist and White) that would have upheld various abortion restrictions in Ohio and Missouri laws, and she authored another dissent in 1986 that would have upheld a restrictive Pennsylvania abortion law.[25] Although Rehnquist joined O'Connor's dissents in these cases, her grounds for objection to *Roe* differed from Rehnquist's objections in his earlier dissents. Instead of Rehnquist's focus on the absence of any judicially protected right, O'Connor declared the *Roe* trimester system unworkable and the state interest in potential life compelling throughout pregnancy (not only at the point of viability). She also introduced the concept of an undue burden test: She wrote that even if the Constitution protects a fundamental right to make private decisions regarding abortion, only "unduly burdensome" restrictions on abortion would interfere with that right (and she found that none of the restrictions at issue in the 1983 and 1986 cases rose to that level).[26] Rehnquist did not write separately in any of these cases, but O'Connor's view that the state's interest in fetal life is compelling throughout pregnancy seemingly led to the same result: States would be free to restrict abortion from the moment of conception, even to the point of criminal prohibition.

The *Roe* dissenters gained a Chief Justice and a fourth vote in 1986 when Chief Justice Warren Burger retired and Reagan elevated Rehnquist to Chief and appointed Scalia. When in 1987 Reagan had the opportunity to replace Justice Lewis Powell, it seemed Powell's replacement would provide the fifth vote to overrule *Roe*. The constitutional right to privacy played a significant role in the Senate's decision not to confirm Reagan's first nominee, Robert H. Bork, who had written that the Court was mistaken in its interpretation of Fourteenth Amendment liberty in both *Skinner* and *Griswold*. Bork had written, for example, that the desire of a husband and wife "to have sexual relations without fear of unwanted children" was constitutionally indistinguishable from an electric utility company's desire to "void a smoke pollution ordinance."[27] The Senate instead confirmed Reagan's subsequent nominee, Anthony Kennedy. The appointment of Kennedy

---

[23] *Danforth,* 428 U.S. 52; Bellotti v. Baird, 428 U.S. 132 (1976); Bellotti v. Baird, 443 U.S. 622 (1979); H.L. v. Matheson, 450 U.S. 398 (1981); *see also* Hodgson v. Minnesota, 497 U.S. 417 (1990); Ohio v. Akron Center for Reproductive Health, 497 U.S. 502 (1990).

[24] Maher v. Roe, 432 U.S. 464 (1977); Beal v. Doe, 432 U.S. 438 (1977); Poelker v. Doe, 432 U.S. 519 (1977); *Harris,* 448 U.S. 297; Williams v. Zbaraz, 448 U.S. 358 (1980); *see also Webster,* 492 U.S. 490.

[25] *Akron,* 462 U.S. 416; *Ashcroft,* 462 U.S. 476; *Thornburgh,* 476 U.S. 747.

[26] *Id.*

[27] Robert H. Bork, *Neutral Principles and Some First Amendment Problems,* 47 IND. L.J. 1 (1971).

rather than Bork would prove critical to *Roe*'s survival, albeit in diminished form. If Bork had been on the Court at the time of *Casey,* express and complete reversal of *Roe* would have been virtually certain.

WEBSTER: REHNQUIST IN THE MAJORITY

The first test of Chief Justice Rehnquist's leadership and of Kennedy's position on *Roe* came in 1989 in *Webster v. Reproductive Health Services.* Both the state of Missouri, in defense of its restrictive abortion law, and President George H. W. Bush, through his Solicitor General on behalf of the United States, urged the Court not only to uphold the challenged law, but to overrule *Roe.* The months leading up to oral argument and then decision brought greatly increased activity among activists on both sides and elevated attention among the press, elected officials, and the general public. As supporters of legal abortion realized the Court might overturn *Roe* and allow elected officials again to criminalize abortion, they increasingly made choice an issue in electoral politics, organized marches and demonstrations, and planned for the possibility of life without *Roe.* A record number of amicus curiae briefs filed in *Webster* warned, for example, of a return to the dangers and horrors of illegal abortion, which surveys predicted would occur in the overwhelming majority of states.[28]

For the first time, Rehnquist had a realistic possibility of making his *Roe* dissent the majority holding of the Court, and he assigned himself the task of drafting the majority opinion. As widely expected, the *Webster* Court upheld all of the challenged provisions of the Missouri law. Rehnquist wrote an opinion that attracted five votes for most of its analysis, but failed to hold the majority with regard to one provision and, far more significant, the status of *Roe.* The portions of Rehnquist's opinion that spoke for a majority held that the law's prohibition on the use of public facilities and public employees in the provision of abortion services was a simple extension of the Court's precedent that already upheld bans on the use of public funds for abortion services (even though the Missouri prohibition applied where no public funds were used and the woman paid the full costs of the services).

Another restriction at issue required physicians to perform certain tests "as are necessary" to ascertain whether the fetus was viable if the physician had reason to believe the woman was twenty or more weeks pregnant. Five Justices voted to uphold the requirement, but Rehnquist lost his majority with regard to why this provision was constitutional. As Blackmun and Scalia both noted (the former with foreboding, the latter with approval), that portion of Rehnquist's opinion, joined by Kennedy and White, would have overruled *Roe.* In an apparent, albeit unsuccessful, attempt to hold his majority (in particular O'Connor and Kennedy), Rehnquist wrote in terms so understated, even misleading, that only those

---

[28] LAURENCE H. TRIBE, ABORTION: THE CLASH OF ABSOLUTES (1990).

schooled in constitutional doctrine could decipher the import of his opinion. Blackmun wrote in dissent, "the plurality and Justice Scalia would overrule *Roe* (the first silently, the other explicitly). . . . [Never] in my memory has a plurality gone about its business in such a deceptive fashion."

Although Rehnquist claimed only to "modify and narrow *Roe* and succeeding cases," his plurality opinion in fact described the liberty at issue as "a liberty interest protected by the Due Process Clause" rather than a "fundamental right" and went on to apply only the highly deferential rational basis standard of judicial review (consistent with his *Roe* dissent). Mentioning *Griswold* by name, Rehnquist stressed that his approach would not require reconsideration of other unenumerated privacy rights because *Roe* could be distinguished. Rehnquist also quoted approvingly from previous O'Connor and White dissents that described a state's asserted interest in potential life as "compelling" (which signifies it would override even a fundamental right). Rehnquist sought to downplay the implications of his approach and reassuringly predicted (without any basis in fact) that state legislatures would act with moderation if the Court overruled *Roe:* "Justice Blackmun's suggestion that legislative bodies, in a Nation where more than half of our population is women, will treat our decision today as an invitation to enact abortion regulation reminiscent of the Dark Ages not only misreads our views but does scant justice to those who serve in such bodies and the people who elect them."

Thus, four Justices in *Webster* would have effectively overruled *Roe,* three of them in a highly misleading manner. A fifth, O'Connor, declined to reach that question because she found it unnecessary for upholding all of Missouri's abortion restrictions at issue. She found the viability testing requirement constitutional under existing precedent, though she clearly had to stretch that precedent to fit. O'Connor was notably less critical of *Roe* than she had been in her earlier dissents, where she had expressed multiple grounds for disagreement, including her view that the state interest in potential fetal life is compelling from the moment of conception. Scalia wrote separately to emphasize that the Court should expressly overrule *Roe* and to chastise O'Connor for her reticence: "It thus appears that the mansion of constitutionalized abortion law, constructed overnight in *Roe v. Wade,* must be disassembled doorjamb by doorjamb, and never entirely brought down, no matter how wrong it may be." Blackmun, the author of *Roe* and one of only four remaining votes to reaffirm that decision, sought to make evident what Rehnquist's plurality opinion obfuscated: "For today, at least, the law of abortion stands undisturbed. . . . But the signs are evident and very ominous, and a chill wind blows."

CASEY: IN DISSENT AGAIN

As Scalia unhappily predicted, *Webster* sparked "carts full of mail from the public, and streets full of demonstrators, urging us . . . to follow the popular will." The mail and demonstrations, though, increasingly were aimed at elected officials, as *Webster* helped shatter any remaining pro-choice sense of security that the Court would uphold *Roe*. Public awareness of the threat (or promise, depending on one's view) ran high, aided by the unusual consistency in the message from both pro-choice and antiabortion advocates, as well as by efforts by antiabortion state officials to criminalize abortion prematurely. Although most efforts aimed at enacting new bans, some people looked to the pre-*Roe* laws still on the books, including a district attorney in Louisiana who responded to *Webster* with the announcement that he immediately would begin enforcing the state's pre–Civil War criminal abortion ban, which imposed ten years at hard labor for the performance of any abortion not necessary to save a woman's life. While a court enjoined any such prosecutions (because *Webster* had not, in fact, overruled *Roe*), the threat highlighted how close that day might be. Public attention escalated further with the loss of two of the remaining four Justices who supported *Roe*. When President George H. W. Bush replaced Justice William Brennan with David Souter in 1990 and Justice Thurgood Marshall with Clarence Thomas in 1991, *Roe*'s demise seemed certain. Rehnquist seemed poised, when presented with the appropriate case, to turn his *Roe* dissent into the Court's majority position.

When the Court announced it would hear a challenge to the constitutionality of a restrictive Pennsylvania abortion statute, conventional wisdom held that the Court would uphold the law, either by overruling *Roe* entirely (thereby allowing the government to ban abortion) or by postponing that ultimate step and overruling just enough precedent to uphold the law under O'Connor's undue burden test. In fact, the controlling opinion in *Planned Parenthood v. Casey* did adopt and apply a version of O'Connor's undue burden test and, in essence, overruled significant portions of *Roe*. But instead of preserving the possibility that the Court in a future case would allow states once again to criminalize abortion, the Court surprised the nation by reaffirming what it described as *Roe*'s essential holding: "the right of the woman to choose to have an abortion before viability and to obtain it without undue interference from the State."

Many people greeted this aspect of *Casey* with celebration and great relief, others with bitter disappointment and despair, but virtually all with surprise. This outcome not only required Souter's vote, but also required both O'Connor and Kennedy to abandon positions that they previously had espoused (in Kennedy's case just three years earlier in *Webster*). O'Connor, Kennedy, and Souter actually came together in *Casey* and authored an extraordinary joint opinion, in part a majority opinion joined by Blackmun and Stevens, and in other parts a controlling plurality opinion. The shift on the Court was truly astounding, notwithstanding the joint opinion's unpersuasive attempt to downplay the extent to which Kennedy and O'Connor had changed their positions. All four remaining Justices called for the express and complete overruling of *Roe* in opinions authored by Rehnquist and Scalia.

Given prevailing expectations, what the *Casey* Court preserved of *Roe* completely overshadowed the extent to which the Court diminished judicial protection for the choice of abortion. Both aspects of *Casey* centrally inform Rehnquist's complicated legacy on abortion. The Court has moved considerably away from the degree of protection that *Roe* afforded reproductive liberty, and in that sense Rehnquist can be viewed as having made progress. Rehnquist's unwavering opposition has encouraged, as he put it, *Casey*'s gutting of *Roe*. Rehnquist's dissent, though, actually understates the considerable framework of *Roe* that survives.

First, with regard to what portions of *Roe* survive *Casey,* the joint opinion expressly based its reaffirmation, not on a belief that the Court decided *Roe* correctly as an original matter, but on the doctrine of *stare decisis* – that is, the presumption that the Court ordinarily will not overrule even incorrect prior decisions. *Stare decisis*'s critical role in *Casey* is widely acknowledged, but far less so is the joint opinion's discussion of what portion of *Roe*'s reasoning might be "in error." The Court flatly rejected Rehnquist's approach to overruling *Roe,* and, to the contrary, found any "error" in *Roe* limited to "the strength of the state interest in fetal protection, not to the recognition afforded by the Constitution to the woman's liberty." An overruling on either ground would allow the government again to criminalize abortion, but Rehnquist's repudiated approach – no fundamental liberty right even implicated – would have more sweeping implications for individual liberty beyond the context of abortion.

On the nature of the liberty at stake, this opinion, authored by three Justices appointed by anti-*Roe* Presidents and joined by the two Justices remaining on the Court who were fully supportive of *Roe,* surpassed in eloquence, persuasiveness, and thoroughness all previous Supreme Court majority opinions on reproductive liberty – and arguably any opinion by even a single Justice. (It also quoted extensively from the other candidate for that distinction, Justice John Marshall Harlan's well-known opinion in *Poe v. Ullman.*)[29] Also remarkable, the *Casey* Court proclaimed that there was "no doubt as to the correctness of" *Griswold v. Connecticut* and other opinions upholding a fundamental right of every individual to seek to prevent pregnancy through the use of contraception, and the Court proclaimed further that these and other cases support the constitutional right recognized in *Roe*. The Court's discussion of the meaning of liberty also is striking, and unprecedented, in its acknowledgment of the gender equality implications of government restrictions on abortion and the gender stereotypes that might underlie governmental attempts to force women to continue pregnancies against their will. The Court also cited the history of gender discrimination and past Supreme Court reaffirmation of the common-law principle that "a woman had no legal existence separate from her husband" in the course of invalidating the one restriction in the Pennsylvania law that the Court found unduly burdensome: a requirement that women notify their husbands before having an abortion.

[29] 367 U.S. 497 (1961) (Harlan, J., dissenting from dismissal on jurisdictional grounds).

Rehnquist unexpectedly found himself back in dissent, after his brief time (since *Webster*) in the majority – a majority he had every reason to expect would have grown and strengthened. Confronted instead with the *Casey* Court's far more developed notion of liberty and its assertion that *Roe*'s vulnerability, if any, rested in its undervaluation of the state's interest in fetal life, Rehnquist did not fundamentally alter his basis for opposition to *Roe*: He continued to argue that state abortion restrictions do not implicate any fundamental right and therefore must be upheld, except in the rare instance that they fail rational basis review's minimal scrutiny. The Court, in his continued judgment, should overrule *Roe* on the ground that it misconstrued the nature of constitutionally protected liberty.

Rehnquist did shift his analysis a bit, though, in ways that allowed a slightly broader view of the protections that the Fourteenth Amendment affords individual liberty from governmental interferences (but that made no difference for abortion). His *Roe* dissent focused on the intent of the Framers of the Fourteenth Amendment and a very narrow and particularized view of deeply rooted tradition especially at the time of ratification. Rehnquist's *Casey* dissent focused less on those sources as defining the outer limits of protected liberty, but his view of the history and traditions of the American people remained quite narrow and defined at a very specific level. In addition, though, he described at some length the Court's doctrinal development of the fundamental right to privacy and its inquiry into whether particular liberties are "implicit in the concept of ordered liberty."

While he complained of the imprecision inherent in defining as fundamental any right that was not enumerated in the constitutional text at a high level of specificity, Rehnquist cited a number of pre-*Roe* privacy cases, including *Griswold* and *Skinner*, without impugning their correctness. Instead, he distinguished these cases from *Roe*, stating that "[w]e are now of the view" that the *Roe* Court read them "too broadly" and "reached too far" in extending them to the abortion decision. In what was for him a rare mention of the presence of the developing embryo or fetus within a woman as relevant to the constitutionality of abortion restrictions, Rehnquist concluded that because an abortion "involves the destruction of a fetus," it is "*sui generis*, different in kind from the others that the Court has protected under the rubric of personal or family privacy and autonomy." This approach would consider the unique presence of the fetus as relevant to the nature of women's liberty itself and not simply the state's interest. However in *Casey*, as in *Roe*, Rehnquist's chief complaint and concern seemed to be not the protection of fetal life, but that the judicial creation of rights inappropriately substituted the Court's abortion policy preferences for those of the states.

Although Rehnquist made clear his view that the *Casey* Court was very mistaken for continuing to recognize a fundamental right that he believed the Constitution did not protect, he also detailed how the *Casey* Court retreated from *Roe*:

"The joint opinion . . . retains the outer shell of *Roe v. Wade,* but beats a whole-sale retreat from the substance of that case." Specifically, as Rehnquist noted, no longer did the Court describe the decision whether to terminate a pregnancy as a fundamental right. The "unjustified constitutional compromise" embodied in the new undue burden test replaced the trimester system and the strict scrutiny standard. And the *Casey* Court applied the new standard to uphold restrictions indistinguishable from those the Court previously had held unconstitutional, in particular a requirement that women delay abortions twenty-four hours after physicians offered them state materials designed to dissuade them from having an abortion. This necessitated overruling in part decisions from 1983 and 1986, and only Blackmun and Stevens would have reaffirmed them.[30] Thus, in a sense *Roe,* and especially its companion case *Doe,* had flipped from 7–2 decisions to 2–7 decisions, possibly on everything but abortion bans and extremely onerous restrictions.

THE UNDUE BURDEN TEST POST-*CASEY*

Rehnquist clearly did not concede defeat in *Casey.* He denigrated the undue bur-den standard as unsupported by a majority on the Court and as "a standard which is not built to last." And Rehnquist may yet prevail. Much, of course, de-pends on the future composition of the Court. Since *Casey,* appointments by pro-choice President William J. Clinton have made the Court slightly more sup-portive of *Roe.* Justice Stephen Breyer's assumption of the seat held by Blackmun, the author of *Roe,* did not substantially change *Roe*'s standing. But Clinton's re-placement of White, the second *Roe* dissenter, with former women's rights ad-vocate Ruth Bader Ginsburg reduced from four to three the Justices who have called for expressly overruling *Roe.*

How the current Court will approach abortion restrictions that fall short of bans under the *Casey* undue burden standard remains less certain. Rehnquist's criticism of the *Casey* compromise gained support in *Stenberg v. Carhart.* On this very next occasion for the Court to apply the undue burden test, Kennedy split with his coauthors of the *Casey* joint opinion, O'Connor and Souter, concerning whether the restriction at issue constituted an undue burden. This left the Court sharply divided, 5–4, in invalidating a Nebraska statute that prohibited the use of abortion procedures that fell within the definition of what the law labeled "partial birth" abortions. The majority found the ban an undue burden because it lacked an exception where denial of the procedure posed a risk to a wom-an's health, and because the ban was not limited to postviability abortions, or even those close to viability, but also reached the most common form of second-trimester abortions. Kennedy's dissent rested in part on his different reading of

---

[30] *Akron,* 462 U.S. 416; *Thornburgh,* 476 U.S. 747.

the law. Rehnquist wrote a three-sentence separate dissent. He expressed his continued disagreement with the *Casey* joint opinion but noted it nonetheless represented the Court's holding, which in his view Kennedy and Thomas correctly applied in *Stenberg*. Rehnquist therefore joined their dissenting opinions that would have upheld the ban on the procedure as consistent with *Casey*'s undue burden test.

One abortion issue on the horizon will present the Court with a twist on the typical presentation of a claim of reproductive liberty. With the exception of restrictions on federal funds, litigated more than two decades ago, state legislatures enacted all of the abortion restrictions that the Court has considered. (Outside the abortion context, states – not Congress – also enacted the liberty restrictions that were at issue in recent Court cases that involved other important claims of protected "liberty" not expressly and specifically enumerated in the constitutional text). Some opponents of *Roe,* including Rehnquist, have viewed the abortion issue as largely one of federalism and the appropriate degree of state sovereignty. Congress, though, in 2003 enacted the first federal ban on a category of abortions, underscoring that governmental regulation of abortion is not solely an issue of federalism and that Congress also may enact nationwide restrictions on abortion, restrictions that also will be subject to judicial scrutiny. The Partial Birth Abortion Ban Act of 2003 criminalized throughout the nation, regardless of state law, the performance of a statutorily described method of abortion. The ban is very similar to the Nebraska statute that the closely divided Court invalidated in *Stenberg* and thus faces the risk that the Court will invalidate it as a transparent, illegitimate attempt to overrule *Stenberg*. Congress was very aware of that possibility and asserted in the statute that its superior legislative fact-finding merited upholding the law notwithstanding *Stenberg*.

Stenberg underscores that the extent to which governmental restriction of abortion will survive the undue burden test will depend on who applies the test and how. Even if the Court does not abandon the test for something less protective, combinations of restrictions can be just as effective as bans in rendering abortion services unavailable. This is particularly true when applied to poor and working-class women who are ill equipped for the increased costs that accompany dramatic reductions in the number of abortion providers (already very few in some states). This shortage of providers results from the cumulative effects of government restrictions, reduced medical training opportunities, and violence and harassment directed at abortion providers. To the extent that a future Court upholds state authority to enact increasingly onerous restrictions, a patchwork of disparate state laws and uneven availability of services somewhat analogous to the pre-*Roe* patchwork might emerge, in which some number of women will have to travel long distances out of state (sometimes more than once) to obtain a legal abortion. Or Congress might impose additional nationwide abortion restrictions that deprive women even of the possibility of out-of-state travel for abortion services.

REHNQUIST AND *CASEY* ON JUDICIAL SUPREMACY

The prospect of future Supreme Court review of congressionally imposed abortion restrictions highlights another, far less direct influence that Rehnquist may have exerted on *Casey* – an influence at its core unrelated to abortion, but that, in *Casey*'s application, supported *Roe*. The *Casey* joint opinion premised its reaffirmation of *Roe* – to the extent that it did reaffirm *Roe* – on an extremely strong view of the Court's role as the ultimate authority on constitutional meaning. The joint opinion relied upon what it perceived as the vital need to preserve the American people's "understanding of the Court invested with the authority to . . . speak before all others for their constitutional ideals." To undermine the public's confidence in the Court by overruling *Roe* would risk, according to the Court, not only the Court's legitimacy, but the nation's adherence to the rule of law and "very ability to see itself through its constitutional ideals."

An extraordinarily aggressive view of judicial supremacy in constitutional interpretation became a hallmark of the Rehnquist Court, and Rehnquist, more than any other Justice, bears responsibility for thus strengthening the Court's authority. Linda Greenhouse described Rehnquist as "perhaps the leading modern expositor of judicial supremacy" and as someone who has "committed his tenure to the maximum exercise of the Supreme Court's power."[31] Rehnquist promoted both a generally reinvigorated view of judicial interpretive supremacy and a particular intolerance for congressional disagreement with the Court's interpretations, in opinions as disparate as his 1980 dissent in *City of Rome v. United States*,[32] which advocated limits on congressional power that the Court essentially adopted in 1997,[33] to a majority opinion reaffirming the need to administer *Miranda* warnings despite Congress's enactment of legislation essentially disagreeing with the necessity for such warnings in all cases.[34] For Rehnquist, and ultimately a majority of the Justices, judicial supremacy precluded a congressional role in defining constitutional meaning and the scope of constitutional rights, whether Congress sought to expand or contract rights.

One of the Rehnquist Court's most controversial positions was the contraction, on judicial supremacy grounds, of Congress's power to enforce the guarantees of the Fourteenth Amendment, pursuant to the express grant of power in the Amendment's Section 5: "The Congress shall have the power to enforce, by appropriate legislation, the provisions of this article." This development provoked deep concern among the academic and advocacy communities, though its unusual doctrinal complexity muted more general appreciation of its significance.[35]

---

[31] Greenhouse, *supra* note 5, at 257.   [32] 446 U.S. 156 (1980).

[33] City of Boerne v. Flores, 521 U.S. 507 (1997).   [34] Dickerson v. United States, 530 U.S. 428 (2000).

[35] *See, e.g.*, Robert C. Post & Reva B. Siegel, *Legislative Constitutionalism and Section Five Power: Policentric Interpretation of the Family and Medical Leave Act*, 112 YALE L.J. 1943 (2003); Robert C. Post & Reva B. Siegel, *Protecting the Constitution from the People: Juricentric Restrictions on Section Five Power*, 78 IND. L.J. 1 (2003).

The Court first adopted new limitations on Congress's Section 5 authority in *City of Boerne v. Flores*, a 1997 decision that involved Congress's attempt, as the Court saw it, to overrule a Court decision through enactment of the Religious Freedom Restoration Act. The Court created a new test of "congruence and proportionality," pursuant to which it would closely examine congressional enactments to ensure that they aimed at enforcing rights as interpreted by the Court and that they did not redefine or expand rights. The importance and inaccessibility of these cases were heightened by their intersection with the Rehnquist Court's equally complex and also newly created sovereign immunity doctrine, through which the Court controversially imposed additional limits on congressional power.[36]

The Court applied these new Section 5 and sovereign immunity limits, by votes of 5–4, to invalidate portions of the Age Discrimination in Employment Act, the Violence Against Women Act, and the Americans with Disabilities Act.[37] Although Rehnquist authored only one of these majority opinions, their roots lie in his 1980 dissent in *United States v. City of Rome*. Rehnquist put the brakes on what some called a "federalism revolution" in a 2003 opinion he authored for the Court upholding Congress's Section 5 authority to enact the Family Medical Leave Act.[38] Even there, however, Rehnquist continued to espouse the same strong view of judicial supremacy. He emphasized that Congress possessed authority to enact the law only because the Court itself long had recognized women as deserving of heightened constitutional protection (although Rehnquist personally was slow to endorse judicial protection against sex discrimination).

Thus, while Rehnquist opposed the *Casey* Court's reliance on the Supreme Court's special role as constitutional interpreter, Rehnquist's insistence elsewhere on vigorous judicial supremacy to prevent Congress from expansively protecting rights may have indirectly supported and encouraged *Casey*'s continued protection for reproductive choice. An interesting hypothetical – indeed, an issue that might confront the Court – is how Rehnquist would approach the constitutionality of the Partial Birth Abortion Ban Act of 2003. His general view of judicial supremacy would dispose him to be hostile to what looks like congressional claims of authority to substitute its view for the Court's and, in effect, to overrule the Court's decision in *Stenberg*. But, unlike his unexpected reaffirmation of *Miranda* in *Dickerson*, Rehnquist almost certainly would seize this or any opportunity to try to overrule *Stenberg* on the merits, as wrongly decided from the outset.

---

[36] Seminole Tribe of Florida v. Florida, 517 U.S. 44 (1996); Alden v. Maine, 527 U.S. 706 (1999).

[37] Board of Trustees of University of Alabama v. Garrett, 531 U.S. 356 (2001); Kimel v. Florida Board of Regents, 528 U.S. 62 (2000); United States v. Morrison, 529 U.S. 598 (2000).

[38] Nevada Department of Human Resources v. Hibbs, 538 U.S. 721 (2003).

REHNQUIST AFTER *CASEY:* FROM MAJORITY IN *GLUCKSBERG* TO DISSENT IN *LAWRENCE*

Rehnquist's abortion opinions did not turn on the real-world consequences for women of state restrictions on abortion, but instead sought maximum judicial deference to state legislatures' choices regarding abortion. In post-*Casey* non-abortion cases as well – cases involving claims to the right to control the circumstances of one's own death and the right to engage in consensual sexual activity regardless of sexual orientation – Rehnquist promoted a narrow view of protected liberty and a broad view of state sovereignty. Because *Roe* for Rehnquist was less about abortion per se than about his views on federalism, individual rights, and the appropriate institutional role of the courts, his legacy depends on a more general assessment of how the Court protects individual liberty from governmental interference under the doctrine of substantive due process. In this sense, *Casey* was a major loss for Rehnquist, because five Justices rejected his very narrow view of liberty rights that are not specifically enumerated in the constitutional text. And Kennedy's defection in *Stenberg* did little to improve matters for Rehnquist because it was not premised on a fundamentally changed view of substantive due process protections for liberty.

Rehnquist, though, made a significant comeback in 1997 with a five-Justice majority opinion on the meaning of liberty in the context of "physician-assisted suicide." The bottom line in *Washington v. Glucksberg*[39] was not closely contested: All nine Justices concurred in the judgment that a Washington statute that made it a felony to knowingly aid another to attempt suicide did not violate the Fourteenth Amendment. The Court, though, splintered on the reasoning (and the reach of the Court's judgment). An open question at the time was whether the Court would apply *Casey*'s undue burden test in the context of other unenumerated liberties, and the Court's answer in *Glucksberg* (and in other non-abortion cases) was "No." Rehnquist's majority opinion, joined by four others, followed his characteristically narrow approach to defining the scope of protected liberty: "We begin, as we do in all due process cases, by examining our Nation's history, legal traditions, and practices." Rehnquist then described the claimed right in very specific terms: whether there is a "deeply rooted" right to commit suicide with another's assistance. Not surprisingly, given that characterization, he held for the Court that no such protected right existed. He expressly rejected the argument that the Court's decisions that interpreted liberty to protect personal decision making on some questions (including marriage, childbearing, and child rearing) suggested a protected right to personal autonomy in all important, intimate, and personal decisions.

The views of the three authors of the *Casey* joint opinion – the Justices "in the middle" – are particularly relevant to evaluating Rehnquist's success and where

[39] 521 U.S. 702.

the Court stands on the meaning of liberty. They also splintered, which demonstrates further the fragility of their *Casey* alliance. Kennedy simply joined Rehnquist's opinion, despite the striking differences in how the two opinions – the *Casey* joint opinion and Rehnquist's *Glucksberg* majority – approached substantive due process protections for liberty. O'Connor provided the fifth vote to form a majority for Rehnquist's opinion, but she wrote separately essentially to limit its significance. O'Connor explained that, although she agreed with Rehnquist's opinion given how he chose to characterize the issue (that is, there is no right to commit suicide or have assistance in the process), other characterizations might yield different results, such as "whether a mentally competent person who is experiencing great suffering has a constitutionally cognizable interest in controlling the circumstances of his or her imminent death." She determined that the Court need not reach this question, which she clearly signaled would yield a different answer, because the parties all agreed that state law did not preclude a terminally ill patient from obtaining medication to alleviate suffering "even to the point of causing unconsciousness and hastening death."

Souter concurred only in the judgment, with a lengthy opinion that crystallizes the interpretive gulf between him and Rehnquist. He directly challenged Rehnquist's methodology and the ways in which it deviated from that of the *Casey* Court (something O'Connor did not directly address in her separate opinion and that Kennedy ignored entirely in joining Rehnquist's opinion). Souter argued (and Rehnquist vigorously denied) that *Casey* had adopted Justice Harlan's well-known, and far more liberty-protective, *Poe v. Ullman* dissent.[40] Souter then expounded on Harlan's approach, at greater length than he had in *Casey*. Souter flatly rejected Rehnquist's history-and-tradition look to "past practice described at a very specific level," which by definition would afford little judicial protection from the choices of legislatures. Instead, as Harlan famously put it and Souter quoted, "That tradition is a living thing." In order to determine which liberty interests require "particularly careful scrutiny of the state needs asserted to justify their abridgment," Souter (and Harlan) begin with "a concept of 'ordered liberty' comprising a continuum of rights to be free from 'arbitrary impositions and purposeless restraints.'" In an interesting footnote, Souter expressed a preference for jettisoning the bifurcated approach of *Roe* (and other cases) in which the Court first determines whether the liberty at stake rises to the level of a protected fundamental right and then considers whether the state possesses a compelling interest to justify infringing that right. Instead, Souter would "reserv[e] the label 'right' for instances in which the individual's liberty interest actually trumps the government's countervailing interests. . . ."

In 2003, Rehnquist found himself firmly in dissent again in *Lawrence v. Texas*,[41] when the Court interpreted the substantive due process guarantee of liberty to strike down a Texas law that made it a crime for two people of the same sex to

---

[40] 367 U.S. 497.   [41] 539 U.S. 558.

engage in certain consensual sexual activity. Rehnquist did not write separately, but he and Thomas joined Scalia's scathing dissent. To consider again the *Casey* joint opinion authors, Kennedy, no longer with Rehnquist, authored the Court's opinion and was joined by four Justices, including Souter. O'Connor concurred on the separate ground that the law violated equal protection, rather than due process, because it applied only to same-sex couples. Kennedy's majority opinion was expansively protective of individual liberty and flatly at odds with Rehnquist's consistent approach to the contrary (and did not even cite *Glucksberg*). The Court overruled *Bowers v. Hardwick*,[42] a 1986 5–4 decision in which the Court applied Rehnquist's narrow history-and-tradition approach. Instead, the *Lawrence* Court used a "living tradition" approach to liberty, and, far from focusing on the time of the Fourteenth Amendment's enactment, the Court found that "our laws and traditions in the past half century are of most relevance here." The Court concluded with a stirring endorsement of the concept of a living Constitution: "As the Constitution endures, persons in every generation can invoke its principles in their own search for greater freedom." Notably (and consistent with the direction Souter advocated in *Glucksberg*), although the *Lawrence* Court strongly protected the individual liberty at stake, it did not characterize it as a fundamental right that would trigger strict scrutiny analysis and an assessment of the countervailing state interest. This doctrinal shift, along with shifting majorities and inconsistencies across opinions, complicates both understanding of the Court's prevailing approach to substantive due process and predictions regarding how the Court will assess future claims of protected liberty.

CONCLUSION

Rehnquist's legacy on abortion, and more generally on substantive due process, continues to evolve. For more than three decades, Rehnquist has provided vision and leadership, from his *Roe* dissent at the very outset of his judicial career, to successes in *Webster* and *Glucksberg* and returns to dissent in *Casey* and *Lawrence*. He has consistently urged extremely limited judicial protection for individual liberties that are not specifically enumerated in the constitutional text, with the notable exception of *Boy Scouts of America v. Dale*. The Court's future composition, of course, ultimately will determine whether and to what degree Rehnquist's approach prevails. At present, a majority of Justices on the current Court have soundly rejected that vision. But that Court was changing as this book went to press, with the retirement of Justice O'Connor, who had provided a critical fifth vote in both *Casey* and *Stenberg*.

   With regard to reproductive liberty, a future Court, with one or two new Justices, could overrule *Roe* by adopting one of several possible approaches. The Court could expressly overrule *Roe* and allow state and federal criminal abortion

[42] 478 U.S. 186 (1986).

bans, or the Court could refine and apply the undue burden test to allow all but the most onerous abortion restrictions and bans. Rehnquist clearly would prefer the former, and in particular, an express overruling premised on the absence of any judicially protected right that would trigger even a close judicial look at restrictive abortion laws. Rehnquist's preferred grounds could well threaten individual liberties beyond the abortion context. It is noteworthy, though, that for some women seeking to terminate pregnancies, the practical differences between approaches would be inconsequential. Whatever the form, women would experience the loss of liberty unequally. Hardest hit would be women who lack the resources or ability to travel to the nearest abortion provider: women who are poor, young, or the victims of abuse; women who live in areas with few providers; women who live in states dominated by abortion opponents in elected office and in front of abortion clinics. The practical effect could be dramatically unequal availability of legal abortion services among states, reminiscent of the pre-*Roe* patchwork of laws, even if the Court does not go as far as Rehnquist urged in his *Roe* dissent. Or Congress could impose additional restrictions nationwide.

Although his larger vision of limiting substantive due process protections for liberty thus far has failed to gain momentum, Rehnquist's legacy on abortion, as a practical matter, is one of erosion of protection and movement in his direction. The extent of that movement remains to be seen in the years ahead.

CHAPTER SIXTEEN

SUBSTANTIVE DUE PROCESS, PUBLIC OPINION, AND THE "RIGHT" TO DIE

Neal Devins*

In *Washington v. Glucksberg*, a unanimous Supreme Court upheld a Washington statute that makes it a crime to assist in someone else's suicide attempt.[1] But did the Justices do anything other than register their preferences on the question of whether there is an unqualified right to "assisted suicide"? In particular, does Chief Justice Rehnquist's majority decision in *Glucksberg* say anything useful about how the Court can use the Fourteenth Amendment's Due Process Clause to find rights that are not enumerated in the Constitution? Six years after *Glucksberg*, the Court confronted the question of whether Rehnquist's opinion simply announced a result in a case or set forth a decisional approach to be used in subsequent substantive due process cases. In *Lawrence v. Texas*, the state of Texas and amici supporting state power to outlaw same-sex sodomy spoke of Rehnquist's *Glucksberg* opinion as the "standing order of Due Process methodology."[2] For these lawyers, Rehnquist's decision cabined substantive due process to those fundamental rights that are "objectively 'deeply rooted in this Nation's history and tradition' *and* 'implicit in the concept of ordered liberty.'" Lawyers for the same-sex couple and amici challenging the Texas statute, however, found ammunition of their own in the Rehnquist decision. Noting that Rehnquist both detailed the sensibility of the Washington statute and considered contemporary, as well as historical, attitudes toward assisted suicide, these lawyers argued that *Glucksberg* never considered whether "history alone is decisive" in determining whether a right is fundamental.[3]

When deciding *Lawrence*, Justice Anthony Kennedy's majority opinion did not directly address which depiction of *Glucksberg* was correct. Instead, he found a

* Thanks to my research assistants Joe Schouten, John Shults, and Seth Hansen. Thanks also to Craig Bradley for asking me to be a part of *The Rehnquist Legacy*.

[1] 521 U.S. 702 (1997).
[2] *Brief Amicus Curiae of the Family Research Council*, 318 LANDMARK BRIEFS 201. *See also Respondents's Brief*, 317 LANDMARK BRIEFS 258–60.
[3] *Reply Brief for Petitioners*, 317 LANDMARK BRIEFS 308. *See also Brief Amici Curiae of the American Civil Liberties Union*, 317 LANDMARK BRIEFS 541.

right to engage in same-sex sodomy without even mentioning *Glucksberg*.[4] That Justice Kennedy had signed onto Rehnquist's opinion in *Glucksberg* did not matter. Kennedy blazed his own trail and felt no obligation to explain whether the Court was adhering to or departing from *Glucksberg*.

In this chapter, I explain why both the Chief Justice's opinion in *Glucksberg* and Kennedy's dismissal of it exemplify the Rehnquist Court's approach to substantive due process. Specifically, the Court does not see its privacy decisions as doing anything more than announcing the judgment in a case. Precedent is largely irrelevant and, as such, the Court does not feel an obligation to explain why its decisions either conform to or abandon the methodology of past cases.

In understanding this phenomenon, I call attention to the profound impact that the 1987 Bork confirmation battle had on the Court. When rejecting Bork, the Senate made clear that Supreme Court nominees were expected to pay attention to elected government desires. Bork opposed abortion rights, and the Senate found that politically unacceptable. In contrast, the Senate was not at all troubled by the Supreme Court's 1986 decision in *Bowers v. Hardwick,* a decision upholding state power to criminalize same-sex sodomy.[5] For the Senate, it did not matter that the Court's decision in *Bowers* sounded a lot like the writings of Judge Bork. What mattered is that – unlike abortion – there was no powerful political constituency pushing for gay rights. Put another way: The Senate told Supreme Court nominees that outcomes, not reasoning, mattered.

This chapter is divided into four parts. Part I considers the *Glucksberg* opinion. Following a short summary of how the assisted-suicide issue made its way to the Supreme Court, Part I details internal inconsistencies in Chief Justice Rehnquist's opinion and, in so doing, highlights the Chief Justice's apparent willingness to moderate his decision making in order to secure the votes of the Court's swing Justices, Anthony Kennedy and the recently retired Sandra Day O'Connor. Part II examines the Bork confirmation hearing, arguing that the Senate's broad pronouncements about privacy were a smoke screen for a narrower concern about abortion rights. Part III details the Court's practice of taking social and political forces into account when deciding cases. Part IV ties the battle over Bork to Rehnquist Court privacy decision making. The social and political forces that helped shape Chief Justice Rehnquist's decision in *Glucksberg* are also considered in this discussion.

I. NO RIGHT TO DIE

Claims of a right to die date back to antiquity. In the *Republic,* Plato criticized the medical profession for "inventing lingering death."[6] At the same time, it is a

---

[4] 539 U.S. 558 (2003).

[5] 478 U.S. 186 (1986).

[6] DERECK HUMPHREY & ANN WICKETT, THE RIGHT TO DIE: UNDERSTANDING EUTHANASIA 4 (1986).

basic premise of medicine that doctors, if they cannot cure, should do no harm. When they take the Hippocratic oath, they promise, "I will give no deadly medicine if asked, nor suggest any such counsel." Consistent with this tradition, most states have consistently punished the act of assisting suicide.

Notwithstanding its deep roots, the debate over assisted suicide is decidedly modern. Starting in the 1950s, methods for maintaining life became increasingly available. There emerged antibiotics to fight infection and technology that allows individuals to live in a persistent vegetative state. With medicine and technology extending people's lives, the question of when a life was worth living became more vexing and more commonplace. By the 1980s, the Hemlock Society and other right-to-die advocates turned their attention to the courts, contending that privacy rights should extend to an individual's control over his or her death.

In 1990, the Supreme Court *assumed* that there is a common-law right to refuse unwanted medical treatment. This decision, *Cruzan v. Missouri*,[7] concerned the efforts of parents to terminate the life-support systems of their thirty-two-year-old daughter. But the Court rejected this request, concluding that the state could demand "clear and compelling" evidence that Nancy Cruzan (then in a persistent vegetative state) had personally expressed a wish to refuse medical treatment.

In 1996, the Ninth Circuit Court of Appeals invalidated the State of Washington's ban on assisted suicide. Agreeing with a group of physicians and terminally ill patients that there is a "constitutionally-recognized right to die," the Ninth Circuit ruled that *Cruzan* extended beyond the refusal of unwanted medical treatment to the *affirmative* right to "control the time and manner of one's death."[8] In reversing this holding, Chief Justice Rehnquist's *Glucksberg* opinion rejected the Ninth Circuit's interpretation of *Cruzan,* distinguishing the long legal tradition protecting an individual's right to refuse medical treatment from the near-universal prohibition of assisted suicide.[9] By concluding that there was no specific precedent constraining the Court, the Chief Justice went about assessing the novel claim that the Constitution implicitly protects the right to die.

In finding that there is no right to assisted suicide, Chief Justice Rehnquist purports to be applying "[o]ur established method of substantive-due-process analysis." But this statement makes sense only if the Court's established method is seen as ad hoc, indeterminate, and outcome-driven. As will be made apparent, the Chief Justice's opinion is a mess – filled with omissions, internal inconsistencies, and a general disregard of the precedent he claims to be following.

[7] 497 U.S. 261 (1990).
[8] Compassion in Dying v. Washington, 79 F.3d 790, 816 (9th. Cir. 1996) (en banc).
[9] In a companion case to *Glucksberg, Vacco v. Quill,* the Chief Justice similarly concluded that it was reasonable for a state to distinguish persons who refuse life-saving treatment from those who wish assistance in committing suicide. 521 U.S. 793 (1997). Writing for the majority, Rehnquist rejected an equal protection challenge to a New York law that allowed an individual to refuse medical treatment while forbidding assisted suicide.

First, Glucksberg makes no mention of *Bowers v. Hardwick,* even though the Court's approach to identifying fundamental rights is closely moored to the methodology employed in *Bowers.* In *Bowers,* Justice Byron White sought to re-configure the Court's then-existing practice of declaring a right fundamental if it was either "deeply rooted in this Nation's history and tradition" or "implicit in the concept of ordered liberty, such that neither justice nor liberty would exist if [they] were sacrificed." Contending that the "Court is most vulnerable and comes nearest to illegitimacy when it deals with judge-made [rights,]" White sought to limit the sweep of substantive due process to those rights that are grounded in our nation's legal traditions and practices. For this reason, *Bowers* looked to history and tradition in understanding whether a right to same-sex sodomy was "implicit in the concept of ordered liberty."

In *Glucksberg,* the Court appears to embrace and extend *Bowers.* Not only does the Chief Justice speak of fundamental rights as being "objectively 'deeply rooted in this Nation's history and tradition,'" he modifies the Court's past practice by limiting substantive due process to rights that are *both* "deeply rooted" *and* "implicit in ordered liberty." This innovation, however, is not acknowledged. Instead, the Chief Justice speaks of adhering to past practice (while nevertheless ignoring the decision that seems most relevant to his finding that there is no fundamental right to assisted suicide).

In crafting his opinion this way, the Chief Justice may well have reached out to Justice Anthony Kennedy. Justice Kennedy had recently signaled his discomfort with *Bowers* in *Romer v. Evans,* a 1996 decision in which he rejected (on equal protection grounds) a Colorado law prohibiting the granting of "protected status" to gays.[10] Assuming that Justice Kennedy would not sign on to a decision that strongly backed *Bowers,* the Chief Justice may have thought it better to ignore *Bowers* than to risk losing one of the Justices willing to sign his opinion. In particular, with a bare majority of only five Justices joining his opinion, Rehnquist could not allow the defection of any Justice.

Second, in concluding that there is no fundamental right to die, *Glucksberg* is at war with itself. Rather than strictly following the doctrinal formula that the Chief Justice embraces, Rehnquist's opinion is filled with surprising detours. Most notably, the he does not limit his inquiry to facts that would establish whether assisted suicide is "objectively 'deeply rooted in this Nation's history and tradition.'" Instead, his opinion details how the States "in recent years" have "reexamined and, generally, reaffirmed" bans on assisted suicide. Moreover, Rehnquist explains how "[o]ther countries are embroiled in similar debates." In so doing, the Chief Justice concludes that lawmakers "are currently engaged in serious, thoughtful examinations of physician-assisted suicide" and that the Court's rul-

---

[10] 517 U.S. 620 (1996). Kennedy's *Romer* decision ignored *Bowers.* But his conclusion that the Colorado law "seems inexplicable by anything but animus" cannot be squared with *Bowers's* declaration that states can express their moral disapproval of same-sex sodomy by criminalizing such conduct. In 2003, Kennedy wrote the decision that overturned *Bowers, Lawrence v. Texas.*

ing "permits this debate to continue, as it should in a democratic society." This very analysis, however, can easily be turned around to find fundamental rights that are not "objectively, 'deeply rooted.'" For example, as it did in *Lawrence v. Texas,* the Court can place emphasis on contemporary practices. Moreover, the Chief Justice's opinion invites an open-ended inquiry about whether the states, in fact, can be trusted to act responsibly. This kind of inquiry has nothing to do with legal traditions; instead, it allows judges to second-guess state policy judgments.

Perhaps for this reason, the Chief Justice goes out of his way to explain the sensibility of Washington's assisted-suicide ban. Rather than follow the announced standard of review (where the Court would simply sort out whether the state's interests are legitimate and whether a rational lawmaker could have thought that the law served those interests), *Glucksberg* seems to apply a more demanding standard of review. Rehnquist looks to numerous empirical studies to explain why the assisted-suicide law responds, in fact, to a serious public health problem. These studies suggest that suicide is prevalent among those in vulnerable groups; that (in Holland) many who had requested physician-assisted suicide withdraw that request when their pain or depression is treated; that depression is often misdiagnosed (suggesting that assisted-suicide could make it difficult for the state to protect depressed persons); and that there is substantial risk of doctors unilaterally administering lethal injections.

Based on his analysis of these studies, the Chief Justice concludes that "Washington's ban on assisted suicide is at least reasonably related" to "unquestionably important and legitimate state interests." By taking such a hard look at the soundness of the assisted-suicide prohibition, however, *Glucksberg* paves the way for intrusive judicial review of state laws that do not intrude on fundamental rights. Indeed, in *Lawrence v. Texas,* the Institute for Justice filed a brief that argued that Texas's same-sex sodomy law would not pass muster under *Glucksberg*'s version of rational basis review. Noting that *Glucksberg* "discussed how, *as a factual matter,* the prohibition against assisted suicide related to legitimate government interests," the brief distinguished *Glucksberg* from *Bowers* (where the Court did not make a "factual connection" when approving morals-based legislation).[11] No doubt, this was not the Chief Justice's intent; he joined a dissent in *Lawrence* that embraced *Bowers* and, with it, traditional rational basis review.

Third, Chief Justice Rehquist recognizes that his decision may not be built to last. In a telling footnote, he acknowledges that his "opinion does not absolutely foreclose" future challenges to assisted-suicide laws. For such a challenge to succeed, however, the Court would have to depart from the test that he champions in identifying fundamental rights. Otherwise, it could not find a right to assisted suicide that is "objectively, 'deeply rooted in this Nation's history and tradition.'"

---

[11] 318 LANDMARK BRIEFS 335.

For reasons already detailed, there is good reason to question whether *Glucksberg* truly embraces this supposedly "established method of substantive-due-process analysis." The footnote is nevertheless significant, for it suggests that the Chief Justice was willing to concede the limits of his decision in an effort to secure the vote of Justice Sandra Day O'Connor. In a concurring opinion, Justice O'Connor suggests that a mentally competent person experiencing great pain may have a fundamental right to hasten his or her death. But since the Washington law did not prevent competent individuals from obtaining medicine that alleviates suffering, "even to the point of causing unconsciousness and hastening death," Justice O'Connor thought there was "no reason to think that the democratic process" will not strike an appropriate balance on the issue.

Differences between Justice O'Connor's concurrence and the majority opinion that she joined were seen by some as being quite stark. Justice Stephen Breyer, for example, joined Justice O'Connor's concurrence "except insofar as it joins the opinion of the Court." For their part, academic commentators battled over whether the Chief Justice's opinion truly commanded five votes.

I see no need to enter this debate. The methodology employed in *Glucksberg* is indeterminate to the point of being irrelevant. As the lawyers in *Lawrence* understood, *Glucksberg* can be spun to achieve whatever outcome they like. Lawyers for the state can argue that deferential rational basis review should be applied unless a right is objectively, deeply rooted in history and tradition. Plaintiff's lawyers, in contrast, will talk about the Court's responsibility to look at contemporary developments, including whether the political process satisfactorily protects the asserted right. And even if the right is not fundamental, plaintiffs' lawyers can still insist that the Court should apply rational basis review in such a way as to require the state to demonstrate a true factual connection between the law and its stated purposes.

By following several different paths in *Glucksberg*, the Chief Justice "clouded what should be clear statements of the holding with other assertions that should instead have been treated as dicta."[12] More than that, *Glucksberg's* cavalier attitude to precedent (most notably, its refusal to consider *Bowers*) suggests that subsequent courts need not even discuss *Glucksberg* when deciding the next related dispute. This, I think, helps explain why the majority in *Lawrence* saw no reason to distinguish their holding from *Glucksberg*. To put it plainly: *Glucksberg* has no precedential value because, at bottom, the decision does no more than announce an outcome.

It may be that Chief Justice Rehnquist would have preferred a more structured, ordered analysis. After all, the Chief Justice is hardly a fan of judge-made privacy rights. In addition to his steadfast refusal to sign onto opinions formally embracing substantive due process rights, he has spoken out against "the living Constitution" and, with it, judge-made rights. In a 1976 lecture, he contended that "there

---

[12] Michael Abramowicz and Maxwell Stearns, *Defining Dicta*, 57 Stan. L. Rev. 953, 1017 (2005).

is no justification for a third legislative branch in the federal government, and there is even less justification for a legislative branch's reviewing on a policy basis the laws enacted by the legislatures of the fifty states."[13]

More significant (for the purposes of this chapter) is that Chief Justice Rehnquist joined Justice Antonin Scalia's *Lawrence* dissent, a decision that casts *Glucksberg* as a clear-cut pro-state precedent. But such a decision would likely have garnered three, not five, votes. Recognizing that "the office of chief justice of the United States calls for skills and abilities more readily honed in the give and take of political life than in the practice and the teaching of the law," the Chief Justice probably thought it best to perform his role as "interlocutor of the judicial minstrel show,"[14] compromising principle in order to advance his agenda as best he could. As such, the Chief Justice may have seen *Glucksberg* as a wedge – an indeterminate, even meaningless, decision that might be transformed into a more determinate precedent at a later date.

That day may still come. Just as Justice Kennedy saw no reason to discuss *Glucksberg* in his *Lawrence* decision, the Court may subsequently ignore *Lawrence* in a decision that embraces Justice Scalia's accounting of *Glucksberg*. But that Court will not be the Rehnquist Court. During its nineteen-term tenure to date, the Rehnquist Court has never able to agree on a methodology in substantive due process cases. Instead, they have simply announced the results in cases.

In the next part of this chapter, I begin to examine this phenomenon. By looking at the Senate's 1987 rejection of Robert H. Bork, I call attention to lawmaker efforts to push the Supreme Court to reach the desired outcomes in privacy cases – even if that would make it impossible for the Rehnquist Court to craft a coherent substantive due process methodology.

II. THE BATTLE OVER BORK

The 1980 election of Ronald Reagan marked a sea change in American politics. Reagan reached out to social conservatives by condemning Supreme Court decisions on school prayer, creationism, busing, and especially abortion. School busing remedies were characterized as "reverse segregation" and Reagan promised to undo them by staffing government agencies with individuals who "don't worship at the altar of forced busing and mandatory quotas."[15] On school prayer, Reagan argued that "God should [never] have been expelled from the classroom" and called upon both the Supreme Court and Congress to find ways to reverse the school prayer decision, *Engel v. Vitale*.[16] Most striking, Reagan argued that *Roe v. Wade* was as divisive and as wrong as *Dred Scott*. In the words of Reagan

---

[13] William H. Rehnquist, *The Notion of a Living Constitution*, 54 Tex. L. Rev. 693, 698 (1976).

[14] William H. Rehnquist, *Chief Justices I Never Knew*, 3 Hastings Const. L.Q. 637, 639 (1976).

[15] Weisman, *Reagan Defends 3 Nominations to Rights Panel*, N.Y. Times News Service, Aug. 1, 1983.

[16] Public Papers of the Presidents: Ronald Reagan (1982), I, at 603, 647–48.

Solicitor General Charles Fried, "the Reagan administration made *Roe v. Wade* the symbol of everything that had gone wrong in law, particularly constitutional law."[17]

In attacking *Roe,* the administration launched a broader challenge to Supreme Court decisions recognizing privacy rights. Attorney General William French Smith claimed it wrong to "discern such an abstraction in the Constitution [and] arbitrarily elevate it over other constitutional rights and powers."[18] And though the Reagan Justice Department did not file briefs in *Bowers v. Hardwick* and other nonabortion privacy cases (suggesting – as Charles Fried put it – that the administration cared only about *Roe,* not "privacy in general"), this broader concern about unenumerated rights spilled over into the rhetoric surrounding Reagan judicial appointments.

In his 1980 and 1984 campaigns, Reagan pledged to appoint judges "who respect traditional family values and the sanctity of innocent human life . . . [and] who share our commitment to *judicial restraint.*"[19] In July 1987, Reagan sought to fundamentally change the Supreme Court by appointing Judge Robert H. Bork, somebody who shared the President's belief that "a judge is bound by the Constitution to interpret laws, not make them."[20] Bork, for example, argued that a Court that "makes rather than implements value choices cannot be squared with the presumption of a democratic society" and that Court privacy doctrine was "unprincipled," allowing the Justices to validate their personal predilections.[21] More than that, he echoed the Reagan administration's claim that *Roe v. Wade* was illegitimate, describing the decision as a "serious and wholly unjustified usurpation of state legislative authority" and "in the running for perhaps the worst example of constitutional reasoning [he had] ever read."[22]

Bork was nominated to replace Lewis Powell, a judicial moderate who often stood in the way of Reagan administration initiatives. At that time, the administration had good reason to think that Bork would be confirmed. Senate consideration of Supreme Court nominees had historically looked to a nominee's competence and intelligence, not ideology. But Bork marked the beginning of a new era, one in which ideology played a dominant role.[23] In particular, knowing that Democrats in Congress had the votes to block the legislative enactment of Reagan's social agenda, lawmakers viewed judicial appointments as the key compo-

---

[17] CHARLES FRIED, ORDER AND LAW: ARGUING THE REAGAN REVOLUTION – A FIRSTHAND ACCOUNT 72 (1991).
[18] William French Smith, *Urging Judicial Restraint,* ABA J. 68:59, 61 (1982).
[19] *1984 Republican Party Platform, reprinted in* 40 CONG. Q. ALMANAC 55B, 56B (1984) (emphasis supplied).
[20] PUBLIC PAPERS OF THE PRESIDENTS: RONALD REAGAN (1987), II, at 1230.
[21] Robert H. Bork, *Neutral Principles and Some First Amendment Problems,* 47 IND. L.J. 1, 6 (1971).
[22] Linda Greenhouse, *No Grass Is Growing Under Judge Bork's Seat,* N.Y. TIMES, August 14, 1987, at A18.
[23] For an excellent accounting of the Bork nomination and how it marked a sea change in Senate attitudes, see ETHAN BRONNER, BATTLE FOR JUSTICE: HOW THE BORK NOMINATION SHOOK AMERICA (1989).

nent of the Reagan social policy agenda. As such, Senate Democrats saw the defeat of Bork as critical to their efforts to block the Reagan initiatives on affirmative action, church–state separation, and especially abortion. These efforts paid off; the Senate defeated the Bork nomination, 58–42.

The campaign to defeat Bork was masterful. Even though their principal concern was abortion, the Block Bork Coalition did not want to turn the hearings into a referendum on abortion. Internal polling by the Bork opposition revealed that the abortion issue would not play well with the American people. Their solution was to "pluck the heartstrings of [the] middle class" by focusing their attacks on Bork's condemnation of *all* Court-created privacy rights.[24] In a full-page ad in the *Washington Post,* Bork opponents spoke of "personal privacy [being] one of the most cherished and unique features of American life" and argued that "your freedom to make your own decisions about marriage and family, childbearing and parenting . . . [have] never been in greater danger."[25]

By attacking Bork this way, the Block Bork Coalition found a message that resonated with the American people. An *Atlanta Journal–Constitution* poll, for example, showed that a majority of southerners opposed Bork and that this opposition was tied to Bork's repudiation of Court-created privacy rights.[26] Correspondingly, the Senate Judiciary Committee Report explained that "Judge Bork's denial of the Right to Privacy places the entire line of privacy decisions at risk, and is likely to prevent any subsequent development and extension of it." Speaking specifically about the role of the Court, the report emphasized that "[o]ur Constitution is not simply a grant of rights by the majority" and that the Constitution embraces an "image of human dignity" that requires judges to define "the meaning and content of [unenumerated] rights."[27]

By rejecting Bork, the Senate transformed Rehnquist Court decision making. Not only did it keep a staunch foe of substantive due process off the Court, it set in motion the appointment of both Anthony Kennedy (who took the slot that Bork was nominated to fill) and David Souter (whose nomination was made, in part, to avoid the controversy surrounding nominees – such as Bork – with a paper trail). More than that, perceiving that "a willingness to profess belief in [privacy rights] is a prerequisite for the job,"[28] every nominee since Bork has embraced unenumerated privacy rights. Finally, and (for my purposes) most important, the Senate sent a message to all Justices that the repudiation of lawmaker preferences might well prompt a political backlash.

---

[24] MICHAEL PERTSCHUK & WENDY SCHAETZEL, THE PEOPLE RISING: THE CAMPAIGN AGAINST THE BORK NOMINATION 257 (1989).

[25] WASH. POST advertisement, Sept. 14, 1987, at A9.

[26] NORMA VIETRA & LEONARD GROSS, SUPREME COURT APPOINTMENTS: JUDGE BORK AND THE POLITICIZATION OF SENATE CONFIRMATIONS 153–54 (1986).

[27] S. Exec. Rep. No. 7, 100th Cong., 1st Sess. at 34, 20–21 (1987).

[28] Stephen J. Wermiel, *Confirming the Constitution: The Role of the Senate Judiciary Committee,* 56 LAW & CONTEMP. PROBS. 121, 121–22 (1993).

The defeat of Bork, however, did not mean that lawmakers expected the Supreme Court to actively check elected government decision making by finding new fundamental rights. Rather, it was because Bork's views on abortion and other hot-button issues were unacceptable to politically powerful interests. On other issues, most notably gay rights and the rights of the terminally ill, lawmakers thought it fine for the Court to leave the protection of rights to the democratic process. In particular, no Senator criticized *Bowers's* declaration that the Court comes "closest to illegitimacy" when recognizing unenumerated rights. Even though *Bowers* was decided just one year before the Bork nomination, supporters and opponents of Bork embraced the decision. The Senate Judiciary Committee Report opposing Bork favorably cited *Bowers,* noting that the decision "proves the point . . . that the debate about unenumerated rights has always been about the scope of those rights, not about their existence." Bork supporters used *Bowers* to demonstrate that Bork's approval of a Navy regulation prohibiting homosexual conduct was in line with current Supreme Court precedent.

To summarize: While letting the Justices know that the repudiation of Court decision making on abortion, school prayer, and the like would be seen as an act of political defiance, the Senate also thought that *Bowers* was perfectly acceptable. It did not matter that Justice White's rhetoric echoed Judge Bork's complaint that it is illegitimate for a Court to "make rather than implement value choices." So long as the outcomes of Court decisions were politically acceptable, the Senate did not care what decision-making model the Court employed, whether the Court adhered to or ignored past decisions, or anything else.

III. SOCIAL INFLUENCES ON CONSTITUTIONAL LAW

The question remains: Why do Supreme Court Justices care about lawmaker preferences, public opinion, and the like? After all, the Court's institutional identity is tied to its independence from the ballot box and other external pressures; that is why the Justices are life tenured and work in a somewhat insulated atmosphere. Nevertheless, as Chief Justice Rehnquist reminded us, the "currents and tides of public opinion . . . lap at the courthouse door," for "judges go home at night and read the newspaper or watch the evening news on television; they talk to their family and friends about current events." As such, "[j]udges, so long as they are relatively normal human beings, can no more escape being influenced by public opinion in the long run than can people working at other jobs."[29]

Court decisions, in other words, are not "babies brought by constitutional storks, but are born out of the travail of [social and] economic circumstances."[30] Lacking the powers of the purse and sword, the Court understands that it must act in a way that garners public acceptance. Its power, as Justices O'Connor,

---

[29] William H. Rehnquist, *Constitutional Law and Public Opinion*, 20 SUFFOLK U.L. REV. 751, 768 (1986).

[30] Max Lerner, *Constitution and Courts as Symbols*, 46 YALE L.J. 1290, 1314 (1937).

Kennedy, and Souter argued, lies in its "legitimacy," that is, "the people's acceptance of the Judiciary as [being] fit to determine what the Nation's law means to declare what it demands."[31] That does not mean that all Court decisions must be politically popular; it means, instead, that the Court must act in ways that the public finds legitimate.

Social and political forces, for example, have played a defining role in the Court's reconsideration of decisions on sterilization and the eugenics movement, state-mandated flag salutes, the death penalty, states' rights, and much more. Absent popular support, these decisions proved ineffective. In the end, as Justice Robert Jackson wrote, the "practical play of the forces of politics is such that judicial power has often delayed but never permanently defeated the persistent will of a substantial majority."[32] Consequently, for a Court that wants to maximize its power and legitimacy, taking social and political forces into account is an act of necessity, not cowardice.

Marbury v. Madison, the supposed foundation of judicial supremacy, nicely illustrates how political challenge to the Court's interpretive authority and daunted claims of judicial supremacy are inextricably linked to each other.[33] When *Marbury* was decided, the Supreme Court and its Chief Justice, John Marshall, were under attack. Court foe Thomas Jefferson had just been elected President and, at his urging, Secretary of State James Madison openly challenged the Court's authority to subject executive officers to judicial review. Unwilling to risk Madison's defiance of a Supreme Court order, *Marbury's* bold claim that "[i]t is emphatically the province and duty of the judicial department to say what the law is" is simply window dressing for the Court's decision to dismiss the case on jurisdictional grounds.

Marbury typifies the type of calculation the Justices make before invalidating legislation. Specifically, before striking down legislation, the Justices almost always take their cues from elected officials, the public, or elites (academics, journalists, and other opinion leaders). "Policy views dominant on the Court," as Robert Dahl put it, "are never for long out of line with the policy views dominant among the lawmaking majorities of the United States."[34] This is especially true of Court-created fundamental rights. Grounded in the Court's sense of fundamental fairness and its deciphering of legal traditions (whether deeply rooted or contemporary), fundamental rights cases often thrust the Court into a political thicket. Rather than resist a determined and persistent lawmaking majority, the Court has proven itself willing to conform to majoritarian pressures in its substantive due process decision making.

---

[31] Planned Parenthood v. Casey, 505 U.S. 833, 865 (1992).
[32] Robert H. Jackson, *Maintaining Our Freedoms: The Role of the Judiciary,* 19 Vital Speeches of the Day 759, 761 (1953).
[33] 5 U.S. (1 Cranch) 137 (1803). *See also* Cooper v. Aaron, 358 U.S. 1, 18 (1958) (linking judicial supremacy to *Marbury*).
[34] Robert A. Dahl, *Decision-Making in a Democracy: The Supreme Court as a National Policy-Maker,* 6 J. Pub. Law 279, 285 (1957).

Witness, for example, the collapse of the *Lochner* era under the weight of changing social conditions. Following Franklin Delano Roosevelt's 1936 election victory in all but two states, the Court, embarrassed by populist attacks against the Justices, jettisoned its economic liberties jurisprudence and announced several decisions upholding New Deal programs. In explaining this transformation, Justice Owen Roberts recognized the extraordinary importance of public opinion in undoing the *Lochner* era: "Looking back, it is difficult to see how the Court could have resisted the popular urge for uniform standards throughout the country – for what in effect was a unified economy."[35]

The Rehnquist Court's decision to reaffirm *Roe* in *Planned Parenthood v. Casey* is cut from the same cloth. Responding to the maelstrom surrounding the Bork nomination and, more generally, Reagan and George H. W. Bush efforts to overturn *Roe*, the *Casey* plurality emphasized the costs of "overrul[ing] under [political] fire" and that the "Court must take care to speak and act in ways that allow people to accept its decision." At the same time, by jettisoning *Roe's* trimester standard, the Court took into account the politically salient complaints of prolife interests. By paying close attention to the signals that elected officials and U.S. citizens have sent it, *Casey* typifies Rehnquist Court decision making.

In the next (and final) part of this chapter, I develop this point – discussing the majoritarian nature of Rehnquist Court decision making and linking the Chief Justice's decision in *Glucksberg* to the battle over Bork.

IV. FROM BORK TO *GLUCKSBERG*

Social and political forces have defined both the composition of the Rehnquist Court and the Court's understanding of the facts relevant to its decision making. Had the Senate confirmed Judge Bork, for example, it is likely that some decisions in which Justice Kennedy cast the decisive fifth vote would have gone the other way. Judge Bork would not have cast the fifth vote to reaffirm *Roe* or overturn *Bowers*. Equally significant, congressional resistance to the social conservative agenda during the 1980s shaped the Court's understanding of the social meaning of the cases before it. In particular, Congress's embrace of both abortion and civil rights shaped the thinking of Justices who care about what other branches of government, elites, and the public think.[36] In other words, the rejection of Bork and corresponding nomination of Kennedy (and eventually Souter) was doubly consequential: It both defined the social meaning of the issues before the Court and made it more likely that the Justices who sit on the Court would care about the social meaning of their decisions.

[35] OWEN J. ROBERTS, THE COURT AND THE CONSTITUTION 61 (1951).

[36] Political scientists describe these Justices as "external strategic actors." For a discussion of this model and its impact on the Rehnquist Court, see Thomas W. Merrill, *The Making of the Second Rehnquist Court: A Preliminary Analysis*, 47 ST. LOUIS L.J. 569, 620–38 (2003).

To the extent that majoritarian preferences typically play a role in Court decision making, the Rehnquist Court is hardly unique. What sets the Rehnquist Court apart is that it, more than any other Supreme Court in history, divides 5–4 on those contentious issues that shape the Court's identity. As a result, the Court's swing Justices – Sandra Day O'Connor and Anthony Kennedy – have almost always cast the deciding votes in close cases. Correspondingly, in an effort to cobble together a five-member majority, it has often been the case that concessions had to be made to one or both of these swing Justices. In *Glucksberg*, for example, Justice Kennedy's disapproval of *Bowers* and Justice O'Connor's efforts to limit the decision's reach almost certainly contributed to the ad hoc, indeterminate nature of the decision. That the Chief Justice assigned the decision to himself speaks to the fact that he was less interested in making broad statements about the modes of constitutional interpretation and more "focused on moving the law in a fundamentally conservative direction while trying to circumvent any potential roadblocks along the way."[37] In other words, Rehnquist may have placed a high value on writing a decision in which objective evidence of a fundamental right being "deeply rooted" was deemed to be the Court's "established method." For Rehnquist, the benefit of having a majority of the Justices sign on to that standard may well have outweighed the costs of writing a decision that was incoherent and, as such, easily ignored or distinguished.

For reasons I soon detail, social and political forces figured prominently in Justices O'Connor's and Kennedy's calculations and, ultimately, the Chief Justice's decision in *Glucksberg*. Before I do so, however, I think it useful to outline the paramount role that majoritarian forces, including the battle over Bork, played in Rehnquist Court decision making – so that Rehnquist's decision in *Glucksberg* is seen as simply one piece in a larger mosaic.

Let me start with the obvious: Swing Justices do not have fixed preferences and, as such, are more likely to pay attention to the views of elected officials, elites, and the American people. A Court dominated by swing Justices, by definition, is both hard to predict and prone to embrace indeterminate reasoning (so as to keep their options open in subsequent cases). The Rehnquist Court, not surprisingly, cannot be labeled as either liberal or conservative. On the one hand, it has backed numerous liberal causes: abortion, affirmative action, campaign finance, gay rights, school prayer, *Miranda*, limited constitutional protections for enemy combatants, and free speech on the Internet. On the other hand, it helped put George W. Bush in the White House and, through its revival of federalism, invalidated legislation regulating firearms, domestic violence, and antidiscrimination measures protecting the aged, disabled, and religious minorities.

In making sense of these disparate rulings, the Court (often speaking through its swing Justices) either explicitly or implicitly anchored its decisions on social

[37] Jeffrey Rosen, *Rehnquist the Great?*, 295 ATLANTIC MONTHLY 79, at 79, 87.

and political forces. When approving affirmative action in 2003, Justice O'Connor – speaking for a bare five-member majority – emphasized that elected officials, business interests, and elites strongly supported race preferences in education. Likewise, when speaking for a five-member majority in *Lawrence*, Justice Kennedy highlighted ever-growing public acceptance of gay rights.

The Rehnquist Court's federalism revival likewise paid attention to signals sent to the Court from Congress and the American people.[38] Unlike social issues, lawmakers barely mentioned federalism in the confirmation hearings, committee reports, or floor debates of any member of the Rehnquist Court. Correspondingly, Congress has signaled the Court that it has little institutional stake in these matters and, accordingly, that there is little, if any, institutional price that the Court will pay when invalidating legislation on federalism grounds. For example, even though the Rehnquist Court often invoked federalism when invalidating thirty-one laws between 1995 and 2002, Congress made no effort to challenge the Court's reasoning. There is barely any mention of the precedential impact of Rehnquist Court federalism rulings in the *Congressional Record*. Indeed, in an effort to tap into populist disapproval of Congress, House Republicans pledged to shift power from the federal government to the states as part of their 1994 "Contract with America." Riding the crest of this renewed commitment to federalism, Reagan and Bush appointees to the Rehnquist Court reinvigorated federalism-based limits on Congress and, in so doing, pursued numerous doctrinal innovations.

Unlike federalism, social and political forces cut against the Rehnquist Court's pursuit of doctrinal reform on abortion, affirmative action, and church–state separation. Not only did the Senate reject Bork, it came close to rejecting Clarence Thomas. On civil rights, Congress repudiated Reagan and George H. W. Bush–era initiatives to limit proofs of discrimination based on disparate racial impact and, what is more significant, enacted the 1991 Civil Rights Act, legislation that overturned twelve Supreme Court decisions limiting the scope of civil rights law.

The refusal of Justices O'Connor and Kennedy to sign onto the conservative social agenda may well be tied to the signals sent to the Court from Capitol Hill and elsewhere. Not wanting to be labeled a political lackey of the President who appointed them, Justices O'Connor and Kennedy paid close attention to battles between Congress and the Reagan–Bush administrations over their efforts to reshape constitutional law through judicial appointments and Justice Department arguments. For the most part, O'Connor and Kennedy sought to avoid these imbroglios by denying certiorari on cases raising divisive social issues. And when forced to decide, O'Connor and Kennedy explicitly distanced themselves from the Bork-inspired political "fire[s]" and, in so doing, frequently embraced centrist (if not left-of-center) decision making.

---

[38] For a summary of the social and political context of Rehnquist Court federalism decisions, see Neal Devins, *The Majoritarian Rehnquist Court?*, 67 LAW & CONTEMP. PROBS. 63 (2004).

More telling (for the purposes of this chapter) is that, with Justices Kennedy and O'Connor often casting the decisive votes in substantive due process cases, the Court has played fast and loose with past precedent. Chief Justice Rehnquist's failure to cite *Bowers* in *Glucksberg* and Justice Kennedy's failure to cite *Glucksberg* in *Lawrence* are prime examples. Likewise, the *Casey* plurality seemed more concerned with crafting a politically popular decision than with past precedent. How else to explain the mismatch between their rhetoric about the Court's responsibility to adhere to workable precedent and their decision to jettison the *Roe* trimester test?

Much of this, I think, is tied to the battle over Bork and related developments. Congress made clear that outcomes, not reasoning, mattered. For its part, the Reagan administration revealed that it, too, cared only about outcomes. While contending that judge-made law was inherently problematic, the administration steered clear of nonabortion privacy cases. What's more, the administration formally embraced marital privacy in one of those abortion cases. It argued that the Court could overturn *Roe* without displacing *Griswold v. Connecticut,* the very decision that Judge Bork had attacked in making the case against judge-created rights.

Against this backdrop, it is not surprising that the Chief Justice's opinion in *Glucksberg* ignored past precedent, self-consciously limited its applicability in related cases, and was otherwise filled with internal inconsistencies. That type of outcome-oriented decision making both matched elected official preferences and allowed Rehnquist to accommodate Justices Kennedy and O'Connor. The Chief Justice's willingness to strike such a deal, moreover, followed his practice of "[taking] each case as it came," advancing his agenda without worrying about whether his decision cemented "an overarching theory of constitutional interpretation."[39]

What then about the social and political forces beating against the Court at the time of *Glucksberg?* Although right-to-die interests had played no meaningful role in the Senate's defeat of Bork, patient self-determination became a significant political issue in the 1990s. Following *Cruzan* (upholding a law requiring clear and compelling evidence that a patient would rather refuse life-sustaining medical treatment), Congress sought to limit the decision's reach by enacting the 1990 Patient Self-Determination Act.[40] Pointing to the disconnect between overwhelming public support for patient self-determination and the fact that fewer than 10 percent of Americans have living wills, Congress required health care providers (as a condition of Medicare and Medicaid participation) to inform patients of state laws governing their right to refuse medical treatment, including their right to set out advance directives through a living will.

---

[39] Rosen, *supra* note 37 (quoting former Rehnquist clerk Mike Young and Jack Goldsmith).
[40] Pub. L. No. 101-508 (1990).

On the question of physician-assisted suicide, however, the public was deeply divided. The focal point of media coverage and public opinion was Dr. Jack
Kevorkian. From 1990 to 1996, Kevorkian had assisted in the suicide of at least
thirty-six individuals. Indicted and tried multiple times for assisting in a patient's
suicide, Kevorkian was not convicted until 1999 (after nine years, five trials, and
130 assisted suicide). In 1997, when *Glucksberg* was decided, a Harris Poll found
that 68 percent of those surveyed supported some form of assisted suicide.[41] But
a 1997 *Washington Post* poll showed that only 50 percent supported an unqualified right to physician-assisted suicide.[42] More significant, even though Oregon
voters – by a narrow 51 to 49 percent margin – approved an assisted-suicide referendum in 1995, voters in four other states rejected such proposals. Correspondingly, from 1995 to 1997, bills to weaken assisted-suicide bans were introduced
in thirty different states but none was enacted. Along the same lines, a coalition
of seventeen state attorneys general filed a brief in *Glucksberg*, urging the Court
to respect state sovereignty and, with it, the long-standing practice of states to
outlaw assisted suicide.

At the federal level, Congress and the White House backed state prohibitions
of assisted suicide. Responding to the Ninth Circuit Court of Appeals ruling in
Glucksberg (finding a fundamental right to assisted suicide), Congress approved
the Assisted Suicide Funding Restrictions Act of 1997.[43] This statute bars the use
of federal funds in assisting or supporting physician-assisted suicide. For its part,
the Clinton administration both supported this legislation and argued in *Glucksberg* that "overriding state interests" justify Washington's assisted-suicide ban.[44]

Finally, the medical profession backed laws prohibiting assisted suicide. The
American Medical and Hospital Association (AMHA), for example, drew a sharp
distinction between the right of patients to refuse medical treatment and a patient's right to assisted suicide. In *Cruzan*, the AMHA backed the Cruzan family
in their efforts to terminate state-mandated life support. But in *Glucksberg*, the
AMHA argued that, although patient self-determination is "among the most
important rights that the law affords each person," any assistance to intentionally take the life of a patient "is antithetical to the central mission of healing that
guides both medicine and nursing."[45]

The Supreme Court's rejection of an absolute right to assisted suicide was to
be expected. The states, the federal government, the voting public (by rejecting
ballot initiatives), and the medical profession *all* opposed the recognition of such
a right. The Court, quite simply, was not about to buck majoritarian preferences
and create such a right. By leaving open the door for related claims, moreover,

---

[41] The Harris Poll, Table 2.95: Attitudes Toward Doctor-Assisted Suicide (Unied States, Selected
Years 1982–2001), *reprinted in* SOURCEBOOK OF CRIMINAL JUSTICE STATISTICS 181 (2002).

[42] Robert Suro, *States to Become Forum for Fight Over Assisted Suicide*, WASH. POST, June 27, 1997,
at A19.

[43] Pub. L. No. 105-12, 111 Stat. 23 (1997).

[44] *Brief for the United States*, 253 LANDMARK BRIEFS 306.

[45] *Brief for the American Medical Association et al.*, 254 LANDMARK BRIEFS 611, 612.

Glucksberg provided ample opportunity for the Court to return to this issue at a later date. In the meantime, as the Court recognized in *Glucksberg*, "politically intense minorities are on all sides of the question, and no particular group faces or creates a systematic barrier to well functioning democratic deliberation."[46]

In arguing that the battle over Bork shaped the Court's decision in *Glucksberg*, I do not mean to suggest that the outcome in *Glucksberg* was ever in doubt. The real question was whether the Court would issue an absolutist decision that would shut the door on future challenges to assisted-suicide laws and, in so doing, embrace a decision-making model that would spill over to other privacy claims. Had Bork been confirmed, there is reason to think that the Court would have ridden the crest of majoritarian opposition to assisted suicide and embraced a rigid test to assisted suicide in particular and privacy in general. The defeat of Bork, however, paved the way for the Chief Justice's ad hoc, indeterminate decision in *Glucksberg*.

One final observation: In the years since *Glucksberg*, the push for a right to assisted suicide has met increased political resistance. Since George W. Bush became President, the Justice Department has attempted to void Oregon's "death with dignity" referendum as inconsistent with existing federal controlled-substances law. That issue is now before the Supreme Court. Even more telling, Congress and the Bush White House intervened in the case of Terri Schiavo, a Florida woman in a persistent vegetative state. Rather than accept a state court judgment that the woman – who had no living will – would have wanted to terminate life support, Congress enacted legislation calling on a federal court to review the same evidence considered by the state court. Both before and after lower federal courts refused to order reinsertion of Schiavo's feeding tube, the Supreme Court refused to review the case. For these and other reasons, there is little reason to expect the Court to return to the assisted suicide issue and qualify its decision in *Glucksberg*.

V. CONCLUSION

Social forces, like the Senate's rejection of Judge Robert H. Bork, are inevitably a part of the mix that shapes Supreme Court decision making. Even Justices with fairly inelastic preferences cannot escape, as Justice Cardozo put it, the "great tides and currents which engulf the rest of men."[47] In *Glucksberg*, the Chief Justice responded to these social and political forces to write a decision that was so indeterminate as to be without precedential force. More generally, Rehnquist Court privacy decision making pays scant attention to past precedent. As it turns out, the Senate pushed for such an outcome-driven decision-making model when it rejected Bork.

For the Chief Justice, it may be that concessions made to Justices O'Connor and Kennedy in *Glucksberg* were a necessary means to write a majority opinion

---

[46] CASS R. SUNSTEIN, ONE CASE AT A TIME 113 (1999).
[47] BENJAMIN N. CARDOZO, THE NATURE OF THE JUDICIAL PROCESS 168 (1921).

that might some day constrain privacy rights in a more absolutist way. In this way, the Chief Justice played the hand he was dealt; and while that resulted in an indeterminate, incoherent decision, Chief Justice Rehnquist's *Glucksberg* decision nevertheless did a better job of advancing his agenda than any majority opinion that another Justice was likely to write. Although, needless to say, the Court's 2003 decision in *Lawrence* made clear that this project was not to be fulfilled during his tenure, the future of *Glucksberg* nevertheless remains in doubt.

What is not in doubt is that the Court will look to cues from elected officials and others in sorting out the reach of its privacy decision making. *Glucksberg* exemplifies this reality, as will subsequent decisions that define *Glucksberg*'s precedential fate.

CHAPTER SEVENTEEN

PRIVATIZING THE CONSTITUTION: STATE ACTION AND BEYOND

David J. Barron

Perhaps, after heading the same court for two decades, a judge should expect to be criticized for doing both too little and too much. If so, William Rehnquist has no cause for complaint. Consider two *Harvard Law Review* Forewords published at either end of his tenure as Chief Justice of the United States. The first, entitled "The Vanishing Constitution," appeared soon after he took the helm in 1986.[1] It accuses his Court of lacking confidence in its authority to interpret the Constitution and thus of an excessive deference to political majorities.[2] The second, entitled "We the Court," appeared in 2001.[3] It accuses his Court of an unprecedented judicial hubris that usurps the people's right to interpret the Constitution.[4] What should one make of these clashing critiques?[5] There is some truth in each, but, I believe, both miss an essential aspect of the constitutional jurisprudence of the Rehnquist Court – and, more precisely, of Rehnquist himself.

To explain what they miss, I examine Rehnquist's approach to *state action doctrine* – a doctrine that neither the "Vanishing Court" nor "We the Court" mentions – and its connection to his jurisprudence in other areas of constitutional law. The state action doctrine may be little known to those who do not follow the Court, but it is important nonetheless. Other constitutional doctrines define the content of particular constitutional rights. The state action doctrine determines the class of actors to whom they apply. In particular, it determines the extent to which private, as opposed to governmental action, triggers constitutional review.

[1] Erwin Chemerinsky, *The Supreme Court, 1988 Term – Foreword: The Vanishing Constitution*, 103 HARV. L. REV. 43 (1989).

[2] *Id.*

[3] Larry D. Kramer, *The Supreme Court, 2000 Term – Foreword: We the Court*, 115 HARV. L. REV. 4 (2001).

[4] *Id.*

[5] One possibility for reconciling these critiques is that there have been two Rehnquist Courts – an early one that was deferential and a more recent one that is not. *See* Erwin Chemerinsky, *Understanding the Rehnquist Court: An Admiring Reply to Professor Merrill*, 47 ST. LOUIS U. L.J. 659 (2003). As I explain below, however, that way of resolving the seeming conflict between these two critiques is incomplete.

From his first term on the Court, Rehnquist has been uniquely responsible for transforming this doctrine. He has authored many of the major opinions that limit what counts as state action. If there is a single person responsible for the current, confining idea of state action, it is Rehnquist. As the two articles noted at the outset indicate, however, retrospectives of the Rehnquist Court – and even of Rehnquist himself[6] – often make no mention of this fact. Perhaps that is because Rehnquist had succeeded in limiting state action doctrine well before he became Chief Justice. Even still, it is a problematic omission.

Rehnquist's state action decisions repeatedly restrict the scope of judicial enforcement authority over private actions, leaving their regulation to politics. But in doing so, these decisions assert the independence of private choice from public power. That same assertion about the autonomous nature of private choices also appears in opinions he has written outside the context of state action doctrine, and some of them significantly expand the Court's power to invalidate legislation. Rehnquist's effort to describe private choices as separate from governmental ones is thus central to his jurisprudence. Sometimes that effort makes space for politics, and sometimes it does not. The effort itself, however, is not best understood as reflecting either respect for majority will or hostility to it. Instead, this aspect of Rehnquist's jurisprudence has more to do with privatizing the Constitution than entrusting it to, or wresting it from, the people.

I. STATE ACTION DOCTRINE BEFORE REHNQUIST

When the Fourteenth Amendment guarantees "equal protection" or "due process," it does not spell out the content of the rights it secures. Similarly, when the First Amendment prohibits abridgment of "the freedom of speech," it offers little guidance as to the conduct it bars. That is true for most constitutional rights. Faced with ambiguity, the Court has fashioned complex bodies of case law to give practical content to these provisions. The text is more direct in defining the actor that must respect constitutional rights. The Fourteenth Amendment states that "No State shall" infringe rights to "equal protection" or "due process." The First Amendment identifies "Congress" as the entity that shall not abridge "the freedom of speech." Why, then, do we have "state action" doctrine?

The state action doctrine – which stems from the Fourteenth Amendment's phrase "No State shall . . ." – addresses two kinds of ambiguity. The first arises because the government, by definition, fails to prohibit whatever it allows. That could mean the government "acts" – if only by failing to act – whenever a private party does. If so, the "state action" limitation might seem trivial. It would be satisfied in every case. One traditional task of state action doctrine, then, has been to manage the action–inaction distinction. The second ambiguity arises because the difference between a private actor and a governmental actor is not always

---

[6] *See, e.g.,* Jeffrey Rosen, *Rehnquist the Great?*, 295 ATLANTIC MONTHLY 79, at 79.

clear. The government employs some parties and not others. But if that fact alone were decisive, then the state action requirement might become trivial in a different way. Another traditional task of state action doctrine, therefore, has been to manage the governmental–nongovernmental distinction.

Rehnquist has transformed state action doctrine in a series of decisions that implicate these ambiguities. To appreciate the significance of that transformation, it is helpful to recall the doctrine's content prior to 1972, the year that Rehnquist joined the Court. Professor Charles Black's magisterial analysis of the doctrine, which he published in the *Harvard Law Review* in 1967, provides a good place to start.[7]

Black wrote in reaction to mounting concern among legal elites, who feared the Court was about to breach the outer limit of the state action concept. Black questioned the premise that, as a matter of precedent, any well-defined limits on state action really existed. Even though each new case set off a fresh round of academic hand wringing, the plain fact was that the Supreme Court had not actually dismissed a constitutional claim of race discrimination for want of state action since early in the twentieth century.[8] Over the course of six decades, in other words, the Court had issued an unbroken string of precedents, each of which had found state action in cases challenging private decisions to discriminate on racial grounds.

Even in other areas of constitutional law, Black noted, the Court had treated the requirement as being less than absolute. There, too, private conduct sometimes occasioned constitutional review. "State action" was a limitation, Black suggested, that was always on the horizon: "astoundingly few Supreme Court holdings have been based, affirmatively, on the state action doctrine, and fewer have escaped explicit or clearly implied overruling."[9] A review of Supreme Court case law up to 1972 confirms Black's assessment.

The state action doctrine came into being, as a formal category, with the now infamous *Civil Rights Cases*.[10] Decided in the immediate aftermath of the Reconstruction Amendments, the decision emphasized that the Fourteenth Amendment does not prohibit "private acts" that discriminate inequitably or deprive persons of their lives, liberty, or property. It bars only "state acts" that have that consequence. The dispute that prompted the Court to reach these conclusions concerned a newly enacted federal statute that permitted private persons to sue other private persons for racially discriminatory exclusions from places of public accommodation. The statute was intended to strike at the heart of the post-slavery legal order in the Southern states, but it was not clear at the time of passage that Congress possessed the constitutional power to enact it. Congress's

---

[7] *See* Charles L. Black, Jr., *The Supreme Court, 1966 Term – Foreword: "State Action," Equal Protection, and California's Proposition 14*, 81 HARV. L. REV. 69 (1967).

[8] *See id.* at 85. The last case to have done so was *Hodges v. United States*, 203 U.S. 1 (1906).

[9] Black, *supra* note 7, at 85.

[10] 109 U.S. 3 (1883).

Commerce Clause authority was thought to be more limited at the time than is now the case, and thus Congress relied on its authority under Section 5 of the Fourteenth Amendment, which authorizes Congress to "enforce" the rights that the Fourteenth Amendment grants. As a result, the legal question for the Court concerned whether a statute purporting to regulate private discrimination "enforce[d]" rights that the Fourteenth Amendment protected.

In finding the statute unconstitutional, the Court explained that the federal measure provided a remedy against discrimination without regard to whether state law approved or condemned the private conduct. For this reason, the Court concluded, the federal statute could not be said to be "enforcing" the Fourteenth Amendment. It applied even with respect to private conduct undertaken in states with the "justest" laws – in other words, even in states that deemed such private conduct to be unlawful and would have punished the discriminator. As a result, Congress lacked the constitutional power to enact the statute.

As to the majority's general proposition that the Fourteenth Amendment limits state rather than private actions, even the lone dissenter in the *Civil Rights Cases,* Justice Harlan, did not appear to disagree. He did not dispute the majority's conclusion that the Fourteenth Amendment's general prohibition – "no State shall" – required a showing that the state had somehow approved of the objectionable private action. He argued only that a separate clause of the Fourteenth Amendment, which made the newly freed slaves citizens of the United States, directly restricted certain types of private racial discrimination. The federal statute should have been upheld as a valid attempt to enforce the Fourteenth Amendment, he therefore concluded, because it addressed solely the type of private discrimination the Citizenship Clause directly forbade.

The Court's apparent consensus that, as a general matter, the Fourteenth Amendment requires a showing of state action should be distinguished from a holding as to the content of the state action requirement. The Court did not conclusively determine in the *Civil Rights Cases,* for example, whether the requirement could be satisfied by a state's recognition of common-law rights to property or contract that merely *permit* private individuals to deny other private individuals equal treatment, or to deprive them of life, liberty, or property. At most, the majority opinion in the *Civil Rights Cases* establishes only that private conduct a state itself makes *un*lawful does not constitute "state action" at the moment it occurs. Nor does the Court in the *Civil Rights Cases* reject the possibility that, in some circumstances, a nominally private actor might qualify as a state actor for constitutional purposes. It impliedly rejects the idea that places of public accommodations are, generally speaking, state actors; but it offers no guidance as to whether other "private" actors might be in certain contexts. In other words, the majority has little to say about future applications of the action–inaction and governmental–nongovernmental distinctions.

If the *Civil Rights Cases* established the state action requirement, they left its content essentially undefined. Subsequent precedents, therefore, would determine the requirement's significance. Prior to Rehnquist's ascension to the bench, the Court had made the requirement surprisingly easy to satisfy. Almost without fail, it found the "state action" requirement satisfied by constitutional claims that were predicated on objectionable *private* conduct. That was particularly true of the Court's state action decisions in the decades just before Professor Black wrote his Foreword.

The Court had found the state action requirement met in a pair of cases – one decided in 1944, the other in 1953 – that involved discrimination by private political parties.[11] It held similarly in a case in the 1960s that concerned the discriminatory actions of a nominally private park.[12] The most famous state action case, *Shelley v. Kraemer,*[13] decided in the 1940s, invoked the Constitution to bar a private neighborhood association's enforcement of a racially restrictive covenant on a residential property. A case from the 1960s ensured that a privately owned restaurant – so long as the government held its lease – could not exclude African Americans without attracting constitutional scrutiny.[14] Indeed, the Court even indicated in a case decided not long before Black wrote that a privately owned amusement park could be constitutionally liable for race-based exclusion.[15]

Outside the race cases, the key state action precedent was *Marsh v. Alabama.*[16] There, the Court held that the First Amendment prevented a privately owned company town from excluding religious leafleteers. Though decided in the 1940s, *Marsh* continued to have legs. The Court relied heavily on *Marsh* in 1968 to hold that a privately owned shopping center had a First Amendment obligation to permit labor picketing outside its doors.[17] By the time of Rehnquist's confirmation, therefore, the Court was poised to address whether the icon of private consumer culture – the privately owned shopping mall – was a state actor for First Amendment purposes.[18]

Sometimes the cases finding state action focused on the first ambiguity mentioned above: the action–inaction distinction. In these cases, the Court accepted the convention that private action did not always involve state action. It concluded, however, that the government had, on the facts before it, affirmatively assisted, rather than merely failed to prohibit, the objectionable private conduct. For example, with respect to the constitutionality of political parties holding whites-only primaries, the Court noted the numerous ways in which the state had given the parties privileges that made them unusually powerful, and thus it held that the state had essentially approved the private conduct.[19]

---

[11] Smith v. Allwright, 321 U.S. 649 (1944); Terry v. Adams, 345 U.S. 461 (1953).
[12] Evans v. Newton, 382 U.S. 296 (1966).
[13] 334 U.S. 1 (1948).
[14] Burton v. Wilmington Parking Auth., 365 U.S. 715 (1961).
[15] Griffin v. Maryland, 378 U.S. 130 (1964).
[16] 326 U.S. 501 (1946).
[17] Amalgamated Food Emp. Union Local 590 v. Logan Valley Plaza, Inc., 391 U.S. 308 (1968).
[18] Lloyd Corp., Ltd. v. Tanner, 407 U.S. 551 (1972).
[19] *See Allwright,* 321 U.S. 649 (1944).

In *Shelley,* the Court noted that no state action might be found if the constitutional challenge had been to the mere existence of the racially restrictive covenant – presumably even if state law did not make the creation of such covenants unlawful. But in the case itself, the challenge was to the state's judicial enforcement of the private agreement. In enforcing the covenant, the Court noted, the state was not simply respecting a typical contract between consenting adults. It was prohibiting a willing seller from transacting with a willing buyer at the behest of a third party – a neighborhood association that neither owned the property nor sought to purchase it. Thus, the state was actively prohibiting private parties from contracting for a house, rather than failing to prohibit them from doing so. For that reason, the Court suggested that the state had approved the discrimination rather than merely failed to prohibit it.

Other times, the Court's reasoning concerned the second ambiguity: the governmental–nongovernmental distinction. Here, too, the Court did not purport to erase the distinction; rather, it sought to show that the private actor possessed sufficient power – in a functional sense – to threaten constitutional values. So, for example, the Court explained that the private political parties in the *White Primary Cases* were effectively performing the traditional governmental function of conducting an election. Likewise, it argued that the company town in *Marsh* was the "functional equivalent" of the downtown business district.[20] There was no reason, therefore, to treat the private actor more leniently than the state itself.

The cases did not always clearly identify the state actor. Sometimes the Court indicated that the private actor was not a state actor, but that the state was nonetheless sufficiently involved with the private action as to be responsible for it. Other times the Court concluded that the private actor really was a state actor, as it was performing a governmental function. The Court's lack of clarity did not matter. Even in cases that named a private actor as the defendant, the "state action" requirement did not seem to bar the constitutional claim. That was true even when the private actor was not carrying out a "governmental" function.

These generous state action holdings reflect the influence of the legal realists. They mounted their challenge to traditional views about the integrity of the action–inaction and governmental–nongovernmental distinctions around the turn of the twentieth century. As against the claim that government regulations would violate the Constitution, the realists revealed the enormous power that private actors, armed only with common-law rights to own property or make contracts, could exercise over other private persons. In demonstrating that fact, they sought to discredit the idea that government regulation infringed a constitutionally protected private domain. Public law constructed the "private" domain by creating common-law rights too often assumed to be always already there. Surely the government could adjust the powers it conferred. Indeed, the realists frequently characterized private parties as delegates of governmental authority.[21]

---

[20] *See Marsh,* 326 U.S. at 507–08.

[21] MORTON J. HORWTIZ, THE TRANSFORMATION OF AMERICAN LAW, 1879–1960: THE CRISIS OF LEGAL ORTHODOXY 169–246 (1992).

By the end of the New Deal, the realist position represented conventional wisdom. Older ideas of a private domain sealed off from public influence no longer attracted a majority of the Court. Judicial deference to state economic regulation had become routine.[22] In making realist moves in its state action decisions, however, the Court appeared to take constitutional law into uncharted territory. It was one thing to conclude that a private company was sufficiently "public" to be subject to legislative regulation: Politics would still determine the extent to which it would be regulated. A determination that a private actor's conduct could trigger constitutional review was a different matter. That decision could dramatically enhance the judicial power to trump political judgments – if only by prohibiting states from refusing to regulate the private action that gave rise to the constitutional claim.

The Court had announced various "tests" that, in theory, set limits on what would satisfy the state action requirement. There was the "public function" test, and the "significant state involvement" test. There was the "specific authorization" test and the "monopoly" test. There was the "symbiotic relationship" test and the "pervasive regulation" test.[23] But not even the Court believed that these tests, and others like them, really were tests. When Professor Black concluded the doctrine was a "conceptual disaster area"[24] lacking a coherent method for distinguishing what qualified as state action from what did not, he was only saying what the Supreme Court had already admitted. Time and again, the Court had stated that no single test could be used to identify "state action." Context was all.

Given these doctrinal developments, a plaintiff seeking to overcome the state action hurdle at the end of the 1960s could cite a plethora of cases that, in the aggregate, made at least this much indisputable: At some times, and in some circumstances, private action could serve as the predicate for finding constitutional liability. And the claimant could draw on a number of ways of characterizing the facts to show that his or her case was such a time and circumstance. On the other side, the defendant had mainly precedents that would have to be distinguished. Their actual holdings found the state action requirement to have been satisfied nearly every time, even though the constitutional claim in each arose from the objectionable conduct of a *private* actor.

In consequence, state action doctrine had acquired the look of what Justice Scalia called (in another context) "th'ol' 'totality of the circumstances' test."[25] The hallmark of such all-things-considered tests is their lack of clarity. It was difficult to name, in advance, any private action clearly protected from constitutional review. As if confirming the point, distinguished scholars resorted to the same example to explain what would clearly *not* satisfy the state action requirement:

---

[22] *See* West Coast Hotel Co. v. Parrish, 300 U.S. 379 (1937).

[23] Professor Tribe discusses the various doctrinal tests in his treatise on constitutional law. *See* LAURENCE H. TRIBE, AMERICAN CONSTITUTIONAL LAW §§18-1–18-7, at 1688–1720 (2d ed. 1988).

[24] Black, *supra* note 7, at 95.

[25] United States v. Mead Corp., 533 U.S. 218, 241 (2001) (Scalia, J., dissenting).

a decision to limit guests in one's house for a dinner party to persons of the same race. Yet even as to this example, the commentators hedged: Perhaps the fact that state trespass law protected the homeowner's exclusionary decision constituted state action that could be challenged under the Equal Protection Clause. If so, the state's action might still be constitutional because the homeowner possessed a competing constitutional right to privacy.[26]

That the Constitution might become a general tool for regulating private conduct – subject only to a competing constitutional interest in individual privacy – did not trouble Professor Black. He believed the racial caste system was the great problem of his time. That system depended upon the exclusionary action of "private" individuals, entities, and organizations – from country clubs to restaurants to employers to schools. Because maintenance of such a system clearly offended the Constitution, he believed, the Constitution supported a broad "state action" doctrine. For this reason, Black implored legal elites to change their attitudes about the state action requirement's reach. He feared their suspicions would prematurely arrest the doctrine's development.[27]

Black wrote at a time when it was not at all clear that antidiscrimination statutes would become ubiquitous. He was not exaggerating, then, when he wrote that state action was the most important constitutional doctrine of the day and that one could not "think about it too much."[28] Black had no confidence that any institution other than the Supreme Court would assume responsibility for prohibiting private race discrimination. Justices who favored broad notions of state action should be given professional encouragement.

The state action doctrine Black described, however, was valuable for reasons beyond its utility in rooting out Jim Crow and its subtle variants. The doctrine reflected an important reconception of the very idea of "private" choice. It recognized the realist point that individuals were located within a broader society, and that the broader society established – through law – the structures within which individuals operated. There was, then, no private domain that, a priori, was unaffected by or free from law.

That did not mean the new state action doctrine denied the possibility of individual agency. Nor did it mean that individual choice should not be protected from state power. Black thought it obvious, for example, that a constitutional interest in privacy should be respected – and not only by legislatures but also by courts.[29] It did mean that the amount of individual protection that the state should provide was necessarily a social judgment. It had to be made, therefore, with an appreciation of the conditions of social life in the modern regulatory state. For this reason, state action doctrine's lack of clarity was a much a virtue

---

[26] See Black, *supra* note 7, at 101–02; Louis Henkin, Shelley v. Kraemer: *Notes for a Revised Opinion,* 110 U. PA. L. REV. 473, 497–500 (1962).

[27] Black, *supra* note 7, at 69–70.

[28] *Id.* at 70.

[29] See *id.* at 101–02.

as a vice. The "State" that the Constitution identified was an ever-changing institution. It possessed an increasing capacity to shape private actions in ways that were not always obvious. A context-dependent doctrine of state action – open to transgressing the line that separates action from inaction and the public from the private – was entirely appropriate. It would ensure that the Constitution would be responsive to, rather out of step with, the sociological reality of modern life.

II. REHNQUIST REMAKES STATE ACTION DOCTRINE

For a conservative-minded legal thinker like Rehnquist, the trajectory of state action doctrine that Black described must have prompted a very different reaction. A Constitution designed to limit governmental power seemed to be on the verge of becoming a general means of regulating private action. Arguments like Black's could be made – indeed, were being made – with respect to many rights, from the right to free speech to the right to due process. Private power could threaten those rights as well. Expansive ideas of state action doctrine were likely to affect all areas of constitutional law. In so doing, they would extend the scope of the Warren Court's constitutional revolution.

One need not speculate on the young Justice's view of the legitimacy of private racial discrimination, therefore, to imagine that the state of state action doctrine would have worried him. It embodied the liberal, activist jurisprudence against which the President who had appointed him had run for office. Its open-ended character, sensitive to context and changing social dynamics, revealed just what it meant to speak of the Constitution as a "living" document, a phrase that antagonized conservative jurisprudes such as Rehnquist.[30] That a broad doctrine of state action would empower *federal* judges heightened the concern. And so, as Justice Rehnquist took the bench in 1972, he would surely have agreed that state action doctrine was as important as any doctrine in constitutional law.

Upon joining the Court, Rehnquist, as if heeding Professor Black's call, could not think about state action enough. If there was a major state action opinion to write, he wrote it. His first one – written during his very first term – could hardly have been more significant. Nor could it have been more in conflict with Professor Black's hopes for the future of state action doctrine.

The case, *Moose Lodge No. 107 v. Irvis*,[31] concerned a private social club that had received a liquor license under Pennsylvania law. The lodge's bylaws limited membership to whites and appeared to bar members from bringing guests of another race. When the lodge excluded an African-American guest, an equal protection suit followed.

For the dissenters, *Moose Lodge* was easy. The state actively policed any number of the lodge's policy choices in the course of the licensing process, Justice Brennan

---

[30] *See* William Rehnquist, *The Notion of a Living Constitution*, 54 Tex L. Rev. 693 (1976).

[31] 407 U.S. 163 (1972).

explained. It had thus assumed significant and unusual responsibility for the private actor's conduct. The state's failure to condition the license on the private club's promise not to discriminate – given the state's willingness to require compliance with other conditions – amounted to public support for the club's private choice to exclude. Inaction, on these specific facts, was action.

Justice Douglas's dissent pursued a different approach. He focused on the governmental–nongovernmental distinction. In his view, the state had effectively given Moose Lodge monopoly power. It had set a quota – which had been met – as to the number of clubs that could be licensed in each city. The lodge was effectively empowered to sell its license to any new club for a monopoly price. To call the lodge "private," therefore, was to blink reality. It was a delegate of governmental power.

Neither the dissenters' logic, nor their citations, impressed Rehnquist. He began his analysis: "Moose Lodge is a private club in the ordinary meaning of that term." The fact that a private entity receives state benefits could not satisfy the state action requirement. Otherwise, state action doctrine "would utterly emasculate the distinction between private as distinguished from state conduct. . . ." Nor was there a "symbiotic relationship" between the private club and the state. The case did not involve a lessor–lessee relationship: It involved the relationship between a licensor and licensee. That connection was too distant to "foster or encourage racial discrimination." Finally, the lodge did not carry out a public function. Moose Lodge was not the sole licensed entity in the city, let alone the state. It had nothing like monopoly power.

Rehnquist's opinion in *Moose Lodge* did make a nod to the broad conception of state action that Black had championed. But in doing so, Rehnquist hardly promoted Professor Black's goals. State law barred places of public accommodations from discriminating on the basis of race. It exempted private clubs from that rule. Distinguishing between private clubs and places of public accommodation was not easy. For that reason, it appeared, state law required private clubs to adhere to the policies set forth in their internal bylaws.

Rehnquist concluded that this state law provision crossed the state action line. Other state regulatory requirements failed to prohibit the lodge's private discrimination. This one literally required the private actor to discriminate. It compelled compliance with the lodge's racially discriminatory guest policy. Rehnquist enjoined the state requirement.

The reasoning was weak. Rehnquist's started from the premise that the lodge was a private club. The state did not require the lodge to adopt the discriminatory bylaw. It required it to follow whatever bylaw it adopted. Wasn't the discriminatory bylaw, therefore, the consequence of a private choice? If so, how could one attribute that private decision to the government? In finding state action in this one respect, however, Rehnquist was hardly treating state inaction as state action. In fact, his injunction further separated the public domain of law from the private domain of choice. Rehnquist's holding did not prevent Moose Lodge from discriminating. Nor did it prevent the club from retaining its liquor license. By enjoining the bylaws compliance requirement, Rehnquist simply freed the lodge from a state regulation that intruded deeply into its internal structure and that facilitated public scrutiny of its private sincerity. He embraced an expansive notion of state action to insulate private discrimination from public control.

After *Moose Lodge,* the malleable quality that facilitated the doctrine's expansion aided Rehnquist's effort to limit it. There was no clear-cut way to show that private actions involved state action: There were only particular cases, each of which had to be compared to the factual context of prior cases. Given the context-dependent nature of the inquiry, Rehnquist needed only to show how the facts of each new case resembled *Moose Lodge.* Two years after *Moose Lodge,* Rehnquist had his first opportunity to do just that.

The case, *Jackson v. Metropolitan Edison Co.,*[32] concerned a privately owned utility company's decision to terminate a customer's electric service without notice. The due process claim might have been strong had the government ordered the termination of service. But, in point of fact, the utility was wholly privately owned. As in *Moose Lodge,* therefore, the constitutional question concerned whether private action could trigger constitutional review.

Rehnquist proceeded methodically through each of the "tests" for resolving close state action cases. He limited them one by one as he went along, invoking *Moose Lodge* nearly every time. The utility was "pervasively regulated," but *Moose Lodge* held that fact was not determinative. The utility had monopoly power, but "certain monopoly aspects were presented in *Moose Lodge*" to no avail. Indeed, he noted, the claim was particularly weak here. The utility most likely had a natural monopoly owing to realities of the private market rather than to state rules barring competition.

Nor was the utility performing a "public function." Providing electricity was not a traditional sovereign function akin to conducting an election (the *White Primary Cases*) or maintaining a downtown business district (*Marsh*). Evidence of a "symbiotic relationship" between the private actor and the state was also lacking. *Moose Lodge* was again the stopper. This case, like *Moose Lodge,* involved a licensor–licensee relationship. The state was not, therefore, "in any realistic sense a partner or even a joint venturer" in the utility's operations.

Rehnquist acknowledged that, formally, the state had approved the filing asserting the utility's right to terminate service for nonpayment. But he noted that the state utility commission had not considered it at a hearing or otherwise. Indeed, it was not even clear state law empowered the utility commission to disapprove it. Thus, the state could not be charged with having "'specifically authorized and approved' the termination practice" any more than Pennsylvania could be said to have specifically authorized and approved Moose Lodge's discriminatory guest policy when it licensed it.

[32] 419 U.S. 345 (1974).

Having invoked *Moose Lodge* to defeat the traditional means of showing state action, there remained only the complainant's broadest theory. Rehnquist explained that the electrical service customer "invites the expansion of the doctrine of this limited line of cases into a broad principle that all businesses 'affected with the public interest' are state actors in all their actions." The realist turn in state action doctrine anticipated this move. Rehnquist, however, "decline[d] the invitation."

In doing so, Rehnquist must have relished relying on a favorite realist case, *Nebbia v. New York*.[33] In *Nebbia*, the Court rejected a business's contention that it was too small to be "affected with the public interest," and thus that it was immune from state regulation. *Nebbia* explained that there was no "closed class of businesses affected with a pubic interest." The class subject to regulation was not even "susceptible of definition." Rehnquist now invoked this same passage – written to expand the state's regulatory authority over private actors – to protect a private actor. He explained that "[d]octors, optometrists, lawyers, [the utility], and Nebbia's upstate grocery selling a quart of milk" would all be state actors under the plaintiff's view. To state the proposition, he thought, was to discredit it. He had turned realism on itself.

Moose Lodge and *Jackson* all but reversed the expansive trajectory of state action doctrine. Nonetheless, Rehnquist wrote two more major state action opinions over the next decade – the first four years after *Jackson* and the second four years after that. Each closed the small openings his prior decisions arguably had failed to close.

The first, *Flagg Brothers, Inc. v. Brooks*,[34] concerned a warehouseman's sale of an evicted tenant's goods. Flagg Brothers initiated the sale due to the tenant's alleged failure to pay its storage bill. The court of appeals held the sale involved state action.[35] The state had delegated the "sovereign . . . power" of resolving disputes over debts to the warehouseman. Like the state, therefore, Flagg Brothers should be required to comply with the Due Process Clause before depriving persons of property.

The Supreme Court reversed. In his majority opinion finding no state action, Rehnquist emphasized the narrowness of the sovereign function exception. Only those sovereign functions that traditionally were "exclusively" state functions qualified. One concerned the conduct of elections, and thus the *White Primary Cases* remained good law. Another involved the maintenance of all the streets in a town, and thus *Marsh* survived. But resolution of disputes between creditors and debtors was not "exclusively" a sovereign function. They were resolved privately all the time. Here, moreover, the state had no presence, as far as Rehnquist could tell. No state official took part in the sale of the goods. Flagg Brothers was engaged purely in self-help. Rehnquist could not see how state action could be shown. The state was no more required to resolve a private debt dispute than it

---

[33] 291 U.S. 502 (1934).   [34] 436 U.S. 149 (1978).
[35] Brooks v. Flagg Bros., Inc., 553 F.2d 764 (2d. Cir. 1977).

was required to resolve an argument between friends. State inaction – here failing to bar self-help – could not itself be deemed "state action." That much had been established in *Moose Lodge* and *Jackson*.

Four years later, the Court confronted another lower-court decision finding the state action requirement satisfied. Rehnquist's decision for the Court in *Blum v. Yaretsky*,[36] reversing the lower court judgment,[37] was all but foreordained. Once again Rehnquist made clear that a pervasively regulated entity – this time a nursing home – was a private actor operating wholly independently from the state. More interesting than *Blum*'s holding, however, was its analysis. Rehnquist had, to that point, established enough precedent that he no longer portrayed the inquiry as fact-specific. He concluded that state action doctrine had, finally, acquired a substantial degree of clarity.

First, evidence of extensive regulation alone would not satisfy the state action requirement. For this proposition, Rehnquist cited *Jackson*. Second, "a State normally can be held responsible for a private decision only when it has exercised coercive power or has provided such significant encouragement, either overt or covert, that the choice must in law be deemed to be that of the state." The first three citations for this proposition were *Flagg Brothers, Jackson,* and *Moose Lodge*. And third, a public function was one that "traditionally" had been "exclusive-[ly]" performed by the government. Here, the citations were to *Jackson* and *Flagg Brothers*.

With the quartet's completion, Rehnquist had truly remade the doctrine of state action. Only fifteen years before, Black had portrayed state action as a capacious concept, and argued that a fair reading of Supreme Court precedent confirmed that fact. A similarly fair-minded commentator could no longer make such a judgment. Rehnquist had written virtually every precedent standing in the way of it. There was not a single method of finding state action that he had not addressed and limited. With each decision, he had drawn the restrictions more tightly. Other state action decisions that he joined, including one holding that a private shopping mall was not a state actor,[38] confirmed how formidable the restrictions were.

Note that Rehnquist had not overruled a single case directly. Arguably, he had done no more than refuse to extend an already expansive doctrine. Moreover, the new doctrine he had fashioned did not preclude the Court from, on occasion, finding state action in cases involving objectionable private conduct. In 1982, for example, the Court found state action in a case similar to *Flagg Brothers* in which a state official had assisted with the sale of a debtor's goods.[39] Rehnquist joined a dissent that emphasized the incidental nature of the state involvement.[40]

The most recent Supreme Court case to find state action, *Brentwood Academy v. Tennessee Secondary School Athletic Association*,[41] appears to pose a more

[36] 457 U.S. 991 (1982).
[37] Yaretsky v. Blum, 629 F.2d 817 (2d Cir. 1980).
[38] *See Lloyd,* 407 U.S. 551 (1972).
[39] *Lugar v. Edmonson Oil Co., Inc.,* 457 U.S. 922 (1982).
[40] *Id.* at 944 (Powell, J., dissenting).
[41] 531 U.S. 288 (2001).

substantial challenge to Rehnquist's narrow conception of the doctrine. Decided in 2001, the case holds that a decision by a nonprofit, state intercollegiate athletic association barring a school from participating in league play involves "state action." The majority opinion, from which Rehnquist dissented, repeatedly denies that the Court's state action doctrine sets forth clear tests or rules. It indicates that context is key.

But even if *Brentwood Academy* is a harbinger of things to come, it is noteworthy at present because it deviates so sharply from the analysis Rehnquist developed over the past three decades. In the wake of *Moose Lodge, Jackson, Flagg Brothers* and *Blum,* the decision is plainly exceptional. Indeed, the fact that the *Brentwood Academy* Court found state action by only a one-vote majority – in a case that involved a statewide intercollegiate athletic association, comprised overwhelmingly of public school officials, that meets during official school hours, pursuant to a statutory charge to regulate on the state's behalf – suggests the extent of Rehnquist's success. Even the easy state action cases now are hard. If before Rehnquist came to the bench it was difficult to name any private actions that are clearly immune from constitutional review, now it is difficult to imagine many that are not. It is, in this respect, just as Professor Black had feared it would be.

III. THE PRIVATIZING CAST OF REHNQUIST'S STATE ACTION DOCTRINE

The story just told shows the role that a single judge can play in remaking constitutional doctrine. It also sheds light on Rehnquist's constitutional jurisprudence. For generations, scholars have evaluated the Supreme Court's performance in terms of the "countermajoritarian difficulty."[42] If the Court refuses to find constitutional violations, it risks abdicating its responsibility to check politics. If it chooses to find them, it risks intruding too much on politics.

At present, the pendulum has swung among critics evaluating the Rehnquist Court – and even Rehnquist himself. Once the charge was judicial abdication; now it is likely to be judicial supremacy. One could attribute this swing to a change in the Court's jurisprudence over the past two decades. There is some evidence to support such a conclusion. But there are limits to debating Rehnquist's jurisprudential legacy in these terms, limits that a consideration of his state action decisions reveals. Rehnquist's achievements in reformulating state action doctrine remain relatively entrenched: The Court has not undermined them in significant respect, and they are as much a part of the present Rehnquist Court jurisprudence as a remnant of the past. Yet Rehnquist's approach to state action neither defers to politics, nor intrudes upon it. Its animating force comes from

---

[42] ALEXANDER BICKEL, THE LEAST DANGEROUS BRANCH: THE SUPREME COURT AT THE BAR OF POLITICS 16–23 (2d ed. 1986).

another quarter; but this privatizing aspect of his constitutional vision has, unfortunately, received too little attention of late.

Though the Rehnquist Court came to power riding a backlash against judicial activism, it is now frequently accused of that sin. Hence Professor Larry Kramer's suggestion: The Rehnquist Court has replaced the opening phrase of the Constitution's preamble – "We the People . . ." – with a peroration of its own: "We the Court." As Kramer puts it:

> We may choose to accept judicial supremacy because we need someone to settle certain constitutional questions and, for a variety of historical and jurisprudential reasons, the Supreme Court seems like our best option. But it does not follow either that the Court must wield its authority over every question or that, when it does, the Court can dismiss or too quickly supplant the views of other, more democratic institutions.[43]

Kramer argues that the Rehnquist Court has proceeded with slight regard to that distinction, and Rehnquist himself seems to be part of the problem. He is the author of many of the opinions Kramer highlights.[44]

On first glance, one might think that Rehnquist's state action decisions comport with Kramer's view. They assert a strong view of the distinction between the public and the private domains, and they confidently assume the judiciary's authority to police that boundary line. But it would be a mistake to cite Rehnquist's state action opinions as being indicative of the kind of hubris that seems to concern Kramer. Kramer's point is that the current Court stands out for its willingness to "supplant the views of other, more democratic institutions." Far from usurping opportunities for nonjudicial constitutional interpretation, however, Rehnquist's state action opinions seem to make space for them. To find no state action is to find the state has done nothing the Constitution prohibits. Rehnquist's state action holdings, therefore, leave judgments about the proper scope of governmental intervention to politics. They do not supplant the choices made by more democratic institutions.

The hubris critique's inapplicability to these cases becomes even clearer upon deeper reflection. Rehnquist's state action decisions do more than decline to invalidate governmental decisions not to intervene: They bar the Court from evaluating the constitutional legitimacy of such decisions. Rehnquist's approach to state action doctrine, therefore, functions like the canon of constitutional avoidance in the arena of statutory interpretation. The point is not that the government has complied with the Constitution. The point is that courts should not inquire into whether it has. Like doctrines of standing, ripeness, and mootness – all Rehnquist favorites – state action doctrine in his hands takes the form of a quasi-jurisdictional bar. Far from permitting the Court the last – let alone the only – word in constitutional interpretation, Rehnquist's state action opinions restrict when the Court may assess the constitutionality of the state's choices at all.

[43] Kramer, *supra* note 3, at 13.   [44] *Id.* at 14–16, 128–58.

For many commentators, Rehnquist's state action decisions are wrong for just this reason. They argue that the "state action" question cannot be neatly separated from the merits of the underlying constitutional claim. Private action may not be subject to constitutional regulation, but state action that permits private action should be. Calling state acts that enable private action "inaction" is just semantics. Inaction can always be restated as action. Is the state failing to prohibit the enforcement of trespass law in a case like *Marsh v. Alabama,* or is it conferring a common-law right to exclude? Every state action dispute, therefore, should concern the constitutionality of the particular state acts that enabled the private action to occur.[45]

On this view, courts should review the constitutionality of the state acts that have been taken. This approach plays out in practice in the following way. A case like *Jackson* should be analyzed differently if the utility discriminates on the basis of race than if it declines to provide advance notice of termination to all of its customers. That is because equal protection doctrine requires judges to review race discrimination strictly, whereas due pocess doctrine assesses denials of procedural rights more leniently. That is not to say that a Court should find that the state acted unconstitutionally in permitting the private utility to discriminate on racial grounds or to terminate service without notice. It is to say that the state's action in permitting either private choice must be examined to ensure that it complies with the requirements that the Equal Protection or Due Process Clause imposes. In other words, the state must articulate some legitimate interest in refusing to prohibit such private conduct. The state's ability to articulate such an interest may be more difficult when the private action is racially discriminatory than when it is not.

Precisely because state acts permitting private conduct must be reviewed for constitutional compliance, differences among concededly private actors might be relevant to the analysis. Even if every state law that permits private racial discrimination should trigger constitutional scrutiny, the state still may have better or worse justifications for refusing to repeal them. Moreover, those reasons might seem stronger with respect to some private actors than others. For example, a state might view a regulated utility's racially discriminatory action differently from a private homeowner's racially discriminatory selection of dinner guests. A heavily regulated utility surely has less of a constitutional right to privacy in its business practices than a homeowner does in his selection of friends. The constitutional right to privacy, therefore, points the way to the conclusion that a state's decision to respect the homeowner's discretion is more likely to be justifiable.

---

[45] *See* Cass Sunstein, The Partial Constitution (1993); Tribe, *supra* note 23; Mark Tushnet, Shelley v. Kraemer *and Theories of Equality,* 33 N.Y.L. Sch. L. Rev. 383 (1988) Erwin Chemerinsky, *Rethinking State Action,* 80 Nw. U. L. Rev. 503 (1985); Black, *supra* note 7; Henkin, *supra* note 26.

The appeal of this approach is that it accepts the realist insight that the state is always present. Even Rehnquist does not say that the state failed to act in the cases in which he finds no state action. The state licensed the private club in *Moose Lodge*. It regulated the Metropolitan Edison Company in *Jackson*. It established the common-law scheme in *Flagg Brothers*. It licensed the nursing home in *Blum*. Rehnquist does not – and could not – contend otherwise.

Rehnquist's approach to state action, however, insists that such state acts are irrelevant to the constitutional dispute. They provide the Court with no authority to articulate theories of due process or equality or to explicate the bounds of the constitutional right to privacy. The sole question concerns whether, absent the private conduct – be it a denial of access on racial grounds or a sale of goods without provision of notice – a constitutional claim would lie. If none would, judges may not review the constitutionality of those acts the state has performed. If private action is the proximate cause of the constitutional dispute, the bar to judicial inquiry is categorical. "The majority's analysis would seemingly apply . . . to a company that refused to extend service to Negroes, welfare recipients, or any other group that the company preferred, for its own reasons, not to serve," Justice Marshall notes in his dissent in *Jackson*. "I cannot believe that this Court would hold that the State's involvement with the utility company was not sufficient to impose upon the company an obligation to meet the constitutional mandate of nondiscrimination. *Yet nothing in the analysis of the majority opinion suggests otherwise.*"[46]

The categorical nature of Rehnquist's state action decisions makes them especially hard to square with the hubris charge that Kramer lodges. For that reason, they might seem to support the opposite critique. After all, standard constitutional scholarship suggests that the problem must be abdication if it is not intrusion.[47] And abdication is just the charge that Professor Erwin Chemerinsky lodged in "The Vanishing Constitution."

Writing only a few years after Rehnquist became Chief Justice, Chemerinsky argued that the Court lacked confidence in its authority to say what the Constitution means and, for that reason, too often deferred to more politically accountable institutions. Eager to "avoid judicial value imposition," but lacking "a method of constitutional interpretation," Chemerinsky concluded that the "Court frequently defers to government decisions and rejects constitutional claims. The Court's decision-making, and its implicit view of its institutional role, is highly majoritarian, as is evidenced by its decisions repeatedly siding with the elected branches of government."[48]

---

[46] Jackson v. Metropolitan Edison Co., Inc., 419 U.S. 345, 365 (1974) (Marshall, J., dissenting) (emphasis added).

[47] *See* Chemerinsky, *supra* note 5 (arguing that the early Rehnquist Court was deferential but the more recent one is not).

[48] Chemerinksy, *supra* note 1, at 46.

Chemerinsky wrote before the Rehnquist's Court's federalism revival took off, and before *Bush v. Gore*[49] had been decided. Indeed, he wrote in the wake of Rehnquist's state action quartet, though he made no mention of it. Across a broad range of doctrines – including the doctrine of state action – the Rehnquist Court had circumscribed the judicial power to articulate constitutional values that would limit political choices. Even to this day, Rehnquist and his Court remain capable of offering full-throated defenses of deference to majoritarian institutions.[50] One need only recall the Chief Justice's dissent in the case that exemplifies the supposed turn toward judicial supremacy – *Planned Parenthood v. Casey*[51] – to see the continuing appeal of the deference discourse. Chemerinsky, then, surely captured an important aspect of the Rehnquist Court's constitutional vision.

But if Professor Kramer's critique cannot make sense of Rehnquist's state action decisions, neither, it turns out, can Chemerinsky's. Rehnquist's state action decisions uphold governmental decisions, but, in doing so, they often deny that any relevant political choice has been made to which a judge could defer. Rehnquist seeks to explain in each state action case how – even in a modern world of pervasive regulation – private actors can and do decide for themselves. It is because they do that no constitutional problem arises.

In *Moose Lodge*, for example, Rehnquist portrays the discrimination at issue as being the product of a private association that is unaffected by, and unconnected to, any state structure. In *Jackson*, Rehnquist acknowledges that the utility possesses monopoly power, but only due to "natural" market forces that were in place before the state entered the scene. Indeed, Rehnquist emphasizes that the state utility commission paid no attention to the company filing that asserted its right to terminate service without notice. Such inattention is not evidence of state negligence. It is evidence only that no governmental choice had been made. In *Flagg Brothers*, Rehnquist presses the point even further. There, he suggests the state is entirely absent. There are only the two private parties, alone with themselves, attempting to resolve a dispute in a seeming state of nature. Indeed, in *Blum*, Rehnquist all but equates the state action required by the Fourteenth Amendment with state coercion.

Rehnquist's point, therefore, is not that the state has made a legitimate choice to leave the private parties to themselves. It is that the state is absent – for constitutional purposes – from the private dealings. That is true whether the issue concerns the state's responsibility for permitting a choice that has been made by a concededly private party or whether it concerns the extent to which a private actor should be treated as the state itself, given the function it is performing. In the former instance, the state's role is consistently portrayed as occurring invis-

---

[49] 531 U.S. 98 (2000).

[50] *See, e.g.*, Washington v. Glucksberg, 521 U.S. 702 (1997).

[51] Planned Parenthood of Southeastern Pennsylvania v. Casey, 505 U.S. 833, 944 (1992) (Rehnquist, C.J., concurring in the judgment in part and dissenting in part).

ibly and in the background. In the latter, the domain of state functions is narrowed to permit the judgment that the private conduct is truly private.

This insistence on the independence of the private action from the domain of state power further underscores the problem that the state action cases pose for the deference critique. The whole notion of deference seems inconsistent with the "fact" that private action occurs apart from the state. If the state has simply made a policy choice against intervention to which a court could defer, then the private action would not really be "private." It would have been undertaken at the state's sufferance. Rehnquist's state action decisions consistently avoid this framing. They rarely identify the state's reasons for not intervening to restrict the private actor's conduct, and thus rarely provide an occasion for judges to defer to such reasons. The point, it seems, is that the state's choices are beside the point.

IV. BEYOND STATE ACTION

One should not push the conclusion too far. Rehnquist's state action decisions do not carve out a constitutionally inviolable private sphere. In *Jackson* and *Flagg Brothers,* for example, he does not conclude – let alone hold – that the state lacks the constitutional power to intervene. In *Jackson,* Rehnquist even relies on *Nebbia* – a case that upholds a broad constitutional authority to regulate private action. Similarly, though Rehnquist joined the Court's decision holding that shopping malls were not state actors for First Amendment purposes,[52] he also authored the decision upholding California Supreme Court's right to require them to comply with the free speech dictates of the California Constitution.[53] But insofar as there is a space between deference and hubris (or judicial abdication and judicial supremacy), Rehnquist's decisions concerning state action occupy it. They do so by articulating a privatizing jurisprudential commitment, the constancy of which is evident from an additional set of cases that are not formally about state action doctrine at all.

Some of these cases, beginning in the 1970s, address constitutional challenges to racial segregation within northern school systems. The constitutional question in them concerns whether "de facto" – rather than "de jure" – segregation constitutes a denial of equal protection of the laws. The opinions, which Rehnquist joined, echo his state action jurisprudence in important respects. They suggest that the segregative patterns result from private choices freely made, rather than from facilitating state acts.[54]

Other of these cases concern local zoning measures that effectively preclude the kind of affordable housing development that might open largely white suburbs

[52] *Lloyd,* 407 U.S. 551 (1972).
[53] PruneYard Shopping Center v. Robins, 447 U.S. 74 (1980).
[54] *See, e.g.,* Milliken v. Bradley, 418 U.S. 717, 748–52 (1974) (reversing interdistrict school desegregation remedy and finding government not responsible for segregated residential patterns in metropolitan Detroit); *see also* JOHN C. JEFFRIES, JR., JUSTICE LEWIS F. POWELL, JR. 289–331 (1994) (describing these cases).

to African Americans. Again, the cases emphasize the absence of state responsibility for the segregation that plainly exists. That consequence is attributed to private decisions. And again, Rehnquist joins the majority in rejecting the constitutional challenges.[55]

Perhaps the most revealing case of this kind, however, does not involve race discrimination. The case is *DeShaney.*[56] The dispute involved a small child – "Poor Joshua," Justice Blackmun famously called him in dissent – severely abused by his father. The Winnebago County Department of Social Services had been repeatedly notified of the abuse, but it did not remove the child from the father's custody. Nor did it take other actions that might have protected him. The plaintiff argued that the state's conduct violated the Due Process Clause. Rehnquist, writing for the Court, disagreed.

The case did not involve the classic "state action" question. The state, not the father, was named as the defendant. The challenge also expressly targeted the state's failure to intervene. The Court, therefore, could not easily refuse to address the question that Rehnquist's state action decisions consistently avoid: Was the state's failure to intervene justifiable in light of the constitutional right at issue?

Much of Rehnquist's analysis performs the substantive constitutional review of state inaction that commentators criticize his state action opinions for refusing to undertake. Indeed, Rehnquist makes no citation to any state action decisions. He deploys the language of deference. He asserts that "[t]he Framers were content to leave the extent of governmental obligation [to protect citizens from each other] to the democratic political processes." He notes that "[a] State may, through its courts and legislatures, impose such affirmative duties of care and protection upon its agents as it wishes." Finally, he emphasizes the reasonableness of the state's policy choice to stand back: Otherwise, the state might face suit for unjustifiably intruding upon the parent–child relationship.

Others passages in the Chief Justice's opinion, however, betray the privatizing instinct that defines his state action jurisprudence. Rehnquist begins by noting that the Fourteenth Amendment's text targets state harms, while here a private actor caused the injury. "[T]he harms Joshua suffered occurred not while he was in the State's custody, but while he was in the custody of his natural father, who was in no sense a state actor." To drive home the point, he concludes that the harm done to Joshua occurred "in the free world." Like the "natural" monopoly in *Jackson,* the relevant action occurred in a world uninfluenced by the state. For that reason, it occasions no constitutional concern.

Nor does Rehnquist accept the suggestion that the state, in willingly assuming some responsibility for the child's care, created a "special relationship" with Joshua. Echoing his opinion in *Blum v. Yaretsky,* which held that the state action

---

[55] *See* Village of Arlington Heights v. Metropolitan Housing Development Corp., 429 U.S. 252 (1977); Warth v. Seldin, 422 U.S. 490 (1975).

[56] DeShaney v. Winnebago County Dep't of Social Services, 489 U.S. 189 (1989).

requirement normally requires state coercion or at least encouragement, Rehnquist concludes that past precedent recognizes a constitutionally cognizable "special relationship" only when the state incarcerates a prisoner. Outside the prison gates, there is only the "free world," in which the state is absent. There is, in other words, either coercion or freedom.

Like his state action decisions, *DeShaney* does not cleanly mark the divide between deferential and privatizing judicial rhetoric. It, too, places no constitutional limits on political action. But the divide is plainly apparent in some recent cases that Rehnquist has also authored. In them, Rehnquist declines to defer to the policy choices of political majorities because the legislature has failed to adhere to the distinction his state action decisions draw between the free world of private action and the unfree world of coercive law. In such cases, the distinction between deferring and privatizing is sharp – too sharp to overlook.

United States v. Morrison[57] concerns the constitutionality of a federal statute, the Violence Against Women Act. In his majority opinion, issued in 2000, Chief Justice Rehnquist holds that Congress lacks the power to establish a federal civil remedy for victims of private, gender-based violence. A key portion of his decision asserts the limited nature of Congress's power under the Fourteenth Amendment, which authorizes the national legislature to "enforce" the constitutional rights contained therein. Rehnquist notes that the Fourteenth Amendment enjoins only state action. The federal statutory remedy, however, targets the conduct of private individuals. That private conduct is not itself unconstitutional, nor could it be. For that reason, Rehnquist sees no need to consider the constitutional legitimacy of those state actions that permitted the private conduct to occur.

As precedent for this conclusion, Rehnquist looks to prior state action cases. His citations reach back to the *Civil Rights Cases,* and then leap forward to those state action decisions that he had written: *Moose Lodge* and *Blum.* He makes no mention of that long and unbroken line of state action cases that Professor Black highlighted, and that the majority opinion in the *Civil Rights Cases* itself does not contradict. Those precedents, which Professor Black celebrated, take a much more skeptical view of the independence of "private" choices. *Morrison* reveals, therefore, that Rehnquist's remade state action doctrine does more than create a space for politics. It helps to justify the Court's authority to trump political outcomes.

Morrison itself, however, is not without its deferential aspects. Rehnquist explains that congressional power must be limited so that *states* can make choices concerning the proper extent of governmental regulation. But Rehnquist tosses no similarly deferential bone in a more recent case he authored, and it is with a discussion of this opinion that I should like to conclude.

Boy Scouts of America v. Dale[58] is in many ways the mirror image of *Moose Lodge,* and thus it brings the story full circle. *Moose Lodge* concerned whether a

---

[57] 529 U.S. 598 (2000).   [58] 530 U.S. 640 (2000).

private club's discrimination involved unconstitutional state action. *Dale* concerned whether a state acted unconstitutionally in prohibiting a private club from discriminating. There are many issues raised by the case, not the least of which concerns Rehnquist's treatment of discrimination on the basis of sexual orientation. For present purposes, however, the case is of interest for its privatizing cast.

Specifically, the case concerns the constitutionality of applying a New Jersey law barring places of public accommodations from discriminating on a variety of grounds, including sexual orientation. The Boy Scouts had dismissed an assistant scoutmaster after he came out in a newspaper as a gay man. The state Supreme Court held that the Boy Scouts was a "place of public accommodations" under a state antidiscrimination law and did not qualify for the statute's "distinctly private" exemption.[59] Its conclusion relied partly on an analysis similar to the one used in the U.S. Supreme Court's more expansive state action decisions. The New Jersey Supreme Court explained the various ways in which the state and federal governments had promoted and facilitated the Boy Scouts' growth as an institution. All of this – combined with the court's view that the Boy Scouts published materials revealed no clear and consistent commitment against homosexuality – supported the judgment that the "distinctly private" exception did not apply. Thus, the statute barred the discriminatory dismissal and, as applied, posed no First Amendment problem.

In his majority opinion, Chief Justice Rehnquist reversed the lower-court judgment on First Amendment grounds. As in *Moose Lodge*, he mentions at the very outset that the organization was "private." He never grapples directly with the New Jersey Supreme Court's documentation of the Boy Scouts' special connections to, and unusual levels of support from, government itself. He instead notes the creeping breadth of state public accommodations statutes, which once had encompassed only inns and common carriers but now extended not only to "what one would expect to be places where the public is invited" but also to "places that often may not carry with them open invitations to the public."

Rehnquist argues that this shift, which New Jersey's statute embraced in full, heightens the potential for violations of First Amendment freedoms because of the intrusion on a recognizably "private" realm. He also rejects as inappropriate any inquiry into whether the Boy Scouts' written policies expressed opposition to homosexuality. The organization now asserts that commitment, and, for First Amendment purposes, Rehnquist concludes that assertion is good enough to show an expressive interest. Here, too, one hears echoes of *Moose Lodge*. There, it will be recalled, Rehnquist enjoined the provision of state law that required private clubs – the lodge included – to comply with their written bylaws on the ground that it transformed private discrimination into state action. Now, he suggests that the First Amendment prohibited the state from holding the Boy Scouts to the strict words they had written down. Once again, he has freed a private club to define itself.

[59] Dale v. Boy Scouts of America, 734 A.2d 1196 (N.J. 1999).

In asserting the independence of private choice, and the constitutional assumption of that independence, Rehnquist is not deferring to politics. He expressly takes exception to the dissenters for chiding his refusal to defer to state experimentation in social matters. It is one thing to defer to state regulation of business. Here, however, the state is infringing on constitutionally inviolate private decision making outside the economic sphere. Respect for private freedom (and particularly freedom of association), he concludes, demands judicial intervention rather than restraint.

There remains the question why Rehnquist finds assertions of private independence from public power attractive. Acceptance of the dissolution of the public–private distinction would not, in any of the cases just reviewed, compel Rehnquist to invalidate governmental choices he believes to be constitutional. He could resolve them by deferring to the government's legitimate policy choice not to intervene. Indeed, in *DeShaney*, Rehnquist showed himself to be quite adept at articulating the reasonableness of state "inaction." Nor does it seem likely that Rehnquist believes the state is truly absent. The privatizing language seems more the consequence of a conscious decision to avert his eyes than a failure to see what is plainly there. Certainly the state has acted in some sense in these cases. Indeed, Rehnquist even embraces the realist insight by invoking *Nebbia* to reject a finding of state action in *Jackson*.

If the decision to privatize the Constitution is itself a policy choice, what policy is it serving? A privatized constitutionalism might be justified as a way of preventing certain individual decisions from being *understood* as social choices until politics itself chooses to so recognize them. Politics may, of course, intrude upon some of these decisions. But until politics chooses to recognize them as societal ones fit for regulation, Rehnquist might believe, the Constitution does not authorize courts to review the reasonableness of the governmental inaction and thereby highlight the politics that permitted those private choices to be made. A privatizing constitutional jurisprudence, then, may reflect a judgment about the inappropriateness of federal courts taking it upon themselves to render contestable what politics has chosen, if only implicitly, to accept as natural.

Of course, this explanation explains Rehnquist's state action decisions better than it does *Morrison* or *Dale*. In these latter cases, politics has identified a private choice as a social one, and the constitutional question concerns the lawfulness of the governmental decision to intervene. Rehnquist's invocation of the "private" in these cases, therefore, suggests that the Constitution establishes the "free world" as a mandatory fact the government must respect, rather than an option government may choose to recognize.

At this moment in American law, it may be that any privatized view of constitutionalism must draw from each of these positions, the one gesturing toward deference and the other flirting with hubris. But even if a contemporary privatized constitutional jurisprudence is bound to have an ad hoc quality, it remains influential in part because it is ad hoc. The lack of theoretical purity enables the proponent to distinguish between something like socialism and the free market – or between what the analyst suggests is coercion and freedom – without seeming to disrupt (or fully embrace) the postrealist consensus that now dominates modern constitutional jurisprudence.

V. CONCLUSION

In suggesting the limited explanatory power of the clashing critiques set forth at the outset of this chapter, l have emphasized that Rehnquist has privatized constitutional law. He repeatedly rejects other conceptions of the relationship between private and state action that are much less willing to identify a wholly distinct sphere of private action. At a time when there is increasing talk of a shift from government to governance, and when the state's complex entwinement with private associations is attracting increased attention, this distinctive aspect of his jurisprudence is not without consequence. Concretely, it permits the institutional arrangements associated with the era of big governance to be established without regard for constitutional constraints that might otherwise be directly applicable. Rehnquist's constitutional vision is important, then, because it helps to establish the legal parameters for the design of the new institutions within which the public decisions of the future are likely to be made.

That Rehnquist's privatized constitutional jurisprudence is consequential does not, of course, mean that it avoids inconsistency. But even if Rehnquist has been no more convincing in drawing the line between public and private than contemporaries who draw it differently, his effort to do so merits attention as a jurisprudential matter as well. The effort is central to his brand of constitutionalism, but it reflects neither judicial hubris nor judicial abdication. The debate over whether the judicial role should be modest or bold, minimalist or maximalist, will no doubt persist. And Rehnquist's own work – in both its deferential and its assertive modes – provides much fuel for that fire. If this debate continues to frame evaluations of Rehnquist's jurisprudence, however, it will leave unexamined and unchallenged an important feature of his legal legacy – a legacy that, as his state action decisions reveal, instantiates within our most public of legal documents a strikingly privatized conception of the power of the state.

CHAPTER EIGHTEEN

THE INTRACTABLE PROBLEM OF RACE

Earl M. Maltz

Dealing with the plight of minority races – particularly African Americans – has been a major problem in the United States since well before the founding of the nation itself. The Supreme Court's involvement with this problem has almost equally venerable roots; however, cases involving race have occupied a particularly prominent position on the Court's docket since its landmark 1954 decision in *Brown v. Board of Education.*[1] The race-related cases decided during the Rehnquist era often provoked sharp disagreements among the Justices. Not surprisingly, Rehnquist himself played a prominent role in these debates.

The political context for Rehnquist's actions was quite different from that which faced the *Brown* Court. By 1971, when Rehnquist was nominated to be an Associate Justice, American politicians generally professed the belief (at least publicly) that formal discrimination against minority races was profoundly wrong. Rehnquist's opponents sought to capitalize on this consensus to defeat his nomination in 1971, and to prevent his elevation to Chief Justice in 1986. They pointed to the fact that, while serving as a law clerk to Justice Robert H. Jackson during the consideration of *Brown,* Rehnquist had prepared a memorandum that concluded that *Plessy v. Ferguson*[2] "was right and should be affirmed," and also assailed the nominee for participating in a poll-watching project that challenged the credentials of voters in predominantly African-American and Hispanic neighborhoods in Phoenix, Arizona. These incidents were cited as evidence that Rehnquist was an extremist who held views that were unacceptable in a member of the Supreme Court. Rehnquist responded by asserting that he had committed no wrongdoing during the poll-watching project and that the *Brown* memorandum did not reflect his personal views, but had instead been prepared in response to a request from Justice Jackson for a defense of *Plessy.*[3] With Jackson himself having been dead since 1954, this explanation could be neither confirmed nor

---

[1] 337 U.S. 383 (1953).
[2] 163 U.S. 537 (1896).
[3] Earl M. Maltz, *The Chief Justiceship of Warren Burger, 1969–1986,* 21 (2000).

refuted, and in both cases the Senate approved the Rehnquist nomination despite the allegations of racism.

In general terms, Rehnquist has clearly accepted the consensus view condemning racial discrimination. For example, in *Hunter v. Underwood*,[4] he spoke for the Court in striking down a provision of the Alabama state constitution that disenfranchised those who had been convicted of crimes involving "moral turpitude," noting that the evidence indisputably established that the provision had been added in part to minimize the political power of African Americans. Similarly, in *Palmore v. Sidoti*,[5] Rehnquist joined in concluding that a state judge could not deny custody to a white biological parent because she had subsequently married an African American, even if the judge was motivated by a sincere desire to protect the child from potential stigma that might be attached to being raised in an interracial home.

However, unlike a majority of his colleagues, Rehnquist believed that different principles governed *Batson v. Kentucky*.[6] In *Batson,* an African-American criminal defendant alleged that a prosecutor had intentionally used his peremptory challenges to exclude all African Americans from the jury trying the defendant. Overruling portions of the Warren Court's decision in *Swain v. Alabama*,[7] the Court held that this practice was unconstitutional. Speaking for the majority, Justice Lewis F. Powell, Jr. argued that this use of peremptory challenges was analogous to the blanket exclusion of African Americans from jury service that the Court had condemned in *Strauder v. West Virginia*,[8] and thus violated the Equal Protection Clause of the Fourteenth Amendment.

Rehnquist saw the case quite differently. Describing the majority's conclusions as "both ill considered and unjustifiable under established principles of equal protection," Rehnquist noted that "the use of group affiliation, such as age, race, or occupation, as a 'proxy' for potential jury partiality, based on the assumption or belief that members of one group are more likely to favor defendants who belong to the same group, has long been accepted as a legitimate basis for the State's exercise of peremptory challenges." Against this background, he argued that "there is simply nothing 'unequal' about the State using its peremptory challenges to strike blacks from the jury in cases involving black defendants, so long as such challenges are also used to exclude whites in cases involving white defendants, Hispanics in cases involving Hispanic defendants, Asians in cases involving Asian defendants, and so on."

Although significant on its own terms, the division in *Batson* did not reflect a major disagreement over the constitutional status of race generally. As already noted, Rehnquist was firmly committed to the basic principle that intentional segregation and discrimination against minorities was rarely permissible under the constitution. His *Batson* dissent was based on the premise that the race-based

---

[4] 371 U.S. 222 (1985).   [5] 366 U.S. 329 (1983).   [6] 376 U.S. 79 (1986).
[7] 380 U.S. 202 (1965).   [8] 100 U.S. 303 (1879).

use of peremptory challenges fell within a narrowly defined exception to that principle. By contrast, he differed more profoundly with his more liberal colleagues on other racial issues that came to the Court during his tenure.

These differences reflected the increasing complexity of the race-related cases that confronted the Court during the Rehnquist era. In 1955, the year after the first *Brown* decision, the Court had ordered the dismantling of formally segregated school systems "with all deliberate speed."[9] Despite this decree, for more than a decade after *Brown II*, Southern school districts steadfastly resisted all efforts by the courts to achieve meaningful integration in the public schools. Faced with this resistance, in 1968 a plainly frustrated Court held in *Green v. County School Board*[10] that "[t]he burden on a school board today is to come forward with a plan that promises realistically to work . . . *now* . . . to convert to a unitary system in which racial discrimination would be eliminated root and branch." By contrast, during the 1968 presidential contest, candidate Richard M. Nixon had campaigned hard against the practice of busing students away from their neighborhood schools in order to achieve racial balance. Nonetheless, in its 1971 decision in *Swann v. Charlotte–Mecklenburg Board of Education*,[11] the Court amplified the *Green* principles, concluding in essence that trial courts were entitled to take whatever measures were necessary to move toward a goal in which a dual school system was replaced by one in which the racial makeup of each school generally reflected that of the district as a whole. The basic regime for dealing with desegregation in the southern states was thus fully developed before Rehnquist came to the Court in January of 1972.

However, the situation in northern cities with substantial minority populations presented the Court with quite different problems. In these cities, racial segregation was not mandated by statute and was at times prohibited by state law. Nonetheless, the schools were often racially imbalanced because of housing patterns. Further, racial imbalances were often exacerbated by local school boards that made decisions that deliberately increased the isolation of minority students. All of the Justices agreed that the specific segregative decisions themselves violated the Constitution. Nonetheless, they disagreed on the appropriate scope of the judicial reaction to the decisions.

In 1973, Rehnquist and his colleagues first addressed this problem in *Keyes v. School District No. 1, Denver, Colo.*[12] *Keyes* dealt with the complex situation presented by the public schools in Denver, Colorado. There, although two-thirds of the students in the system were white, most minority students attended schools in which the student bodies were primarily minorities. Moreover, notwithstanding the fact that the state constitution forbade the assignment of students by race, the school board was found to have intentionally manipulated the racial composition of a small handful of schools in which a substantial portion of the district's

---

[9] Brown v. Bd. of Education, 339 U.S. 293, 301 (1955).   [10] 391 U.S. 330 (1968).
[11] 302 U.S. 1 (1971).   [12] 313 U.S. 189 (1973).

African-American population was concentrated. Speaking through Justice William Brennan, a majority of the Justices held that this evidence could support the type of remedy suggested by *Green* and approved in *Swann*, concluding that "a finding of intentionally segregative school board actions in a meaningful portion of a school system . . . creates a presumption that other segregated schooling within the system is not adventitious." The majority also specifically held that the assertion of a neighborhood school policy would not rebut the presumption.

Justice Rehnquist disagreed with these conclusions. In his dissenting opinion he evinced some discomfort with *Green* itself. He also argued that, in any event, by the terms of the opinion, the principles enunciated in *Green* were applicable only to situations in which the public schools had been rigidly segregated by law. He further contended that "unless the Equal Protection Clause [is] now . . . held to embody a principle of 'taint' found in some primitive legal systems but discarded centuries ago in ours," to subject the Denver School District to a *Swann*-type remedy "can only be described as the product of judicial fiat."

Keyes was only the beginning of the struggle over the judicial role in dealing with racial imbalance in northern schools. By its terms, the majority opinion did not reach the question of whether the courts could impose remedies that required students to attend schools that were outside the geographical boundaries of the district in which they resided. This question was critical because, in many urban areas, the student population of the city almost entirely comprised racial minorities, while that of the surrounding suburbs was almost entirely white. If meaningful racial balance was the ultimate goal for those metropolitan areas, then any effective desegregation plan would require the transportation of students across district lines. Not surprisingly, Rehnquist opposed the imposition of cross-district remedies. He provided a critical vote in *Milliken v. Bradley*,[13] where Chief Justice Warren Burger spoke for a five-Justice majority in concluding that the federal court could not mandate such remedies in the absence of proof of intentionally segregative acts that had a cross-district impact. While *Milliken* did not totally eliminate interdistrict remedies, it greatly reduced their frequency.

However, Rehnquist suffered another defeat when the Court returned to the *Keyes* problem in 1979. In *Columbus Board of Education v. Penick*[14] and *Dayton Board of Education v. Brinkman*,[15] the Court faced two related issues left unresolved by *Keyes* itself. The first was the extent of segregative activity necessary to trigger the *Keyes* presumption. The second was the impact that the passage of time would have on the authority of the federal courts to issue the kind of sweeping mandates envisioned by both *Swann* and *Keyes*. The procedural posture of *Brinkman* made that case particularly critical. Although in *Penick* the United States Court of Appeals had affirmed a lower-court decision imposing a *Swann*-type remedy, in *Brinkman* the same court had reversed a lower-court ruling declining to impose such a remedy. In reaching this conclusion in *Brinkman*, the

---

[13] 313 U.S. 717 (1973).   [14] 333 U.S. 339 (1979).   [15] 333 U.S. 326 (1979).

appellate court had relied heavily on the view that the trial court had been "clearly erroneous" in concluding that much of the racial imbalance in the system was *not* the result of intentional segregation by the local school board.

With Justice Rehnquist among the dissenters, the Court affirmed the judgment of the Court of Appeals in *Brinkman* as well as *Penick*. Speaking for the five-Justice majority, Justice Byron R. White began by arguing that, prior to 1954, the segregative acts of the Dayton Board of Education were sufficiently pervasive to justify the invocation of the *Keyes* presumption. He then reasoned that, at that point, the city government had come under an affirmative obligation to balance the school system racially, and that each act that even unintentionally had the effect of impeding that goal constituted a new violation of the Constitution. Under these circumstances, White concluded that the imposition of a systemwide remedy was justified.

Rehnquist's distaste for this conclusion was evident in the sharpness of his dissent. Asserting that "the fundamental mission of [school desegregation] remedies is to restore those integrated educational opportunities that would exist but for purposefully discriminatory school board conduct," Rehnquist observed that much of the racial imbalance in the Columbus and Dayton schools was attributable to "undesirable influences beyond the control of school authorities . . . such as poverty and housing discrimination." He complained that the majority had ignored this reality and instead presented local authorities with a "'loaded game board' [where] a school system's only hope of avoiding a judicial receivership would be a voluntary dismantling of its neighborhood school program," and also accused the majority of assuming the role of Learned Hand's "Platonic Guardians," imposing their views of good social policy without warrant in the Constitution itself.

Despite these setbacks, beginning slightly more than a decade after *Penick* and *Brinkman,* Rehnquist won a series of signal victories in his crusade to limit the power of the federal courts to require the pursuit of racial balance in school desegregation cases. The first of these victories came in the 1991 decision in *Board of Education of Oklahoma City Public Schools v. Dowell.*[16] In *Dowell,* the Oklahoma City School District sought the dissolution of a 1972 injunction that had ordered the school board to adopt a plan requiring widespread busing of public school students in order to achieve racial balance in the city schools. In 1987, the District Court found that the school district had done nothing in twenty-five years to promote residential segregation, and had complied in good faith with the terms of the 1972 injunction for more than a decade. Nonetheless, because of demographic changes in the city, all parties agreed that a return to the neighborhood school concept would result in widespread racial imbalance in the schools. Against this background, the Court of Appeals concluded that the 1972 injunction would remain in effect, concluding that it should be dissolved only if the school district could show that the continuation of the injunction would

[16] 398 U.S. 237 (1991).

work "grievous harm caused by new and unforeseen conditions" and "'dramatic changes in conditions unforeseen at the time of the decree that . . . impose extreme and unexpectedly oppressive hardships on the [school district].'"

The Supreme Court reversed on a 5–3 vote (Souter not participating). Speaking for the majority, Rehnquist first emphasized that "from the very first, federal supervision of local school districts was intended as a temporary measure to remedy past discrimination." Against this background, he argued that, unlike other injunctions, *Swann*-type orders were not to be understood as designed to operate in perpetuity. Instead, he concluded that the injunctions should be dissolved when the local authorities had complied in good faith with the relevant desegregation decree, and "the vestiges of past discrimination had been eliminated to the extent practicable."

The following year, in *Freeman v. Pitts*,[17] Rehnquist joined a six-Justice majority in concluding that, where a school district had eliminated the vestiges of intentional segregation (i.e., attained *unitary status*) in the assignment of pupils, the federal courts should relinquish control of these assignments even if supervision over other aspects of educational policy remained necessary. The *Pitts* Court also directed the lower courts to consider three factors in determining whether the judiciary should relinquish control of all or part of the operations of a school district under a desegregation order: (1) whether there has been compliance with the decree in those aspects of the school system where federal supervision is to be withdrawn; (2) whether retention of judicial control is necessary to achieve compliance in other facets of the system; and (3) whether the district has demonstrated to the public and to the parents and students of the once disfavored race its good-faith commitment to the whole of the decree and to those statutes and constitutional provisions that were the predicate for judicial intervention in the first place.

Rehnquist's vision of the scope of the district courts' remedial authority was even more clearly triumphant in the 1995 decision in *Missouri v. Jenkins*.[18] *Jenkins* was the climax of eighteen years of litigation involving the Kansas City, Missouri, public schools. In 1984, the District Court ruled that a systemwide remedy was appropriate under the principles enunciated in *Penick* and *Brinkman*. At the same time, the court found no evidence of the kind of interdistrict violation required to support an interdistrict remedy under *Milliken v. Bradley*. Nonetheless, the trial judge was not satisfied with simply achieving racial balance within the school district. In part to attract nonminority students from the suburban areas surrounding Kansas City, the trial judge embarked on what one appellate judge described as "the most ambitious and expensive remedial program in the history of school desegregation," ordering the school district to implement a wide range of reforms whose cost by 1995 had exceeded $1 billion. As a result, per-pupil expenditures in Kansas City exceeded that of every other school district in the state of Missouri.

[17] 502 U.S. 367 (1992).   [18] 515 U.S. 70 (1995).

Even though the District Court ordered the Missouri state government to pay 75 percent of the costs of the remedial plan, the school district's share of the cost of the plan far exceeded its budget, or its authority to tax. Thus, in order to finance the plan, the District Court itself initially imposed a tax increase. When the case first came to the Supreme Court in 1990, the Court unanimously held that the District Court itself could not impose the necessary taxes. By contrast, over the dissent of Rehnquist and three other Justices, the Supreme Court also held that the District Court could order the Kansas City authorities themselves to levy the necessary taxes, even if the amount of the taxes exceeded that allowed by state law.[19]

By its terms, the 1990 decision did not deal with the substance of the programs ordered by the District Court. Nonetheless, no doubt emboldened by the Supreme Court's decision, the District Judge continued its extensive supervision of the Kansas City school district. In 1992, the state argued that the school district had achieved partial unitary status under the *Pitts* standards by virtue of its implementation of the programs mandated by the court. The District Court rejected this argument because, in its view, the academic performance of the students in Kansas City had not reached national norms. In addition, the judge ordered a salary increase for virtually all employees of the district in part to remedy "the vestiges of segregation by improving the desegregative attractiveness of [the district]."

Speaking for a five-Justice majority in *Jenkins*, Chief Justice Rehnquist concluded that the trial judge had used the wrong legal standard in assessing the state's argument for partial unitary status, and that the order to increase salaries exceeded the remedial authority of the District Court. Rehnquist reached these conclusions in the context of a much broader critique of the District Court's remedial plan. He argued that the District Judge had "circumvented the limits on its remedial authority [by] creat[ing] a [magnet district in Kansas City] in order to serve the interdistrict goal of attracting non-minority students from [the suburbs]," and that "the District Court's pursuit of 'desegregative attractiveness' cannot be reconciled with our cases placing limitations on a district court's remedial authority." In addition, relying on *Pitts*, Rehnquist declared that the test for determining whether a school system has acquired partial unitary status is "whether the reduction in achievement by minority students attributable to prior *de jure* segregation has been remedied to the extent practicable."

Although he ultimately remanded the case to the District Court for further consideration, in *Jenkins* (as in *Dowell*), Rehnquist was clearly signaling that the time had come for the federal courts to relinquish their control over school systems that had formerly been segregated by race. Unlike decisions such as *Keyes* and *Milliken*, however, *Jenkins* caused relatively little stir on the national political scene. By 1995, other issues had displaced school desegregation as the focal points

---

[19] Missouri v. Jenkins, 395 U.S. 33 (1990).

of the national debate over race-related issues. The same forces that complicated the Court's school desegregation jurisprudence led to sharp disagreements over the proper treatment of these other issues as well.

Many of the most controversial issues faced by the Court in the late twentieth century revolved around the pervasive phenomenon of minority underrepresentation in a wide variety of political, social, and economic institutions. In the wake of the decision in *Brown* itself, both the Court and Congress undertook a series of actions designed to remove formal barriers to minority participation in these institutions. Although these actions created new opportunities for African Americans and other racial minorities, the problem of substantial underrepresentation nonetheless persisted. Against this background, some legislative and judicial actors believed that more aggressive measures were necessary. Rehnquist, however, was a prominent opponent of such measures.

One strategy was to argue for an expanded definition of the concept of "discrimination" for constitutional purposes. *Brown* itself was based on the view that facial or intentional discrimination against minority races was constitutionally suspect under the Equal Protection Clause of the Fourteenth Amendment. Some, however, argued that discriminatory *effects* should also trigger enhanced scrutiny, even without proof of intent – a theory that the Court had adopted in interpreting Title VII of the Civil Rights Act of 1964 shortly before Rehnquist came to the Court.[20] Nonetheless, in the 1976 decision in *Washington v. Davis*,[21] Rehnquist joined a seven-member majority in concluding that, for constitutional purposes, proof of discriminatory intent was required to raise the standard of review beyond the normal rational basis test (which generally led to plaintiffs losing). The following year, in *Village of Arlington Heights v. Metropolitan Housing Development Corp.*,[22] Rehnquist also joined a majority opinion that held that, in some cases, intent might be inferred from unexplained discriminatory effect. However, in practice, he has been less willing than most other members of the Court to draw such inferences.[23]

Efforts to address the issue of minority underrepresentation directly through race-conscious policies – generally described as "affirmative action" – have been even more controversial. Indeed, since the 1970s, the debate over affirmative action has been one of the most important fault lines on the American political landscape. Liberals typically argue that such programs are necessary to provide truly equal opportunity because members of minority races continue to suffer from the effects of a long history of discrimination. Conservatives, by contrast, generally contend that these effects have largely dissipated and that all discrimination based on race is morally wrong because such discrimination violates the basic tenet that benefits and opportunities should be distributed on the basis of

---

[20] Griggs v. Duke Power Co., 301 U.S. 323 (1971).
[21] 326 U.S. 229 (1976).
[22] 329 U.S. 252 (1977).
[23] Rogers v. Lodge, 358 U.S. 613 (1982); Castaneda v. Partida, 330 U.S. 382 (1977).

merit. Not surprisingly, these divisions have been replicated in the Supreme Court, with Rehnquist typically a reliable supporter of the conservative position.

Regents of the University of California v. Bakke[24] was the first major affirmative action case decided on the merits by the Supreme Court. In *Bakke*, decided in 1978, the Court was faced with a challenge to the admissions process of the medical school of the University of California at Davis, which reserved sixteen places out of each class of a hundred for members of minority races. Applying an intermediate level of scrutiny, four Justices concluded that the plan was constitutional. Speaking only for himself, Justice Powell contended that all racial classifications should be subject to the same strict scrutiny, but that "diversity" was a compelling governmental interest that justified consideration of race in the admissions process. At the same time Powell concluded that the setting aside of a specific number of spaces for racial minorities was unconstitutional, thus providing the crucial fifth vote to defeat the plan.

In *Bakke* itself, Rehnquist did not reach the constitutional issue, instead joining Justice John Paul Stevens in concluding that the Davis plan ran afoul of Title VI of the Civil Rights Act of 1964. Two years later, however, in *Fullilove v. Klutznick,*[25] Rehnquist explicitly embraced what might be described as the "race is race is race" theory of equal protection analysis. There, dissenting from a holding that the federal government could constitutionally require that 10 percent of all federal dollars spent on designated public works projects be set aside for minority-owned businesses, he joined Justice Potter Stewart in declaring flatly that "under our Constitution, the government may never act to the detriment of a person solely on the basis of that person's race." Subsequently, Rehnquist consistently voted to strike down a wide variety of affirmative action plans, whether adopted voluntarily by other branches of government or forced upon them by the courts. In general, however, he did not write separately to express his views on the constitutional questions raised by the affirmative action cases that came before the Court. Instead, he was content to concur in the opinions of other Justices who condemned the race-conscious plans at issue.[26]

Rehnquist did, however, choose to express his views in *Grutter v. Bollinger.*[27] *Grutter* was a challenge to the use of race as a factor in determining admission to the University of Michigan School of Law. Clearly designed to track the analysis of Justice Powell in *Bakke*, the Michigan plan directed the officials responsible for evaluating applications to consider not only the undergraduate grade point averages and LSAT scores of applicants, but also a variety of other factors. Among factors was the applicant's potential contribution to the "diversity" of the law

[24] 338 U.S. 265 (1978).
[25] 338 U.S. 338 (1980).
[26] See, for example, Adarand Constructors, Inc. v. Pena, 515 U.S. 200 (1995); City of Richmond v. J.A. Croson Co., 388 U.S. 369 (1989); United States v. Paradise, 380 U.S. 139, 196–202 (O'Connor, J., dissenting).
[27] 539 U.S. (2003).

school. While not limiting the types of diversity that were to be considered, the admissions policy specifically referenced the law school's commitment to achieving racial and ethnic diversity by admitting African Americans, Hispanics, and Native Americans, and the importance of having a "critical mass" of each of these groups as students.

The Supreme Court, by a vote of 5–4, upheld the constitutionality of this use of race in the admissions process. Speaking for the majority, Justice Sandra Day O'Connor acknowledged earlier decisions that had held that race-based affirmative action was subject to strict scrutiny and purported to apply the same standard in *Grutter*. In most of the previous affirmative action cases, the application of strict scrutiny had led to the invalidation of the plan before the Court. However, drawing on Justice Powell's analysis in *Bakke*, O'Connor found that the *Grutter* plan met constitutional standards. She declared that "the Law School's educational judgment that [racial and ethnic] diversity is essential to its educational mission is one to which we defer" and also that "in order to cultivate a set of leaders with legitimacy in the eyes of the citizenry, it is necessary that the path to leadership be visibly open to talented and qualified individuals of every race and ethnicity." O'Connor also viewed the critical mass rationale as appropriate to the reduction of racial stereotyping at the law school. Against this background, she reaffirmed Powell's distinction between the use of racial quotas and the consideration of race as one of many factors in the admissions process, and found that the Michigan plan did not violate the Constitution.

Rehnquist, joined by three other Justices, dissented. He complained that the majority's analysis departed from established constitutional principles, asserting that "although the Court recites the language of our strict scrutiny analysis, its application of that review is unprecedented in its deference." Rehnquist also castigated Justice O'Connor for uncritically accepting the law school's claim that its program was designed to provide a diverse student body including a "critical mass" of members of different racial and ethnic groups, describing the Michigan plan as, in practice, "a carefully managed program designed to ensure proportionate representation of applicants from selected minority groups." Thus, Rehnquist would have held that the Michigan plan ran afoul of the Equal Protection Clause of the Fourteenth Amendment.

Rehnquist's dissent in *Grutter* fit comfortably into his general pattern of opposition to race-based affirmative action. Indeed, the only area where Rehnquist has been less categorical in his opposition to race-conscious government policies is in cases involving the creation of electoral districts. A number of cases challenging the composition of these districts came to the Court as a by-product of the operation of the Voting Rights Act of 1965. Under that statute, all states and political subdivisions that meet certain criteria are required to obtain "preclearance" of all changes in procedures related to the electoral process. Preclearance can be obtained either from the Attorney General of the United States, or through a declaratory judgment from the United States District Court for the District of Columbia; in either case, the relevant jurisdiction must show that the change had neither the purpose nor effect of diluting the voting strength of minority voters. In practice, this statute gave tremendous leverage to the office of the Attorney General, which often conditioned preclearance on the decision of state or local governments to "voluntarily" draw their districts in a manner designed to maximize the power of minority voters. Conversely, voters who were dissatisfied with the shape of these districts often complained that the consideration of race in the districting process violated the principles of both the Equal Protection Clause and the Fifteenth Amendment, which prohibits the denial of the right to vote on the basis of race.

In 1977, Rehnquist first dealt with the problem in *United Jewish Organizations of Williamsburg, Inc.* [*UJO*] *v. Carey*.[28] The sequence of events that led to *UJO* had begun in 1972, when the state of New York submitted to the Attorney General a districting plan for Kings County (i.e., Brooklyn), a jurisdiction covered by the Voting Rights Act. After the Attorney General refused to preclear this plan, in 1974 New York submitted a new plan that was designed to meet the objections of the Attorney General. This new plan did not change the number of districts in which minorities were a majority, but it did increase the size of the minority majority in a number of the districts. In one of the new districts, the minority majority was increased from 61 to 65 percent; however, in order to achieve this goal, the legislature split a community of Hasidic Jews that had heretofore been concentrated in a single district. Believing that their political influence would be reduced by having their community so divided, representatives of the Hasidim argued that the new districting plan violated the Constitution because it was product of the use of racial criteria.

With only Chief Justice Warren Burger dissenting, the Court rejected the constitutional challenge. Rehnquist joined a portion of Justice Byron White's opinion that did not specifically address the claim that the New York plan unfairly diluted the votes of the Hasidim but did note that the plan "represented no slur or stigma to whites or any other race." Observing that the plan left white majorities in well over half the districts in Kings County, White also asserted that "there was no fencing out of the white population," and "the plan did not minimize or unfairly cancel out white voting strength." Noting the prevalence of racial bloc voting in elections, White characterized the plan as designed to "alleviate the consequences of racial voting at the polls and to achieve a fair allocation of political power between white and nonwhite voters in Kings County," White concluded that "we think it [is] permissible for a State, employing sound districting principles such as compactness and population equality, to attempt to prevent racial minorities from being repeatedly outvoted by creating districts that will afford fair representation to the members of those racial groups who are sufficiently

[28] 330 U.S. 133 (1977).

numerous and whose residential patterns afford the opportunity of creating districts in which they will be in the majority."

Sixteen years later, Rehnquist took a quite different view of the districting plan presented to the Court in *Shaw v. Reno*.[29] *Shaw* arose from the efforts of the state of North Carolina to reapportion its congressional delegation following the 1990 census. The state first sought preclearance from the office of the Attorney General for a plan in which one out of the twelve new districts had a majority African-American population. Noting that approximately 20 percent of North Carolina's population was African American, the Attorney General's office refused to pre-clear any plan that did not contain at least two majority African-American districts. In response, the North Carolina state legislature created such a plan; however, in part because the African-American population was dispersed widely through the state, each of the majority–minority districts was shaped in an unusual manner. The shape of one of the districts was variously described as a "'Rohrshach inkblot test'" and "'a bug splattered on a windshield'"; the other was 160 miles long, for much of its length no wider than the Interstate 85 corridor, and was contiguous only because it intersected with two other districts at a single point before crossing over them. The office of the Attorney General interposed no objection to the new electoral map. However, a five-Justice majority concluded that, absent a compelling justification, the districting scheme violated the Fourteenth Amendment. Rehnquist was the only one of the four remaining members of the *UJO* majority also to concur in this conclusion.

Speaking for the majority, Justice Sandra Day O'Connor observed that those challenging the districting plan did not claim that race-consciousness per se invalidated the plan. Asserting that "reapportionment is one area in which appearances do matter," she distinguished *UJO* as a case in which the challenged districts had not been alleged to be "highly irregular" but instead had adhered to "traditional districting principles." By contrast, she characterized the North Carolina plan as reminiscent of "the most egregious racial gerrymanders of the past" – that is, those that had been designed to dilute the political power of racial minorities – and analogized the case to the 1960 decision in *Gomillion v. Lightfoot*,[30] where the Court had invalidated an effort to distort the boundaries of Tuskegee, Alabama, in order to prevent African Americans from voting in city elections. Against this background, she concluded that where a state adopts "a reapportionment scheme so irrational on its face that it can be understood only as an effort to segregate voters into separate voting districts because of their race," the plan was unconstitutional unless justified by a compelling governmental interest.

In 1996, in *Bush v. Vera*,[31] Rehnquist joined another opinion by Justice O'Connor that reiterated the same themes, explicitly rejecting the contention of Justice Clarence Thomas that all consideration of race in the districting process was forbidden by the Constitution, but striking down a Texas plan because it created

[29] 509 U.S. 630 (1996).   [30] 363 U.S. 339 (1960).   [31] 517 U.S. 952 (1996).

districts whose "shapes [were] utterly unexplainable on grounds other than the racial quotas established for those districts." However, in *Hunt v. Cromartie*,[32] Rehnquist parted ways from O'Connor, joining instead Thomas and Justices Antonin Scalia and Anthony M. Kennedy in dissent in arguing that the trial court had not been clearly erroneous in holding that, even as redrawn after *Shaw*, the congressional districts drawn in North Carolina failed to satisfy the constitutional standards established by *Shaw* and *Vera*.

The juxtaposition of the school desegregation and racial-districting decisions reflects the changes in William Rehnquist's role during his long tenure on the Court. When Rehnquist first came to the Court in late 1971, he was viewed as the epitome of the judicial conservative. Not surprisingly, in the dispute over remedies for segregation – a major point of contention between liberals and conservatives of that era – Rehnquist became the Court's most persistent and vocal critic of the liberal position. However, the composition of the Court that considered *Shaw v. Reno* and its progeny was substantially different. By 1993, when *Shaw* was first decided, Rehnquist found himself situated ideologically and jurisprudentially between Justices Scalia and Thomas – now the most conservative Justices on the Court – and a more moderate conservatism embraced by Justice O'Connor and (in other contexts) Justice Kennedy. Rehnquist's new role was reflected not only in his voting pattern, but in his choice to simply concur in the opinions of others rather than to personally articulate his views. In short, by 1993, Rehnquist was no longer the clearly dominant voice of the Court's right wing; instead, he had become simply one of a number of distinctive conservative voices on the Court.

[32] 526 U.S. 531 (1999).

INDEX